Complex Processes in New Languages

Creole Language Library (CLL)

A book series presenting descriptive and theoretical studies designed to add significantly to the data available on pidgin and creole languages.

Editors

Miriam Meyerhoff
University of Edinburgh

Umberto Ansaldo
The University of Hong Kong

Editorial Advisory Board

Mervyn C. Alleyne
Kingston, Jamaica

Marlyse Baptista
Ann Arbor, USA

George L. Huttar
Dallas, USA

John Holm
Coimbra, Portugal

Silvia Kouwenberg
Kingston, Jamaica

Susanne Michaelis
Leipzig, Germany

Salikoko S. Mufwene
Chicago, USA

Pieter Muysken
Nijmegen, The Netherlands

Peter Mühlhäusler
Adelaide, Australia

Shobha Satyanath
Delhi, India

John Victor Singler
New York, USA

Norval Smith
Amsterdam, The Netherlands

Sarah G. Thomason
Ann Arbor, USA

Tonjes Veenstra
Berlin, Germany

Volume 35

Complex Processes in New Languages
Edited by Enoch O. Aboh and Norval Smith

Complex Processes in New Languages

Edited by

Enoch O. Aboh
University of Amsterdam

Norval Smith
University of Amsterdam

John Benjamins Publishing Company
Amsterdam / Philadelphia

The paper used in this publication meets the minimum requirements of American National Standard for Information Sciences – Permanence of Paper for Printed Library Materials, ANSI z39.48-1984.

Library of Congress Cataloging-in-Publication Data

Complex processes in new languages / edited by Enoch O. Aboh, Norval Smith.
    p. cm. (Creole Language Library, ISSN 0920-9026 ; v. 35)
Includes bibliographical references and index.
1. Creole dialects. I. Aboh, Enoch Oladé. II. Smith, Norval.
PM7831.C69   2009
417'.22--dc22
                                                    2009036623
ISBN 978 90 272 5257 9 (Hb ; alk. paper)
ISBN 978 90 272 8877 6 (Eb)

© 2009 – John Benjamins B.V.
No part of this book may be reproduced in any form, by print, photoprint, microfilm, or any other means, without written permission from the publisher.

John Benjamins Publishing Co. · P.O. Box 36224 · 1020 ME Amsterdam · The Netherlands
John Benjamins North America · P.O. Box 27519 · Philadelphia PA 19118-0519 · USA

Table of contents

Acknowledgments — VII

Simplicity, simplification, complexity and complexification: Where have the interfaces gone? — 1
Enoch O. Aboh and Norval Smith

Part I. Morphophonology

Initial vowel agglutination in the Gulf of Guinea creoles — 29
Tjerk Hagemeijer

Simplification of a complex part of grammar or not? What happened to KiKoongo nouns in Saramaccan? — 51
Norval Smith

Reducing phonological complexity and grammatical opaqueness: Old Tibetan as a *lingua franca* and the development of the modern Tibetan varieties — 75
Bettina Zeisler

Part II. Verbal morphology

Verb allomorphy and the syntax of phases — 99
Tonjes Veenstra

The invisible hand in creole genesis: Reanalysis in the formation of Berbice Dutch — 115
Silvia Kouwenberg

Complexification or regularization of paradigms: The case of prepositional verbs in Solomon Islands Pijin — 159
Christine Jourdan

Part III. Nominals

The Mauritian Creole determiner system: A historical overview   173
   Diana Guillemin

Demonstratives in Afrikaans and Cape Dutch Pidgin: A first attempt   201
   Hans den Besten

Part IV. The selection of features in complex morphology

Contact, complexification and change in Mindanao Chabacano structure   223
   Anthony P. Grant

Morphosyntactic finiteness as increased complexity in a mixed
negation system   243
   Peter Slomanson

Contact language formation in evolutionary terms   265
   Umberto Ansaldo

Part V. Evaluating simplification and complexification

Economy, innovation and degrees of complexity in creole formation   293
   Marlyse Baptista

Competition and selection: That's all!   317
   Enoch O. Aboh

Complexity and the age of languages   345
   Umberto Ansaldo and Sebastian Nordhoff

Part VI. Postscript

Restructuring, hybridization, and complexity in language evolution   367
   Salikoko S. Mufwene

Language index   401
Subject index   405

Acknowledgments

This book is the second of a series of two volumes that grew out of the Sixth Creolistics Workshop in Giessen 2006. The first volume, *Simplicity and Complexity* is edited by Nicholas Faraclas and Thomas B. Klein.

In addition to a selection of papers presented at the workshop, the editors of this volume invited a number of other scholars to reflect on the question of complexity and simplicity, and implications of this for creole grammars and creole studies. We are grateful to all the contributors to the volume, the series editors, and all the reviewers for helping evaluate the work presented here.

Simplicity, simplification, complexity and complexification
Where have the interfaces gone?

Enoch O. Aboh and Norval Smith

This volume grew out of selected papers from the Sixth Creolistics Workshop in Giessen 2006 and a number of invited contributions. The theme of this workshop was "simplicity and complexity in pidgins and creoles", and part of the call for abstracts read as follows:

> A basic assumption, shared by *virtually all creolists* [emphasis is ours], is that pidgins are structurally simple, while creoles are more complex languages. In generalizing statements such as this, simplicity and complexity are of course ill-defined notions, but most of us would accept the basic truth of the above. For example, while a few TMA markers are found in pidgins, combinations of two preverbal markers seem to be unattested in any pidgin prior to it acquiring native speakers. Also, pidgins tend to lack progressive/nonpunctual markers. Both observations appear to confirm the status of pidgins as simple languages in comparison to creoles. *Creoles, in turn, are arguably less complex than so-called natural languages* [emphasis is ours], although there are certainly fewer scholars supporting this claim. One aim of the workshop will be to investigate in how far empirical data drawn from a range of restructured languages confirm or disconfirm the pidgins-are-simple-and-creoles-are-complex-but-less-complex-than-natural-languages equation.

Considerations of this sort go beyond the creolist community. Indeed, a near-universal idea prevalent in the linguistics family at large is that creolization involves the simplification or pidginization of the colonial languages they are based on. Accordingly, creole languages, being developed from pidgins, are simple, or at least simpler than (all?) other languages. A development of creole languages that would fit in this scenario can be found in Hall's (1962: 152ff.) characterization of pidgins and creoles as indicated in (1):

(1) a. Pidgins [are] "*minimal*" *languages*, and, from their basically improvisatory character, 'make-shift' languages. In the contact situation, by the very definition of the term pidgin, all its speakers have full-sized '*normal*' *languages*..."
b. "From the structural point of view, a pidgin represents the *very first stage of rudimentary language learning*, with the development of *linguistic structure and lexicon arrested at this level*..."
c. "*Usually*, since pidgins do not enjoy any degree of social esteem, they *go out of use rapidly* once the special contact situation which called them into existence has disappeared..."
d. There is, however, one type of use in which *a pidgin can achieve the transition to the status of a 'normal' language*, and thereby escape extinction when the contact situation disappears: this is, of course, *when the pidgin is creolized, i.e., becomes the first language of a speech community*."

Recent work by McWhorter (2001, 2005) who revived Bickerton's (1988) original "creolization as backward process" has attempted to theorize over this developmental path, and how it could have set creole languages typologically apart from other 'normal' or 'older' languages. In terms of Bickerton (1988: 268), the emergence of creoles is a consequence of catastrophic language change "new languages are produced *ab ovo* within the space of, at most, one or two generations". Under this approach, while slaves brought to the colonies during the homestead period had enough opportunities of to achieve "a reasonable second language fluency in the target language" (p. 270), the cohort of African slaves who were deported to the colonies during the plantation phase had a very limited access to the model language. Given that these slaves did not speak a common language, they had to learn the target language from each other. This process in turn led to a dilution of the model language that ended in a macaronic pidgin which could not feed first language acquisition. Accordingly, children born on plantations had to develop a new L1 *ab ovo*, recycling the degenerate input they were faced with. According to Bickerton (1988: 274), this scenario is compatible with the widespread idea that creoles are simpler than older languages. In terms of this author,

> "the present viewpoint accounts very naturally for this 'simplicity'. In older languages, the universally shared set of syntactic principles is added to, and complicated by, a wide range of lexical and morphological properties acquired from the universal inventory of possible properties, as a result of millennia of diachronic change. But the process of dilution of the model language […] had, as one of its results, the loss of a large number of these properties".

Accordingly, the conclusion that pidgins and creoles are simpler than older languages is a logical consequence of their developing from a diluted target language, where dilution means loss of large numbers of lexico-semantic and syntactic properties. This analysis obviously reminds us of McWhorter's (2001: 132) typology of creole languages which assumes that "creoles, in being recently born of communication vehicles deliberately designed to eschew all but the functional central (pidgins), are unique examples of natural languages with much less contingent accumulation of "ornamental" elaboration than older grammars drag along with them".

While many recent publications react to McWhorter's complexity metrics, it is important to recall Muysken's (1988) warnings on this issue. In his reaction to Bickerton's (1988) theory of creolization and his conclusions that creole languages are somehow simpler than older languages, Muysken (1988: 288) rightly points out that the notion of simplicity as evoked in the creole literature involves two levels of analysis: morphology and syntax. On the morphological level, simplicity is taken to mean that creole languages display a rather poor morphology, whether inflectional or derivational, and mainly resort to compounding – itself a third type of morphology, of course. The rationale here is that such a lack of morphology would favor a semantic transparency not found in other natural languages. On the level of syntax, it is assumed that "the overall grammar of creole languages is less complex than that of other languages". This view is particularly transparent in Bickerton's and McWhorter's work reported on in this chapter. Yet, as Muysken (1988: 288) points out, "the idea that absence of morphology is related to grammatical simplicity needs to be evaluated in the context of contemporary research into morphology-syntax interactions, and the grammatical status of inflection. [...] Even more importantly, the idea that the creole languages are not grammatically complex in general only makes sense if one has a theory of grammatical complexity to fall back on." Some authors (e.g., McWhorter 2005) have tried to take this observation to heart and develop a metric of complexity. However, what has been forgotten on the way is Muysken's observations about the role of the interfaces (in his words the morphology-syntax interactions), and the relation (if any) between morphological expression and syntactic complexity.

Consider, for instance, McWhorter's (2001: 135ff.) metric defined in the following terms:

(2) an area of grammar is more complex than the same area in another grammar to the extent that it encompasses more *overt* distinctions and/or *rules* than another grammar.

With regard to syntax, the author further suggests that:

(3) a. a syntax is more complex than another to the extent that it requires the processing of more rules, such as asymmetries between matrix and subordinate clauses (e.g., Germanic verb-second rules), or containing two kinds of alignment rather than one (i.e., ergative/absolutive and nominative/accusative).
  b. Third, a grammar is more complex than another to the extent that it gives overt and grammaticalized expression to more fine-grained semantic and/or pragmatic distinctions than another.

c. Fourth, inflectional morphology renders a grammar more complex than another one in most cases [….] Inflection more often than not has wider repercussions in a grammar [...], which are complexifying factors in terms of exerting a load upon processing.

In a sense, this view reminds us of Bickerton's idea that language dilution results in the loss (that is the silencing) of certain categories. Accordingly, a new language that develops from a diluted model (i.e., a creole) is by necessity simpler than older languages because the former will fail to overtly express all the muted categories.

Morphological complexity

Let us first examine the claim for morphological simplicity. What this usually refers to is two aspects that are really completely disconnected from each other. One aspect of morphological complexity/simplicity refers strictly to the roundabouts-and-swings relationship between morphology and syntax, together a.k.a. morphosyntax.

The other aspect of morphological complexity refers to the degree of inflectional (and derivational) irregularity in the lexicon. We will return to this aspect below.

Morphosyntactic complexity: Morphology versus syntax

Although no reliable measure of the trade-off between morphology and syntax has ever been constructed, we may uncontroversially assume that the combination of above-word morphosyntax (a.k.a. syntax) and below-word morphosyntax (a.k.a. morphology) results in similar overall complexities in all languages.

We can picture this in approximate terms in the table below. Here we see a table of real languages with varying degrees of emphasis on "below-word" and "above-word" morphosyntax, from the polysynthetic West Greenlandic to Sranan with no inflectional morphology at all.

The only real difference among these languages is where the word-level is situated – Selkirk's X_0-level (Selkirk 1986). Note that this table illustrates the priority of syntax over (inflectional) morphology. There is no language that has no above-word morphosyntax. In other words, there is no language where *all* the "sentences" consist of a single word – hyperpolysynthetic word-cum-sentences do not exist. It is true that many more sentences can consist of single words in polysynthetic languages than in synthetic languages, and the same applies even more so in respect of isolating languages.

Non-existent	West Greenlandic	Sanskrit	Ancient Greek	Latin	French	English	Sranan
hyperpoly-synthetic	polysyn-thetic	synthetic	synthetic	synthetic	synthetic	weakly synthetic	isolating/analytic
Inflectional Morphology	Syntax	Syntax	Syntax	Syntax	Syntax	Syntax	Syntax
	Inflectional Morphology						
		Inflectional Morphology					
			Inflectional Morphology				
				Inflectional Morphology			
					Inflectional Morphology		
						Inflectional Morphology	

So we have one-word sentences in West Greenlandic like:

(4) naalaa-qqissaa-qqu-aa
listen-**carefully**-**tell_to**-3SG.3SG.INDIC
'He told him to listen carefully' (Fortescue 1984: 43)

Because of the widespread possibility in polysynthetic languages like West Greenlandic of incorporating more than one lexical morpheme – indicated in this example with bold type – into the word, the number of such one-word sentences will obviously be much larger than in a synthetic language like Latin where we are restricted to a single lexical morpheme in (non-compound) words.

(5) cant-a-v-era-t
sing-CLASS_MARKER-PERFECT-PAST-3SG
'He had sung'

In isolating languages the number of one-word sentences will be even more limited. We have ordered the other languages in terms of the complexity of their below-word morphosyntax. So a verb in Sanskrit has in excess of a thousand forms in its paradigm Ancient Greek somewhere in the order of 250. Latin in excess of a hundred, French a much smaller number, English less than ten, and Sranan only one. An increasing amount of work is left to the above-word morphosyntax as we progress from left to right in the above table.

What emerges from this discussion is that one cannot evaluate the complexity of grammars by just counting overt distinctions. Indeed, when comparing a language to another, absence of morphological expression (e.g., inflectional morphology) in one as opposed to the other does not tell us anything about the interface properties (morphology vs. syntax) in both languages. Yet, it is only at this level that we can say anything sensible about complexity. Consider for instance the following three examples from French, Russian, and Gungbe (Kwa):

(6) a. Jean a acheté une maison [French]
John has bought a house
b. Džon kupi-l dom [Russian]
John buy-PST.SG.MASC house.ACC.SG
'John has bought a house' [Vadim Kimmerman, p.c.]
c. Ján xɔ̀ xwé [Gungbe]
John buy house
'John has bought (a) house(s)'

Apart from the fact that all these languages are SVO, it appears that Russian overtly marks case on the nouns while both French and Gungbe lack such morphological distinctions. In the case of Russian, it is important to note that accusative case on the direct object *dom* 'house' in example (6b) is expressed by absence of morphology. This illustrates a situation where covertness is linked to meaning distinction (i.e., nominative versus accusative). Put together, these facts indicate that, morphology-wise, Russian displays a more contrastive (or distinctive) case system than French and Gungbe (though French displays more morphology than Gungbe). In terms of current metrics of complexity, the conclusion would be that Russian has a more complex case system than both French and Gungbe.

However, another distinction that comes into play here is that despite Russian rich case morphology, the language lacks articles and therefore allows bare nouns in argument positions. This is not the case in French, where common nouns require a determiner to occur in argument positions. Gungbe, which exhibits a complete lack of nominal morphology, clusters with Russian. It has no determiner of the French type (e.g., *le/un*), and bare nouns occur in all argument positions. If we make the reasonable assumption that there is an interface between morphology and syntax, what we observe here is that this aspect of human language does not seem to be particularly affected by the distinctions between Gungbe, which has completely undressed (to use a McWhorterian term) and Russian, which refuses to do so. Accordingly, noun phrases have the same distributions in these three languages, though they have distinct morphological properties.

Under the assumption that noun phrases are predicates, it is commonly assumed that some operation of type-shifting has to take place for such predicates to be turned into arguments. In the relevant generative literature, it is proposed that this operation is performed by the determiner in Romance and Germanic (e.g., Longobardi 1994; Cherchia 1998). If we make the uniformitarian hypothesis that the same operation applies cross-linguistically, we are led to conclude that this operation applies to Russian and Gungbe as well, though covertly. This would mean that the Gungbe and Russian bare nouns are syntactically strictly equivalent to the Romance article-noun phrases.

We therefore reach the situation where these three languages rely on the same underlying syntactic machinery to license noun phrases, but this syntactic machinery does not seem to tie up to any specific morphological effect cross-linguistically. Clearly therefore, expression of morphosyntactic distinctions does not tell us anything about syntactic computation (i.e., how syntax is structured and how compositional semantics arises from that structure), or what this means vis-à-vis computational complexity and processing. Put differently, before we claim that Russian has a more complex grammatical system in the domain of the noun phrase than French and Gungbe, we will have to show that richness of morphology correlates with computational complexity at the level of the interfaces. Various experiments can be conducted to determine this – one that comes to mind is the following. If we can show for different languages that the time it takes a speaker to parse a sentence is unambiguously related to levels of morphological complexity of that sentence (e.g., case, agreement), then we may ask whether in the context of the examples under (6) a Russian speaker takes more time to parse the sentence than a French speaker, who should take more time than a Gungbe speaker. To the best of our knowledge no such study on computational complexity and its relations to morphological exuberance has been conducted.

The issue is not trivial and it relates to fundamental questions about the human language faculty. Indeed, we are reminded of Vergnaud's (1977) seminal observation that when it comes to the distribution of noun phrases (NPs), even languages with virtually no case morphology pattern with case-morphology languages. Put another way, case-marked NPs have the same distribution as unmarked NPs in languages with no case morphology. Whatever the technical implementation of this observation is, the generalization seems to be that the distribution of noun phrases in syntax interacts with case assignment (overt or covert) which itself may interact with finiteness (e.g., nominative case in English), see Chomsky (1995), Marantz (2000) for some suggestions.

Remarkably, however, languages like Gungbe, which obviously fall under this generalization, do not exhibit any case morphology on NPs headed by lexical nouns (6c). The only reflection of case that we find is confined to a corner of the pronominal system (i.e., 1SG and 2SG as in *ùn* 1SG-NOM versus *mì* 1SG-ACC, or *à* 2SG-NOM versus *wè* 2SG-ACC, see Aboh 2004, Chapter 4). Jamaican creole and a number of other creoles display no case distinction at all, and the same forms and set of pronouns occur both in nominative and accusative positions. Despite their complete lack of case morphology, the syntax of case assignment in case marked languages should extend to Gungbe-type languages as well as creole languages, since these do not show any relevant syntactic difference from languages with case morphology: In both groups, NPs have the same range of distribution. What this discussion shows is that while it might be interesting to count overt morphological distinctions in languages, the differences in number of types of morphemes make no sense in terms of morphosyntactic complexity, unless they tell us exactly how overt morphemes and covert morphemes interact at the interfaces, and how they may burden or alleviate syntactic processing by virtue of being overt or covert.

To use an analogy from the biological world, that some spiders have eight eyes, while others have six represents a morphological difference that does not necessarily imply that the former have a more complex or advanced vision system. The same, it seems to us, would hold of languages. Accordingly, one cannot talk of complexity in language in any informative way if one does not tie this notion to issues of the interface and to computational complexity.

This is precisely the problem encountered in the studies in Miestamo, Sinnemäki & Karlsson (2008). They are restricted by and large to observations on the surface structures of the languages studied. As such they miss much of the complexities introduced by syntactic relations like movement or agreement. Sinnemäki (2008:75), for instance, describes how languages vary in the number of features of the argument that are determined by the predicate – person only (Urubú-Kaapor), person and number (Somali), or person, number and gender (Kannada). But in generative terms these are only superficial differences which do not necessarily bring about syntactic complexity. Even so, Siewierska (1998) with a sample of 171 languages finds a statistically significant correlation between case-marking and freedom of word-order. Gil (2008) notes however that Siewierska still finds languages which clearly go against the correlation. Nine languages have case-marking *and* fixed word-order, and five have no case-marking *but* free word-order. Though these statistical differences may be interesting from a typological perspective, it is important to realise that these results clearly indicate that there is no one-to-one correlation between surface morphology and computational complexity. The following section focuses on issues of apparent complexity and information structure.

Complexity and information structure

In the previous section we argued that the fact that a language (e.g., a creole) may lack certain morphological distinctions should not be equated with simplicity. The discussion there mainly referred to aspects of languages where creole languages typically appear to lack certain grammatical properties found in older languages. In this section, we will turn to an aspect of the grammars of creoles which, on the surface, show more distinctions than many older languages. In the context of this discussion, consider again McWhorter's complexity metric cited in (3b) repeated here for convenience.

(3) b. Third, a grammar is more complex than another to the extent that it gives overt and grammaticalized expression to more fine-grained semantic and/or pragmatic distinctions than another.

Under this description, a language with more grammaticalized expression of topic and focus constructions will appear to be more complex than a language without such distinctions. Keeping to this line of thought, it is interesting to observe that nearly all the Atlantic creoles develop distinct morphosyntactic means to express topic and focus constructions. In many of these languages topic or focused constituents must necessarily move to the sentence-initial position. Consider the following examples from Saramaccan.

As discussed in Byrne (1987), Byrne & Caskey (1993), Smith (1996), and Aboh (2006), Saramaccan displays focus constructions rules where the focused category, here in square brackets, must move to the left periphery, in the space between the complementizer *táa* 'that' and the subject (7a). The example of long extraction in sentence (7b) shows that focusing is not restricted to main clauses.

(7) a. A   sábi   táa [dí píngo]$_i$ dí   wómi bi   hondi t$_i$.
       3SG know   that DET pig   DET   man   ANT hunt
       'S/he knows that the man hunted THE PIG.'

  b. [Dí wómi]$_i$ (hen) a   sábi   táa t$_i$ bi   hondi dí   píngo.
       DET man   3SG-S 3SG know that   ANT hunt DET pig
       'S/he knows that THE MAN had hunted the pig.'
                                          [Adapted from Byrne 1987: 149]

Like an old language, Saramaccan displays contrastive focus constructions which involve a focus marker – *wὲ* – as in (8a). The example in (8b) further indicates that the focus rule also applies to wh-questions. In this case, the wh-phrase occurs to the position immediately to the left of the focus marker.

(8) a. [Di mujɛɛ] wɛ   mi bi   bɛl,   naa di   womi.
       DET woman FOC   1SG ANT phone   NEG DET man
       'I phoned THE WOMAN not the man.'   [Smith 1996: 118]
  b. Andí wɛ   i   bói?
       What FOC 2SG cook
       'What did you cook?'   [Smith 1996: 117]

In contrasting the examples in (7) and (8) to those in (9), we realize that the focus rule is obligatory in Saramaccan because the language disallows focus in situ and wh-in-situ strategies where the focus marker occurs in sentence-initial position.

(9) a. (*Wɛ) mi   bi   bɛl   [dí mujée], náa dí   wómi.
       FOC 1SG ANT phone DET woman   NEG DET man
       'I phoned THE WOMAN not the man.'
  b. (*Wɛ) i   bói   andí?
       FOC 2SG cook what
       'What did you cook?'

These examples indicate that focused categories and wh-phrases occur in the same position in Saramaccan. Following Aboh (2006), this would mean that the Saramaccan left periphery can be described as in (10), where the fronted category is represented by XP.

(10) [$_{\text{ForceP}}$ táa.... [$_{\text{FocP}}$ XP$_{[+f/+wh]i}$ [$_{\text{Foc}°}$ wɛ [$_{\text{FinP}}$ [t$_i$ ...]]]]]

Quite interestingly, this strategy applies to predicates as well. In this context, the fronted verb, adjective or modal is doubled inside the proposition.

(11) a. Sì   Kòfi sì   dì   mujée bi   tà   woòkò a   di   kéiki.
         See   Kofi see   DET   woman PAST PROG   work   LOC   DET   church
         'Kofi SAW the woman working at the church.'
     b. Go   Amato bi   **go** na   wooyo.
         go   Amato ANT   go   LOC   market
         'Amato WENT to the market.'

Put together, these examples show that Saramaccan is a language where notions of information structure are built into syntax such that focused categories must front to the sentence-initial position. In terms of the metric in (3b), this would mean that Saramaccan has a more complex syntax than, say English where such a distinction is not made systematically and it is not always clear whether a fronted element represents a focus or a topic. In addition, new information focus in English typically occurs in-situ, though with appropriate intonation.

If we were to stick to the metric of complexity in (3b), we would conclude that Saramaccan is more complex than English in the domain of information structure and its correlations to syntax. Yet, that English can achieve the same results as in Saramaccan either by means of stress or word order alternation clearly suggests that such characterization would be inconclusive. Indeed, Aboh (2007) has shown that morphology aside, languages behave similarly when it comes to the syntax-discourse interface. Three patterns are mainly found across languages:

(12) Information status is signalled by:
   a. Dislocation
   b. Marking of the relevant category (prosodic or morphological)
   c. Any combination of the above two

Crucially, there does not seem to be any language known to us which does not display any of the options under (12). This leads us to conclude that the options in (12) are expressions of the same syntactic principle, which requires information bearing units to be licensed structurally. Be this as it may, morphology or the number of syntactic rules cannot help us distinguish a language like English (with no grammaticalised focus marker) from a language like Saramaccan, when it comes to the 'complexity of information-structure-sensitive' constructions. What we see here is that there is a constraint imposed by the interface properties, and languages resolve this constraint differently. However, nothing about the outer form of the expression that languages choose hinges on issues of computational complexity, which is the relevant level for calculating complex grammars as opposed to simple ones (assuming that the distinction makes sense).

Lexical "complexity"

The other aspect of so-called morphological complexity/simplicity is really an aspect of lexical complexity, or the complexity of lexical entries. This again has two aspects, parallel to the two aspects of the morpheme, as De Saussure (1916) first described them. We have a form side, connected with the phonological shape of words, but also a semantic side, connected to the meaning of words. First we turn to the question of the phonological complexity of lexical items. This is basically concerned with paradigmatic irregularity, either as regards to the unforecastable phonological aspects of words or the constituent morphemes of words, and less commonly to suppletion.

Phonological complexity of lexical items

Note that questions of the phonological complexity of lexical items are controlled by two opposing forces. The first is the tendency of child-learners of language to overgeneralize irregularities out of the language. There is however also a countervailing tendency working to preserve irregularities in frequently-used lexical items. These two tendencies can be directly related to Markedness and Faithfulness constraints in an Optimality Theory view of phonology. Under creolization, however, when relexification may take place, a single form from a superstrate language may be selected to replace a single form in an isolating substrate language.

We will take as an example the Strong verb system in Germanic languages. This system in Germanic languages goes back to Proto-Indo-European (PIE). According to the archaeologists PIE was originally spoken in a small area north of the Black Sea 7000 years ago. Soon afterwards the area occupied by Indo-European languages began to grow larger, and the individual subgroups came into existence/split off, thus destroying the unity of Proto-Indo-European. By the time that (cuneiform) Hittite was first recorded, nearly 4000 years ago, a very considerable divergence in the verb system had already taken place. However, remnants of the ablaut patterns present in the original verb system remain functional to this day in the Strong verb systems of the various Germanic languages. This system has been irregular for an extremely long time – approaching 2000 years have passed since the competing Weak verb system took over the leading role in verb conjugation, but the Strong verb system is still propped up by the frequency of occurrence of many strong verbs. The loss of verbs to the competing regular weak verb system in Germanic is extremely slow, although steady, despite the fact that the strong verb system has been recessive for so long.

The nature of this *morpholexical irregularity* has however no bearing at all on the questions of morphosyntactic structural complexity/simplicity, which as we have stated above, can be regarded as balancing out between morphological and syntactic expression.

It is even clear that traces of the strong verb system must have been present – at least as variant stem-forms – during the creolization of Sranan and Saramaccan in 17th century Surinam.

(13) The verb 'sink' in the Surinam creoles
    a. Sranan: súɲu   <   Early Modern English *sunk*
    b. Saramaccan: síŋgi <   Early Modern English *sink*

In Sranan, it is likely that a substandard past tense form was selected (rather than the past participle form), while in Saramaccan apparently the present tense form was selected.

It is however difficult to see to what extent this kind of lexical irregularity contributes to the complexity of non-creole languages. Any isolating language – like the Surinam creoles – excludes irregular inflectional forms by definition, inasmuch as isolating languages lack inflectional paradigms. What is possible is suppletion, which does occur for instance in Ndyuka, in some uses of the copula, with context-determined alternation between the two forms /de/ and /da/. McWhorter seems to be correct in referring to such lexical irregularity as detritus. We would argue that the loss of a strong verb form like in (14), and its replacement by the regular form in (15) does not really contribute much to the simplicity of the English verb in dialects which have changed their lexical entry for *thrive* from something like (14) to something like (15).

(14) thrive, throve, thriven

(15) thrive, thrived, thrived

The explanation lies presumably in a reduction of frequency of usage of the verb *thrive*.

This said, we also have to ask ourselves how lexical irregularity arises in the first place. Consider the major aspects of the Germanic strong verb system as it is evidenced in Gothic, the oldest recorded Germanic language. Note that the formation of preterites had been replaced as the regular pattern by a formerly periphrastic formation based on the past tense form of the verb *dōn* 'do' (the most satisfying account of this can be found in Kiparsky 2003). By the time of our earliest Germanic records this had become fused to the verb stem. The strong verb pattern had clearly been replaced as the regular one well before the Gothic period (4th century A.D.). There are seven subclasses of Germanic strong verb, but we will only take account of the first four here.

	Infinitive	Preterite Sg.	Preterite Pl.	Past Participle	Gloss
Class I	bīd-an	báiþ	bid-um	bid-ans	'await'
Class II	-biud-an	-báuþ	-bud-um	-bud-ans	'bid'
Class III	bind-an	band	bund-um	bund-ans	'bind'
Class IV	nim-an	nam	**nēm-um**	num-ans	'take'
	baír-an	bar	**bēr-um**	baúr-ans	'bear'

In Proto-Indo-European the infinitive (and present indicative) forms of athematic verbs are typically in the *e*-grade. The forms in the "Infinitive" column in the table are historically derived from the combination of /e/ with various glides and consonants. Note that the phonological products in this column may not be directly recoverable from the original historical forms.

The preterite singular is derived from the Indo-European *perfect* forms. These forms are in the so-called *o*-grade in the singular, where it has been replaced by /a/, in the Germanic languages. The preterit plural forms in bold type are however derived from the Indo-European *aorist* plural (according to Lockwood 1969). Those not in bold type correspond to old perfect plural forms in the so-called *zero*-grade. Here neither /e/ nor /o/ is present. In Class III the original nasal was syllabic between consonants, and was replaced in Gothic by /un/.

The past participle represents the historical *zero*-grade right through. In terms of Proto-Germanic the vocalic alternations represented in this table come out as:

	Infinitive	Preterite Sg.	Preterite Pl.	Past Participle
Class I	īC	aiC	iC	iC
Class II	euC	auC	uC	uC
Class III	iNC	aNC	uNC	uNC
Class IV	eN	aN	ēN	uN

This has obvious reflexes in the Gothic system of alternations, but is more regular in terms of vocalic relationships.

But the original Proto-Indo-European system was different. Here the /ē/ of the Class IV plural is absent from the Proto-Indo-European perfect plural. The original reconstructed system is completely regular.

	Infinitive	Perfect Sg.	Perfect Pl.	Past Participle
Class I	eiC	oiC	iC	iC
Class II	euC	ouC	uC	uC
Class III	eNC	oNC	NC	NC
Class IV	eN	oN	ØN	ØN

In Old English however, we see a more "modern" development of the Proto-Germanic system than we saw in Gothic. Here much of the systematicity still observable in that language has been lost.

	Infinitive	Preterite Sg.	Preterite Pl.	Past Participle	Gloss
Class I	bīd-an	bād	bid-on	-bid-en	'await'
Class II	bēod-an	bēad	bud-on	-bod-en	'bid'
Class III	bind-an	band	bund-on	bund-en	'bind'
Class IV	nim-an	nōm	nōm-on	num-en	'take'
	ber-an	bær	bær-on	bor-en	'bear'

A mixture of regular sound change and analogical morphological replacements is on its way to destroying any systematic relations there might have been in the system, increasing the need for lexical specification/irregularity.

By the time we get to Modern English the classes have become totally irregular.

	Infinitive	Preterite	Past Participle	Gloss
Class I	drive	drove	driv-en	'drive'
Class II	forbid	forbad	forbidd-en	'bid'
Class III	bind	bound	bound(-en)	'bind'
Class IV	steal	stole	stol-en	'steal'
	break	broke	brok-en	'break'

The original regular system has now been irretrievably lost. The question now is whether the cost to pay for this irregularity is complexity such that modern English speakers will have more trouble learning and speaking English than their ancestors?

Semantic complexity of lexical items

Now we turn briefly to questions of semantic simplicity or complexity in terms of word-meaning. We repeat here our comment above:

> On the morphological level, simplicity is taken to mean that creole languages display a rather poor morphology whether inflectional or derivational and mainly resort to compounding [...]. The rationale here is that such a lack of morphology would favor a semantic transparency not found in other natural languages.

The connection assumed here between compounding and semantic transparency is in fact completely erroneous. A word formed by the morphological process of compounding does not have a meaning construable from the composition of the meanings of the words compounded. This is not a relevant description of typical compounding strategies in any language. In other words the assumption that compounding is form-driven is wrong. It is not the case that the primary operation is controlled by forms, and that the meanings accompany these in piggy-back fashion.

In fact the rules governing compounding are similar to those governing derivational morphology. A new word is created when a new concept is required to be articulated. The lexical item *comput-er* does not bear all the possible meanings of *compute + er*. It is not 'someone who counts', although there is nothing to prevent such a word from being created if there was a need for that concept in English. Nor does it even refer to all 'instruments that count'. An *adding machine* has a different meaning from *computer*. Similarly, the compound word *goal kick* only refers to a kick carried out by a goalkeeper into a football field. It does not bear other possible meanings resulting from the composition of the meanings of *goal* and *kick*. So the word cannot be used to describe a situation where a goalkeeper kicks his goal in frustration at allowing balls to slip past him. This is so, despite the fact that there is nothing about the word *goal kick* that inhibits this. So, derivation and compounding are both concept-led processes.

Because of this, derivations and compounds are inherently *irregular* in semantic terms! Compounding more so than derivation, because the nature of lexical meaning and the free nature of the compounding relationship, provides scope for a great variety of potential meanings, most of which are not utilized. So we can see that the meaning of *goal kick* is actually very irregular in that the majority of the potential meanings are not utilized, and therefore are not associated with the (new) lexical item.

Thus a new compound only enters a language when there is a need for it. Compounds in creole languages are just as irregular *from the very moment of their creation* as they are in any other language. They do not start out regular in semantic terms, and then wander off into syntactic disorder, as McWhorter suggests. No, they are irregular from their very beginnings. And inasmuch as compounding is a morphological process of word-formation more accessible to creoles than derivation, creoles are by this measure, *more* irregular/complex than other languages.

Complex lexica

Kusters (2008) finds difficulty in imagining how the lexical knowledge of all languages can be equated. He makes the comparison between languages with a large lexicon and those with a small one. To quote him (p. 11):

> For, example, knowing approximately 66,000 words, as Shakespeare had allegedly at his disposal (cf. Efron & Thisted 1976), would in some way have to be equally complex as knowledge of a very rudimentary lexicon restricted to, say, small-village pre-modern agrarian life. One might be inclined to argue that indeed these two kinds of knowledge are equally complex, because with both kinds of lexicons it is possible to *function* in certain niches in society. However, in that case we reach the bottom-line of argumentation, since this entails that all languages that exist must be equally complex just because they exist, and therefore "function". According to my definition of complexity, however, a large lexicon, ceteris pribus, is probably more complex than a smaller lexicon, since an outsider has less problems in acquiring and using a smaller lexicon, ...

Kusters is overlooking one very important fact here. At the same time as Shakespeare was writing his plays in English, with his 66,000-word lexicon, the vast majority of his fellow English-speakers were precisely the small-village pre-modern toilers on the soil that he refers to. The size of one's lexicon tells us nothing. Speakers vary enormously in the size of their active lexica. Some speakers have access to technical jargon, others do not; this has a purely social explanation. It is the social context then that determines the size of a speaker's lexicon, not the language one speaks. Unless, of course, Kusters wants to distinguish the Early Modern Standard English dialect used by Shakespeare as "complex", from the majority of local dialects of English, to be characterized as "very rudimentary" in terms of their lexica.

In fact, the size of one's lexicon tells us nothing about complexity. Considering the ease with which some languages borrow words from another – the current situation in Dutch with regard to English – should this be interpreted as increasing the complexity of Dutch? It seems unlikely. The number of vocabulary items in languages varies tremendously, but languages seem capable of expanding their lexica to cope with new circumstances very easily. This would seem to be a case where the vast storage-capacity of the brain makes any talk of simplicity or complexity nonsensical.

Phonological complexity

Let us now turn to a consideration of phonological complexity. Can we not refer to the one phonological system as being more complex than the other? Strictly speaking, yes. However, the complexity of inventories is by no means the only aspect of phonological complexity.

In fact, just as we can refer to above-word morphosyntax and below-word morphosyntax, we can also refer to below-segment phonology (a.k.a. segmental phonology) and above-segment phonology (a.k.a. suprasegmental phonology). The complexity of segments (as measured in possible combinations of features), or segmental structure, is not the only relevant consideration in phonology. There are various suprasegmental conditions influencing phonological complexity. For instance, Hawaiian has a very small inventory of consonants (10), in addition to its 5 vowels. Because of severe restrictions (simplicity) on syllable structure, the typical Hawaiian morpheme is two syllables in length. In other words the simple consonant system of the language, and its simple range of syllable types is compensated for by longer (more complex) typically bisyllabic morphemes.

There is less necessity for such "measures" in English or Dutch, where monosyllabic morphemes are vastly commoner because of the greater variety (complexity) of possible syllables. Another option is chosen in Mandarin Chinese where the possible syllables are simpler (fewer) in segmental type, but where the number of possible syllables is augmented by the additional (suprasegmental) dimension of tone. The occurrence of four tones in this form of Chinese multiplies (complicates) the number of possible syllables by four.

Some segments are complex by virtue of the fact that they are more difficult to articulate, or distinguish in perception. Such complex segments are also subject to roundabout-and-swing effects. They may only be present in the salient initial position of morphemes. Bisyllabic morphemes may have drastically reduced possibilities. In !Xóõ, a click language of Botswana, there are 122 possible initial consonants in words

(Traill 1985). The second onset consonant in a (non-compound) word is restricted to being one of only 6 simple (non-click) consonants. In other words, the largest number of phonemic distinctions is restricted to the most salient position, the beginning of the word, while succeeding consonants allow very few distinctions at all. Another case of roundabouts and swings.

In other words complexity in one department of phonology will be offset by simplicity in another. In one sense the situation as regards complexity and simplicity is more complicated than in morphosyntax, because of the greater variety of possible dimensions of complexity: number of syllables, syllable structure possibilities, segmental complexity, the occurrence of distinctions of tone, etc. Creole languages vary considerably in terms of all these aspects. So-called complex phonological structures of many types are to be found.

A few words on complexity/simplicity and language acquisition

An aspect of language that we haven't discussed thus far is that of language complexity/simplicity and its relation to language acquisition. If one takes the notions of complexity and simplicity as possible defining properties of language types, a simple question that arises is whether such notions correlate with ease or difficulty of language acquisition. Put another way, does the equation simple language = easy and fast acquisition hold? In the case of creoles, the prediction would be that creole children learn their language effortlessly and faster. In terms of Bickerton's Language Bioprogram Hypothesis (LBH), also adopted in Adone (1994) for instance, the rationale is the following: Given that creole languages reflect UG default settings, the hypotheses made by the creole L1 learners will match those provided by UG, and the children will face no contradictory input from the adult language. Accordingly, the creole child will always find her learning hypotheses positively confirmed by adult speakers. In older languages, however, things are less straightforward. These languages have drifted away from UG and do not always reflect its default settings. Accordingly, L1 learners of such languages may start with wrong hypotheses about their languages even though these hypotheses may be prompted by UG. Such wrong hypotheses will be source of errors and will require some effort from the L1 learner to fix the relevant parameter correctly. If we follow this rationale and accept that simplicity correlates with easy and fast acquisition, while complexity goes hand in hand with slow and difficult acquisition, we could expect creole children to achieve a very high level of proficiency (maybe adult-like) very early (e.g., by the age of four) compared to Dutch children who themselves should be ahead of Xhosa children who should in turn be ahead of Mohawk children.

In her work on the acquisition of Mauritian creole, Adone (1994), for instance, reports that children make no mistake in the acquisition of negation and correctly place the negative marker *pa* in preverbal position. Similarly, children correctly place the negative marker in contexts where the verb is preceded by TMA particles. On the basis of similar data, Adone (1994: 108) remarks that "the fact that there are no mistakes in the placement of negation in early Mauritian grammars [...] shows that as soon as I [i.e., INFL] has been developed, NEG is adjoined to I, as in adult grammar". What this means is that as soon as children acquire distinctions between contexts where the verb is finite and contexts where it is not, they also use negation correctly. Adone further concludes that her findings can be interpreted in terms of Bickerton's LBH, which assumes that creole languages are closer to UG and therefore display an overall simpler grammar than older languages (see previous discussion). Accordingly, Adone (1994: 111) concludes that "Mauritian creole has retained the typical creole negation pattern. Since this pattern is consistent with the Bioprogram, one would expect an effortless and early acquisition, which is exactly what happens."

As DeGraff (1995) demonstrates in his review, Adone's conclusions about the acquisition of MC and its implications for Bickerton's LBH are not without problems. The acquisition of negation in general appears to be one of the most studied phenomena in L1 acquisition. Meisel (1997) reports studies of the acquisition of negation in English, French, Spanish, Basque, German and English. It appears from these studies that the acquisition of negation proceeds rather smoothly and fast as soon as children acquire the structure of INFL and can decide whether NEG is a head or a phrase. As this author puts it

> one can, indeed, argue that, besides the fact that NEG may have to be cliticized to the finite verb, the syntax of negation merely consists in the implementation of NEG into the phrase structure. This explains why the acquisition of sentence negation happens *fast and virtually without errors in the languages studied so far, in spite of the fact that the surface properties of negative constructions in these languages differ significantly.* [the emphasis is ours] (p. 239)

Obviously, any metric of complexity that is designed to single out creole languages as involving overall simpler and young grammars reflecting bare properties of UG (e.g., Bickerton 1988; McWhorter 2001), will put Mauritian creole on a lower complexity scale than the languages reported in Meisel (1997): Spanish, French, Basque, English, and German. Yet, children acquiring these languages perform just as well as the Mauritian kids, not better, but crucially not worse. Putting Adone's findings together with Meisel's, what we may conclude is that the acquisition of INFL (that is, certain aspects of the clause structure) allows a fast and effortless acquisition of negation, though the latter may involve different categories (e.g., phrases, heads, clitics) and display different distribution cross-linguistically. In terms of the current discussion, this is strong evidence in favor of the hypothesis we put forward in this text that, unless we can evaluate its interaction with structure, an irregular or apparently complex *morphology* does not necessarily relate to a complex structure and therefore should not automatically count as index of complexity or computational complexity. We conclude that what matters most is the weight of presence or absence of morphology at the morphology-syntax interface.

Conclusion

The discussion in the preceding sections shows that the notion of complexity as conceived of in creole linguistics (and in typology) mainly centers on weighing outer manifestations of creoles against the so-called 'older languages'. While this exercise may prove to be useful in establishing the exact phenotypes of creoles in terms of their degrees of analyticity, agglutination or synthesis, the endeavor appears hopeless in evaluating the 'overall complexity' of creole grammars (or grammars *tout court*) because it fails to address the properties of the inner rules of these grammars and how these relate to the computational system that governs human language capacity. Put simply, issues of complexity should not be confused with surface patterns of grammars. Instead, they should be concerned with inner properties and how these properties (some of which have no clear overt manifestation) shed light on our cognitive systems.

With regard to overt manifestations so important to proponents of the equation "rich morphology = complex structure", it will become clear from the papers contained in this book that the creole languages identified here, though they cannot be equated with polysynthetic languages, do not display a simpler grammatical system than so-called old languages. In other words, creolization (i.e., the formation of a creole or new language) cannot be equated with simplification.

The chapters in the book

The book is organized into five thematic parts:

1. Morphophonology

This part includes three chapters that deal with vowel agglutination in Gulf creoles (Hagemeijer), morphological and phonological regularization in Saramaccan (Smith), and in Old Tibetan (Zeisler).

Hagemeijer discusses the Gulf of Guinea creoles (GGCs). These languages sometimes exhibit initial vowel agglutination to etymologically consonant-initial words in the lexifier, Portuguese. In comparing these agglutinated items in the four GGCs, the author analyses their diachronic development and shows the linguistic combinations that came out of the different linguistic patterns that were in contact. It is argued that prosthetic vowels are phonetically calqued on the Portuguese definite article system, which bleached and became generalized.

Smith, in his article approached the question of the morphological reanalysis that accompanied the incorporation of a large number of KiKoongo vocabulary items into Saramaccan. The point of discussion here is what happens when the emerging creole, possessing no noun-class system or number marking, had to absorb many words from KiKoongo where such a system was present. This chapter examines KiKoongo borrowings belonging to three classes: 3/4, 5/6, 7/8. It appears from the analysis that: (i) the slaves learned African languages (or words) from each other, (ii) such L2 acquisition makes it possible that a certain degree of morphological complexity was apparently retained in Saramaccan word classes, even though the prefixes had lost their (Kikongo) semantics.

Zeisler's chapter on Old Tibetan shows that this language displayed a high degree of complexity in its syllable structure (CCC)CV(CC) as well as a highly complex and irregular verb morphology. Yet, modern central Tibetan dialects have a remarkably simple syllable structure: CV(C). The irregularities observed in Old Tibetan with regard to the alternations of prefixes, consonants and vowels in verb stem formation were leveled out and replaced by regular systems of periphrastic constructions in the western and central varieties. Both developments can be described as processes of simplification that were triggered in a linguistic contact situation, where Old Tibetan served as a *lingua franca* for various non-Tibetan peoples. Yet, not all irregularities were wiped out by the contact situation. The question then is why this did not happen.

2. Verbal morphology

This part includes three chapters on INFL-related morphology in French-based creoles (Veenstra), Berbice Dutch (Kouwenberg) and a new variety of Solomon Islands Pijin (Jourdan).

Veenstra discusses long versus short verb form alternations in certain French-related creoles. The author argues that this alternation is a reflex of French inflectional morphology that has survived the creolization process. Comparing the creole data to varieties produced by French learners, the author concludes that the creole long versus short verb forms can be accounted for in terms of learner strategies in L2 acquisition of French. It is therefore proposed that the alternation started out as a phonological/prosodic phenomenon conditioned by the morphology-syntax interface.

Kouwenberg discusses the historical context in which Berbice Dutch was formed before turning to the significance of the presence in that language of function words derived from the Eastern Ijo substrate. Close inspection of the tense-mood-aspect and negation markers in Berbice Dutch reveals, important areas of divergence or discontinuity between the creole and its substrate languages. These discrepancies suggest that the creators of Berbice Dutch had reanalyzed certain substrate-derived functional material. This new finding runs counter to the view that Eastern Ijo speakers played a central role in the formation of Berbice Dutch. Accordingly, it is argued that another group, possibly the mixed progeny of the plantation population, which included Dutch, Eastern Ijo and Arawak speakers, could be the source of this reanalysis. While this chapter shows that L2 acquisition in this case involves Ijo as target and not just

Dutch, it also indicates that the routes to creolization are many and do not necessarily involve simplification as the result of dilution of the European target language.

Jourdan discusses a new development in Honiara, capital city of the Solomon Islands, where speakers of the local variety of Pijin make extensive usage of the transitive suffix *-em* (and its variants *-im* and *-um*) to transform prepositions into prepositional verbs. For instance, *daon* 'down' gives *daonem* 'to lower'; *ap* 'up' gives *apum* 'to raise'; *insaet* 'inside' gives *insaetim* 'to insert, to take inside'; *aot* 'out' gives *aotim* 'to remove', etc. In her account of this type of complexification, the author hypothesizes that the formation of prepositional verbs in Solomon Island Pijin (SIP) is best understood as an instance of paradigmatic regularization that is also present in other parts of the morphosyntax. She concludes that: (1) simplification and complexification are not the only types of linguistic changes affecting Pidgin and Creole languages; and (2) regularization is internally-induced and may not be linked to any external linguistic factor (e.g., substrate or superstrate effect).

3. Nominals

This part discusses the nominal morphosyntax of Mauritian creole (Guillemin) and Afrikaan (den Besten).

Guillemin's chapter deals with the development of determiners in Mauritian Creole (MC). As is generally the case in creoles, MC exhibits bare nouns in argument positions. These bare nouns can be interpreted as (in)definite, singular, plural or generic depending on context and the predicate they occur with. In addition, MC involves a determiner-like element (i.e., *la*) which encodes specificity. It is argued in this chapter that bare nouns in MC are comparable to English bare plurals: they are argumental kind-denoting terms that do not require a determiner in argument positions. Accordingly, the singular indefinite article *enn* and the plural marker *bann* serve to derive instances of kinds. The differential behaviour of MC count and mass nouns is attributed to the feature of number, which must be checked for count nouns. What emerges from this study is that while MC creole involves a system of bare nouns which does not require overt expression of definiteness, the language has also developed a series of nominal markers that are more specialized than determiners in French (e.g., *le/la*).

Den Besten discusses the development of demonstratives in Afrikaans. It is shown that this language did not retain the Dutch independent demonstrative *dat* 'that', the pronoun *het* 'it', and the attributive element *deze* 'this, these'. On the other hand, the independent *dit* 'this' was kept and appears to have taken over the functions of *dat* and *het*. Similarly, attributive *die* 'that, those' took on a proximate reading (Afr. *dié week* 'this week'). The author further argues that, as the weak pronoun *het* eventually disappeared, *dat* and *dit* could not be functionally distinguished any longer. It is proposed that these changes in the system of attributive demonstratives are due to developments in Cape Dutch Pidgin.

4. The selection of features in complex morphology

The chapters in this section are concerned with the issue of what feature may be retained in a situation of language contact and how. The discussion includes phonological and structural restructuring in Mindanao Chabacano (Grant), the morphosyntax of negation in Sri Lanka Malay (Slomanson) and the emergence of a new case system in this language (Ansaldo).

Grant's chapter examines several instances of phonological and structural complexification in Mindanao Chabacano, a predominantly Spanish-lexifier creole of southwestern Mindanao, which have arisen as the result of the interaction of elements of Philippine languages (especially Tagalog and the Bisayan languages), Spanish and English.

Slomanson's chapter deals with negation in Sri Lanka Malay (SLM) and shows that this language converged typologically on the grammar with Sri Lankan Muslim Tamil and to some extent of Sinhala. SLM involves syntactic patterns from two typologically distinct sources. For instance, SLM negation exhibits greater inflectional complexity than its lexifier by encoding finiteness and tense features. Contrary to other Sri Lankan languages, SLM has also developed a strict morphological contrast between all non-finite negation contexts (infinitives, participles, and imperatives), and finite negation contexts (tensed verbs).

Ansaldo analyses the evolution of case markers in a variety of Sri Lanka Malay. The data discussed are particularly interesting as they could be seen as 'complex', 'marked' or at least 'unexpected' instances of contact-induced change. According to the evolutionary framework adopted in this chapter, it is proposed that these developments are natural acts of linguistic replication in multilingual settings. It is further concluded that overall structural complexity, however defined, does not change as a result of contact language formation: a new grammar is simply the result of a recombination of grammatical features of the input languages.

5. Evaluating simplification and complexification

This part includes three chapters which evaluate (though differently) the concept of simplification or complexification in the study of language. The discussion is based on Cape Verdean Creole and Guinea-Bissau Creole (Baptista), the Suriname creoles (Aboh), and Sri Lanka Malay (Ansaldo and Nordhoff).

Baptista explores the idea that in contact situations, there exists a process whereby what would appear to be an instance of morpho-syntactic simplification is correlated to semantic complexification. In examining this process in the verbal and nominal domains, the author shows that a given morpheme in Cape Verdean Creole (CVC) and Guinea-Bissau Creole (GBC) may carry a cluster of semantic feature values where the European lexifier only has one. In order to measure degrees of simplification versus complexification, the author adopts Kusters' (2003) complexity evaluation metrics of inflectional morphology. This chapter further investigates to what extent two sister creoles (i.e., CVC, GBC) may display distinct morphological properties.

Aboh's chapter also deals with the issue of simplicity. This author demonstrates that the notion of *simplicity* as often used in creole studies is irrelevant to the understanding of the structure, as well as the genesis, of creole languages. This is because creole languages are linguistic hybrids in the biological sense. They emerge from the recombination of linguistic features from different languages. Given this perspective, it appears that what could be of some relevance to the study of language change is rather the notion of complexity. Adopting Mufwene's framework of Competition and Selection, this chapter shows that creole languages develop opaque syntactic and semantic features, which could not have arisen only in the context of their source languages. The author therefore concludes that the common claim that creoles are simplified versions of their sources is a fallacy, just as it would be to claim in biology that hybrids are genetically simplified children of their parents.

Ansaldo and Nordhoff discuss the issue of complexity in language creation and the time it takes for 'complex' structures to emerge in the history of a language. The presence of morphological material is often equated to a certain degree of complexity or is taken to signify a certain time-depth in the history of a language. Though this assumption appears misleading in the absence of a theoretically-based definition of complexity, the authors decided to put it to a test by looking at morphological development in a relatively 'young' language: Sri Lanka Malay (SLM). SLM is a mixed language which shows considerably rich morphology and displays other signs which are commonly attributed to old languages rather than young languages such as creoles. Based on these observations, the authors propose that (a) the structural output in language genesis is partially determined by the typology of the input languages, and (b) our understanding of the rate of change needs to be revised to take into account ecological matters.

6. Postscript

Given the importance of the issue of simplicity and complexity in creolistics, the editors of this volume decided to invite **Salikoko Mufwene** to write a postscript. We are grateful that he accepted the invitation to contribute to the volume. In his overview, Mufwene addresses aspects of the chapters in the book and puts them into a challenging perspective so as to address the bigger picture of language change, language contact and language evolution that is, the ecology of language change and its theoretical implications for creolistics. In this regard, Mufwene raises important questions such as the notion of "complexity" and its relations to exceptionalist views on creolization and creole typology. In this context, he addresses the question of whether creoles form a uniform type that can be evaluated in terms of simplicity vs. complexity, and whether, as some creolists claim, there could be a set of "creole features", which would distinguish them typologically from other languages whose origins are assumed not to be contact-based. This raises the related question of whether there exists a human language that could be claimed to have developed in a 'contact-free' context. Other issues that Mufwene discusses have to do with the recombination of linguistic features, i.e., "hybridization" in a situation of language contact, and how this relates to the emergence of new varieties. As he concludes:

> The evolution of the structures of creoles and other so-called "contact language varieties" is far from reflecting a simple, straightforward, and (uni-)linear trajectory. As new studies such as in this volume contribute more facts about the sociohistorical ecologies of the emergence of some of these vernaculars in the Caribbean, the Indian Ocean, and elsewhere [....], the complexity of the evolutionary scenarios increases more obviously, although it remains difficult to interpret unequivocally. There is no single local or regional history for which the informed reader could not think of alternative interpretations of the same facts. This simply means that an honest debate must go on that may shed better light on the significance of various ecological factors.

References

Aboh, Enoch O. 2004. *The Morphosyntax of Complement-head Sequences: Clause Structure and Word Order Patterns in Kwa*. Oxford: OUP.
Aboh, Enoch O. 2006. Complementation in Saramaccan and Gungbe: The case of c-type modal particles. *Natural Language and Linguistic Theory* 24(1): 1–55.
Aboh, Enoch O. 2007. La genèse de la périphérie gauche du saramaka: Un cas d'influence du substrat? In *Grammaires Créoles et Grammaire Comparative*, Karl Gadelii & Anne Zribi-Hertz (eds), 73–97. Saint-Denis: Presses Universitaires de Paris.
Adone, Dany. 1994. *The Acquisition of Mauritian Creole* [Language Acquisition & Langauge Disorders 9]. Amsterdam: John Benjamins.
Bickerton, Derek. 1981. *Roots of Language*. Ann Arbor MI: Karoma.
Bickerton, Derek. 1988. Creole languages and the Bioprogram. In *Linguistic Theory: Extensions and Implications. Linguistics: The Cambridge Survey* 2, Frederick Newmeyer (ed.), 268–284. Cambridge: CUP.
Byrne, Francis. 1987. *Grammatical Relations in a Radical Creole. Verb Complementation in Saramaccan* [Creole Language Library 3]. Amsterdam: John Benjamins.
Byrne, Francis & Caskey, Alexander F. 1993. Focus emphasis and pronominals in Saramaccan. In *Focus and Grammatical Relations in Creole Languages* [Creole Language Library 12], Francis Byrne & Donald Winford (eds), 213–230. Amsterdam: John Benjamins.
Chierchia, Gennaro. 1998. Reference to kinds across languages. *Natural Language Semantics* 6: 339–405.
Chomsky, Noam. 1995. *The Minimalist Program*. Cambridge MA: The MIT Press.
DeGraff, Michel. 1995. Kids, Creoles, and UG. Review of The Acquisition of Mauritian Creole by Dany Adone. *Glot International* 1(3): 18–20.
Efron, Bradley & Thisted, Ronald. 1976. Estimating the number of unknown species: How many words did Shakespeare know? *Biometrika* 63(3): 435–437.

Fortescue, Michael D. 1984. *West Greenlandic*. Beckenham: Croom Helm.
Gil, David. 2008. How complex are isolating languages? In *Language Complexity: Typology, Contact, Change*, Matti Miestamo, Kaius Sinnemäki & Fred Karlsson (eds), 109–131. Amsterdam: John Benjamins.
Hall, Robert, A. Jr. 1962. The life cycle of pidgin languages. *Lingua* 11: 151–156.
Kiparsky, Paul. 2003. The Germanic weak preterite. (Draft submitted to Wurzel memorial volume).
Kusters, Wouter. 2008. Complexity in linguistic theory, language learning and language change. In *Language Complexity: Typology, Contact, Change*, Matti Miestamo, Kaius Sinnemäki & Fred Karlsson (eds), 3–22. Amsterdam: John Benjamins.
Lockwood, William Burley. 1969. *Indo-European Philology*. London: Hutchinson University Library.
Longobardi, Giusepe. 1994. Reference and proper names: A theory of N-movement in syntax and logical form. *Linguistic Inquiry* 25: 609–665.
Marantz, Alec. 2000. Case and licensing. In *Arguments and Case*: *Explaining Burzio's. Generalization* [Linguistik Aktuell/Linguistics Today 34], Eric Reuland (ed.), 11–30. Amsterdam: John Benjamins.
McWhorter, John. 2001. The world's simplest grammars are creole grammars. *Linguistic Typology* 5: 125–165.
McWhorter, John. 2005. *Defining Creole*. Oxford: OUP.
Miestamo, Matti, Kaius Sinnemäki & Fred Karlsson (eds). 2008. *Language Complexity: Typology, Contact, Change* [Studies in Language Companion Series 94]. Amsterdam: John Benjamins.
Meisel, Jürgen, M. 1997. The acquisition of the syntax of negation in French and German: Contrasting first and second language development. *Second Language Research* 13: 227–263.
Muysken, Pieter. 1988. Are creoles a special type of language? In *Linguistics*: *The Cambridge Survey*, Vol. 2: *Linguistic Theory: Extensions and Implications*, 285–301. Cambridge: CUP.
Saussure, Ferdinand de. 1916. *Cours de linguistique générale*, Charles Bally & Albert Sechehaye (eds). Lausanne & Paris: Payot (Translated by Wade Baskin as *Course in General Linguistics*. Glasgow: Fontana/Collins, 1977).
Selkirk, Elisabeth. 1986. On derived domains in sentence phonology. *Phonology* 3: 371–405.
Siewierska, Anna. 1998. Variation in major constituent order: A global and a European perspective. In *Constituent Order in the Languages of Europe, Empirical Approaches to Language Typology* [Eurotyp 20-1], Anna Siewierska (ed.), 475–551. Berlin: Mouton de Gruyter.
Sinnemäki, Kaius. 2008. Complexity trade-offs in core argument marking. In *Language Complexity: Typology, Contact, Change*, Matti Miestamo, Kaius Sinnemäki & Fred Karlsson (eds), 67–88. Amsterdam: John Benjamins.
Smith, Norval. 1996. Wɛ-focus in Saramaccan: Substrate feature or grammaticalization? In *Changing Meanings, Changing Functions. Papers Relating to Grammaticalization in Contact Languages* [Westminster Creolistics Series], Philip Baker & Anand Syea (eds), 113–128. Westminster: University of Westminster Press.
Traill, Anthony. 1985. *Phonetic and Phonological Studies of !Xóõ Bushman*. Hamburg: Helmut Buske.
Vergnaud, Jean-Roger. 1977. Letter to Noam Chomsky and Howard Lasnik. In *Foundational Issues in Linguistic Theory: Essays in Honor of Jean-Roger Vergnaud*, Robert Freidin, Carlos P. Otero & Maria Luisa Zubizarreta (eds), 3–15. Cambridge MA: The MIT Press.

PART I

Morphophonology

Initial vowel agglutination in the Gulf of Guinea creoles*

Tjerk Hagemeijer

The Gulf of Guinea creoles (GGCs) exhibit a number of cases of initial vowel agglutination to etymologically consonant-initial words in the lexifier, Portuguese. This property is especially common in Lung'ie (Principense). Comparing agglutinated items in the four GGCs not only sheds light on their diachronic development, it also shows the linguistic compromise made between the different strata that gave rise to this feature. It will be argued that prosthetic vowels are phonetically calqued on the Portuguese definite article system, which bleached and became generalized as something else than a gender/number system, whereas the African contribution consists of creating vowel-initial items that are guided by rules of vowel harmony.

1. Introduction

Reinterpretation of morpheme boundaries is a well-attested phenomenon in contact linguistics and language-internal diachronic change. Examples of agglutination have been noted in a wide array of creole languages (e.g. Holm 1988:97; Parkvall 2000:81–83) and especially in French-based creoles (e.g. Baker 1984; Grant 1995). This paper focuses on the Gulf of Guinea creoles (GGCs), where a number of etymologically consonant-initial words in the lexifier language, Portuguese, exhibit an

---

* I am truly grateful to Norval Smith for comments on draft versions of this paper. I would also like to thank the audience of the ACBPLE 2005 Orléans meeting, where I first presented this paper, especially Thomas Klein. I want to express especial gratitude to Philippe Maurer and Armando Zamora for comments and for letting me have access to their unpublished work on Lung'ie and Fa d'Ambô, respectively. Finally, a word of thanks to Marike Post and Ota Ogie for helping me out with the Fa d'Ambô and Èdó data, respectively. After sending a final draft version to the editors, it came to my knowledge that John Ladhams was awaiting the publication of a paper called "Article Agglutination and the African Contribution to the Portuguese-based Creoles" (see references), which deals with the same topic but in a distinct fashion.

agglutinated vowel lacking a morphological function. This property is particularly common in Lung'ie (Principense Creole). My aim is to answer the following interrelated questions:

i. Is there evidence for diachronic layering of agglutination in the GGCs?
ii. What are the principles that underlie agglutination in the GGCs?
iii. What are the origins of agglutination in the GGCs?

In a nutshell, the four GGCs are the 16th century offspring of a proto-GGC (e.g. Ferraz 1979; Hagemeijer 1999; Schang 2000; Hagemeijer & Parkvall 2001), a contact variety spoken on the island of São Tomé that resulted from contact between Portuguese and African languages, in particular from the Niger Delta and the Congo/Angola area. The proto-GGC evolved into what is presently Santome (São-Tomense). Lung'ie is the historical result of a variety or varieties of the proto-GGC whose speakers settled on the island of Príncipe, located to the north of São Tomé. The settling of creole speakers from São Tomé on the island of Annobón, located to the south of São Tomé, created an isolated variety now known as Fa d'Ambô (Annobonese). Finally, Ngola (Angolar), spoken on S. Tomé, is arguably the historical outcome of a society of runaway slaves (Lorenzino 1998).

This paper has the following outline. Section 2 discusses the agglutination data in Appendix 1. In Section 3 I will provide an overview of how agglutination in the GGCs has been treated in previous literature. Section 4 considers the role of the Portuguese article system with respect to prosthesis. Section 5 is concerned with vowel assimilation and harmony processes that play a role in agglutination. In Section 6 I will address the putative role of the different strata that contributed to the formation of the GGCs with regard to the topic under consideration.

2. Overview of the data

A full list of agglutinated items in the GGCs and the sources they were drawn from can be found in Appendix 1, which shows that agglutination is an outstanding feature of Lung'ie. Note that this does not pretend to be an exhaustive list of items.

Since diffusion of the GGCs took place from the proto-GGC that evolved into Santome, I will first consider to what extent the agglutinations found in this language are also found in the other GGCs. The results are listed in Table 1.[1]

First, it can be observed that in most cases agglutinated items in Santome have a corresponding form in Lung'ie and to a certain extent in Fa d'Ambô and Angolar as well. It should be noted that some items in Ngola, such as *mionga* and *nvumbu*, have a Bantu origin, which is expected in the particular scenario of relexification proposed

---

1. Note that for writing purposes closed mid-vowels are written *ê* and *ô* and open mid-vowels *e* and *o*.

Table 1. Instances of agglutination in Santome with matches in the other GGCs[2]

Santome	Lung'ie	Fa d'Ambô	Ngola	Portuguese etymology	Meaning
afe	afe	fe	fe	*fé (fem.)*	'faith'
apa	apa		anpa	*pá (fem.)*	'spade, shovel'
ase	(gêêza)-ase	[gɛ̃za]	[ngeedha]	*sé (fem.)*	'cathedral'
aglasa	nomi	galasa, nomi	nomi	*graça (fem.)*	'name'
ope	ope	ope	ope	*pé (masc.)*	'foot, leg'
opo	opo	opo	ompo	*pó (masc.)*	'dust'
ose	ose	ôsê	onthe	*céu (masc.)*	'sky, heaven'
ono	ono	ono		*nó (masc.)*	'knot'
odo	odo		odo~oro	*dó (masc.)*	'mourning'
ôlhô*	ôryô	[lubela]	[awa]	*rio (masc.)*	'river'
oali	uari	[oventu]	[ventu]	*ar (masc.)*	'air'
omali	umwe(n)	omal	[mionga]	*mar (masc.)*	'sea'
uku	uku		[ndagu]	*cu (masc.)*	'arse'
unu	*unu*	[*dodyi*]		*nu (masc.)*	'naked'

* This item occurs in Negreiros (1895) but is absent in contemporary speech.

by Lorenzino (1998). The open cells in Table 1 simply reflect the lack of available data. Except for *aglasa* 'name', it follows that these shared items involve essentially etymologically monosyllabic words with an agglutinated [a], [ɔ], [o], or [u]. It can be concluded that these forms reflect an early diachronic stage and were lexicalized in the proto-GGC, prior to the spatio-temporal diffusion into four different creoles sketched in Section 1.

Fa d'Ambô, on the other hand, exhibits several cases of agglutination that are shared with Lung'ie but are not found in Santome nor Ngola, as illustrated in Table 2.

The main difference is that in these cases Lung'ie exhibits almost exclusively prosthetic [u] and Fa d'Ambô typically an agglutinated [o] or [ɔ]. It follows from Table 2 that at this point agglutination is no longer restricted to items whose etymology is monosyllabic. This raises the question as to why these agglutinated forms are not found in Santome as well, under the assumption that they spread from the proto-GGC, especially given the lack of historical evidence for direct contact between Lung'ie and Fa d'Ambô. I will return to this issue in Section 6.3.

---

2. I did not include the item *arê~alê* 'king', which is common to the four GGCs, because it is presumably derived from Old Portuguese expression *el-rei* 'the king' rather than form *rei*.

Table 2. Instances of agglutination common to Lung'ie and Fa d'Ambô

Fa d'Ambô	Lung'ie	Santome	Ngola	Portuguese etymology	Meaning
ôzôyô	ôzê (n)~ôzên~uzên	zê	[m'puna~puna]	*joelho*	'knee'
onfenu	unfenu	nfenu	nfenu	*inferno*	'hell'
ôlatu	uratu	latu	latu	*rato*	'rat, mouse'
olemu	uremu	lemu	lemu~lêmu	*remo*	'oar'
oventu	uventu	ventu	ventu	*vento*	'wind'
onfelu	ufew	felu	felu~fêlu	*ferro*	'iron'
ampan	umpan	mpon	pon	*pão*	'bread'
ônũa, ônũya	unwan	nw̃a	[mbêi~mbêzi~mêzi]	*lua*	'moon'
ôman	uman	mon	mo~mon	*mão*	'hand, lower arm'
ôpa	upa	po	po	*pau*	'stick, tree'
ôbôyô	ubwê	bwê	buê	*bói*	'cow'

The numerous remaining cases involving agglutination listed in Appendix 1, i.e. the cases not listed in Tables 1 and 2, are exclusive to Lung'ie, encompassing [u] and [i]-agglutination. Note that the latter type is not attested in any other GGC.

In sum, in the light of the data above, initial vowel agglutination first affected items with a monosyllabic etymology but spread to items with a disyllabic etymology. It is therefore suggestive that in the case of *omali* 'sea' (from Ptg. *mar*) and *oali* 'air' (from Ptg. *ar*) agglutination preceded resyllabification: *mar* > **omar* >* *omari* > *omali*.

3. Previous literature on agglutination in the GGCs

Several scholars mention or seek to explain the existence of agglutination (Barrena 1957; Ferraz 1979, 1984; De Granda 1986; Parkvall 2000; Schang 2000).

In his work on Santome, Ferraz states that Portuguese monosyllabic nouns are sometimes integrated in the creole by agglutination of a non-nasal vowel, which he suggests is derived from the Portuguese definite article. He further suggests some sort of relation between the agglutinated forms and massive imports of Bantu-speaking slaves, but does not elaborate on this.

In a similar vein, De Granda (1986: 118) argues that prosthetic vowels in Fa d'Ambô are formally identifiable with the Portuguese singular definite *o* for masculine and *a* for feminine (cf. Section 4). However, the two cases of [a]-agglutination listed by the author are attached to two items with a masculine etymology, *ampan* 'bread' (from *(o) pão*) and *alê* 'king' (from *el-rei*, see Note 2). De Granda provides a number of examples of etymologically monosyllabic items that exhibit agglutination and argues that the purpose of this process is to produce dissyllabic items. However, this claim cannot be upheld given the number of agglutinations to items in Fa d'Ambô (v. Appendix 1) whose etymology is dissyllabic.

Parkvall (2000) introduces a different approach to agglutination by suggesting that the Edoid cluster is a putative substratum, since nouns are obligatorily vowel-initial[3] and Edoid influence on the GGCs is well attested. Following Ferraz' (1979) claim that all verbs are consonant-initial in Santome, Parkvall sees in this a further link with the equally consonant-initial nature of verbs in this cluster.

Schang (2000) provides the most exhaustive discussion so far on prosthetic vowels in the GGCs, adopting the Bantu perspective summarily proposed in Ferraz. First, he considers that the influence from Bantu noun classifiers cannot be responsible for [i] and [u]-agglutination because a semantic overlap with the respective noun classes cannot be recovered.[4] Instead, the hypothesis to explain [u]-agglutination in Lung'ie is based on the assumption that Portuguese lexicon massively relexifies Kimbundu lexicon, and that therefore Portuguese vocabulary was arguably incorporated into noun class 9 (loanwords) and additionally prefixed with Kimbundu's definite article [o]. Schang further suggests that the similarities between Portuguese definite article [u] and Kimbundu [o] may have conflated into the pattern observed in Lung'ie. As a piece of supporting evidence for the relevance of the Bantu substrate, he argues that [i] and [u]-agglutination resemble [o], [ɔ] and [i]-prefixation of Portuguese lexicon produced by Angolan Tonga's,[5] who are essentially the descendants of contract labourers that arrived during the coffee and cacao boom in the 19th and 20th century, and in that sense unrelated to the creolization process that took place in the 16th century.

There are, however, several arguments that cast serious doubts on the alleged influence of Bantu on prosthesis. Foremost, it is relatively uncontroversial that Lung'ie exhibits a number of properties that clearly reflect a stronger impact from a Niger delta substrate than the other GGCs (Section 6.3). And since these creoles exhibit a stronger Bantu impact, especially at the level of lexicon and phonology, one would expect more pervasive agglutination under the Bantu hypothesis. Ngola, in particular, exhibits an exceptionally high percentage of Kimbundu items (Maurer 1992, 1995;

---

3. In this respect, note that Portuguese (or English) loanwords are/were integrated in Edo with an initial vowel (a, e, ɛ, i) in order to comply with the rule that all nouns should be vowel initial. All the oral vowels in Edo may serve as prefixes and their choice is generally not predictable (Agheyisi 1990: 32). A few examples of Portuguese nouns in Edo are: *efɛ̄rhinyɛ* 'a dish from unsifted cassava' (Ptg. farinha), *ekuyɛ* 'spoon' (Ptg. colher), *esara* 'saw' (Ptg. serra), *etuheru* 'scissors' (Ptg. tesoura), *ɛpipa* 'keg, barrel' (Ptg. pipa), *ibata* 'shoe, boot' (Ptg. bota), *isāhɛ̄* 'key' (Ptg. chave) and *itaba* 'tobacco' (Ptg. tabaco) (Melzian 1937).

4. Although agglutination in the GGCs is not restricted to specific semantic classes, it should be noted that some semantic fields are overrepresented, which is especially the case for body-related items and mass nouns. The latter type, for instance, is clearly overrepresented in the small group of [i]-agglutination.

5. On Tonga Portuguese, see Rougé (1992) and Baxter (2004).

Lorenzino 1998), but yet shows the lowest degree of agglutination.[6] The lack of correlation between agglutination and a Bantu substrate is underscored by cross-linguistic evidence. Colombian Palenquero creole, for example, is heavily influenced by a Kikongo substrate (e.g. Schwegler 2006) but exhibits no agglutination of the type under discussion (Schwegler, p.c.).[7]

Furthermore, the morpho-syntax of the GGCs shows a greater deal of similarities with its Nigerian substrate than with its Bantu substrate (Hagemeijer 1999; Hagemeijer & Parkvall 2001; Hagemeijer & Ogie in prep.). The claim that Portuguese lexicon massively replaced Kimbundu lexicon in SLA is also unwarranted because the evidence suggests that Kimbundu played essentially an adstratal role at a stage when the creole(s) had already started crystallizing. The fact that the Tonga Portuguese samples do suggest some morpho-semantic transfer of a Bantu noun class system therefore sharply contrasts with the findings for Lung'ie, where this relation cannot be established.

Finally, if conflation of Bantu [o] and Portuguese [u], which both have a semantic function (definiteness), were responsible for the agglutinated forms, one would actually expect the agglutinated items to exhibit a semantic function as well, contrary to fact.

In sum, contrary to previous claims, the available evidence does not support a decisive role of Bantu in the agglutination patterns found in the GGCs in general and in Lung'ie in particular. On the other hand, the highlighted importance of Portuguese gender for the agglutinated forms appears to be motivated and will be addressed in the next section.

4. (Mis)calquing on gender and number

In other creoles, especially French-based creoles, cases of agglutination typically involve the lexifier's determiner. In Portuguese, the lexifier language of the GGCs, definite articles bear gender and number features, as shown in Table 3.

Under the hypothesis that [o], [ɔ] and [u]-agglutination are potentially related to instances of Portuguese singular masculine *o*, and [a] to instances of Portuguese singular feminine *a*, it follows that agglutinations in the oldest diachronic layer, which corresponds to the items listed in Table 1, are, without exception, correctly calqued on the superstrate's gender distinction.

In the diachronic stage where similar agglutinations are found in Lung'ie and Fa d'Ambô (see Table 2), but crucially not in Santome and Ngola, several gender

---

[6]. Note, however, that Maurer (1995:26) proposes that nasal sonorants in Angolar can be interpreted as class-prefixes.

[7]. Norval Smith [p.c.] brings to my attention that Palenquero does exhibit a single case of functional nominal prefixation directly reflecting the Bantu class prefix *ma-*.

Table 3. Number and gender marking in Portuguese

	Masculine	Feminine
Singular	o [u]	a [ɐ]
Plural	os [uʃ]	as [ɐʃ]

Table 4. The role of Portuguese number-marking in agglutination

Form	Portuguese etymology	Meaning
zonda (LU)	*as ondas*	wave(s)
Zawa (ST)	*as águas*	urine (lit. the waters)
zalima (LU, ST), *zalma* (FA)	*as almas*	souls

mismatches can be found, namely *unwan/ônũa* 'moon' (Ptg. *a lua*) and *uman/ôman* 'hand, lower arm' (Ptg. *a mão*) and *ampan* 'bread' (Ptg. *o pão*). These mismatches are also attested in agglutinated items that are exclusive to Lung'ie (see Appendix 1), for instance *ubuka* 'mouth' (Ptg. *a boca*), *ufaka* 'knife (Ptg. *a faca*) and *usuva* 'rain' (Ptg. *a chuva*). Furthermore, the [i]-agglutination patterns exclusive to Lung'ie are unrelated to Portuguese gender distinctions.

Calquing on Portuguese is not limited to the relation between the agglutinated vowel and Portuguese gender, but also applies to agglutination of Portuguese plural forms. This follows from the few cases where creole items reanalyzed a Portuguese plural article. These forms are listed here in Table 4.

In these cases, unvoiced fricative [ʃ] in the Portuguese plural article *as* becomes voiced [z] in intervocalic environments, namely *as ondas* [ɐzɔ̃dɐʃ] 'the waves', *as águas* [ɐzagwɐʃ] and *as almas* [ɐzalmaʃ]. This pattern was transferred into the GGCs. In his manuscript on Fa d'Ambô, Zamora (MS) brings to attention crucial data showing that in this creole number plays a role not attested in the other GGCs. Some examples are:

(1) a. *úbêlê d'öbóyo*   udder of a cow (lit. udder of-cow)
    b. *zúbêlê d'öbóyo* udders of a cow
(2) a. *opè bálba*   hair of the beard (lit. foot beard)
    b. *zópi bálba*   hairs of the beard (lit. foot beard)

Zamora's phonological explanation for these cases is identical to the explanation above. Since the pluralizing *z* is etymologically related to Portuguese,[8] it raises the question whether a pluralizing rule existed in the proto-GGC or whether this is a local innovation. I will leave this issue for further research.

The general conclusion of this section is therefore that, except for [i]-agglutination in Lung'ie, prosthetic vowels in the GGCs started out as an etymological reflex of

---

8. An etymological link to the Spanish definite article system (*lo(s)*, *la(s)*) is unlikely, since we would expect preservation of the initial *l*.

the Portuguese article system, which became semantically bleached and generalized as something else than a gender/number system. The gender mismatches that start to show after the oldest diachronic stage support that the Portuguese masculine article became generalized, whereas the use of the agglutinating feminine article (*a*) was abandoned. Less access of these two creoles to Portuguese after diffusion and isolation may have accelerated the loss of the gender-calquing rule.[9] In the next section I will argue that, in addition to the morphological relation with Portuguese outlined in this section, agglutination in the GGCs is also phonologically conditioned.

5. Harmony processes in the GGCs

The GGCs exhibit seven oral vowels,[10] as illustrated in Table 5.

Assimilation in the vowel and consonant system of Santome was first reported by Ferraz (1979), who claimed that "[v]owel harmony is a consistent feature of ST phonology." Some of Ferraz's examples of Santome are:

(i) Vowel Harmony spreading from a tonic vowel (Ferraz 1979):

		Portuguese		Santome	
(3)	Progressive:	pɔ́rtɐ	→	pɔ́tɔ	'door'
		fógu	→	fógo	'fire'
(4)	Regressive:	ʀalɔ́ʒyu	→	lɔlɔ́zu	'watch'
		dəgrédu	→	dlɛgédu	'exile'

(ii) Vowel Harmony in clitic groups (Hagemeijer 2005: 87):

(5) a. gɔlɔ e (search + 3SG) → [gɔlɔɛ] 'search it'
    b. volo e (get angry + 3SG) → [voloe] 'get angry at him/her'

Table 5. Oral vowel inventory of the GGCs

	Front			Central	Back		
	High	Close-Mid	Open-Mid	Low	High	Close-Mid	Open-Mid
Oral	i	e	ɛ	a	u	o	ɔ

---

9. Although the historiography of the island of Annobón is still incomplete in many respects, old documents suggest that the island was settled by slaves from São Tomé, with very limited European presence (e.g. Caldeira 2005).

10. For the status of nasal vowels, I refer the reader to Günther (1973: 36–37), Ferraz (1979: 20) and Maurer (1995: 23).

Note that the type of VH in (5) is restricted to 3sg object pronouns. Ferraz (1979: 25) describes vowel harmony (VH) in Santome as "a tendency for the same vowel to occur in two consecutive syllables within a morpheme" and provides examples for each of the vowels in Table 5 above. In fact, this tendency exists and can be seen in, for instance, cases of epenthesis (e.g. Ptg. *largo* 'wide' > Santome *lalugu* 'wide'). However, these cases should rather be described as instances of vowel assimilation. VH in the GGC is a more restricted phenomenon that occurs in the mid-vowel domain, as follows from Table 6.

Table 6. Dissyllabic words in Santome

V_1 \ V_2	i	u	e	ɛ	o	ɔ	a
i	ligi	migu	izê	mile	libô	jinklo	mina
u	buli	mulu	ubwê	kume	–	–	uswa
e	sêji	dêsu	vêndê	–	–	–	zêma
ɛ	peli	petu	–	vede	–	tebo	bega
o	sôtxi	wôdu	ômê	–	pôvô	–	lôpa
ɔ	doxi	mosu	–	love	–	kodo	bola
a	mali	matu	padê	manse	kasô	avo	faka

Although VH is still an understudied area in the phonology of the GGCs, Table 6 shows that the low and high vowels in general do not impose any co-occurrence restrictions on neighbouring vowels.[11] This, however, stands in sharp contrast with the co-occurrence restrictions on mid-vowels. Very clearly, Santome exhibits a solid rule of mid-vowel stem harmony in at least disyllabic words, meaning that open-mid vowels and close-mid vowels never co-occur in these cases.[12] Upon inspection of the available literature, I found this rule to apply to Ngola and Lung'ie as well. It is therefore expected to apply to Fa d'Ambô as well, although this distinction cannot be determined from the orthographies used in the available literature (e.g. Barrena 1957; Post 1995).

The tendency toward assimilation, especially in the vocalic domain, raises the question as to whether agglutinated vowels are also subject to constraints imposed on the vowel quality and/or other phonological constraints. It can readily be shown that this is indeed the case.

The first observation is that, in agreement with Table 6, mid-vowel stem harmony is always obeyed in the GGCs. If we follow the hypothesis of diachronic layers with respect to agglutination, the following can be observed (✓ in the table means attested and is followed by an example).

---

11. I did not find any data for a high round vowel in the first syllable and a high-mid or low-mid round vowel in the second syllable, which may indicate a rule of vowel elevation.

12. This situation is also attested in Saramaccan (Norval Smith, p.c.).

Table 7. Agglutination in the oldest diachronic layer (according to the data in Table 1)

V V_aggl.	a	ɛ	e	ɔ	o	i	u
a	✓ (apa)	✓ (afe)	–	–	–	–	–
ɔ	✓ (omali)	✓ (ope)	–	✓ (ono)	–	–	–
o	–	–	✓ (ôsê)	–	✓ (ôlhô)	–	–
u	–	–	–	–	–	–	✓ (unu)

Table 8. Agglutination in Fa d'Ambô (according to the data in Table 2)

V V_aggl.	a	ɛ	e	ɔ	o	i	u
a	✓ (ampan)	–	–	–	–	–	–
ɔ	✓ (olatu)	✓ (olemu)	–	–	–	–	–
o	✓ (ôman)	–	–	–	✓ (ôbôyô)	–	✓ (ônũa)
u	–	–	–	–	–	–	✓ (udum)

Table 9. Agglutination in Lung'ie (according to the data in Table 2)

V V_aggl.	a	ɛ	e	ɔ	o	i	u
o	–	–	✓ (ôzê)	–	–	–	–
u	✓ (upa)	✓ (uremu)	✓ (ubwê)	–	–	–	–

Despite the low number of tokens, it follows that in this proto-GGC stage agglutination is strongly associated to vowel height. Low and low-mid vowels in the stem trigger agglutination of a low or low-mid vowel, high-mid vowels occur with high-mid vowels and high vowels occur with high vowels. It is therefore suggestive that Portuguese gender and a reduced ATR-system determined the outcome of agglutinated vowels in proto-GGC. According to Van der Hulst & Van de Weijer (1995: 512), ATR-systems often lack the low [+ATR] vowel or the high [–ATR] vowels, or both.

In the following diachronic stage (Table 2), where the cases of agglutination in Lung'ie and Fa d'Ambô overlap, separate treatment of the data is required.

The Fa d'Ambô data in Table 2 are consistent with the patterns found in the oldest diachronic layer (Table 1 and 7). For the etymologically identical items in Lung'ie, however, the situation is quite different, as shown in Table 9.

These data are no longer in agreement with the findings of Table 7 and 8 and strongly suggest that while the cases of agglutination in Fa d'Ambô can arguably still be related to harmony processes found in proto-GGC, [u]-agglutination in Lung'ie was a local development that may have replaced other, previously existing, types of agglutination.

Table 10. Agglutination in Lung'ie (remaining items, cf. Appendix 1)

V V$_{aggl.}$	a	ɛ	e	ɔ	o	i	u
i	–	✓ (ite)	✓ (izêtxi)	–	–	✓ (irixi)	–
u	✓ (upanu)	✓ (uremu)	✓ (upêtu)	✓ (usolu)	✓ (ufôgô)	–	✓ (uzuntu)

Now consider the agglutination patterns found in items exclusive to Lung'ie, which only involve [u] and [i]-agglutination.

Quite clearly, the instances of [i]-agglutination exclusive to Lung'ie clearly involve front harmony with a tonic vowel (i, e, ɛ). However, if this rule is correct, cases such as *upêtu* 'chest', *ufew* 'iron' or *uwê* 'eye' should also receive [i]-agglutination. Therefore, another constraint on the distribution of [i] and [u] is required. This constraint, I argue, is roundness. If there is a front vowel in the stem and no round material (vowels or glides) elsewhere in the stem, [i]-agglutination is triggered; in all the other cases, [u]-agglutination occurs by default.

Cases where Lung'ie exhibits variation, namely *idêntu~udêntu* 'inside', *ifi~ufu~ifu* 'thread, wire', *usolu~isolu* 'sun', *ônôtxi~unôtxi*, *ôzên~uzên* 'knee' show that other agglutination patterns in this creole may have been more widespread and became replaced by [u]. In fact, this hypothesis can also be adopted for the differences between Fa d'Ambô and Lung'ie in Table 2. Thus, [u]-agglutination in Lung'ie must be the most recent diachronic agglutination process.

6. What triggers harmony processes in the GGCs?

In this section I will discuss the relevance of the different strata that contributed to the formation of the proto-GGC in the phonological conditioning of the agglutination process.

6.1 Portuguese

Standard Portuguese exhibits essentially the same oral vowel inventory as the GGCs. VH is well-attested in the GGCs' lexifier, European Portuguese (e.g. Mateus & d'Andrade 2000), and even more so in Brazilian Portuguese (e.g. File-Muriel 2004). The following types of assimilation are found in Portuguese:

i.   assimilation in the verbal domain (all conjugations)
ii. assimilation in the nominal domain: especially with certain suffixes in BP (height assimilation)

iii. metaphony: a tonic vowel harmonizes with post-tonic vowels

However, the processes found in the GGCs are considerably distinct from the processes above, which should therefore be dismissed as the putative trigger.[13]

6.2 Western Bantu

The impact of certain Western Bantu languages on the formation of the GGCs has been addressed by Ferraz (1979). In addition to Kongo lexicon in Santome, Ferraz also argues that a number of grammatical features can be assigned to this stratum. The lexical role of Kimbundu (Mbundu) for Ngola is also uncontroversial (Maurer 1992; Lorenzino 1998). As to Lung'ie, which is crucial to the present discussion, Ferraz (1975) briefly discusses the possible substrata for a number of phonological properties in this creole. For instance, he links palatalization and syllable structure to Bantu; voiced velar stops are assigned to the impact of West-African languages other than Bantu. In the light of historical and linguistic evidence, this latter feature must be original from the Nigerian substrate.[14] The presence of trills in Lung'ie and their absence in Santome and Fa d'Ambô, as well as less widespread prenasalization in Lung'ie as compared with Santome or Ngola, is also suggestive of less impact from Bantu and the retention of more Nigerian-related phonology. Although Lung'ie shares with the other GGCs some typical Nigerian syntactic features, such as substantial serialization (Hagemeijer 2000, 2001; Hagemeijer & Ogie in prep. for Santome), the presence of Bantu is possibly felt in the final negation patterns (Güldemann & Hagemeijer 2006; Hagemeijer 2007).

Kongo languages exhibit five oral vowels with phonemic status and significant VH (e.g. Hyman 1999). Ferraz (1979:49) states that "Kongo exhibits vowel harmony in the same way as ST as a tendency for the same vowel to occur in two consecutive syllables.". I have claimed above that there is a rule of VH in the GGCs' mid-vowel domain, but no other consistent rule can be found, only cases of vowel assimilation. As to Kongo languages, Bentley (1967:524) mentions the so-called "euphonic preferences", where [e] patterns with [o] and [i] with [u]. However, Bentley's use of the term 'preferences' should arguably not be related to a 'tendency' (in the sense of Ferraz) but to phonological rules that apply with "ideal regularity and consistency", as Bentley himself points out. In other words, this author refers here to an instance of vowel height harmony, which is well attested across Bantu in general, as well as Kongo lan-

---

13. Note that in Indo-Portuguese creoles VH is related to Portuguese (Clements 2004).

14. For instance, some of the items exhibiting co-articulated stop /gb/ in Lung'ie also exist in the other GGCs, but in the form of /kw/ or /bw/, which is arguably related to the massive imports of Bantu slaves on S. Tomé when the island shifts from a *societé d'habitation* to a *societé de plantation*.

guages in particular (Hyman 1999),[15] where VH between stem and perfective suffixes occurs. It is also obvious that five vowel systems (*i, u, e, o, a*) lack mid-vowel stem harmony.

Since prosthetic vowels in the GGCs typically harmonize with the stressed vowel, it is important to observe how Bantu noun classifiers behave with respect to the stem. According to Hyman (1999), prefix harmonization is uncommon across the Bantu cluster and only applicable to some noun classes. Languages that do exhibit this type of harmony, though, typically have a seven vowel system. The relevant Western Bantu languages do not pattern among this type.

In sum, while it cannot be denied that certain Bantu-related phonological processes do play a role in the GGCs in general, a number of phonological traits in Lung'ie strongly suggest that the impact of Bantu was more reduced in this creole than in the other GGCs. In addition, there is no obvious reason to believe that the type of VH found in the Western Bantu was crucial to pervasive mid-vowel stem harmony and to the observed agglutination patterns.

6.3 Edoid

The impact of Edoid on the formation of the GGCs has been addressed since Ferraz (1979), for lexicon and grammar. In a nutshell, a strikingly high percentage of African lexicon in Lung'ie has its origin in Edoid (Maurer 2009) and many syntactic properties in the GGCs can be traced back directly to Edoid (Hagemeijer 1999; Hagemeijer & Parkvall 2001; Hagemeijer & Ogie in prep.). Although Edoid displays many typological similarities to, for instance, Yoruboid and Kwa languages, both historical and linguistic evidence do not underscore a major role for these clusters in the formation of the GGCs. In fact, the available linguistic and historical evidence strongly suggests that Edoid had a founder effect on the formation of the proto-GGC, preceding in time the massive imports of Bantu slaves from the Congo and Angola.

Nouns in the Edoid cluster are vowel-initial and exhibit either the same oral vowel system as the GGCs or more complex 9/10 vowel systems. VH is substantial in the verb and noun system of many Edoid languages (Delta, South-Western and North-Western Edoid), according to Elugbe (1989). In 7-vowel systems, such as Ẹdọ, however, VH is much more restricted and, when it occurs, it is typically limited to nouns. Elugbe considers VH a feature of reconstructed proto-Edoid. The relevant feature for VH in Edoid is [±ATR], yielding the two following mutually exclusive sets of vowels.

---

15. According to Hyman (1999), southern Kongo languages are unusual in the sense that they exhibit a five vowel system and symmetric height harmony, i.e. harmony whereby *i* and *u* are lowered after *o* and *e*. In asymmetric height harmony, which is very common throughout the Bantu cluster, *u* is only lowered after *o*, but not after *e*.

(6) [Expanded]   [Non-expanded]
     i   u   ɪ   ʊ
     e   o   ɛ   ɔ
             ə   a

Although the 7-vowel chart of the GGCs could not copy a full-fledged ATR-system, it was able to retain the essence of Edoid's mid-vowel harmony.[16] ATR is also present in the neighbouring language clusters, namely Defoid (Van der Hulst & Van de Weijer 1995: 515–516), Ijoid (Clements & Rialland, 2008; Williamson 1965) and Igboid (Emenanjo 1987), which makes it an important areal feature. There is at least evidence that these clusters left some lexical imprints on the GGCs. Mid-vowel ATR stem harmony in the GGCs can thus be safely related to Nigerian language clusters with a special role for Edoid.

Furthermore, a noun class system can be reconstructed for proto-Edoid, although most Edoid language only show vestiges hereof (Elugbe 1983, 1989). Ẹ̀dó, for instance, only exhibits a vowel prefix alternation for only a few items (e.g. òkpìa > ikpìa 'man-men' (Dunn 1968), whereas Dẹgẹma, a delta-Edoid language, exhibits a complex noun prefixation system for plural formation that obeys rules of VH (Elugbe 1976; Kari 2007). In the typical contemporary Edoid language, however, the vestiges of prefixes do not indicate semantic classes and are the result of "assimilation, vowel harmony, class shifting and levelling" (Elugbe 1983).[17] All the oral vowels can generally be prefixes (i.e. word-initial). In footnote 3, it could be seen that Portuguese words in Ẹ̀dó are often prefixed by e and ɛ, which are the only patterns that are not found in the GGCs. In fact, from the available literature, no direct relation semantic or formal relation can be established between prefixation in Edoid and the agglutination patterns in the GGCs. Basically, VH in these languages must have operated as a trigger for the agglutination patterns in the GGCs. In Ẹ̀dó, for instance, nouns with an [ɔ]-prefix are also likely to have ɔ, ɛ or a in the stem (Elugbe 1989: 78), which is exactly the pattern that obtained in the oldest diachronic stage of the GGCs (see data in Table 1 and the findings of Table 7) and falls into non-expanded in (6) above.

In sum, despite the fact that there are substantial differences between prefixation in Edoid and agglutination in the GGCs, several findings, in addition to other linguistic and historical evidence, favour an Edoid substratum:

i.   Edoid nouns are obligatorily vowel-initial;
ii. Edoid languages generally exhibit ATR harmony or did so in older stages;

---

16. Note, however, that in Edoid languages with seven-vowel systems, there are only vestiges of VH. For instance, Ọlọma (North-Central Edoid) underwent a reduction from a nine-vowel system to a seven-vowel system, but retains VH (mid-vowels) with singular/plural prefixation (Elugbe 1989).

17. Rules of VH also apply to past and plurality suffixes (Aikhionbare 1989).

iii. Edoid languages typically exhibit vestiges of noun prefixation which is (or was) constrained by rules of VH;
iv. agglutination is most pervasive in Lung'ie, which is the GGC that exhibits the strongest Edoid impact.

A particular role for Edoid in agglutination may also provide an explanation for the problem presented in Section 4, namely the unexpected fact that Fa d'Ambô and Lung'ie have a number of agglutinated items that do not occur in Santome or Ngola. In fact, while it is quite uncontroversial that Lung'ie underwent the strongest impact from Edoid, the impact of Western Bantu was comparatively more significant on São Tomé, not only because of the sugar production but also because of the island's key position in the trans-Atlantic slave trade. The question is therefore whether the proto-GGC exhibited more agglutination at some diachronic stage, or whether a significant part of the agglutination data should be considered coincidental independent innovations in Fa d'Ambô and Lung'ie.

To answer this question, note first that Fa d'Ambô and Lung'ie share several other features not shared by Santome and Ngola, such as the following:

i. Portuguese nasal diphthong *-ão* yielded *-an* in FA and LU and *-on* in ST and NG;
ii. Several items in FA and LU exhibit /v/ where ST and NG exhibit /b/;
iii. Less widespread prenasalization in LU and FA than in ST and NG.
iv. Syntax of the Noun Phrase:
    – Universal quantifier *tudu* 'all' occurs to the right of the head noun in LU and FA and to its left in ST and NG;
    – Numerals in FA occur typically to the right of the head noun, which is also the case for 'one' and 'two' in LU;[18] in ST and NG numerals typically precede the head noun;

I therefore assume that at least a number of common features in LU and FA must have existed in the proto-GGC. Since it can hardly be coincidence that the agglutinated items found in Fa d'Ambô, but not in Santome/Ngola, also exist in Lung'ie, I argue that at least these forms must have existed in (varieties of) the proto-GGC and that the diachrony of the substrata involved in the formation of the GGCs provides an explanation for what might have happened.

I propose that the early proto-GGC is essentially the result of Edoid slaves acquiring Portuguese. Since this period corresponds by and large to the *société d'habitation*, there was arguably better access to the Target Language (TL) and therefore phonetic calquing upon Portuguese gender was additionally able to satisfy the Edoid constraint that nouns are vowel-initial. The fact that the [u], in Lung'ie, and the [ɔ] and [o], in Fa d'Ambô, became so generalized means that the vowel-initial constraint was still active, but also that reanalysis phonetically based on the Portuguese gender distinction

---

18. In more archaic varieties of Lung'ie, all numerals could follow the noun (Maurer 2009: 42).

was lost and that the Portuguese masculine definite article was retained as input for agglutination.

In this scenario, Lung'ie was the first to branch off the proto-GGC and become isolated at an early stage of creolization and therefore retained a greater number of Edoid features, including agglutination.[19] The direct import of Niger Delta slaves to Príncipe under the contract to Antonio Carneiro (1514–1518), and possibly for some years after that, underlines the importance of this area for Lung'ie (Ladhams 2003). This, of course, would account for the heavier influence from Edoid languages in Lung'ie. The fact that a number of words with [u]-agglutination in Lung'ie also have agglutination in Santome and especially Fa d'Ambô, but with a different initial vowel, strongly suggests that [u]-agglutination in Lung'ie locally absorbed previously existing patterns in this creole. This also follows from the items that show variation between [i] and [u]-agglutination.

Fa d'Ambô became isolated between 1543, when a royal charter was requested, and 1565 (Caldeira 2006).[20] Thus, the time span reaching between the isolation of Lung'ie and Fa d'Ambô may well correspond to a decrease in agglutinated items in the proto-GGC. Historically, this time span overlaps to a more significant extent with the expansion of the plantation stage (from approx. 1517 on) and the massive arrival of Bantu slaves. However, it is not obvious that Bantu slaves can be held directly responsible for the breakdown of agglutination in the proto-GGC. Nouns, including (singular) prefixes, are to a great extent consonant-initial in the relevant Bantu languages and it can be hypothesized that Bantu speakers learning the proto-GGC related agglutination to the Bantu definite article *o* and therefore reanalyzed the morpheme boundary. It is, however, more likely that Portuguese was responsible for lexical restructuring. Santome, the direct descendant of the proto-GGC, is nowadays the only GGC that exhibits, for instance, widespread consonant clusters, especially with a liquid in C_2, which is a non-typical feature of Edoid and Western Bantu, but well-attested in Portuguese. Furthermore, Zamora [p.c] informs me that several agglutinated items in contemporary Fa d'Ambô have counterparts that lack the agglutinated vowel, namely *(o)po, (ô)bôyô, (o)man* and *(am)pan*. It is not clear whether this is a recent process or part of a larger process that decisively affected more items in the past.

Irrespectively of what explanation one adopts for the fact that Santome only exhibits agglutinated items from the oldest diachronic stage, the absence of this feature in Ngola suggests that this creole still remained in contact with Santome after the spread of the Proto-GGC to Príncipe and Annobón.

---

19. Permanent settlement of São Tomé occurred in 1493. The island of Príncipe was officially settled from 1500 on, but there is documentary evidence that some slaves left for the island before the turn of the century.

20. Settlement of Annobón arguably started in 1503. The island was claimed to have 9 European inhabitants (moradores) in 1507. However, a 16th century letter states that Annobón was uninhabited in 1543.

7. Concluding remarks

Although it was shown that agglutination was far more productive in Lung'ie than in any of the other GGCs, only cases involving prosthetic [i] are exclusive to this creole. The remaining patterns, namely with agglutinated [u], [o], [ɔ] and [a], are also attested in the other GGCs. Since both the islands of Príncipe and Annobón were settled from São Tomé, I assume that agglutination must have existed and spread from the proto-GGC.

At least the following diachronic layers should be distinguished. First, etymologically monosyllabic items in the proto-GGC were restructured through agglutinating an initial vowel corresponding to the Portuguese definite masculine and feminine article, following at least phonetically the Portuguese gender distinction, as well as rules of VH from the substrate. Second, agglutination spread to disyllabic items (Lung'ie and Fa d'Ambô) and the Portuguese gender distinction was abandoned, while the rules of VH in the oldest diachronic stage were still active in Fa d'Ambô. Third, Lung'ie exhibits some [i]-agglutination and generalized [u]-agglutination, with an important role for the features [Front] and [Round]. I further argued that in addition to the Portuguese article system, the earliest substrate cluster, Nigerian language clusters and Edoid in particular played a major role in this process of morpho-phonological restructuring.

References

Agheyisi, Rebecca N. 1990. A Grammar of Edo. Ms, Unesco.
Aikhionbare, Matt. Osayaba. 1989. Defining the domain of nasality in Edo. *Studies in African Linguistics* 20(3): 301–315.
Baker, Philip. 1984. Agglutinated nominals in Creole French: Their evolutionary significance. *Te Reo* 27: 89–129.
Barrena, Natalio. 1957. *Gramatica Annobonesa*. Madrid: Consejo de Investigaciones Cientificas.
Baxter, Alan. 2004. The development of variable NP plural agreement in a restructured African variety of Portuguese. In *Creoles, Contact and Language Change: Linguistics and Social Implications* [Creole Language Library 27], Geneviève Escure & Armin Schwegler (eds), 97–126. Amsterdam: John Benjamins.
Bentley, William Holman. 1967 [1887]. *Dictionary and Grammar of the Kongo Language*. London: Baptist Missionary Society.
Caldeira, Arlindo. 2005. A 'república negra' de Ano Bom: Invenção de um 'Estado' entre duas colonizações. In Centro de Estudos da Universidade do Porto (coord). *Trabalho forçado africano: Experiência coloniais comparadas*. Porto: Campo das Letras – Editores, S.A.
Caldeira, Arlindo. 2006. Uma ilha quase desconhecida. Notas para a história de Ano Bom. *Studia Africana – Revista Interuniversitària d'Estudis Africans* 17: 99–109.

Clements, J. Clancy. 2004. La armonización vocálica en los criollos indo-portugueses. In *Los criollos de base ibérica: ACBLPE 2003*, Mauro Fernández, Manuel Fernández-Ferreiro & Nancy Vázquez Veiga (eds), 33–40. Frankfurt/Madrid: Vervuert/Iberoamericana.

Clements, Nick & Rialland, Annie. 2008. Africa as a Phonological Area. In *A Linguistic Geography of Africa*, Bernd Heine & Derek Nurse (eds), 36–85. Cambridge: CUP.

Dunn, Ernest F. 1968. *An Introduction to Bini*. East Lansing MI: African Studies Center, Michigan State University.

Elugbe, Ben. 1976. Noun class vestiges in Dẹgẹma. *Afrika und Übersee* LIX(3): 224–233.

Elugbe, Ben. 1983. Noun class prefixes in proto-Edoid. In *Current Approaches to African Linguistics*, Vol. 1, Ivan R. Dihoff (ed.), 59–83. Dordrecht: Foris.

Elugbe, Ben. 1989. *Comparative Edoid: Phonology and Lexicon*. Port Harcourt: University of Port Harcourt Press.

Emenanjo, E. Nolue. 1987. *Elements of Modern Igbo Grammar: A Descriptive Approach*. Ibadan: University Press.

Ferraz, Luiz Ivens. 1975. African influences on Principense Creole. In *Miscelânea luso-africana*, Marius Valkhoff (ed.), 153–164. Lisbon: Junta de investigacoes cientificas do ultramar.

Ferraz, Luiz Ivens. 1984. The substrate of Annobonese. *African Studies* 43: 119–136.

Ferraz, Luiz Ivens. 1979. *The Creole of São Tomé*. Johannesburg: Witwatersrand University Press.

File-Muriel, Richard J. 2004. An OT approach to vowel height harmony in Brazilian Portuguese. *Indiana University Linguistic Club Working papers* 4: 1–16.

Graham, Steve & Graham, Trina. 2004. West Africa Lusolexed Creoles Word List File Documentation. SIL Electronic Survey Reports. <http://www.sil.org/silesr/2004/silesr2004-012.html>.

Granda, German de. 1986. Retenciones africanas en la fonética de criollo portugués de Annobón. *Revista de Filología Románica* 4: 111–124.

Grant, Anthony P. 1995. Article agglutination in creole French: A wider perspective. In *From Contact to Creole and Beyond*, Philip Baker (ed.), 149–176. London: University of Westminster Press.

Güldemann, Tom & Hagemeijer, Tjerk. 2006. Negation in the Gulf of Guinea creoles: Typological and historical perspectives. Talk delivered at the 2006 ACBLPE meeting, Coimbra.

Günther, Wilfried. 1973. *Das Portugiesische Kreolisch der ilha do Príncipe* [Marburger Studien zur Afrika- und Asienkunde, Serie A, 2]. Marburg an der Lahn: Selbstverlag.

Hagemeijer, Tjerk. 1999. As ilhas de Babel: A crioulização no Golfo da Guiné. *Revista Camões* 6: 74–88.

Hagemeijer, Tjerk. 2001. Semi-lexicality and underspecfication in serial verb constructions. In *Semi-lexical Categories: The Functions of Content Words and the Content of Function Words*, Norbert Corver & Henk van Riemsdijk (eds), 415–451. Berlin: Mouton de Gruyter.

Hagemeijer, Tjerk. 2005. Going in the clause: *Ba* and *be* in Santome. *Journal of Portuguese Linguistics* 3(2): 71–95.

Hagemeijer, Tjerk. 2007. Clause Structure in Santome. PhD dissertation, Universidade de Lisboa.

Hagemeijer, Tjerk & Ogie, Ota. In preparation. Ẹ̀dó influence on Santome: Evidence from verb serialization.

Hagemeijer, Tjerk & Parkvall, Mikael. 2001. The development of the Gulf of Guinea creoles. Talk delivered at the 2001 ACBLPE annual meeting, Coimbra.

Holm, John. 1988. *Pidgins and Creoles*, Vol. 1. Cambridge: CUP.

Hulst, Harry van der & van de Weijer, Jeroen. 1995. Vowel harmony. In *The Handbook of Phonological Theory*, John A. Goldsmith (ed.), 495–534. Cambridge MA: Blackwell.

Hyman, Larry M. 1999. The historical interpretation of vowel harmony in Bantu. In *Bantu Historical Linguistics: Theorical and Empirical Perspectives*, Jean-Marie Hombert & Larry M. Hyman (eds), 235–295. Stanford CA: CSLI.

Kari, Ethelbert E. 2007. Vowel harmony in Degema, Nigeria. *African Study Monographs* 28(2): 87–97.

Ladhams, John. 2003. The Formation of the Portuguese Plantation Creoles. PhD dissertation, University of Westminster.

Ladhams, John. Forthcoming. Article agglutination and the African contribution to the Portuguese-based creoles. In *Black through White*, Angela Bartens & Philip Baker (eds). London: Battlebridge.

Lorenzino, Gerardo. 1998. The Angolar Creole Portuguese of São Tomé: Its Grammar and Sociolinguistic History. PhD dissertation, City University of New York.

Mateus, Maria Helena & d'Andrade, Ernesto. 2000. *The Phonology of Portuguese*. Oxford: OUP.

Maurer, Philippe. 1992. L'apport lexical bantou en Angolar. *Afrikanische Arbeitspapiere* 29: 163–174.

Maurer, Philippe. 1995. *L'Angolar: Un créole Afro-Portugaise parlé à São Tomé*. Hamburg: Helmut Buske.

Maurer, Philippe. 2009. *Principense: Grammar, Texts, and Vocabulary of the Afro-Portuguese Creole of the Island of Príncipe, Gulf of Guinea*. London: Battlebridge.

Melzian, Hans Joachim. 1937. *A Concise Dictionary of the Bini Language of Southern Nigeria*. London: Kegan Paul, Trench Trubner & Co.

Negreiros, Almada. 1895. *Historia Ethnographica da ilha de S. Tomé*. Lisbon: Antiga Casa Bertrand – José Bastos.

Parkvall, Mikael. 2000. *Out of Africa*. London: Battlebridge.

Post, Marike. 1995. Fa d'Ambô. In *Pidgins and Creoles: An introduction* [Creole Language Library 15], Jacques Arends, Pieter Muysken & Norval Smith (eds), 191–204. Amsterdam: John Benjamins.

Rougé, Jean-Louis. 1992. Les langues des Tonga. In *Actas do colóquio sobre crioulos de base lexical portuguesa*, Ernesto d'Andrade & Alain Kihm (eds). Lisbon: Colibri.

Schang, Emmanuel. 2000. L'émergence des créoles portugais du Golfe de Guinée. PhD dissertation, Université de Nancy 2.

Schwegler, Armin. 2006. Bantu elements in Palenque (Colombia): Anthropological, archeological and linguistic evidence. In *Confronting Social Issues of the African Diaspora*, Jay B. Haviser (ed.). London: Routledge.

Williamson, Kay. 1965. *A Grammar of the Kolokuma Dialect of Ịjọ* [West African Language Monographs 2]. Cambridge: CUP.

Zamora, Armando. Ms. *Gramática descriptiva del fa d'ambô*.

Appendix 1. Prosthetic vowels in the GGC*

Lung'ie	Santome	Fa d'Ambô**	Lunga Ngola	Portuguese etymology	Meaning
afe	afe	fe		fé	'faith'
apa	apa	[pala]	anpa	pá	'spade, shovel'
(gêêza-)ase	ase	[geza]	[ngeedha]	sé	'church, cathedral'
[nomi]	aglasa	galasa		graça, nome	'name'
ope	ope	ope	ope	pé	'foot, leg'
opo	opo	opo	ompo	pó	'dust'
ose	ose	ôsê	onthe	céu	'sky, heaven'
ono	ono	ono	[nvumbu]	nó	'knot'
odo	odo	dôl	odo~oro	dó	'mourning'
ônôtxi~unôtxi	nôtxi	notsyi	[n'thuku]	noite	'night'
ôryô 'river'	ôlhô***	[lubela]	awa	rio	'river'
ôzê (n)~ôzên~uzên	zê	ôzôyô	[m'puna~puna]	joelho	'knee'
uari	oali	oventu	ventu	ar, vento	'air'
ubaaku	blaku, kobo	[fuladu]	[kobo]	buraco, furado, cova	'hole'
ubaasu	[mon]	bazu, baasu	[mon]	braço, mão	'upper arm'
ubanku	banku	banku	banku	banco	'bank'
ubasu	basu	basu	[kosi]	baixo	'under(neath)'
ubudu	budu	budu, buudu	buru	?	'stone'
ubuka	boka	boxo	boka	boca	'mouth'
udedu	dedu	dedu(-oman)	reru	dedo	'finger, (toe)'
udôdô	dôdô	dôdô	[toto]	doido, tótó	'idiot'
udumu	dumu	udum		Edo (u)dumu	'pestle'
udyabu	[demono]	[damon(o)]	[romono]	diabo, demónio	'devil'
ufaka	faka	faxa	faka	faca	'knife'
ufatu	fatu	[bitsyidu]		fato, vestido	'suit'
ufôgô / ufôgu	fôgô	fogo	fôgô	fogo	'fire'
ufunda	funda			Kikongo fúnda	'parcel made of leaves'
ufundu	fundu	fundu	fundu	fundo	'depth'
ugaafu	galufu	gefa	ngalufu	garfo	'fork'
ugagu	gagu	gagi	ngagu	gago	'stutterer'
ugalu	galu	galu	[n'kombo]	galo	'cock'
ugatu	gatu	gatu, ngatu		gatu	'cat'
uguya	guya	guya, gunha	ngunha	agulha	'needle'
ukabu				cabo	'end'
ukagu	[luge]	xálgu		cargo, lugar	'responsability'
ukalu	kalu	ekuza		? caldo	'broth'

ukampu	kampu		kampu	campo	'field'
ukanu	kanu			cano	'pipe'
ukantu	[kantxin]		[tia]	canto	'corner'
ukaru	karu	[moto]	karu	carro	'car'
ukuru	kulu	kulu	[n'thuku]	escuro	'darkness'
ukuru	kulu	kulù	kuru	cru	'raw'
ukwatu	kwatu	[xotchian]		quarto	'room'
uladu	[bodo]	ladu		lado	'side'
ulalu	lalu	lalu		?	'skin disease'
ulasu	lasu	lasu	[n'vumbu]	laço	'knot'
ulatu				lato(?)	'footpath'
ulensu	lensu	lensu(-zubela)		lenço	'handkerchief'
umari, umwe(n)	omali	omal	[mionga]	mar	'sea'
umatu	matu	**omatu**, matu	matu	mato	'bush-bush, jungle'
umundu	mundu	mundu		mundo	'world'
unfenu	nfenu	**onfenu**	nfenu	inferno	'hell'
upanu	panu	panu	panu	pano	'cloth'
upasu	pasu			passo	'step'
upetu	petu			espeto	'fork, spit'
upêtu	petu	[boxo-kusá]	[pota-kotho]	peito	'chest'
urabu	labu	**labu**	[inkila~n'kila]	rabo	'tail'
uramu	[aba]	[aba]	[n'thala, tango]	ramo	'branch'
uratu	latu	**ólatu**	latu	rato	'rat, mouse'
uremu	lemu	**olemu**	lemu~lêmu	remo	'oar'
urôsô	lôsô	alôsô	lôthô	arroz	'rice'
usaku	saku	saku	thaku	saco	'bag'
usalu	salu	salu	thalu	sal	'salt'
usolu (isolu)	solo	solo	tholo	sol	'sun'
usuva	suba	[awa]	thuba	chuva	'rain'
utabu	taba	taba	taba	tábua	'plank'
utasu	tasu	tasu	tathu	tacho	'bowl'
utempu	tempu	tempu	tepu	tempo	'weather'
uventu	ventu	**oventu**	ventu	vento	'wind'
uzuntu	zuntu	zuntu	[dhunta]	junto	'next to'
ubaw	balu	[lama]	[mavu]	barro	'soil, clay'
ubwê	bwê	**òbôyô**	buè	bói	'cow'
ubên	bên	ben		bem, riqueza	'richness, possessions'
ufew	felu	**onfelu**	felu~fêlu	ferro	'iron'
uga	lwa	**ólua**	lua	rua	'street', 'outside'
ufya	fya	fala	fia	folha	'leaf'
uku	uku	[zanga]	[ndagu]	cu	'arse'
umpan	mpon	**ampan**	pon	pão	'bread'
unu	unu	[dodyí]		nu	'naked'
unwan	nw̃a	ônũa, ônũya	[mbêi~mbêzi~mêzi]	lua	'moon'

uman	mon	ôman, man	mo~mon	*mão*	'hand, lower arm'
upa	po	ôpa	po	*pau*	'stick, tree'
usan	son	san	thon	*chão*	'ground'
uwê	wê	ôyô	wê	*olho*	'eye'
idintxi	dêntxi	denchi	rêtxi~dêtxi	*dente*	'tooth'
ifi (ufi, ufu)	fi	filu	fi	*fio*	'thread, wire'
ijinjibi	jijimpli	yimbil		*gengiva*	'gum'
imin	min	milu	minhu	*milho*	'maize'
injizu	jinzu			*jejum*	'religious fasting'
irixi	lixi	lichi	lisi~risi~disi	*nariz*	'nose'
ise	sela	[xama]	[kama]	*esteira, cama*	'bed'
isengi	sangi	sangi	thangi	*sangue*	'blood'
ite	tela	[lama]	tela	*terra, lama*	'soil, clay'
ivin	vin	vin	vi	*vinho*	'wine'
ixima	xima (also [liba])	[liba]	[riba~diba]	*(em?) cima, arriba*	'on top'
ixize	xinza	chinza	txindja	*cinza*	'ashes'
izêtxi	zêtê	zete(-palm)	[mazi]	*azeite*	'palm oil'
idêntu (udêntu)	glêntu	dentulu, dantulu	lêtu	*dentro*	'inside'
ipin	pyan	pina, pyan	pinha	*espinha*	'thorn'

* Sources: Lung'ie – Günther (1973), Maurer (2009); Santome – Ferraz (1979), my own corpus; Fa d'Ambô – Barrena (1957), Graham & Graham (2004), De Granda (1986), Marike Post [p.c.], Armando Zamora [p.c.]; Angolar – Maurer (1995). Fricative [ʃ] is represented as *x* in Santome, Lung'ie and Ngola. In Fa d'Ambô, [ʃ] is *ch* and [x] is *x*. The bracketed items are not related to the etymology of the agglutinated form.

** I have drawn the Fa d'Ambô from written sources, namely Barrena (1957), De Granda (1986) and Graham & Graham (2004). However, the data pieces are often contradictory, especially with respect to the vowel qualities. I have therefore submitted these forms to a native speaker, Armando Zamora, whose judgements are ultimately reflected in the table.

*** Form attested in Negreiros (1895).

Simplification of a complex part of grammar or not?
What happened to KiKoongo nouns in Saramaccan?

Norval Smith

In this article I attempt to approach the question of what effect the incorporation of a large number of KiKoongo vocabulary items by the creole languages of Surinam had vis-a-vis notions of simplification or complexification. So, we have the situation of a language lacking an extensive noun-class system with number marking having to absorb many words possessing such a system.

An examination of the KiKoongo borrowings belonging to three classes is performed: 3/4, 5/6, 7/8. Each class appears to display a different constellation of singular and plural prefixes. 3/4 appears to represent only singular forms, either with an explicit prefix, or with no prefix. 5/6, where the KiKoongo dialect which seems to be best represented in Surinam has no explicit prefix in the singular, has a large preponderance of plural prefix forms. 7/8 has mixed results, possibly indicating KiKoongo dialect mixture. Most items occur without a prefix – presumably representing singulars, while a smaller number have explicit singular or plural prefixes.

A surprisingly large number of forms display the wrong prefix. The common prefixes /ma-/ (pl.cl. 6) and /mu-/ (sg.cl. 3) seem to be involved frequently.

I hypothesize that KiKoongo speakers initially used the relevant prefix in words borrowed from KiKoongo. This is however redundant given that the definite article is marked for number. Fongbe speakers would not know the correct number agreement, but would be able to recognize KiKoongo morphemes because of word length. In class 5/6 the preferred option was for a prefixed form (plural). The next stage is the loss of knowledge that KiKoongo loans contain a prefix at all.

The loss of number distinctions, then gender distinctions, then parsability into discrete morphemes takes place in the lack of any meaningful function for the prefixes. The number distinctions presumably initially encoded by KiKoongo speakers would be redundant in any case. Gender distinctions play no role in the larger Surinam Creole lexica. And meaningless prefixes cease to have any role. The complexity that is lost in this corner of the lexicon never played a significant role in these creoles.

1. Introduction

The title of this article refers to a hypothesis on the changing morphological status of a body of KiKoongo-derived nouns present in the creole languages of Surinam. It has become very clear in the last fifteen years that the dominant substrate for the three Surinam creoles, Saramaccan, Sranan, and Ndyuka (Aboh 2005, to appear; Muysken & Smith, to appear), is not KiKoongo, an impression that was created by the valuable study of Daeleman (1972) on the KiKoongo element in Saramaccan, but Fongbe and closely-related Eastern Gbe languages originating on the West African 'Slave Coast', (henceforth just Fongbe).[1] However, KiKoongo (a Bantu language) does provide a very significant proportion of the recognizable African element in the Surinam creoles.

One reason for the dominance of Fongbe as the main substrate language for the above-mentioned creoles is presumably the fact that during the first 60–70 years of the existence of the colony of Surinam more slaves of Slave Coast origin were imported to Surinam than slaves of West Central African origin. In this period arose then a new language – Sranan – to allow communication among the slaves of different origins.

While the recorded slave imports from the Slave Coast (among whom Fon slaves appear to have been linguistically very significant), and from West Central Africa (who were probably mostly KiKoongo speakers on the basis of the known Bantu vocabulary in Saramaccan, in particular), do not differ terribly much in numbers, the West Central African imports were more concentrated into a small number of periods, especially towards the end of the 17th century. Slaves from the Slave Coast came in a more constant stream.

2. The source of the slaves

A glance at the Table 1 below will confirm what I have just stated: that more slaves from the Slave Coast were imported between the years 1675–1714 (52.6%) than from West Central Africa (the coastal regions of the Congo, in the table subsumed under the name *Loango*) during the same period (40.5%), ignoring slaves of unknown origin (Arends 1995). For the period 1658–1674 no separate figures for Surinam have been published, but source-identified slaves in the general Dutch slave trade (including trade to Surinam) come out at 49.5% from the Slave Coast as against only 24.6% from the Congo. This suggests a significant increase in the slave-imports from the Congo to the figure for the period 1675–1714 (40.5%), but in fact the supply was very erratic. In fact without the peak 5-year period 1685–1689, their proportion over this period would only have been 33.9%.

---

[1]. The nucleus of the Slave Coast corresponds to the coastal areas of Togo, Benin and Western Nigeria.

Table 1. Slave imports to Surinam (based on data in Postma 1990: 35, 308–348)

	Gold Coast	Slave Coast	Loango	Other	Unknown	Total
1658–1674 (general Dutch trade)	10.4% (18.4%)[2]	28.0% (49.5%)	13.9% (24.6%)	(W) 4.3% (7.6%)	43.4%	
1675–1679			710 61.2%		450 38.8%	
1680–1684	150 5.6%	1289 47.8%	679 25.0%		582 21.6%	
1685–1689	175 2.5%	1721 24.3%	3882 54.9%	844 (B) 11.9%	450 6.4%	
1690–1694		950 45.8%	615 29.6%		511 24.6%	
1695–1699		2197 41.7%	2384 45.2%		692 13.1%	
1700–1704		2397 68.6%	568 16.3%		528 15.1%	
1705–1709	657 14.6%	3250 72.4%	579 12.9%			
1710–1714		1360 65.9%	705 34.1%			
1675–1714	892	13164 52.6%	10122 40.5%	844	3213 ignored	28235 25022

W = Windward Coast; B = Bight of Biafra.

What can we conclude from these figures? It is fairly safe to say that there was a consistently larger importation of slaves over most of this period from the Slave Coast than from the Loango/Congo area. The predicted linguistic effect would be that there would be greater substrate influence from Fongbe than from KiKoongo. There is now a large body of work that bears this out (cf. Smith 1987a, 1987b; Articles in Muysken & Smith, to appear). At present solid evidence of the KiKoongo substrate in the Surinam creole languages is limited to a body of lexical items, and the differential nasal effects from the Fongbe and KiKoongo substrates treated in Smith (2004).

We can immediately base a hypothesis on these observations. There are numbers of identified lexical items in Saramaccan – the creole language I will largely utilize here because of its much greater known African lexical resources – from both Fongbe and KiKoongo. If, as we have reason to believe, both from the demographic data, *and* the presence of a number of non-lexical substrate features in Saramaccan, that Fongbe was indeed dominant over KiKoongo, then we would expect to maybe find indications of Fongbe influence on KiKoongo-derived items, but not so many indications of

---

2. The figures in brackets in this and following cells represent the percentages obtained by ignoring the slaves of unknown provenance.

KiKoongo influence on Fongbe-derived items. In the following sections I will attempt to show that this hypothesis is supported by the facts.

3. Fongbe and KiKoongo word shapes

Fongbe and KiKoongo are strikingly different in morphological typology. Fongbe is very poor in inflectional morphology. The situation in KiKoongo is precisely the reverse. This language can be described as having a rich agglutinative structure in its inflectional morphology. In particular the verbal morphology is highly complex.

In the Surinam creoles the most common part of speech among words of African origin is the noun. Nominal structure is strikingly different in the two African languages as might be expected from the foregoing, although the surface differences are considerably less obvious than in verbs. Little of the verbal morphology has survived in Surinam however, and that little is opaque. Virtually only the underived stems of KiKoongo verbs have made it into the Surinam creoles, while Fongbe-derived verbs appear in root and reduplicated stem forms (Aboh 2005, to appear). The reduplicated forms themselves display certain substrate effects (Aboh 2007; Aboh & Smith, to appear).

Fongbe noun roots are typically monosyllabic. Compounds can be quite complex in structure although fewer of these appear to occur in Surinam, most compounds being limited to two stems. The rollcall of African vocabulary items in Surinam is incomplete in the sense that new words are still being discovered – our knowledge of the Saramaccan lexicon, for instance, is clearly incomplete, and this may well also be true of Ndyuka and Sranan. Our knowledge of rural forms of Sranan, for example, is practically non-existent.

Monosyllabic noun roots in Fongbe may have a non-functional noun-class prefix. Fongbe actually has the poorest such system among the Gbe languages, only opposing an /a-/ class to a /Ø-/ class. Other Gbe lects have up to 4 classes marked by different vowels. Unlike the more familiar noun-class systems of Bantu languages, these noun-classes are vestigial (non-functional) in the sense that no singular-plural pairs occur (as *is* the case in some West African Niger-Congo languages, for example certain Edo languages, and also in the Akan languages), and also in that there is no relationship with any semantic categories.

By contrast KiKoongo noun roots are typically disyllabic, and come with class prefixes which nearly always involve a prefix consisting of a consonant-vowel syllable. These prefixes normally come in singular-plural pairs, and represent a number of "genders" with vaguish semantic core-meanings.

So we find two radically different patterns in the prototypical noun stems derived from these two languages. The contrast manifests itself in terms of overall length, syllable structure, and segment types. Consider the noun-templates in (1).

(1) *Basic word templates in Fongbe and KiKoongo*
Fongbe: (V) - C (L/G)   V(~)
KiKoongo: ((C) V) - N C (G)   V N . C V

[(~) = possible vowel-nasalization]

The peoples' names Fon[3] and BaKoongo themselves are good illustrations of these differences in structure. Fon is phonologically /fõ/, ignoring vowel height, while BaKoongo is phonologically /bakoongo/, ignoring tones in both cases. The most striking difference is in overall length – KiKoongo words are usually quite a bit longer.

In both languages we have the possibility of noun class prefixes. These are different in function and form in the two languages. Fongbe only has the option of functionless /a-/ versus /Ø-/ (the lack of a prefix). Other Gbe languages have more choices, but all of the overt markers consist of a single vowel, and are functionless. The class-membership is (apparently) arbitrary. KiKoongo, on the other hand, nearly always has an overt class prefix, and they come in singular-plural pairs, one or both of which will always be overt, usually both. The membership of classes is not completely arbitrary – human nouns are mostly in Class 1/2, for instance.

Onset possibilities in the two languages differ. KiKoongo allows nasal clusters in onsets – /NC-/, optionally followed by a glide /G/, while the Eastern Gbe languages allow liquid clusters – /CL-/, as well as /CG-/ but not nasal clusters. Modern KiKoongo also allows syllabic nasals initially, but these derive historically from prefixes /mu-, mi-/, and this former stage is represented in KiKoongo items in Saramaccan.

The nucleus in both languages is usually a short vowel, but in both Fongbe and KiKoongo a minority of roots can have a long vowel. In KiKoongo these long vowels are sometimes derived by rule, and sometimes in phonological contrast with short vowels. Phonologically nasalized vowels are possible in Fongbe, but forbidden in KiKoongo.

Root morphemes are usually monosyllabic in Fongbe, although disyllables are possible. In KiKoongo things are the other way around. Root morphemes are usually disyllabic, although monosyllables also occur, as also longer forms.

4.   Fongbe and KiKoongo speakers in early Surinam

I have written elsewhere on my ideas of how the development of a creole language (Sranan) took place in Surinam (Smith 2006). Briefly summarized, my views are as follows:

The first stage in the development of interethnic communication would have been a MIC (medium of interethnic communication) (cf. Baker 1990). Such a

---

3. The name of the people is Fon, and Fongbe – literally 'Fon-tongue' – is the name of the language.

communication system probably already existed prior to the foundation of the colony, in Barbados (Smith 2001). This was necessary because there were slaves of various origins represented there, and then in Surinam, right from the beginning.

I differ from Baker on two important points. Firstly, I don't agree with him that each plantation in Surinam would have had its own MIC. Arends (2001: 301–304, drawing on Muyrers 1993: 99–108) provides a whole list of opportunities for slaves to develop what he terms "external network relations". There is no reason to doubt that the totality of Surinam plantations should be considered as forming one overall slave society, particularly in the mid-17th century, before the plantations had grown larger, and the population more one-sided in ethnicity.

Secondly, I consider it highly likely that the slave MIC would have been restricted to the slave proto-ethnic group. The story of the formation of the Surinam creole language (Sranan) would seem fairly obviously to be the story of the development of an in-group code. As I have attempted to show in Smith (2009), there is every reason to assume that many slaves could have and would have had a fair command of English in the early period, as the conditions for sufficient exposure to that language to make that possible prevailed up till 1685 or so. And we have no conceivable reason for assuming that 17th century Africans would be any worse at acquiring second languages than anyone else in any place at any time. In particular the language density in West Africa is such that many slaves from the Slave Coast would already certainly have known more than one language, albeit often closely related languages. And the situation in early Surinam was such, as I have claimed, that sufficient exposure to English was available to enable the acqusition of adequate English fairly rapidly (cf. also Mufwene 2008).

My position is then as follows. If English had become the primary language of the slave population, as proponents of gradual creolization argue, there is in fact no reason for assuming it would not have remained so. As we know that English did not end up as the primary language of the slave population, it is not likely that this was ever the case, given the above. To put this in a stronger fashion, the very fact that (a form of) English is not the primary language of the descendants of the slaves, can in fact be regarded as an argument that it never achieved that status, or had had it but subsequently lost it.

A report from a Dutch traveller to Surinam in 1693 (Van Alphen 1962) claims the language of the slaves was English. Presumably a Dutch traveller would be able to distinguish English (quite similar to Dutch after all) from Sranan, which is obviously totally different.

(2) "De Engelse hebben hier een colonie gemaeckt en wort die tael daer nog meest bij de slaven gesproken."
[The English have made a colony here, and that language is still most spoken there by the slaves, NS.]

Our first written record of Sranan dates from 1707 (Van den Berg 2007). The 1693 report has been interpreted to mean that Sranan had not yet developed, but had been preceded as the primary slave language by English (cf. Smith 2009). I would rather interpret it to mean that English was (widely) spoken by the slave population. Only *not* as their primary language, for sociological reasons connection with resistance (cf. DeGraff 2002; Jourdan 2008; Smith 2009). Sranan must have existed in a well-developed form fairly shortly after the beginning of the 18th century in any case since this was when plantation Sranan gave rise to the language of the Ndyuka tribe through marronnage. But even previous to this, in the 1690's, we have the large-scale marronnage that gave rise to Saramaccan (Price 1983; Smith 2009). This must represent not the creation of a new creole in the jungle, as envisaged by Bickerton, but the carrying-off of a previously existing mixed creole, formed on the basis of Sranan and Portuguese (creole) – what was referred to as Dju-Tongo ('Jew(ish) language') – from the Jewish plantation area on the Middle Surinam River (Smith 1999).

The lack of contact with English speakers which is often claimed to have resulted in the creation of Sranan *at a later date*, is always posited on the basis of the lack of linguistic contact between the main body of slaves and whites *at this later date*, when the former group had greatly expanded in size, making intimate contact with whites the exception rather than the rule. As I have argued in Smith (2006), this is a false premise. It is a mistake to work purely on the premise that the proportions of Europeans and slaves *at any given moment* should necessarily reflect the respective proportions of English speakers and speakers of other languages.

To cut a long story short, I conclude that the development of Sranan must have taken place fairly early on – I have argued (Smith 2002, 2006) for the first half of the 1660's (see also McWhorter (1998) for a similar viewpoint). In other words the development of Sranan did not follow a period in which English language-learning took place – it overlapped with it, in a period when Fongbe and KiKoongo were both widely spoken as mother-tongues. One reason for insisting on the earliness of this period is the necessity to allow sufficient time for the development of the precursor of Saramaccan (Dju-Tongo or 'Jew(ish) language') in the second half of the 1670's, as a mixed creole language created from *Sranan*, and either Portuguese or a Portuguese-lexifier creole or conceivably both. That Saramaccan is basically a mixed creole, rather than a Portuguese-based one, or basically an English-based one with a lot of Portuguese lexical borrowings, has gradually become clearer (cf. Smith & Cardoso 2004). A surprising finding was that verbs of European (but non-Dutch) origin were more frequently of Portuguese than English origin.

A less fundamental question, but the crucial one in relation to this article, is that of KiKoongo and Fongbe/Eastern Gbe language use in the formative period of Sranan, and thereafter, of Saramaccan. In this period we can assume that the two above-mentioned African languages would be the only African languages used to any extent in the slave community, considering the provenance of the vast majority of slaves.

What would this mean in practice? Conversations involving any number of interlocutors would be in the community language (Sranan, or later also Saramaccan, in the Jewish plantation area). The smaller the number of people involved the greater the chance that Fongbe or KiKoongo would be used. At the level of mother-child interactions we can imagine either a monolingual African language interaction, or a bilingual African language-Creole language interaction. As time went on there would presumably be more of the second type, and less of the first type. We do know however that African languages remained spoken for some time.

There are still three ritual languages of African origin used in Surinam, going under various names, such as Papa (Gbe), Ampuku (KiKoongo), and Kromanti (Akan). The last of these we can safely ignore here, as the Gold Coast, where it hailed from, only began to be a significant source of slaves in the 1700's.

Further early Dutch colonial records speak of maroon settlements with qualifications like *Papadorp*, i.e. 'Gbe village'. And some of the clans making up the Saramaccan maroon tribe have specifically Gbe associations, like the Abaísa and Matjáu (cf. Price 1983), while others are clearly of KiKoongo origin, like the Lángu (Loango).

For the mid-1660's I proceed from the following model (Figure 1) of language interactions.

The degree to which Fongbe-speakers had full active competence in KiKoongo or vice versa is unclear. The facts we will describe below would tend to suggest that the above was not generally the case. The most probable situation is that the interaction between Fongbe and KiKoongo was largely mediated by Sranan/Saramaccan.

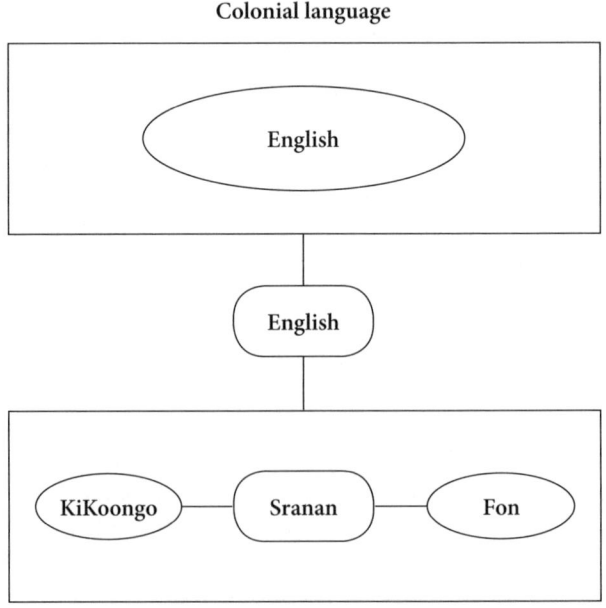

Figure 1. A model of possible mid-1660's language interaction

In the light of the previous paragraph, I will provide evidence in the following section for a number of phenomena involving KiKoongo lexical items that together suggest that Fongbe speakers were aware of the fact that KiKoongo nouns had class-prefixes, but largely through their employment by KiKoongo speakers in the context of the Surinam creole languages. I hypothesize then that this knowledge would be indirectly acquired through the medium of the new slave-language, Sranan. I will return to this point below.

5. Bantu noun class morphology preserved in Saramaccan

As stated above, we find a large body of KiKoongo-derived nouns incorporating class prefixes in Surinam. Similar to what we find in the English-derived vocabulary, sporadic plural forms occur among the majority singular nouns in most classes. Unlike the English plural forms, which may be explicable as forms normally encountered in the plural with collective reference, most KiKoongo forms with plural prefixes are not susceptible to such an explanation. This suggests that we have a case of petrification, with the prefixes not being understood, or perhaps ceasing to be understood, by a large body of speakers of the incipient creole languages.

In what follows I discuss first the examples of noun prefixes used in KiKoongo loans in the Surinam creole langages. The greater part of these lexical items come from Daeleman (1972), but others are from my own research, and that of Huttar (1985). A number of new etymologies for plant names were found by comparing Van 't Klooster, Lindeman & Jansen-Jacobs (2003) with Daeleman & Pauwels (1983).

KiNtandu, the KiKoongo variety Daeleman identified as closest to the KiKoongo elements in Saramaccan, has the following noun-class system:[4]

(3) | Nomenclature | Singular prefix | Plural prefix | |
| --- | --- | --- | --- |
| 1/2 | mu/N/mw- | ba- | |
| 3/4 | mu/N/mw- | mi/N/my- | (N is syllabic) |
| 5/6 | di/Ø/dy- | ma/m- | |
| 7/8 | ki/ky-[5] | bi/by- | |
| 9/10 | N- | N- | (N is non-syllabic) |
| 11/12 | lu/lw- | tu/tw- | |
| 11/10 | lu/lw- | N- | (N is non-syllabic) |
| 11/14 | lu/lw- | bu/bw- | |

The Ø-reflex of noun class 5, the singular marker in gender 5/6, will play a significant role in what follows. This is the default allomorph of this marker in KiNtandu.

---

4. I ignore rare "genders" involving unusual combinations of singular and plural prefixes.
5. In other forms of KiKoongo the singular prefix may have no surface representation.

Clearly, KiNtandu does not tell us the whole story. The class 7 prefix is also often realised as Ø in other forms of KiKoongo, as is noted in Note 7, but not in KiNtandu. I will suggest that a dialect of this type was also spoken among the slaves imported to Surinam.

There is such a dialect in Laman's Central KiKoongo (identified as Mazinga[6] by Söderberg 1985). Thilo Schadeberg (pers.comm.) informs me that about 45 nouns in Laman (1938) are class 7 nouns from Central KiKoongo, only nine of which display an explicit prefix, in specific morphophonemic contexts.[7] Examples of bare singulars in Mazinga are (from Laman 1938):

(4) *Mazinga bare singulars*

	singular	plural	gloss
cl. 5/6	dyaba	ma-dyaba	sp. medicine
	fúndi	ma-fúndi	muscle
	kéke	ma-kéke	twig
	dunguta	ma-dunguta	sp. basket
cl. 7/8	dóngo	bi-dóngo	side
	dóngo	bi-dóngo	rifle
	kàka	bi-kàka	sp. dish
	kéke	bi-kéke	end of palm root

As we will also see from the KiKoongo words in the Surinam creoles, there is a large group of class 5/6 words which have a plural prefix in their Surinam creole form. A smaller group of class 7/8 words share this feature. A few words of other classes also occur in the plural form. However, some of these can be explained in semantic terms.

5.1   The reflexes of KiKoongo class prefixes in the Surinam creoles

I will restrict myself to an examination of three noun-classes: 3/4, 5/6 and 7/8. These are the best illustrated of the noun-classes, and will suffice to make my point. My examples will be drawn from Saramaccan in large part, but also from Sranan, Ndyuka and Kwinti.

Noun-class 3/4 (Swartenbroekcx class 4)
Words deriving from KiKoongo noun-class 3/4 frequently illustrate the continuation of the singular prefix /mu-/ in the Surinam creoles. No case is known displaying the plural prefix /mi-/. This noun-class occurs eight times in our data.

---

6.   Spoken in the area of Mukimbungu.

7.   These are ki- with monosyllabic stems; ky- with vowel-initial stems; and ki- before nasal clusters (Schadeberg, pers.comm.).

Table 2. KiKoongo noun-class 3/4 lexical items in the Surinam creoles

Lang./Source	Form	1778	KiNtandu[8]	Gloss [Sur]	Pref.	Nr.
Sa-D	mukangá	*mokwango*	N-kwaangá	sp. plant	mu-	sg
Sa-D	mutyáma	*mutjamma*	n-kyaamá;	rainbow	mu-	sg
Nd-H	muntyama		N-kyáma (Laman)			
Sa-D	muungá	*mulungà*	N-luungá	armband	mu-	sg
Sa-D	mutete		N-tete	basket	mu-	sg
Nd-H	mutete			backpack		
Sr-S	musoyo	*müssunja, sunja*		sp. grass	mu-	sg
Nd-H	musokóo		N-sókó	palm leaf	mu-	sg

Sa-D = Saramaccan-Daeleman, Nd-H = Ndyuka-Huttar, Sr-S Sranan-Smith.

Other words do not show any trace of a prefix (Table 3).

These two cases could be explained in terms of their length. The standard noun of KiKoongo origin has a disyllabic stem with a monosyllabic prefix – three syllables in all. These examples are trisyllabic, so that the first syllable could have been presumed to have been a prefix by Fongbe speakers. See below for further support. This explanation cannot however apply in the following six cases (Table 4).

Table 3. Prefixless noun-class 3/4 lexical items in the Surinam creoles

Lang./Source	Form	1778	KiNtandu	Gloss [Sur]	Pref.	Nr.
Sa-D	sakusu		N-sakusu	bellows	Ø-	
Sa-D	séngɛɛ		N-séngele	knife blade	Ø-	
Nd-H	sengee					

Table 4. More prefixless noun-class 3/4 lexical items in the Surinam creoles

Lang./Source	Form	1778	KiNtandu	Gloss [Sur]	Pref.	Nr.
Sa-S	wandú		wandú	pigeon pea	Ø-	sg
Sa-S	kumbá	*gumbà*	N-kúumba (KiKoongo)	navel	Ø-	sg
Al-S	kumba					
Nd-H	kumba					
Kw-H	kuumba					
Sa-D	mbulu		mbúlu (Ndibu)	hairless corners	Ø-	sg
Sa-D	bungi		N-buungi	mildew	Ø-	sg
Sa-D	lalú		N-lalú	hibiscus	Ø-	sg
Sa-D	yundú		N-yuundú	otter	Ø-	sg
Nd-H	nyuundú					

Al-S = Aluku-Smith, Kw-H = Kwinti-Huttar.

---

8. n = nonsyllabic nasal; N = syllabic nasal.

Why these lack a prefix is as yet unclear. One thing is clear however, that a plural prefix is never found with words of this class. At least /wandú/ of this group occurs in KiNtandu too without an explicit prefix.

Class 5/6 (Swartenbroekcx class 6)
The KiKoongo words from this class in the Surinam creoles present a completely different picture. Nearly every form represents a KiKoongo plural form (Table 5).

Table 5. KiKoongo noun-class 5/6 lexical items in the Surinam creoles

Lang./Source	Form	1778	KiNtandu	Gloss [Sur]	Pref.	Nr.
Sa-D	manungú	madungu	(ma-)dúungu	hernia	ma-	pl
Nd-H	manungu					
Sa-D	mayaya		(ma-)dyaadya	sp. grass	ma-	pl
Sa-D	makobo		(ma-)kubu	sp. fish	ma-	pl
Sa-D	makpánya		(ma-)kwaansya	pimple	ma-	pl
Sa-D	makúku	makúku	(ma-)kúku	potstand	ma-	pl
Sa-S	mapápi		(ma-)pàpi	wing point	ma-	pl
Nd-H	mapaapí			wing		
Sa-D	masiá	massila	(ma-)síila	second crop	ma-	pl
Sa-D	masisá	massisà	(ma-)sisa (Yombe)	sp. plant	ma-	pl
Nd-H	masisá					
Sr-D	masusá		(ma-)susá		ma	pl
Sa-D	masuá		(ma-)swá	fishtrap	ma-	pl
Nd-H	masúa					
Sa-D	matutu		(ma-)tutu	sp. rat	ma-	pl
Sa-D	matungá		(ma-)tunga nyundu	sp. plant (Myila)	ma-	pl
Nd-H	matungá máka					
Sa-D	(**mamá**)kóngo		(ma-)kóongo	kind of *kándu*	ma-	pl
AP-S	makaya		(ma-)káya	magic remedy	ma-	pl
Sr-S	makanda		(ma-)kanda	clan	ma-	pl
Nd-H	makonkón		(ma-)kónko	grasshopper	ma-	pl
Nd-H	masanga		(ma-)sanga	hut	ma-	pl
Nd-H	mántama		(ma-)táma	cheek	ma-	pl
Sa-D	**mu**tama	mattamma			**mu-**	
Sa-D	**mu**venda	lovenda	(ma-)véénda	receding hairline	**mu-**	

Sa-S = Saramaccan-Smith, AP-S = Aluku (Papa)-Smith.

All in all we note nineteen such forms – all originally using what was the plural prefix form (Table 6).

A small number of singular forms occur. The Kwinti form /isangá/ conceivably retains a prefix which has other disappeared from singular forms in KiNtandu.

Table 6. Prefixless noun-class 5/6 lexical items in the Surinam creoles

Lang./Source	Form	1778	KiNtandu	Gloss [Sur]	Pref.	Nr.
Kw-S[9]	isangá		?-sanga		i-	sg?
Sa-D	yangá		yaangá	mockery	Ø-	sg
Sa-D	tutú	tutù	túutu	trumpet	Ø-	sg
Sr-S	kundú		kúndu (KiKoongo)	lump	Ø-	sg

Kw-S = Kwinti-Smith.

Bentley notes the class 5 prefix as /e-/, and when it does occur in KiNtandu, it appears in the form /di-/ – before a nasal cluster, and /dy-/ before a vowel.

Some words that belonged to class 5/6 historically appear to now bear prefixes belonging to other classes). I will discuss these cases later.

Class 7/8 (Swartenbroekcx class 5)

Here we see a mixed result. Four items occur with the plural prefix /bi-/, four more with an explicit singular prefix /ki-, ky-/, but the majority appear with no explicit suffix, and are presumably singular forms (Table 7).

Table 7. KiKoongo noun-class 7/8 lexical items in the Surinam creoles

Lang./Source	Form	1778	KiNtandu	Gloss [Sur]	Pref.	Nr.
Sa-D	ambolo		ki-mboolo	large lizard		?
Sa-D	tyalí		ky-aadí	regret	ki-	sg
Sa-D	tyanga		ky-anga	ritual area	ki-	sg
Sa-D	kiná/tyiná	kjina/tchina	ki-ina (Yombe)	taboo	ki-	sg
Sa-D	tyubɛngɛ	kibenge	ki-béenga	girdle for cassava	ki-	sg
Sa-P	biɔ́ngɔ		bi-lóongo	ritual ingredients	bi-	pl
Sa-D	bisaka	bisakka	bi-saka	reed fishtrap	bi-	pl
Sa-S	bilolí		bilolí	sp. moss	bi-	pl
Sa-D	bingúngu		ngúúngú (Yombe); ki-ngungu (Laman)	bug	bi-	pl
Nd-H	búngú		ki-búungu; búngu (Laman)	earthenware jar	Ø-	sg
Sa-D	búngu	bungu			Ø-	sg
Sa-D	gangá		ki-gáanga	head load rest	Ø-	sg
Sa-D	kándu	kandu	ki-káandu; kándu (Laman)	curse	Ø-	sg
Sa-D	gobo-gobo	gobbogobbo	ki-nguba-ngubá	sp. large peanut	Ø-	sg

Sa-P = Saramaccan-Price.

---

9. This form is taken from Van der Elst (1975).

With the exception of /tyubɛngɛ/ – older *kibenge*, the only forms displaying an explicit singular prefix /ki-/ are items corresponding to forms in KiKoongo where the /ki-/ precedes vowel-initial stems. Other words deriving from this class either display no trace of a KiKoongo prefix, and some of these are recorded from Laman's Central KiKoongo (i.e. Mazinga) dialect), or exhibit the plural prefix /bi-/.

5.2 Summary of class prefix presence/absence

Class 3/4 illustrates two variants: forms reflecting the old singular prefix /mu-/, or no prefix at all. At least one of these prefixless forms occurs in a parallel prefixless form in KiNtandu. The plural prefix /mi-/ does not appear at all.

Class 5/6 is illustrated by a large majority of forms reflecting the old plural prefix /ma-/. A few isolated prefixless forms presumably reflect old singular cases.

Class 7/8 is illustrated by a number of forms derived from old prefixed forms with /ki-/. Most of these are in prevocalic position. A group of prefixless singulars also occur, while another group of words reflects forms with the plural prefix /bi-/.

To conclude, class 5/6 appears in the large majority of cases in the plural form with a prefix. Class 3/4 exhibits no forms at all with plural prefixes. Class 7/8 exhibits an explicit singular prefix in KiNtandu, but not in Mazinga. At least some of the prefixless forms in this group correspond to prefixless forms in the latter dialect. This occurrence of bare singulars may have triggered the appearance of some forms with explicit plural suffixes.

6. KiKoongo words with the "wrong" prefixes in Surinam

There are about a dozen KiKoongo nouns which display a reflex of the wrong prefix in the Saramaccan version of the KiKoongo word. This reflex always corresponds however to one of the KiKoongo class prefixes, except for a single isolated case. Among these are two cases where what looks like a double KiKoongo class 6 prefix where /ma-ma-/ appears optionally in the Saramaccan form. One of these is a class 5/6 noun, where we would expect /ma-/ anyway as the plural class marker, the other, however, is a class 9/10 noun. In both cases there are alternate forms lacking any reflex of the plural prefix.

Confirmation of the fact that the class markers ceased to have any class meaning is further indicated by a form like /kamamba/ 'scar', corresponding to a plural form in KiKoongo /ma-kaamba/. Here the first two syllables have been switched – a putative earlier form /**ma**ka**m**ba/ has become /ka**ma**mba/ (Table 8).

Table 8. Surinam creole forms with the "wrong" prefix

Lang./Source	Form	1778	KiNtandu	Gloss [Sur]	Pref.	Nr.
Nd-H	**má**ntama		(ma-)táma	cheek	ma-	pl
Sa-S	**mu**tama	*mat*tamma			mu-	
Sa-S	**mu**venda	*lo*venda	(ma-)véénda	receding hairline	mu-	
Sa-D	(**mamá**)kóngo		(ma-)kóongo	kind of *kándu*	ma-	pl
Sa-D	(**mama**)sakusaku		n-saku-n-saku sákú-saku lu-sákú-saku[10]			
Sa-D	**ma**fengé[11]	*ma*fingè	m-fingí[12]	small rat		
Sa-D	**ma**séngé [13]					
Sa-S	**ma**lembe(lembe)		ki-léémbé	sp. plant		
Pa-S	**mu**lomba		ki-lóomba	sp. plant		
Sa-S	**ka**mambá		ma-kámba	scars	ma-	pl
Sa-D	**mu**zega[14]		ki-zíka (Yaka)	sp. grass		
Sa-D	**ma**zigaziga		ki-zika-zíka (")			

For at least two lexical items we have evidence of change in "prefix" in Saramaccan during the last two hundred years.

(5) 20th century 18th century KiKoongo   prefix   gloss
    mutama   *mat*tamma   **ma**-táma   ma > mu   cheek
    muvenda   *lo*venda   **ma**-véénda ma > lu > mu   receding hairline

Rather than a series of two replacements in the second case, it is also possible that the /ma-/ was replaced by /lu-/ and /mu-/ in different variants of Saramaccan.

Other cases illustrate the possible replacement of other prefixes by the more familiar /mu-, ma-/. Examples include 9/10 (N-) and 7/8 (ki-). Curious are the two cases of optional double /ma-/ prefixation.

6.1 Trisyllabicity

In some cases quadrisyllabic nouns are reduced to three syllables.

---

10. Class 11/10.
11. Lombe village.
12. Class 9/10.
13. Golio village.
14. Golio village.

(6) | Saramaccan | KiKoongo | gloss |
|---|---|---|
| pukusu | **lu**-mpukusu | bat |
| sakusu | **mu**-sakusu | bellows |
| séngɛɛ | **mu**-séngele | handleless blade |
| bukɔkɔ, mukɔkɔ | mbulu-koóko | black ibis |

In three out of these four cases the syllable lost is the KiKoongo prefix syllable.

7. Provisional conclusions

(7) a. KiKoongo-speaking slaves were not only present in large numbers in Surinam but contributed in a significant degree to the lexicons of the creole languages, in particular to that of Saramaccan. Both these aspects have already been established by the efforts of previous scholars. My only contribution has been to point out the "smoother" nature of the importation of Fon slaves vis-à-vis the "lumpier" nature of the KiKoongo slave traffic. This is more clearly revealed by examining the importation of slaves in terms of half-decades.

b. As far as nouns are concerned, KiKoongo differs typologically from Fongbe in a significant manner. Fongbe nouns are (V).CV while KiKoongo nouns are CV.CV.CV (ignoring clusters and long vowels).

c. The initial (prefix) syllable of the prototypically trisyllabic KiKoongo noun is normally preserved, although not always. When altered, the replacement syllable usually corresponds to another Kikongo prefix.

d. Disyllabic noun stems lacking a class prefix in the singular tend to be adopted in their plural form with an overt prefix. This occurs most clearly in class 5/6, but also to a lesser degree in class 7/8.

e. That initial prefix syllables in KiKoongo may be replaced in historical Saramaccan records implies that they have progressively lost whatever vague meanings they possessed in that language.

f. That quadrisyllabic words are sometimes reduced to three syllables, often with the loss of the class prefix, indicates again that the class prefixes have gradually lost their original function in KiKoongo nouns, and in addition indicates that the general prototypical KiKoongo noun no longer necessarily involved a class prefix as such in the eyes of Sranan speakers, but perhaps merely came to consist of a trisyllabic structure.

8. Sranan as a mediating language

What does this tell us about what role Sranan had with respect to the two main groups, the Fon and the Bakoongo? It suggests in itself that Sranan (and later Saramaccan) acted as intermediary or mediator in the contact between the two groups.

I hypothesize that when KiKoongo mother tongue speakers first used nouns from their own language *in Sranan* they employed them with the relevant native language *inflectional* morphology.[15] What would this mean for the word that was adopted into Saramaccan as /mutyáma/? In the light of this hypothesis we would then have an original singular/plural paradigm as follows:

(8) a. di   mu-tyáma
       DEF   CL3-rainbow
       'the rainbow'
    b. den   mi-tyáma
       DEF.PL CL4-rainbow
       'the rainbows'

Note that we have a redundant situation. That the (a) NP is singular was already indicated sufficiently by the singular definite article /di/. To indicate singularity again by the *contrastive* use of a class 3 prefix as against a class 4 prefix is unnecessary. Similarly that the (b) NP is plural was already sufficiently indicated by the plural definite article /den/. To indicate plurality again by the *contrastive* use of a class 4 prefix as against a class 3 prefix is once again unnecessary.

However, the normal class 5/6 singular/plural pair would present a different picture.

(9) a. di   kúku
       DEF   potstand (CL5)
       'the potstand'
    b. den   ma-kúku
       DEF.PL CL6-potstand
       'the potstands'

(8) and (9), taken together, give us with the basis for a credible scenario of how the present situation of KiKoongo-derived items could have developed. A first step would involve the selection of a number-neutral prefix. This would preserve the KiKoongo noun-classes with KiKoongo nouns, but get rid of the redundant extra number distinctions involved.

---

15. Note that plural marking in Fongbe is in the form of a clitic, and so would not be preserved.

(10) a. **di** **mu**-tyáma >> **di** *mu*-tyáma
DEF CL3-rainbow DEF MU-rainbow
'the rainbow'
b. **den** **mi**-tyáma >> **den** *mu*-tyáma
DEF.PL CL4-rainbow DEF.PL MU-rainbow
'the rainbows'

(11) a. **di** kúku >> **di** *ma*-kúku
DEF potstand (CL5) DEF MA-potstand
'the potstand'
b. **den** **ma**-kúku >> **den** ma-kúku
DEF.PL CL6-potstand DEF.PL MA-potstand
'the potstands'

In (10) the most frequent form would be adopted, that of the singular (class 3) form. While in (11) the expectation among Fongbe speakers that a prefix be present would ensure the adoption of the plural (class 6) form. So, I am arguing here for the staged loss of the number-gender aspect of the prefixes. In favour of this are the various cases given above where the prefix has been replaced by a "wrong" prefix.

As a result of the neutralization of number, even this grammatical meaning would then be lost, resulting in apparently "simpler" structures:

(12) a. **di** mutyáma
DEF rainbow
'the rainbow'
b. **den** mutyáma
DEF.PL rainbow
'the rainbows'

(13) a. **di** makúku
DEF potstand
'the potstand'
b. **den** makúku
DEF.PL potstand
'the potstands'

What we see here is, I hypothesize, the following development in the morphology of KiKoongo items in Saramaccan/Sranan:

(14) class.number-N >> class-N >> N

These changes can only be seen as "local" simplifications – in the context of the KiKoongo lexical stratum in the Surinam creoles, and then only for KiKoongo speakers. The number-marking aspect of the prefix would be redundant for most creole speakers, and simply disappeared. I hypothesize that the class-marking as-

Table 9. Morphological analysis and meaning

	Functional	Functional	Morphotactic	Frozen
Formally parsed	+	+	+	−
Semantically parsed	+	±	−	−
	KiKoongo	17th c. Saramaccan	18th c. Saramaccan	20th c. Saramaccan

pect lasted longer, but ultimately disappeared as something that was non-functional in the larger vocabulary. In addition I had raised the possible existence of a tendency towards a trisyllabic canonical form in KiKoongo words in the Surinam creoles. In hindsight this may be partially accounted for by the development towards a semantically empty class-marker system in KiKoongo items in18th century Saramaccan/Sranan (see Table 9).

The claim is that in 18th century Saramaccan these Bantu prefixes had a status similar to Latinate prefixes in English like: *de-ceive, re-ceive, con-ceive, de-fer, re-fer, con-fer* etc. The words as a whole have a meaning in Modern English, but we cannot attach any particular meaning to the parsable prefixes *de*, *re*, and *con*. The numerous cases of the occurrence of the plural *ma-* prefix in noun-class 5/6 rather than the singular zero-prefix argues for the tendency to have an explicit prefix with disyllabic KiKoongo stems. The forms had come to represent an isolated MA-gender. In addition the frequent forms with "wrong" prefixes witness to the loss of functionality of these prefixes.

That things have changed in modern Saramaccan as compared to the 18th century is indicated by the possibility of a form like /kamamba/ instead of /*makamba/ 'scar' (cf. KiKoongo /ma-kaamba/). Although a form /*makamba/ is not evidenced from earlier Saramaccan, we can be fairly sure that such a form existed. No prefix /ka-/ exists in nominal inflection in KiKoongo,[16] indicating that these forms had ceased to be "morphotactically parsable". The original functional load of the KiKoongo prefixes became redundant in the Surinam creoles due to the presence of determiners bearing number features.

What does this tell us about simplification and/or complexification? It tells us that restricted strata in the lexicon, while they may well enter a creole language exemplifying complex morphological patterns, will tend to lose these if they are redundant. An apparently redundant irregularity introduced in a small part of the lexicon will just tend to disappear. A purely distributional remnant set of morphemes, which no longer correspond to functional meanings, will then also tend to disappear as parsable entities. All that will remain will be certain phonological bits and pieces, with no guarantee of any stability (cf. the example in the previous paragraph).

---

16. Although this did exist in Proto-Bantu, as the marker of class 13, with diminutive meaning.

It is not completely clear at what date these KiKoongo items entered the various creole languages. However, it is certainly striking that four cases in noun class 3/4, six cases in noun class 5/6, and one class in class 7/8 out of the examples are shared between Saramaccan and Ndyuka. This could be seen as an argument for putting the adoption of these items back before the formation of Saramaccan in 1680. The fact that these items are all lacking in (Paramaribo) Sranan (if our data for Sranan are relevant in this context) could be attributed to cultural factors. It must not be forgotten that Ndyuka derives from a plantation variant of Sranan, One form does show up in modern Sranan (*masusa*) but with a different KiKoongo dialect origin. It is difficult to know how to interpret this case. An argument for the shared adoption of these words into Ndyuka and Saramaccan is provided by the form *manungu* displayed a shared, and irregular, innovation as compared to the original KiKoongo form.

We cannot determine whether the incorporation of these words predated the formation of Sranan, i.e. happened during the MIC (medium of interethnic communication) phase. Note that we do have evidence suggesting that the basis of this MIC was already an expanded pidgin, a general Caribbean Plantation Pidgin English (Smith 2001), already possessing a number of complex morphosyntactic structures, which are still shared among Caribbean-area creole languages today.

None of this provides any evidence for any kind of general simplification in creole languages. And in fact there seems to be little for any correspondance between the creole-pidgin dichotomy and the simplicity-complexity dimension. If the facts in Smith (2001) hold, then the only time and place in the Caribbean where a truly simple jargon pidgin could have existed was during the first few years in Barbados.

As I said above, the facts of the adoption of a significant number of KiKoongo lexical items into the Surinam creoles is only evidence of a "local" kind of simplification – ridding the language(s) of an irregular redundancy likely introduced by the borrowing of a number of lexical items from the same source language – KiKoongo. What we see here then is a nice example of the ironing-out of a limited irregularity introduced from another language – something that is precisely interpreted as an irregularity because of its limited nature, and therefore disappears.

Acknowledgements

I am very grateful to Enoch Aboh and Umberto Ansaldo for their very useful commentary on versions of this paper. Together they managed to persuade me to write a very different, and I am sure more interesting, article than the one I had originally envisaged. I am solely responsible for any errors. I am also grateful to Thilo Schadeberg for his enthusiastic assistance with KiKoongo.

References

Aboh, Enoch O. 2005. Object shift, verb movement and verb reduplication. In *The Oxford Handbook of Comparative Syntax*, Guglielmo Cinque & Richard Kayne (eds). Oxford: OUP.

Aboh, Enoch O. 2007. A 'mini' relative clause analysis for reduplicated attributive adjectives. *Linguistics in The Netherlands* 24: 1–13.

Aboh, Enoch O. To appear. The left periphery in the Surinamese Creoles and Gbe: On the modularity of substrate transfer. In *The Transatlantic Sprachbund: Benin and Surinam*, Pieter C. Muysken & Norval Smith (eds).

Aboh, Enoch O. & Smith, Norval. To appear. Non-iconic reduplications in Eastern Gbe and Surinam. In *The Transatlantic Sprachbund: Benin and Surinam*, Pieter C. Muysken & Norval Smith (eds).

Arends, Jacques. 1995. Demographic factors in the formation of Sranan. In *The Early Stages of Creolization* [Creole Language Library 13], Jacques Arends (ed.), 233–285. Amsterdam: John Benjamins.

Arends, Jacques. 2001. Social stratification and network relations in the formation of Sranan. In *Creolization and Contact* [Creole Language Library 23], Norval Smith & Tonjes Veenstra (eds), 291–307. Amsterdam: John Benjamins.

Baker, Philip. 1990. Off Target? *Journal of Pidgin and Creole Languages* 5: 107–120.

Daeleman, Jan. 1972. Kongo elements in Saramacca Tongo. *Journal of African Languages* 11: 1–44.

Daeleman, Jan & Pauwels, Luc. 1983. Notes d'ethnobotanique Ntándu (Kóongo): Principales plantes de la région de Kisaántu: Noms Ntándu et noms scientifiques [Africana Linguistica IX]. Tervuren: Koninklijk Museum voor Midden-Afrika.

DeGraff, M. 2002. Relexification: A reevaluation. Anthropological Linguistics 44: 321–414.

Huttar, George. 1985. Sources of Ndjuka African vocabulary. New West Indian Guide 59: 45–71.

Jourdan, Christine. 2008. The cultural in PC genesis. In *The Handbook of Pidgin and Creole Languages*, John Singler & Silvia Kouwenberg (eds). Oxford: Blackwell.

Laman, Karl E. 1938. *Dictionary of the Kongo Language*. Brussels.

McWhorter, John H. 1998. Identifying the creole prototype: Vindicating a typological class. Language 74: 788–818.

Mufwene, Salikoko S. 2008. *Language Evolution: Contact, Competition and Change*. London: Continuum.

Muyrers, Sabine. 1993. Het netwerk van de slaaf: Een onderzoek naar contacten van Surinaamse plantageslaven in de achtiende en negentiende eeuw. MA thesis, Erasmus University Rotterdam.

Muysken, Pieter C. & Smith, Norval. To appear. *The Transatlantic Sprachbund: Benin and Surinam*.

Postma, Johannes M. 1990. *The Dutch in the Atlantic Slave Trade 1600–1815*. Cambridge: CUP.

Price, Richard. 1983. *First-time: The Historical Vision of an Afro-American People*. Baltimore MD: Johns Hopkins University Press.

Smith, Norval. 1987a. Gbe words in the creole languages of Surinam. Paper given at the *Amsterdam Creole Workshop*, University of Amsterdam, 1987.

Smith, Norval. 1987b. The Genesis of the Creole Languages of Surinam. PhD dissertation, University of Amsterdam.
Smith, Norval. 1999. Pernambuco to Surinam 1654–1665? The Jewish slave controversy. In *Spreading the Word: The Issue of Diffusion among the Atlantic Creoles*, Magnus Huber & Mikael Parkvall (eds), 251–298. London: University of Westminster Press.
Smith, Norval. 2001. Reconstructing Proto-Caribbean Pidgin English. Paper given at *Pidginfest*, University of Westminster, 19–21 April, 2001.
Smith, Norval. 2002. The creole languages of Surinam: Past and present. In *Language Atlas of Surinam*, Jacques Arends & Eithne Carlin (eds), 131–151. Leiden: KITLV Press.
Smith, Norval. 2004. A case of creole substrate allophony 350 years on: Nasality in Saramaccan. Paper given at *Montreal Dialogues: Processes in L2 Acquisition and in Creole Genesis*, Université du Québec à Montréal, 29 August, 2004.
Smith, Norval. 2006. Very rapid creolization in the framework of the Restricted Motivation Hypothesis. In *L2 acquisition and creole genesis: Dialogues* [Language Acquisition & Language Disorders 42], Claire Lefebvre, Lydia White & Christine Jourdan (eds), 49–65. Amsterdam: John Benjamins.
Smith, Norval. 2009. English-speaking in early Surinam? In *Gradual Creolization: Studies Celebrating Jacques Arends* [Creole Language Library 34], Rachel Selbach, Margot C. van den Berg & Hugo Cardoso (eds). Amsterdam: John Benjamins.
Smith, Norval & Cardoso, Hugo. 2004. The origin of the Portuguese words in Saramaccan: Implications for sociohistory. *Journal of Portuguese Linguistics* 3: 115–147.
Smith, Norval, Robertson, Ian E. & Williamson, Kay. 1987. The Ijo element in Berbice Dutch. Language and Society 16: 49–90.
Smith, Norval & Veenstra, Tonjes. 1998. Synthetic compounds in a radical creole: Abrupt versus gradual change. International Symposium on Degrees of Restructuring in Creole Languages, University of Regensburg, 26 June, 1998.
Söderberg, Bertil. 1985. *Karl Edvard Laman, missionär, språkforskare, etnograf* (Karl Edvard Laman, missionary, linguist, ethnographer). Stockholm: Svenska Missionsförbundet.
Swartenbroekx, Pierre. 1973. *Dictionnaire Kikongo et Kituba-Française.*Bandundu: Ceeba.
Van Alphen, G. 1962. Suriname in een onbekend journaal van 1693. *West-Indische Gids* 42: 303–313.
Van den Berg, Margot C. 2007. A Grammar of Early Sranan. PhD dissertation, University of Amsterdam.
Van der Elst, Dirk H. 1975. The Coppename Kwinti: Notes on an Afro-American tribe in Surinam. *Nieuw West-Indische Gids* 50: 7–17, 107–122, 200–211.
Van 't Klooster, Charlotte I.E.A., Lindeman, Jan Christiaan & Jansen-Jacobs, Marion J. 2003. *Index of vernacular plant names of Suriname* [Blumela: Journal of Plant taxonomy and Plant Geography, Supplement 15]. Leiden: National Herbarium Nederland.

Eighteenth-century data sources

Schumann, Christian L. 1778. Saramaccanisch Deutsches Wörter-buch. (Published in Schuchardt, Hugo. 1914. *Die Sprache der Saramakkaneger in Surinam*. Amsterdam: Johannes Müller).
Schumann, Christian L. 1783. Neger-Englisches Wörterbuch. (Published in Kramp, Alwin André. 1983. Early Creole Lexicography: A Study of C. L. Schumann's Manuscript Dictionary of Sranan. PhD dissertation, Universiteit Leiden).

Reducing phonological complexity and grammatical opaqueness
Old Tibetan as a *lingua franca* and the development of the modern Tibetan varieties*

Bettina Zeisler

Old Tibetan shows extraordinary complexity in its syllable structure as well as highly complex or rather opaque verb morphology. The syllable structure (CCC)CV(CC) has broken down completely in the modern Central Tibetan dialects to CV(C), while the opaque alternations of prefixes, consonants and vowels in verb stem formation were levelled out and replaced by regular systems of periphrastic construction in the western and central varieties. Both developments can be described as processes of simplification that were triggered in a linguistic contact situation, where Old Tibetan served as a *lingua franca* for various non-Tibetan peoples.

Preliminary remarks

Pidgins and creoles were for a long time defined as phonologically, lexically, and syntactically more or less reduced languages, but recent research seems to indicate that many features of pidgins and creoles are less 'simple' than in earlier, possibly biased descriptions. As a consequence, the specialists in the field suggest that the equation of pidginisation = simplification and creolisation = (re-) complexification does not hold, not even as a general tendency. This change of perspective made it almost impossible to write the present article. Even more so as this terminological problem has quite different facets.

---

*   This article is a by-product of my 2005 field work in Ladakh, conducted within a DFG sponsored research project as part of the SFB 441: 'Linguistic Data Structures: On the Relation between Data and Theory in Linguistics' at the University of Tübingen, see our project page: http://www.sfb441.uni-tuebingen.de/b11/index-engl.html.

The first difficulty is that the notions of simplicity and complexity have been burdened with inadequate judgements about mental abilities or social advancement of the respective speech communities. From a more or less naive Eurocentric evolutionary perspective it was taken for granted that an inflectional language is more complex *and* more advanced than, say, an agglutinative or even analytic language.

The main problem lies in the association of two unrelated facts (complexity and social advancement). Taking an anti-colonial stance by merely exchanging the labels thus does not really help, since any die-hard could subscribe to a logical reversal, namely that inflection or any kind of syntactification is, in fact, a means of simplification, while at the same time insisting that the resulting simplicity is reflecting a 'higher sense of abstraction', and thus again only to be found in languages of 'higher civilisations'.[1]

Unfortunately, any replacement by expressions, such as *more* or *less* 'economic', 'structured', or 'syntactic', faces exactly the same difficulty, as such new terms can again be misused for socio-political judgements in terms of 'primitiveness' or 'advancement'. Besides, they might reflect the speaker's socio-economic background rather than the linguistic facts. In this paper, the use of the words 'simple' and 'complex' and related terms is meant to be solely descriptive and does not license any evaluation in terms of 'more' or 'less advanced'.

A further difficulty, at the philosophical level, is to define and measure complexity (or related notions). Depending on the conceptual or technological model(s) behind these notions, the respective judgements might turn out to be incompatible if not contradictory. From an information-processing perspective, e.g., large irregular, if not chaotic sets of entities appear to be more complex than smaller sets governed by a hierarchy of syntactic rules, whereas from a perspective of biological morphology or organisation theory, rules and hierarchies certainly add to the structural complexity of the 'organism' language.

Related to this is the selection of what to count. This might be exemplified with the seemingly uncomplicated matter of phonemic inventories. Apparently, pidgins, and creoles do not differ significantly from other languages in their basic phonetic inventory, i.e. the overall number of consonants and vowels (Bakker 2006; Uffmann 2006). Some pidgins might even show a larger inventory, especially with respect to suprasegmental features (Faraclas 2006).

---

1. This can be exemplified with the stance taken against lexical complexity: lack of generic terms and richness of concrete terms were often enough interpreted as a symptom of mental "primitiveness". Almost as frequently, "primitiveness" becomes the object of romanticisation. I might recall here the usual exaggeration concerning the number of expressions for 'snow' in Inuit. Indigenous generic terms probably often went unnoticed (as they did not present themselves to the European mind, not being, so to speak, in the questionnaire) or they were again rejected (or acclaimed) as being "primitive" whenever going against the European classifications (cf. Borghes' satirical "Chinese classification of animals", which made its way even into modern philosophy as a real fact).

Nobody, however, would deny that languages differ essentially with respect to syllable or word structure, such as the number of consonants that can combine at a certain position or the overall length of a semantic unit. It is thus important to discuss all these features together in order to avoid contradictory results. In Modern Lhasa Tibetan, e.g., one can observe a dramatic rise in the phonemic inventory, but at the same time an even more dramatic reduction in the number of possible syllables (cf. Section 1.1 below). And it is likewise important not to lose sight of the general background.

According to Uffmann (2006), a few West African creoles have more complex onset and coda clusters than their substrates, though still below the level of the superstrate (nothing being said about the overall word length). But in the context of the languages discussed, this is not really surprising. Given the very basic syllable structure of the substrate languages (CV, CVC_{nasal}, or $CC_{glide/liquid}V$), it is difficult to imagine how this structure could be even further simplified. Moreover, the abstract structural patterns alone do not tell us much about the combinatory possibilities of a language, especially since the more complex combinations typically allow less variation, due to articulatory restrictions, and a language with only CC clusters could, in principle, show more variation than another one allowing CCC clusters. Finally, if a given variety has more complex consonant onsets or codas than its sub- or superstrate, this could be due to contractions of originally syllabic elements (hence the necessity to compare the word or morpheme length).

The last and perhaps most vexing difficulty is that the terms 'simplicity' and 'complexity' and even more all possible substitutes are highly context-dependent. There will always be at least one perspective under which a given feature is 'simple' or at least 'economic', 'easy to process' or 'acquire', etc. and at the same time there will be at least one perspective under which the opposite holds true. What might be syntactically economic and hence speeding up the mental processing of information might be difficult to acquire or leading to an undesired loss of semantic precision while, on the other hand, semantic precision is costly in terms of utterance length and thus also mental processing. The needs of efficient language acquisition, utterance production, and utterance processing are to a certain extent conflicting, and their different strategies make the notions of 'complexity' and 'simplicity' somewhat arbitrary. But without these notions we lack an essential motivation for changes in language, and ultimately we might no longer be able to argue about whether a particular change is triggered by more internal processes or through language contact.

It is the latter question that is essential for my own research into the history of the Tibetan languages. The development that I am going to describe, especially the extreme simplification of syllable onsets, has long been taken by Tibetologists as an internal development starting in the centre of the Tibetan region and spreading slowly to the peripheral areas without reaching the westernmost areas of Baltistan and Ladakh and the easternmost areas of the nomadic populations in Amdo and Kham. However, with respect to the Balti and Ladakhi varieties, the historical facts are not in accordance with this assumption and with respect to the second feature to be discussed, i.e. verbal morphology, it turns out that the reorganisation is even further developed in the westernmost periphery than in the 'centre'.

The development of the misleadingly so-called 'archaic' or 'conservative' West Tibetan varieties can only be explained as an outcome of a long lasting contact situation between primarily Tibeto-Burman and Indo-Iranian languages and a gradual shift to the then *spoken* Old Tibetan *lingua franca*. Even the development of the Central Tibetan varieties is better explained as a result of linguistic contact than as a result of internal development.

While the idea of Old Tibetan as a *lingua franca* in Central Asia might not be entirely new, my suggestions concerning contact-induced simplifications might come as a surprise for most scholars in the field of Tibetan philology. What I am presenting here is not much more than a hypothesis, which, quite probably, cannot be proved, but which seems to have more explanatory force than previous assumptions.

1. Old Tibetan (OT; ca. 650 C.E. – ca. 1050)[2]

Tibet and her language left the darkness of prehistory at the moment when a petty kingdom or a confederacy of diverse tribes started to expand into Central Asia under a centralised power, the Tibetan emperors (*brtsanpo*-s). At the same time, in the first half of the 7th century, the Tibetan script was officially introduced for administrative purposes. With the conquests of oasis towns in Eastern Turkistan, Tibet gained control over essential parts of the Silk Route, and this apparently led to the development of a particular *Archaic Tibetan variety[3] into a *lingua franca*, or rather to the adoption of an already existing *lingua franca* as the language of administration and commerce in the new empire. The Central Asian elites obviously adopted OT also as a cultural *lingua franca* and started transmitting their own mythology as well as Indian epics in OT. During the second half of the 8th century, when Buddhism became the state religion in Tibet, OT finally became the *lingua franca* of religion.

The Tibetan Empire came to an end in 848. OT, however, remained in use in Central Asia during the next two centuries, particularly as *the* language of religion, but it can be assumed that it also continued as a colloquial language of commerce. The Dunhuang caves (where most of the OT documents were found) were sealed off at the beginning of the 11th century in the course of an Arab invasion, and this event seems to indicate the beginning of the end of the oral OT *lingua franca* in Central Asia, as well.

---

2. As this paper is written for a general linguistic audience, discussion of the cultural and historical background is reduced to a minimum. More details will be found in a monograph addressing the Tibetan studies audience (Zeisler, to appear b).

3. An asterisk is used whenever I refer to a merely hypothetical language state.

1.1 Phonological complexity of Old Tibetan

Written OT shows extremely complex syllable onsets of up to 4 consonants and syllable codas of up to 2 consonants, CCCCVCC. Of course, there are restrictions on the combinations (see Beckwith 2006), and the extreme case of four initial consonants can only be found in combination with velar radicals.[4] In the writing system,

---

[4]. The 30 consonants or radicals of the Tibetan alphabet are: k, kh, g, ŋ, c [tɕ], ch [tɕʰ], j [dʑ], ñ [ɲ], t, th, d, n, p, ph, b, m, ts, tsh, dz, w, ḥ [ɦ/ɣ], y [j], r, l, ž [ʒ], z, š [ʃ], s, h, a [ʔ]; all of them representing basic phonemes, but the phoneme /ɬ/ is represented by the cluster superscript *l* plus radical *h*. It is an open question whether the aspiration contrast was fully phonemic in *Proto-Tibetan, but it is so in Classical Tibetan, although most voiceless non-aspirated initials appear to be restricted to marginal vocabulary (onomatopoetic words, adverbs, and loan words), or might be phonetically conditioned (reduplicated words). Only the following onset combinations are attested in OT and CT (R = radical, p = prescript, sup = superscript; s = subscript; [0] = unproductive, singular; [1] = marginal vocabulary (onomatopoetic forms, clitics, adverbs, possible loans); [2] = only in loans; [3] = not attested in OT; [4] = OT spelling conventions; [5] = only attested in OT, but not necessarily with phonemic status (cf. Beckwith 2006: 53–54; because of diverging assumptions, his list is not complete):

Table I. Classical (and Old) Tibetan onset clusters

2 elements			3 elements				4 elements
R s	p R	sup R	R s s	p R s	sup R s	p sup R	p sup R s
[1]ky, [1]kr, kl, [0,2]kw	dk, bk,	rk, lk, sk		dky, dkr, [3]bky, [3]bkr, [0,3]bkl	rky, sky, skr	[3]brk, bsk	bsky, [3]bskr
khy, khr, [0,3]khw	mkh, ḥkh, [5]bkh			mkhy, mkhr, [3]ḥkhy, ḥkhr			
gy, gr, gl	dg, bg, mg, ḥg	rg, [3]lg, sg	[0,3]grw	dgy, dgr, bgy, bgr, mgy, mgr, ḥgy, ḥgr	rgy, sgy, sgr	brg, bsg	brgy, bsgy, bsgr
	dŋ, mŋ	rŋ, lŋ, sŋ				[3]brŋ, bsŋ	
	gc, bc	[5]rc, lc, [5]sc					
	mch, ḥch, [5]bch, [5]gch						
	mj, ḥj	rj, lj,				brj	
	gñ, [5]bñ, mñ	rñ, sñ				brñ, bsñ	
[2]tr	gt, bt	rt, lt, st				brt, blt, bst	
[2]thr	mth, hth, [5]bth, [5]gth						
dr	gd, bd, md, ḥd	rd, ld, sd		[0]bdr, ḥdr		brd, bsd	
	gn, [5]bn, mn	rn, sn				brn, bsn	
[0,4]pr	dp, sp		[0]pyw	dpy, dpr, spy, spr			
phy, phr	ḥph			ḥphy, ḥphr			
by, br, bl	db, ḥb	rb, [0]lb, sb		dby, dbr, ḥby, ḥbr	sby, sbr		
my	dm	rm, sm		dmy	rmy, smy, [0]smr		
	gts, bts	rts, sts			[0]rtsw	brts, bsts	
[0]tshw	mtsh, ḥtsh						

possible slots			example syllable	transliteration	translation
b/g/d/m/ḥ	i/e/o/		b s bs བསྒྲུབས་	bsgrubs	'accomplished'
	r/l/s	[a] C s/d	g		
	C		r		
	r/y/l/w		u		
	/u				

Figure 1. The structure of the graphic representation

the clusters are represented by consonant signs that are written before, above, or below the radical or basic consonant.[5] All consonants are arranged relative to an invisible upper line. Superscribed consonants thus 'push' the radical consonants 'down'. Among the prescripts, only *b-* can combine with the superscripts. The vowel *a* is not represented in the script; it follows the onset by default if no other vowel sign is written. A graphically syllabic notation with the help of a final dot, the possibility of vertical combinations, and a few combinatory rules guarantee that the inherent vowel *a* can always be located at the right place.

As can be seen in Figure 2, the phonological complexity of OT was already somewhat reduced in the written language of Classical Tibetan (CT, ca. 11th–19th century), by the loss of post-final *-d*. The syllable structure is almost completely reduced to CV(C) in present day Central Tibetan (CtrT), particularly in Lhasa Tibetan (LT). Only the combination velar plus palatal glide (though commonly treated as simple phoneme) survived the simplification process, whereas the original complexity is retained to a large extent in West Tibetan (WT), where one can still find syllables of the CCCVCC type, and, to a lesser extent, in some Amdo Tibetan (AT) varieties, where the maximally complex syllable takes the form CCCVC (cf. Haller 2004: 30).

2 elements			3 elements			4 elements	
	mdz, ḥdz	rdz			brdz		
	gž, ⁵dž, bž						
zl	gz, ⁵dz, bz		bzl				
	g.y						
rl, ⁰rw			brl				
	gš, bš						
sr, sl	gs, bs		bsr, bsl				
³hr							

5. The Tibetan grammarians take the basic consonant as the root consonant. But the graphic analysis does not always reflect the historical linguistic facts. E.g. subscribed *-l-* (except perhaps in the combination *zl-*) must have been an original root consonant (Beyer 1992: 74–79), and there is some evidence that this holds also for (at least some) combinations with subscribed *-r-* and of labial with subscribed *-y-* (cf. Beyer 1992: 73; Zeisler in preparation).

pre-radical pre- and super-scribed[6]		radical	post-radical subscribed		coda	
					'final'	'post-final'
OT	b- -r,l,s-	$C_{1,3,4}$	-y,r,l,(w)	V	-g,ŋ,b,m	-s
	g,d,b-	C_{1-4}			-n,r,l	-d
	m-	C_{2-4}			-d,s	
	ḥ-	$C_{2,3}$				
CT	b- -r,l,s-	$C_{1,3,4}$	-y,r,l,(w)	V	-g,ŋ,b,m	-s
	g,d,b-	$C_{1,3,4}$			-n,r,l	traces of -d
	m-	C_{2-4}			-d,s	
	ḥ-	$C_{2,3}$				
WT		C_2	-y,(r)[7], ▮(w)[8]	V	-g,ŋ,d,n,b,m,r,l	-s
	g,b, ▮ r,l,s-[9]	$C_{1,3,4}$			-s	
LT		$C_{1,2+tone}$	-y ▮▮▮	V	-g,ŋ,b,m	
					traces of -d,n,r,l,s	
AT	nasal	C_{2-4}	▮▮▮ (w)[10]	V	-g,ŋ,n,b,m,r,l(<d,l)	
	g,(d),b,r-▮ ▮[11]	$C_{1,3,4}$			traces of -s	

C_1: [–voice, –aspiration]; C_2: [–voice, +aspiration]; C3: [+voice]; C4: nasal.

Figure 2. The development of syllable structure

---

6. The light grey tone highlights combinatory features or elements that have been slightly changed or reorganised, the dark grey tone is used for elements that have been completely lost. The presentation is a gross simplification, and the combinatory rules for C refer only to the preceding consonants.

7. In most modern Tibetan varieties, combinations with the alveolar trill have become what is somewhat unfortunately described as 'retroflex' stop or affricate. It is typically treated as a single consonant. Except for the manner of articulation, the Tibetan 'retroflexes' have nothing in common with the retroflexes of Indian languages. The West Tibetan 'retroflexes' might perhaps be better described as affricates, or clusters of alveolar stops with the alveolar trill [tr̥/tr̥ʰ/dɻ]. Some Western Sham dialects have preserved the combination of labial stop plus alveolar trill, most of the Purik and Balti dialects even preserve the combination velar plus alveolar trill.

8. Not a continuation of the OT/CT semivowel, and only found in the westernmost varieties, where it replaces the vowels *o* or *u* as first element of diphthongs.

9. The former pre-radicals *g*- and *b*- have been preserved only in Balti as /χ-/, /ɣ-/, and /b-/, /ph-/, of which only χ- combines with nasals. In the other Shamskat dialects, the former pre-radicals *g*-, *d*-, and *b*- have merged with r- as /r̥-/ and /r-/. The feature [±voice] is conditioned by the feature [±voice] of the radical.

The loss of complexity in the syllable structure was only partially compensated by the development of suprasegmental features, although the phonemic inventory increased considerably in the tonal varieties. These might thus be far more 'complex' than OT, showing a sixfold (in some varieties even eightfold) articulatory distinction of consonants: high tone: k, kh, ŋ versus low tone: k, kh, (g, ⁿg), ŋ in place of the fourfold distinction of OT/CT: k, kh, g, ŋ.[12] But the new opposition between the low tone aspirated and non-aspirated consonants and the low and high tone nasals only reflects the difference between bare radicals and radicals preceded by pre-radicals. It neither reflects the qualitative differences of the eight pre-radicals nor does it reflects the possibility of combining two pre-radicals. With respect to all possible CT onsets, the tonal varieties have preserved only about a third or less of the original complexity.[13] The simplification of the syllable structure naturally leads to an increase in homophones.

If one compares the syllabic structure of the modern varieties, it looks as if the reduction of phonological complexity was a process that started in the centre of Tibet (i.e. in Lhasa), and spread towards the periphery, but did not reach the most peripheral areas in the west and in the east (cf. *inter alia* Jäschke 1881:xii; Bielmeier 1998). It was always taken for granted that the reduction was an internal development, particularly "erosion through use" (Stein 1962:212). The hypothesis of concentric spread is certainly valid for more marginal features or for developments in smaller areas, but with respect to the two features described here there are some serious problems.

First of all, the hypothesis contains some silent assumptions about where to locate the political or cultural 'centre' and why the 'periphery' should be delinked from the processes in the centre. We do not know enough about early Tibetan history to

---

10. Likewise not a continuation of the OT/CT semivowel, but triggered by an original labial pre-radical.

11. In Themchen, e.g., the former pre-radical d- is preserved only as a trace of the former clusters *dp* and *db* /χ/, /ʁ/ and has otherwise merged with *g*- /ɕ/, /γ/ or, together with *l*- and *s*-, with *r*- /ʂ/, /r/; *b*- may be realised as /p/, /φ/, or /b/.

12. Actually an increase by 77% from 31 to 55 consonantal phonemes in Modern Lhasa Tibetan, for speakers using prenasalisation even by 100% to 62 consonantal phonemes (cf. Tournadre 1996:60–61). One may well question the inclusion of a suprasegmental feature in the consonantal inventory, particularly as it is realised with the following vowel. However, pitch and voice are very closely related features and in the case of Tibetan, pitch distinction developed from voice distinction. Furthermore, if suprasegmental features should be ignored, I would go on to ask whether manner of articulation should then be considered, at all. If not, the difference between Old and Modern Tibetan would be quite marginal. If yes, the exclusion of the pitch distinction would lead to a reduction of the original inventory by almost one third. Simplification without apparent compensation.

13. 178 initial combinations can be added to the simple consonants of Classical Tibetan (see also Table I, note 4 above), but none in Modern Lhasa Tibetan.

locate the socio-political 'epicentre' of the imperial period. The silent assumption that there was only one main centre and that it was necessarily located at the imperial court in Lhasa could be a projection from modern (nation-state) conceptions of European medieval history. We also do not know much about the ethnic composition of the Tibetan empire, let alone which languages were spoken in which region. It could well be the case that Central Tibet was, linguistically as well as politically, the peripheral area.

A second problem concerns the time schedule. If the phonological development was endogenous, it should have been rather gradual and slow. But this assumption is in conflict with the historical facts (see Section 1.3 below). A third problem concerns the development of verbal morphology, which does not show a pattern of concentric spread. The OT verbal 'system' is preserved almost completely in the northeast (Amdo), partially in the east (Kham), but is totally reorganised from the centre to the west, following the same lines in the reorganisation process. Even more, in contrast to the phonetic development, the changes turn out to be somewhat more complete in the so-called periphery than in the so-called centre.

1.2 Verbal morphology

OT shows an extremely opaque 'system' consisting of up to four verb stems, based on the distinction of non-causative verbs (1–2 stems if non-agentive, 1–3 if agentive) vs. causative verbs (1–4 stems). Stem I indicates non-anteriority (simultaneity or unmarked posteriority, by default present tense), stem II anteriority (by default past tense), stem III modal (necessitative) posteriority. Stem IV originally indicated ability, but became conventionalised as expression of request. The connotations of necessity and ability presuppose an intentional agent and, therefore, stems III and IV are (with very few exceptions) only found with agentive verbs. The formation of the verb stems is highly unpredictable, and less than half of the verbs show regularities with respect to the number of stems and the formative elements. The original function of most of the formative elements cannot be reconstructed, but it appears that the general arrangement of two plus four stems results from the reorganisation of an earlier derivational pattern with up to eight (with the *s*-causative, nine) slots (cf. Zeisler 2001). In the most complex causative paradigm 1a, the stems are derived by prefix alternation, suffixes, and vowel and consonant alternations (cf. Table 1 below).

The development of the modern varieties can be summed up as follows:

- All modern varieties have lost stem III.
- CtrT and WT have lost all grammatical prefixes as well as vowel and consonant alternations for stems I and II.
- Stem IV shows a tendency towards loss of ablaut $a \rightarrow o$ in CtrT and WT, its aspiration was lost in WT.
- CtrT has lost the suffixes, but WT shows over-generalisation of suffix -s.

Table 1. Main features of some OT and CT causative paradigms

Causative paradigm 1a (ca. 50 verbs):

stem	I	II	III	IV
prefix	ḥ	b	g ~ d	ø
radical	voiced	OT: [±]voiced CT: voiceless	voiced	aspirated
vowel[14]	e (~ o)	a	a	o
suffix	d (s)	ø ~ s (d)	ø	ø ~ s (d)

Causative paradigm 1b (ca. 10 verbs):

prefix	g	b	g ~ d	ø
radical	OT: [±]aspirated CT: non-aspirated	OT: [±]aspirated CT: non-aspirated	OT: [±]aspirated CT: non-aspirated	aspirated
vowel[14]	o	a	a	o
suffix	ø	ø ~ s (d)	ø	ø ~ s (d)

Causative paradigm 2a (ca. 220 verbs with clusters of superscript plus radical):

stem	I	II	III	IV
prefix	ø	b	b	ø
vowel[14]	o (~ e)	a	a	o
suffix	ø (~d (s))	s (d)	ø	s (d)

Causative paradigm 2b (ca. 30 verbs):

stem	I	II	III	IV
prefix	ḥ	b	b	ø
radical	aspirated	OT: [±]aspirated CT: non-aspirated	OT: [±]aspirated CT: non-aspirated	aspirated
vowel[14]	o (~ e)	a	a	o
suffix	ø	s (d)	ø	s (d)

The assimilation of verb stems was typically oriented towards stem II, infrequently also towards stem I. The assimilation of vowels and consonants must have taken place at different times, because in rare cases they went in different directions (cf. Table 3, p. 91).

---

14. The *ablaut* rules are given relative to the second and third stem. There is another *ablaut* uŋ + -d > in*d. While there are only few exceptions concerning the *ablaut* feature for stem I in paradigms 1, the feature is somewhat less frequent in the other paradigms.

Table 2. Development of the verbal morphology[15]

Causative paradigm 1a:				
	I	II	III	IV
OT	gaŋ	–	–	–	'be full (of), get filled up (with)'
	ḥ-kheŋs	kheŋs	–	–	'be full (of), get filled up (with)'
	ḥ-**g**-**e**-ŋ-**s**	**b**-**k̲**-aŋ	**d**-gaŋ	**k̲h**-**o**-ŋ	'make full (of)'
AT	/kaŋ/	–		–	'be full (of), get filled up (with)'
	II	/**k̲**-**w**-aŋ/		/**k̲h**-**u**-ŋ/	'make full (of)'
St.I: < OT St.II; St.II: prefix b- → infix /-w-/ after /k/ before /a/ or /i/ (< as)					
OT stem II: consonant k & vowel a					
LT	/khaŋ/	–		–	'be full (of), get filled up (with)'
	/khēŋ/~/k̲hāŋ/	–		–	'be full (of), get filled up (with)'
	/**k̲ēŋ**/	–		(I)	'make full (of)'
St.I: C < OT St.II, V < OT St.II or I; (St. IV other verbs also: C & V < OT St.IV)					
WT	gaŋ	–		–	'be full (of),get filled up (with)'
	/**k̲**aŋ/	–	/**k̲**aŋ-**s**/	/**k̲**-**o**-ŋ/	'make full (of)'
St.I: C, V < OT St.II; St.II: /-s/ < OT prdgm.2 St.II; St.IV: C < OT St.II, V < OT St.IV					
OT	ḥ-khep	khep-s	–	–	'be covered, spread over'
	ḥ-**g**-**e**-p-**s**	**b**-**k̲**-ap	**d**-gab	**k̲h**-**o**-b	'cover, spread over'
AT	/ŋ-**g**-**e**-p/	/**k̲**-**w**-ap/		/**k̲h**-**o**-p/	'cover, spread over'
St.II: prefix b- → infix /-w-/ after /k/ before /a/ or /i/ (< as)					
OT stem II: consonant k & vowel a					
LT	/khēp/	–		–	'be covered, spread over'
	/**k̲ēp**/~/**k̲āp**/	–		(I)	'cover, spread over'
St.I: C < OT St.II, V < OT St.II or I; (St. IV other verbs also: C & V < OT St.IV)					
WT	/khep(s)/	(I)		–	'be covered, spread over'
	/**k̲**ap/	–	/**k̲**ap-**s**/	**k̲**-**o**-p	'cover, spread over'
St.I: C, V < OT St.II; St.II: /-s/ < OT prdgm.2 St.II; St.IV: C < OT St.II, V < OT St.IV					
Causative paradigm 2a:				
	I	II	III	IV
OT	ḥ-grub	grub	–	–	'get accomplished'
	s-grub	(**b**)-**s**-grub-**s**	**b**-**s**-grub	**s**-grub-**s**	'make accomplished'
AT	**n**-dzəp	(I)		–	'get accomplished'
	/**ɣ**-dzəp/	(I)		(I)	'make accomplished'
LT	/tṣup/	–		–	'get accomplished'
	/tṣup/	–		(I)	'make accomplished'
WT	/drup/~/grup/	–		–	'get accomplished'

---

15. Prefix, consonant and vowel alternations in relation to the root form are emphasised by bold face, additionally by non-italics or italics for vowel ablaut and underlining for consonant ablaut. Light shading is used for the causative verb forms.

1.3 Historical background

In the so-called Lhasa treaty, a bilingual inscription dating from the year 821/22, Chinese transcriptions of Tibetan names demonstrate an advanced simplification of syllable onsets in Old Lhasa Tibetan almost to the extent of present day LT (Laufer 1914: 77–94).[16] This is all the more interesting, as speakers tend to treat personal or place names more conservatively than other items.

Baltistan and western Ladakh, although nominally part of Zhangzhung, belonged culturally to the Indo-Iranian sphere of influence, and were inhabited by a predominantly Iranian or Indo-Aryan speaking population. Zhangzhung and its western provinces were annexed by the Tibetans around 644, but they remained semi-autonomous and were only loosely integrated into the military administration of the Empire. The impact of the new administrative language was felt in the western provinces probably only at the beginning of the 8th century, when larger military units, bound to attack Gilgit, passed through Ladakh and Baltistan.[17]

If the population had shifted over to the then spoken language in Lhasa shortly after the annexation, this would have left a time frame of maximally 200 years for the phonological development in Old Lhasa Tibetan. But no annexation necessarily or automatically involves a language shift, even more if the annexed entity retains a certain amount of autonomy. A linguistic shift under high pressures typically takes three generations to complete. We should also allow at least one or two generations for the sound changes in Old Lhasa Tibetan to have affected the names and titles. If we count each generation with 30 years,[18] this leaves a time frame of about 150 years or maximally 5 generations for the sound changes in Old Lhasa Tibetan. This would still be quite fast (especially in relation to the phonetical stability of the outer-most varieties during the next 1200 years). Such dramatic changes could no longer be described as a language internal process of erosion but would point to high pressures and thus to a very sudden change in the linguistic and ethnic composition of the population in Central Tibet. There is no necessity, however, that the changes in Old Lhasa Tibetan occurred only after the annexation of Zhangzhung.

---

16. This is not just because Middle Chinese had fewer onsets. In transcribing foreign names, clusters were typically analysed with two or more graphemes, but exactly this kind of analytical representation is missing for the word onsets in question. It is not missing for clusters in word-medial position, a position at which, under certain conditions, clusters survived to the present day.

17. This is an extremely condensed representation of a highly complex and geographically quite problematic situation. The interested reader is referred to the discussion in Zeisler (to appear b), Chapter 2).

18. Generation distance is defined by the average distance of all children to both of their respective parents. Thus even in times of war, hunger or epidemics, the average hardly ever goes down below 30 years.

From a sociolinguistic or political perspective, one would like to ask why the people of Ladakh and Baltistan should have adopted an obviously outdated version of Tibetan instead of the prestigious language of the political elites at the imperial court. A possible answer could be that the political elites that were instrumental in the administration of the conquered areas (and for the administration of the empire in general) spoke a different variety and possibly a more widely accepted variety, than their contemporaries at the Lhasa court.

In my opinion, however, the Tibetanisation of western Ladakh (i.e. the adoption of Tibetan as L1) took place much later. Possibly it started at the end of the 10th or at the beginning of the 11th century, when a branch of the former imperial family established themselves as kings of Western Tibet (Ngari) and consequently of Ladakh. This is also the time of the so-called second spread of Buddhism, and it is not unlikely that this religious movement encouraged the language shift. Baltistan might have been Tibetanised even later, but this process must have been completed before the conversion of the whole area to Islam in the 15th or 16th century.

2. An alternative explanation: Old Tibetan as an imported *lingua franca*

This section contains in parts some conjectures about a distant past on which we do not have reliable information. I will use italics to indicate when historical evidence is unavailable.

The problem with the time frame may be solved, if one gives up the idea that OT developed in Central Tibet, but accepts that it was introduced by military elites migrating from the north-eastern areas to the central region *and taking over power some time before the Tibetan empire came into being. A possible date could be around the 4th or 5th century, when the Tuyuhun and associated tribes migrated from the Chinese borderland into the Kokonor area. They might have pushed some of the so-called Qiang (Ch'iang) tribes (generally identified with the speakers of *Proto-Tibetan) from the Sino-Tibetan borderland into Central Tibet. Alternatively, the speakers of *Archaic Tibetan may have been among the associated tribes, and moved on into Central Tibet. In that case, the speakers of *Archaic Tibetan might have constituted a particular socio-economic class (e.g. traders) of mixed ethnic or linguistic background, and their language might have evolved as a trade language in the area of their former activity or more generally as an in-group language.*[19]

Whatever the scenario, although *Archaic Tibetan apparently originated from the Tibeto-Burman family, it must have been heavily influenced by one or several

---

19. 'Tribes' are not necessarily ethnically homogeneous entities. Cf. the modern Golok, i.e. 'Rebel' tribe in northeastern Tibet. As the name suggests, this tribe constituted itself as an outlaw community. The members came from various Tibetan, Mongolian, and other tribes, and chose one regional Tibetan variety as their common language, although their leader was a Mongolian (cf. Roerich 1931).

non-Tibeto-Burman languages. The above-described OT verbal morphology, especially the causative derivation pattern 1a is absolutely unique among all Tibeto-Burman languages, and the overall opaqueness and the hardly even half-developed paradigms indicate that whatever the original verbal morphology looked like, it must have been reorganised under the pressure of external influences.

Contact with the indigenous populations (especially speakers of Tibeto-Burman, i.e. West Himalayan languages, but also of Indo-Iranian languages, Burushaski and perhaps other languages) might have set off the process of phonological simplification in Central Tibet.[20]

It is clear that speakers of an East Tibetan variety were central to the administration of the empire, *most likely because they were either instrumental in the conquests in Central Asia, or controlled the Central Asian trade*. They left their dialectal imprint on the language of the early Tibetan documents (e.g. the OT palatalisation of the labial nasal in front of the palatal vowels *i* and *e*, as in OT *mye*, CT *me* 'fire' is due to an innovation that affected only the eastern varieties, likewise the palatalisation of the cluster velar plus alveolar trill as in the word CT *ralgri*, OT *ra(l)gyi* 'sword', is an innovation affecting only the Amdo varieties). One may thus safely say that *Old East Tibetan was the administrative and military *lingua franca* of the empire.

One has to differentiate, however, between OT as a *written* language, used only by elites, and OT as a *spoken* language, used by the common people. The written language became quickly petrified and reflects dialectal or diachronic variation only in rare cases. In particular, grammarians and scholarly revisers strove to standardise CT spellings more and more (as can be seen in repeated re-editions of the same work). These continuous efforts can be taken as indirect evidence for the growing distance between the spoken and the written language. Whatever subtle differences between OT and CT are attested, they all show a certain tendency towards phonological simplification, cf.:

> OT *-s-ts* > CT *-s* (~ *-s-ts* > WT *s*): OT *-la(s)stsogs* > CT *-lasogs* 'etc.';
> OT *gstsand* > CT *gsan* 'shall listen'; OT, CT *stsol, bstsal* > WT /sal/ 'give (hon)'.

Although the spoken *lingua franca* was never documented, its development can be reconstructed in part from the evidence found in the WT varieties.

---

20. Given the fact that the linguistic contact with the Indo-Iranian languages in West Tibet did not lead to such a radical simplification of the clusters, language contact between languages of different affiliation cannot be the sole reason for this process. I would thus hypothesise that the process was triggered by the contact of two rather closely related languages, such as West Himalayan and *Archaic Tibetan. The medieval West Himalayan language Zhangzhung, and Old Tibetan seem to have many words in common, differing sometimes only in the prefixes. During cross-language interactions, the insecurity of the speakers about which prefix to use might have led to neutralisation, and eventual loss of these prefixes. Alternatively, one may take recourse to a large-scale immigration of sinicised people, without, however, being able to explain why the area of passage, East Tibet, was not much affected.

3. The development of West Tibetan[21]

In the case of Baltistan and the western parts of Ladakh (where the lexico-phonetically conservative dialects of the Shamskat group are spoken), there cannot be any doubt that there was a situation of language contact between Indo-Iranian (and possibly other languages) and Tibetan, and the subsequent development of modern WT is best explained as a process of interaction with, and final adaptation of, the spoken OT *lingua franca*.

As one might have realised from the above charts, the OT/CT verbal morphology is completely opaque for non-native speakers, and the first thing a second language learner would happen to do is to over-generalise the few regularities that seem to be obvious.

Generally, one might expect that learners pick up a verbal form which is either least marked, such as the bare root or an infinitive, or which is most common in situations of social interaction. Since the OT verb roots were opaque, and, by consequence, also no true infinitive was available, the most common form should have been stem I or its verbal noun, expressing simultaneity and, by an implicature, present time reference. As a matter of fact, this is not the chosen form in the case of causative verbs, but there are various reasons for picking up stem II for causative verbs:

- The majority of OT verbs do not show vowel or consonant alternation; the reason for an alternation as in the causative paradigm 1a is not intelligible.
- Almost all the verbs that show vowel alternation between stems I and II/III, have vowel *a* in stem II.
- All verbs that show consonant alternation have a non-aspirated voiceless consonant in stem II.
- Most of the causative verbs have a *b-* prefix in stem II, many also in stem III.
- The [±causative] distinction is most obvious in stem II, while it is somewhat blurred in stem I.
- Verbal nouns of stem I and III of causative verbs display a kind of diathesis (agent vs. patient orientation), while stem II is neutral.

Therefore, if one does not know which form to use, stem II would be at least formally correct, even though the temporal deixis might be wrong.

Evidence for the neutralisation of vowel and consonant alternations in the direction of stem II was already given for WT as well as CtrT (cf. Table 2, p. 10 above). The

---

[21]. The WT dialects can be divided into at least two main groups: (a) Shamskat (the language of Lower Ladakh), including the dialects of the lower Indus region (Sham proper), western Nubra, Purik, and Baltistan, and (b) Kenhat (the language of Upper Ladakh), including the upper Indus region and Zanskar. Kenhat shows a strong affinity with neighbouring Tibetan varieties in Himachal Pradesh, e.g. Spiti. The differences between the two dialect groups might reflect different linguistic or ethnic affiliations. For more details see Zeisler (to appear a).

suggested over-generalisation of the verbal *b-* prefix is certainly less evident, since both CtrT and WT have lost this prefix at the word-initial position. But prefixes are, under certain conditions, preserved in word-medial position, at morpheme boundaries, particularly in compounds. This feature has been observed in all Tibetan varieties (including 9th century Old Lhasa Tibetan), cf. e.g. my favourite example from eastern Ladakhi (Kenhat):

/burfe go**p**-tri/ < *sburpaḥi mgo-bkrus* 'beetles' head-washing' (said jokingly of a rainy day, when the beetles come out of the earth)[22]

Another quite unique and rather accidental finding from a village of bi-lingual Shina and Purik speakers at the border with Pakistan indicates that the *b-* prefix was not only generalised for stems I and II, but also for stem IV, before it was eventually lost. As the *b-* prefix leads to deaspiration, this explains why stem IV does not show aspiration in West Tibetan. It is interesting to note that the *b-* prefix showed up only in one single verb, only in the negated form (thus at a morpheme boundary),[23] and that the prefix form is already alternating with the 'regular' prefixless form:

/ma**p**-sot!/ < *ma-bsod* 'don't kill' from the verb /sat, sats, sot/ 'kill'; cf. CT *ma-gsod* (i.e. negation marker plus stem I; OT also with stem II or III) from the CT/OT verb *gsod, bsad, gsad, sod* 'kill'

Furthermore, the former grammatical *b-* prefix has lexicalised in some 20 verbs in Balti, cf. e.g. Khapulu /ptul/ 'please, make happy' (Sprigg 2002) ~ Skardo /phtul/ 'calm someone, make agree' (Bielmeier, in preparation) < CT *ḥdul, btul (thul), gdul, thul* 'subdue, discipline'.

It is thus possible to reconstruct the development of the West Tibetan verbal system as follows: as stem II of causative verbs became something like a semantic base form, the new root or infinitive, its prefix was exported to stems I and IV, either leading automatically to de-aspiration and devoicing of the corresponding initials, or leaving this assimilation to a subsequent stage.[24] While Balti vowel assimilations always follow the same direction as consonant assimilations, in Shamskat, the assimilation of vowel alternations must have happened independently and at times in different directions as the following two verbs 'do' and 'make go out' show.

Although the direction of change of vowels and consonants is different (and indeed opposite) for the two verbs, the trigger was apparently in both cases the behaviour of the initial clusters in the context of different vowels: The palatal vowels *i* and

---

22. More examples can be found in Zeisler (2005) and Zeisler (in preparation).

23. It may be noted that the prohibitive, which has stem I in all Tibetan varieties, was regularised with stem IV in the two western-most Balti and Purik varieties.

24. Compounds like /zap-thuŋ/ *za-bthuŋ* 'eating and drinking' or /šap-tshoŋ/ *ša-btshoŋ* 'butcher, meat seller' show that the deaspiration of stem I did not follow automatically.

Table 3. Asymmetric assimilation of vowels and consonants

Stem	'Root'	I	II	IV	Meaning
OT/CT	*(b)ya	byed (<bya + d)	byas	byos	'do, make, perform'
Balti	< II	bya	byas		
	< IV			byos	
Shamskat[25]		*be(t) <*byet	*byas	*byos	
	C I		→bas	→bos	
	V II	→ba		(→bas)	
OT/CT	*byuŋ	ḫbyind (<ḫ + byuŋ + d)	phyuŋ (< b + pyuŋ)	phyuŋ	'make go out'
Balti	< II	phyuŋ	phyuŋs	phyuŋ	
Shamskat		*biŋ < *byiŋ	*phyuŋs	*phyuŋ	
	V I		→phiŋs	→phiŋ	
	C II	→phiŋ			

e lead to a neutralisation of the palatal post-radical in all WT dialects. In the Kenhat dialects this leads to an even more 'intolerable' differentiation of the stem initials, because the clusters of labial radical plus palatal post-radical became palatal affricates when followed by the non-palatal vowels *a*, *u*, and *o*. The verb stems would thus have been */be(t)/ vs. */cas/ and */biŋ/ vs. */cuŋs/. As a consequence, both verbs (as well as the intransitive counterpart of the second one) were lost and substituted in the Kenhat dialects by /ce/ (Zanskar /co, coe/) 'do' < OT/CT ḫcho, bcos, bco, chos 'construct' and /tōn/ 'make go out' < OT/CT ḫdon, bton, gdon, thon. The mixed Leh dialect likewise substituted the forms /co, cos/ for the verb 'do' but retained the forms /phiŋ, phiŋs/ for the verb 'make go out'.

It seems thus that at least in Ladakh vowel assimilation towards stem I started earlier than consonant assimilation, but when consonant assimilation towards stem II became more prominent, vowel assimilation towards stem I was given up in favour of assimilation towards stem II.

4. The Old Tibetan *lingua franca* and the development of Modern Tibetan

The CtrT verbal morphology shows almost the same development as WT: reduction of vowel and consonant alternations, and over-generalisation of the *b-* prefix (as can be seen in compounds, cf. Shirai 1999). It follows that this should have had the same motivation as in WT, namely to get rid of an opaque complexity, alien to the original linguistic substrate.

---

25. The verb /ba, bas, (bos)/ is productive only in the Purik dialects; in the Western Sham dialects it is restricted to particular phrases. As a light verb it is replaced by /co, cos/, obviously due to the influence of the Leh dialect.

Of course, both processes might be seen as independent developments, merely canalised in the same direction by the available options, which, rather accidentally, were the same. However, if one compares the CtrT and the WT dialects in more detail, one can observe that the CtrT dialects retained more traces of the OT system than WT: a few verbs are left showing alternations between stem I and II, cf. LT /cè̠, cä̠, cö̠/ CT *byed, byas, byos* 'do', Dingri: /ʈö̀ˀ (ʈȫt-), ʈä̀ˀ (ʈǟt-)/ CT *sprod, sprad* 'give' (Herrmann 1989: 60, cf. also p. 29), Shigatse: /toè̠, tiè̠/ CT *sdod, bsdad* 'sit, stay'; /ʈʂœ̀, ʈʂiè/ *sprod, sprad* 'give'; /ɕœ̀, ɕiè/ CT *šod, bšad* 'speak' (Haller 2000: 80). In WT these alternations are only reflected in nouns derived from the original stem I (cf. Zeisler 2004: 876–877). One can further observe that Ladakhi has a few more verbs showing assimilation or partial assimilation towards stem I than Balti (cf. the above case of the verbs 'do' and 'make go out').

As mentioned before, the Tibetanisation, i.e. the shift within, or the abandonment of, a bilingual or multilingual situation in favour of Tibetan as L1 may have taken place gradually, and it seems to have started in western Ladakh as late as the end of the 10th or the beginning of the 11th century, progressing slowly to the western border (a few villages in the farthest west of Ladakh are still bilingual or rather multilingual with Shina and a Purik variety as L2 or L1). The difference in stem form assimilation between Balti and Shamskat (described in the last section) and the assimilation of the prohibitive to stem IV in Balti and Purik (mentioned in note 23) indicate that the language shift took place even later in Baltistan and certain areas of Purik. I would thus argue that the observable differences between the WT dialects as well as between WT and CtrT reflect an ongoing process of morphological simplification in the donor language, the spoken OT *lingua franca*.

But while morphological simplification was a process within the OT *lingua franca*, phonological simplification initially affected only the CtrT varieties (but may have been caused by an earlier pidginisation/creolisation process). When CtrT became dominant as the intra-Tibetan *lingua franca*, its simplified phonology might have triggered or reinforced similar processes in the neighbouring varieties.

The reduction in morphological complexity in the central and particularly in the western varieties, however, is the result of the long-lasting linguistic contact of various peoples, speaking Indo-Iranian and West Himalayan languages, among others, with a dominant and prestigious language used for trade, administration, and religion. From the viewpoint of Indo-Iranian, the adaptation of Tibetan results in a certain loss of paradigmatic complexity (nominal and verbal inflection), while from the viewpoint of West Himalayan, the loss of complexity in some parts might have been balanced by the increase of complexity in other parts. But given that the modern varieties are "truly Tibetan", in so far as the greatest part of the lexicon and the grammatical structure can be linked to OT or CT, one cannot avoid seeing the development as a process of overall simplification from the viewpoint of Old (East) Tibetan.

I would further argue that the development of the modern CtrT and WT varieties was highly complex, involving not just one single donor language and one single receiving language. Moreover, different influences are involved in different registers,

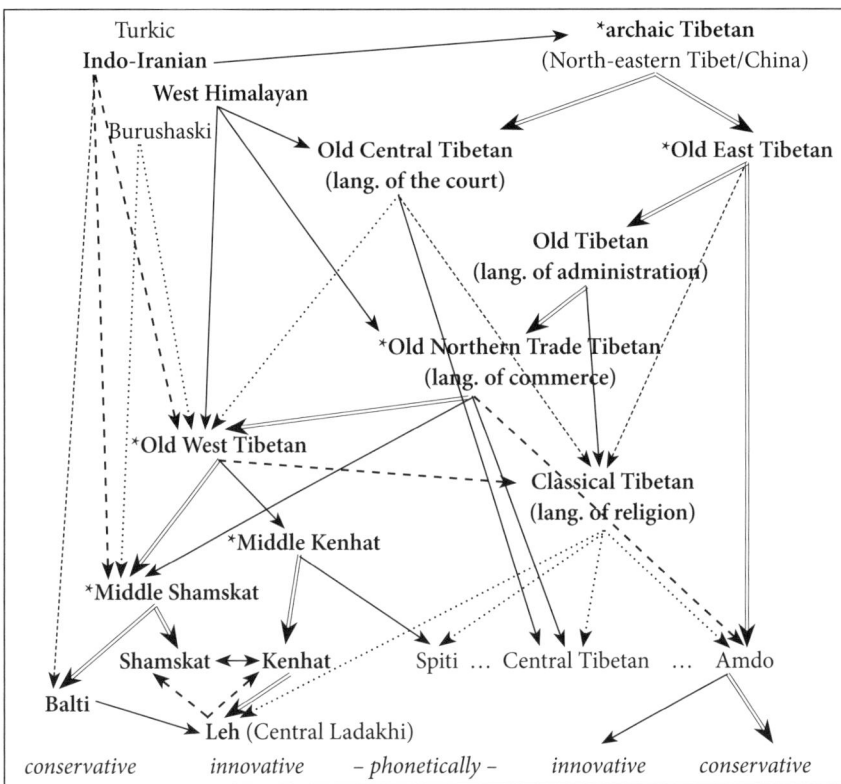

Figure 3. A network of linguistic influences

and influences vary over time (in their intensity as well as in their direction). The relationship between the varieties would thus correspond to a network, as tentatively modelled in Figure 3, rather than to a genealogical tree.

I do not want to claim that language contact in general or, more particularly, the formation of a *lingua franca* necessarily leads to simplification or only to simplification, despite such developments in *the* Lingua Franca itself. The extent of simplification might not only depend on the structures of the donor and recipient languages, but also on sociolinguistic factors. The high prestige of OT as a language of religion, as well as a certain pride in participating in the cultural heritage of the Tibetan Empire together with normative pressures, might have prevented a further break down. It is perhaps noteworthy in this context that none of the modern varieties was able to develop into a literary language, because CT is still seen as the only standard for writing. Modern Literary Tibetan, as used in Lhasa or in exile is more or less only a lexically expanded version of CT.

Furthermore, the loss of morphological complexity was counterbalanced in all varieties by the systematisation of periphrastic expressions with the help of specific morphemes and verbal auxiliaries. In the case of verbs this also leads to a tremendous increase of length in the verb syntagm. With only one exception, the auxiliaries and morphemes had already been in use in Old Tibetan (an indication that the process of morphological simplification must have started earlier), but were not grammaticalised, except for the 'progressive' forms. The modern varieties (including Amdo Tibetan) have developed these periphrastic expressions into new paradigms. I would take this paradigmatisation, in contrast to Meyerhoff's mathematical approach, as a kind of complexification on a 'higher' (or, if you prefer: 'deeper') level, comparable to the introduction of an administrative layer. The new paradigms, however, must have developed independently in the various dialect groups, with the effect that in several cases different auxiliaries are chosen for the same function or identical constructions are used for different functions. It is thus possible that the main process of paradigmatisation started only after the OT *lingua franca* became extinct.

Not all of the changes induced through linguistic contact are instances of simplification or complexification. This can be observed in the Tibetan case system. Here it seems that a few additional morphemes were introduced into early Tibetan, while the modern varieties have dropped (or never accepted) some of the resulting functional doublets (cf. Zeisler to appear a, Section 8). Apart from this, the West Tibetan dialect groups show a fundamentally different system of case markers: the regular experiencer-subject construction for 'transitive' non-agentive verbs is quite probably inherited from the Indo-Aryan languages, while the use of the comitative case for instruments and the Kenhat use of the genitive case for agents (both instead of the instrumental case) might well be inherited either from original *Proto-Tibetan or from an indigenous Tibeto-Burman language.

References

Bakker, Peter. 2006. Phonological complexity in pidgins (and creoles). Paper presented at the 7th Creolistics Workshop, University of Giessen, Germany, 6–8 April 2006.

Beckwith, Christopher I. 2006. The sonority sequencing principle and Old Tibetan syllable margins. In *Medieval Tibeto-Burman languages II. PIATS 2003: Tibetan Studies: Proceedings of the Tenth Seminar of the International Association for Tibetan Studies, Oxford 2003* [Brill's Tibetan Studies Library 10(1)], Christopher I. Beckwith (ed.), 45–55. Leiden: Brill.

Beyer, Stephan V. 1992. *The Classical Tibetan Language*. New York: State University of New York. Reprint 1993, [Bibliotheca Indo-Buddhica Series 116]. Delhi: Sri Satguru.

Bielmeier, Roland. 1998. Balti Tibetan in its historical linguistic context. In *Karakorum-Hindukush-Himalaya: Dynamics of Change* [Culture Area Karakorum Scientific Studies 4], Irmtraud Stellrecht (ed.), Part II: 583–610. Köln: Köppe.

Bielmeier, Roland. In preparation. *Comparative Dictionary of Tibetan Dialects*.

Faraclas, Nicholas, 2006. Suprasegmentals and the myth of the simplicity continuum from 'pidgin', to 'creole', to 'natural' languages. Paper presented at the 7th Creolistics Workshop, University of Giessen, Germany, 6–8 April 2006.

Haller, Felix. 2000. *Dialekt und Erzählungen von Shigatse* [Beiträge zur tibetischen Erzählforschung 13]. Bonn: VGH Wissenschaftsverlag.

Haller, Felix. 2004. *Dialekt und Erzählungen von Themchen* [Beiträge zur tibetischen Erzählforschung 14]. Bonn: VGH Wissenschaftsverlag.

Herrmann, Silke. 1989. *Erzählungen und Dialekt von Dinri* [Beiträge zur tibetischen Erzählforschung 9]. Bonn: VGH-Wissenschaftsverlag.

Jäschke, Heinrich August. 1881. *A Tibetan-English Dictionary. With Special Reference to Prevailing Dialects*. London. (4th reprint 1992, Delhi: Motilal Banarsidass).

Laufer, Berthold. 1914. Bird divination among the Tibetans. Notes on document Pelliot No. 3530, with a Study of Tibetan Phonology of the Ninth Century. *T'oung Pao* 15: 1–110.

Meyerhoff, Miriam. 2006. Empirical problems with domain-based notions of 'simple'. Paper presented at the 7th Creolistics Workshop, University of Giessen, Germany, 6–8 April 2006.

Roerich, Georges de. 1933. Les Goloks et leur caractère ethnique. *XVe Congrès International d'Anthropologie et d'Archéologie Préhistorique, 1931*, 736–741. Paris: Nourry.

Shirai, Satoko. 1999. Chibettogo gendai Rasa hogenno 2 onsetsukanni arawareru -b- nitsuite (On the inter-syllabic -b- in Modern Lhasa Tibetan). *Gengogaku Kenkyu (Linguistic Research)* 17–18: 59–72.

Sprigg, Richard Keith. 2002. *Balti-English English-Balti Dictionary*. London: RoutledgeCurzon.

Stein, Rolf A. 1962. *La civilisation tibétaine*. Paris: Dunod.

Tournadre, Nicolas. 1996. *L'ergativité en tibétain. Approche morphosyntaxique de la langue parlée* [Bibliothèque de l'information grammaticale 33]. Leuven: Peeters.

Uffmann, Christian. 2006. Simplicity vs. unmarkedness in creole phonology. Paper presented at the 7th Creolistics Workshop, University of Giessen, Germany, 6–8 April 2006.

Zeisler, Bettina. 2001. The development of temporal coding in Tibetan: Some suggestions for a functional internal reconstruction. Part II: The original semantics of the 'past stem' of controlled action verbs and the reorganisation of the Proto-Tibetan verb system. *Zentralasiatische Studien* 31: 169–216.

Zeisler, Bettina. 2004. *Relative Tense and Aspectual Values in Tibetan Languages. A Comparative Study*. Berlin: Mouton de Gruyter.

Zeisler, Bettina. 2005. *Skaddi ḥgyurcanaŋ / rdobaḥi mentogtsogsla luskanni sŋonḥjug baḥi rdzessiskorla //* – Language change and the fossilization of the Old Tibetan *b-* prefix in Ladakhi and Balti. Paper presented at the 12th Colloquium of the International Association for Ladakh, Kargil (Ladakh), 12th–15th July 2005. [For a more easily accessible version cf. also http://www.sfb441.uni-tuebingen.de/b11/languageArchaeology.pdf.]

Zeisler, Bettina. To appear a. Kenhat, the dialects of Upper Ladakh and Zanskar – an introduction. Paper given at the 11th Himalayan Languages Symposium, Chulalongkorn University Bangkok, 6–9 December, 2005.

Zeisler, Bettina. To appear b. Ethnic diversity, language contact, and the Old Tibetan lingua franca: Early Tibetan history and the development of the modern Tibetan languages.

Zeisler, Bettina. In preparation. West Tibetan verbal morphology and the reconstruction of the Proto-language: The Shafer hypothesis revisited.

PART II

Verbal morphology

Verb allomorphy and the syntax of phases

Tonjes Veenstra

In a number of French-related creoles a distinction is made between long and short forms of verbs. We argue that the alternation is a reflex of French inflectional morphology that has survived the creolization process, showing that the result is a long-short opposition of verb forms, similar to the formal variation in the learner varieties, and therefore ultimately due to learner strategies in the acquisition of French as a second language. We further discuss the potential role of substrate and argue that the alternation started out as a phonological/prosodic phenomenon (as it basically still is in Haitian Creole). We conclude that the alternation (or verb allomorphy) can be seen as a morphological reflex of the Spell-Out domain at the vP-level.

1. Introduction

In a number of French-related creoles a distinction is made between long and short forms of (some classes of) verbs, as shown in (1) through (3) for Louisiana Creole, Haitian Creole, and Mauritian Creole respectively:

(1) a. Fo tuzhu kupe zerb-la.   (Louisiana Creole)
       FO always cut   grass-DET
       'It's always necessary to cut the grass.'
    b. Fo to kup tuzhu zerb-la.
       FO 2SG cut always grass-DET
       'You always have to cut the grass.'

(2) a. Mwen fé   kabann lan rapid-rapid maten an. (Haitian Creole)
       1SG make bed   the fast-fast   morning the
       'I made the bed very quickly this morning.'
    b. Kabann lan fét rapid-rapid maten   an.
       Bed   the made fast-fast   morning the
       'The bed was made very quickly this morning.'

(3) a. Mo pe mãze. (Mauritian Creole)
    1SG ASP eat
    'I'm eating.'
 b. Mo pe mãz dipen.
    1SG ASP eat bread
    'I am eating bread.'

This paper deals with the following issues:

(4) a. where does this alternation come from?
 b. what are the grammatical underpinnings of this alternation?
 c. where do these underpinnings come from?
 d. theoretical implications.

We argue that the alternation is the reflex of French inflectional morphology that survived the creolization process, showing that the result is a long-short opposition of verb forms, much akin to the formal variation in the learner varieties, therefore ultimately due to learner strategies in the acquisition of French as a second language (Section 2). The alternation is shown to correlate with syntactic properties. Interestingly, the syntactic correlate differs in (almost) each French creole. Thus, as we show in Section 3, it correlates with the finiteness of the verb in Louisiana Creole (Rottet 1992). In Haitian Creole as well as Mauritian Creole, on the other hand, it has been argued to depend on the theta-theoretic status of the phrase following the verb, basically argument vs. adjunct (DeGraff 2001; Seuren 1990; Syea 1992). Whereas the factor determining the grammatical underpinning of this alternation might come from the superstrate language in the case of Louisiana Creole (see Becker & Veenstra 2003 for arguments that only late adstrate influence is involved here), superstrate influence cannot account for the other pattern. Therefore, it can only be due to either substrate influence or universal processes in creolization. We discuss the potential role of substrate influence in Section 4. In the rest of the paper we mainly focus on the pattern as found in Mauritian Creole. We argue that the alternation started out as a phonological/prosodic phenomenon (as it basically still is in Haitian Creole). We propose that Mauritian Creole has gone one step further than Haitian Creole and has grammaticalized the long/short alternation to only superficially mark the argument/adjunct distinction. We argue that the form of the verb is determined at each Phase (Chomsky 2001). If the verb ends up in the final position of a Phase, it will be spelled out in the long form. Two contexts are identified where this occurs: (i) when the internal argument has undergone leftward movement; (ii) when there is no internal argument. Adjuncts, on the other hand, are merged after completion of the Phase, and therefore do not induce the short form. Thus, the alternation (or verb allomorphy) can be seen as a morphological reflex of the Spell-Out domain at the vP-level.

2. Second language acquisition

There is general agreement in SLA that verbal morphology constitutes a major acquisition problem for adult learners (Meisel 1994; Prévost & White 2000; Schlyter 2002). The following presentation of the acquisition of verbal morphology in French learner varieties is based on the findings of the ESF-project "Second Language Acquisition of Adult Immigrants" (Klein and Perdue 1992, 1997; Dietrich, Klein, and Noyau 1995; Starren 2001). The study included L2 learners of French whose L1s were Moroccan Arabic and Spanish.

In untutored L2 acquisition learners have to segment and analyze the lexical and functional information encoded on the verb mainly on the basis of oral input. The learners' task is especially difficult in the acquisition of French for two basic reasons. First, there are a number of homophonous forms that carry different values (e.g., tense, aspect, mood, person, and number). Second, relevant functional information is often encoded in a preverbal cluster consisting of an auxiliary and one or more clitic pronouns, which is in most cases perceived as a single prosodic unit (Dietrich et al. 1995). We limit the discussion to the first problem area. The distinction of morphological variants of a verb has been retained in the orthographic representation of French, but the number of audibly distinctive forms in colloquial French is severely reduced (Harris 1987). This can be illustrated by the present indicative forms of the class of -er verbs, exemplified by the verb parler 'to speak'. The majority of French verbs belongs to this conjugation class, as shown in (5):

(5) 1SG   je parle   /parl/
     2SG   tu parles   /parl/
     3SG   il/elle parle   /parl/
     1PL   on parle   /parl/
     1PL   nous parlons   /parlõ/
     2PL   vous parlez   /parle/
     3PL   ils/elles parlent /parl/

There is no audible contrast between the singular forms and the third-person-plural form. Furthermore, the unambiguous first-person-plural marking -ons/õ/is rare in casual speech as the function of the subject pronoun nous 'we' has largely been taken over by the originally impersonal pronoun on (literally 'one'). As a consequence, only the second-person-plural form is distinctive. The same holds by and large for the other verbal paradigms of French (Veenstra 2003).

As can be seen in the paradigm in (5), the verb appears either in the root form or with a final /-e/. The latter form has two more functions. First, it serves as an infinitive that appears, for instance, in frequently used periphrastic verb constructions including 'je viens de parler' (literally I come from speaking, 'I just spoke') or 'je vais parler' ('I am going to speak'). Second, it carries the value of a past participle that is required in French in a broad range of compound verb constructions like the passé composé (e.g., 'j'ai parlé, literally I have spoken', 'I spoke'). Thus, a form like /parle/ can have the following functions:

(6) /parle/ vous parlez 2PL present indicative
    /parle/ parlé   past participle
    /parle/ parler   infinitive

The conclusion is that the multifunctionality of a single form confronts the learner with a serious problem in form-function-assignment. In the remainder of this section we discuss how the learners of the ESF project cope with this problem.

In the Basic Variety of both the Moroccan and the Spanish learners, verbs mainly appear in two formal variants with respect to their endings: as a short form V-/i/ or as a long form V-/e/. Some verbs show up in both forms but the variation does not have any functional value. The same observation has been made for Swedish-speaking learners of French (Schlyter 2002):

(7) a. et après la-dame l'autre /lerogard/ la-dame le-volur
       and after D-lady D.other look   D-lady D-thief
    b. et après charlot /irogarde/ la-dame
       and then Charly look   D-lady
       (Klein & Perdue 1992: 242, 243)

(8) a. la police /ʃerʃ/ à-la-fille (…)
       D-police look.for-D-girl
    b. et après (…) la-dame /eleʃerʃe/ à-la-maison
       and then   D-lady look.for-D-house
       (Klein & Perdue 1992: 238, 247)

(9) a. tous les deux après /ipart/ à-la-campagne
       both of them then depart to-D-countryside
    b. /leparti/ tou les deux à-la-campagne
       depart   both of them to-D-countryside
       (Klein & Perdue 1992: 247)

The variation in the form is not motivated by person or number marking. The examples in (7) and (8) all have a third person singular subject, but the examples in (9) have a third person plural subject. It can also be excluded that the different forms express a temporal contrast. In the following examples, the same form refers to states/events situated in the present (10a), the future (10b) and the past (10c):

(10) a. et maintenant /rest/ la-France la-femme
        and now   live   D-France D-wife
     b. /ileparti/ le-maroc et après /res/ la-dame du   maroc
        depart   D-Morocco and then stay D-lady from Morocco

c. le-maroc;   /res/ le-maroc   avec les enfants
    D-Morocco;   stay   D-Morocco with D-children
    (Noyau et al. 1995: 162–164)

The examples illustrate a general trait of the Basic Variety: temporal relations are not expressed by means of inflectional morphology (cf. Dietrich et al. 1995; Klein & Perdue 1997). Starren (2001) shows that the verb suffix -e is not the context that shows acquisitional progress. Instead, the overt marking of temporal information etc. emerges on a newly created protoauxiliary:

(11)   SUB AUX V-{Ø,e}

We propose that at this stage in the creolization process a target shift takes place from French to the Basic Variety (see Becker & Veenstra 2003 for details). The proto-auxiliary can be seen as the fore-runner of the TMA system. It functions as a kind of bottleneck where the different continuities (from the superstrate as well as substrate languages) pass through on their way into the creoles.

In summary, we can say that at the stage of L2 acquisition identified as the Basic Variety the learners' output exhibits formal variation in the verb forms, but they do not have attached to it the functions found in the target language. In essence, there exists formal variation without functional differentiation, i.e. the co-existence of various morphological forms without appropriate functions. Within such a highly variable system, there are two possibilities: either you get rid of this functionless variation, or you use and reinterpret it. As we show in the next section, both options can be found in the different French-related creoles.

3. Long/short opposition in French-related Creoles

Corne (1999:132) observes that verb forms in the Lesser Antillean Creoles (the different varieties as spoken in Guadeloupe, Martinique, St. Lucia, Dominica, a.o.) are invariable, and what little variation there is has no semantic correlates. In a number of other creoles, however, the long/short opposition have survived. It basically comes in two guises: (i) in some creoles, it is a Tense distinction (present/past); (ii) in other creoles, there is a context-sensitive rule that deletes the -e when the following element is selected by the verb.

The first pattern is found in Louisiana Creole. As Neumann (1985) and Rottet (1992) show, long and short verb forms have different temporal/aspectual (TMA) interpretations. The short form occurs in the (habitual) present, the second person imperative and in the complement of 'fo' (a predicate derived from 'il faut que' 'it is necessary that':

(12) a. Sop-la   frem a sez-er.
       Shop-DET close at six-o'clock
       'The shop (always) closes at six o'clock.'
    b. Sop-la   freme a sez-er.
       Shop-DET close at six-o'clock
       'The shop closed at six o'clock.'

In addition to this interpretative difference, the long/short opposition also correlates with V-to-I movement:

(13) a. Mo pa monzhe/*monzh.   Negation Placement
       1SG NEG eat   (Rottet 1992:268)
       'I did not eat.' OR 'I have not eaten.'
    b. Mo monzh/*monzhe pa.
       1SG eat   NEG
       'I don't eat.'

(14) a. Fo tuzhu kupe/*kup zerb-la.   Adverb Placement
       FO always cut   grass-DET   (Rottet 1992:266)
       'It is always necessary to cut the grass.'
    b. Fo to kup/*kupe tuzhu zerb-la.
       FO 2SG cut   always grass-DET
       'You always have to cut the grass.'

An additional argument for the correlation between the long/short opposition and V-to-I movement is the incompatability of short forms and preverbal TMA markers. If these markers are present, only the long form can surface:

(15) Le   klosh ap sone/*son aster.   TMA marker
     DET bell ASP ring   now   (Rottet 1992:267)
     'The bells are ringing now.'

Thus, we arrive at the following structures for Louisiana Creole.

(16) a. [TP DP V-Ø [VP <V> DP]]
    b. [TP DP   [VP V-e DP]]

The second pattern is found in Haitian Creole and Mauritian Creole. The broad generalization that emerges from the studies of Corne (1981), Seuren (1990), Baker & Syea (1991), and Syea (1992) on the long/short opposition in Mauritian Creole, is that verb syncopation applies whenever the verb in question is followed by some material of its own VP. Elements that induce this rule of syncopation include direct objects, indirect objects, measure phrases, selected adverbials, etc. The relevant factor is argumenthood. Arguments induce the short form, adjuncts the long one:

(17) a. Pyer ti   manz/*manze min. [Theme]
       Peter TNS eat   Chinese.noodles
       'Peter ate Chinese noodles.'
    b. Pyer ti   manze/*manz Rozil. [Locative]
       Peter TNS eat   Rose-Hill
       'Peter ate at Rose-Hill.'

If Locatives are arguments, the short form appears, as in (18):

(18) Pyer ti   al/*ale Rozil. [Locative]
     Peter TNS go   Rose-Hill
     'Peter went to Rose-Hill.'

The application of this syncopation-rule is post-syntactic. If the object of a verb undergoes wh-movement, the verb spells out as the short form, exemplified in (19):

(19) Question: Ki   Pyer ti   manze/*manz?
                What Peter TNS eat
                'What did Peter eat?'
     Answer: Pyer ti   manz/*manze dipen.
                Peter TNS eat   bread
                'Peter ate bread.'

Thus, we arrive at the following structure for Mauritian Creole:

(20) a. [TP DP [VP V-Ø XP$_{ARG}$]]
    b. [TP DP [VP V-e (XP$_{ADJ}$)]]

DeGraff (2001) summarizes the pattern for Haitian Creole as follows. The long verb-form shows up when the object of a verb is questioned, or the verb is the last overt element in the VP. The short verb-form appears when the verb is followed by its complement. Thus, Haitian Creole has a pattern reminiscent to that of Mauritian Creole. But there are reasons to believe that they are not (necessarily) identical. Factors that complicate the picture in Haitian Creole are: (i) the status of the object: full NPs, but not pronominal objects, induce the short form; (ii) emphasis which disfavors the occurrence of the short form; (iii) there appears to be variation among the different dialects of Haitian Creole. In Mauritian Creole, on the other hand, the distribution of the long and short forms is categorial and not subject to dialectal variation.

Whereas the factor determining the grammatical underpinning of this alternation might come from the superstrate language in the case of Louisiana Creole (see Becker & Veenstra (2003) for arguments that only late adstrate influence is involved here), superstrate influence cannot account for the other pattern. Therefore, it can only be due to either substrate influence or universal processes in creolization.

4. Conjoint/disjoint opposition in Bantu languages

The long/short alternation in Mauritian Creole is reminiscent of the conjoint/disjoint (CJ/DJ) distinction in Bantu languages (Meeussen 1959; Creissels 1986). Speakers of Bantu languages have been argued to be part of the substrate group for Mauritian Creole. Setting aside potential problems involved in the precise determination of the relevant substrate language due to the absence of precise demographic evidence, (e.g. who, when, from where, see Arends 2007 for a recent assessment of some of the difficulties involved in socio-historic research on contact languages in general), Makhuwa, Yao, Mwera and Bemba are among the Bantu languages that have been suggested (see Baker & Corne 1986).

The CJ/DJ distinction refers to verb allomorphy found in some tense-aspect paradigms that is conditioned by the verb's relation to other elements in the clause. The DJ-form is obligatory used when the verb is clause-final, while the CJ-form needs some clause-internal constituent to follow the verb. Thus, in Kinyarwanda the CJ-form cannot occur in intransitive contexts (21d). The presence vs absence of the DJ-form here marks an aspectual distinction (habitual vs nonhabitual), compare (21a) and (21c):

(21) a. A-kora   mu-mulimá.   CJ   Kinyarwanda
        AGR-work LOC-farm   (Cadiou 1985:65f.)
        'She works on the farm.'   [habitual]
    b. A-ra-kóra.   DJ
        AGR-DJ-work
        'She is working/about to work.'
    c. A-ra-kóra   mu-mulimá.   DJ
        AGR-DJ-work LOC-farm
        'She is working/at work on the farm.' [non-habitual]
    d. *A-kora.   CJ
        AGR-work

The CJ/DJ opposition is considered a classic topic in Bantu linguistics, and its description, characterization, analysis and explanation is still one of the most vexing problems. There appears to be a bewildering amount of variation among the different languages (cf. Schadeberg 2004 for an overview). Thus, Meeussen (1959:251) notes for Kirundi that it marks a thetic/categoric distinction:

(22) a. Imuúngu zi-rya ig0ti.   CJ
        9.termite 9-eat 11.door
        'The termite eats wood.'
    b. Imuúngu zi-ra-rya' uruugi   DJ
        9.termite 9-DJ-eat 11.door
        'The termite eats the door.'

Creissels & Robert (1998), on the other hand, argue that the distribution of the DJ and CJ forms are the result of the interplay between structural and information-structural factors, schematically summarized in (23) and exemplified in (24) for Setswana:

(23) $V_{CONJOINT}$ X || [X = part of clause & (part of) Rheme ~ COMMENT]
     $V_{DISJOINT}$ || X [X = post-clausal & Theme ~ TOPIC]

(24) a. Mphó ó-tsámaile.   DJ   Setswana
         'Mpho$_{THEME}$ has gone.'   (Creissels 1996; McCormack 2006)
     b. ó-tsámaile Mphó.   DJ
         'He has gone, Mpho$_{THEME}$ that is.'
     c. Gó-tsámailé Mphó.   CJ
         'There has gone Mpho$_{RHEME}$.'   [locative inversion to focus subject]

Another line of research links the opposition to Focus. Givón (1975) and, more recently, Ndayiragije (1999) and Güldemann (2003), have all argued that it is directly related to Focus. The verb appears in the CJ-form if the element immediately following the verb is in focus:

(25) a. Ba-ya-dlal-a   phandle   DJ   Zulu
         1.SBJ-ya-play-FV   outside   (Buell 2006)
         'They're playing outside.'
     b. Ba-dlal-a   phandle   CJ
         1.SBJ-play-FV   outside
         'They're playing OUTSIDE.'

Interestingly, the only Bantu language that has been mentioned as a possible substrate language of Mauritian Creole, and for which we found reliable data, is Makhuwa (van der Wal 2006). According to her description, there is a strong correlation with Focus:

(26) a. The verb appears in its conjoint form when a focal element occupies the Immediate After Verb (IAV) position;
     b. The verb appears in its disjoint form when the IAV position is empty.

As shown in the previous section, the long/short opposition in Mauritian Creole is related to the argument/adjunct distinction, and not to Focus. Thus, the following example can be an answer to the out-of-the-blue question 'What happened?', showing that Focus on the object is not involved:

(27) Pyer ti   manz dipen.   (Mauritian Creole)
     Peter TNS eat bread
     'Peter ate bread.'

Buell (2006) has also argued against the Focus-analysis on the basis of Zulu. He discusses two different Focus-analyses. The first type is the analysis as proposed by van der Wal (2006) for Makhuwa:

(28) THE POSTVERBAL TERM FOCUS HYPOTHESIS (Creissels 1996)
The element following a conjoint form is in focus, while the element following a disjoint form is not in focus.

Evidence against this analysis comes from broad focus contexts. Although the object in the answer in (29) is not in focus, the verb still appears in the CJ-form:

(29) Question: Kw-enzek-e-ni? CJ Zulu
17.SBJ-sing-FV-what (Buell 2006)
'What happened?'
Answer: Ngi-cul-e i-ngoma CJ
1S.SBJ-sing-FV DET-9.song
'I sang a song.' [no focus on the object]

The other type of analysis has been advanced by Güldemann (2003):

(30) THE VERB FOCUS HYPOTHESIS
The verb appearing in a disjoint form is in focus, while a verb appearing in a conjoint form is not.

Buell (2006) shows that focused verbs in Zulu can occur in the CJ-form:

(31) A-ngi-dans-i kahle, kodwa ngi-cul-a kahle. CJ
NEG-1S.SBJ-dance-FV well but 1S.SBJ-sing-FV well
'I don't dance well, but I sing well.' [verb focus]

The conclusion is that in Zulu there is no strict correlation with Focus. Buell (2006) argues that the CJ/DJ distinction relates to different phrase structure configurations, a proposal at least going back to van der Spuy (1993), and reminiscent of Creissels & Robert (1998) (see (23) above):

(32) a. $[V_{CONJOINT} \ X \ ]_{AgrSP}$ (Y)
b. $[V_{DISJOINT}]_{AgrSP}$ (X) (Y)

If a constituent is adjacent to the verb in the AgrSP-domain, it surfaces in the CJ-form, otherwise the DJ-form is chosen.

In summary, we have seen there is considerable variation between the different Bantu languages with respect to the CJ/DJ alternation. There does not seem to be a direct parallel in any of the Bantu languages with Mauritian Creole, only a partial one at best. In Zulu, there is an adjacency requirement between the verb and an object in a certain domain, reminiscent of the pattern in Mauritian Creole. Two remarks are pertinent here: (i) the adjacency in Zulu is in derived positions, not in base-generated positions; (ii) the adjunct/argument distinction does not play a role. In Mauritian Creole, on the other hand, there has to be adjacency between the verb and its argument within the VP domain, since it does not have V-movement (Adone 1994). In Makhuwa, one of the substrate languages of Mauritian Creole, the CJ/DJ opposition is closely linked to Focus, unlike Mauritian Creole. Thus, the grammatical underpinnings of the alternation in Mauritian Creole and the Bantu languages, Makhuwa in particular, is just not similar enough to enable us to come up with a realistic scenario on the emergence of the long/short opposition in Mauritian Creole in terms of substrate influence.

5. Phonological origin of the alternation and phase syntax

Neither superstrate nor substrate influence seems to have played an important role in the emergence of the grammatical underpinning of long/short alternation. The superstrate language only provided the raw material. The role of the substrate languages seems to be even less important. On the other hand, we argued in Section 2 that universals of second language acquisition have played an important role in the emergence of the long/short alternation. The enslaved population consisting of second-language learners picked up a phonetic alternation from the input (superstrate language) without the appropriate functions. We have shown that in Basic Varieties of French we find a similar situation. The acquisition of the form precedes the acquisition of the function. Whereas beyond the Basic Variety, learners seem to eventually converge on the properties of the target language (French), this has not happened in the case of the French-related creoles. At the moment that the superstrate language stopped playing an important role as the target language in the colonial setting (target shift from superstrate language to the Basic Variety thereof, Baker 1990; Becker & Veenstra 2003 for details), the alternation began to lead its own life, but in essence was only a highly variable pattern of phonetic/phonological variation.

We propose that the ultimate origin of the alternation lies in its phonological nature. A number of studies have shown that semantic factors play an important role in phonological phrasing, especially argument/adjunct asymmetries (Gussenhoven 1983, 1992; Selkirk 1984; Uhmann 1991; Winkler 1997; etc.). If a head-argument structure is in focus, accent can be realized on the argument only, but if a head-adjunct structure is in focus, accent must be realized on the head and the adjunct (examples from German):

(33) a. Hans ist [VP [im Zelt] [V geblieben]]$_F$ argument
(Hans ist) (im Zélt geblieben)
'Hans stayed in the tent.'
b. Hans hat [VP [im Zelt] [VP geraucht]]$_F$ adjunct
(Hans hat) (im Zélt) (geráucht)
'Hans smoked in the tent.'

The head-argument configuration constitutes a phonological phrase, whereas the head-adjunct configuration does not. We could interpret this for French-related creoles as follows. If the verb receives the accent, it surfaces in the long form, otherwise the short one surfaces. This captures the distribution of the long and short form:

(34) a. V ARG [V ARG]   (V ARG*) short form of V
     b. V ADJ [V] [ADJ] (V*) (ADJ*) long form of V

The pattern as exhibited by Haitian Creole can be taken strong evidence for such a direct relationship between accent placement, argument/adjunct asymmetries and the long/short alternation. As DeGraff (2001) shows, prosodic factors play an important role in the long/short alternation in Haitian Creole. Thus, full NPs induce the short form, but not pronominal objects. The latter are phonological clitics and cannot receive the accent, therefore, the accent must be realized on the verb, hence the long form has to surface. Furthermore, emphasis disfavors the occurrence of the short form. The pattern of Mauritian Creole is different in one important respect: here prosodic factors do not seem to play a role.

We, therefore, propose that Mauritian Creole has gone one step further than Haitian Creole and has grammaticalized the long/short alternation to only superficially mark the argument/adjunct distinction. In particular, we argue that the form of the verb is determined at each Phase. We hereby follow recent proposals by Chomsky (see Chomsky 2000, 2001, 2005) in assuming that the syntactic derivation is split up into Phases, where each phase is identified by a particular category that is merged (little v, C and D have been argued to be the relevant categories). On the construction of each phase, the complement of the phasal head is spelled out, so it is this category that is interpreted by the A-P component of the grammar.[1] If the verb ends up in the final position of a Phase, it will be spelled out in the long form. Two contexts are identified where this occurs:

i. when the internal argument has undergone leftward movement, as in (35d);
ii. when there is no internal argument, as in (35a). Adjuncts, on the other hand, are merged after completion of the Phase, and therefore do not induce the short form (35b):

Spell-out @ v-Phase

(35) a. Mo pe mānze.   long form   intransitive V   [vP v+V]
     b. Mo pe mānze Rosil   long form   V+ adjunct   [vP v+V]
     c. Mo pe mānz dipen   short form V+ object   [vP v+V DP]
     d. Ki Pye ti mānze?   long form   V+ wh-object
                                                          [vP WH [vP v+V <WH>]

---

1. See Adger (2006) and Legate (2003) for more details.

When the vP-Phase plays such an important role in the long/shortalternation, the question arises whether we also see such effects at other Phase edges, e.g. the CP-Phase. The following data indicates that this is indeed the case. If the embedded is a full CP (36a) or an embedded full infinitive (36b), the matrix verb surfaces in the expected long form. These Spell-Out domains have been sent out to the A-P interface and do not count anymore in the derivation. Embedded bare infinitives, on the other hand, have not been sent off yet (due to the missing CP-level), therefore are still syntactically active and induce the short form, as in (36c):

(36) a. Mo pāse ki zot pu vini dime. (Syea 1992)
     1SG think that 3PL MOOD come tomorrow
     'I think that they will come tomorrow.'
  b. Mo pa kone kuma pu eksplik tua sa.
     1SG NEG know how FOR explain 2SG DEM
     'I don't know how to explain this to you.'
  c. Zot kon kwi dipen.
     3PL know bake bread
     'They know how to make bread.'

The long/short alternation in Mauritian Creole can then be best analysed as a morphological reflex of a Spell-Out domain at the Phase level. As such, it can be construed as an argument in favour of the Multi-Spell-Out architecture of Uriagereka (1999).

References

Adger, David. 2006. Stress and phasal syntax. Ms.
Adone, Dany. 1994. *The Acquisition of Mauritian Creole* [Language Acquisition & Language Disorders 9]. Amsterdam: John Benjamins.
Arends, Jacques. 2007. A demographic perspective on creole formation. In *Handbook of Pidgin and Creole Languages*, John Singler & Silvia Kouwenberg (eds), 309–331. Malden MA: Blackwell.
Baker, Philip. 1990. Off Target? *Journal of Pidgin and Creole Languages* 5(1): 107–119.
Baker, Philip & Corne, Chris. 1986. Universals, substrata and the Indian Ocean Creoles. In *Universals versus Substrata in Creole Genesis* [Creole Language Library 1], Pieter Muysken & Norval Smith (eds), 163–183. Amsterdam: John Benjamins.
Baker, Philip & Syea, Anand. 1991. On the copula in Mauritian Creole, past and present. In *Development and Structures of Creole Language* [Creole Language Library 9], Frank Byrne & Tom Huebner (eds), 159–175. Amsterdam: John Benjamins.
Becker, Angelika & Veenstra, Tonjes. 2003. The survival of inflectional morphology in French-related creoles: The role of SLA processes. *Studies in Second Language Acquisition* 25(2): 283–306.
Buell, Leston. 2006. The Zulu conjoint/disjoint verb alternation: Focus or constituency? *ZAS WPiL* 43: 9–30.

Cadiou, Yves. 1985. Sur ùn problème de syntaxe: La relation verbe-complément en kinyarwanda. In *Le kinyarwanda: études de morpho-syntaxe,* Yves Caudio (ed.), 65–83. Leuven: Peeters.

Chomsky, Noam. 2000. Minimalist inquiries: The framework. In *Step by Step: Essays on Minimalist Syntax in Honour of Howard Lasnik,* Roger Martin, David Michaels & Juan Uriagereka (eds.), 89–115. Cambridge MA: The MIT Press.

Chomsky, Noam. 2001. Derivation by phase. In *Ken Hale: A Life in Language,* Michael J. Kenstowicz (ed.), 1–52. Cambridge MA: The MIT Press.

Chomsky, Noam. 2005. Three factors in language design. *Linguistic Inquiry* 104: 1–61.

Corne, Chris. 1981. A re-evaluation of the predicate in Ile-de-France Creole. In *Generative Studies on Creole Languages,* Pieter Muysken (ed.), 103–124. Dordrecht: Foris.

Corne, Chris. 1999. *From French to Creole.* London: University of Westminster Press.

Creissels, Denis. 1996. Conjunctive and disjunctive verb forms in Setswana. *South African Journal of African Languages* 16: 109–115.

Creissels, Denis & Robert, Stéphane. 1998. Morphologie verbale et organisation discursive de l'énoncé: l'Exemple du tschwana et du wolof. In *Faits de Langues* [Revue de Linguistique 11/12], Suzy Platiel & Raphael Kabore (eds), 161–178. Paris : Ophrys.

DeGraff, Michel. 2001. Morphology in creole genesis: A prolegomenon. In *Ken Hale: A Life in Language,* Michael J. Kenstowicz (ed.), 53–122. Cambridge MA: The MIT Press.

Dietrich, Rainer, Klein, Wolfgang & Noyau, Colette (eds). 1995. *The Acquisition of Temporality in a Second Language* [Studies in Bilingualism 7]. Amsterdam: John Benjamins.

Givón, Talmy. 1975. Focus and the scope of assertion: Some Bantu evidence. *Studies in African Linguistics* 6: 185–205.

Güldemann, Tom. 2003. Present progressive vis-à-vis predication focus in Bantu: A verbal category between semantics and pragmatics. *Studies in Language* 27: 323–360.

Gussenhoven, Carlos. 1983. Focus, mode, and the nucleus. *Journal of Linguistics* 19: 377–417.

Gussenhoven, Carlos. 1992. Sentence accents and argument structure. In *Thematic Structure. Its Role in Grammar,* Iggy M. Roca (ed.), 79–106. Berlin: Foris.

Harris, Martin. 1987. French. In *The World's Major Languages,* Bernard Comrie (ed.), London: Routledge.

Klein, Wolfgang & Perdue, Clive (eds). 1992. *Utterance Structure. Developing Grammars Again* [Studies in Bilingualism 5]. Amsterdam: John Benjamins.

Klein, Wolfgang & Perdue, Clive. 1997. The basic variety (or: Couldn't natural languages be much simpler?). *Second Language Research* 13: 301–347.

Legate, Julie. 2003. Some interface properties of the phase. *Linguistic Inquiry* 34: 506–516.

McCormack, Anna. 2006. A further look at conjunctive and disjunctive forms in Setswana. *ZAS WPiL* 43: 123–141.

Meeussen, Achille Emiel. 1959. *Essai de Grammaire Rundi* [Série Sciences Humaines 24]. Tervuren: Annales du Musée Royal du Congo Belge.

Meisel, Jürgen. 1994. Getting FAT: finiteness, agreement and tense in early grammars. In *Bilingual First Language Acquisition* [Language Acquisition & Language Disorders 7], Jürgen Meisel (ed.), 89–129. Amsterdam: John Benjamins.

Ndayiragije, Juvenil. 1999. Checking economy. *Linguistic Inquiry* 30: 399–444.

Neumann, Ingrid. 1985. *Le créole de Breaux Bridge, Louisiane: Étude morphosyntaxe, textes, vocabulaire.* Hamburg: Helmut Buske.

Noyau, Colette, Et-Tayeb Houdaïfa, Vasseur, Marie-Thérèse & Véronique, Daniel. 1995. The acquisition of French. In *The Acquisition of Temporality in a Second Language*, Rainer Dietrich, Wolfgang Klein & Colette Noyau (eds), 145–209. Amsterdam: John Benjamins.

Prévost, Philippe & White, Lydia. 2000. Missing surface inflection or impairment in second language acquisition? Evidence from tense and agreement. *Second Language Research* 16(2): 103–133.

Rottet, Kevin. 1992. Functional categories and verb raising in Louisiana Creole. *Probus* 4: 261–289.

Schadeberg, Thilo. 2004. Conjoint and disjoint – an enigmatic category from Bantu. Paper presented at the University of Bayreuth, June 15, 2004.

Schlyter, Suzanne. 2002. Development of verb morphology and finiteness in children and adults acquiring French. In *Information Structure, Linguistic Structure and the Dynamics of Learner Language* [Studies in Bilingualism 26], Christine Dimroth & Marianne Starren (eds). Amsterdam: John Benjamins.

Selkirk, Elisabeth O. 1984. *Phonology and Syntax: The Relation between Sound and Structure: Current Studies in Linguistics*. Cambridge MA: The MIT Press.

Seuren, Pieter. 1990. Verb syncopation and predicate raising in Mauritian Creole. *Linguistics* 28(4): 809–844.

Starren, Marianne. 2001. The Second Time. PhD dissertation, Catholic University of Brabant.

Syea, Anand. 1992. The short and long form of verbs in Mauritian Creole: Functionalism versus formalism. *Theoretical Linguistics* 18(1): 61–97.

Uhmann, Susanne, 1991. *Fokusphonologie. Eine Analyse deutscher Intonationskonturen im Rahmen der nicht-linearen Phonologie* [Linguistische Arbeiten 252]. Tübingen: Niemeyer.

Uriagereka, Juan. 1999. Multiple spell-out. In *Working Minimalism*, Samuel David Epstein & Norbert Hornstein (eds), 251–282. Cambridge MA: The MIT Press.

Van der Spuy, Andrew. 1993. Dislocated noun phrases in Nguni. *Lingua* 90: 335–355.

Van der Wal, Jenneke. 2006. The disjoint verb form and an empty Intermediate After Verb position in Makhuwa. *ZAS WPiL* 43: 233–256.

Veenstra, Tonjes. 2003. What verbal morphology can tell us about creole genesis: The case of French-related creoles. In *Phonology and Morphology of Creole Languages,* Ingo Plag (ed.), 293–314. Tübingen: Niemeyer.

Winkler, Susanne. 1997. *Focus and Secondary Predication*. Berlin: Mouton de Gruyter.

The invisible hand in creole genesis
Reanalysis in the formation of Berbice Dutch*

Silvia Kouwenberg

This paper considers the historical context in which Berbice Dutch was formed before turning to the significance of the presence in that language of function words derived from the Eastern Ijọ substrate. The view that transfer of Eastern Ijọ grammatical properties took place in the formation of Berbice Dutch, is subjected to detailed scrutiny for tense-mood-aspect marking and negation. Despite similarities, important areas of divergence or discontinuity between Berbice Dutch and its substrate are identified – areas which point to reanalysis of substrate-derived functional material in the genesis of Berbice Dutch. This runs counter to the view that Eastern Ijọ speakers played a central role in the formation of Berbice Dutch, and suggests that 'the invisible hand' in its genesis must have been another group, possibly the mixed progeny of the plantation population, which included Dutch, Eastern Ijọ and Arawak speakers.

1. Introduction

The question of the identity of those involved in the formation of the creole languages of the Caribbean links substratist research with historical research on the plantation societies of the Caribbean. In some cases, the historical record helps in finding an answer to that question. Thus, research on the historical demographic context of creole formation in Suriname has identified the numerical dominance of different ethnolinguistic groups in the slave population over different time periods – corresponding to contributions to the lexicon of Suriname creole languages, in particular in the

---

* For the data presented in this paper, I am indebted to the Berbice Dutch and Kalaḅarị speakers who willingly worked and shared with me, and to the Netherlands Foundation for the Advancement of Tropical Research (WOTRO), which funded my fieldwork in Berbice and in the Niger Delta. I wish also to thank the editors for valuable comments, and especially Norval Smith for pointing me to useful Okrika data. Finally, I thank Darlene LaCharité for her hospitality during the fall of 2007, when I wrote most of this article.

Maroon creoles, and to the survival of remnant African languages in esoteric contexts (Arends 1995).

In other cases, however, the historical record fails. The Berbice Dutch (BD) case is in the latter category, as will be discussed in more detail below (Section 2). But here, it appears that the linguistic record provides an answer. Since the publication of Smith, Robertson & Williamson (1987), we know that Eastern Ijọ (EI) varieties contributed around 38% of BD basic vocabulary (using the Swadesh 100-word list as the basis for this assessment; see Kouwenberg 1992, forthc.). From this significant single-substrate contribution to basic lexicon, it is a natural step to the view that speakers of EI varieties constituted an early dominant presence in the Berbice colony, and were the agents in the formation of BD (Kouwenberg 1996d). On first consideration, this conclusion appears to be supported by a number of features in BD grammar which seemingly reflect the pronounced tendency in EI towards surface syntactic strings which are head-final. These BD features include locative postpositions, clause-final negation, and various grammatical suffixes. Moreover, in each case at least some if not all of the morphemes involved in these constructions are of EI etymology.

Despite this apparently strong case for a single dominant substrate in the genesis of BD, Smith et al. (1987) argue that EI speakers were not the sole agents in the formation of BD. This article aims to substantiate the linguistic evidence in favor of that position, although I ultimately do not agree with the scenario adopted by Smith et al., as will become evident when I return to it below. The evidence presented here comes from the treatment which functional morphemes of EI etymology have received in BD, ranging from reanalysis to utter loss. In no case did EI functional morphemes make it into BD 'unscathed', so to speak. The reinterpretation which EI material, including functional material, has undergone in the formation of BD suggests strongly that EI speakers could not have been involved in this process. It seems unlikely that Dutch speakers could have had this kind of profound impact in the formation of BD, and in any case, none of the cases of reanalysis brought the language closer to Dutch. This means that the question posed at the beginning of this paper is wide open. I will speculate on possible answers to it in Section 6.

But first I consider what is known of the historical demographics of the Berbice colony – which is precious little, as we shall see (Section 2). In Section 3, I will briefly review the significance of the presence in BD of functional morphemes of EI etymology (3.1). There, I also consider the significance of 15 BD words whose EI etymon is a phrasal expression (3.2); we shall see evidence that reinterpretation and back-formation gave rise to BD simplex forms in ways which cannot be attributed to EI speakers. In Sections 4 and 5, I will describe two grammatical subsystems in detail, tense-mood-aspect marking and negation, respectively, and I will turn to the question of the extent to which transfer of EI properties can be said to have been part of the emergence of these BD subsystems. We will see that, at best, partial transfer obtained.

2. The Berbice colony and its slave population

Berbice Dutch was the creole vernacular of the plantation populations of the Berbice and Canje Rivers which jointly constituted the privately-owned Berbice colony (now part of Guyana, South America). It is the last known Dutch-lexifier creole to have become extinct, Skepi Dutch and Negerhollands having gone before. BD was documented in its pre-language-death-form by Robertson (1979) and Kouwenberg (1994a, 2007). Its demise can be considered to have started during the mid-to-late eighteenth century, when plantations shifted from their upriver locations to the coast (Kramer 1991). Here, we will survey the development of the colony, as it emerges from historical sources, and consider the provenance of its slaves.

2.1 The development of the Berbice colony

Berbice was established as a private colony in 1627 by Abraham van Pere, with permission of the Zeeland chamber of the Dutch West India Company. Van Pere dispatched a party consisting of sixty whites and six blacks to establish the colony (Robertson 1993: 298; Postma 1990: 13).[1]

Nearly a hundred years later, the 1720 contract for the transfer of ownership of the colony to a new joint stock company, the 'Sociëteit van Berbice' (the Berbice Association),[2] lists 895 slaves (adults and children) among the colony's assets (Hartsinck

---

1. According to Robertson (ibid.), less than ten years later, in the mid 1630s, the white population numbered 40, the black population 25. It appears, however, that these figures may not be reliable. Robertson (1993: 313, n.1) attributes this information to Anna Benjamins, who obtained it from an unspecified archival source. That source is now available in English translation (Ishmael 2001). One Don Pedro de Vivero, Magistrate of Santo Tome de la Guayana, writes in April 1637 of the presence of various European competitors to the Spanish; his report includes a statement that "...they are strongly fortified in that of Essequibo with one hundred and twenty Dutch and a large body of negroes; **in that of Berbiz with forty Dutch and twenty-five negroes**" (ibid.; emphasis mine). What makes this source less than reliable is the fact that these figures recur in a memorandum of November 19, 1637, by Don Juan Desologuren "as to the powers of the Dutch in the West Indies." The memorandum provides an account of the taking of the island of Tobago from the Dutch, which runs as follows: "He then proceeded to the Island of Tobago, where they [= the Dutch] had cultivated land and built a fortress with twenty-eight pieces of cannon and a quantity of arms and ammunition, and 150 Dutch, whom he conquered and dislodged, and they finally settled on the River Essequibo, 100 leagues off, with 120 Dutch and many negroes, **and on the River Berbice, 90 leagues off, with forty Dutch and twenty-five negroes**, both in the direction of Brazil" (ibid.; emphasis mine). Here, it appears that the figures do not refer to the entire population of Berbice, but rather to the number of Dutchmen and slaves which joined that population after the taking of Tobago by the Spaniards.

2. The Association's main shareholders were Amsterdam merchants. In 1732 it was granted a charter by the West India Company.

1770: 327). Robertson (1993: 299) takes this figure to represent the total number of slaves in the colony, but it appears that the figure does not take into account the number of slaves belonging to privately owned plantations. That it is probable that there were privately established plantations, whose slaves were not counted among the colony's assets, is supported by a comparison with Smith's (2000) claim that twelve years later, in 1732, there were ninety-three private plantations in the Berbice river and twenty in the Canje Creek, *in addition to* the estates of the Berbice Association. It is likely, then, that the eight plantations (6 sugar, 2 cacao) listed among the colony's assets in 1720, alongside the aforementioned 895 slaves, only represent the plantations owned by Van Pere and his associates, which were transferred to the newly formed Berbice Association.

Nonetheless, a comparison with Kramer's later figures suggests that the total slave population of Berbice may not have been very much greater than 895:[3] almost 30 years later, in 1749, when the colony consists of 111 plantations, the black slave population – according to taxation counts – has not quite reached 1,500 (Kramer 1991: 60). Kramer points out, though, that numbers derived from taxation documents cannot be taken to be absolutely reliable: planters would have profited from low counts. This means that it is likely that the figures underestimate the number of enslaved on the plantations. Table 1 shows the growth of the population of enslaved Africans over the period to 1782 according to Kramer's figures.[4]

---

3. From the listed figure of 895 slaves, 6 sugar plantations, 2 cacao plantations, a fort, several outposts, a smithy, and a church, Robertson concludes that the average number of slaves was 90 per plantation – a figure which is rather high and which suggests the possibility of inflation: the figure is part of a bid to sell shares in the new company, and may have been inflated for this purpose. However, slave ownership varied considerably based on the size of plantations and their crops, and since sugar plantations were typically the largest and most labor- and capital-intensive plantations, it is true that the plantations operated by the Association (and before that, by Van Pere and his associates) must have averaged more slaves than the private plantations, which mostly grew cacao, coffee and cotton – and continued to do so throughout the history of Berbice as a Dutch colony. For instance, according to Hartsinck's description of the colony in the 1760s, only five of more than 100 plantations along the Berbice River were sugar plantations; of this number, four belonged to the Association, while one was privately owned (1770: 288). In short, the six sugar plantations are more than likely responsible for the relatively high number of slaves in the inventory, although the possibility of an inflated figure should not be discounted.

4. Kramer's table covers the period 1740–1782. He provides population figures for subdivisions of the colony; I only provide totals. Slaves aged between 3 and 10 years were apparently counted as half for the purpose of assessing taxes owed; this means that the totals underrepresent the real numbers, although probably not by more than a few percentage points. As pointed out before, planters' interest in underestimated numbers is more likely to be a source of misrepresentation. During 1763–1764, a slave uprising resulted in the abandonment of around a third of plantations. It also reduced the slave population by almost one third (Kramer 1991: 53). This accounts for the fact that the 1771 figures are below those of 1762.

Table 1. Plantations and slave populations in Berbice during the mid-eighteenth century, based on tax assessments (source: Kramer's (1991: 60) Table 5 'Berbice plantations and slaves')

Year	Plantations	Black slaves	Amerindian slaves
1749	111	1,466.5	199.5
1753	139	1,712	234
1760	118	2,226	213.5
1762	126	2,622.5	203.5
1771	117	2,597.5	36
1774	111	5,582	–
1779	118	5,250	
1782	111	5,318	

Where the white population is concerned, Robertson (1993: 299) cites a 1735 source,[5] which mentions a total of 60 planters, suggesting that the white population grew but slowly. But this number is hard to reconcile with Smith's (2000) claim that there were ninety-three private plantations in the Berbice river and twenty in the Canje Creek in 1732 – figures which suggest a good deal more than 60 planters, although the possibility of multiple plantation ownership can't be ruled out. Smith (2000) further claims that by 1762, the population of the Berbice colony had reached 346 whites, 3,833 Negro slaves, and 244 Indian slaves.[6]

Noteworthy is the fact that the Dutch distinguished, for taxation purposes, between black slaves and Amerindian slaves. The latter category disappears from the records after the slave uprising of 1763–1764, but from the very small number recorded in 1771, it is clear that the enslavement of Amerindians was abandoned even before. It is well-known from later sources that the Dutch were keen to maintain good relations with the indigenous population. Thus, Hartsinck (1770: 290) says that "[w]e have made friendship pacts with all these peoples [= Amerindians], forbidding their sale as slaves."[7] These pacts were motivated by the planters' need for Amerindian allies in tracking runaway slaves and preventing slave uprisings.

---

5. That source is Galbo Elephantus's *A voyage to the new colony of Berbice in 1735*, translated and published in 1877. As far as I am aware, nothing is known of the author, and the credibility of the information provided in this source cannot be reliably assessed.

6. Note that Smith's figures for the slave population exceed those of Kramer, who, as noted earlier, indicates that his figures are probably low, due in part to the fact that children aged 3–10 are counted as half, and due in (probably larger) part to the efforts of planters to evade the payment of taxes on the slaves in their possession.

7. The original text is as follows: Wy hebben met alle deeze Volken Verbonden van Vriendschap geslooten, mogende dezelve niet tot Slaaven verkocht worden.

2.2 The provenance of African slaves in the Berbice colony

There appear to be no surviving records of slave shipments to Berbice or of the sale of slaves in Berbice for the entire seventeenth century.[8] This means that nothing is known from the historical record of the provenance of slaves in the Berbice colony during that crucial period.

Based on the linguistic evidence which they unearthed, Smith et al. (1987:66–68) searched for evidence of Dutch slave trade in those locations in the Bight of Biafra from which EI slaves may have been traded (now part of Rivers State, Nigeria). Because of their coastal location, the Eastern Ịjọ were in fact among the first to engage in the slave trade with European buyers in the Bight of Biafra. Smith et al. quote Dapper (1668), who describes the Dutch presence in the Calabar River. According to Dapper's description, the Dutch were engaged in the purchase of slaves from traders in Elem Kalaḅarị and in Ḅile – both of which then traded in slaves from raids on competing neighboring villages. In other words, the presence of EI speakers in the mid-seventeenth-century Dutch slave trade is historically supported.

That the Berbice colony received slaves from the Bight of Biafra is further confirmed by Postma (1990), although he is unable to identify more precisely the source of these slaves. He points out that slaves from the Bight of Biafra were generally referred to as 'Calabaries' (p. 106) – a term which does not allow us to distinguish between Ijo, Delta-Cross River, or Igbo ethnicities. According to Postma, Calabary slaves "were invariably considered undesirable by most Dutch colonists" (ibid.), but during the early stages of their development, small settlements like Berbice, Essequibo, Eustatius and Saba "were forced to accept shipments of Calabary slaves" (p. 107).

2.3 Summary

To sum up, the very slow growth of the colony surmised by Robertson (1993) is based on unreliable sources, and it is likely that the Berbice colony grew quite a bit faster, both in terms of the number of plantations, and in terms of the size of the white and black population. Also, the very low proportion of whites to blacks assumed by Robertson (1993) appears unjustified, although it is clear that the white population

---

8. This is based on consultation of the Eltis et al. (1999) database of the trans-Atlantic slavetrade. The earliest voyage in the database which disembarked slaves in Berbice is of 1714. Despite a reference in Van Kampen (1831), cited by Smith et al. (1987:74), to "an agreement between the Company of Berbice and the Dutch West Indian Company in 1714 for the supply of 250 slaves from Angola by the latter", the earliest records in the database of slave shipments to Berbice originating in Angola date to the 1760s. This does not mean, of course, that such shipments did not take place, just that we have no evidence of it. Postma (1990:189) points out that the first regular slave consignment by the WIC for either Essequibo or Berbice had to wait until 1720, and that prior to that, the WIC was reluctant even to set aside portions of Suriname consignments for Essequibo and Berbice.

was outnumbered by blacks at least at the start of the eighteenth century, and in all likelihood much earlier.[9]

Despite evidence that slaves were shipped to Berbice from the Bight of Biafra during the early years of the Berbice colony, there is no direct evidence that these slaves originated in EI-speaking communities. However, we can marry that observation with the linguistic evidence, which we will consider in some detail below.

3. The Eastern Ịjọ contribution to Berbice Dutch

3.1 The significance of EI function words in BD

As pointed out earlier, the linguistic record very clearly identifies one or several lects in the Eastern Ịjọ cluster as the source of the majority of lexical Africanisms[10] in BD, as first documented by Smith, et al. (1987). Their list of possibly EI-derived BD forms numbers 101. Additional data which I collected in fieldwork between 1986 and 1990 has since brought that number to a total of 184 wholly or partially EI-derived forms, consisting of 85 verbs, 65 nouns, 14 adjectives, 4 adverbs, and 16 function words (Kouwenberg forthc.).

Almost all other BD words of African origin – whether identified as such, or suspected to be of African origin – are shared with Creolese, Guyana's English-lexifier creole. Since BD as documented in its final stages before language death includes many more Creolese forms, it is clear that quite a bit of borrowing from Creolese has taken place. Creolese vocabulary does not include words of EI origin, showing that borrowing has been unidirectional: from Creolese into BD, inclusive of forms which are ultimately of African origin. This means that a non-EI source can be ruled out for lexical Africanisms which date back to the formative period of BD. Lokono or 'true' Arawak is a third important contributor to BD lexicon, alongside Dutch and EI; it has furnished several hundred forms, in particular in the domains of flora and fauna, but is negligible as a contributor to basic lexicon. (See Kouwenberg 1996c for discussion.)

---

9. Hartsinck (1770:299ff.) describes a 1712 French raid on the Berbice colony, where the planters were forced to pay off the French in both cash and kind; payment in kind included 259 black slaves, specified as 153 male slaves, 91 female slaves, and 15 boys (p. 302). There being no report of the abandonment of plantations as a result of this loss, I surmise that the slave population of Berbice cannot have been substantially smaller in 1712 than the figure of 895 reported for 1720. This, in turn, suggests that the black slave population of Berbice numbered at least in the several hundred around 1700.

10. The term 'lexical Africanism' is owed to Joseph Farquharson's work on the African contribution to the lexicon of Jamaican Creole.

In short, the etymologies of BD forms point to an initial contact situation involving three parties: speakers of Dutch, speakers of EI, and speakers of Arawak. The language which resulted from this contact situation can be considered untypical of Caribbean creole languages in several respects: in its employment of grammatical morphemes which are mostly African in origin rather than European; in its display of word order patterns which diverge in some ways from an expected preference for head-initial order; and most importantly, in the link between the former and the latter: African-origin grammatical morphemes are associated with the divergent word order patterns.[11] Functional morphemes of EI origin in BD include pronouns, aspect markers, the focus marker, the resultative auxiliary, and the standard negator, inter alia. All this strongly suggests pervasive EI substrate transfer in the formation of BD. But BD is typologically different from its EI substrate, and diverges from it in each module of grammar. In other words, BD is morphosyntactically independent from EI, despite the resemblances. We will see that the concept of 'transfer' is too simple and undifferentiated to account for the full range of facts, including both the resemblances and the differences.

In the following sections, I will survey aspect marking (Section 4) and negation (5) in BD and EI in this light. Here, I will first look briefly at some BD forms whose EI source is a complex expression – an exercise which reveals reanalysis of the EI source material in each case.

Kalaḅarị (KA) data will be used to represent EI throughout. Smith et al. (1987) tentatively identify KA as the main source of EI forms in BD, but point out that some BD forms are more clearly cognate with other EI lects. Be that as it may, no or insufficient data are available for other EI lects. Whether the lexical and syntactic patterns of KA are fully representative of other EI lects may, of course, be questioned.[12]

---

11. One should note that head-final surface orders, while uncommon, do appear in several other Caribbean creoles. For instance, postpositions appear in the Suriname creoles (Muysken 1987), and a clause-final negator appears in Palenquero.

12. There is, of course, the possibility that these languages have undergone significant change since the period of the formation of BD – a possibility which makes comparisons based on modern material suspect. Unfortunately, only modern material is available for EI, and only a few sentences of the early and mid nineteenth century are available for BD. However, where BD is concerned, those few early sentences contain grammatical patterns which are identical with those of the language as documented in the late twentieth century (Kouwenberg 1996c). Where EI is concerned, it is relevant to point out that Ijoid languages are typologically unusual within Niger-Congo. Surrounded by Benue-Congo languages, Ijoid is classified outside of Benue-Congo, on a separate branch within Atlantic-Congo (two levels removed from Benue-Congo, and only one level below Niger-Congo itself; Williamson 1989:21). Despite centuries-long contact with Benue-Congo languages belonging to Edoid, Defoid, Igboid and Delta-Cross River subbranches, it appears that Ijoid has moved no closer to Benue-Congo, pointing to remarkable historical stability. I would think that the use of modern material for the comparison is legitimate, therefore.

3.2 BD forms with complex EI etyma

Unusual for Caribbean creole languages, verbs constitute the largest number of BD substrate-derived vocabulary (85 out of a total of 184 wholly or partially Ịjọ-derived forms; see Kouwenberg forthc.). The cases that are of interest here are those where a BD verb derives from a KA complex expression. There are 7 verbs of this kind in BD. Additionally, there are several simplex adjectives and nouns whose source is also a KA complex expression. The data in Table 2 show that these forms have been subject to some amount of reanalysis in BD.[13]

Table 2. BD forms derived from KA phrasal etyma

BD form		KA source form
V	*bi, bifi* 'say, speak'	*bíbí fíé* [language speak] 'speak', frequently reduced to *bí fíé* in connected speech
V	*bionto* 'believe, remember'	*bíó tọn* [inside arrange] 'think in one's mind'; *bíó* 'inside' is commonly used with reference to mental activity, feelings, moods, etc.
V/N	*jefi* 'eat', also: 'food'	*yé fí* [thing eat] 'to eat (something)'; *yé* 'thing' acts as dummy complement; compare *fíyé* < *fí yé* [eat thing] 'food', litt. 'thing to eat'
V	*pama* 'tell'	*ẹ́kụ́ẹ́n páká-ma* [speech come.out-CAUSE], *ḍuko páká-ma* [tell come.out- CAUSE] 'to speak out'
V	*poko* 'to like'	*pọkọ tárí* [throat thirst/ hunger] 'to feel like, long for'
V	*tumbi* 'to visit, see a person'	*tom-bọ́ bi* [person greet] 'to greet (a person)'
A	*fiku* 'deceased'	*fị kọn* [die have] 'dead, having died'
V/N	*kori* 'work'	*kọrí namá* 'work, job' / *namá kọ́rí* 'to work'
A/V	*potε* 'old, ripe, mature,' also 'become old etc.'	*kpọ́-tẹ* [be.old/ mature-PF] 'old, mature'
A/V	*tarki* 'strong, hard, thicken (of liquid)'[14]	*tọ́rụ́ kụrọ́, tọ́rụ krọ* [eye be.hard/strong] 'to be fierce, ruthless'
A	*kali* 'small'	*kálá-yē* 'small thing', normally pronounced *káliē*
N	*lukuba* 'fable'	*ílúkú gba* [story tell] 'to tell a story'
N	*mangiapu* 'runaway slave'	*mangị bọ* / *mangị apụ* [run person/persons] 'escaped person/persons'; *mangị omoni bọ* 'run-away slave'
N/V	*dondo* 'breast (n), suck (v)'	*índó ńdó* [breast suck] 'to suck breast'
N	*baratwa* 'ring', *beritwa* 'earring', *pokotwa* 'necklace'	*bárá sụá yé, bẹri sụa yé, pọkọ sụa yé* [hand / ear / throat put thing] 'ring, earring, necklace'

---

13. KA entries can be sourced from Anon. (n.d.).

14. It is possible that the BD form was influenced also by Dutch *sterk* 'strong' (with loss of initial s, which is attested for some – but not all – Dutch-derived forms with initial s-Consonant clusters).

The BD forms in Table 2 do not reflect their EI etyma in a straightforward way. Thus, we see the incorporation of a dummy object (*jefi*); the formation of a simplex form from idiomatic combinations of a verb and its preposed argument (*bifi, bionto, tumbi, tarki*); the formation of a simplex form from a combination of a main verb and an auxiliary (*fiku*); and from a combination of a verb and an aspect suffix (*potɛ*); the reinterpretation of one element in a complex expression as carrying the main content (*kori*,[15] *poko*) – in the case of *poko* in fact of the 'wrong' part of that expression; the reinterpretation of a light verb as a content verb (*pama*); the reinterpretation of a verbal expression as a noun (*lukuba, dondo, jefi*); the reinterpration of a plural nominalization as a simplex form (*mangiapu*);[16] the reinterpretation of a verbal stem as a noun (*baratwa, beritwa, pokotwa*); and backformation from a surface form (*kali*).

BD *pama* is of particular interest, as KA *páká-ma* is the causative of KA *páká* 'come out, emerge', which we find in BD as *paka* of the same meaning. Furthermore, there is evidence that KA causative formation was productive in the earliest contact stages, witness its application to a form of Dutch origin, i.e. BD *sɛrɛma* 'to hurt' < Dutch *zeer* 'pain' + KA *-ma* [CAUSE]. The reinterpretation in BD of KA *páká-ma* as unrelated to KA *páká* suggests that productive causative formation ceased very early on, and that the ability to recognize causative forms was lost with it; this in turn suggests that the reinterpretation which led to BD *pama* was not carried out by the EI speakers who ultimately provided the vocabulary.

A similar point can be made for the fact that BD *jefi* is not only a verb, but is also used as a noun, to mean 'food'. In KA, 'food' is *fíyé* < *fí yé* [eat thing], litt. 'thing to eat'.[17] It is inconceivable that EI speakers could be responsible for the multifunctionality of BD *jefi* as both verb and noun. In the same vein, it is hard to see how KA or other EI speakers could have picked out *poko* to mean 'like'.

In the case of BD *potɛ*, the KA source form is the perfective of *kpó / kpóo* 'to be old, mature,' which did not make it into BD, despite the fact that the perfective suffix was retained separately. In fact, BD *potɛ* can take the perfective suffix: *potɛ-tɛ* 'to have grown old, ripe, mature.'

The reinterpretation of complex sequences as simplex forms in creole formation has been noted in the creole literature mainly with regards to the French-lexifier creoles, which all have a number of nouns which derive from combinations of an article and noun in the lexifier (e.g. Haitian *nom* 'man' < French *un homme* 'a man'; *lari* 'street' < *la rue* 'the street', *ze* 'eye' < *les yeux* 'the eyes' etc.). It is usually assumed that

---

15. It is not entirely clear which part of the KA complex expression refers to 'work'. The contemporary meanings of *kọrị* ('to burn, weed') and *námá* (to build) suggest that it is the latter which has the more general meaning, but I have observed the use of *kọrị* to refer to 'work', as in example (21) in this paper.

16. Along the same lines, we may point to BD *jɛrma* 'woman' which derives from an irregular plural: KA *éré-me* 'women'; compare *ẹ́rẹ́-bọ́* 'woman').

17. Infinitival relatives are right-headed in EI.

this is evidence that those who created the creole had insufficient access to the lexifier to be able to interpret the French input as complex.

A similar point may be made here for the fate of these EI complex forms in BD: those who were responsible for the reanalysis which is evident in BD forms such as *jefi, fiku, potɛ* etc. must have had insufficient knowledge of KA (or other EI lects). In other words, this is evidence that those responsible for the formation of BD were not EI speakers.

4. The Berbice Dutch tense-mood-aspect system

4.1 Kalab̩ari̩ tense-aspect and modality

From Jenewari's (1977: 461ff.) description, the KA tense-aspect system emerges as aspect-dominant; in other words, there are no tense markers *per se*. I will restrict my discussion to what may be considered the core tense-aspect system, which consists of the forms in Table 3.[18] My terminology is not the same as that of Jenewari (1977), as indicated here:[19]

Table 3. Kalab̩ari̩ tense-aspect and mood markers

Affix	Jenewari's (1977: 440ff.) characterization	Characterization used here (+ gloss)
-ḿ	factative: marks present or past state on statives, past completed on non-statives	factative (FACT)
-tɛ́	completive: marks past, present and future completed	perfective (PF)
-b̩a	future: marks future or likelihood; suppletive forms: -b̩e in embedded clauses, -b̩i in negative clauses, -b̩ari̩ in relative clauses	irrealis (IRR)
-ári̩	general: marks progressive, habitual, and (on a limited class of verbs) present state	imperfective (IPF)
-b̩ete	future-completive: expresses known or certain future	imminent (IMM)

---

18. Also relevant to a fuller discussion of KA tense-aspect – which I will not attempt here – are the clause-final auxiliary *wɛ́rári̩* [STATE], seen in example (71), which historically incorporates the imperfective suffix, and does not cooccur with other tense-aspect material, and the modal auxiliary *íné* 'be able', as in (44)–(46), i.a.

19. Jenewari's characterization of the interpretation of the factative marker is actually quite unsatisfactory. There are many instances where a bare verb appears where the presence of the factative marker would be predicted, and v.v. The examples in 4.3 illustrate this problem. Since BD has not inherited this marker, I will not be concerned with this issue here.

Of most interest to us are the perfective and imperfective suffixes which BD inherited. The examples below illustrate the perfective and imperfective markers in KA;[20] the imperfective here is a habitual.[21]

(1) KA *wa, oḅori, ama-yana-(ḅ)ọ   fi-tẹ,   wa mu, pẹlẹ-ḅa*
    1P goat town-own-person die-PF 1P go cut-IRR
    'When the town chief dies, we sacrifice a goat.' [T.0402]

(2) KA *polo   mẹ   yana-ḅọ   ẹrẹ   mẹ,   miẹ   n   kẹ*
    compound DEF own-person name DEF DEM-thing 3P OBJ
    polo   mẹ   sin-arị
    compound DEF call-IPF
    'The name of the compound's founder (lit.: its owner), is what they call the compound' [T.0402]

The following examples illustrate some of the different mood forms; (5) below contains the suppletive form *-ḅi*, and (5)–(7) are examples of the factative marker:

(3) KA *jen,   í   gbola-ḅarị   ye   pik(ị)   emi?*
    other 2s ask-IRR thing also be.there
    'Is there something else you wanted to ask?' [T.0402]

---

20. KA data are mostly drawn from recordings made during fieldwork carried out in 1995; the source is identified by an initial which identifies the speaker, and by the date of recording. Syllable structure in KA is strictly CV(N). Nonetheless, suppression of vowels in connected speech frequently results in closed syllables (...VC) or in consonant clusters (CCV...). In the data presented here, suppressed vowels are indicated in parentheses. For instance, *or(i)* is /ori/, articulated as *or*. In a few cases, the surface form has undergone additional processes; in those cases, the underlying form is provided in square brackets, e.g. *jọnkọ* [< *jen ọkọ*]. Commas are used to mark intonation breaks. The fieldwork data is supplemented here and there by examples drawn from Jenewari (1977), with glosses adapted to the conventions established here (see Note 21).

KA lexical tone is largely overridden in the syntax (Harry 2004); as a result, tone is of limited relevance in the interpretation of surface strings. In the data presented here, only high tone is marked, and only on a small number of function words. These include the negator, tense-aspect material, the subordinator *tẹ́*, and pronouns which are distinguished from segmentally identical pronouns by a high tone.

21. Abbreviations used here: BE = copula, CAUSE = causative, COMP = complementizer, COND = conditional, CONJ = conjunction, DEF = definite article, DEM = demonstrative, EXCL = exclamative, F/M/N (for pronouns and determiners) = feminine/masculine/neuter, FACT = factative, FOC = focus marker, GEN = genitive, HAB = habitual, IND = indefinite article, INDEP = independent (for pronouns), IMM = imminent mood marker, IPF = imperfective, IRR = irrealis mood marker, NEG = negation, NOM = nominalizer, OBJ = object marker, PAST = past tense, PF = perfective, PL = plural, PROHIB = prohibitive, RESULT = resultative, S/P = singular/plural (in pronouns), STATE = stative auxiliary, SUB = subordinator.

(4) KA *elem sakị mẹ,   ọmụ bọ-bẹtẹ   (b)ẹbẹẹ, ...*
     old time DEF.N war come-IMM   COND, ...
     'In the olden days, if war was upon us, ...' [T.0402]

4.2 Berbice Dutch TMA

The BD system of tense, aspect and mood marking depends in part on preverbal particles, as is the case for creole languages more generally, but also includes aspectual suffixes, as set out in Table 4.[22]

As we can see here, BD inherited its aspect suffixes from EI, and they appear to carry largely the same interpretations as the KA forms: perfectivity in Comrie's (1976) sense of "a complete situation" (p. 18) and imperfectivity as refering "to the internal temporal structure of a situation" (p. 24); the KA and the BD imperfectives both cover imperfective interpretations such as durative, progressive, habitual, iterative. In addition, BD inherited a restricted version of a constraint in KA which disallows tense-aspect marking in the scope of negation: the BD perfective aspect marker is not acceptable under negation, but other markers are (see Section 5 for more detailed discussion).

The preverbal particles either have a superstrate source or result from a language-internal development. Preverbal *wa* and *sa* derive from Dutch auxiliaries, provided here in their modern Dutch orthographic forms. The most likely source of preverbal *ma* is neither the superstrate nor the substrate, but a language-internal development (Kouwenberg & Robertson 1988; Kouwenberg 1994a).[23]

Table 4. Berbice Dutch TMA markers

Berbice Dutch form	Interpretation (and gloss)	Source
-tɛ	perfective aspect (PF)	KA -tẹ́
-a (short), -arɛ (long form)	imperfective aspect (IPF)	KA -ári
wa	past tense (PAST)	Dutch auxiliary *was* 'was'
sa	irrealis mood (IRR)	Dutch auxiliary *zal* 'shall, will'
ma	irrealis mood (IRR)	language-internal < *mu-a* [go-IPF]

---

22. Modal and other auxiliaries are not considered here, but see Section 5.6 for a brief discussion of resultatives, and example (10) for a completive serial verb construction. Additional to the preverbal forms in Table 4, BD in its pre-extinction stage also uses two preverbal habitual aspect markers (tense-neutral *das*, inherently past *justu*), borrowed from Guyana's English-lexifier creole. An illustration of *das* can be seen in examples (8), (13).

23. See Kouwenberg (1994a: 70f.) for a discussion of the different interpretations of the two preverbal mood markers *sa* and *ma*. For modal auxiliaries, which are not discussed here, see Kouwenberg (1994a: 74–85).

4.3 The relevance of transfer for the BD TMA system

Why BD did not inherit the full system of tense-aspect and mood marking of KA is anybody's guess. Smith et al. (1987: 62) and Kouwenberg (1992: 286) point to the resemblance between the KA perfective suffix and the Dutch past suffix -*də/-tə* (affixed to verbs which take regular inflection);[24] I have even argued that this furtuitous similarity caused the retention of the KA perfective suffix (p. 288), but no such account can be given for the imperfective marker, which was also retained. Possible considerations in regard to the loss of other markers include the fact that the KA factative marker is not phonologically salient, and that the suppletive variation in the irrealis mood marker – dependent as it is on the status of the clause in which it appears – made it too complicated for survival during the formation of BD. The KA imperfective marker, on the other hand, is phonologically salient and not subject to allomorphy.

In short, BD has inherited part of the substrate's system of tense-aspect marking in the form of the perfective and imperfective suffixes. It is clear that the distinctions marked by these forms in the substrate were inherited with the forms themselves. But, by and large, it is unusual to see the transfer of aspects of substrate grammar through substrate functional material in creole languages. It is far more common for the transfer of grammatical properties of the substrate to take place via their association with superstrate-derived forms. In other words, it is possible that the functions of the KA tense-aspect and mood forms which are not seen in BD are performed by superstrate-derived items. However, a comparison of the distinctions made in KA and BD does not support this view. In particular, the realization of tense stands out as a significant difference: where KA does not have any marker whose sole function it is to mark tense, BD does. The KA factative marker comes closest to having a tense interpretation – as seen in Jenewari's characterization in Table 3 – but examples such as the following make it clear that tense marking is not its primary function: in both (5) and (6), where the factative marks a stative predicate and a nonstative predicate, respectively, tense reference is generic. In (7), the factative marker appears in a future counterfactual context.

(5) KA *a ine-tẹ́ bẹ-bi-á wamịna ye mẹ kụrọ*
 1s be.able-SUB say-IRR-NEG 1P.INDEP thing DEF.N be.strong
 tẹin-m.
 surpass-FACT
 'I could not say (that) our thing [our oracle] is stronger.' [T.0402]

---

24. Smith et al. (1987) consider BD -*tɛ* to be a past tense marker, and suggest that while its form is indebted to EI, its interpretation is Dutch-derived. In subsequent work, I established that it is, in fact, a perfective marker, like its EI etymon (e.g. Kouwenberg 1994a).

(6) KA *tomi, kẹ ḅ(o) ama mẹ gb(ẹ)-ar(ị), kẹ ḅ(o) oru mẹ*
people OBJ come town DEF.N pay-IPF OBJ come juju DEF.N
pịr(ị)-ar(ị), sime k(ẹ) ama mẹ pịrị-m
give-IPF remain OBJ town the give-FACT
'People come pay the town, come give to the juju, which means give to the town.' [T.0402]

(7) KA *o ḅó-m ḅeḅéẹ, wá mú-ḅa*
3s come-FACT COND 1p go-IRR
'If he comes, we shall go.' (Jenewari 1977:467)

Compare BD preverbal *wa* in (8), which contains an example of both a stative predicate (adjectival *kali*) and a nonstative predicate (*ku*, also premodified by the Creolese habitual marker *das*); it has a straightforward past interpretation in both cases.[25]

(8) BD *titi ɛkɛ* **wa** *kal(i) in(i)* **wa** *das ku di bok(o)-ap(u)*
time 1s PAST small 3P PAST HAB catch DEF Amerindian-PL
an ba in(i) an jefi in(i)
and kill 3P and eat 3P
'When I was small they would catch the Amerindians and kill them and eat them' [EK050688]

Another striking difference is in the possible combination of markers and the additional distinctions made by these combinations. As seen in Table 3, Jenewari claims the "known future" mood marker to be a combination of mood and perfective markers; it is quite possible that the suppletive form *-ḅarị* (restricted to relative clauses) is also historically complex, combining mood and imperfective aspect. However, neither of these forms is transparent to modern speakers, and modern KA allows no other combinations of markers.

BD on the other hand, allows combinations of preverbal and postverbal TMA material, as in Table 5.

The following illustrates the combination of the tense and perfective aspect markers, which obtains a past-before-past interpretation:

(9) BD *en(i)-di* **wa** *plan(di)-tɛ bom bat di kui-ap(u) sei-t(ɛ) o*
3P-DEM PAST plant-PF tree but DEF COW-PL damage-PF 3s
'They had planted trees, but the cows destroyed it.' [BB260288]

---

25. BD data are drawn from recordings made during fieldwork carried out in 1986, 1988, 1990, identified by the initials of the speaker and the date of recording; ! before the speaker's initials indicates that the example was elicited. In the absence of such a mark, the example represents 'spontaneous' production, i.e. production during free conversations with me. Kouwenberg (1994a) provides details of the fieldwork methodology employed. The representation here indicates reduction in the same way as done for the KA data (see Note 20). Abbreviations are those listed in Note 21.

Table 5. Combinations of BD TMA markers

Preverbal	Postverbal	Interpretation
wa	-tɛ	past-before-past
wa	-a(rɛ)	past imperfective
wa ma / wa sa	(-tɛ)	future-in-the-past (often counterfactual)
ma	-tɛ	posterior perfective (rarely used)

Another quite obvious difference is related to the word order differences between the two languages. In (10) and (11), we see where in both languages, a single marker marks a tense-aspect domain which contains several verbs combined in a completive serial verb construction. However, where the marker appears on the first verb in the series in BD, it appears on the last verb in KA. Elicited judgments confirm that BD serial *fama* does not accept aspectual suffixes, although its interpretation is clearly within the scope of the perfective marker:

(10) BD o   spɛn-tɛ   ʃi   boki   fama
         3s spend-PF 3s.GEN money finish
         'He had spent all of his money.' [BB110788]

(11) KA mįę na iḅi   a-ye,   á   ḍugo fan-tę [< fama-tę], ịn mįę-arị,
         do GEN good PL-thing 3s.F tell finish-PF,   3P do-IPF
         ama mę ḅio
         town DEF.N inside
         'Once she has told of all the good things which are to be done, they do them in the town.' [S2803]

The different placement of the perfective suffix clearly derives from the different word order facts of the two languages: whereas tense-aspect is marked clause-finally in KA, hence on the final verb in this SOV language, it is predicate-medial in BD, where basic word order is SVO.

In addition to the combination of preverbal and postverbal markers in BD, verbs in a serial verb construction frequently display agreement for aspect, resulting in repeated occurrences of an aspect suffix within a single clause. This is especially frequent for the perfective suffix (12), and rarer for the imperfective (13). (But note that some serial verbs do not particpe in this type of agreement, such as serial *fama* in (10); see Kouwenberg 1994a: 389–421 for discussion.)

(12) BD o   dek(i)-t(ɛ)   o   mja-tɛ   ʃi   papa
         3s take-PF   3s make-PF 3s.GEN father
         'She took him as her father.' [BB040388]

(13) BD A. das dok(o)-a   di   balahu fan   so   bringi-a   tutu hiri
        A. HAB paddle-IPF DEF punt   from there bring-IPF until here
        'A. (habitually) paddles the punt from overthere to here.' [BB090488]

In KA, we see that tense-aspect is only marked once, clause-finally. Nonetheless, it is possible that the BD practice of aspectual agreement has a precursor of sorts in a KA pattern: Consider (14), a fairly typical example illustrating several occurences of the KA subordinating particle *tẹ́* [SUB], in a sequence of clauses describing consecutive events.[26] As can be seen here, *tẹ́* is enclitic.[27] Its occurrence after the negative marker in the second clause clearly shows it to be on the periphery of the clause. Other examples in this chapter which illustrate occurrences of *tẹ́* include (30), (36), and examples in 5.2, although in most cases, it only occurs once.

(14) KA *Kugbo o   fị-ye   ẹrị-tẹ́   fị-á-tẹ́   so-m.*
     Kugbo 3S.M eat-thing see-SUB eat-NEG-SUB leave-FACT
     'Kugbo did not see food to eat and left.' [H2304]

Enclitic *tẹ́* [SUB] is homophonous with the perfective suffix. Hence, constructions containing repeated occurrences of *tẹ́* [SUB] may have been misinterpreted as containing repeated occurrences of perfectivity instead, providing a model for the pattern of aspectual agreement in serial verb constructions in BD. However, a reinterpretation of this kind once again points to a crucial role for non-EI speakers.

4.4 Summary

While the perfective and imperfective aspect suffixes of BD and the distinctions that they mark appear to be a straightforward result of transfer from the Ijọ substrate source, one can hardly argue that the BD system of TMA marking provides evidence of transfer. The BD tense distinction, its use of preverbal markers, and the possibility of cooccurrence of markers, all point to developments independent of a substrate model. So does the existence of BD preverbal *ma* [IRR], its most likely origin being the language-internal grammaticalization of *mu-a* [go-IPF], a combination of the verb *mu* 'go' with imperfective inflection. To the extent that the BD practice of aspectual agreement in serial verb constructions has a possible precursor in KA, it is in a subordinating construction, introduced by an enclitic marker which happens to resemble the perfective suffix. If that is indeed the model of the BD pattern, it can only have resulted from reanalysis by non-EI speakers. Alternatively, it too, represents an independent development.

---

26. Constructions involving the subordinator *tẹ* are discussed in more detail in 5.5.

27. Cliticization depends on the phonological environment. There are cases where *tẹ́* is preceded by an intonation break. Jenewari (1977:118) describes it as a conjunction, translated as 'and (then)'.

5. Negation

5.1 Introduction

We now turn to standard negation, which is clause-final in both KA and BD, as illustrated in (15) and (16), respectively: [28]

(15) KA *ama ogbo mẹ, si ḅaka-áa*
 town square DEF be.bad exceed-NEG
 'The town square was not too bad.' [C0702.p5]

(16) BD *en(i) kan sɛtɛ danga ka*
 3P can stay there NEG
 'They can't stay there you know.' [AH210390]

One problem is immediately obvious when considering the form of the standard negator in the two languages: BD *ka* (short form) or *kanɛ* (long form) is quite clearly not derivable from modern KA *-á*. There is, however, evidence that an earlier KA form contained a dorsal obstruent. Additionally, modern Okrika seems to offer a better source. There are, then, both historical and modern forms in EI which may explain the form of BD *ka*, as will be discussed in 5.8 below. There, I also consider the further possibility that a KA negative tag is its source.

Other problems emerge as we consider negation in the two languages in more detail. In the following, I will consider the clitic status of negation (5.2), the interaction between negation and aspect (5.3), negation and indefinite quantifiers (5.4), negation and embedding (5.5), resultative negatives (5.6), and miscellaneous issues (5.7). In each section, I will first consider the salient characteristics of negation in KA, then turn to a comparison with BD, and consider the implications for a scenario which calls on substrate transfer. Finally, I return to a consideration of the source of the BD form (5.8).

5.2 Clitic status

Since surface word order in KA is OV, the negator is normally encliticized unto a verb. This surface word order is accounted for by assuming movement, prompted by the phonological dependence of the KA negator, of its TP complement into the [SPEC, NegP] position:

(17) [$_{NegP}$ [$_{TP}$ ...]$_i$ [$_{NegP'}$ NEG [$_{TP}$ t$_i$]]]

---

[28]. BD negation is discussed in more detail in Kouwenberg (1994a, 1994b, 2000).

The addition of a boundary tone in a negative declarative has the effect of lengthening the negator, as can be seen in (15), and in many of the examples which follow.[29]

In KA, it is possible for a predicate to be non-verbal. As seen in the following examples, in such cases, the standard negator is encliticized on non-verbal material: on a noun in (18), on a pronominal in (19).

(18) KA *oyibo be   na, ala-bo   ye   me   na, gboru b(a)ra-áa*
        man DEF.M and chief-person thing DEF.N and one   manner-NEG
        'An (ordinary) man's and a chief's (burial customs) are not the same.'
        [V2901]

(19) KA *árị-áa*
        3S.INDEP.F-NEG
        'It is not her.' [F2504]

In the following example, the direct object of *nimí* 'know', a relativized noun, appears in a non-canonical position, following the verb. As a result, the negator directly follows the head noun *ángá* 'place'. Note that the adverb *bari* 'anymore' marks the left edge of the scopal domain of negation.

(20) KA *gberi so, o   bari   nimi o   sim(e) anga-áa*
        one FOC 3S.M anymore know 3S.M remain place-NEG
        'Not even one thing, he no longer knew where he was.' [M2801]

The encliticization of the KA negator on non-verbal material, as in these examples, supports its treatment as an enclitic rather than a suffix, which would be expected to be more restricted in its distribution. Example (21), where the host is a tense-aspect marker, further supports its enclitic status. (21) is a case of constituent negation, not of sentential negation; tense-aspect marking would otherwise be unacceptable under negation (see Section 5.3).

(21) KA *gbal(a) i   kor(i)nama. a   kori-té   fi-ari-á*
        as.if   1s work   1s work-SUB   eat-IPF NEG
        'Like my work. Not what I make a living with.' (Context: asked about his work, T. responds by requesting clarification that the question is about his work as the town father, not about his source of income.)
        [T0402]

Additionally, while in conversation, my production of a negative utterance was once corrected by someone along the lines of 'not [MY UTTERANCE]', in other words:[30]

---

29. Jenewari (1977: 140) refers to this tonal morpheme as "non-interrogative sentence marker", as it is absent in interrogatives.

30. Unfortunately, this conversation was not recorded.

(22) KA [...-áa] -áa
    [...-NEG] -NEG

Like (21), this type of utterance involves constituent negation; a sequence of sentential negators is not otherwise attested in my data.

BD standard negation is also clause-final, but is only optionally enclitic. Because of its VO order, the BD negator usually follows nonverbal material – something which is also possible in KA, as we have just seen, in cases where the predicate is nonverbal, or where an object appears in a noncanonical position. BD does not allow nonverbal predicates;[31] nominal predicates similar to those seen in the KA examples (18)–(19) correspond to verbal predicates, headed by a copula, in BD:

(23) BD eni da datʃ kɛnɛ-ap(u) ka, da arwa(k) kɛnɛ-ap(u)
     3P BE Dutch person-PL NEG BE Arawak person-PL
     'They are not Dutch people, they are Arawak people.' [BB260288]

Moreover, constituent negation is not acceptable in BD. In Kouwenberg (1994a: 90–91, 1994b: 255–257), I argue that spontaneous utterances which look like negated constituents, as in (24), are in fact sentence fragments. Evidence of this comes from cases such as (25) and (26), which include negation even though in each case, the fragments consist solely of a nominal which is not negated.

(24) BD da gu-gu-jɛ-apu   ju nintɛ (< nimi-tɛ), kal(i)-kal(i) tau   ka
     BE big-big-NOM-PL 2s know-PF   small-small snake NEG
     '(Those) are big ones you know, (those are) not small snakes.'
     [AK2602090]

(25) BD ɛk(ɛ) 'ID card' hab(u) di det ka, di det wanɛr(ɛ) ɛk(ɛ)
     1s   ID card   have DEF date NEG DEF date when   1s
     ban-tɛ   ka
     born-PF NEG
     'My ID card doesn't have the date, (it doesn't have) my date of birth.'
     [HA140788]

(26) BD ju mu kaʃi di en 'window' ka, di fɛnsrɛ ka,
     2s must close DEF one window NEG DEF window NEG
     wɛl di   doro ka
     well DEF door NEG
     'You mustn't close the one window, the window, or the door.'
     [BB260288]

---

31. I will not discuss the status of predicate adjectives here. Suffice it to say that there are arguments in favour of distinguishing a class of adjectives separate from the class of stative verbs in BD (see Kouwenberg 1994a, 1996a). I assume that the +V feature of predicate adjectives enables their occurrence without a copula.

In sum, BD and KA share the clause-final position of the standard negator. Also, in both languages, the negator is enclitic on any preceding material – obligatorily in KA, optionally in BD – irrespective of the syntactic status of that material. Differences can be seen in the fact that a predicate must be verbal in BD, but not in KA, and that KA allows constituent negation, where BD does not. In short, there are subtle differences despite a general resemblance.

5.3 Tense-aspect and mood under negation

No tense-aspect marking is acceptable under negation in KA, unless in confirmative questions, as in these examples:

(27) KA *ár(i̧) bu̧ru̧-tę a-ye   m(a)   o̧ki̧   su̧a-tę-á?*
     3S.F rot-PF PL-thing DEF.PL take wear-PF-NEG
     'Isn't it true that she put back on her rotten things (i.e., clothes)?' [F2504]
     Not: 'Didn't she put back on her rotten things?'

(28) KA *ani̧ tręrę,   ḍiri ḅio,   im [<i̧ni̧] pi̧ki̧, ęri̧-ari̧-á?*
     that before book inside, 3P   also   see-IPF-NEG
     'Otherwise, isn't it true that they were also seeing (the names) in books?' [D1803]
     Not: 'Otherwise, weren't they also seeing (the names) in books?'

The suppletive irrealis mood marker *-ḅi* is the only marker which is acceptable under negation in non-rhetorical contexts, as in (29)–(30); it appears as *-ḅa* in non-negative contexts, as also seen in (30).

(29) KA *n fi̧-ye   k(ę) á   p(i̧)ri̧-ḅi-áa*
     3P eat-thing OBJ 3S.F give-IRR-NEG
     'They won't give her food.' [F2504]

(30) KA *męni̧ ḍu̧ku̧-tę́   minji mę   fi̧e-ḅi-áa,   á   ḅile-ḅa*
     then agree-SUB water DEF.N produce.sound-IRR-NEG 3S.F dive-IRR
     'Then, not allowing the water to make a sound, she will dive.' [V2901]

In BD, perfective aspect inflection does not appear in the scope of negation, but, like in KA, this constraint is not relevant to confirmative questions:[32]

(31) BD *O no-ko   ku-tɛ   en toko dang(a) ka?*
     3S not-RESULT catch-PF IND child there   NEG
     'Didn't it catch a child overthere?' [BB090488]
     Not: 'It didn't catch a child overthere.'

---

32. Note the presence in (31) of a preverbal negator *no*, which marks the resultative construction to which we will return in 5.6.

There are no constraints on the cooccurrence of negation in BD with other tense, aspect and modal markers. This is illustrated below for tense (32), imperfective aspect (32), and mood (33):

(32) BD ɛk(ɛ) **wa** noiti ni(mi) **ka**, solok(o) bɛr(ɛ) kɛk(ɛ) di sa hapn
1s PAST never know NEG such story like this IRR happen
'I never knew such things could happen.' [AK010390]

(33) BD o suku-a danʃ(i) ababa **ka**
3s want-IPF dance anymore NEG
'She doesn't want to dance any more.' [HH.lukuba1]

(34) BD en **ma** kar(a) ɛkɛ **ka**
one IRR be.enough 1s NEG
'One will not be enough for me.' [AT190386]

In summary, BD and KA share a constraint on tense-aspect marking under negation. They also share the 'lifting' of this constraint in confirmative questions. But while the constraint is limited to perfective aspect in BD, it applies to all tense-aspect marking in KA, allowing only a suppletive mood marker under negation. In other words, to the extent that the BD constraint can be said to result from the transfer of a KA constraint, transfer was incomplete.

5.4 Indefinite quantifiers under negation

KA has no inherently negative quantifiers. Instead, an indefinite quantifier is usually interpreted as non-referential under negation. This is seen for a subject in (42), an object in (43).

(35) KA anị mẹ, **tombọ** niim-ḅi-áa [< nimi-ḅi-áa]
DEM DEF.N person know-IRR-NEG
'That, noone can know.' [I1704]

(36) KA Anịẹ sue mẹ, tẹ́ ị ẹrị sue mẹ, dein, ḅarị **kịnị**
DEM-thing well DEF.N SUB 2s see well DEF.N quiet anymore person
ḅa-áa
kill-NEG
'That well, that is, the well that you saw, (has become) peaceful, and doesn't kill anyone anymore.' [S2803]

In contrast, as seen here, it is also possible for an indefinite to be referential under negation:

(37) KA *ịmbọ̇ paka   bọ-bị-áa*
person emerge come-IRR-NEG
'The person wouldn't come out.' (context: describing an old mourning custom whereby the widow of a chief was kept in isolation for a prolonged period of time) [V2901]

(38) KA *tomi   ngeri-áa*
person.PL alone-NEG
'Not only people.' [context: talking about a situation where spirits walk among the people, in other words, not only people were present.] [S2803]

Similarly, in BD, indefinites in a negative clause usually receive an interpretation which shows them to be within the scope of the negative operator. In this manner, constituent negation is achieved. Thus, in (39), the subject is negated, while in (40), it is the direct object which is negated. Elicited judgements and occasional spontaneous use show that it is possible for the indefinite quantifier to take higher scope. Example (34) in the preceding and (41) below are spontaneous examples of this kind. Elicited judgements show that wide scope of negation is prefered.

(39) BD *en   kɛnɛ   kan kap(u) o   ka*
IND person can cut 3s NEG
'Nobody can cut it (i.c., a certain tree) down.' [AH210390]

(40) BD *ɛk(ɛ) ma ha(bu) en   gut(u) moi fu prusinti ju fortit(i) ju mu ka*
1s IRR have IND thing good for present 2s before 2s go NEG
'I will have nothing nice to give you before you go.' [AK120788]

(41) BD *alm(a) ɛk(ɛ) aka   moi (a)baba-ka, so ɛk(ɛ) suk(u)-a nun(u) alma*
all 1s tooth good anymore-NEG so 1s want-IPF pull all
'All of my teeth are no good anymore, so I want to have them all extracted.' [AK030688]

BD has several Dutch-derived negative quantifiers (*neks* 'nothing,' *nimdali* 'for nothing, gratis,' *noiti* 'never'), but except for *noiti*, these are rarely used. Thus, to express the meaning 'nothing,' Dutch-origin *en gutu* 'a thing, something' is used in a negative utterance – where it is potentially ambiguous – in preference to *neks*. Other BD indefinite quantifiers which are subject to negative attraction include *(en) kɛnɛ* '(a) person, someone' (of KA origin), *(en) plɛkɛ* '(a) place, somewhere' *en* 'one', *alma* 'all', *idri* 'every' (all of Dutch origin), and *musu* 'much'.

In short, BD and KA are quite similar in regards to the interpretation of indefinite quantifiers in negative contexts, despite the existence in BD of negative quantifiers.

5.5 Negative scope and embedded clauses

Despite KA's predominant OV order, only nominal objects and subjectless infinitival complements may precede a main verb. Subject-containing clausal complements follow it, resulting in VO-type word orders. In (42), the main verb *ḍụkụ* 'agree, allow' takes a subjectless infinitival complement, which appears in the canonical position for objects, to its left. Negation clearly has scope over the main clause rather than the embedded clause. In contrast, in (43), *ḍụkụ* takes a subject-containing clause as its complement; that clause appears to its right, introduced by the enclitic subordinating particle *tẹ́*. Here, negation has scope over both the main clause and the embedded clause; the appropriate form of the mood marker appears (see Section 4.1).

(42) KA *sonio so-t(ẹ́)   ori   o   so   ḍụkụ-áa*
     six leave-SUB 3S.M.INDEP 3S.M leave agree-NEG
     'Six had left, (but) he did not agree to leave.' [A2803]
     Not: '…he agreed not to leave.'

(43) KA *a   ḍụkụ-tẹ́, gbọrụ bọ   sọ, gbọrụ (bọ)   s(ọ) inuma-bị-áa*
     1S agree-SUB one person FOC one (person) FOC cheat-IRR-NEG
     'I will not allow anyone, anyone to cheat.' [T0402]
     Not: 'I will not allow someone to cheat.'

Constructions which use *tẹ́*-subordination are of several different kinds: (a) subcategorized, where *tẹ́* introduces a complement clause in a postverbal position, as seen in (43) above; (b) consecutive action, where each clause describes one of a sequence of events; (c) subevents, where the events of the clauses 'linked' by *tẹ́* constitute subevents of a single complex event.[33]

Below, example (44) illustrates both the first and second type: main verb *íné* 'be able' takes a complement clause introduced by *tẹ́*; that complement clause describes a sequence of two events (*ọ́lọ̄* 'hold', *ḅá* 'kill'), the second event again introduced by *tẹ́*. (45) and (46) are two further examples involving subcategorization; (46) shows that although in the majority of cases, the complement of *íné* is introduced by *tẹ́*, it can appear without an overt subordinator. Negation clearly has wide scope in all these cases. Note that in (44) and (46), the negative polarity item *bạrị* 'anymore' appears, and that the mood marker in (44) and (45) takes the appropriate suppletive form; note also that the repeated occurrence of the direct object in (44) shows that it is not a serial verb construction.

---

33. *tẹ́* also introduces nominalized relative clauses, which appear in a non-canonical postnominal position (Kouwenberg 1996b).

(44) KA *o   mu la-t(ẹ́)   anga mẹ,   kịnị   bạrị   **ine-tẹ́**,*
     3S.M go reach-PF place DEF.N person anymore be.able-SUB,
     bọ   ọr(ị)   ọlọ-tẹ́,   ọ   ba-bị-áa
     come 3S.INDEP.M hold-SUB 3S kill-IRR-NEG
     'Where he went, nobody would be able to come and catch him and kill him anymore.' [M2801]

(45) KA *á   **ine-tẹ́**   ala tọrụ dọkụ   trẹrẹ   bọ   o   sim(e)*
     3S.F be.able-SUB salt sea paddle before come 3S.M remain
     anga la-bị-áa
     place reach-IRR-NEG
     'She would not be able to paddle the sea to reach to where he was.' [M2901]

(46) KA *n   bạrị   **ine**,   sue mẹ   bio,   sọ   mu-áa*
     3P anymore be.able well DEF.N inside enter go-NEG
     'They cannot go back into the well again.' [M2901]

The following examples illustrate consecutive action (47), and subevents (48)–(49). Once again, negation has wide scope:

(47) KA *Kugbo o   fị-ye   ẹrị-tẹ́   **fị-á-tẹ́**   so-m*
     Kugbo 3S.M eat-thing see-SUB eat-NEG-SUB leave-FACT
     'Kugbo did not see food to eat and left.' [H2304]

(48) KA *wa ị   b(a)ra igbigi tol(ụ)-tẹ́, **fị-bị-áa***
     1P 2S hand money bore-SUB eat-IRR-NEG
     'We will not pressure you financially' (lit.: bore money from your hand and eat) [M2901]

(49) KA *anịẹ   gbalaa, oyibọ   be,   bạrị   bọ-tẹ́   bọ,   ị*
     DEM-thing as.if man DEF.M anymore come-SUB come, 2S
     na   gboloma-bị-áa
     with connect-IRR-NEG
     'It is as if the man will not come to bother you anymore.' [V2901]

Here we see that where negation is to be restricted to one of the events in a sequence, this is achieved by marking negation within the relevant clause:

(50) KA *In oru kur(o)   ẹrẹbọ   wari   **mu-á-tẹ́**   k(ụ)rọ-tẹ́ a-ye*
     3P juju descend woman house go-NEG-SUB strong-PF PL-thing
     sụn-tẹ́   kuroma   kụrọ   laan-tẹ́ [<lama-tẹ́] bẹ(b)ẹe, ...
     go.far-SUB put.down strong reach-PF   COND, ...
     'If they fail to go to the female juju-carrier's place and danger has reached far, ...' [E2803]

(51) KA an(i̩) ai̩   ma   mi̩ẹ-áá t(ẹ́) á i̩ngani̩-á   bẹbẹẹ, ...
        DEM PL-thing DEF.PL do-NEG SUB 3s anger-NEG COND
        'But if (we) don't do these things and she does not get angry ...' [M2901]

A different picture emerges when we consider verbs such as ḍugó 'tell', bẹ 'say', nímí 'know', which subcategorize for full clausal complements. These examples show that negation has scope only over the embedded clause:

(52) KA a ḍugo k(ẹ) i̩na p(i̩)ri̩ in iy(i)-áa
        1s tell OBJ 3P give   3P bear.child-NEG
        'I told them (that) they didn't have children.' [M2901]
        Not: * 'I didn't tell them...'

(53) KA ini   bẹ-m   in ḅari̩   oru ya-áa (<ye-áa)
        3P.INDEP say-FACT 3P anymore   juju do-NEG
        'They say they don't deal with juju anymore.' [S2803]
        Not: * 'They don't say...'

Negation of the main proposition rather than the embedded one is achieved by a surface order such that the clausal complement follows negation. This is illustrated here for the complement of bẹ 'say' and nímí 'know':

(54) KA a ine-tẹ́   bẹ-ḅi-á,   wami̩na ye   mẹ
        1s be.able-SUB say-IRR-NEG 1P.INDEP thing DEF.N
        kụrọ   tẹin-m
        strong surpass-FACT
        'I could not say (that) our thing [i.c., our oracle] is stronger.' [T0402]

(55) KA Kalaḅari̩ nimi-á   mi̩nẹsọ, ọdụm ma   anịẹ   ama sue
        Kalaḅari̩ know-NEG CONJ   boa   DEF.PL DEM-thing town well
        m(ẹ)   emi-t(ẹ́)   i̩n ọkọ k(ẹ) i̩na ḅ(a)-ar(i̩)
        DEF.N be.there-SUB 3P thus OBJ 3P   kill-IPF
        'The Kalabari didn't know that the pythons were in the well and killing people like that.' [M2901]

The contrast in the negative scope properties seen in the preceding can be accounted for by considering the status of the embedded clause. The examples in (52)–(55) involve full clauses, and behave as expected: since CP is a boundary for negative scope, negation scopes only over the clause in which it is contained. This suggests that the complement of íné 'be able' and the clauses involved in consecutive action constructions and complex events are not full clauses: as seen in the preceding, they are transparent for negation. This difference is not tied up with the presence or absence of the subordinator tẹ́: whereas examples of tẹ́-clauses in the preceding involved wide scope, in (56) we see where negation has narrow scope over the tẹ́-clause, the complement of mi̩ẹ 'make, cause.' In other words, tẹ́ also introduces full clauses.

(56) KA *anị mịẹ-tẹ́*   wa si   kẹ   jumo   tọn-tọn-áa
        DEM make-SUB 1s bad OBJ each.other measure-measure-NEG
        'Therefore we do not fear each other.' [W2801]
        Not: 'That does not cause us to fear each other.'

At first blush, BD presents a similar picture. In accordance with its SVO word order, embedded clauses follow the main verb, and normally precede the standard negator immediately. In (57), negation has wide scope, over both the main and the embedded propositions; the latter is a subjectless infinitival:

(57) BD *ɛkɛ suku mu titi   ori jɛnda   ka*
        1s want go time 3s be.there NEG
        'I don't want to go when he is not there.' [BB110190]

Both spontaneous usage and elicited judgements show that negation can scope narrowly over the main clause only, as in (57)', where the complement clause is outside the scope of the negative operator. These different interpretations of the same utterance were confirmed with different informants, and were also occasionally seen in spontaneous production. There is complete reliance on discourse context to disambiguate these kinds of utterances.

(57)' BD *ɛkɛ suku mu titi   o jɛnda   ka*
          1s want go time 3s be.there NEG
          'I don't want to go when she is there.' [!AK250190]

Similar ambiguity is found where the embedded clause is a full CP. Thus, in (58), negation has scope over main verb *nimi*, whereas in (59), it has scope over the embedded clause. But here, the absence or presence of perfective aspect, which is unacceptable under negation, signals its scope:[34]

(58) BD *ɛkɛ ni(mi) hos(o) eni nim(i)-tɛ dida ka*
        1s know how   3p know-PF DEM NEG
        'I don't know how they knew that.' [AH210390]

(59) BD *ju nimi-tɛ ɛkɛ kan nimi dida ka*
        2s know-PF 1s can know DEM NEG
        'You know I cannot really know that.' [AH060588]

In (60), perfective aspect marking on *pama* 'tell' in the main clause similarly indicates that negation scopes only over the embedded clause.

---

34. BD *nimi* is an event verb, better translated as 'acquire knowledge, obtain knowledge' than as 'know'. For convenience sake, I will continue to gloss it as 'know'.

(60) BD *dakta* **pan-tɛ** [< *pama-tɛ*] *bi   o   mo* [< *muti*] *jefi   musu sautu ka*
doctor tell-PF   say 3s must   eat   much salt NEG
'The doctor told him he mustn't each much salt.' [BB260288]

The following illustrate cases where negation has scope only over the main clause (61), or over both the main clause and one of a pair of embedded conjuncts (62). Once again, the absence of perfective marking on *nimi* makes it clear that the main clause is within the scope of negation, but as seen in (62), despite its absence in the embedded clause, that clause is not fully within the scope of negation:

(61) BD *ɛkɛ* **nimi** *wi-sa   bu-t(ɛ)   o fama ka*
1s know who-FOCUS drink-PF 3s finish NEG
'I don't know who emptied it.' [BB160488]

(62) BD *wɛl ɛkɛ* **ni(mi)** *aw(i) ju ma laki   ar ju ma laki   ka, ...*
well 1s know   if   2s IRR laugh or 2s IRR laugh NEG
'Well I don't know whether or not you will laugh, ...' [HH.lukuba2]

Although perfective marking frequently disambiguates scope where propositional verbs such as *nimi* 'know' and *pama* 'tell' take a clausal complement, it clearly does not help where the main verb is a stative verb such as *suku* 'want' in (57); nor does it help for verbs such as *bifi* 'say' and perception verbs *kiki* 'see' and *horo* 'hear', which rarely accept perfective marking:

(63) BD *en(i)* **bi(fi)** *dat(i) ju mu   jef(i) aboko   ka*
3p   say   COMP 2s must eat   chicken NEG
'They say that you shouldn't eat chicken.' [AK220290]
Not: 'They don't say ...'

(64) BD *... wanga ju* **kik(i)** *di   mingi strom ka*
where 2s see   DEF water stream NEG
'...where you see the water doesn't run.' [AK190488]
Not: '...where you don't see ...'

The following examples illustrate the presence of a negative adverbial, which marks negative scope over the main clause in (65), the presence of a negative resultative in (66) which has a similar effect, here ensuring that both the main clause and the embedded clause are negated, and right-dislocation of the embedded clause, which puts it outside the scope of the negative operator in (67):

(65) BD *ɛkɛ* **noiti** *hor(o) en(i) jefi dida ka*
1s never hear   3p   eat DEM NEG
'I have never heard that they eat that.' [AC090488]
Not: 'I have never heard that they don't eat that.'

(66) BD ɛkɛ ni(mi) hos(o) ifi **no-ko** kjant ka
    1s know how 1P NEG-RESULT topple NEG
    'I don't know how we didn't topple.' [BB110788]
    Not: 'I don't know how we toppled.'

(67) BD ɛk(ɛ) wa noiti ni(mi) **ka**, solok(o) bɛr(ɛ) kɛk(ɛ) di sa hapn
    1s PAST never know NEG such story like DEM IRR happen
    'I never knew that this kind of thing could happen.' [AK010390]

In short, embedding under negation entails quite a bit more ambiguity in BD than it does in KA, where the linearly closest CP is a bounding node for negative scope. In BD, the relation between linear order and scope properties is not as clear-cut. Considering a surface string of the form in (68), where V2 is contained in an embedded complement clause which has the status of a CP, and the standard negator appears in absolute final position, we note that this can be derived from three different underlying strings in BD, but has only one possible derivation in KA:

(68) $[_{CP} ... V1 [_{CP} ... V2 - NEG$

(68)' BD (i) $[_{CP} [_{NEGP} NEG ... V1 [_{CP} ... V2]]]$
      (ii) $[_{CP} [_{NEGP} NEG ... V1 [_{CP} [_{NEGP} NEG ... V2]]]]$[35]
      (iii) $[_{CP} ... V1 [_{CP} [_{NEGP} NEG ... V2]]]$

(68)" KA $[_{CP} ... V1 [_{CP} [_{NEGP} NEG ... V2]]]$

In conclusion, negative scope in clausal embedding is a clear case of mismatch between BD and KA patterns. All too often, surface similarities between creoles and their substrates have been taken as sufficient indication of substrate transfer. We see here that surface similarities may evaporate as we consider the details of grammar.

5.6 The BD resultative

The BD resultative construction affirms or negates the fact that a particular event or state obtains. The affirmative resultative uses a preverbal auxiliary *kon*, combined with a perfective verb form. Its most likely source is the KA auxiliary *kọn*, rather inaccurately translated as 'have'. It is in fact a light verb, which combines with lexical verbs or nouns, which normally precede it.[36] The following examples illustrate; *kọn* appears as matrix verb in (69), in a prenominal relative clause in (70):

---

35. BD does not allow two consecutive occurrences of the negator to surface; a constraint to this effect at PF may be assumed.

36. We saw earlier, in Section 3.2, that an expression using the KA auxiliary *kọn* preceded by a lexical verb is the source of BD *fiku* 'deceased'.

(69) KA *Mọkụ in ti   kọn-arị-té,* ...
         now   3P play have-IPF-SUB
         'Now, as they are having a masquerade, ...' [D1803]

(70) KA ... *ini   na,   tu(b)o kọn-a(rị) sakị,* ...
             3P.INDEP with trade have-IPF time
         '... when (they) were trading with them, ...' [D1803]

However, I have also come across fairly frequent preverbal use of *kọn*, as in (71)–(72). It is this usage of *kọn* which may be considered the source of the BD resultative construction.

(71) KA *anịẹ   ị̀   kọn ni(mi) wẹrarị?*
         DEM-thing 2s have know   STATE
         'Did you know that?' [I1704]

(72) KA *a ḍugo ye   ị̀   kọn na-té?*
         1s tell thing 2s have hear-PF
         'Do you understand what I told you?' [I1704]

Compare this with the BD affirmative resultative: *kon* precedes the main verb, which appears in a perfective form; it is used to refer to specific occasions where the event denoted by the main verb obtained:

(73) BD *ɛkɛ sosro **kon**   do(to)-tɛ lasan-tɛ, dan o **kon**   trou-tɛ*
         1s   sister RESULT die-PF   leave-PF   then 3s RESULT marry-PF
         en   kurkur(u) jɛrma   nau
         IND black   woman now
         'My sister died (and) left (him), (and) then he married a black woman.'
         [BB230288]

(74) BD *en(i) **kon**   drai-t(ɛ) o fi domni nau*
         3P   RESULT turn-PF 3s for pastor now
         'Then they ordained him as pastor.' [BB260288]

Its negative counterpart uses preverbal *no-ko*, a combination of a negator (*no*) and a reduced form of the resultative auxiliary (*ko*), preceding a bare verb. The preverbal negator *no* is restricted to the resultative construction, and requires the presence of the standard negator. Examples here include stative (75) and nonstative predicates (76)–(77):[37]

---

37. There are cases where it is used without the standard negator; these can be considered performance errors (Kouwenberg 2000).

(75) BD *ɛkɛ nis **no-ko** sɛtɛ bot dri jari ka o doto-tɛ*
     1s niece NEG-RESULT stay about three year NEG 3s die-PF
     'My niece hadn't spent more than about three years (in that house) (when) she died.' [BB150190]

(76) BD *fi di hɛlɛ weki o **no-ko** kori ka*
     for DEF whole week 3s NEG-RESULT work NEG
     'He hasn't worked for the entire week.' (talking of someone unable to go to work after he met with an accident at the work place) [BB110386]

(77) BD *di(da) da nju plɛkɛ wanga en(i) noiti **no-ko** la ka*
     DEM BE new place where 3P never NEG-RESULT reach NEG
     'That is a new place where they never went before.' [AH210390]

The BD affirmative resultative seems clearly related to the KA light verb – although some influence from Dutch expressions in which *komen* 'to come' introduces a purposive cannot be completely discounted. A seventeenth-century example follows:

(78) DU ... *hoe dat ons Boot aen het Eylandt Sylon, en het volck*
     ... how that our boat at the island Ceylon and the people
     *negen sterck wesende, met een Schip aen Batavia waren **komen***
     nine strong being with a ship at Batavia were come
     te landen
     to land
     '... how our vessel (had come) to the island of Ceylon, and (how) the crew of nine had landed with a ship at Batavia.' (Stokram 1991 [1663]: 43)

BD *kumu* 'come', derived from Dutch *komen*, is frequently reduced to *kon,* and the reduced form appears as connective verb in the purposive construction (Kouwenberg 1994a: 308). In other words, the reduced form of the BD auxiliary does not point conclusively to EI, as opposed to the possibility of the joint influence of EI and Dutch.

What makes a Dutch contribution somewhat less likely is the variation in the form of the verb (cf. participle *gekomen*, inflected *komt*), as well as, more importantly, its variable placement relative to its complement, which – thanks to scrambling effects – displays far more variation than is the case for KA *kǫn*. An example follows, which shows that *ons te pas* has been separated altogether from *komen*:

(79) DU ... *dan soude **ons** die drooghe visch wel **te pas** moghen **komen***
     then would us the dry fish surely of use may come
     '... the dried fish would then be useful for us.' (Stokram 1991 [1663]: 43)

The source of the negative form *no-ko* is even less clear. One possibility is the reanalysis of a form derived from the Dutch adverbial *nog* [nɔx] 'still, (not) yet'. Its BD reflex *noko* 'still, (not) yet' is final in the predicate, different from its Dutch source, which typically appears in predicate-initial position. Perhaps variation in its early BD usage, in both preverbal and predicate-final position, gave rise to reanalysis of the preverbal form. This scenario has the advantage that it accounts for the fact that the negative resultative *ko* differs from the affirmative form *kon* in that it lacks a final nasal. The following example illustrates the negative resultative in a construction which also includes the adverbial *noko*:

(80) BD *di   tok(o) mu-tɛ, tut(u) fandak(a) o   no-k(o)   pak(a)   no(ko) ka*
         DEF child go-PF   until   today   3s NEG-RESULT come.out   still NEG
     'The child is gone, to date he hasn't come back out.' (i.e. from the bush, where he disappeared) [AK270190]

In short, while the BD resultative construction finds its most likely origin in a KA construction, the BD auxiliary does not have the same function as its KA counterpart, and the negative form of that construction is not derivable from the substrate.

5.7 Miscellaneous negatives

KA prohibitives use an enclitic suppletive negative marker *má* (81)–(82). This formative is not found in BD, which forms negative imperatives by using the standard negator (83):

(81) KA *sime-má-o!*
         remain-PROHIB-EXCL
     'Don't stay!' (i.e.: 'Come right away!') [F2504]

(82) KA *á   ḍuku-té,   fị   na fa   na ḅio,   í   mu sọ-má*
         3s.F allow-SUB death and loss and inside 2s go enter-PROHIB
     'She [the guardian spirit of Kalaḅarị] should not allow for you to suffer death and loss.' [A0102p2]

(83) BD *feṣi bi: ... ba ɛkɛ ka!*
         fish say   kill 1s NEG
     'Fish said: "don't kill me!"' (in the context of a fable) [HH.lukuba2]

Finally, the KA verb *ófórí* 'be absent, not be there' is an inherently negative verb; it does not cooccur with the standard negator, as seen in (84). Its BD reflex is *furi*, with the same meaning as its etymon, but it appears most commonly as *furda*, which incorporates a dummy complement *da*. Different from its EI etymon, BD *furi/furda* normally cooccurs with the standard negator (85):

(84) KA *omongi ap(ụ)   tẹ́ mịẹ ḅẹ   ọku   ofori   ḅẹ omongi apụ...*
         old   persons SUB do GEN livelihood be.absent GEN old   persons
     'Elderly people with no source of income ... ' [F1404]

(85) BD *en   kɛn(ɛ) mɛr(ɛ) **fur-da**   ka*
       IND person more be.absent-there NEG
       'There is nobody else.' [AK180190]

Summarizing, BD fails to replicate the KA prohibitive. Moreover, while BD has inherited a KA negative verb, it is used in utterances marked as negative by the standard negator in BD, but not in KA, suggesting that it is a purely lexical negative in KA.

5.8 The source of BD *ka, kanɛ*

The BD long form of the standard negator, *kanɛ*, consists of a combination of the short form *ka* with **nɛ*, the latter derived from the Dutch independent negator 'nee.' That negator has also found its way into BD in *nɛnɛ* 'no' (independent negator), but the clause-final position of BD *kanɛ* rather suggests that **nɛ* derives not from the independent negator but from its use in Dutch as an emphatic negative tag, as in the following modern example:

(86) DU *Dat mag niet, **nee!***
       that can not, no
       'That's not allowed, **no**!'

Of more interest here is the origin of the BD short form *ka*. Although it is clearly EI-derived, identifying its source is not straightforward. Here, I will consider three possibilities – none of which is entirely satisfactory: that it derives from an Okrika negator; that it derives from an earlier form of the negator which may have varied between *ka ~ ga*, and which must have been widespread in Ịjọ; finally, that BD *ka* is related to an EI negative tag.

5.8.1 An Okrika source for BD *ka*

Smith et al. (1987) list three negative forms for Okrika (Kịrịkẹ): *-ka* (question), *-áā* and *-kẹ* (statement) (p. 85, based on Sika 1995). Note that the second form is listed without qualification; it is this form which is the standard negator. Unfortunately, Okrika grammar remains largely undescribed. Sika (1995) is a wordlist preceded by some brief notes on Okrika grammar, and the grammar notes do not include any negatives. On the other hand, the wordlist contains around five dozen apparently lexicalized phrasal expressions which contain *-ka*. Some examples follow; morpheme divisions and morpheme glosses are mine:

(87) OK *àlà-pẹ́lẹ̣́-ká* [salt.water-cut-NEG] 'bronze; brass metal'
        fúrú-ká [steal-NEG] 'honest; honesty'
        kárá-kà [suffice-NEG] 'incomplete, not correct'

nyàná-ká-bọ̀ [have-NEG-person] 'expression pointing to oneself or another in enlisting sympathy for some happening; another expression meaning 'poor me' or 'poor you''
yé-lá-ká [thing-reach-NEG] 'cheap; unworthy'

George (1989) contains a single example of a negative. It happens to be an interrogative, hence uses *-ka*:[38]

(88) OK *che   goye   ị   fẹ   mu-ká?*
    what reason 2s   market go-NEG
    'Why did you not go to the market?' (George 1989: 48)

Smith (in prep.) points out that the best cognates with BD forms are not always found in KA. What it comes down to is that the linguistic evidence does not allow us to identify with complete certainty which EI lect (or lects) was represented in the early Berbice colony. In other words, it is entirely possible that an EI lect other than KA, such as Okrika, is the source of some, many, or even all BD forms of EI derivation. However, if the modern distribution of negatives reflects the historical distribution, it requires that exposure in the context where BD was formed was predominantly to negative interrogatives rather than to negative declaratives, where *áā* would have appeared instead, and that the BD development involved the generalization of an erstwhile specialized form. We could speculate, instead, that the lexicalized negatives represent an earlier standard strategy, and that its current restriction to interrogative contexts is a relatively recent development.

5.8.2 *An early EI source for BD* ka

The Ịjọ lects Nembe (Eastern Ịjọ) and Kolokuma (Central Ịjọ) also seem to offer a better source than does KA: the standard negator appears as *ya* in both. Moreover, as pointed out by Smith et al., Nkọrọọ – a 'deviant' dialect of EI (1987: 54), has *ka* as well as *ya*, and KA drum language, which presumably represents archaic usage, has *ya*. In other words, a form containing a dorsal obstruent is by no means restricted to Okrika. It is historically widespread in EI, including KA, and may have been in common use at the time of first contact in Berbice. The question then is of the precise form of this obstruent. Williamson (1979) sheds some light on this question. Her Proto Ịjọ consonant system does not include ɣ, but includes both k and g (1979: 74). She points out that a clear k/g contrast in medial position cannot be established for Proto Ịjọ, and reconstructs all medial velar stops as G – unspecified for voice (1979: 81). The relevance of this is in the fact that *ya* is not a good candidate as a source of BD *ka*, as its expected BD reflex would be **ga*, retaining voice. In other words, we need the EI source form to contain voiceless *k*. The historical indeterminacy of voice noted for medial obstruents

---

[38]. For tonemarking and glossing I have followed the conventions established earlier for KA (see Notes 20, 21).

does not extend to initial obstruents. But the clitic status and clause-final position of the negator means that it is always preceded by other material, on which it is phonologically dependent. It is conceivable that, historically, this initial obstruent patterned with medial k/g (no clear contrast) rather than with initial k/g (contrast). In that case, the fact that the modern varieties include forms such as *ya* and *ka* simply reflects the historical indeterminacy of the medial stops. This would allow us to postulate a development, at least for KA, along the lines of: early *ka* ~ *ga* > more recent *ya* > modern *a*. Crucially, both steps of this historical development must postdate the founding of the Berbice colony by the Dutch. We have, of course, no independent way of verifying the time depth of this change.

5.8.3 *A negative tag as source for BD* ka

As an alternative possibility, I point, speculatively, to the existence of an almost identical form in KA, which occurs as negative tag in (89). In (90), the negative tag is followed by the appropriate response.

(89) KA *'stroke' mẹ aniẹ bekin bibi, aniẹ 'stroke', ọk(ọ)-aá?*
stroke DEF DEM-thing English speech DEM-thing stroke thus-NEG
'Stroke' is English language, that is stroke, isn't it? [C 0702.p2]

(90) KA *ọk(ọ)-á? ọk(ọ)-áa!*
'Isn't it? True!'

The usual suppression of the final vowel of *ọkọ* yields *ọká? ọkáa!* – forms which, I suggest, may have been reanalysed in the Berbice contact situation as *o ka*, in other words as [3s NEG], giving rise to the BD form *ka*. That the source of BD *ka* could be a negative tag is supported by its combination with the Dutch emphatic negative tag in the long form *kanɛ*. In other words, the clause-final position of BD *ka* / *kanɛ* may be due to its origins in a combination of KA and Dutch tags and not to the clause-final position of the KA negator. The evidence for reanalysis of phrasal expressions presented in 3.2 suggests that the reanalysis required for this derivation of *ka* is certainly not unparalleled in the history of BD.

5.8.4 *Conclusion*

In short, although modern Okrika provides a form which most closely resembles BD *ka*, it is a form which is restricted to interrogative contexts. On the other hand, the standard negators of modern EI lects have historical precursors which resemble the BD form *ka* closely. Nevertheless, questions remain as to whether those historical precursors were available at the time that we need them. Absent early documentation of any EI variety, these questions shall remain unanswered. An alternative derivation of BD *ka* from a negative tag assumes the reinterpretation of a KA phrasal expression – not so far-fetched, considering the evidence in 3.2. In conclusion, the EI source of the BD standard negator remains uncertain.

5.9 Summary

On first consideration, BD negation looks very similar to KA. The similarities can be enumerated as follows:

a. The position of the standard negator is clause-final in both BD and KA.
b. BD disallows the perfective aspect marker in the scope of negation, except in rhetorical questions; a similar constraint exists in KA.
c. Negation has scope over indefinite quantifiers in both languages.
d. The BD negative verb *ofori* 'be absent' is an inherited form.

But on closer inspection, there are a number of differences which should not be ignored:

e. The BD clause-final standard negator may not be a direct reflex of an EI standard negator.
f. While BD imposes a restriction on the perfective suffix only, KA disallows all tense-aspect markers, allowing only a suppletive mood marker in negative contexts.
g. Where the clause-final standard negator is directly preceded by an embedded CP in KA, the string-adjacency reflects the scope of the negator; not so in BD, where it may have scope over the main clause instead of or in addition to the embedded clause, resulting in some amount of ambiguity which can only partially be resolved by perfective marking and other devices which interact with negation.
h. BD *ofori* cooccurs with the standard negator where its KA etymon does not.
i. BD developed a preverbal negator which is not of substrate origin and which appears only in the resultative construction.
j. BD fails to replicate the KA prohibitive.

In all, this shows that BD negation has developed its own dynamics and does not simply replicate an EI model. To the extent that it replicates EI patterns at all, it does so incompletely.

6. The invisible hand in the formation of Berbice Dutch

The BD lexicon clearly identifies three sources: Dutch, Eastern Ijo, and Arawak. These lexical contributions represent the three groups of persons who were present in the early contact situation from which BD emerged. Dutch is the most important contributor to content vocabulary, Arawak to vocabulary pertaining to elements of the natural environment, and EI, in addition to a significant contribution to content vocabulary, dominates in functional vocabulary. We have seen that EI-derived function words are central to predication, having furnished aspect markers and the standard negator. These are of special interest in that they appear to be associated with unusual word order patterns – unusual, that is, for creole languages: postverbal aspectual modification, and clause-final negation.

However, we have also seen that verbal modification overall in BD looks more like a creole system, seeing that it employs preverbal particles (and auxiliaries, which we have not considered here). Moreover, BD is unlike EI in that it marks past tense. BD has also developed a preverbal irrealis marker which has no precursor in any of the lexical source languages, and it has an independently developed preverbal negative. Finally, BD fails to replicate the restrictions and scope properties of negation in EI in all its details, and deviates significantly from those properties in some respects.

In short, the overall evidence for L1 transfer by KA speakers or speakers of other EI lects is not as strong as a superficial survey of EI-derived function words and grammatical patterns suggests. As we have seen in the preceding sections, at best, there is evidence for partial transfer only.

Nor do the findings point to a central role for Dutch speakers, although they do suggest that Dutch speakers did more than merely furnish content vocabulary. After all, Dutch is the main contributor to the preverbal TMA material of BD, it is a partial source of the standard negator, and it may even have provided the source of the preverbal resultative negator. But it is evident that not only the EI-derived functional material but also that derived from Dutch has been subject to reanalysis, and has been incorporated into a system which differs in important respects from both its sources. In other words, there is clear evidence for discontinuity, both with regards to the superstrate elements and with regards to the substrate elements in BD.

The reanalysis that we have seen ample evidence of points away from either EI speakers or Dutch speakers as the agents in this process. For instance, it seems extremely unlikely that Dutch speakers would have turned a Dutch adverbial into a negative marker, or a Dutch tag into a standard negator – just as unlikely as EI speakers adopting preverbal markers rather than continuing to use a system of suffixed verb modifiers, or changing the restrictions on tense-aspect marking under negation and on scope over embedded clauses. The evidence gained from BD words whose source is an EI phrasal expression has further underscored that point.

'The invisible hand' at work in BD genesis is that of a third group of speakers – sufficiently important in numbers that the reanalysis imposed by this group formed the grammar of BD, but somehow not in a position to contribute functional or lexical material during this process. Who might this all-important group be? Several possibilities come to mind. First, there is the third group of contributors to BD lexicon, the speakers of Arawak. A second possibility is that a new group of enslaved Africans, possibly of various linguistic backgrounds, arrived into a situation where only the three groups mentioned earlier had been present. And the third and last possibility is that a locally-born, creole population was responsible. Let us review these in turn.

For Arawak speakers to have been responsible for the formation of BD grammar requires that they were present in large enough numbers during the early years of the Berbice colony. There were, of course, Arawak communities in the Berbice area, but the language of those communities remained Arawak into the 20th century. It is the Arawak speakers on the plantations who were in the best place to exert this kind of influence: they would have been in the right place, and would have had need for a contact variety for their interactions with the Dutch proprietors and with enslaved Africans. That there was an Arawak population on the plantations we already know: we saw earlier that Amerindian slaves were used by the Dutch during the early colonial period. Unfortunately, the earliest figures available are for the mid-eighteenth century. At that time, active enslavement of Amerindians is no longer practiced, and Amerindian slaves number only a few hundred. Dutch colonists must have relied much more on Amerindian slaves during the earliest years of the colony, although we will probably never know to what extent this was the case. In other words, a substantial presence of Amerindian (i.e. Arawak) slaves on the plantations during the earlier, undocumented period, is highly likely.

But aside from the question of numbers, there are problems with this scenario. One is the fact that Arawak speakers, in all likelihood, did not enter the plantation context *after* EI speakers, but *before*. In other words, Arawak speakers did not constitute a population confronted with a makeshift contact variety waiting to be expanded, they were a presence during the development of that makeshift variety. But if they were such a significant presence from the start, then why did Arawak fail to contribute *any* functional material to BD? And why do we find only a handful of non-peripheral Arawak contributions in BD lexicon? (a few kin terms, some other words of common use, and a few words which designate spiritual elements; see Kouwenberg 1996c.) While the absence of functional material could perhaps be explained by its agglutinative character and allomorphy, which would have made Arawak functional material difficult to interpret for the contact groups, far more pervasive contributions to non-peripheral lexicon would certainly have been expected.

Another problem is the motivation of Arawak speakers for the job. If Arawak slaves were indeed a substantial presence on the plantations, then they would have had ample opportunity to continue to speak Arawak with fellow Arawak slaves even in the unlikely case that they were cut off from the Arawak communities in the Berbice colony. The interactions of Arawak slaves with plantation owners and enslaved Africans would surely have been too limited for them to go to the extraordinary effort of developing a fully fledged creole language.

In short, although Arawak speakers may have been in the right place in the right numbers, they were there at the wrong time (too early) and are unlikely to have been sufficiently motivated to create a new language.

The second possibility is that a new group of enslaved Africans, of various linguistic backgrounds, arrived in a situation where, up to that time, only speakers of Arawak, EI lects, and Dutch had been present. In this scenario, the rudimentary system of communication worked out by these three groups was transformed into a full-fledged language by the newly arrived. This is one of the scenarios considered and rejected by Smith et al. (1987:72ff.). I concur, although for different reasons. In my opinion, the main problem for this scenario is in the fact that this group must be assumed to have abstained from the option of adding at least some content vocabulary of its own.[39] That this is unlikely is seen elsewhere in the Caribbean, where the sequential presence of different African ethnicities translates into substantial lexical contributions by each of the groups. This has been demonstrated for contributions by Kikongo, Gbe and Twi to the vocabularies of the Suriname creoles (see Smith 1987; Arends 1995). More recently, I have argued that Akan speakers made a substantial lexical contribution to an already fully formed Jamaican Creole during the eighteenth century (Kouwenberg 2008). For new groups of enslaved Africans in the Berbice colony not to have added some amount of vocabulary makes sense only if they were confronted with a full-fledged language on their arrival.

Smith et al. (1987) explore the possibility that a new, linguistically diverse group of slaves may have triggered the formation of BD by EI speakers rather than carry out that process. They suggest that Skepi Dutch (SD), the Dutch-lexifier creole of Essequibo, of which only remnant knowledge has been documented (Robertson 1989), in fact represents a 'unified' Dutch creole spoken by slaves not only in Essequibo, but also in Berbice during the early colonization period. The incorporation of EI elements, they claim, took place when EI-speaking slaves in interaction with newly arriving slaves sought, through language, to express a new ethnic identity; relexification of Dutch creole with EI forms is then thought to have led to the formation of BD.

However, a comparison of Dutch-derived vocabulary in SD (based on Robertson 1980) and BD (based on Kouwenberg 1994a) turns up some problems for this scenario. That SD should have a number of Dutch-derived forms which correspond to EI-derived forms in BD is as expected. But mismatches in Dutch-derived forms are harder to account for under this hypothesis. Those mismatches are of two kinds. The first kind takes the form of cases where the Dutch etymon is the same for the SD and BD items but the creole reflexes differ; the second kind consists of cases where the SD and BD forms have different Dutch etyma altogether.

The difference between SD forms such as *blut* 'blood', *gaut* 'gold', *ɛk* [1s], *stat* 'town', *mɛt* 'with', and BD *blutu, gautu, ɛkɛ, stati, mɛtɛ*, all of the same meaning, is of the first kind. These all correspond to Dutch consonant-final forms. This contrast does not constitute a problem for Smith et al., as it can be postulated that 'unified' Dutch creole had vowel-final forms throughout, and that SD subsequently lost most of these. But there are some other differences in cognate items which are harder to account for. Thus, the contrast between SD *drag* 'carry', *drʌg* 'dry', and the corresponding BD forms *draki, droko*, suggests that the Dutch items which formed the input in the formation of SD and BD were consonant-final in one case, but not in another. Thus, the voiceless stops in BD *draki* and *droko* require that the creators of these languages

---

39. There are but a handful of forms in modern BD of unknown origin, which cannot be ascribed to Dutch, EI, Arawak, or the more recent influence of Creolese. While it is possible that these forms originate in other languages spoken at one time or another among the enslaved Africans in Berbice, it is equally possible that their etyma will eventually turn up when better vocabularies of Arawak and/or EI varieties become available.

Table 6. Mismatches in Dutch etyma of Skepi Dutch and Berbice Dutch forms

Skepi Dutch	Dutch etymon	Berbice Dutch	Dutch etymon	Gloss
lɛnt	lende	atri	achter	'back'
bɛnɛr	beneden	ondro	onder	'beneath'
kluk	kloek	gu	goe(d)	'big'
fut	voet	bautu	bout	'leg'
murg	morgen	daki	dag	'good day'
mʌker	moker	hamburu	hamer	'hammer'
brai	braai(en)	brandi	branden	'roast'
kʊmbus	kombuis	kambru	kamer	'room'
slanka	slang	tau	touw	'snake'
wɛl	willen	suku	zoeken	'want'

were exposed to Dutch stem forms *draag* and *droog*, respectively, where the final obstruent devoicing rule of Dutch would have ensured the perception of these forms as containing a final voiceless obstruent. On the other hand, the voiced stops in SD *drag* and *drʌg* require exposure to Dutch *dragen* and *drogen*, where the presence of a final schwa (the articulation of -*en*) would have allowed the preservation of voice in the articulation of the obstruent, hence in the creole reflex.

To account for the contrast in these SD and BD forms, we either need to assume that 'unified' Dutch creole included forms derived both from Dutch consonant-final articulations and from Dutch vowel-final articulations, or that 'unified' Dutch creole included only one of each pair, and that SD or BD adopted a different form at a later stage. Neither of these explanations strike me as terribly convincing.

The second type of mismatch is also hard to explain. The relevant forms are listed in Table 6.[40] As can be seen there, in the development of SD and BD vocabulary from Dutch source forms, very different selections were sometimes made. Once again, this either requires that we postulate variation in the 'unified' Dutch creole, or else that one of the creoles later changed its mind about a particular selection. Again, this simply seems unlikely.

The third and final option which I will consider here, and the one that I adopt, is that BD was formed by creole slaves and/or by the mixed descendants of the three populations. In other words, the agents in the formation of BD were children, who adopted as their own a makeshift variety to which speakers of Dutch, EI and Arawak had contributed. Whether this variety was adopted as a mark of a new identity, or simply because of accessibility and usefulness will not concern me here.

That there were children in the colony is known, although not in what numbers. It is well known that Dutch plantation proprietors were usually single males, and early nineteenth-century sources show that they frequently cohabited with Arawak women;

---

40. Dutch etyma are provided in their modern orthographic forms. Note that the glosses are for the SD and BD forms, and may not accurately reflect the meaning of the Dutch etyma.

indeed, relationships with Arawak women were encouraged as part of a strategic alliance with Arawak communities. Of relevance is also the recognition in modern-day Guyana of a mixed ethnic group whose members are called 'Boviander'. Bovianders are the descendants of mixed relationships, involving Amerindian, Afro-Guyanese and/or white forebears. Allsopp (1996: 113) derives the word from Dutch *bovenlander* (upriver dweller) – an appropriate term, considering that this mixed population is typically associated with the former upriver plantation areas. Finally, the progeny of mixed white-black relationships and of relationships among slaves completes the picture. In other words, locally-born children included creole slaves and the mixed off-spring of the three populations. We may add to this that it is likely that there were children among the enslaved Africans that arrived in the Berbice colony.

I submit that it is the population of (mostly locally born) children who should be considered responsible for the large-scale reanalysis of functional material which took place in the genesis of BD. The range to which these children were exposed would have included versions of the makeshift contact variety used by adults of the three ethnic groups, and must have been quite varied. EI speakers were clearly sufficiently dominant that reanalysis did not affect some properties that align BD with aspects of EI grammar, but not sufficiently dominant that BD emerged with an essentially EI grammar.

These children had no linguistic material to add to the contact variety other than that proferred by their parents, i.e. members of the three ethnic groups which had formed the contact variety in the first place. This scenario thus accounts both for pervasive reanalysis and for the fact that no fourth-language material was added by the group responsible for the reanalysis. This scenario supposes that locally-born children were a significant presence in the Berbice colony *before* the advent of other groups of enslaved Africans, while the three groups mentioned earlier were still dominant in the colony. One may object to this that what is generally known of reproductive patterns and child mortality in Caribbean colonies suggests that this is unlikely. But we should take into account that the provision of basic food stock by local Arawak communities, and their solid knowledge of healing practices based on the resources of the natural environment may have made this a healthier population than was the norm elsewhere. Indeed, Robertson (1993: 299) claims that there was heavy reliance on creole slaves throughout the history of the Berbice colony.

7. Conclusion

Veenstra (2006), in his discussion of Saramaccan synthetic compounds, argues that an account of the grammatical properties of creole languages cannot rely on continuities from the contributing languages only. He argues that discontinuities, "grammatical properties that diverge from all the languages that were present in the original contact situation" (62), provide evidence of the role of nativization in producing these innovations.

I have essentially argued here for a similar account of BD formation. EI speakers were clearly not the primary agents in the formation of BD, even though EI lects constitute the main source of BD functional material. A detailed comparative study of aspects of BD and EI grammar shows that surface similarities cannot be taken as sufficient indication of substrate transfer. Such similarities evaporate as we examine the details of grammar.

Considering that only the three languages EI, Dutch and Arawak contributed to BD lexicon, that none of these groups could have been responsible for the processes which led to the formation of BD, and that it is unlikely that a fourth ethnic group was involved, I suggest that children in the population, both slave children and mixed-descent children, carried out the reanalysis which led to the emergence of BD. From the point of view of EI speakers, we see mixed patterns, at times recognizably aligned with EI, at other times quite divergent from it. In other words, BD is characterized by discontinuities at least as much as it is by apparent continuities.

References

Allsopp, Richard. 1996. *Dictionary of Caribbean English Usage*. Oxford: OUP.
Anon. n.d. *Kalabari Dictionary*. <http://www.rogerblench.info/Language%20data/Niger-Congo/Ijoid/Kalabari%20dictionary.pdf>.
Arends, Jacques. 1995. Demographic factors in the formation of Sranan. In *The Early Stages of Creolization* [Creole Language Library 13], Jacques Arends (ed.), 233–285. Amsterdam: John Benjamins.
Comrie, Bernard. 1976. *Aspect*. Cambridge: CUP.
Dapper, Olfert. 1668. *Naukeurige beschrijvinge der Afrikaensche gewesten*. Amsterdam: Jacob van Meurs.
Eltis, David, Behrendt, Stephen D., Richardson, David & Klein, Herbert S. (eds). 1999. *The Trans-Atlantic Slave Trade: A Database on CD-Rom*. Cambridge: CUP.
George, Boma Odunayo. 1989. Focus Constructions in Okrika. BA thesis, University of Port Harcourt.
Harry, Otelemate. 2004. *Aspects of the Tonal System of Kalaḅarị-Ịjọ*. Stanford CA: CSLI.
Hartsinck, Jan Jacob. 1770. *Beschryving van Guiana, of de Wilde Kust in Zuid-America*. Amsterdam: Gerrit Tielenburg. <http://www.dbnl.org/tekst/hart038besc01_01/index.htm>.
Ishmael, Odeen (ed.). 2001. *Guyana's Western Border: Background Historical Documents*. <http://www.guyana.org/Western/Cover.htm>, July 29, 2007.
Jenewari, Charles E. 1977. Studies in Kalaḅarị Syntax. PhD dissertation, University of Ibadan.
Kouwenberg, Silvia. 1992. From OV to VO. Linguistic negotiation in the development of Berbice Dutch Creole. *Lingua* 88: 263–299.
Kouwenberg, Silvia. 1994a. *A Grammar of Berbice Dutch Creole* [Mouton Grammar Library 12]. Berlin: Mouton de Gruyter.
Kouwenberg, Silvia. 1994b. Berbice Dutch. In *Typological Studies in Negation* [Typological Studies in Language 29], Peter Kahrel & René van den Berg (eds), 237–266. Amsterdam: John Benjamins.

Kouwenberg, Silvia. 1996a. The relationship between adjectives and verbs, with special reference to Berbice Dutch Creole. In *Caribbean Language Issues Old and New: Papers in Honour of Professor Mervyn Alleyne on the Occasion of his Sixtieth Birthday,* Pauline Christie (ed.), 27–40. Barbados: The Press University of the West Indies.

Kouwenberg, Silvia. 1996b. Grammaticalization and word order in the history of Berbice Dutch Creole. In *Changing Meanings, Changing Functions: Papers relating to Grammaticalization in Contact Languages* [Westminster Creolistics Series 2], Philip Baker & Anand Syea (eds), 207–218. London: University of Westminster Press.

Kouwenberg, Silvia. 1996c. Berbice Dutch Creole. In *Atlas of Languages of Intercultural Communication in the Pacific, Asia, and the Americas,* Stephen A. Wurm, Peter Mühlhäusler & Darrell T. Tryon (eds), 1347–1356. Berlin: Mouton de Gruyter.

Kouwenberg, Silvia. 1996d. Substrate or superstrate: What's in a name? *Journal of Pidgin and Creole Languages* 11(2): 371–375.

Kouwenberg, Silvia. 2000. Loss in Berbice Dutch Creole negative constructions: An examination of competence and performance of the last speakers. *Linguistics* 38(5): 889–923.

Kouwenberg, Silvia. 2007. Berbice Creole (Creole Dutch). In *Comparative Creole Syntax,* John Holm & Peter Patrick (eds), 25–52. London: Battlebridge.

Kouwenberg, Silvia. 2008. The problem of multiple substrates: The case of Jamaican Creole. In *Roots of Creole Structures: Weighing the Contribution of Substrates and Superstrates,* Susanne Michaelis (ed.), 1–27. Amsterdam: John Benjamins.

Kouwenberg, Silvia. Forthcoming. The Ijo-derived lexicon of Berbice Dutch Creole: An a-typical case of African lexical influence. In *African Words and Calques in Creoles and Transplanted European Languages,* Angela Bartens & Philip Baker (eds). London: Battlebridge.

Kouwenberg, Silvia & Robertson, Ian E. 1988. The marking of tense, mood and aspect in the Berbice Dutch Creole language. In *Beiträge zum 4. Essener Kolloquium über 'Sprachkontakt, Sprachwandel, Sprachwechsel, Sprachtod',* Norbert Boretzky, Werner Enninger & Thomas Stolz (eds), 151–174. Bochum: Brockmeyer.

Kramer, Klaas. 1991. Plantation development in Berbice from 1753 to 1779: The shift from the interior to the coast. *New West Indian Guide* 65(1–2): 51–65.

Muysken, Pieter. 1987. Prepositions and postpositions in Saramaccan. In *Studies in Saramaccan Language Structure,* Mervyn C. Alleyne (ed), 89–101. Amsterdam/Kingston: University of Amsterdam/University of the West Indies.

Postma, Johannes. 1990. *The Dutch in the Atlantic Slave Trade, 1600–1815.* Cambridge: CUP.

Robertson, Ian E. 1979. Berbice Dutch: A Description. PhD dissertation, University of the West Indies.

Robertson, Ian E. 1993. The Ijọ element in Berbice Dutch and the pidginization/ creolization process. In *Africanisms in Afro-American Language Varieties,* Salikoko S. Mufwene (ed.), 296–316. Athens: University of Georgia Press.

Robertson, Ian E. 1989. Berbice and Skepi Dutch: A lexical comparison. *Tijdschrift voor Nederlandse Taal- en Letterkunde* 105: 3–21.

Sika, Levi. 2005 [1995]. *Kirikeni okueingbolu diri: Okrika dictionary* <http://www.rogerblench.info/Language%20data/Niger-Congo/Ijoid/KIRIKE%20dictionary.pdf>, February 1, 2006.

Smith, Norval. 1987. The Genesis of the Creole Languages of Surinam. PhD dissertation, University of Amsterdam.

Smith, Norval. In preparation. From Ijo to Berbice Dutch vowels: A phonological study.

Smith, Norval, Robertson, Ian E. & Williamson, Kay. 1987. The Ijọ element in Berbice Dutch. *Language in Society* 16: 49–90.

Smith, Raymond T. 2000 [1962, 1980]. *British Guiana*. London: OUP; reprinted 1980, Connecticut: Greenwood Press. <http://home.uchicago.edu/~rts1/chapter_ii.htm>, October 20, 2007.

Stokram, Andries. 1991 [1663]. *Korte Beschryvinge van de Ongeluckige Weer-om-reys van het Schip AERNHEM*. Amsterdam: Terra Incognita.

Veenstra, Tonjes. 2006. Modeling creole genesis: Headedness in morphology. In *Structure and Variation in Language Contact* [Creole Language Library 29] Ana Deumert & Stephanie Durrleman (eds), 61–83. Amsterdam: John Benjamins.

Williamson, Kay. 1979. Medial consonants in Proto-Ịjọ. *Journal of African Languages and Linguistics* 1: 73–94.

Williamson, Kay. 1989. Niger-Congo overview. In *The Niger-Congo Languages: A Classification and Description of Africa's Largest Language Family*, John Bendor-Samuel (ed.), 3–45. Lanham MA: University Press of America.

Complexification or regularization of paradigms

The case of prepositional verbs in Solomon Islands Pijin

Christine Jourdan

In Honiara, capital city of the Solomon Islands, speakers of the local variety of Pijin are making extensive usage of the transitive suffix *-em* (and its variants *-im* and *-um*) to transform prepositions into prepositional verbs: *daon* /down/ becomes *daonem* /to lower/; *ap* /up/ becomes *apum* /to raise/; *insaet* /inside/ becomes *insaetim* /to insert, to take inside/; *aot* /out/ becomes *aotim* /to remove/, etc. Looking at data gathered in Honiara since 1981, this paper will hypothesize that the formation of prepositional verbs in Solomon Island Pijin (SIP) is best understood as an instance of paradigmatic regularization that is also present in other parts of the morphosyntax. The paper will argue that: (1) simplification and complexification are not the only types of linguistic changes affecting the life of PCs (Pidgin and Creole language); and (2) that regularization is internally-induced, and may not be linked to any substrate or superstrate effect.

1. Introduction

In Honiara, capital city of the Solomon Islands, speakers of some urban varieties of Pijin have made extensive usage of prepositions (*daon* /down/; *ap* /up/; *insaet* /inside/; *aot* /out/) to qualify verbs of movement and action. Traditionally, these prepositions used to be positioned after verbs, e.g. *tekem aot* /take out, remove/; *putim ap* /raise/; etc. Over the years, some of them have become affixed to verbs and bear the transitive marker (*em, im, um*) whenever appropriate; *filim ap* becomes *filimapum*; but *tekem aot* becomes *tekaotem*. In the first case, the stem keeps the transitive suffix, in the second it does not. Over the years some prepositions such as *of*; *ap*; *daon*; *antap*; *insaet*; *atsaet* have been used increasingly without the support of preposed action verbs, and are used as roots of transitive verbs: *tekaotem* becomes *aotem*; *tekem insaet* becomes *insaetim*; *tekem daon*, or *daon* becomes *daonem*; *of* becomes *ofum*. Compare examples (1) and (2) below:

(1) Mami   bae **tekem** kaleko **insaet** from   ren.
    S   FUT V   OBJ   PREP   PREP
    Mother will take   cloth inside   because rain.
    'Mother will bring the laundry in because of the rain.'

(2) Mami   bae **insaetim** kaleko from   ren.
    S   FUT PREP V   OBJ   PREP
    Mother will take inside laundry against rain.
    'Mother will bring the laundry inside because of the rain.'

This pattern, which looks simpler than the 'classic' periphrastic construction, is increasingly found in the speech of young urbanites. It is rarer in the speech of older speakers, particularly in rural areas where periphrastic forms, which look more complex, are more common.

Looking at data gathered in Honiara since 1981, this paper will hypothesize that the formation of prepositional verbs in Solomon Island Pijin (SIP) is best understood as an instance of paradigmatic regularization that is also present in other parts of the morphosyntax. The paper will argue that: (1) simplification and complexification are not the only types of linguistic changes affecting the life of PCs (Pidgin and Creole language): in practice, regularization is a form of simplification of the morphosyntax of Pijin that does not involve loss; (2) that this change is internally-induced and not linked to any substrate or superstrate effect. It may, in the process, reinforce patterns originating from substrates or lexifiers (Sankoff 1991); and (3) that, so far, regularization is a process of language change that is initiated by the adults of the community, and carried through by children. The role of teenagers in language change remains to be better understood. We know that in an effort to differentiate themselves from the generation of their parents, they seek ways of speaking that are different. We do not know, for PC-speaking communities at least, whether some form of feedback exists from the speech of teenagers to that of their parents, or whether their linguistic innovations make it into the system. The reader should keep two things in mind: (1) Solomon Islands Pijin is one of the extended pidgins of Melanesia. It remained in use as a pidgin (that is as a secondary language in the speech community) for close on 80 years before creolizing; (2) by creole, I am referring here to a PC that has become the primary language of a speech community, and has acquired cultural depth, with or without concomitant nativization.

2. On simplification and complexification

In his 2004 paper *Morphological simplicity in pidgins and creoles,* Siegel reminds us that there is no agreement in the field of creolistics as to what simplicity really refers to

(Siegel 2004: 140). This begs the question. If the specialists do not agree on what they mean by simplicity, do they agree on what they mean by simplification? Not so either (Siegel 2000 : 2).[1] Yet everyone probably agrees that the word 'simplification' implies a comparison. In creolistics, the terms of the comparison depend on a scholar's theoretical position on the genesis of PCs and usually involve reference to the relevant substrate and/or the superstrate language. Is the PC considered to be simpler than the substrate (Bakker 1995), or the superstrate (Chaudenson 1994), or both (Foley 2006)? Some theorists, such as Keesing (1988) proposed a middle ground for the PC he was studying: the PC is not the result of any form of simplification either of the substrate, or of the superstrate, but rather, a simple reflection, a 'calque' of the substrate.[2] In substance, this is also the premise of relexification theory (Lefebvre 1998). In all cases, simplification, as the term indicates, implies a loss. It is seen as the result of the interaction of universal constraints and local factors (Foley 2006). Overall, according to the PC literature, the pidginization that is associated with simplification is a form of contact-induced linguistic change that is exogenous (see Thurston 1987; Crowley 2000), a negotiation (Thomason 2001); 'linguistic accommodations with linguistic others' (Foley 2006: 41), and a linguistic accommodation to cultural circumstances (Jourdan 2000).

Complexification is another matter. Once again, the term implies a comparison. Here clearly, the comparison is with the very language that is being transformed. In some cases, the comparison is made with a pidgin, and in cases where the pidgin already functions as a creole for the speech community, with the creole itself. Throughout the field of creolistics, however, the matter of complexification is most often addressed with reference to a pidgin, and discussion most often takes place with regard to creolization and decreolization.[3] In the former case, complexification is seen as an endogenous form of linguistic change (Thurston 1987; Crowley 2000) taking place when the contexts of pidgin usage expand, or in other terms, when it 'matures socially'; in the latter case, it is still seen as an exogenous form of linguistic change due to continuous contacts with the lexifier within the same speech community (see Rickford 1987). Important questions have been asked in that regard as to the possible

---

1. Nevertheless, he endeavors to tackle the question and divides the processes of simplification into four groups that most scholars will agree upon: (1) reduction; (2) increased regularity; (3) greater transparency; and (4) lack of markedness. More recently, Foley (2006) revisits this issue, and proposes that it is possible to reduce these 4 groups to even to 'still more general principles': (1) the restriction of words to generic terms; (2) the elimination of allomorphy; (3) the use of parataxis rather than embedding; and (4) the adoption of invariant word order.

2. We are aware of the debate surrounding the origin of SIP (Solomon Islands Pidgin), but we will not enter into that here.

3. As reported in the literature (see Rickford 1987 among others) decreolization implies a comparison of the creole with the lexifier with which it coexists. The creole changes in the direction of the lexifier.

effects that these changes have on the typology of PCs. Does the pidgin become a creole simply because it exhibits more internal complexity? Does the pidgin become more complex because it is used societally as a creole or because it has acquired native speakers? In view of the increasingly diverse forms in which pidgins and creoles appear, in view of the diversity of their social history, and given the blurring of linguistic boundaries between the pidgins and creoles that are now being unearthed (Jourdan 1991), it is currently impossible to come up with a unifying theory that would do justice to them all. As a result, many scholars have opted to use the acronym PCs to refer to them.

We will take up this lead and ask a series of questions. If indeed complexification occurs, what is/are its outcome/s? A more complex phonology? A more complex morphosyntax? A more complex lexicon? More complex pragmatics? Historical linguists have shown that the answers to these questions are not to be found painted in black and white: while some complexification may take place in some parts of the language, some simplification may take place in other parts.[4] And oftentimes, the types of changes that take place result neither in simplification nor complexification (see Trask 1996; Crowley 1992; Crowley 2000: 176). These questions will not be answered here. Yet, they are useful in that they force our attention to the fact that we are talking of language change.

As Crowley reminds us:

> Language change can clearly not be unidirectional if it is accepted that relatively simple and relatively complex languages exist, and we need to recognize that relatively simple languages can become structurally more complex over time.
>
> (2000: 176).

In between these two extremes of language change represented by simplification and complexification, are there other ways of thinking about the types of changes that affect P/Cs in the course of their history? Are there other processes at play? In this short note on the development of prepositional verbs in Solomon Islands Pijin, I will propose that regularization of paradigms is happening across the language and is a form of change that is internally induced.

3. The data

Pijin has a limited number of prepositions: locatives, possessive and completive. Beimers (2008) makes a distinction between what he calls simple prepositions such as *long, blong, fo* and complex prepositions such as *antap long, atsaet long, fastaem long*, etc. Note that complex prepositions, with the exception of *fastaem long* are usu-

---

4. I do not imply that a causal relationship exists between the two processes. They are independent principles of change.

Table 1. Prepositions

Abaot	About, around
Agens	Against
Andanit	Underneath
Antap	Above
Aot	Out
Ap	Up
Atsaed	Outside
Bihaen	Behind
Blong	Possession
Daon	Below
Fastaem	Ahead
From	From, because
Insaet	Inside
Kolsap	Close
Long	At, to, about
Raon	Around
Wetem	With

ally composed of locatives (*atsaed, insaet, antap*) followed obligatorily by *long*. These prepositions, simple or complex, introduce the NP and the PP. We can also make a distinction between the fully lexicalized prepositions such as *insaet, atsaed* and the more suffixial prepositions such as *of, on, aot, ap*.

The complete set of prepositions is as in Table 1.

Interestingly, only some of these prepositions, a subset of the locatives, can function as verbs with the adjunction of the transitive suffix *-em, -im, -um*.[5] Note that the transitive marker is the preferred mark of transitivity in Pijin, and that it is extremely productive. When added to nouns, adjectives or prepositions, it transforms them into verbs. Note also that in some serial verb constructions, most notably with auxiliary (*go, bin*) or modals (*maet, save*), the verb does not bear the transitive marker. Note finally that the canonical object does not need to be expressed in some constructions. Compare examples (3) and (4).

(3) *Dadi   blong mi   no   save   kaekae suka.*
    SUBJ   POSS   PRO   NEG   MODAL   VERB   OBJ
    Daddy mine   not   eat   sugar
    'My father does not eat sugar.'

---

5. The transitive suffix has been widely discussed in the literature on Bislama (see Charpentier 1979; Crowley 1990) and Pijin (Jourdan 1985, 2004; Keesing 1988). Meyeroff (1996) analyzes the role of the transitive suffix in the contact Englishes of the Pacific.

(4) Mi   bae   mi   no   save   kaekaem   tu.
    PRO   FUT   PRO   NEG   MODAL   eat   PREP
    I   shall I   not   eat   also
    'I shall not eat (it) also.'

Note that the transitive suffix varies according to a rule of vocalic harmony that links the verb stem and the suffix. Yet, a great deal of variation exists among speakers, and sometimes, the same speaker may use a *-em* ending with a verb on one occasion, and a *-im* ending the next time. Table 2 indicates the most common usage and shows the prepositions and their extension as verbs.

In addition, the preposition *ap* can be cliticized onto verb stems to form a single lexical unit. For instance we have *bagarap, wekap, stanap, laenap* but we never have *bagar, wek, stan, laen* (as verb). This is a direct reanalysis of English 'bugger up' 'wake up', 'stand up', 'line up', etc. In turn, some of the verbs constructed with *ap* can become transitive. There are two options. The first one involves inserting the transitive marker between the verb stem and the preposition as in {verb stem} + {transitive marker} + {preposition}: *bagaremap, wekemap, stanemap; laenemap, klamap*. The TM, normally a suffix, becomes in fact an infix. The second involves the addition of the transitive suffix after the preposition, as per the following model: {verb stem} + {transitive suffix}. Table 3 gives a series of examples.

Table 2. Prepositional verbs in SIP

Preposition			Transitive verb	Gloss
Abaot	About	Em	*Abaotem*	1) To concern, 2) about
Agens	Against	Em	*Agensem*	1) To lean, 2) to oppose
Antap	On top of	Em	*Antapem*	1) To climb on top of
Aot	Out	Em	*Aotem*	1) To remove, 2) to reveal
Ap	High	Um	*Apum*	1) To raise, 2) to praise
Atsaed	Outside	Im	*Atsaetim*	1) To take outside
Bihaen	Behind	Em	*Bihaenem*	1) To follow, 2) to come second
Daon	Below	Em	*Daonem*	1) To lower, 2) to denigrate
Insaet	Inside	Im	*Insaetim*	1) To take inside
Raon	Around	Em	*Raonem*	1) To surround, 2) to circle

Table 3. Two ways of marking transitivity

Intr./stat. verb	Gloss	Transitive 1	Transitive 2	Gloss
Bagarap	'broken down', ruined	*Bagaremap*	*Bagarapem*	'to ruin', 'to damage'
Wekap	'awaken'	*Wekemap*	*Wekapem*	'to wake up someone'
Stanap	'stand'	*Stanemap*	*Stanapem*	'to stand something up'
Laenap	'lined up'	*Laenemap*	*Laenapum*	'to line something up'
Miksap	'confused'	*Miksimap*		'to confuse'

We will have to allow for lexifier influence to explain some of these Transitive 1 constructions – clearly these are calques of non-standard English. We can imagine a plantation overseer telling his labor to 'line 'em up' or 'wake 'im up', or again 'stand 'em up'. The Transitive 2 constructions, however, follow the classical Pijin rule for the construction of transitive verbs. These two systems coexist, even though the second one seems to be more recent. Whereas older speakers may have used serial verb constructions of the type {aux} + {verb} as in *hem save klaemap fens* /he climbs the fence/ or *hem mekem olketa boe save laenap* /arrange it so that the boys line up/; or again *mekem disfala pos hem stanap* /hold this post straight/. I have heard young urbanites, adults and children, say: "hem *klaemapum fens*; hem *laenapum okete boe*; *stanapum pos ia*!" Granted, these constructions are rare, so rare in fact that they did not appear in my 1983 corpus of Pijin, and still barely occur in my 1993 corpus of urban Pijin.[6] But just as with the prepositional verbs, which too are rather recent innovations, they are increasingly heard in Honiara. The very small, and statistically insignificant test of acceptability that I conducted with a random sample of 15 speakers around town in 1997 shows that while some speakers, across generation and gender, prefer *wekemap* to *wekapum*, others prefer *laenapum* to *laenemap*. Yet, my intuition is that this is a change in progress.

4. Discussion

Looking at the data presented above, one must acknowledge that some changes are taking place in the syntax of verbs and prepositions. These changes are not the only ones that are found in contemporary Pijin: others have been documented in Jourdan (1985, 2002), Jourdan and Keesing (1997), Jourdan and Selbach (2004), Keesing (1988), Selbach (2000), and Beimers (2008), and include a great increase in rate of speech, extensive phonological reduction, a "progressive disappearance of old Oceanic patterns of subject-marking" (Jourdan and Keesing 1997: 414), associated with a reconfiguration of the pronoun systems, the development of relative clause markers, the grammaticalization of the 3rd person pronoun plural, and the dropping of 'old' particles such as *-fala*. These changes are more or less pervasive in the speech of urbanites according to speakers, and contribute to the increasing differences found between the rural and urban registers of Pijin, and within urban Pijin, between the speech of younger urbanites and that of their parents. Yet one question remains: are the changes I have witnessed particular to the process of creolization, defined socially, or are they simply instances of language change at play in linguistic communities undergoing rapid social flux? In other words, are these changes typologically different from those associated with 'ordinary' language change? I will not seek to answer these questions here as they are beyond the scope of this article,

---

6. We are aware of the limitations of corpus based research.

but they bear clearly on the analysis I am making of the changes taking place in the prepositional system of Pijin.

How to analyze this state of affairs? The data presented above do not reveal much complexification of the system of transitive verbs. Rather, we observe some regularization of paradigms, as is also found in other areas of morphosyntax. The syntactic resources already available to speakers are used to create new words in the same way as before, and not only that, but to 'smoothen out' the irregularities found in the system. Here, and as with other parts of Pijin syntax, the transitive marker is called upon, and appended to words or verbal stems to transform them into other parts of speech. This is already the case for active verbs, for statives, and for nouns, and now also for prepositions (see examples (5) to (6)).

Statives:

(5) a. *Kaleko blong mi lo laen hem **tuwet** fogud.*
SUBJ POSS PRO PREP line PRO STAT ADV
Clothes mine   on line it wet very.
'My clothes on the cloth line are very wet.'

b. *Ren nao **tuwetim** kaleko blong mi lo laen.*
SUBJ ACT V OBJ POSS PRO PREP line
Rain drench clothes mine on line
'The rain drenched my clothes on the cloth line.'

Nouns:

(6) a. *Puskat hotim bodi blong hem long **san**.*
SUBJ V OBJ POSS PRON PREP sun
Cat warm body his in sun
'The cat warms up his body in the sun.'

b. *Puskat **sanim** bodi blong hem.*
SUBJ V OBJ POSS PRON
Cat sun body its
'The cat suns its body.'

As Keesing (1988) has remarked, it is also possible to create active verbs in the substrate languages by the adjunction of the TM to statives, adjectives and prepositions (Keesing 1988: 76). Yet one cannot help but remark that the syntax of English, the lexifier language, and the official language of the country, also allows these types of constructions for the same syntactic elements.

It is hard at this point to decide whether the regularization of prepositional verbs is reinforced by patterns of the substrate language or the lexifier language. But is it necessary to invoke the influence of one or other to understand the types of changes that are taking place in Pijin? Not really. I am arguing here that PCs can also develop independently from their contributing languages: This happens when speakers identify the resources that can be used for development, and exploit these resources outside of their 'habitual' linguistic niche. In the case of Pijin, the TM is a good example of such a resource. Its productivity is not only linked to its function, but also to the fact that the speakers recognize it as a malleable feature of the language. This is what has been called a system-internal innovation, which, as Andersen (1988; see also Wolfram 2003) has claimed, has been overlooked by researchers as a source of language development, in comparison with language contact. For a long time, it was de rigueur in the field of creolistics to describe varieties of creole languages with reference to their lexifiers, and to claim that in general, changes took place in the direction of the lexifiers, still regarded by many theorists as the targets. The following quote, taken from Muhlhausler's thesis on Tok Pisin (1979:19), is an example in point:

> It suffices, for the present argument, to point out that any description of Urban Pidgin must be made with reference to English, since Urban Pidgin cannot be regarded as an independent linguistic system.

To be fair, Muhlhausler (private communication February 2007) recognized that this comment was only of historical relevance, and did not correspond to the present situation of Tok Pisin. It is possible today to argue that linguistic changes in PCs take place without reference to the patterns of substrate or lexifier languages, even though some of the changes found are directly parallel to structures present in either. For instance, in contemporary SIP, social and linguistic distance from substratal influences leads to contradictory results: On the one hand, it leads to the disappearance of some substrate-like features (the dropping of so-called predicate marker -*i*); and on the other, to the increased frequency of use of the transitive marker -*em* to create verbs. Yet, the data show that 'proximity' to English leads to the development of morphological plural marking on nouns that are clearly English in terms of phonology. Yet, when it comes to innovations and extensions – the processes that lead to regularization – SIP shows that it is an autonomous language.

Even though I have not yet collected hard data to confirm this, my observations in Honiara show that the regularization of the prepositional verb paradigm is spreading fast in the young urban community. What factors influence such a rapid spread? Saliency is one of them: the TM is easily recognizable, phonologically and syntactically, as a productive marker, and is being picked up by the younger Honiara crowd. Tuite (1998) presents Lightfoot's (1997:37) position:

> Pour qu'une nouvelle génération d'enfants choississe pour un paramètre quelconque une valeur différente, il est nécessaire, selon le modèle de Lightfoot, que certaines variables linguistiques de la parole, les 'primary linguistic data', aient subi un changement suffisamment significatif par rapport à celles des generations précédentes pour que l'organe linguistique de chaque nouveau locuteur remarque et encode ces différences.

Children and young people in Honiara have probably noticed that the TM was used haphazardly, but constructively, by young urban adults in a way that agreed with its traditional place in the morphosyntax of verbs, but was also slightly different. They recognize its saliency, both in the speech of their parents, and in the system in general, identify it as a verb ending, and apply it across the board, thus regularizing the system. This process is nicely explained in Slobin (1974), Mufwene (1999), and Liceras et al. (2006), and corroborates similar observations made for PCs by Jourdan (1985), Sankoff (1991), Smith (2002), and Singler (2006).

We can conceive of regularization as a form of overgeneralization of rules associated with the learning of language by children. The essential difference here lies in the fact that the children I am talking about range between 7 and 13 years of age. They are not toddlers who are in the process of acquiring language: they know Pijin well. Their regularizations of -*em* are not a form of overgeneralization of the rules, but rather a form of extension of the rules across categories. Heine and Kuteva (2006: 35) argue that:

> Not uncommonly, context extension involves a grammaticalization process whereby the use of an item belonging to some open word class is extended to serve as a modifier of another open-class paradigm.

This is very similar to what Trask (1996: 105) is calling analogical levelling. The result is regularization.

But the linguistic organ mentioned by Trudgill above does make not a language and cannot explain the acceleration of the process of regularization. Social processes are central to this process. As I have explained above, and as Wolfram and Schilling-Estes (2003: 223) state regarding the spread of the feature 'weren't' in American southern enclaves communities 'a special set of historical and social circumstances is necessary to ensure the survival and spread of levelling' of a given feature. The special social condition mentioned by Wolfram and Schilling-Estes is marginality. Here, the 'special set of circumstances' that affect the development of Pijin includes: (1) urbanization (and with it the development of an urban culture of which Pijin is the linguistic medium) and (2) 'the need of young people to differentiate themselves from adults' (Chambers 2003: 275) in this new social milieu. When these factors coalesce, innovations appear.

Regularization and leveling take place later with diffusion of the new traits in the linguistic community. What are the advantages of regularization? From the cognitive point of view, it decreases the overload caused by the variability of dialects. Chambers (2003) remarks that 'forms do not need to be memorized anymore, they can simply be generated.' From a social point of view, regularization and leveling are made possible by and contribute to the reinforcement of group-belonging. To some extent, they may serve as a springboard from which communicative norms may develop.

References

Andersen, Henning. 1988. Center and periphery: Adoption, diffusion, and spread. In *Historical Dialectology*, Jacek Fisiak (ed.), 39–83. Berlin: de Gruyter.

Bakker, Peter. 1995. A Grammar and Dictionary of the Timucua Language. *Journal of Pidgin and Creole Languages* 10: 363–365.

Beimers, Gerry. 2008. A Grammar of Solomon Islands Pijin. PhD dissertation, the University of Armidale.

Chambers J. K. 2003. *Sociolinguistic Theory: Linguistic Variation and Its Social Significance*. Oxford: Blackwell.

Charpentier, Jean-Michel. 1979. *Le pidgin bislama(n) et le multilinguisme aux Nouvelles-Hébrides*. Paris: Société d'Etudes Linguistiques et Anthropologiques de France.

Chaudenson, R. 1994. Are French creoles simplified forms of French? *Cahiers du Francais Contemporain* 1: 41–54.

Crowley, Terry. 1990. *Beach-la-Mar to Bislama: The Emergence of a National Language in Vanuatu*. Oxford: Clarendon Press.

Crowley, Terry. 1992. *An Introduction to Historical Linguistic*. Oxford: OUP.

Crowley, Terry. 2000. Simplicity, complexity, emblematicity and grammatical change. In *Processes in Language Contact: Studies from Australia and the South Pacific*, Jeff Siegel (ed.), 75–193. Montréal: Fides.

Foley, William. 2006. Universal constraints and local conditions in pidginization. *Journal of Pidgin and Creole Languages* 21(1): 1–44.

Heine, Bernard & Kuteva, Tania. 2006. *Language Contact and Grammatical Change*. Cambridge: CUP.

Jourdan, Christine. 1985. Sapos Iumi Mitim Iumi: Urbanization and Creolization in the Solomon Islads. PhD dissertation. Australian National University, Canberra.

Jourdan, Christine. 1991. Pidgins and creoles: The blurring of categories. *Annual Review of Anthropology* 20: 187–209.

Jourdan, Christine. 2000. 'My nephew is my aunt': Features and transformation of kinship terminology in Solomon Islands Pijin. In *Processes of Language Change*, Jeff Siegel (ed.), 99–122. Montreal: Fides.

Jourdan, Christine. 2002. *Pijin: A Ttrilingual Cultural Dictionary: Pijin-Inglis-Franis, Pijin-English-French, Pijin-Anglais-Français*. Canberra: Pacific Linguistics, Research School of Pacific and Asian Studies, Australian National University.

Jourdan, Christine. 2004. Morphology and syntax of Solomon Islands Pijin. In *Varieties of English*, Bernd Kortmann & Elisabeth Closs-Traugott (eds), 161–178. Berlin: Mouton de Gruyter.

Jourdan, Christine & Keesing, Roger M. 1997. From Fisin to Pijin: Creolization in process in the Solomon Islands. *Language in Society* 26: 401–420.

Jourdan, Christine & Selbach, Rachel. 2004. Solomon Islands Pijin: Phonetics and phonology. In *A Handbook of Varieties of English: A Multimedia Reference Tool*, Edgar W. Schneider & Bernd Kortmann (eds.), 690–706. Berlin: Mouton de Gruyter.

Keesing, Roger M. 1988. *Melanesian Pidgin and the Oceanic Substrate*. Stanford CA: Stanford University Press.

Lefebvre, Claire. 1998. *Creole Genesis and the Acquisition of Grammar: The Case of Haitian Creole*. Cambridge: CUP.

Liceras, Juana M., Martinez, C., Pérez-Tattam, R., Perales, S. & Fernandez Fuertes, Raquel. 2006. L2 Acquisition as a process of creolization: Insights form child and adult code-mixing. In *L2 Acquisition and Creole Genesis*, Claire Lefebvre, Lydia White & Christine Jourdan (eds), 113–144. Amsterdam: John Benjamins.

Lightfoot, David. 1997. *How New Languages Emerge*. Cambridge: CUP.

Meyerhoff, Miriam, 1996. Transitive marking in contact Englishes. *Australian Journal of Linguistics* 16: 57–80.

Mufwene, Salikoko S. 1999. Creoles. The State of Our Knowledge. *Anthropologie et Societes* 23: 149–173.

Mühlhäusler, Peter. 1979. *Growth and Structure of the Lexicon of New Guinea Pidgin* [Series C.52]. Canberra: Pacific Linguistics.

Rickford, John R. 1987. *Dimensions of a creole continuum: History, texts and linguistic analysis of Guyanese Creole*. Stanford CA: Stanford University Press.

Sankoff, Gillian. 1991. Using the future to explain the past. In *Development and Structures of Creoles Languages: Essays in Honor of Derek Bickerton* [Creole Language Library 9], Francis Byrne & Thom Huebner (eds), 61–74. Amsterdam: John Benjamins.

Selbach, Rachel. 2000. Oketa in Solomon Islands Pijin: Homophony or conceptual link between the third person plural pronoun and nominal plurality? Paper presented at SPCA, LSA, Chicago.

Siegel, Jeff. 2000. Introduction: The processes of language contact. In *Processes in Language Contact: Studies from Australia and the South Pacific*, Jeff Siegel (ed.), 1–11. Montréal: Fides.

Siegel, Jeff. 2004. Morphological simplicity in pidgins and creoles. *Journal of Pidgin and Creole Languages* 19: 139–162.

Singler, John V. 2006. Children and creole genesis. *Journal of Pidgin and Creole Languages* 21: 157–173.

Slobin, Dan I. 1974. *Psycholinguistics*. Glenview IL: Scott, Foresman.

Smith, Geoff. 2002. *Growing up with Tok Pisin. Contact, Creolization and Change in Papua New Guinea's National Language*. London: Battlebridge.

Thomason, Sarah. 2001. *Language Contact: An Introduction*. Edinburgh: University of Edinburgh Press.

Thurston, William R. 1987. *Processes of Change in the Languages of North Western New Britain*. Canberra: Pacific Linguistics, B99.

Trask, R. L. 1996. *Historical Linguistics*. London: St. Martin's Press.

Tuite, Kevin. 1998. Au delà du Stammbaum: Théories modernes du changement linguistique. In *L'Ethnolinguistique*, Christine Jourdan & Claire Lefebvre (eds). Special issue of *Anthropologie et Sociétés* 23: 15–52.

Wolfram, W. & Schilling-Estes, Natalie. 2003. Language change in 'conservative dialects': The case of past tense be in southern enclave communities. *American Speech* 78(2): 209–228.

PART III

Nominals

The Mauritian Creole determiner system
A historical overview

Diana Guillemin

The process of article incorporation early in the genesis of Mauritian Creole (MC) resulted in the occurrence of a bare nouns in argument positions with ambiguous interpretations between [±definite], [±specific] singular, plural and generic. A new determiner system gradually emerged, but MC continues to admit bare nouns in argument positions. It is argued in this paper that the process of article incorporation triggered a shift in noun denotation from predicative in French to argumental in MC. Like English bare plurals, MC nouns are argumental kind-denoting terms that do not require a determiner in argument positions. The MC singular indefinite article *enn* and the plural marker *bann* serve to derive instances of kinds. The differential behaviour of MC count and mass nouns is attributed to the number feature which must be checked for count nouns, and provides evidence for a phonologically null definite determiner which is licensed in subject position by the specificity marker *la*.

1. Introduction

MC is a French lexifier creole whose main substrates in the early stages of creolization included the Gbe languages of West Africa, Bantu languages of East Africa, as well as Malagasy (Baker 1982). Most of the MC lexicon is from French and the creole has retained the strict SVO word order of its lexifier, as well as the count mass distinction of its nouns, but, unlike French, it does not grammaticalize Gender and its nouns do not inflect for number.

Early in the genesis of MC, the French definite articles *le/la* ('the'), which is used with count and mass nouns, and the partitive determiner *du* (the contracted form of *de le*, literally 'of the'), which is used with mass nouns were incorporated into a large number of the nouns that they modified. Determiners in French serve to mark the semantic features of (in)definiteness, number and gender. Their function was not recognized, and they were taken to be an integral part of the nouns (Baissac 1880; Chaudenson 1981; Baker 1984; Grant 1995; Strandquist 2005). The process of article

Table 1. The ambiguous interpretations of early MC count and mass nouns

	Features	French	Early MC	English
Count noun	sg [−definite]	une patte	lapat	a paw
	sg [+definite]	la patte		the paw
	pl [−definite]	des pattes		paws
	pl [+definite]	les pattes		the paws
Mass noun	[−definite]	du sel	disel	(some) salt
	[+definite]	le sel		the salt

incorporation is represented in (1a) for count nouns, and (1b) for mass nouns. In both cases, a French quantified noun phrase yields a bare common noun in MC:

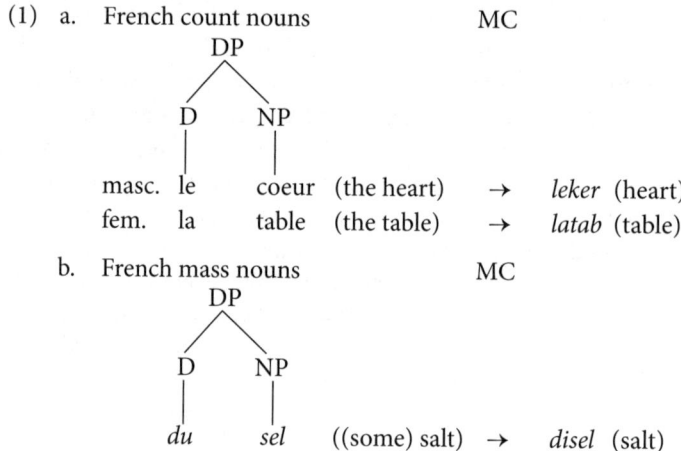

(1) a. French count nouns → MC
    masc. le coeur (the heart) → leker (heart)
    fem. la table (the table) → latab (table)

 b. French mass nouns → MC
    du sel ((some) salt) → disel (salt)

The immediate consequence of article incorporation was that bare nouns occurred in various syntactic configurations, yielding [±definite] interpretations for mass nouns, and [±definite] singular or plural interpretations for count nouns, as shown in Table 1.

New determiners gradually emerged in MC over a period of some 150 years from the mid 18th century to the end of the 19th century. They comprise the following:

a. The deictic markers, which modify both count and mass nouns, namely:
   - The postnominal specificity marker *la* which marks only [+definite] NPs. It is derived either from the French distal demonstrative reinforcer *là* or from the homophonous locative adverb.[1]
   - The demonstrative *sa*, which is generally used in conjunction with *la*. It is derived from the demonstrative pronoun *ça* used determinatively, in lieu of

---

1. The term 'demonstrative reinforcer' was coined by Bernstein (1997). They are proximate *ci* and distal *là*. The proximate vs. distal contrast of demonstratives is not marked in MC.

the French *ce/cet/cette/ces ... là* when used to point to referents that are established in the situation of discourse as in the following sentence from Grant (1749), *ça blanc là li beaucoup malin* (this/white/there/Pro/really/clever: these white men are very clever), see also example (8) below.
b. The quantificational determiners which modify only count nouns, namely:
   - The indefinite singular article *enn*, derived from the French *un/une* (a/an).
   - The plural marker *bann*, derived from the French lexical noun *bande* (group).

The grammaticalization of these lexical items resulted in a determiner system which differs from that of the lexifier in the following respects:

- While French does not admit bare nouns in argument positions (bar a few exceptions), MC freely admits bare nouns as arguments.[2]
- French overtly marks the [±definiteness] contrast of all nouns whilst bare nouns in MC can be [±definite].
- While all determiners in French are pre-nominal, the MC specificity marker *la* is post nominal.

On the points listed above, MC seems to pattern with its substrate languages. The Gbe languages, for example, display poor inflectional morphology. Their nouns do not inflect for number, and are not specified for gender. Bare nouns can be ambiguous between [±definite] and [±plural] interpretations and their meaning is derived from the context. While "Gungbe nominal expressions are unmarked with respect to definiteness, they are always unambiguously specific or non specific" (Aboh 2004: 77). Furthermore, specificity markers are post nominal. Similarly, we have some Bantu languages, (e.g. Bemba) where "there is no provision for the definite/indefinite distinction, but only for that of referential vs. non-referential" (Givon 1978: 300).

In Section 2 I provide a brief overview of my syntactic framework, and Section 3 comprises the semantic definitions used for my analysis. In Section 4 I look at the gradual emergence of the deictic and quantificational determiners. Section 5 is my analysis, and Section 6 concludes this paper.

---

2. The exceptions include:
   - The predicative use of bare nouns that denote a role or profession, e.g.: *Paul est charpentier* (Paul is a carpenter)
   - In fused expressions, such as proverbs, e.g. *Pierre qui roule n'amasse pas mousse* (A rolling stone gathers no moss)
   - In coordinated bare plurals, e.g. 'Un bateau transportant des réfugiés vient d'arriver à Puglia. *Marins et passagers* sont Albanais; le capitaine est Italien.' (Roodenburg 2004: 309, italics in original). (A ship carrying refugees has just arrive in Puglia. *Sailors and passengers* are Albanian; the captain is Italian).

2. Syntactic framework

2.1 Minimalist assumptions

My syntactic analysis is within the framework of Chomsky's (1995) Minimalist Program (MP), which assumes that humans are biologically endowed with a Universal Grammar (UG), and that languages differ as a consequence of parametric variations.

A basic assumption of the MP is that the lexicon comprises *substantive* items, such as lexical verbs, nouns and adjectives, and *functional* items, such as complementizers, tense and determiners. Items selected from the lexicon enter a derivation fully inflected with their phonological, semantic and formal features. Sentences are formed by the recursive application of the operations *Merge*, *Move* and *Agree* The operation *Merge* concatenates two syntactic objects and projects the categorial feature of the head, e.g. the determiner (D) *the* and the noun (N) *cat* merge to form the Determiner Phrase (DP) *the cat*. The operation *Move* is triggered by the feature checking requirement of a lexical resource. *Agree* is the operation that establishes a relation between lexical items.

Representations and derivations must be optimal and economical, i.e. there are no superfluous morphemes, and movement is a 'last resort' operation, triggered strictly by the need to check and eliminate features. Lexical items have interpretable features while functional items have 'uninterpretable' features that must be checked and eliminated for convergence at the interface. Only two levels of representation are assumed, namely, Phonetic Form (PF) and Logical Form (LF), which correspond to the phenomena of sound and meaning respectively.

2.2 The structure of the MC noun phrase

I propose the following structure for the modern MC noun phrase (omitting the projections not discussed in this paper, such as the Possessive Phrase):

(2)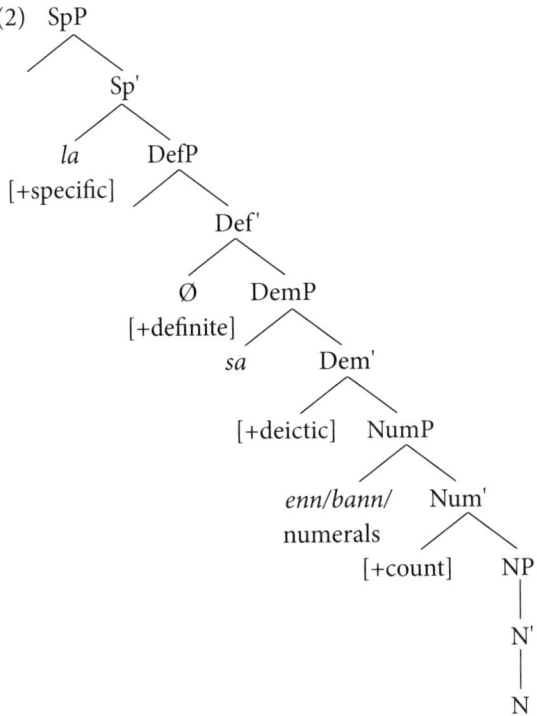

Where:

- The highest projection is the Specificity Phrase (SpP), whose head is specified for the feature [+specific], morphologically realized as *la* for [+definite] noun phrases only.
- The head of Definiteness Phrase (DefP) is specified for the feature [+definite]. The definite determiner in MC is a phonologically null element, represented as Ø.
- The head of the Demonstrative Phrase (DemP) is specified for the feature [+deictic]. The demonstrative *sa* is merged in Spec,DemP. (I follow Bernstein (1997) and Giusti (1997) in my assumption that demonstratives are merged in a specifier position.)
- The head of the Number Phrase (NumP) is specified for the feature [+count]. This projection is realized only for common count nouns. The indefinite singular article *enn*, the plural marker *bann*, and cardinal numerals are merged in Spec,NumP.
- The lowest projection is the NP.

Note that each projection is specified for a single feature and not binary features, such as [±definite] or [±specific].

2.3 Predicates and arguments

I adopt Zamparelli's (2000) proposal for a 'Multi-Layer DP Hypothesis', whereby numerals are interpreted as cardinality predicates in a lower position in the DP, and as strong quantifiers (or referential elements) in a higher position' (2000:5). This is represented in the schema below:

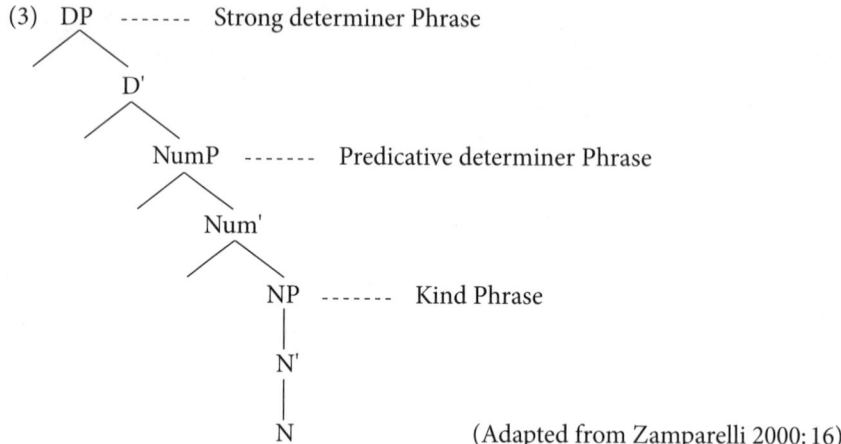

(Adapted from Zamparelli 2000:16)

Zamparelli proposes that languages select their base denotation first and type shift accordingly, and he assumes, as do Stowell (1989) and Longobardi (1994) that the basic denotation of a noun in N is that of a kind. Determiners fall into two categories, 'weak' and 'strong' (Milsark 1979; Barwise and Cooper 1981). Weakly quantified NPs are cardinality predicates that can occur in existential sentences (Milsark 1979), while strongly quantified NPs can function as arguments. These include both specific and non-specific definites as well as specific indefinites, i.e. all noun phrases that are interpreted at the DefP or SpP level, either at PF or LF.

2.4 DPs and NPs

In his typological study of 'Articles', Himmelmann comments that "count nouns cannot be used in core argument positions without a marker for definiteness or specificity" (2001:832), a view shared by Longobardi (1994, 2001) who derives the principle that "DP can be an argument, NP cannot", though D can be a phonologically null element (1994:628).[3] If this is indeed the case, then the occurrence of bare nouns that yield a definite interpretation provides evidence for a phonologically null determiner in MC, equivalent to the English and French definite articles.

---

3. The main contrast between the two points of view is that Longobardi differentiates between singular vs. plural count nouns, and points out that only plural count nouns and mass nouns tolerate a null determiner in some languages.

However, the view that only DPs can occur in argument positions is challenged by Chierchia (1998a), who argues that the denotation of nouns varies across languages, and that this variation may be responsible for the different distribution of bare nominal arguments. In some languages, for example Chinese, all nominals are by default argumental, and they can occur in argument positions without a determiner. In others, such as the Romance languages, all nominals are predicates, and "since predicates by definition cannot function as arguments, such a language should disallow bare nominal arguments altogether" (1998a: 355). There are also languages like English, in which nouns can freely be predicative or argumental – singular count nouns need a determiner, while mass nouns and bare plurals can occur without a determiner.

2.5 The feature Argumental [Arg]

While Longobardi (1994) and Stowell (1989) agree that head nouns in the N position always refer to kinds, they differ from Chierchia (1998a) in their claim that all NPs are predicates. They analyze determiners as operators binding a variable, whose range is the extension of the natural kind referred to by the head noun. The function of a determiner is to convert a predicative NP into a referential expression.

Determiners also serve to assign to their complement NPs the semantic features of (in)definiteness, specificity and deixis, amongst others. These are features of DPs not NPs. Consequently, I assume Stowell's (1989) and Longobardi's (1994) theory that only DPs can be [+ referential] (i.e. definite or specific or both), and when bare nouns occur in argument positions, they are DPs not NPs.

Building on the work of Chierchia (1998a), who proposes that nouns vary with respect to the opposing parameters argumental [±arg] vs. predicative [±pred], I postulate only the feature Arg for D and N, on a par with Agreement [Agree] for Inflection (Infl) and verbs (V). In line with Pollock's (1989) theory that strong Agree features can attract full verbs (as in French), while weak Agree features of Infl can only attract auxiliaries (as in English), I propose that, in MC, D and N have matching strong Arg features that must be checked via movement in the syntax. In languages whose nominals have strong Arg features, referential N can raise and substitute into D, in a move analogous to that proposed by Longobardi (1994, 2003) for proper nouns in Romance.

The shift in nominal parameters from weak Arg in French to strong Arg in MC was triggered by the loss of the French determiners, which resulted in the occurrence of bare nominal arguments. These 'bare' nouns were interpreted as DPs, i.e. either null D + N, or N in the D position. I argue that both are attested in MC. Whilst bare mass nouns can occur in any argument position without D, singular definite count nouns require the specificity marker *la* in subject position. The differential behaviour of count and mass nouns is attributed to the number feature which must be checked for count nouns. A count N raises to Num^0, where it is interpreted as a cardinality predicate. When the NP is [+definite], the null definite determiner projects and selects a NumP. The specificity marker surfaces as a 'last resort' to licence the null determiner in some syntactic environments. I return to how the various interpretations are derived in Section 5.

3. Semantic definitions

3.1 Definiteness

Within the framework of both the Familiarity theories of definiteness (Jespersen 1933; Christophersen 1939; Karttunen 1971; Heim 1983, 1988) and the quantificational theories of definiteness (Russell 1905; Hawkins 1978) the contrast between indefinite and definite noun phrases relates to the notion of 'identifiability'. Jespersen (1933) Christophersen (1939) classified definite descriptions in terms of the contexts in which objects are referred to, namely, *explicit contextual basis*, *implicit contextual basis* and *situational basis*. Hawkins (1978) builds on their work, and identifies eight usage types of the definite article, ranging from the most familiar, which is 'direct anaphora' to 'unfamiliarity uses'.

In (4), for example, an 'unfamiliar', or new referent is introduced in the discourse by an indefinite NP, and (5) is the second mention of the referent. I provide MC and French translations in line 2 and 3 respectively:

(4) Fred was discussing an interesting book in his class. (Hawkins 1978: 86)
Fred ti pe diskit **enn liv** *interesan dan so klas.* MC
Fred discutait d'un livre intéressant dans sa classe. French

(5) I went to discuss *the book* with him afterwards. (Hawkins 1978: 86)
Mo'n al diskit **liv la** *ek li apre.* MC
J'ai été discuter *du livre* avec lui après. French

In (5) 'the book' is understood as referring to the same referent as the preceding indefinite description, and is part of a singleton set. We have here a case of direct anaphora, or a [+specific] [+definite] noun phrase. While English and French use definite determiners, MC has the post-nominal specificity marker *la*.

Other 'familiar' uses of definite descriptions include unique nouns, such as 'the sun', 'the moon', or referents that are shared knowledge in a particular universe of discourse, e.g. 'The Queen of England', 'The Post Office'. In all these cases, MC uses bare nouns: *later, lalin, larenn Langleter, lapost*, respectively.

Strawson (1950) and Donnellan (1966) differentiate between two main uses of definite descriptions: the referential (or identifying) use, and the attributive (or denoting) use. French and English use a definite article with all definite descriptions, regardless of whether they serve to refer or simply to denote. In the latter cases, it could be argued, as suggested by Lyons, that "*the* is not lexically specified as definite – it is a minimal Det with no semantic content, which acts as a semantically empty filler of the

DP specifier in the absence of any other occupant" (1994: 29, emphasis in original). MC has no such overt 'expletive' determiner.

3.2 Specificity

Following Ishane and Puskás (2001), Von Heusinger (2002) and Ionin (2006), I assume definiteness and specificity to comprise different categories of meaning, defined as follows:

(6) a. Definiteness: selects one object in the class of possible objects
 b. Specificity: relates to pre-established elements in the discourse
 (Ishane and Puskás 2001: 40)

This view is share by Pesetsky (1987) who coins the term *d-linking* (discourse linking) to define the phenomenon of specificity. In current literature, however, the feature specificity has more commonly been associated with indefinites when these occur as complements of opacity inducing predicates. For example, English 'a/an', French *un/une* and MC *enn* respectively can be ambiguous between [±specific] readings, as in:

(7) a. When you see *a dog*, are you frightened? (non-specific)
 b. When you saw *a dog*, were you frightened? (specific)
 (Bickerton 1981: 130)

In (7a) *a dog* denotes a type of individual, whilst *a dog* in (7b) has a presupposition of existence. Note, however, that *a dog* can be understood as non-specific if the past tense is taken as habitual in the past, but it is [+specific] in a reading, describing a punctual event.

The non-specific and specific readings correspond to what Quine (1960) termed 'opaque' and 'transparent' readings, and what Fodor & Sag (1982) define as an 'existential' (quantificational) and a 'referential' reading, respectively. A specific noun phrase refers to a particular individual, while a non-specific noun phrase simply denotes a class of objects, and by extension may refer to any individual fitting the description denoted by the NP.

3.2.1 'Noteworthy' specific indefinites

Ionin (2006) identifies two fundamental properties of specificity as expressed by indefinite *this*, namely the speaker's intent to refer and the concept of noteworthy property. The use of indefinite *this* in contrast to the indefinite article *a* in the case of a 'noteworthy' referent and as a trigger for additional information was also noted by Givon (1978) and Perlman (1969).

In the case of newly introduced, 'noteworthy' referents which will become the subject of ongoing discourse, MC uses *sa ... la*, English uses the proximate demonstrative *this*, and French uses the neutral *ce/cet(te)/ces* (without the demonstrative reinforcers *ci* or *là*).

3.2.2 Specific indefinites vs. specific definites

The contrast between specific and non-specific indefinites is akin to the contrast between referential and attributive definites respectively. Note, however, that, in the case of indefinites, the feature specificity is associated with a presupposition of existence, and in the case of definites, the feature specificity relates to the discourse. In MC the specificity marker *la* is used to mark only anaphoric definiteness, i.e. to recall a topic from the previous discourse.

3.2.3 Deixis

The feature deixis is expressed by means of demonstratives. Diessel (1999) proposes that "demonstratives might form a class of deictic expressions that belong to the basic vocabulary or every language ... they serve a particular pragmatic function that sets them apart from all other linguistic expressions" (1999: 9). Demonstratives serve a number of pragmatic functions, namely, to point to objects in situational context, and to organize the information flow in the ongoing discourse. When they refer to objects outside the discourse, they have an exophoric use (they are referred to as 'pointers'), and when they serve to track referents in the discourse, they have an endophoric use.

4. Historical data

In this section I look at the ambiguous interpretations of bare nouns in early MC, prior to documenting the occurrences of deictic and quantificational determiners.

4.1 Bare count nouns in early MC

In early MC, the interpretation of bare nouns was generally derived from the context, as shown in the following examples, where I provide French translations in line 4 and modern MC translations in line 5:

(8) *tirez cet homme moi n'a pas vouler la guerre avec **camarade***   (1793)
     pull DEM man 1.SG NEG want DET war with friend
     'Take away this man, I don't want to fight with a friend.'
     'Enlever cet homme de là, je ne veux pas me battre avec un ami.'
     *tir sa bug la mo pale lager ek **(enn) kamwad***   Modern MC

(9) *...remué comme ça disi **chaise***   (Milbert 1812)
     wriggle like this on chair
     '...wriggled like this on the chair'
     '...remué comme ça sur la chaise'
     *buz-buze kumsa lor **sez***   Modern MC

(10) ça   qui   y en a   *lé-zaile*   (Chrestien 1831:73)
     DEM   COMP   have   wing
     'That which has wings.'
     'Celui qui a des ailes.'
     *saki ena **lezel***   Modern MC

(11) *a soir   **loulous**   vine   dansé*   (Baissac 1888:149)
     at night   wolf   come   danse
     'At night the wolves come to dance.'
     'La nuit les loups viennent danser.'
     *aswar **bann lulu** vin danse*   Modern MC

The bare nouns have the following interpretations:

- In (8) *camarade* can be interpreted either as a generic term, used to denote an individual who has the property of being a *camarade*, or it can be a referential indefinite singular NP. In the case of the former, modern MC can have a bare noun, and in the case of the latter the indefinite singular article *enn* is required, as in French.
- In (9) *chaise*, which is referring to an object in the situational context, is [+definite] singular. Modern MC has a bare noun and French requires the definite article *la*.
- In the existential sentence (10) *lé-zaile* is [−definite] plural. Modern MC has a bare noun, while French requires the indefinite plural determiner *des*.
- In (11) where the narrator is referring to a previously mentioned set of *wolves*, *loulous* is [+definite] plural. In modern MC, a bare noun can never be [+definite] plural. For such an interpretation, it must be marked by the plural marker *bann*. French requires the definite plural determiner *les*.

4.2 The deictic markers with count nouns

The process of article incorporation affected only the quantificational determiners, not the demonstratives, which are attested in the earliest texts as prenominal *ça* and post nominal *là*. I argue that *ça* and *là* initially performed a purely exophoric function, and did not start to mark discourse deixis until around 1820, when they started to be analyzed as independent morphemes. Furthermore, the deictic contrast marked by the French deictic particles, proximate *ci*, as in *cet homme ci* ('this man') and distal *là* as in *cet homme là* ('that man') never surfaced in MC, only *là* was used.

4.2.1 *Exophoric deixis: The demonstratives* ça ... là *– 1750 to 1800*

In very early MC, these morphemes seem to pattern exactly as in French in that the demonstrative determiner *ça* precedes the noun, and the demonstrative reinforcer *là* is post nominal. As in French, *là* is initially not used independently of *ça*.

The following sentences were uttered while pointing to referents who were visible in the situation of discourse.[4] I gloss *là* as DEM (for demonstrative), as opposed to SP (for specificity), on the grounds that the marking of discourse deixis with *là* on its own was a later development. Unlike the French demonstratives which inflect for number and gender, MC *ça* is invariable:

(12) ça   blanc là   li   beaucoup malin   (Grant 1749:77)
     DEM white DEM 3.SG much   clever
     'These/those white men are very clever.'[5]
     'Ces blancs là sont très malins.'

(13) Moi   voulé baiser   ça   négresse là.   (1777)
     1.SG want make love DEM negress DEM
     'I want to make love to **this/that** negress.'
     'Je voulais faire l'amour avec **cette** négresse ci/là.'

4.2.2 *Ça without là – 1820 onwards*

Pre-nominal *ça* starts to be used on its own around 1820 and initially occurs only with count nouns, e.g.:

(14) ça   bonne-anné qui   passé   (Chrestien 1822:61)
     DEM year   COMP pass
     'That year that passed.'
     '**Cette** année qui est passée.'

(15) Maziné ça   grand lè Roi!*[6]*   (Vicars 1830:18)
     Imagine DEM great   king
     '(I) picture that great king.'
     '(J')imagine ce grand roi.'

---

4. The following is an extract from a letter written by Grant, Baron de Vaux (1749): "...they will direct their hand to the point where it [Madagascar] lies and exclaim, in their corrupted French, *ça blanc là li beaucoup malin; li couri beaucoup dans la mer là haut; mais Madagascar li là*", reproduced in Baker and Fon Sing (2007:3, emphasis in original). The 3SG pronoun *li* was used as a resumptive pronoun with both singular and plural subjects (Guillemin 2007). Example (2) is from the 'Affaire du Chevalier de la Poëze', which reports an altercation between the Chevalier and a black man who was bothering a certain 'negress', presumably visible to both individuals in the situation of discourse.

5. Baker notes: "it would appear that the slave was probably referring to the crew of the ship collectively in which case *ça blanc là* and the first two examples of *li* would all be plural" (Baker and Fon Sing 2007:4, italics in original).

6. The speaker is referring to God.

The omission of *ça* in (14) and (15) would yield indefinite plural NPs, namely, 'years that have passed' and 'great kings'. Such uses of *sa* without *la* are ungrammatical in modern MC, where post nominal *la* must be used, as shown in (16a) and (16b):

(16) a. *sa banane ki pase la* (The/that year that passed)
     b. *Mo mazin sa gran lerwa la* (I imagine that great king)

4.2.3 *The specificity marker* là – *1820 onwards*[7]

While in French the demonstrative reinforcer *là* cannot be used independently of the demonstratives *ce/ces*, this morpheme starts to be used on its own in MC around 1820. It serves to mark anaphoric definiteness (or specificity), as in (17) and (18), where both *Torti* and *coq* have discourse antecedents:

(17) Et   Torti   *là*   touzour   marcé   (Freycinet 1827: 105)
     and tortoise SP still   walk
     'And **the** tortoise keeps walking.'
     'Et **la** tortue marche toujours.'

(18) Coq   *là*   répondé li   (Chrestien 1831: 73)
     rooster SP answer 3.SG
     'The rooster answers him.'
     'Le coq lui répond.'

Note that when *là* is used without *ça*, it forces a singular reading of the NP – both *Torti* in (17) and *Coq* in (18) are singular and specific.

4.2.4 *A number feature in* ça *and* là?

When *là* is used in conjunction with *ça*, the NPs are either singular or plural, as shown in the following examples, where their interpretation is derived from the context. In (19) reference is being made to one previously mentioned *lé-rat*, and in (20) the speaker is referring to a large number of previously mentioned *di-zefs*:

(19) Et   ça   lé-rat   là   n'apas   bête!   (Chrestien 1831b: 70)
     and DEM rat   SP NEG   stupid
     'And that rat is not stupid!'
     'Et ce rat là n'est pas bête!'
     E sa lera la napa bet   Modern MC

(20) a soir   ça   di-zefs   là   fini   vini   dés-cents   (Chrestien 1831b: 67)
     P night DEM egg   DEM ASP become two-hundred
     '(By) night time **those** eggs had multiplied into two hundred.'

---

7. Freycinet (1827) comprises materials collected in 1818, hence the date '1820 onwards'.

'(Arrivé) le soir, **ces** oeufs (**là**) étaient deux cent.'
*aswar **sa bann** dizef **la** fin vin de san* Modern MC

The omission of *ça* in (20) would yield a singular NP 'that egg'. There would be no ambiguity in modern MC with regard to a [±plural] interpretation, as *bann* would be used with a plural NP as shown in the last line of the example. The plural marker is not attested until the mid 1880's. The first written example of *bann* is found in Anderson (1885) where it has the form *band*.

4.3 Bare mass nouns in early MC

The rare occurrence of deictic markers with mass nouns in the first half the 19th century is notable on two counts. It can mean either that both *ça* and *là* were associated with a number feature in very early MC, or that the denotation of mass nouns made it possible for them to derive [±definite] and [±specific] interpretations without overt modifiers. Examples follow:

(21) *Pour li   gagné **di lait** ein' maman cèvr'* ...   (Lolliot 1855: 134)
       for 3.SG get   milk   a   mother goat ...
      'To get milk, a nanny-goat ...'
      'Pour avoir du lait une chèvre ...'

(22) *Dans ein zoli   l'endroit à còt' **di l'eau** bien claire* (Lolliot 1855: 128)
       in   a   pretty spot   where   water   very clear
      'In a pretty spot where the water is very clear.'
      'Dans un joli endroit où l'eau est bien claire.'

(23) *Li   vide **dileau** làhaut **café***   (Baissac 1880: 142)
       3.SG pour water   on   coffee
      'She pours the water on the coffee.'
      'Elle verse l'eau sur le café.'

- In (21), the bare noun *di lait*, which is a first mention, is [−definite].
- In (22) the speaker is referring to a known body (mass) of water and the NP is [+definite], but not specific (it does not have a discourse antecedent).
- In (23) both *dileau* and *café* are referential NPs that have discourse antecedents.

Whatever the interpretation of mass nouns in the first half of the 19th century, their contrasting features were not overtly marked, and their interpretation was simply derived from the context – they were [+definite] if they had a discourse antecedent, and [−definite] otherwise.

4.4 Use of deictic markers with mass nouns – 1850 onwards

The first occurrence of the deictic markers *sa ... la* with a mass noun is the following:

(24) li   trouve **sa**   **la** farine maille **la**   (de la Butte 1850:122)
      3.SG find   DEM   flour   corn   SP
      'He finds that corn flour.'
      'Il trouve cette farine de maïs (là).'

The first occurrence of *ça* on its own with a mass noun is dated 5 years later:

(25) To   conné **ça**   di vin qui   rend' toi si malin   (Lolliot 1855:147)
      2.SG know DEM   wine   COMP make 2.SG so clever
      'You know that wine that makes you so clever.'
      'Tu connais ce vin qui te rend si malin.'

And, as far as I can ascertain, the first occurrence of *là* on its own with a mass noun is dated 1888, some 30 years after the use of *ça* on its own with a mass noun:

(26) dileau **là**   pour baingné   (Baissac 1888:25)
      water SP   for   bath
      'That water is for bathing.'
      'Cette eau-là c'est pour le bain.'   (Baissac 1888:24)

If these morphemes were, at any stage of the genesis of MC, associated with a number feature, this was no longer the case by the end of the 19th century, when the demonstrative particles *ça* and *la* served to mark deixis and specificity on both count and mass nouns. This did not happen, however, until the late 1880's, following the grammaticalization of the quantificational determiners.

4.5 The quantificational determiners

4.5.1 *The indefinite singular article* enn – *1820 onwards*

The first occurrence of the indefinite singular article *enn* (*enne, eine, ène*, in early MC) is dated 1818. It may well have been used prior to this date, but it is not possible to know for certain, given the relatively small 18th century MC corpus. Evidence that it was not used in very early MC is the fact that it is not attested in Pitot (1805). Modern MC translations in the last line of the following examples serve as a comparison with very early MC:

(27) mô   saclave la guerre   (Pitot 1805:82)
      1.SG slave   war
      'I am a war slave.'
      'Je suis un esclave de la guerre.'
      Mo **enn** esklav lager   Modern MC

In predicative constructions with nominal predicates, modern MC, like French, has bare nouns only when the noun denotes a role or profession, otherwise, the indefinite singular article is required, as in (28):[8]

(28) ça   ti   éne iève!   (Baissac 1888: 5)
     that PST   a   hare
     'That was a hare!'
     'C'était un lièvre!'
     sa ti enn liev (sa)[9]   Modern MC

In the following example, the bare noun *femme* is pragmatically interpreted as singular, but in this existential construction, modern MC requires the indefinite singular article *enn* for a singular reading, as shown:

(29) vous   yena **femme**, oubien vous   tout cèle?   (Pitot 1805: 81)
     2.SG.F have wife   or   2SG.F   all alone
     Mo   yena **femme**.
     1.SG have wife
     'Do you have a wife, or are you on your own? I have a wife.'
     'Est-ce que vous avez une femme, ou est-ce que vous êtes seul? J'ai une femme.'
     *U ena **enn fam** ubyen u tu sel? Mo ena **enn fam***   Modern MC

Although bare count nouns can have a singular generic reading in opaque contexts (as with *camarade* in (8)), the default interpretation for bare nouns in existential constructions is [−definite] plural, e.g.:

(30) té   iéna   **vavangues, papayes, cocos,   mambolos, zanblongues**
     PST   have   vavangue   pawpaw   coconut   mambolo   jambolana
     'There were vavangues, pawpaws, coconuts, mambolos, jambolanas.'
     'Il y avait des vavangues, des papayes, des cocos, des mambolos, des jamblongs.'   (Baissac 1880: 137–138)

---

8. In modern MC, bare nominal predicates are used only for nouns denoting roles or profession. When the predicate is a complex NP, the indefinite article is required, and the use of *li* is optional as shown:

(1) a. *Pol   dokter*   b. *Pol   (li)   **enn** dokter lopital   sivil*
        Paul doctor   Paul 3.SG   a   doctor hospital public
        Paul is **a** doctor   Paul is **a** doctor from the public hospital
        Paul est médecin   Paul est **un** médecin de l'hôpital civil

9. Clause final *sa* ('that', Fr. *ça*) functions like a declarative particle. It can be translated roughly as 'indeed!'.

For a singular reading in an existential construction *enn* must be used, e.g. *Ti ena enn vavang, enn papay*, etc. ('There was a/one vavangue, a/one pawpaw', etc.).

From the time that it is first used, *enne/eine/enn* etc. has served to unambiguously mark the NP that it modifies as singular and [–definite], and, like the indefinite singular article in English and French, it serves to introduce a new referent in the discourse:

(31)   **Ein' torti**   avec lièvre été voulé parié   (Freycinet 1827: 104)
      a   tortoise with hare PST want bet
      'A tortoise wanted to bet with Hare/a hare/the hare/hares.'
      'Une tortue voulait parier avec Lièvre/un lièvre/le lièvre/des lièvres.'
      Enn torti ti ule parye ek (enn) lyev   Modern MC

Note that the unmarked count noun *lièvre* in (31), at first mention, is ambiguous between a definite singular NP, or a categorial term simply denoting an individual who has the property of being a *lièvre*. If reference was being made to a known character in the story, *lièvre* would be singular and definite, and would function like a proper noun. In this case, the bare noun form could also be used in English and French, namely, 'Hare' and *Lièvre* respectively.

4.5.2 *The plural marker* bann – *1885 onwards*

The first occurrence of *band* from the French lexical *bande* (group) as a marker of plurality occurs in Anderson's (1885) translation of the Bible from French into MC. Examples follow, where I provide the original text from the Bible in both English and French:

(32)   **band** cef   prétr avec zans   pharizien   (Anderson 1885: 19)
      PL   chief priest with people pharisee
      'The chief priests and the Pharisees.'
      '**Les** grands prêtres et **les** pharisiens.' (L'Evangile s. S. Matthieu Ch. 21, v. 45)

(33)   *éne dan*   **band** *profet*   (Anderson 1885: 14)
      one among PL   prophets
      'One of the prophets.'
      'Un **des** prophètes.'   (L'Evangile s. S. Matthieu Ch. 16, v. 4)

Note that the French determiners *les* and *des* conflate [±definiteness] and number marking. MC *bann* serves purely to mark the plural and is unspecified for the feature Definiteness, as shown by its co-occurrence with demonstratives:

(34)   *Namcouticouti qui té faire vous tout ça* **bande** *malices là*
      Namcouticouti who PST make you all   DEM PL   mischief SP
      'It is Namcouticouti who has played all these tricks on you.'
                                                                        (Baissac 1888: 107)
      C'est Namcouticouti qui vous a fait tous ces tours-là   (Baissac 1888: 106)

The co-occurrence of the demonstratives *sa ... la* with the plural marker *band* as in (34) coincides with the use of the demonstratives with mass nouns. This happens in the late 19th century, and represents the final stage of their grammaticalization.

5. The analysis

By the end of the 19th century, an effective and economical determiner system had emerged in MC to mark the semantic contrasts of [±definiteness], [±specificity] and number, but modern MC continues to admit bare nouns in argument positions, as illustrated in Tables 2 and 3 for count and mass nouns respectively.

Table 2. Marking [±definiteness] and [±specificity] on count nouns

		Count nouns			
		[−def] [−spec]	[−def] [+spec]	[+def] [−spec]	[+def] [+spec]
sg	MC	N enn +N	enn + N / sa + N + la	N	(sa) + N + la
	Fr	masc.: un + N fem.: une + N	masc.: un + N / ce + N fem.: une + N / cette + N	masc.: le + N fem.: la + N	masc.: le + N/ ce + N + (ci/là) fem.: la + N/ cette + N + (ci/là)
	Eng	a/an + N	a/an + N/ this + N	the + pl N	the/this/that + N
pl	MC	N	sa + bann + N + la	N bann + N	(sa) + bann + N + la
	Fr	des + pl N	des + pl N / ces + N + pl N	les + pl N	les + pl N/ ces + pl N + (ci/là)
	Eng	pl N	pl N / these + pl N	the + pl N	the/these/those + pl N

Table 3. Marking [±definiteness] and [±specificity] on mass nouns

	Mass nouns			
	[−def] [−spec]	[−def] [+spec]	[+def] [−spec]	[+def] [+spec]
MC	N	N sa + N + la	N	(sa) + N + la
Fr	masc.: du + N fem.: de la + N	masc.: du + N/ ce/cet + N fem.: de la + N/ cette + N	masc.: le + N/ fem.: la + N	masc.: le + N/ ce/cet + N + (ci/là) fem.: la + N/ cette + N + (ci/là)
Eng	N	N this + N	the + N	the/that + N

MC bare count and mass nouns share some of the distributional properties of English bare plurals and mass nouns, but there are some significant differences between them, namely:

- MC bare nouns can be [−definite] [±specific] or [±definite] [−specific]. When a bare count noun is definite, it is always singular.
- English bare plurals and bare mass nouns can only be [−definite] [±specific].
- While English bare plurals comprise N + plural morphology, MC bare count nouns are strictly bare and yet have a default plural interpretation (the default being the unmarked indefinite).

Both Carlson (1978) Chierchia (1998a) argue that English bare plurals are not quantified noun phrases, i.e. there is no phonologically null definite determiner quantifying over the noun. They can function as arguments because they are argumental kind-denoting terms. On the grounds of similarities between English bare plurals and MC bare nouns, I propose that, in their base denotation, MC nouns are argumental, kind-denoting nouns.

5.1 The differential behaviour of MC count and mass nouns

When they occur with individual level predicates, bare MC nouns, like English bare plurals and bare mass nouns derive kind denotations, e.g.:[10]

(35) a. *Dodo napli existe*
 dodo NEG exist
 'Dodos are extinct.'
 'Le dodo n'existe plus.'

b. *Diven bon pu lasante*
 wine good for health
 '**Wine** is good for health.'
 'Le vin est bon pour la santé.'

When they occur with stage level predicates, which select 'instances' of the kind as opposed to the kind itself, MC admits bare mass nouns, but not bare count nouns in subject position, as shown in (36a) and (36b) respectively, where * denotes ungrammaticality. Note that English requires a definite determiner:

(36) a. *Diven lor latab*
 wine on table
 'The wine is on the table.'
 'Le vin est sur la table.'

b. **Dodo gagn fem*
 dodo have hunger
 '≠ Dodos are hungry.'
 '≠ The dodo is hungry.'

---

10. The terms 'individual' and 'stage' level predicates were coined by Carlson (1978). Individual level predicates, that express a permanent property of an individual select kind-denoting terms as subject, while stage level predicates that express a temporary property of the subject select a 'stage' or an 'instance' of the individual, i.e. an existentially quantified NP.

In the case of a common count noun (i.e. one which does not function as a proper noun or unique noun), MC requires the specificity marker *la* in subject position:

(37) *Dodo la gagn fem*
 dodo SP have hunger
 'The/that dodo is hungry.'
 'Le/ce dodo a faim.'

The differential behaviour of count and mass nouns is attributed to the number or [+count] feature which must be checked for common count nouns.

Note however, that the bare count noun *latab* in (36a), which is in an internal argument position, does not require *la* for a [+definite] singular reading. This subject-object asymmetry provides evidence for the occurrence of a null definite determiner which must project with definite singular common count nouns in some syntactic environments.

5.2 Kind-denoting nouns in generic contexts

Longobardi observes that: "In order to refer to a kind ..., a noun must head the N projections at S-Structure" (1994: 637). However, in a generic context, the NP is [+definite] on account of being universally quantified. Both kind-denoting count and mass nouns raise and substitute into Def^0 at LF, as shown in (38).

Kind terms refer to the genus and not to instances of the kind, consequently, in a generic context, count nouns pattern like mass nouns and do not check their number feature.

(38)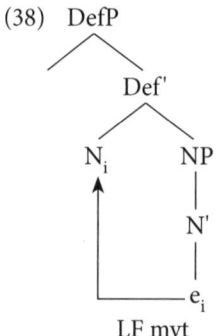
 LF mvt

In an episodic context, as in (36a), where the subject refers to an instance of a kind, mass N raises into Def^0 overtly, a move triggered by the strong Arg features of both D and N. A bare [+definite] mass noun is a DP, i.e. N in the D position.

5.3 The number argument

When reference is made to an 'instance' of a kind, a count noun raises to Num^0 where it is converted into a cardinality predicate. As such, it cannot function as an argument without D. The [+definite] feature of the NP is attributed to null the definite determiner which selects a NumP, as shown:

(39)

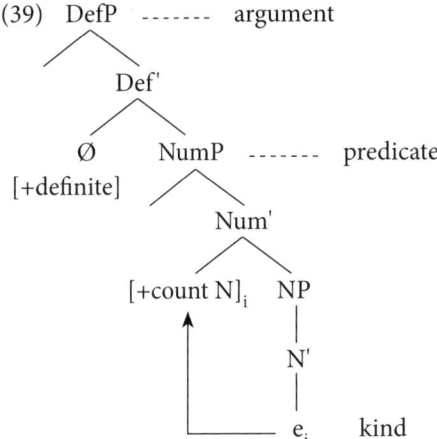

Thus a seemingly 'bare' definite common count noun comprises null D + N.

5.4 Licensing null D

The MC null definite determiner is an 'empty category' (ec), and ec's are subject to certain licensing conditions, namely government by an overt lexical head (Chomsky 1986; Longobardi 1994; Rizzi 1997; Chierchia 1998a; Carlson 1999). This condition is fulfilled when the ec occurs in an internal argument position, e.g. in object position, where it is governed by an overt verb or preposition, but there is no overt lexical head that can govern null D in subject position. In this case, the specificity marker *la* surfaces as a 'last resort' to license the ec. It has strong features which force phrasal movement of DefP to its specifier, deriving the DP final position of *la* as shown:

(40)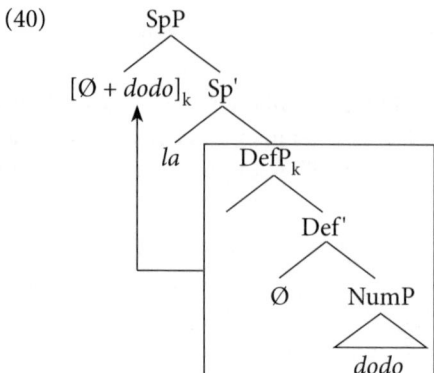

In subject position, the specificity marker is inserted not simply for the semantic function of marking anaphoric definiteness, but for the morpho-syntactic requirement of licensing an ec.

5.5 Deriving instances of the kind – The function of *enn* and *bann*

The fact that MC bare count nouns have a default plural interpretation begs the question; Why does the language need a plural marker?

MC nouns come out of the lexicon as kind-denoting terms, and the function of both the singular indefinite article *enn* and the plural marker *bann* is to assign existential quantification over instances of the kind. Singular *enn* denotes one instance of the kind, and *bann* denotes multiple instances of the kind. *Bann* is simply the lexical realization of the feature [+plural] that agrees with the noun in Num^0. It is in complementary distribution with numerals, and like the indefinite singular article *enn*, it is merged in Spec,NumP. It is roughly equivalent in meaning to English 'some' when used with plural nouns, e.g.:

(41) *Ena   enn / bann dodo dan mize*
 have a/one some dodo in   museum
 'There is a/one dodo in the museum/There are some dodos in the museum.'
 'Il y a un dodo dans le musée/Il y a des/quelques dodos dans le musée.'

Bann + N cannot have a generic interpretation, e.g.:

(42) **Bann dodo napli existe*
  PL   dodo NEG exist
  *Some/the dodos are extinct

5.6 The demonstratives

I suggested in Section 4.2.4 that the demonstratives *ça ... là* in early MC initially occurred only with count nouns and that they may have been associated with a number feature. A more likely explanation is that, prior to the reanalysis of *là/la* as a specificity marker, the occurrence of *ça/sa* was a syntactic requirement to license the phonologically null definite determiner, assuming, as proposed by Giusti (1997), that "Once Spec,DP is filled with an element that has enough features to license the whole projection, no article needs to be inserted" (1997: 108).

The demonstrative *ça/sa* was merged in Spec,DemP and raised to Spec,DefP to license the ec, shown:

(43)
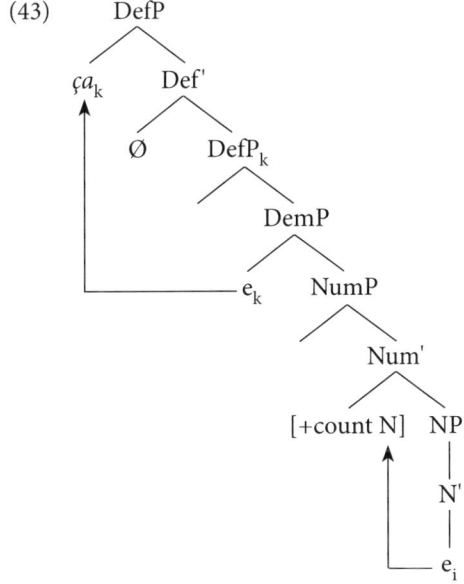

The licensing functions of *ça* and *là* in early MC were not required with mass nouns, which were able to raise into Def⁰ for a definite interpretation (as in modern MC). Following the grammaticalization of *la* as a marker of specificity, which serves to license the null definite determiner, *sa* was no longer required to licence the null D. It weakened into a purely deictic determiner, and started occurring with both count and mass nouns.[11]

---

[11]. The use of *sa* without *là* in early MC is very likely the source of *sa* in Seselwa (Seychellois Creole), where it functions both as definite determiner and demonstrative. The Specificity marker *la* is not attested in Seselwa. The two creoles diverged following the abolition of slavery in 1835, when large numbers of MC-speaking slaves were sent to the Seychelles. The greater presence of the French in Mauritius may have motivated the reanalysis of *là* as a Specificity marker, while *ça* developed into the definite determiner and demonstrative in Seselwa.

6. Motivation for change from French to Creole

The process of article incorporation early in the genesis of MC may have been a case of what Lumsden (1999) describes as 'functional category ellipsis', which is typical of incomplete second language acquisition. Alternatively, the failure to recognize the function of the French determiners may have been motivated by substrate influence. Gungbe admits bare nouns which can have singular, plural or kind denotations (Aboh p.c. 2008).

Whatever triggered the process of article incorporation, the resulting occurrence of bare nouns in argument positions in early MC triggered parametric shift in noun denotation, from predicative in French, to argumental in MC. Chierchia (1998b) claims that the acquisition of a particular setting for a language is made on the basis of positive evidence alone: "In particular, it seems plausible to maintain that the child assumes that the unmarked setting is [+arg, −pred], which is the most restrictive and entails, e.g., the absence of plural marking, the obligatory presence of classifiers with numerals and the absence of articles" (1998b: 94). Encountering plural morphology or articles, on the other hand, would prompt the child to switch to a predicative setting for nominals. Speakers of early MC encountered neither articles, nor plural morphology, and reverted to the unmarked setting for N, the lowest denomination, that of a kind.[12]

The determiner system which emerged over the ensuing 150 years resulted in an effective and economical system which provides the means to express without redundancy the semantic contrasts that could not be expressed immediately following the loss of the French determiners. The singular indefinite article *enn* and the plural marker *bann* are quantificational devices that serve to derive instances of kind-denoting count nouns. The definite determiner is a phonologically null element which projects only for count nouns that must check their number feature, a move which converts them into cardinality predicates. Mass nouns do not need to check a number feature, and, when [+definite] simply raise into Def^0. The specificity marker *la* serves both the pragmatic function of recalling a topic from the previous discourse, and the morphosyntactic function of licensing the null definite determiner in some syntactic environments.

The DP final position of *la* may be attributed to substrate influence. Aboh notes that the marking of specificity in Gungbe "requires fronting of the noun phrase to the left of a designated specificity marker within the determiner phrase" (2006: 222). It could also be due to the fact that the checking of the feature specificity necessarily involves operator movement to a specifier position (see Campbell 1996). Such movement must be overt in MC to license the null determiner, while the checking of the feature specificity can be delayed to LF in both English and French because these

---

12. They did not analyze the French determiners as independent morphemes, and they would not have encountered plural morphology, given that the final s is not normally phonetically realized with French plural nouns.

languages have overt definite articles. The French deictic locative particle *là*, which is post nominal and already encodes deixis, was an obvious candidate for reanalysis as a specificity marker in a 'competition and selection' process which arises in a language contact situation (see Mufwene 2001).

Whatever motivation for the changes in the determiner system from French to creole, be they superstrate or substrate, these changes ultimately complied with universal principles of grammar. They support Chomsky's (1995) minimalist view of language as an economical system, and provide evidence for the universality of semantic features like definiteness, deixis, specificity and number, which must find expression in natural language.

Abbreviations

1.SG	–	1st person singular pronoun	GQ	–	Generalized Quantifier
			Infl	–	Inflection
2.SG.F	–	2nd person singular, Formal form of address	MC	–	Mauritian Creole
			N	–	Noun
Agree	–	Agreement	NEG	–	Negation
Arg	–	Argumental	NP	–	Noun Phrase
ASP	–	Aspect	Num	–	Number
CP	–	Complementizer Phrase	NumP	–	Number Phrase
COMP	–	Complementizer	pl/PL	–	Plural
D	–	Determiner	POSS	–	Possessive
DefP	–	Definiteness Phras	pred	–	Predicative
DEM	–	Demonstrative	PST	–	Past tense
DemP	–	Demonstrative Phrase	sg/SG	–	singular
DefP	–	Definiteness Phrase	SP	–	Specificity
DP	–	Determiner Phrase	Spec	–	Specifier
ec	–	empty category	SpP	–	Specificity Phrase
Eng	–	English	UG	–	Universal Grammar
Fr	–	French	V	–	Verb

References

1777. Affaire du chevalier de la poëze. In *Textes créoles anciens: La Réunion et Ile Maurice. Comparaison et essai d'analyse*, Robert Chaudenson (ed). Hamburg: Helmut Buske.
1793. Mauritius archives, JB 78. In *The Making of Mauritian Creole*, Philip Baker & Guillaume Fon Sing (eds). London: University of Westminster Press.
Aboh, Enoch O. 2004. *The Morpho-syntax of Complement-head Sequences: Clause Structure and Word Order Patterns in Kwa*. Oxford: OUP.

Aboh, Enoch O. 2006. The role of the syntax-semantics interface in language transfer. In *L2 Acquisition and Creole Genesis*, Claire Lefebvre, Lydia White & Christine Jourdan (eds), 221–252. Amsterdam: John Benjamins.

Anderson, Samuel. 1885. *L'Evangile sélon S. Matthié (dan langaz créol Maurice). The Gospel according to St Matthew (in Mauritian creole)*. London: British and Foreign Bible Society.

Baissac, Charles. 1880. *Etude sur le patois créole Mauricien*. Nancy: Imprimerie Berger Levrault.

Baissac, Charles. 1880. Zistoire éne çatte qui té éna botes. In *Textes créoles anciens: La Réunion et Ile Maurice. Comparaison et essai d'analyse*, Robert Chaudenson (ed.), 134–141. Hamburg: Helmut Buske.

Baissac, Charles. 1888. *Le folk-lore de l'Ile Maurice*, Vol. XXVII: *Littératures populaires de toutes les nations*. Paris: G. P. Maisonneuve & Larose.

Baker, Philip. 1982. On the origins of the first Mauritians and of the creole language of their descendants: A refutation of Chaudenson's 'Bourbonnais' theory. In *Isle de France Creole*, Philip Baker & Chris Corne (eds), 131–259. Ann Arbor MI: Karoma.

Baker, Philip. 1984. Agglutinated French articles in creole French: Their evolutionary significance. *Te Reo: Journal of the Linguistic Society of New Zealand* 27: 89–129.

Baker, Philip & Fon Sing, Guillaume (eds). 2007. *The Making of Mauritian Creole* [*Westminster Creolistics Series* 9]. London: University of Westminster Press.

Baker, Philip & Corne, Chris. 1982. *Isle de France Creole: Affinities and Origins*. Ann Arbor MI: Karoma.

Bernstein, Judy B. 1997. Demonstratives and reinforcers in Romance and Germanic languages. *Lingua* 102: 87–113.

Bickerton, Derek. 1981. *Roots of Language*. Ann Arbor MI: Karoma.

Barwise, Jon & Cooper, Robin. 1981. Generalized quantifiers and natural language. *Linguistics and Philosophy* 4: 159–219.

Campbell, Richard. 1996. Specificity operators in SpecDP. *Studia Linguistica* 50: 161–188.

Carlson, Gregory. 1978. *Reference to Kinds in English*. Bloomington IN: Indiana University Linguistics Club.

Chaudenson, Robert. 1981. *Textes créoles anciens: La Réunion et Ile Maurice. Comparaison et essai d'analyse*. Hamburg: Helmut Buske.

Chierchia, Gennaro. 1998a. Reference to kinds across languages. *Natural Language Semantics* 6: 339–405.

Chierchia, Gennaro. 1998b. Plurality of mass nouns and the notion of 'semantic parameter'. In *Events and Grammar*, Susan Rothstein (ed.), 53–103. Dordrecht: Kluwer.

Chomsky, Noam. 1986. *Knowledge of Language, its Nature, Origin and Use*. New York NY: Praeger.

Chomsky, Noam. 1995. *The Minimalist Program*. Cambridge MA: The MIT Press.

Chrestien, François. 1822. Essais d'un bobre africain, 1ère édition. In *Panorama de la littérature mauricienne: La production créolophone*, Vol. 1: *Des origines à l'indépendance*. Robert Furlong & V. Ramharai (eds), 47–63. Petite Rivière, Mauritius: TIMAM.

Chrestien, François. 1831. Les essais d'un bobre africain, 2ème édition. In *Panorama de la littérature mauricienne: La production créolophone*, Vol. 1: *Des origines à l'indépendance*, Robert Furlong & V. Ramharai (eds), 63–77. Petite Rivière, Mauritius: TIMAM.

Christophersen, Paul. 1939. *The Articles: A Study of their Theory and Use in English*. Copenhagen: Einar Munksgaard.

de la Butte, Aristide le Père. 1850. Zistoire Moucié Caraba. In *Textes créoles anciens: La Réunion et Ile Maurice. Comparaison et essai d'analyse*, Robert Chaudenson (ed.), 121–124. Hamburg: Buske.

DeGraff, Michel. 1999. *Language Creation and Language Change: Creolization, Diachrony, and Development*. Cambridge MA: The MIT Press.

Diessel, Holger. 1999. *Demonstratives: Form, Function and Grammaticalization* [Typological Studies in Language 42]. Amsterdam: John Benjamins.

Donnellan, Keith S. 1966. Reference and definite descriptions. *The Philosophical Review* 75: 281–304.

L'Evangile selon Saint Matthieu. 1955. In *La Sainte Bible. Traduite en Français sous la direction de l'Ecole Biblique de Jérusalem*, 1455–1503. Paris: Editions du Cerf.

Fodor, Janet Dean & Sag, Ivan A. 1982. Referential and quantificational indefinites. *Linguistics and Philosophy* 5: 355–398.

Freycinet, Louis de. 1827. Voyage autour du monde. In *Textes créoles anciens: La Réunion et Ile Maurice. Comparaison et essai d'analyse*, Robert Chaudenson (ed.), 100–105. Hamburg: Helmut Buske.

Giusti, Giuliana. 1997. The categorial status of determiners. In *The New Comparative Syntax*, Liliane Haegeman (ed.), 95–123. London: Longman.

Givon, Talmy. 1978. Definiteness and referentiality. In *Universals of Human Language*, Vol. 4, Joseph H. Greenberg, Charles A. Ferguson & Edith A. Moravcsik (eds), 291–330. Stanford CA: Stanford University Press.

Grant, Anthony P. 1995. Article agglutination in Creole French: A wider perspective. In *From Contact to Creole and Beyond*, Philip Baker (ed.), 149–176. London: University of Westminster Press.

Grant, Charles Baron. 1749. Lettre de l'Ile de France (juin 1749). In *Textes créoles anciens: La Réunion et Ile Maurice. Comparaison et essai d'analyse*, Robert Chaudenson (ed.). Hamburg: Helmut Buske.

Guillemin, Diana. 2007. The resumptive pronoun *li* in Mauritian Creole. In *The Making of Mauritian Creole*, Philip Baker & Guillaume Fon Sing (eds), 173–196. London: Battlebridge.

Hawkins, John. 1978. *Definiteness and Indefiniteness: A Study in Reference and Grammaticality Prediction*. London: Croom Helm.

Heim, Irene. 1983. File change semantics and the familiarity theory of definiteness. In *Meaning, Use and Interpretation of Language*, Rainer Bauerle, Christoph Schwarze & Arnim von Stechow (eds.), 165–189. Berlin: Walter de Gruyter.

Heim, Irene. 1988. *The Semantics of Definite and Indefinite Noun Phrases*. New York NY: Garland.

Himmelmann, Nikolaus P. 2001. Articles. In *Language Typology and Language Universals*, Martin Haspelmath et al. (eds.), 831–841. Berlin: de Gruyter.

Ionin, Tania. 2006. This is definitely specific: Specificity and Definiteness in article systems. *Natural Language Semantics* 14: 175–234.

Ishane, Tabea & Puskás, Genoveva. 2001. Specific is not definite. *Generative Grammar in Geneva* 2: 39–54.

Jespersen, Otto. 1933. *Essentials of English Grammar*. London: Allen and Unwin.

Karttunen, Lauri Juhani. 1971. *Discourse Referents*. Bloomington IN: Indiana University Linguistics Club.

Lolliot, Pierre. 1855. Poésies créoles. In *Panorama de la littérature mauricienne: La production créolophone*, Vol. 1: *Des origines à l'indépendance*, Robert Furlong & V. Ramharai (eds), 126–152. Petite Rivière, Mauritius: TIMAM.

Longobardi, Giuseppe. 1994. Reference and proper names: A theory of N-movement in syntax and logical form. *Linguistic Inquiry* 25: 609–665.

Longobardi, Giuseppe. 2001. The structure of DPs. In *The Handbook of Contemporary Syntactic Theory*, Mark Baltin & Chris Collins (eds), 562–603. Oxford: Blackwell.

Lumsden, John S. 1999. Language acquisition and creolization. In *Language Creation and Language Change: Creolization, Diachrony, and Development*, Michel DeGraff (ed.), 129–157. Cambridge MA: The MIT Press.

Lyons, Christopher. 1994. Movement in 'NP' and the DP Hypothesis. *Working Papers in Language and Linguistics* 8. Salford: University of Salford, Department of Modern Languages.

Milbert, Jacques Gérard. 1812. Extracts of 'Voyage pittoresque à l'Ile-de-France'. In *Textes créoles anciens: La Réunion et Ile Maurice. Comparaison et essai d'analyse*, Robert Chaudenson (ed.). Hamburg: Helmut Buske.

Milsark, Gary. 1979. *Existential Sentences in English*. New York NY: Garland.

Mufwene, Salikoko S. 2001. *The Ecology of Language Evolution*. Cambridge: CUP.

Perlman, Alan. 1969. 'This' as a third article in American English. *American Speech* 44: 76–80.

Pesetsky, David. 1987. Wh-in-situ: Movement and unselective binding. In *The Representation of (in)Definiteness*, Eric J. Reuland & Alice G. B. ter Meulen (eds.), 98–129. Cambridge MA: The MIT Press.

Pitot, Thomi C. 1805. Quelques observations sur l'ouvrage intitulé 'Voyage à l'Ile de France par un officier du Roi', presenté à la Société d'Emulation de l'Ile de France, le 3 août 1805. In *Textes créoles anciens: La Réunion et Ile Maurice. Comparaison et essai d'analyse*, Robert Chaudenson (ed.), 80–82. Hamburg: Helmut Buske.

Pollock, Jean Yves. 1989. Verb movement, Universal Grammar, and the structure of IP. *Linguistic Inquiry* 20: 365–424.

Quine, Willard V. 1960. *Word and Object*. Cambridge MA: The MIT Press.

Rizzi, Luigi. 1997. The fine structure of the left periphery. In *Elements of Grammar: Handbook in Generative Syntax*, Liliane Haegeman (ed.), 281–337. Dordrecht: Kluwer.

Roodenburg, Jasper. 2004. French bare arguments are not extinct: The case of coordinated bare nouns. *Linguistic Inquiry* 35: 301–313.

Russell, Bertrand. 1905. On denoting. *Mind* 14: 479–493.

Stowell, Tim. 1989. Subjects, Specifiers, and X-Bar theory. In *Alternative Conceptions of Phrase Structure*, Mark Baltin & Anthony S. Kroch (eds), 232–262. Chicago IL: University of Chicago Press.

Strandquist, Rachel Eva. 2005. Article Incorporation in Mauritian Creole. MA dissertation, University of Victoria, Canada.

Strawson, Peter Frederick. 1950. On referring. *Mind* 59: 320–344.

Vicars. 1830. Hymn. In *The Making of Mauritian Creole*, Philip Baker & Guillaume Fon Sing (eds), 18–19. London: University of Westminster Press.

Von Heusinger, Klaus. 2002. Specificity and definiteness in sentence and discourse structure. *Journal of Semantics* 19: 245–274.

Zamparelli, Roberto. 2000. *Layers in the Determiner Phrase*. New York NY: Garland.

Demonstratives in Afrikaans and Cape Dutch Pidgin
A first attempt

Hans den Besten[1]

Afrikaans seems to have lost the Dutch independent demonstrative *dat* 'that' as well as the pronoun *het* 'it' and the attributive element *deze* 'this, these', while independent *dit* 'this' seems to have taken over the functions of *dat* and *het* and while attributive *die* 'that, those' has acquired a proximate reading (Afr. *dié week* 'this week'). In the present paper it is argued, however, that the weak pronoun *het* was bound to disappear anyway, that *dat* only underwent phonological change (so that *dat* and *dit* couldn't be distinguished any longer) and that the changes in the system of attributive demonstratives are due to developments in Cape Dutch Pidgin.

1. Introduction

While personal pronouns in Afrikaans seem to continue a non-standard Dutch system,[2] Afrikaans demonstratives are quite a different ball-game:

a. The Dutch system seems to be inverted:
   a1. afr. *dit* 'it, that' corresponds to du. *dit* '(independent) this'. (However, see below.)
   a2. afr. *dié* 'this, these' corresponds to du. *die* '(non-neuter) that, those'. (However, see below.)

---

1. Linguistics, University of Amsterdam & General Linguistics, Stellenbosch University.

2. However, note that in addition to the Germanic 2nd person pronouns (*jy* '2SG', *julle* '2PL', *u* '2REV') there is a set of auxiliary 2SG pronouns derived from titles such as *Oom* 'Uncle, Sir', *Pa* 'Dad', *Professor* 'Professor', etc.). Corresponding plurals can be formed by means of the associative marker *-hulle* '-them': *Oom-hulle* 'you, uncle/Sir, and others', etc. This kind of plural formation has minimally affected the Germanic pronominal system in that there is an associative plural of *u* '2REV': *u-hulle* '2REV-them'. Cf. den Besten (1996, 2001).

b. Certain Dutch forms seem to have disappeared:[3]
   b1. *dat* '(independent) that',
   b2. *dat* '(attributive, neuter) that'
   b3. *deze* '(attributive, non-neuter) this, these'
   b4. *dit* '(attributive, neuter) this'. (However, see below.)
c. There are new, un-Germanic formations: *hierdie* (lit.) 'here-the/that' [= 'this, these'] and *daardie* (lit.) 'there-the/that' [= 'that, those'].
d. Afrikaans is moving away from the Dutch dichotomous (proximate ~ distal) demonstrative system: *hierdie* 'this, these' ~ *daardie* 'that, those' to a trichotomous system: *hierdie* 'this, these' ~ *daardie* 'that, those' ~ *doerdie* 'yonder'.

The facts are more complex than this in that (a) and part of (b) must be qualified (which will be done below). Note that about everything in (a) through (d) is discussed in the literature.[4] Yet, for most of the 20th century Afrikaans historical linguistics seems to have taken the surprising semantic swap involving *dié* (distal → proximate) and *dit* (proximate → distal) as a fact of history. This partly changed with the publication of Ponelis (1993). Ponelis took things more seriously but this was mainly "thinking on paper": no clear decision is taken, unfortunately. Since there is quite some in-depth literature on (c) and (d),[5] this paper will be devoted to (a) and (b): the origins of *dit* will be discussed in Section 2, potential evidence from Cape Dutch Pidgin (henceforth: CDP) in Section 3, unexpected uses of *dit* in older Khoekhoe Afrikaans and CDP in Section 4, and the origins of *dié* in Section 5. Section 6, finally, will wrap up the results.

2. The origins of *dit*

2.1 Cautioning remarks

As I indicated above, (a) must be qualified and so must (b). Since the present section concerns the independent demonstrative pronoun *dit*, I will restrict my qualifying remarks to (a1) and (b1), which are repeated here for convenience:

a1. Afr. *dit* 'it, that' corresponds to du. *dit* '(independent) this'.
b1. The Dutch form *dat* '(independent) that' seems to have disappeared.

Both statements are slightly imprecise in that afr. *dit* 'it, that' may also mean 'this' under certain circumstances, while *dat* 'that' may still be used in Afrikaans provided it is

---

3. Dutch nouns are neuter or non-neuter in the singular and non-neuter in the plural. Attributive demonstratives vary according to the gender of the noun.
4. See Ponelis (1993: Ch. 8).
5. See den Besten (1989), Ponelis (1993) and Roberge (2001).

in opposition to *dit* – although in the latter case it is not clear to me whether speakers of Afrikaans interpret *dit* as 'this' and *dat* as 'that'. But let us assume they do. In that case the following example is illustrative both of the occasionally proximate reading for *dit*, and of the residual use of du. *dat* 'that':[6]

(1) *Maar **dit** kon nie gedoen word nie en **dat** kon nie*
But this could not done be not and that could not
gedoen word nie
done be not
[i.e. 'we couldn't do anything at all']

However, apart from examples such as (1) it is difficult to imagine a polysemous lexical analysis for afr. *dit*. *Dit* seems to be a third person pronoun, which speakers of Dutch and English – due to the structure of their respective lexicons – have to interpret as *that*, *this* or *it* (in Dutch: *dat*, *dit* and *het*) – meaning differences that speakers of Afrikaans do not seem to have to worry about since there is only one form, *dit*.

However, some caution is required. On the one hand, it is true that a sentence like (2) is ambiguous for a speaker of English or Dutch while a speaker of Afrikaans seems to be perfectly happy with such a construction:

(2) ***Dit** is my biblioteek / suster*
This / That is my library / sister

However, speakers of Afrikaans are able to express the subtle (and often not so subtle) differences between *this* and *that* (du. *dit* and *dat*) by adding either the demonstrative *hierdie* 'this (one)' or the demonstrative *daardie* 'that (one)' to the sentence:[7]

(3) ***Dit** is my {biblioteek / suster}, {hierdie / daardie}*

But, again, this does not show that afr. *dit* is ambiguous. Example (3) only shows that Afrikaans speakers can make the same distinctions as speakers of English or Dutch, while example (2) shows that they don't have to. Furthermore, we already know that the difference between *dit* in the sense of 'it' and *dit* in the sense of 'this/that' is nonexistent. However, non-referential, abstract *dit* may provide counter-evidence, in that it may not be focused or contrastively stressed:

(4) a. *{*DIT / Dit} reënt*
{*THAT / It} rains
b. *{*DIT / Dit} lyk vir my dat hy jou nie verstaan nie*
{*THAT / It} seems to me that he you not understands not

---

6. Cf. the discussion of *dit* in Ponelis (1979: Ch. 23).
7. Cf. Ponelis (1979) and Donaldson (1993).

For the time being I will assume that these facts can be accounted for under a unitary analysis for *dit*. The question now is how this generalized demonstrative pronoun *dit* came to exist.

2.2 Afrikaans linguistics on the origins of *dit*

Donaldson (1993: 127n, 142) assumes that afr. *dit* 'it, that, this' derives from du. *dit* 'this', which seems to be a bit too simplistic. But note that this is a diachronic side-remark in the context of a synchronic description of Afrikaans. However, Ponelis (1993: 169), a diachronic study of Afrikaans, says roughly the same when he is referring to "[t]he conversion of *dit* 'it' from a demonstrative 'this' to a neutral third person pronoun." However, on the preceding page we find: "The demonstrative pronouns *dit* and *dat* were bleached to third-person pronouns *dit/dat* 'it'." He should have added that *dat* would subsequently disappear. But the latter point is elaborated upon in the next chapter from which I quote the following:

> Currently *dat* has been ousted completely by *dit*. Present-day *dit* 'it' may be the continuation of earlier *dit* 'this', the marked demonstrative. If this is so, then it is puzzling that marked *dit* supervened over unmarked *dat*. What seems to have happened, is that the demonstrative proximate-distal opposition between *dit* 'this' and *dat* 'that' was lost when these demonstratives moved into the territory of neutral reference occupied by *het* 'it'. This entailed the loss of marking: as a neutral referential term *dit* was as unmarked as *dat*, and they competed as free variants. As a neutral referential term, the phonologically weaker form with shwa, *dit*, prevailed over the fuller form *dat*. There remains a further possibility: that original *dit* 'this' disappeared and that Afrikaans *dit* is derived not from earlier *dit* 'this' but from *dat* by weakening of [a] to shwa: *dat* > *dit*.
> (Ponelis 1993: 212)[8]

This is the first serious attempt to come to grips with the emergence of the Afrikaans neuter pronoun *dit*. Although more could be said I will restrict myself to the following comments: (a) In view of the structure of the Dutch pronominal paradigm only distal *dat* could have been substituted for *het* (for which see below). Therefore – and for reasons expounded below – Ponelis' "further possibility" must be on the right track. However, most probably du. *dit* did not disappear. Instead, it was absorbed by the new pronominal element *dit* 'it, that' (<du. *dat* 'that'). The remainder of this paper will be devoted to this alternative hypothesis.

---

8. The suggestion that *dit* is [dət] is in accordance with common practice in Afrikaans phonology to represent the neutralized and schwa-like Afrikaans counterpart of Dutch [ɪ] as a schwa. Donaldson (1993: 4) deviates from this doubtful practice by representing the pertinent vowel as [ï].

Table 1. Singular personal pronouns

			Settlers' Dutch			Afrikaans		
			Nom	Obl	Poss	Nom	Obl	Poss
Sg	1	s	ik	mij	mij(n)	ek	my	my
		w	'k	me	me/m'n	–	–	–
	2	s	jij	jou	jouw	jy	jou	jou
		w	je	je	je	–	–	–
	3M	s	hij	hem	zij(n)	hy	hom	sy
		w	-ie	'm	ze/z'n	–	–	–
	3F	s	zij	haar	haar	sy	haar	haar
		w	ze	d'r/'r	d'r/'r	–	–	–
	3N	s	dat	dat	–	dit	dit	–
		w	't/het	't/het	–	–	–	–

2.3 Personal pronouns and afr. *dit*

An important difference between Dutch and Afrikaans concerns the Dutch weak (that is unstressed, enclitic or proclitic) pronouns. These pronominal forms have completely disappeared in Afrikaans. I will illustrate this point by means of the Dutch and Afrikaans singular personal pronouns, for which see Table 1.[9]

All weak forms – except for *-ie* 'he' – involve a schwa, which is either spelled <e> (in open unstressed syllables) or <'> (in closed monosyllables). The apostrophe is necessary because <e> in closed monosyllables stands for [ɛ].[10] However, in actual writing there is a strong tendency to avoid the use of the apostrophe.

Note that an empty slot indicates the absence of some specialized form, not the absence of the pertinent function as such. E.g. afr. *hom* 'him' can be both stressed and unstressed, as in (5a). The sole difference from Dutch is that Dutch also marks this in the segmental structure of the pronoun.

(5) a. *Ek het {HOM / hom} nie gesien nie*   [Afr.]
    b. *Ik heb {HEM / 'm} niet gezien*   [Dutch]
       I have {HIM / him} not seen (not)

However, in written Dutch the difference between weak and strong forms is often neglected – especially if an apostrophe is required to represent the schwa. So *'m* and *(d)'r* are usually written *hem* and *haar* respectively. Nevertheless, it is *'m* and *(d)'r* in

---

9. 3MSG *-ie* may only show up after a subordinator or a finite verb. – Note that the possessive pronouns *mij* and *zij* are non-standard forms which we may assume were part of the dialectal amalgam that was at the basis of Afrikaans. Most probably *hom* was also part of that amalgam.

10. E.g. *pet* 'cap', *ver* 'far', *rem* 'brake'.

the spoken language, although *hem* and *haar* can also be heard, due to spelling pronunciation.

Also note that weak object pronouns may not be topicalized – or, to say it differently: may not appear in Spec,TopP:

(6) {HEM / hem/ *'m} heb ik daar niet gezien. [Dutch]
 {HIM / him / *him} have I there not seen

This observation is relevant for our understanding of what happened to the 3rd person singular neuter.

Let us now consider the 3rd person singular neuter pronoun *het* and its Afrikaans counterpart *dit*. Strictly speaking the Dutch personal pronoun *het* is weak and does not have a strong variant. So, the demonstrative pronoun *dat* 'that' is used instead. Cf. the following examples:

(7) a. Ik wist {'t / het / dat} niet [Dutch]
 I knew {it / it / that} not
 b. {{*'t / *Het} / Dat} wist ik niet[11]
 {{*It / *It} / That} knew I not

Note that [hɛt], written *het*, is a case of spelling pronunciation. It should be *'t*, i.e. [ət]. But the historical form *het* has been preserved in writing in order to avoid the apostrophe as a grapheme for schwa in a closed monosyllable. Furthermore note that the dummy subject is always *het* and never *dat*:

(8) a. {'t / Het / *Dat} is onduidelijk of hij komt [Dutch]
 {It / It / *That} is unclear whether he comes
 b. {'t / Het / *Dat} regent
 {It / It / *That} rains

In Afrikaans, which only has the strong form *dit* 'it, that', *dit* has taken over all functions of the Dutch pronouns *het/'t* and *dat*:

(9) a. Ek het dit nie geweet nie [Afrikaans]
 I have it/that not known not
 b. Dit het ek nie geweet nie
 That have I not known not

(10) a. Dit is [> Dis] nie duidelik of hy kom nie
 It is not clear whether he comes not
 b. Dit reën
 It rains

---

11. Whenever a sentence starts with a word starting with an apostrophe, the capital marking the beginning of a sentence is realized on the first word that does not start with an apostrophe, usually the second word of such a sentence. E.g. *'t Was waar* 'It was true'.

2.4 Where does afr. *dit* come from?

A quick-and-dirty comparison of Dutch and Afrikaans shows that both du. *'t/het* 'it' and du. *dat* 'that' have disappeared from South African Dutch and that du. *dit* 'this' seems to have taken over. The disappearance of *'t/het* is something to be expected: in the protracted history of L2 acquisition of Cape Dutch the strong forms had the best chances to survive. The only thing that is slightly surprising is the fact that the dummy subject *'t/het*, which does not have a strong counterpart, could survive through *dit*. However, this is only surprising for those who regard the change from the Dutch pronominal system to the Afrikaans one as a case of empoverishment. Note that the other dummy subject of Dutch, *er* 'there', has undergone a similar change: *daar*, *er*'s strong counterpart in the functions, and in fact the etymological source for *er*,[12] has taken over all functions of *er*, among which its function as a dummy subject. Cf. Table 2 and the examples in (11) and (12) below.

(11) a. *Waarom wordt er niet meer gelachen?* [Du.]
     b. *Waarom word daar nie meer gelag nie?* [Afr.]
        Why is there not anymore laughed (not)?

(12) a. *Er zijn hier veel bavianen* [Du.]
     b. *Daar is hier baie bobbejane* [Afr.]
        There are here many baboons

Now note that in Afrikaans it is distal *daar* and not proximate *hier* that has taken over the sub-paradigm of the demonstrative locative elements. So why did *dit* 'this' take over in the case of the 3rd person singular neuter pronoun? I would like to suggest the following answer.

Table 2. Locative-like elements[13]

		Settlers' Dutch		Afrikaans	
		Distal	Proxim.	Distal	Proxim.
Dummy	s	–	–	daar	–
Subj.	w	er/d'r/'r	–	–	–
Locatives	s	daar	hier	daar	hier
	w	er/d'r/'r	–	–	–
R-Pronouns	s	daar + P	hier + P	daar + P	hier + P
	w	er/d'r/'r + P	–	–	–

---

12. Note that *er* is another example of apostrophe avoidance. *Er* "should" be *'r* or *d'r*. (i.e [ər] or [dər]). Due to spelling pronunciation *er* is often pronounced [ɛr].

13. Locative element + P stands for P + pronoun with inanimate reference: P + 'it/that' and P + 'this' respectively.

(13) The *Dit/dat* Hypothesis
Afrikaans *dit* 'it, that' does not derive from du. *dit* '(independent) this' but from du. *dat* '(independent) that' – and only secondarily from du. *dit* '(independent) this'.

Note that this hypothesis slightly differs from the idea that appears almost as an afterthought in Ponelis's discussion of the problem – which I repeat here for convenience:

> There remains a further possibility: that original *dit* 'this' disappeared and that Afrikaans *dit* is derived not from earlier *dit* 'this' but from *dat* by weakening of [a] to shwa: *dat* > *dit*. (Ponelis 1993:212)

It is a pity that Ponelis did not work this out in any detail, but it is clear from the text that for Ponelis this was just an alternative hypothesis and not necessarily his main line of thought, whereas the *Dit/dat* Hypothesis is the core idea of the present paper. Before discussing the phonology of this etymology I would like to expound the bonuses provided by the *Dit/dat* Hypothesis.

First of all, by deriving afr. *dit* from du. *dat* we are getting rid of an otherwise strange semantic development.

Secondly, afr. *dis*, a contracted form of *dit is* 'it/that/this is' can now be derived from du. *das*, a contraction of *dat is* 'that is'. Note that du. *dit is* 'this is' does not contract. Compare:

(14) a. *Das* [< *Dat is*] *waar* [Du.]
     b. *Dis* [< *Dit is*] *waar* [Afr.]
        That's/It's true

Thirdly, the Afrikaans free relative pronoun *wat* 'what' can also be expressed by means of *dit wat* 'that which'. Afr. *wat* and *dit wat* correspond to the Dutch free relative expressions *wat* 'what' and *dat wat* 'that which' respectively, while du. *dit wat 'this which' is ungrammatical. Compare:

(15) a. (*Dat*) *wat hij zegt, is waar* [Du.]
     b. (*Dit*) *wat hy sê, is waar* [Afr.]
        (That) what/which he says, is true

Fourthly, *dat* and *das* are well-known variants of *dit* 'it, that' and *dis* 'it/that is' in Khoekhoe Afrikaans.[14]

Now the question is how the form *dit* may have come about. Let us suppose that in CDP and in Cape Dutch *dat* was used as an independent demonstrative. If my database can be trusted such was indeed the case. A few examples from the pidgin are:

---

14. Cf. Rademeyer (1938).

(16) a. *wat   Capiteyn   [...] is dat!*
    What Captain [...] is that!
    (1668; van Overbeke 1668; 1998:82)[15]
  b. *Dat is doet*[16]
    That is good
    (1673; ten Rhyne 1686; 1933:140)
  c. *is dat braa?*
    Is that right?
    (1705–1713; Kolb 1719:417)

Now it so happens that in non-standard Afrikaans the <a> of function words like *as* 'if', *lat / dat* '(subordinating) that', and *sal* 'will' can be turned into <i>: *is* 'if', *lit / dit* '(subordinating) that', and *sil* 'will'. This type of variation is reported for Namaqualand by von Wielligh (1925:160–161). Similar variation between demonstrative *dat* and *dit* may have created *dit* out of the Dutch demonstrative *dat*.

Supporting evidence may be derived from Grebe (2001), which discusses some phonological phenomena in the Swellendam dialect (which is not a variety of Khoekhoe Afrikaans). On p. 93 Grebe mentions the variant *ken* for the modal auxiliary *kan* 'can'. However, I found more occurrences of *kin* in Grebe's transcripts than occurrences of *ken*, as well as many cases of *sil* (< *sal* 'shall, will') vs. not a single occurrence of **sel*.[17] If (*kan* ~) *ken* ~ *kin* is part of the more general non-standard [ɪ] ~ [ɛ] allophony, as Grebe seems to suggest, the pair *sal* ~ *sil* becomes even more telling. And since the incidence of [ɪ] → [ɛ] seems to be higher than the incidence of its converse, with a nasal coda as a facilitating factor for either change,[18] we might tentatively construe the historical chains *kan* → *kin* → *ken* and *sal* → *sil*.[19]

This implies that kh. afr. *dat* does not derive from afr. *dit* but rather the other way around: afr. and kh. afr. *dit* derives from *dat*. In General Afrikaans the non-standard

---

15. References to the sources of CDP data are structured as follows: year or period in which the sentence was recorded; the original source and – if applicable – the modern edition.

16. *Doet* is a typo. In the 1685 manuscript original we find *goet* 'good'. Cf. den Besten (2007b).

17. In a (fictitious?) letter to the editor of *De Zuid-Afrikaan* in 1831, written by EEN BOER ('a farmer') from the Swellendam district (Nienaber 1971:52) I found three instances of *kan* and six instances of *dit* 'it, that' without phonological variation. However, there is variation in the form of the subordinator *dat* 'that': 6 times *dat*, 6 times *dit*.

18. Cf. le Roux & Pienaar (1927:54) and Links (1989:10–11). – Some examples from Grebe (2001): (a) [ɪ] → [ɛ]: *distrek* 'district', *wenkel-* 'shop', *denk* 'think', *deng* 'thing', *seng* 'sing', *en* 'in', *senk* 'zinc', (b) [ɛ] → [ɪ]: *omtrint* 'about', *ik* 'I', *in* 'and', *mit* 'with'.

19. However, *sel* can at least be found in the documents of the Cape Archives (e.g. Franken 1953:93). So, maybe *sal* → *sil* is a 'syncopated' variant of a chain *sal* → *sel* → *sil*. Consequently *kin* may be an endpoint rather than an intermediary stage. Which scenario is best is something for future research (preferably by a phonologist).

variant *dit* has become the standard form and has absorbed – or rather, ousted – proximate *dit*. The question is of course why. The following scenario seems possible:

Two phonological factors may have played a role here: (a) The Afrikaans [ɪ] is somewhat centralized and so is difficult to distinguish from the schwa, (b) [ɑ] is a well-known colloquial and non-standard substitute for the schwa. So the originally non-standard variant *dit* may have acquired a higher status due to [ɑ]-avoidance. In short: afr. *dit* out of du. *dat* is in a sense a case of hypercorrection.

Now note that the subordinator *dat* 'that' did not change into *dit*. So why is there hypercorrection in the case of demonstrative *dat* and not in the case of the subordinator? In so far as I can see this difference may be due to a difference in sentence prosody, which in its turn is due to the different syntaxes of the subordinator and the demonstrative pronoun. The subordinator *dat* can only appear in clause-initial position and depending upon what follows it will count as a strong or a weak syllable. The demonstrative, however, usually appears in a metrically weak position. Even Spec-TopP, which requires the **strong form** of an object pronoun, is **metrically weak**. So, demonstrative *dat* could be misconstrued as a non-standard variant of [dɪt]/[dət].

Most probably other factors played a role as well. Dutch speakers of Cape Dutch Pidgin may have understood [dɪt]/[dət] as a new variant of the pronoun *'t* ([ət]) 'it' and could have integrated this feature into their vernacular. Furthermore, given the high amount of phonological variation involving [ɪ], [ə] and [ɑ] the old opposition between unmarked *dat* 'that' vs. marked *dit* 'this' must have broken down completely. And thus arose a generalized demonstrative, which – insofar as I know – is not due to substrate influence.

It is important to notice, though, that this may look like simplification – and it is possible that for a short period that was the case indeed – but after the creation of the items *hierdie* 'this (one)' and *daardie* 'that (one)' the Afrikaans demonstrative system was in a way more complex than its Dutch counterpart – and it still is.

3. Potential evidence from CDP

It would be nice if we could find supporting evidence for the *Dit/dat* Hypothesis in our CDP data. And there is indeed some evidence.

First of all, there are two sentences in Kolb (1719) which are identical but for the demonstrative pronouns used (examples (17a) and (18a) below).[20] In both cases Kolb translates the subject with the German proximate demonstrative *dieses* 'this', for which compare (17b) and (18b):

(17) a. **Dat** is Hottentotts Manier, …
       That is Hottentottic custom, …

---

20. The spelling difference *Hottentotts* ~ *Hottentots* is irrelevant.

      b. ***Dieses** ist Hottentotten Manier.*
         This   is Hottentots' custom
         (1705–1713; Kolb 1719: 432)

(18) a. ***Dit** is Hottentots   Manier, ...*
         This is Hottentottic custom, ...
      b. ***Dieses** ist der Gebrauch bey   den Hottentotten.*
         This is the custom   among the Hottentots
         (1705–1713; Kolb 1719: 549)

This may be indicative of phonological variation but a 'correcting hand' (either Kolb's or somebody else's), changing *dit* into *dat* in (17a), cannot be excluded. But we don't need these two sentences to argue for phonological variation in the "Dutch" distal demonstrative *dat* in CDP. At least some of the occurrences of *dat* in our CDP data will be original. What we need is at least one case of *dit* meaning 'that'.

    Example (18a) presents us with such a case. Or – to put it differently – *dit* in (18a) is an early case of afr. *dit* 'it, that, (this)' and my gloss ('this') and Kolb's translation (germ. *dieses* 'this') are misleading. But misleading though Kolb's translation may be, it shows that *dit* in (18a) is original. For a native speaker of Dutch, however, proximate *dit* is more marked, formal, literary, etc. than distal *dat*. (Similarly for germ. *dies / dieses* and *das*.) That is why the 'correcting hand' changed *dit* into *dat* in (17a) – probably in haste, and not noticing *dieses* in the German translation.

    Now consider the 'opposition' between *dat* and *dit* in the following fragment of a monologue concerning a 'medication':

(19) *Vrouw, jou Tover Goeds bra   bytum, **dat** is waar, maar jou*
      Woman, your magic stuff heavily bites, that is true, but   your
      *Tover Goeds ook weer gezond maakum, **dit** is ook waar,...*
      magic stuff also again healthy makes, this is also true, ...
      (1705–1713; Kolb 1719: 439)

Assuming a 'correcting hand' in this case is somewhat unlikely, since – from a Dutch (or German) point of view – two times *dat* is perfect and the textual sequence ... *dat* ... *dit* ... (i.e. distal before proximate) is strange. But if this is genuine CDP *dat* and *dit* may be two representatives of the same generalized demonstrative, "afr." *dit*. And in this case Kolb translates *dat* with germ. *das* 'that', while editing out *dit*: ... *das muß ich bekennen / alleine ich muß auch gestehen* '... I have to confess that'. However, I also have to admit ...'. So the sequence *dat* before *dit* may very well be original.[21] Therefore, example (19) provides evidence for the <a> ~ <i> variation postulated in Section 2.

---

21. The full "translation" runs as follows: *Frau ! euer Zauber-Guth beisset wohl hefftig / das muß ich bekennen : alleine ich muß auch gestehen / daß es herrlich heilet und gesund macht* 'Woman! Your magic stuff is biting heavily; I have to confess that. However, I also have to admit that it is healing splendidly and restores one's health.'

Finally, the following monologue from Langhanß (1705) may provide evidence for the change from *as* 'if, when' to *is* in CDP:[22]

(20) *Hollænder   arbeitem sterbem dem*
　　 [THE] Dutchman　works　　dies　　then (?)
　　 Hottentot　　　sterbem　is　　　　　　　storben
　　 [THE] Hottentot dies　(a) has　[3SGM] died [3SGM]
　　　　　　　　　　　　　(b) when [3SGM] dies
　　 krup　　　　　der ard　　als ock Hollender　　　mann
　　 crawls [IN(TO)] the earth　as also [THE] Dutchman man
　　 'The Dutchman is working and then dies. The Hottentot dies [i.e. without heavy work]. (a) Has he died, OR (b) When he dies, he slips into the earth, as does the Dutchman.' (1694; Langhanß 1705: 119)[23]

This monologue is marred by a couple of Germanicisms and corruptions three of which are important for our understanding of the text. Firstly, *dem* probably is a typo for the Early Modern German temporal adverb *denn* 'then'. Secondly, unless *der* is a typo for *die* 'the' we are forced to read it as the dative feminine singular of the German definite article, which would lead to the undesirable reading 'crawling around in the earth'. Since we don't need the subtleties of German grammar anyway, we had better interpret *der* as another typo.[24]

Finally: *is storben*. This could be read as a V1 conditional on the basis of the perfect of *sterven* 'die'. This interpretation is a bit doubtful but not impossible. But why is the past participle *storben* and not *gestorben*? This is a legitimate question since nonstandard Afrikaans has expanded the use of the participial prefix ge-, e.g. *gevergeet* 'forgotten' as against *(*ge)vergeet* in Standard Afrikaans (du. *(*ge)vergeten*). Therefore, Langhanß may have heard *is sterben* with *is* as a variant of *as* 'if, when'. Being unaware of the change from <a> to <i> in function words he interpreted *is* as a temporal auxil-

---

22. For a discussion of the syntax of this monologue see den Besten (2007a: 159).

23. Note that in Raven-Hart's collection of Cape fragments from travelogues (Raven-Hart 1971: II, 407) the following inaccuracies can be found: (a) *Hollænder* → *Hollaender* (which can hardly be called an error), (b) *storben* → *storbem*, (c) *ard* omitted, (d) *Hollender* → *Hollaender*. The inaccuracies (a) and (d) can also be found in my own transcript of this monologue in den Besten (2007a: 159).

24. In German *in* governing dative case indicates location ('in'), and *in* governing accusative case direction ('into'). – Since early CDP hardly made use of definite articles it is also possible that *der* is a typo for the preposition *onder* 'under'. The German "translation", which I will quote here in full, does not contain any evidence to choose between *die* → *der* and *onder* → *der*: *die Holländer arbeiten und plagen sich sehr / die Hottentotten aber nicht / endlich sterben sie alle beyde / und wird auch einer so wohl als der andere in die Erde begraben*. 'the Dutch work and toil very much; the Hottentots, however, don't. In the end they both die, and one as well as the other is buried in the earth' (Langhanß 1705: 119).

iary and changed the stem-vowel of *sterben*, although he did not dare to add the prefix *ge-* because he had not heard that.²⁵

If this argument can be upheld, the likelihood that we may have early pidgin cases of afr. *dit* 'it, that' in (17)–(19) above is enhanced.

4. More on *dat/dit* in Khoekhoe Afrikaans and CDP

Interestingly, Khoekhoe Afrikaans has introduced further changes, which have never reached General Afrikaans. According to von Wielligh (1925: 109, 141, 163) *dit* could – at least in his days – be used as an attributive demonstrative ('that, those'). It goes without saying that the variant *dat* is also possible:

(21) a. Soos {*dit / dat / det*}²⁶ man kan rook, het ek nog nie
       Such as that   man can smoke have I yet not
       gesien nie   [N]
       seen not
    b. *Ei!* is **dit** meisie nie mooi nie!   [CV]
       Wow! is that girl not beautiful not!

Von Wielligh mentions this use of *dit* for Namaqualand [N] and for the districts of Clanwilliam and Vanrhynsdorp [CV].²⁷

I could find no confirmation for this phenomenon in Rademeyer (1938), Links (1989) or van Rensburg (1984). However there is somewhat unusual confirmation in Jacobs (1942), a book full of "Griqua stories". This book is somewhat problematic in that many of the stories – also those that are supposed to be historical – are clearly stereotyping the Griquas (and the Koranas). This probably explains the heavy use of attributive *dat* 'that, those' (also 'the'). Nevertheless the feature as such seems to be genuine, also in view of the fact that it is restricted to stories about the 19th century. 20th century conversations with Griquas or Koranas reported upon in this book don't provide any evidence for that feature at all.

(22) a. *Kom ons lêe-jnaap* **dat** *gemsbok se boudvleis*   (p. 104)
       Come we ASP-cut   that gemsbok 's haunch-meat

---

25. Further aspects: (a) For Pro-drop under inversion see den Besten (2007a). (b) For [b] instead of [v] see den Besten (1999).

26. The same variation (*dit, dat, dêt*) is mentioned for the complementizer *dat* (Namaqualand).

27. Scholtz (1958 [1963]: 127) found a similar system in letters written by Piet Retief (early 19th century). E.g. *dat nasie* 'that nation', *dat school* 'that school', *dat kraalen* 'those kraals'. Note that the nouns are historically non-neuter.

b. *As jelle-goed se mans te broekbang ees om **dat***
   If 2PL 's men too trousers-afraid are for those
   bobbejaansnetters die nek en te moker, … (p. 47)
   baboon-chatters [i.e. San] the neck in to bash, …

This use of attributive *dat* may well be an old feature of Cape Dutch Pidgin, but this can hardly be proven because nearly all instances of attributive *dat* (or *dit*) in my pidgin database are construed with etymologically neuter nouns, such as *schaap* 'sheep', *beest* 'animal', *koper* 'copper', which would require *dat* (or *dit*) in Dutch anyway.

So we need cases of *dat* or *dit* combined with a historically non-neuter noun. Kolb (1719:358) provides us with one such case in a monologue by Captain Pegu (unfortunately in Dutch, not in CDP): *dit Hals-Band* 'this/that neck-lace'. But this may be due to Kolb's native German, in which *Halsband* is neuter.

Yet, the following mixture of Dutch and German may provide evidence for the use of *dat/dit* + Noun in CDP:

(23) [on eating lice]
  dat Schindhund *u. beidden wier weder*
  That/Those blood-sucker-[PL] 1PL.ACC bite 1PL.NOM again/back
  beidden, unser Blut Suugum, wier weder suugen
  bite, 1PL.POSS blood suck, 1PL.NOM again/back suck,
  unser Blut
  1PL.POSS blood
  (1688; Meister 1692:253)

Meister did not try to write Germanized CDP. He tried to write up what he had heard in a graphemically consistent manner.[28] Apparently he had heard *oens* 'us' and *oens se* (or: *oense*) 'our' (as in later Khoekhoe Afrikaans),[29] and *wi* 'we'. He interpreted these as germ. *uns* 'us' (> *u.*), *unser* 'our' and *wir* (here written *wier*) 'we', which was possible due to the existence of syllable-final r-deletion in CDP as spoken by the Khoekhoen.[30]

What is important for us, however, is the following: Meister didn't remember the second word of this monologue and he used germ. *Schindhund* 'blood-sucker' as a substitute, while keeping the attributive demonstrative *dat* in place. So he had heard *dat* + N and since he did not remember the noun the form of attributive *dat* (*dat* and

---

28. Cf. <uu> (=[y]) in *suugum, suugen* vs. <u> (= [u]) in *u[ns], unser, Blut, -um*. – Graphemic consistency explains why du. *bloed* 'blood' is changed into its homophonous German cognate *Blut*. – Note that graphemic consistency yields an argument for the presence of a (high) back vowel in the CDP "suffix" -*um*. But that is the topic for another paper.

29. Cf. *oens* '1PL' and *oense* 'our' in Khoekhoe-Afrikaans (Rademeyer 1938:45, 69; Links 1989:14).

30. Cf. den Besten (2009:234–235).

not *die*) cannot be due to 'editing'. Furthermore, after inserting the non-neuter (masculine) German noun *Schindhund* he did not edit the text either.

So there was a pattern *dat* + N in CDP and that means that the following example with the historically neuter noun *beest* 'animal' may be genuine:

(24) [concerning a praying mantis]
gy	*dit*	*Beest*	*fangum*	*zoo,*	*en*	*nu*	*dood*	*makum*	*zoo,*	*is*
2	this/that	animal	catch	so,	and	now	dead	make	so,	is

dat braa ?
that proper?
(1705–1713; Kolb 1719: 417)

The same may hold of the following example. But here things are complicated by the fact that the potential pidgin phrase *dat schaap* is embedded in a Dutch sentence:

(25)   *Waarom neem je **dat** schaap, …*
  a. Why take 2 that sheep, …
  b. Why take 2 those sheep-[PL]
(1706; *Minuuten, Just[.] Attest.*, 1706, nr. 30; Franken 1953: 93)

This is a "translation" of what "the Hottentot Lubbert" said to five runaway slaves who were each trying to steal a sheep (so five in total) from Lubbert's kraal. What he meant was: "Why are you guys stealing those sheep?" (reading b). And he probably used the pidgin phrase *dat schaap* with an unmarked plural. In court this phrase was misunderstood as a Dutch singular DP: 'that sheep' (reading a).[31]

Unfortunately, it cannot be excluded that Lubbert actually had said **die schaap*, meaning 'these/those sheep'. After this long intermezzo on aspects of the use of *dat* in Khoekhoe Afrikaans and CDP we return to the main topic of this article and continue with the demonstrative *die*.

---

31. In addition there are the following two early cases: (a) *dat coper* 'that/the copper', said by the Khoekhoe leader Herry (20 September 1655; Muller 1655; 1952: 418). He may have said **die coper* 'this/that/the copper', in which case his "Dutch" has been corrected – due to the fact that his monologue has been turned into Dutch anyway. (b) *dat binnenlandt* 'that/the interior', said by Jan van Riebeeck in a conversation with Herry. Even though he may have spoken pidginized Dutch, and may have had the intention to use the *dat* + N pattern, *dat binnenlandt* does not show anything at all, since *binnenlandt* is a neuter noun in Dutch (14 January 1658; van Riebeeck 1658; 1955: 231).

5. The origins of *dié* 'this, these'

5.1 The various usages of *dié*

Dié can be used both as an attributive and as an independent demonstrative. The definition of its meaning is more complicated than was the case with *dit*. According to Donaldson (1993:143) *dié* can mean both 'this, these' and 'that, those', but there is only an example of the proximate reading:

(26) Die R20-prys   word dié week gewen deur mnr. G. du Toit
      The R20-prize is   this week won   by   Mr. G. du Toit

However, it is not impossible that Donaldson is connecting the distal meaning with the use of *dié* as a kind of third person pronoun, as in:

(27) Dié   het   dorp toe   gegaan
      {He / She / They} {has / have} town towards gone
      [example Donaldson's, slightly adapted]

Note that this is a typically Dutch construction, as are exclamatives consisting of *dié* plus a given name, e.g. *dié Jan!* Now note that Ponelis (1979) – who does not deny the existence of pronominal *dié* – defines attributive *dié* as being equivalent to *hierdie* 'this' (pp. 91, 125). This is un-Dutch. Another example of this proximate usage can be found in the following exchange:

(28) a. Wanneer sal   ons dit doen?
          When   will we it   do?
      b. Dié {week / maand}
          This {week / month}

Also note that the frozen expression *diékant* means '1. (prep.) on this side of, 2. (adv.) on this side'.

5.2 The origins of proximate *dié*

Pronominal *dié* clearly is a superstratal (Dutch) feature of Afrikaans. Proximate attributive *dié* is not, but I cannot link it to any of the known substrate languages (Khoekhoe, Pasar Malay, etc.) either. Therefore, it should be linked to Cape Dutch Pidgin or its successor Cape Dutch Vernacular. However, since our knowledge of these linguistic entities is very limited, any hypothesis will by necessity be speculative. Nevertheless let us try.

Cape Dutch Pidgin made use of attributive *die*. *Die* could be a demonstrative and an article. Let us suppose that *die*, just like independent *dat/dit*, was a generalized demonstrative. However, the "invention" of attributive *dat/dit* may have disturbed this system. If we assume that attributive *dit/dat* acquired a distal reading, then *dié* was free to acquire a proximate reading. This is admittedly very speculative, but maybe this was the way Dutch distal *die* could turn into a proximate demonstrative. Note that this was possible due to the absence of gender in the pidgin and later in Afrikaans. In the Dutch gender-driven system attributive *dat* and *die* are both distal demonstratives, *dat* serving neuter nouns and *die* non-neuter ones. In Afrikaans with its genderless system attributive *dat* and *die* could be redefined.

6. Concluding remarks

In this article I have argued (a) that afr. *dit* 'it, that, this' derives from du. *dat* 'that', and (b) that given the demise of the Dutch weak pronouns in Afrikaans du. *dat* (and so afr. *dit*) had to take over de functions of du. *'t/het* 'it', and (c) that afr. *dit* absorbed du. *dit* 'this'. This generalized demonstrative arose in CDP. Cdp *dit* furthermore developed a new attributive function, which survived until the early 20th century in Khoekhoe Afrikaans. Since both *dit* and *dié* could be used as attributive demonstratives functional specialization became possible. Since attributive *dit* is linked to independent *dit*, it could acquire the unmarked (distal) reading. This left the marked (proximate) reading for *dié*. Although attributive *dit* has disappeared, the specialized meaning of attributive *dié* stuck. Independent *dié* on the other hand clearly continues Dutch usages. However, these usages are such that independent *dié* better be called a generalized demonstrative pronoun, there being no demonstrative element it clearly contrasts with.

Future research must show whether these hypotheses can be upheld: the semantics must be refined, *hierdie* 'this, these' and *daardie* 'that, those' must also be taken into account, and the demise of du. *deze* (non-neuter) 'this, these' must be investigated.

References

A. Linguistic literature

Carstens, Adelia & Grebe, Heinrich (eds). 2001. *Taallandskap. Huldigingsbundel vir Christo van Rensburg*. Pretoria: Van Schaik.
den Besten, Hans. 1989. Universal-Grammatik und/oder Zweitsprachenerwerb: Der Fall Afrikaans. In *Beiträge zum 4. Essener Kolloquium über "Sprachkontakt, Sprachwandel, Sprachwechsel, Sprachtod"*, Norbert Boretzky, Werner Ennninger & Thomas Stolz (eds), 11–44. Bochum: Brockmeyer.
den Besten, Hans. 1996. Associative DPs. In *Linguistics in the Netherlands 1996*, Crit Cremers & Marcel den Dikken (eds), 13–24. Amsterdam: John Benjamins.

den Besten, Hans. 1999. Speculations on [χ]-elision and intersonorantic [ʋ] in Afrikaans. In *Language genesis*, Rudolf P. Botha (ed.), Stellenbosch: Universiteit van Stellenbosch. *Stellenbosch Papers in Linguistics* 32: 45–66.
den Besten, Hans. 2001. The complex ancestry of the Afrikaans associative constructions. In Carstens & Grebe (2001: 49–58).
den Besten, Hans. 2007a. Relexification and pidgin development. The case of Cape Dutch Pidgin. In *Deconstructing Creole*, Umberto Ansaldo, Stephen Matthews & Lisa Lim (eds.), 141–164. Amsterdam: John Benjamins.
den Besten, Hans. 2007b. The manuscript underlying Ten Rhyne's *Schediasma de Promonorio bonae spei*: A comparison of two versions. *Quarterly Bulletin of the National Library of South Africa* 61(4): 33–45.
den Besten, Hans. 2009. In search of a submerged phonology. The case of early Cape Dutch Pidgin. In *Gradual Creolization. Studies celebrating Jacques Arends* [Creole Language Library 34], Rachel Selbach, Hugo C. Cardoso & Margot van den Berg (eds), 219–241. Amsterdam: John Benjamins.
Donaldson, Bruce. 1993. *A Grammar of Afrikaans*. Berlin: Mouton de Gruyter.
Franken, Johan Lambertus Machiel. 1953. *Taalhistoriese Bydraes*. Cape Town: A.A. Balkema.
Grebe, Heinrich. 2001. Overbergs of Transvaals? In Carstens & Grebe 2001: 92–102.
le Roux, Thomas Hugo & de Villiers Pienaar, Pierre. 1927. *Afrikaanse fonetiek*. Cape Town: Juta.
Links, Tony. 1989. *So Praat ons Namakwalanders*. Cape Town: Tafelberg.
Ponelis, Fritz A. 1979. *Afrikaanse Sintaksis*. Pretoria: Van Schaik.
Ponelis, Fritz A. 1993. *The Development of Afrikaans*. Frankfurt: Peter Lang.
Rademeyer, J. 1938. *Kleurling-Afrikaans. Die Taal van die Griekwas en Rehoboth-Basters*. Amsterdam: Swets en Zeitlinger.
Roberge, Paul T. 2001. Diachronic notes on the Afrikaans demonstrative pronouns. In Carstens & Grebe 2101: 124–136.
Scholtz, J. du P. 1958 [1963]. Die ondergang van die nominale tweeklassesisteem in Afrikaans. *Tydskrif vir Wetenskap en Kuns*, Oct. 1958. Reprinted in J. du P. Scholtz, *Taalhistoriese Opstelle. Voorstudies tot 'n Geskiedenis van Afrikaans*, 122–145. Pretoria: Van Schaik.
van Rensburg, M. C. J. (ed.). 1984. *Finale verslag van 'n ondersoek na die Afrikaans van die Griekwas van die tagtiger jare, onderneem met finansiële steun van die RGN, uitgevoer aan die Universiteit van die Oranje-Vrystaat*. Bloemfontein: UOVS.
von Wielligh, Gideon Retief. 1925. *Ons Geselstaal. 'n Oorsig van Gewestelike Spraak soos Afrikaans Gepraat Word*. Pretoria: Van Schaik.

B. Sources

Bosman, D. B. & H. B. Thom (Eds.). 1952–1957. *Daghregister Gehouden by den Oppercoopman Jan Anthonisz van Riebeeck*. 3 vols: I (1952), II (1955), III (1957). Cape Town: A.A. Balkema.
Jacobs, J. F. 1942. *Die Grikwas en hul Bure*. Bloemfontein: Nasionale Pers.
Kolb, Peter. 1719. *Caput Bonae Spei Hodiernum, das ist Vollständige Beschreibung des Africanischen Vorgebürges der Guten Hofnung ...*, Nuremberg: Peter Conrad Monath.
Langhanß, Christoph. 1705. *Neue Ost-Indische Reise*. Leipzig: Michael Rohrlachs seel. Wittib und Erben.

Meister, Georg. 1692. *Der Orientalisch-Indianische Kunst und Lustgärtner.* Dresden & Leipzig: C. Heckel.

Muller, Willem. 1655. (Journal of an expedition by land). In Bosman & Thom 1952: 416–421.

Nienaber, Gabriel Stefanus. 1971. *Afrikaans in die Vroeër Jare.* Johannesburg: Voortrekkers.

Raven-Hart, Rowland. 1971. *Cape of Good Hope 1652–1702. The First Fifty Years of Dutch Colonisation as seen by Callers*, 2 vols. Cape Town: A.A. Balkema.

ten Rhyne, Willem. 1686 [1933]. *Schediasma de Promontorio Bonae Spei; ejusve tractus incolis Hottentottis.* Schaffhausen: J. M. Oswald. With a foreword by B. Farrington in Isaac Schapera, (ed.), *Early Cape Hottentots*, 78–157. Cape Town: VRS.

van Overbeke, Aernout. 1668 [1998]. *Geestige en Vermaeckelijcke Reys-beschryving.* In *Buyten gaets. Twee burleske reisbrieven van Aernout van Overbeke*, Marijke Barend-van Haeften & Arie Jan Gelderblom (eds.), 41–88. Hilversum: Verloren.

van Riebeeck, Jan Antonisz. 1651–1662. *Daghregister Gehouden by den Oppercoopman.* In Bosman & Thom 1952–1957.

PART IV

The selection of features in complex morphology

Contact, complexification and change in Mindanao Chabacano structure*

Anthony P. Grant

This paper examines several instances of phonological and structural complexification in Mindanao Chabacano, a predominantly Spanish-lexifier creole of southwestern Mindanao, which have arisen as the result of the interaction of elements of Philippine (especially Tagalog and the Bisayan languages), Spanish and English origin in the language, which have given rise to contact-induced change in the language's structure.

1. Preliminaries: Mindanao Chabacano and its history

Mindanao Chabacano, a cluster of varieties of Philippine Creole Spanish, is rather unusual among creole languages in as much as it has been in constant contact both with its chief lexifier, namely Spanish, and with the languages which most strongly shaped it typologically, the Central Philippine languages, for most of the 300 or so years of its existence. This paper discusses the effects of this continued contact and also the convergence effects of external contact-induced change on some of the languages which have shaped this creole. It will be seen that a number of changes which have been documented in Mindanao Chabacano have the effect of making it more similar to many of the languages which have influenced it, many of which have undergone the same recent changes.

---

* I would like to thank Aireen L. Barrios, John Green, Paz B. Naylor, Eeva Sippola, Patrick Steinkrüger, Ida Wagner, and R. David Zorc for help and iformation which has found its way into this paper. I first read about the nature of Mindanao Chabacano in Frake (1971) as a teenager when considering a degree in Linguistics, and continued my investigation of the language during my undergraduate years at the University of York as a creolist under the example of Robert Le Page, to whose memory I dedicate this paper.

1.1   Philippine Creole Spanish

Philippine Creole Spanish (or PCS) is itself a cover term for two groups of Spanish-lexifier creoles which are used in two main areas in the Philippines. Use of this term should not be taken as prima facie evidence that these groups of creoles have a common origin. Varieties of Philippine Creole Spanish are generally referred to as *Chabacano* (Chabakano, Chavacano), literally "uncouth". These creoles are supposed by many to have evolved from the interaction of speakers of Spanish with a Portuguese-lexifier creole used by Catholic refugees from the Moluccan island of Ternate in 1655, who fled to Manila Bay. Subsequently they have come into contact with Tagalog and in the case of the creoles used in Mindanao, also with Bisayan varieties and other Philippine languages. They have absorbed many features from Philippine languages.

The first group of creoles is situated on Luzon and specifically in Manila (formerly used in the old suburbs of Ermita and Intramuros) and its outskirts (the towns of Cavite, and Ternate), where these varieties, Caviteño, the obsolete Ermiteño, and Ternateño, are spoken. They are customarily referred to as the Manila Bay Creoles. (However, it may be disputed whether they constitute a historically valid subgroup: Ternateño contains a number of lexical and other features not found elsewhere on Manila Bay[1]).

The second group of creoles is found in cities and rural areas in southern and western Mindanao (especially Zamboanga City and much of Zamboanga del Sur, but to a lesser extent in Cotabato City and in Davao City); these varieties (Zamboangueño, Cotabateño, Davaueño respectively) may be described as Mindanao Chabacano. These varieties (certainly the first two) share a great deal of material[2] and appear to descend from a single creole, which, given that Zamboanga City was the earliest of these settlements to be furnished with a creolophone population (from 1719 or be-

---

1.   These include the use of *yeismo*, in which the earlier Spanish sound *elle* is realised as /j/, a feature which other forms of creole Spanish spoken on Manila Bay do not exhibit, and the presence of a few dozen words of Moluccan Malay, Portuguese and Bahasa Ternate origin (the last is a non-Austronesian Trans New Guinea Phylum language) in the lexicon. At my oral presentation of this paper at the University of Giessen Patrick Steinkrüger pointed out that very many of these words were unknown to the speakers with whom he conducted recent fieldwork in Ternate, but they were certainly used in the 1970s when Carol Hodson Molony conducted her fieldwork on the creole, and Mgr. Eeva Sippola of the University of Helsinki, who has also done fieldwork on this language kindly furnished me with a copy of Tirona (1923) in which many of the selfsame words of these disparate origins which Molony lists are also cited. The creole-speakers in the town of Ternate are supposed to descend from *Márdikas* (literally 'freemen', a name of Malay and ultimately Sanskrit origin which is Christians from the Moluccas who immigrated from Ternate in the 1680s); this matter is discussed in greater depth in Frake (1971). There is no reason for us to assume aprioristically that the origin of creolophone people in Cavite is similar.

2.   Cotabateño contains lexical elements from the local languages Tiruray and Magindanaw which are not found in Zam.

fore, with the establishment of a permanent garrison), is likely to have originated in or around Zamboanga City.

Zamboangueño, henceforth Zam, is the most widely-spoken and deeply-studied PCS variety and has numerous speakers on Basilan Island and elsewhere in the region (Frake 1971). It has over 290,000 native speakers and perhaps as many L2 speakers, whose first languages are Tausug, Samalan languages, Hokkien (among people whose roots go back a long time in the area), and Cebuano and Tagalog among people who have relocated to the area more recently (in the case of Tagalog-speakers, often as a response to heightened military and security concerns in an area disfigured by terrorism). Zam is also spoken in Kampong Air (Malay: "Water Village"), a village in the Semporna region of Sabah, Malaysia.

Davaueño is little-studied and the number of its speakers in Davao is unknown. On the other hand, there is a certain amount of documentation on the endangered language Cotabateño, preeminently in Riego de Dios 1989, a lexical and grammatical work by a native speaker of that variety (but a work which also contains plentiful lexical material, with phonetic transcriptions for each word, from Zam, Ternateño and Caviteño).

In decreasing order the major lexical components of Zam are Spanish, Bisayan languages, Tagalog, and latterly Philippine English. The influence of Bisayan languages and also Tagalog on Zam has been profound and stretches well beyond mere acculturational lexical borrowing, providing the creole with un-Spanish features such as more consistent VSO marking, a distinction between personal and other nouns, three semantically-defined negators (one of them of Philippine origin), and the general zero-marking of copulas. Appendix 1 provides a table of Zam structural features with indications of their origins, while in Appendix 2 the sources of the major features in Zam as a whole are presented according to the linguistics stratum in question, and Appendix 3 presents information on the approximate periods of contact which speakers of Zam had with the relevant languages. Lexical influence from Philippine languages is manifest. About 15% of the items on the Swadesh lists and the 200-item Hudson-Blust list used for classifying Austronesian languages are of non-Spanish origin, and are especially of Philippine origin. The lexical influence of Tausug (an important local lingua franca), Samalan languages (the original languages of the area, including Sinama, the original language of the Zamboanga area), and Hokkien on Zam may also be mentioned,[3] while many people in the rural parts of the provinces of Zamboanga del Sur and Zamboanga del Norte who are conversant with Zam are

---

3. Tausug (which itself borrowed heavily from Samalan languages when its speakers moved westwards: Pallesen 1985) has provided vocabulary dealing with Islam, much of which is itself from Brunei Malay (and much of that is ultimately from Arabic). Hokkien has provided a small number of words, of which *sen* 'money' is the most notable, while Samalan languages have furnished a few terms such as *mundúhin* 'pirate' and they are the source for *Zamboanga* itself, *sambwanggan* menaing 'landing-stage' or 'jetty' (Reid 1971). Some lexical influence has gone in the other direction, as Tausug and Sinama, both of them languages which normally look to Malay

second-language speakers of Zam whose L1 is one of the varieties of Subanen, though this last language group does not seem to have donated any lexical loans to Zam.

Tausug, Tagalog and the Bisayan languages are all classified genetically as Central Philippine languages, together with languages such as Bikol which have not played a part in creole formation (Blust 1991). For its part, Subanen is regarded by Blust 1991 as a small family which is part of what he calls 'the Greater Central Philippine hypothesis' (which includes the Central Philippine languages) but which he does not see as part of Central Philippine as narrowly defined. Samalan languages such as Sinama (the original language of Zamboanga City) and Yakan are seen by Blust as members of the Sama-Bajaw family, which is Western Malayo-Polynesian, like Greater Central Philippine, but these are not among the languages of the Greater Central Philippine Hypothesis.

Zam (and Mindanao Chabacano in general) also contain a number of historically important lexical and structural elements which are shared with creoles such as Caviteño, but which are not found in modern-day Philippine Spanish. In contrast to the diversity of influences on Zam, the sole Philippine language which has influenced the creoles of the Manila Bay area is Tagalog, the language in which the speakers of these creoles are nowadays bilingual and often dominant.

The Mindanao Chabacano variety of Cotabato City, which according to Riego de Dios (1989) may have a partially independent history from that of Zam (with which it later converged), also contains some lexical items from Mindanao languages (specifically from the Danaw language Magindanaw and from the South Mindanao language Tiruray).

1.2 The origins of Zam

The origin of Zam is relevant to a consideration of the nature of its complexification. Two major schools of thought exist on the origins of Zam:

a. that it derives from language varieties (Spanish, probably including restructured Spanish, Manila Bay Creoles, Tagalog and Hiligaynon) which were brought to Zamboanga during the building and reestablishment of Fort Pilar there in the 17th or early 18th centuries (specifically the periods around 1635, when the fort was first established, and 1718–1719, when it was rebuilt after its destruction by the Tausugs). The factor of the Hiligaynon-speaking city of Iloilo serving as an important way-station on the journey from Cavite to Mindanao, including serving as a source of locally-born Catholic wives for the members of the Catholic garrison from Manila Bay on its way to a non-Catholic area (Frake 1971, etc.) is important in this theory, because it accounts for many features of Zam if it arose in house-

---

rather than Spanish for additional vocabulary, nonetheless contain a few loans from Zam, such as *tyangge* 'market' (see footnote 6 for further details).

holds where both restructured or creole forms of Spanish and Hiligaynon were available as home languages for acquisition by children and where a Bisayanised forms of creole Spanish could have emerged as the basis for modern Zam;
b. that it is of much more recent origin, maybe dating only from the late 19th century (before which a less heavily restructured form of Spanish was used), and that it arose then as the result of the interaction between Spanish, Bisayan languages and latterly Tagalog (Lipski 1992; Fernández 2004).

One problem which people who are investigating the history of grammatical constructions in Zam must face is the relative lateness of the first published attestation of Zam, namely Henry Broad's handful of sentences and phrases of 1929. McKaughan's texts (which were published in 1954 but which were probably collected some time earlier) are the first large sample of Zam; Whinnom's 1956 handful of song texts (the only Zam material which he provides in his book) are very different from all other published Zam material. Nonetheless, Broad's and McKaughan's works represent a variety of Zam which is lexically and structurally very similar to what Frake recorded in the 1960s and to the spoken and written Zam data which Forman was to collect a little while later.

The American Hispanist John Lipski's published work on Zam (Lipski 1992, 2001, etc.) and on its origins has been influential but it overlooks certain issues:

a. the presence of some distinctively Hiligaynon and Tagalog lexicon in Zam (including items in materials which were gathered before the past couple of decades) which cannot be explained purely by reference to the effects of recent influence from the incursive Cebuano;
b. the presence of some structural and lexical features (e.g. certain TMA markers, Portuguese-derived prepositional *na*, Portuguese-derived *kilaya* 'how?', *gumitá* 'to vomit',[4] etc.) which link Zam to Manila Bay varieties such as Caviteño which also include these, which cannot be easily explained as being from forms of non-creolised Philippine Spanish, and which look more like shared innovations;
c. the fact that *Bisayan/Visayan* and *Cebuano* are not mutually interchangeable terms to refer exclusively to the language of the island of Cebu, although Lipski seems to use these terms that way. As Zorc (1977) shows, the Bisayan varieties are far from being mere dialects of one language, and what is more, the Bisayan elements in Zam can frequently be safely assigned to particular groups within Bisayan, and these do not always include Cebuano;
d. the question of attestation and publications of materials representing earlier, more hispanised varieties of Zam. Lipski has yet to publish any sizeable tranche of his

---

4. This form, a popular reshaping from Latin *vomitāre*, is found in the 'Manila Bay Creoles', Mindanao Chabacano, Papiamentu, the Portuguese-lexifier creoles of West Africa (both Upper and Lower Guinea varieties) and also, as *gumbitá*, in the Portuguese lexical stratum in Saramaccan.

data from older and more rural speakers of Zam which he has claimed has a far greater number of Spanish features than the material made available by Charles Frake,[5] Michael Forman, etc. It is always possible that the hispanising language in Whinnom's song texts is similar to the hispanised variety recorded by Lipski from his oldest consultants – but until Lipski publishes continuous texts in the 'older' forms of Zam (and some of us have been waiting nigh on two decades for him to do so) we cannot know this for sure.

Lipski (1987) has written of the widespread use of Spanish in official notices in Zamboanga until WWII, decades after it had fallen into disuse in that domain in other parts of the Philippines, and points out that two years' study of Spanish was compulsory in high school throughout the Philippines until at least the 1970s. Non-creolised Spanish, in both spoken and written forms, seems to have had a higher and more persistent profile at a public level in Zamboanga City than elsewhere in the Philippines.

Another paper by Lipski (Lipski n.d.: 28 et seqq.) discusses the origins of Chabacano and limns the probable importance of the role of (Christian) slaves of varying linguistic backgrounds, captives of the Sunni Muslim Tausugs, the major ethnic group of the Sulu Archipelago, at Jolo, Basilan Island, in the 18th century formation of Zam.

There is also the fact that Zam has been in constant contact with speakers of Central Philippine languages (though maybe also being influenced by a Samalan substrate) throughout its history: contact was firstly with Hiligaynon (in the early days of Fort Pilar), then with Tausug (consistently through the years), then with Cebuano (from the late 19th century onwards as Cebuano-speakers gobbled up land in Mindanao), and latterly with Tagalog/Pilipino (especially since post-WWII independence, and even more so given the rise of the Muslim separatist organisation Moro National Liberation Front (and latterly that of the Abu Sayyaf terrorists – the Fathers of the Sword – on Jolo and in the province of Tawitawi), the states of emergency and consequent military intervention on the part of the government and military forces in Manila which have characterised life in this region since the 1970s, but also in the early days inasmuch as Tagalog is a crucial component of Manila Bay creoles such as Caviteño).

Zam is therefore one of a rather small group of creoles which has been in continued contact with its SUBSTRATE languages (Hiligaynon, Tagalog, possibly Caviteño, which itself blends elements of Spanish, Tagalog and a Lusoasian or Malayo-Portuguese creole), with its SUPERSTRATE language(s) (possibly Caviteño and certainly some form of Spanish) and with its ADSTRATE languages (Cebuano, Spanish, Tagalog, English) simultaneously at various times in its history, while the same language has often been both substrate and superstrate language, or both superstrate and adstrate. And this is to say nothing of the possible influences that fluent L2 speakers of Zam, who constitute and who have constituted a sizeable proportion of the Zam speech community

---

5. Let it be noted that Charles Frake (Frake 1980) used Zam as a contact language for much of his anthropological fieldwork among Western Subanen-speakers and members of other ethnic groups in the rural parts of the two Zamboanga provinces.

and who often use Zam on a daily or even an hourly basis, may have wrought on the creole in decades recently past. What these changes through L2 transmission actually are is as yet a matter for speculation. This is because the bulk of the published work on Zam deals with the language as it is used by native speakers of Zam. However, most non-native speakers of Zam speak one or more Philippine languages natively.

The framework for contact-induced change and the creation of mixed languages sketched out in Thomason (2003) enables us to understand how the interplay of these languages can be seen to result in the development of Zam as it was used some decades ago and as it is used now. Thomason identifies seven mechanisms which contribute to the creation of such languages. Of these, deliberate linguistic change seems to have had little role in the development of Zam, and nor do her features of 'negotiation' (which involves creating a compromise between two languages' radically different means for expressing the same construction), code alternation and passive familiarity, whereas first and second language acquisition strategies have certainly been crucial in the development and shaping of Zam and at a later stage intersentential and intrasentential codeswitching among Zam-Bisayan (or Zam-Tagalog, Zam-Spanish) bilinguals have probably been important too, as the plethora of borrowed Philippine discourse particles in Zam (*daw* 'quotative', *ba* 'interrogative yes-no question marker', *pa* 'yet', and many others) attests. However, to a very large extent Zam has undergone metatypy (Ross 1996) in the direction of Central Philippine languages.

1.3 Summary

Given such a diverse and vital linguistic backdrop we may expect to find signs of contact-induced change in the language; we also find some degree of COMPLEXIFICATION in modern Zam. By complexification I refer to the processes by which the structure of language becomes more complex than previously (often with the concomitant addition of variation between structures of similar meaning where there was none before) because of the addition of features which were not previously present and of exceptions to previously exceptionless rules; much of this in Zam comes as the result of contact-induced change. Several such instances of contact-induced complexification could have been exemplified, for instance:

a. the borrowing from Philippine languages and the use with personal names of a 'personal article' which can be distinguished from the definite and indefinite articles,
b. the complexity of the personal pronominal system which has absorbed borrowed material from Hiligaynon,
c. a reconstrual on Central Philippine lines of the semantics of some Spanish personal pronouns.
d. The use of three negators under different syntactic circumstances, as found in Philippine languages, whereas Spanish only uses one.

All of these features make these aspects of Zam structure more complex than what is found in corresponding situations in Spanish.

Because of space constraints I cite just two instances of complexification in some detail, namely some contact-induced changes in Zam segmental and canonical phonology, and the rise and grammaticalisation of an overt copula of Bisayan origin, namely *amo*.

2. Changes in segmental (and canonical) phonology

Zam segmental (and indeed also canonical) phonology is a compromise between those of a variety of Spanish which exhibited *seseo* (see footnote 1) (but not *yeismo*)[6] and Bisayan languages and Tagalog. Words from the two major components (Spanish and Central Philippine, respectively) usually preserve their original pronunciation, though for less well-educated speakers of Spanish. /f/ becomes /p/ in Zam. (de Rivas ed. 1982 uses <f> in his etymological spelling but Riego de Dios 1989 does not), though the unfamiliar Spanish palatal lateral and post-alveolar voiceless affricate remain.

As a result we find a five-vowel system in words from Spanish and a reduced three- or four-vowel system in words of Philippine origin (/e/ is missing). These last items may also use consonant clusters such as /-kd-/, word-final voiced[7] and voiceless plosives and word-final bilabial nasals, in addition to those typically Philippine sounds /ʔ/ and the velar nasal, sounds which are not found at phonemic level in the Spanish component (which does however retain /č/, a sound which is found in Hiligaynon et cetera only in loans from Hokkien, Spanish and English). It should be noted that /b d g/ in Zam are always voiced plosives and are never pronounced as fricatives there as they are in many phonological environments in Spanish; Philippine languages which have contributed to Zam lack voiced fricatives.

Molony (1973) also mentions a few sounds, such as /v, š, dž/, which have been borrowed into some Chabacano varieties from English and which occur primarily in English words /dž š/ occur only secondarily in pre-English words (/ˈdžente ~ ˈdyente/ 'tooth', /ˈšete ~ ˈsyete/ 'seven'. Meanwhile Ing (1967) notes some by-forms, beginning with /sC-/ or sometimes with /sCC-/, of words which are of mostly Spanish origin and which otherwise begin with /esC(C)-/. This represents a change to an onset-type

---

6. Although Mexican Spanish seems to have provided the bulk of the Spanish component which found its way directly or indirectly into Zam (and this is evidenced by the presence of a few Mexicanlisms in Zam, such as *mande*? 'could you please repeat the question?' and *chongo* 'monkey', plus *sakate* 'grass', which derives from Nahuatl, *and tyangge* 'market', a Mexicanism which has all the appearance of a loan from an unknown language into Nahuatl: Kaufman 2001: 12), modern Mexican Spanish at least practises *yeismo*, which Zam does not.

7. These are sometimes devoiced: Zam 'anut 'to float' < Central Philippine languages '*anud*.

which is permissible in English syllable structure but not in Spanish or in the relevant Philippine languages. Ing (1967) also describes the increasing permissibility of complex syllabic consonant codas (not permissible in Spanish and Philippine languages) through numerous borrowings from English such as /kard/ 'card'. The segmental phonology of Zam is more involved and complex than those of Philippine languages or Spanish, because Philippine phonological features have been combined with those of Spanish, and Philippine constraints have been added to what was originally a Spanish phonological system, which has undergone post-creolisation contact-induced complexification. Yet Zam phonology is not exclusively that of Philippine languages: for instance it has five vowels, unlike Philippine languages (which usually have only three vowels in words of native origin) but like Spanish.

One point of difference between Spanish, Zam and Philippine languages is the role of rhotics. Spanish has two rhotic phonemes, one of which is a trill (here written /rr/) which is used word-initially, preconsonantally and sometimes medially, the other being a tap (here written /r/) which is used word-finally and sometimes medially, where it contrasts with /rr/ (hence its phonemic status in Spanish). Before contact with Spanish, most Philippine languages had none; in these languages an [r]-sound, if it occurred, was an intervocalic allophone of /d/. [r] has been promoted to phonemic status in these languages very largely as the result of wholesale borrowing of words from Spanish. Spanish /rr/ is borrowed as /r/ in these languages, and its realisation is therefore no different from modern reflexes of Spanish /r/ in loans into those languages.

At a first reading of the first detailed account of Zam phonology, modern Zam apparently has only one /r/-phoneme and therefore makes no distinction between *karo* ['karoh] 'cart' (< Sp. *carro*) and *karo* ['karoh] 'expensive' (< Sp. *caro*) (Riego de Dios 1989: 102). But this may not always have been the case. A brief article by Ing (1967), the work of a Sino-Filipina fluent in Zam who wrote her unpublished PhD, Ing (1968), on Zam segmental and canonical phonology (at University College London) notes (I quote) that there are several free variants of /r/ including [hr], associated with /rr/ and always used word-initially, but that only the tap-r [ɾ] is used word-medially and only the approximant [ɹ] is used finally. Thus Ing is suggesting that phones of /r/ and /rr/ have been redistributed or amalgamated into the phonetic forms of a new phoneme /r/ which includes some allophonic elements from both previous phonemes.

Yet other sources have a different view. Riego de Dios (1989: 107) gives examples of words with varying pronunciations, such as *kore* 'to run' (< Sp. *correr*), which may have a tap-r or a sound which Riego de Dios represents as [hr] in both Cotabateño and Zam (for which she also provides pronunciations). It appears that merger of the former phonemes /rr/ and /r/ into a single phoneme /r/ was not yet complete by the 1970s among some speakers in Cotabato (who perforce belonged to the older generations of the population) and in Zamboanga City. Nonetheless the current state of affairs, in which a single rhotic has subsumed two preexisting rhotics and their allophones, makes the present situation regarding rhotics in Zam resemble that in Philippine languages (and in English) more closely than it does Spanish, Because more allophones are used in Zam than are used in Spanish for this phoneme, the phonetics underlying this phoneme are more complex than those in Spanish and certainly those corresponding to /r/ in Philippine languages.

3. The source and rise of the copula *amo*

Zam handles equivalents of the verb 'to be' in a number of ways. Locative expressions involving 'be'-verbs, for example, may use *talyí* or *talyá*:

(1) Na principio amo   el   Palabra, y el   Palabra talli   junto
    LOC beginning COPULA the word   and the word   be.at together
    con   el   Dios, y el   Palabra amo   el Dios.
    with the God   and the word   COPULA the God
    'In the beginning was the word, and the word was with God, and the Word was God.' (Gospel of John 1:1: de Rivas ed. 1982, original spelling preserved).

Other contexts in Zam call for other constructions, such as *tyene* (= 'have') 'there is' and its negative form *nway*:

(2) a. Tyene komida
        have food
        'There is (some) food.'   (Frake 1971:235)
    b. nway   komida
        Is.not food
        'There is no food.'   (Frake 1971:235)

Nway in Zam (< Spanish *no hay* 'there is not') is also used to negate anterior statements, That is, it is used to mean 'there is not' and by extension 'there was not', and 'not to have'. Such patterns of copulas and negators correspond very closely with what is found in Hiligaynon, where the form meaning 'have' is negated not by a simple negator but by a particle *dili buut* which means 'there is not').

(3) a. May   kan'un
        There.is food
        'There is food, I have food.'   (Hiligaynon)
    b. Dili buut   kan'un
        Not there.is food
        'There is no food.'   (Hiligaynon)

Another kind of 'be'-construction in Zam involves zero marking with Comment-Topic order, which is what is found for non-locative copulas in earlier Zam texts (and in parallel situations in other Philippine languages).

(4) *Guapo   el   doktor.*
    Handsome the doctor
    'The doctor is handsome.'

Notable among 'be'-constructions is the use of the untensed copular verb *amo*. This feature is discussed in extenso in Aoto (2002), in which the author points out its role in making clear and distinguishing the relations between grammatical and semantic subjects in Zam sentences. It can be used with following NPs, and in pseudo-cleft sentences, but not with following adjectives:

(5) a. *Si   Juan amo rey*
        PERSONAL.ARTICLE John be   king
        'John is/was the king.'
    b. *Esos dos amo el que ta   destrosa el   buen imagen de di atun*
        those two be   he who PRES destroy the good image of of.1PL
        Mayor
        Mayor
        'Those two are the people who are destroying the good image of our Mayor.' (Aoto 2002)

but not

(5) c. **Si*   *Juan amo grande*
        PERSONAL.ARTICLE John be   big
        'John is big.'

The form *amo* derives from a Bisayan language- (it occurs in Hiligaynon). It is first recorded in Zam both as a discourse marker (as it is in Hiligaynon) and (with past reference, in the form *amuyá* in the text in Ing 1967) as a copula. We may note the role of *amo*, which is now mostly construed as a copula, was earlier discharged more as a discourse marker and that it sometimes served as a full lexical item with the idea of 'that's right': Forman (1972: 243) lists *ta-m-pa-amo-amó* as meaning 'to pretend to be correct'.

The generalisation of use of *amo* as a copula in certain syntactic contexts in Zam texts is something which seems to have taken place from the 1970s onwards, and we can note its infrequency as a copula in texts before then (it is absent from contexts in Broad 1929 and McKaughan 1954 where we might nowadays expect it). Even now, some speakers seem to use *amo* as a copula which is placed between noun phrases more than other speakers do (in Zam-medium postings on a well-known Zamboanga website, www.zamboanga.com, in which most postings are in English, zero-marking of the copula predominates). We may further mention also that Frake (1980) does not so much as discuss the *amo* construction in his discussion of Zam verbal expressions, and none of his ca. 150 sentences and phrases contains it in any of its senses. This suggests that the rise and spread of *amo* as a copular form has occurred since the late 1960s and has continued throughout the 1970s. There are strong parallels here between the use of *amo* in Zam and the increasing use in modern Tagalog of the untensed particle *ay* (also sometimes found in Zam sentences), whose primary function is as an inverse marker, as a sort of copula (Aoto 2002 remarks upon this parallelism,[8] as did Grant 1996, 2002).[9] But the isomorphism is not yet complete. This Tagalog construction *ay* was originally a stylistically marked structure in the language, which was seized upon and generalised by Spanish missionaries (from the early 17th century onwards) who were describing Tagalog grammar in terms of a Latinate (rather than a Tagalog) framework (for example Totanes 1745). Such authors favoured this admittedly stylistically marked construction because they felt that sentences containing the construction corresponded point by point to a large extent to sentences with similar semantic content in Latin and Spanish which contained obligatory copulas (in the case of Spanish the parallels were especially strong with *ser*). Its use has since then been promulgated in innumerable schoolbooks and teaching aids, but it is still not the unmarked option in spoken Tagalog to express this concept.

(6) a. Tagalog: (marked): *Ang bahay ay maganda*
the house is lovely
(unmarked) *Maganda ang bahay*
lovely the house

For a translation of this sentence into Zam one can only have the form

(6) b. bonita el kasa;
lovely the house

But a word-for-word Zam parallel to the marked Tagalog structure, namely example (6c) is not (or at least not yet) possible in the language. The negative copula is *nway*, as mentioned above.

(6) c. *el kasa amo bonita
the house COPULA lovely

Borrowing *amo* as a discourse particle from a Bisayan language and regrammaticalising it by extending its range of meanings has added another way of forming one kind of copular sentences, but the borrowed copula cannot be used in all grammatical contexts. The possibilities and strictures that come with the use of *amo* could themselves be construed as a kind of complexification of Zam grammar. This is because the rise of

---

8. He also remarked upon the occasional use of the borrowed Tagalog *ay*, and the more frequent use of Spanish *es*, in the same way in Zam sentences.

9. There are also parallels with the increased use of *se* (< French *c'est* 'that is') in Mauritian Creole in contexts, such as Topic-Comment contexts, where zero copula was formerly used (Diana Guillemin, personal communication, 14 August 2007).

amo as a copular form has brought in extra rules and greater variation into Zam where less variation previously existed. By adding an optional rule to the grammar it has made the rules for copula use and non-use more complex than they previously were.

4. A note on the use of some other verbal forms

In this section I briefly mention two kinds of Zam verbal forms, neither of which has received a great deal of attention but both of which reflect aspects of morphological or syntactic change in the language. These are the non-finite subordinate clause marker in *al + V-r*, and the *man-* prefix which characterises loan verbs.

Longitudinal studies of Zam materials from earlier times (insofar as they are possible) could probably tell us a great deal about the rise and often the fall of certain kinds of constructions which were used more frequently in earlier material than they are now. One thinks of certain non-finite subordinate verbal constructions, such as those involving adverbial clause markers such as *antes de X-r* 'before X-ing' or *al X-r* 'upon X-ing', both of which are clearly paralleled in Spanish, which uses identical *al* plus infinitive constructions, and both of which seem to be much more frequent in McKaughan's texts than they are in the New Testament translation by de Rivas (1982), where finite subordinate clauses introduced by *kwando* 'when' or *ke* 'complementiser' are the preferred means for expressing such ideas.[10] An example provided by R. David Zorc from his ongoing work on a Chabacano concordance and newspaper reader is given in (7) below.

(7) *al sera-r   el   tarde   mucho maga   bata   ta   rekreya   na kanto*
    at close-INF   the evening much PLURAL child PRES relax   on edge
    del la mar hug-ando   y   ta   represka konel   ayre.
    of the sea play-PRESENT.GERUND and PRES refresh   OBJECT.the air
    'At the close of day many children would enjoy themselves playing at the seashore and take in the fresh air.'

Changes have taken place in other parts of the Zam verbal system. We may also note the rise and continuing use of the Philippine-inspired *man-* construction for assimilating verbs into Zam (and indeed into Cotabateño) from Philippine languages and

---

10. One should be careful of reading too much into Creole Spanish parallels with more morphologically complex constructions. For instance, modern Papiamentu frequently uses forms of the Spanish present participle which is realised in Papiamentu as *-ando, -yendo*. This is a fact which might at first lead one to assume that they are continuations from the participial base-forms of verbs, of the sort which have been recorded for certain varieties of Pidgin Spanish in parts of the Amazon. However, this is not the case; the participial forms are the result of secondary hispanisation and are not found in use in early and mid-19th century Papiamentu documents.

from English (*ya man-tuktuk yo* 'I knocked'; *ta man miss yo kon ele* 'I miss her/him') when they are used as finite verbs.[11] This was not always so. Frake (1980) lists the very few verbs of Philippine origin which were absorbed into Zam early enough to be able to be used without the loan-verb prefix *man-* or without being preceded by a dummy verb such as *'ase* 'to make, do', which is used with Philippine stems (*'ase-lugut* 'to wipe, rub'). When the borrowing of verbal forms of Philippine (and latterly other non-Spanish) origins became more frequent, new strategies were drafted in to enable these new verbs to be accommodated in the language's structure. Since the *man-* prefix is not used in imperative contexts, for instance, meaning that verbs with the *man-* prefix lose it in the imperative while other verbs undergo no change in form in order to create their imperatives, one can claim that this too adds an extra layer of complexity to verbal morphology in Zam.

5. Conclusions and a glimpse into the future

What we seem to find, as far as variation within Zam is concerned, is an increasing use and privileging of those features in Zam which are similar to, or which are even isomorphic with, corresponding features in whichever non-creolised Philippine language (e.g. Cebuano or Tagalog) the Zam-speaker knows most fully. This does not just involve issues in typology, but increasingly also particular morphemes. Indeed the impact of Philippine languages upon Zam has to be seen in terms of the totality of all kinds of features which have been borrowed, not just in terms of the morphemes which have been transferred. The *transfer of patterns* from Philippine languages to Zam, a process which has been going on for a long time, is being accompanied more and more by the *transfer of Philippine fabric* into Zam in the form of Bisayan morphemes which are structural rather than lexical in nature.

The absorption of Philippine features into Zam is preserving its distinctness from Spanish, even though the bulk of Zam vocabulary is still of Spanish origin. Zam is retaining its own identity as a creole language with a mostly 'creole' and certainly non-Spanish and non-Philippine predicate structural system (e.g. operating with preverbal markers and without infixation) while at the same time privileging more and more Philippine linguistic features in syntax, morphology, phonology and lexicon insofar as these features are easy enough to borrow. This should not surprise us: Zam has been interacting with Philippine languages for centuries (see the chronological details of the various periods of contact in Appendix 3), and Philippine languages have themselves been changing under the influence of Spanish and now English for centuries,

---

11. I use the term "Philippine-inspired" because the Zam prefix *man-* does not readily correspond to any particular verbal prefix with that shape and meaning in the Philippine languages which have shaped Zam, but seems rather to be a combination of various prefixes of similar shape with a template *ma(C-)* which each serve to indicate that the stem which follows them is verbal in nature.

with the result that many of the same changes (for example the increasing absorption of alloglot sounds) are affecting languages of the Philippines whether they be of Austronesian, Indo-European or creole heritage.

As a result, Zam is becoming metatypised – typologically modified – more and more in the direction of Bisayan languages (see Ross 1996 for a discussion of metatypy). McWhorter (2005) points out that creole languages in the same situation as Zam, that is languages which are not separated from their adstrates, substrates or superstrates will remain potentially open to the absorption of further features from these languages. There are exceptions to this openness to borrowing into Zam. For example, up till now, as Nolasco (2005) points out, Zam and other varieties of PCS have not developed an ergative model of syntax despite the fact that Austronesian Philippine languages, in which many Zam-speakers are fully bilingual, customarily use ergative syntactic models which are more complex than the nominative-accusative syntax which Spanish has and which Zam also illustrates. But even that development may occur in the future.

Another way of looking at the issue is that Zam is following the same direction as the Philippine languages which influenced it, inasmuch as many of them have long since absorbed lots of features from Spanish and English (including vast amounts of lexicon) which have made them seem increasingly homogeneous. In addition, more speakers of Zam know Tagalog (and other languages) than they did 60 years ago. With the post-WWII spread of Tagalog (rebranded *Pilipino* and now *Filipino*) throughout the area as an educational, military and national language, and of course with the spread of English, Filipinos are becoming increasingly polyglot. The result is that the typology of Zam is moving in the direction of Tagalog and other Central Philippine languages, which will entail moving towards greater isomorphism and greater typological similarity with the Austronesian Philippine languages whose millions of speakers surround the Zam speech community.

References

Aoto, Seiichi. 2002. La copula AMO del chabacano de Zamboanga. *Papia* 12: 84–106.
Blust, Robert. 1991. The Greater Central Philippine hypothesis. *Oceanic Linguistics* 30: 73–129.
Broad, Henry Philip. 1929. Chabacano. *The Philippine Magazine* XXVI 142, 160.
De Rivas, Carlos (ed.). 1982. *El buen noticia na Chabacano*. Zamboanga City: Claretian.
Fernández, Mauro A. 2004. Las lenguas de Zamboanga según los padres jesuitas y otros observadores occidentales. Paper presented at the Curaçao Creole Conference, World Trade Center, Willemstad, August 2004.
Forman, Michael Lawrence. 1972. Zamboangueño Texts with Grammatical Analysis. PhD dissertation, Cornell University.
Frake, Charles O. 1971. Lexical origins and semantic structures in Philippine Creole Spanish. In *Pidginization and Creolization of Language*, Dell Hymes (ed.), 223–242. Cambridge: CUP.

Frake, Charles O. 1980. Zamboangueño verbal expressions. In *Language and Cultural Description: Selected Essays of Charles O. Frake,* Anwar S. Dil (ed.), 275–310. Stanford CA: Stanford University Press.

Grant, Anthony P. 1996. Spanish, Portuguese and Beyond: A Sociohistorical, Structural and Typological Comparison of Zamboangueño and Papiamentu. Ms, University of Bradford.

Grant, Anthony P. 2002. El chabacano zamboangueño, una lengua mezclada. *Papia* 12: 7–40.

Ing, Roseller Ortega. 1967. A brief outline of Chabacano phonology. (in IPA). *Le maître phonétique* 45: 26–33 (3rd series).

Ing, Roseller Ortega. 1968. A Phonological Analysis of Chabacano. PhD dissertation, University College London.

Kaufman, Terrence S. 2001. The history of the Nawa language group from the earliest times to the sixteenth century: some initial results. Ms, <http://www.albany.edu/anthro/maldp/Nawa.pdf>.

Lipski, John M. 1987. Modern Spanish once removed in Philippine Creole Spanish: The case of Zamboanga. *Language in Society* 16: 91–108.

Lipski, John M. 1992. New thoughts on the origins of Zamboangueño (Philippine Creole Spanish). *Language Sciences* 14: 197–231.

Lipski, John M. 2001. The place of Chabacano in the Philippine linguistic identity. *Estudios de Sociolingüística* 2: 119–163.

Lipski, John M. n.d. When does "Spanish" become "creole" and vice versa? The case of Chabacano (Philippine Creole Spanish). Ms.

McKaughan, Howard P. 1954. Notes on Chabacano grammar. *University of Manila Journal of East Asiatic Studies* 3: 205–226.

McWhorter, John H. 2005. *Defining Creole.* Oxford: OUP.

Molony, Carol Hodson. 1973. Sound changes in Chabacano. In *Parangal kay Cecilio Lopez,* Andrew B. Gonzales (ed.), 38–50. Quezon City: Linguistic Society of the Philippines.

Nolasco, Ricardo Ma. 2005. The Chabacano challenge to Philippine ergativity. In *Linguistics and Language Education in the Philippines and Beyond: A Festschrift in Honor of Ma. Lourdes S. Bautista,* Danilo T. Dayag & J. Stephen Quakenbush (eds.), 401–433. Manila: De La Salle University Press.

Pallesen, A. Kemp. 1985. *Culture Contact and Language Convergence* [Linguistic Society of the Philippines, Special Monograph Issue 24]. Manila: Linguistic Society of the Philippines.

Reid, Lawrence A. 1971. *Philippine Minor Languages: Phonologies and Word Lists* [Oceanic Linguistics Special Publications 8]. Honolulu HI: University of Hawii Press.

Riego de Dios, Maria Isabelita. 1989. *A Composite Dictionary of Philippine Creole Spanish.* Manila: Linguistic Society of the Philippines.

Ross, Malcolm. 1996. Contact-induced change and the comparative method: Cases from Papua New Guinea. In *The Comparative Method Reviewed: Regularity and Irregularity in Language Change,* Mark Durie & Malcolm D. Ross (eds), 180–217. Oxford: OUP.

Smith, Norval. 1999. Younger languages: Genetically modified? Paper given at the Second International Workshop on Mixed Languages, University of Aarhus, May 1999.

Thomason, Sarah Grey. 2003. Social factors and linguistic processes in the emergtence of stable mixed languages. In *The Mixed Language Debate: Theoretical and Empirical Advances,* Yaron Matras & Peter Bakker (eds), 21–39. Berlin: Mouton de Gruyter.

Tirona, Tomas. 1923. An account of the Ternate dialect of Cavite, P. I. Term paper, University of the Philippines. Filed under Tagalog Paper 487 in the H. Otley Beyer Collection, Philippine National Library, Manila.

Totanes, S. de. 1745. *Arte de la lengua tagala y manual tagalog*. Sápaloc: Convento de la Nuestra Señora de Loreto.
Whinnom, Keith. 1956. *Spanish Contact Vernaculars in the Philippines*. Hong Kong: Hong Kong University Press.
Zorc, R. David Paul. 1977. *The Bisayan dialects of the Philippines*. Canberra: Pacific Linguistics.

Web source

www.zamboanga.com

Appendix 1. The origins of function words in Mindanao Creole Spanish

1	personal pronouns	Spanish in singular, Hiligaynon in plural
1a	possessive pronouns	Spanish in singular, Hiligaynon in plural
1b	nominal possession: NP + NP	NP + Spanish *de(l)* + NP
2	numerals	Spanish (but ordinal morph is Tagalog)
3	other prenominal quantifiers ('all the X')	Spanish
4	quantifier nouns ('a lot of X')	Spanish
5	relative pronouns	Spanish
6	reflexives	Spanish (though construction 'my body' is un-Spanish and un-Philippine)
6a	reciprocals	Philippine verbal circumfix used, or peri-phrasis 'the one with the other' with Spanish morphs in unique pattern
6b	indefinite pronouns	Creole Portuguese *maskín* + Spanish interrogative
7	question words	Spanish; 'why?' < Creole Portuguese
8	'quantifying' adverbs	mainly Spanish (some are Philippine)
9	place adverbs	Spanish
9a	deictic adverbs	Spanish
10	time adverbs	Spanish
10a	phasal adverbs	Spanish, or Spanish + Philippine mixed forms (*nway pa* 'not yet')
11	prepositions/locational nouns	Spanish; core preposition *na* < Cr. Port.
11a	adopsitionf of place	Spanish
11b	adpositions of time	Spanish
12	dative word	Spanish
13	instrumental word	Spanish (also denotes direct object)
13a	'and' conjoining NPs = 'with'?	no; Hiligaynon (or else a Spanish form)
14	coordinators in general	Spanish (few are Philippine)
14a	'and'	Spanish; Hilig. form (13a) links NPs
14b	'or'	Spanish (borrowed into Philippine)

14c 'but'	Spanish (borrowed into Philippine)
15 subordinators in general	Spanish (but Philippine *kay* 'because')
15a complementisers ('that', 'whether/if')	Philippine + Spanish merger *kay ~ ke*
15b 'if'	Spanish, Creole Portuguese *maskin*
15c 'because'	Hiligaynon, Spanish
15d 'in order to'	Spanish (often borrowed into Philippine)
15e 'when' (temporal)	Spanish
16 copulas	mostly zero; Spanish forms for exposed copulas, also untensed *amo* from Hiligaynon
16a 'to have'	Spanish
17 TMA particles	Caviteño Creole Spanish
17a modal verbs	Spanish
18 negative particles	Spanish + Tagalog
18a focus particle	Hiligaynon *amo*; see copula
19 determiners	Spanish
19a definite articles	Spanish, Philippine (indef. art. < Sp)
19b demonstratives	Spanish
20 plural NP markers	Philippine
21 question particle	Philippine
22 adverbs of manner	Spanish
23 'as'	Spanish
24 'very X'	Hiligaynon
25 comparison, superlation of adjectives	Spanish (= Philippine)

Appendix 2. A stratification of elements in Mindanao Creole Spanish, inspired by the technique demonstrated in Smith (1999), and with features distinguished as to whether they constitute pattern or fabric elements in a language

Mindanao Creole Spanish

Basic lexicon (fabric)	Spanish, 10% Philippine (= Hiligaynon and Tagalog)
Peripheral lexicon (fabric)	Spanish, 10% Philippine
Cultural lexicon (fabric)	Philippine (minority from Spanish)
Derivational morphology (fabric)	Philippine (for the most part), Spanish
Function words (fabric)	Spanish, Philippine
Inflectional morphology (fabric)	(Philippine, but TMA markers are Caviteño)
Syntax (pattern)	Philippine in terms of element and constituent order
Suprasegmental phonology (pattern)	Philippine (and Spanish?)
Segmental phonology (pattern)	Philippine + Spanish + increasingly English
Allophonic system (pattern)	Philippine

Appendix 3. Languages which have influenced or contributed to Zamboangueño at various periods of its history

Language	Period of influence
Manila Bay Creole Spanish	pre-1719
Lusoasian Creole	pre-1719 (forms entered Zam indirectly through Manila Bay Creole Spanish)
(Mexican) Spanish	1635–
Tagalog	pre-1719 (via Manila Bay Creole Spanish), post-WWII (as national language)
Hiligaynon	c. 1719
Samalan languages	18th century?
Tausug	after 1719?
Cebuano	20th century
Hokkien	(dates of this influence are uncertain)
Philippine English	post-WWII

Morphosyntactic finiteness as increased complexity in a mixed negation system

Peter Slomanson

This paper presents data from negation in Sri Lankan Malay (SLM), a language whose grammar has converged typologically on the grammar of Sri Lankan Muslim Tamil, and to some extent of Sinhala. SLM negation exhibits greater inflectional complexity than its lexifier, by encoding finiteness and tense features. SLM has also developed independently of the other Sri Lankan languages. It has developed a strict morphological contrast between all non-finite negation contexts on the one hand (infinitives, participles, and imperatives), and finite negation contexts (tensed verbs). This effectively circumvents the Dravidian constraint blocking co-occurring tense and negation morphology, in order to emphasize a contrast which is salient in the discourse structure that is common to the languages in the sprachbund.

1. Introduction

In this paper, evidence will be provided for the development of increased morphosyntactic complexity in a so-called 'mixed' language, Sri Lankan Malay [henceforth SLM], which I claim is the result of linguistic convergence. Specifically, I will discuss a clear and previously undocumented case of complexification in the SLM negation system.[1] SLM is the only Austronesian language spoken natively in South Asia and is highly convergent with Sri Lankan Muslim Tamil [henceforth MT] and with spoken

---

1. This research is based on an extensive corpus of naturalistic field recordings and interviews that I have been collecting since 2003, and in Kirinda and the southeastern dialect area since 2004. I have not yet recorded in all SLM-speaking communities, but have recordings from communities in each of the three major dialect areas, with particular emphasis on Colombo and Kirinda. I would like to express my deepest gratitude to Mohamed Jaffar and to Mohammed Thowfeek Mohammed Rihan, irreplaceable as friends and consultants, and to the American Institute for Sri Lankan Studies, for funding a stimulating and productive research year in Sri Lanka.

Sinhala, in that order. Those languages are typologically quite distant from the Indonesian Malay varieties to which SLM is related (Malay vernaculars spoken in eastern Indonesia and on Java, [henceforth MJ[2]]). Closed as well as open-class items in SLM are primarily drawn from MJ, however the morphosyntax of SLM partly reflects the morphosyntax of other Sri Lankan languages. I will show that a new finiteness contrast, reflected both in morphology and in syntax, is encoded in fused negation morphemes. These fused morphemes have begun to exhibit functional complexification, so as to encode temporal contrasts. This is significant because the juxtaposition of temporality and negation is structurally constrained in agglutinating Dravidian and Dravidian-influenced languages. The SLM solution to the Dravidian constraint involves the reanalysis of the pre-verbal imperative marker *jang* as a negation marker to be used in all non-finite contexts, and only in such contexts.[3] This enables speakers to mark a verb as finite or non-finite, without using tense morphology. The finiteness contrast has a discourse function in SLM, which is why the contrast in the form of negation elements is communicatively salient. The solution also involves the use of different negation markers to mark verb stems in finite contexts, a development which has a parallel in MT. The status of *jang* as a negation marker in all non-finite contexts represents an innovation in the SLM negation system, demonstrating that a mixed language can exhibit both complexification and creativity in morphosyntactic development.

In Section 1, I will briefly refer to facts about other mixed languages, and ways in which those languages differ from SLM. In Section 2, I will introduce the development of increased inflectional complexity in the SLM verb. In Section 3, I will introduce the morphosyntax of the finiteness contrast in SLM negation, potential motivations for this development, and the ways in which the SLM system compares with and differs from analogous systems in the other pertinent members of the Sri Lankan sprachbund, including MT. In Section 4, I will argue for the biclausality of the SLM perfect construction, using diagnostic evidence from the finiteness contrast in SLM negation morphology. In Section 5, I will introduce a further contrast in SLM negation morphology, which facilitates discrimination between negated SLM verbs, and aligns clearly with a contrast found in MT (and not in Sinhala). In Section 6, I will conclude by summarizing the findings.

The global value of SLM to linguistic science stems from what it can potentially tell us about the events which take place in cases of radical linguistic convergence, producing a new grammar. The changes from MJ grammars to the current grammar are collectively so typologically radical given their extent, that gradual processes

---

2. These are Moluccan and Jakartan varieties or MJ, cf. Adelaar (1991) and Paauw (2004), respectively.

3. There is also a post-verbal negative imperative marker, *tussa*, which follows the lexical verb it negates. It is not phonologically dependent on the verb as is *jang*, but rather it is a free-standing modal which can be uttered in isolation.

of incremental change cannot be assumed to have applied in the manner familiar to diachronic grammarians. Rather, minimally, an important modeling function for adult second language grammars must be posited, leading to convergence of L1 and L2 Malay varieties, with the outcome favoring the L2 grammar, i.e. Malay in the mouths of native speakers of South Asian languages in Sri Lanka.[4] Convergence of L1 and L2 grammars has been posited by den Besten (1989) for the development of Afrikaans from Dutch, albeit with evidence of actual pidginization in the relevant L2 grammar(s) that has so far been lacking in the case of SLM.

We have no a priori reason to assume that an early L2 Malay grammar in Sri Lanka was not itself a morphologically complex one, and possibly also a mixed grammar. If the only languages involved were a variety of Malay and MT, with pervasive access to both grammars for consecutive generations of speakers, then there is no need to expect a pidgin stage to have existed in Sri Lanka. MJ, minimally inflected, was brought to Sri Lanka from Java. Such varieties had long facilitated communication between Indonesians of different ethnolinguistic backgrounds. MT speakers who needed to acquire MJ as a result of marriage or domestic service had sufficient access to it, and Sinhala speakers, as non-Muslims, were substantially less likely to be involved in this scenario. Early structural change in Sri Lanka is likely to have involved convergence, rather than pidginization.[5] There was no termination of access to native Malay speakers, given a continuous history of migration from southeast Asia, however it is certainly possible

---

4. I do not subscribe to the view that the grammar of SLM is primarily the result of extreme cultural pressure in Sri Lanka. While such pressure can in principle contribute to morphosyntactic and other forms of structural convergence over extended periods of time, certain facts suggest a significant contribution by L2 Malay speakers who were native speakers of MT. These include the constrained interaction of tense and negation morphology, and what is known of the social history and culture of the Malay-speaking communities in Sri Lanka. It is nevertheless difficult to argue *conclusively* for the primacy of an L2 catalyst over extreme cultural pressure. Determining how little time and how much structural convergence are sufficient to justify designating an antecedent L2 grammar the critical catalyst is a subjective endeavor, although comparisons with other cases of linguistic change can be instructive.

There continues to be substantial intermarriage of native SLM and MT speakers, and a not insignificant number of cases in which the children of such marriages are raised bilingually in SLM and MT, in spite of the residence of these families in predominantly Sinhala-speaking areas in which their children attend Sinhala-medium schools. Marriages involving Muslims of different ethnic backgrounds has not constituted a taboo in SLM communities, historically, and the current situation perpetuates a cultural pattern which existed in earlier periods as well. See Hussainmiya (1987, 1990) on marriages between Malays and native Tamil-speaking Muslims ("Moors") in Sri Lanka. In most SLM-speaking communities, it is exceedingly difficult to find a Malay family with no Moorish members through marriage.

5. The fact that many of the immigrants spoke Austronesian languages other than Malay natively is not particularly relevant, since stable intergroup Malay varieties predate the Indonesian migration to Sri Lanka in the mid-seventeenth century. While these varieties were and remain inflectionally simple, they were not pidgins.

that the original L1 model was less readily accepted than the putative L2-influenced model would have been.[6] This is a reasonable speculation given the sociocultural prestige of MT in the traditional Sri Lankan Muslim world.

Unbroken access to input languages is part of a glottogenetic scenario familiar from other mixed languages, such as Media Lengua in Ecuador, in which access to both Quechua and Spanish was retained by the speakers of the new language. Fluency in MT was universal in SLM-speaking communities until well into the twentieth century, due to residential patterns for the two communities, the role of MT as a process language in Sri Lankan Islam, and the popularity of religious literature in MT in Arabic script. The SLM case is not identical to the Media Lengua case, but is in fact more radical, since *all* bound and free functional elements in SLM are etymologically Austronesian.[7] Media Lengua does not display the same etymological conservatism that SLM displays in its exclusive retention of Malay morphemes in its closed class lexical inventory and most of its open class inventory. Media Lengua retains the phonological shapes of closed class morphemes drawn primarily from Quechua, while its open-class vocabulary draws heavily from Spanish. In this sense, SLM is more reminiscent of a canonical creole, in that most phonological shapes for both open and closed-class morphemes are drawn from a single lexifier. Michif belongs to a still more distant mixed language type, in that its verbal domain draws its closed class phonological shapes from Cree and its nominal domain draws its phonological shapes from French. As we will see, the inventory of negation elements in SLM retain their etymological distinctiveness, remaining obviously Malay, while at the same time undergoing functional and morphosyntactic changes which set them apart from their etymological counterparts in all varieties of Malay spoken outside of Sri Lanka.

Areal convergence in South Asia is familiar to many linguists from the Kupwar convergence scenario described in Gumperz & Wilson (1971), involving Kannada, Telugu, Marathi, and Urdu. The SLM case provides an added dimension of great value, since the languages involved are not merely genetically unrelated, but also exceptionally distant from each other typologically. The MJ lexical source varieties have little in common structurally with the major southern south Asian languages (including Sinhala, which is genetically Indo-Aryan). The typological distance between MJ and the southern South Asian languages renders development and change in convergent grammars visible in a way that they would not otherwise be. According to a view predating the research described in this paper, SLM is essentially relexified Tamil, or

---

6. There is archival evidence that the households of Javanese exiles in Sri Lanka contained MT-speaking servants, and this will have provided further reinforcement of L2 Malay. While there is an extensive literature on the linguistic effect of domestic servants on the language socialization of children in the Dutch colonial world, there is no documented discussion of this phenomenon in the early Sri Lankan Malay household.

7. One closed class element, the directional postposition and dative case marker *nang* (variably reduced to *na*) is from the homophonous directional preposition in Javanese (Slomanson 2006). All other closed class elements are Malay elements from MJ.

Tamil with Malay phonological shapes (Bakker 2000). That view was challenged in (Slomanson 2005, 2006), based on morpheme order in SLM verbs. We still find direct parallels with Malay itself (of which there are few), with South Asian languages (of which there are many), and non-parallels. The non-parallels in SLM are independent developments which nevertheless still result from contact, and not surprisingly follow the direction of the language's typological drift. SLM's contrastive negation elements are one such development.

I will focus on the syntactic significance of the phonological shape and linear distribution of negation elements in SLM. The first descriptive claim is that the phonological shape of SLM negation elements reflects the finiteness contrast which SLM has acquired through language contact. The contrast helps us to determine the syntax of the periphrastic construction in (1), which I analyze as biclausal. The second descriptive claim I will make is that there has been a complexification of morphologically-encoded temporal expression in negated contexts, so that a non-past negative marker *tuma-*, is in fact non-finite, but aspectually 'rich', reflecting the habitual reading with which an analogous element in MT is associated.

(1) *Farida nasi a(bi)s-makan (tr)-aḑa.* (SLM)
    Farida rice ASP-eat (NEG.FIN)-AUX
    'Farida has (not) already eaten rice.'

The morphosyntax of negation is one of the grammatical systems in which all Sri Lankan languages *differ*. In colloquial Sinhala, the shape and distribution of negation morphemes is dependent on the matrix or non-matrix status of a verb, but not on its tense/finiteness status, as we will see in Section 3.2. In MT, the shape and distribution of the negation element *-(I)llɛ* is similarly associated with matrix verbs, however those verbs are infinitival in form. Negation morphology associated with non-matrix verbs in MT differs depending on their syntactic and functional status (i.e. adjuncts versus imperatives). The finiteness contrast in negation is unknown in MJ varieties, as are morphological finiteness contrasts generally. The finite negation element in SLM is *tər(ə)-* and the non-finite element is *jang-*.

2. Increased morphological complexity in the SLM verb

SLM verbs differ strikingly from verbs in MJ. One significant difference is that MJ varieties display little (Jakartan) or no (Moluccan/Ambonese) productive bound inflectional morphology.[8] Temporal elements in MJ varieties are free-standing, optional, and mark aspect rather than tense, as in (2).

---

8. Jakartan varieties display a passive prefix, which is absent from SLM. It is important to note that to the extent that a Jakartan variety or varieties was a substrate, this represents a loss of morphological complexity, a fact which is consonant with the view that changes in the extent of

(2) *Farida ada kurang tido.* (Ambonese Malay)
 Farida ASP less sleep
 'Farida is sleeping too little.'

Conversely, tense in SLM is explicitly marked, as in (3)[9] and (4), and occupies a different position from aspect in relation to lexical verbs, as is visible in (4), in which the tense marker cannot be separated from the verb.

(3) *Farida kurang arə-tidur.* (SLM)
 Farida little PRES-sleep
 'Farida is sleeping (too) little.'

(4) *Farida nasi su-makan-abis.* (SLM)
 Farida rice PAST-eat-ASP
 'Farida has finished eating rice.'

The presence of contrastive tense marking correlates with explicit contrastive finiteness marking, another contact linguistic accretion. The centrality of tense parallels its centrality in MT, and as in that language, SLM also features infinitival morphology, although this is suffixal in MT and a prefix in SLM (5). In the MJ example in (2), the interpretation of the *ada*-marked verb can be present tense or not, but its aspect can only be durative, which is what *ada* explicitly marks. The *ada* element is separated from the verb by an adverb, showing us that it is a free-standing element in MJ.

(5) *Farida nasi mə-makan nang tərə-bolɛ.* (MJ)
 Farida rice NONFIN-eat P NEG.FIN-MOD
 'Farida cannot eat rice.'

In the SLM example in (3), the interpretation of the *aḍa/arə*-marked verb can be durative or not, but the tense can only be present tense, and *aḍa/arə* itself does not mark aspectual meaning. The *aḍa/arə*-element is obligatorily bound to the left edge of the verb, and cannot appear elsewhere in the sentence. This demonstrates the presence of bound pre-verbal tense morphology that has developed in SLM. The analogous morphology in MT is post-verbal. The SLM verb in (4) displays bound temporal marking on both edges of the verb.

In (5), a clause containing the SLM verb in its non-finite form is the infinitival complement of a free-standing predicate modal of ability. As the predicate in the main clause, the modal is independently negated, and comma intonation can easily separate *tərə-bolɛ* from the rest of the sentence, a clue to its status as a phonological word. The phonological shape of the negation element, descriptively a prefix, indicates its

---

inflectional complexity are not monodimensional, and may operate in parallel, even in radical contact languages such as SLM.

9. Pre-verbal *ada* in SLM has a number of allomorphs, the most frequent of which is *arə*.

finite status. The categorial status of the modal is not clear, because many SLM adjectives can be tense-marked.

The MT examples in (7a–b) and (8a–b) demonstrate the absence of temporal prefixation (as opposed to suffixation) in those languages, contra the SLM examples in (6a) and (6b). This contrast in linear ordering similarly extends to infinitival marking, which is also pre-verbal in SLM.

(6) a. *Farida nasi su-makan-abis.* COMPLETIVE PAST (SLM)
 Farida rice PAST-eat-ASP
 'Farida has finished eating rice.'
 b. *Farida nasi su-makan.* SIMPLE PAST
 Farida rice PAST-eat
 'Farida ate rice.'

(7) a. *Farida shoor tin-də-ṭṭ-aa.*[10] COMPLETIVE PAST (MT)
 Farida rice eat-PAST-ASP-3SF
 'Farida has finished eating rice.'
 b. *Farida shor tin-d-aa.* SIMPLE PAST
 Farida rice eat-PAST-3SF
 'Farida ate rice.'

(8) a. *Farida bat kaala ivərayi.*[11] COMPLETIVE PAST (Sinhala)
 Farida rice eat-ASP finished
 'Farida has finished eating rice.' –
 b. *Farida bat kææwa.* SIMPLE PAST
 Farida rice eat-PAST
 'Farida ate rice.'
 (present=*ka-nəwa*)

3. The finiteness contrast and a *sprachbund*-discordant negation contrast

The morphological finiteness contrast in the phonological shape of negation elements is also encoded in syntax, as we will see. Finiteness does not make a consistent semantic contribution to the sentence. It is a pragmatic phenomenon in the Sri Lankan sprachbund that permits sequential temporal embedding, in which the most recent event is ordinarily the temporal focus. In common with infinitival complements, participial adjunct clauses are not finite. The surface relationship of the SLM verb to aspect changes from post-verbal to pre-verbal when the verb is not finite (Slomanson 2005). Both the sequential temporal stacking of verbs and the finiteness

---

10. The aspect marker here is a reduced form of the Tamil affix *viḍu*.

11. The element *ivərə* (*ivərayi*) is a free-standing predicate adjective.

contrast are demonstrated in the SLM example in (9), in which the aspect-marked non-finite forms *abis-pi* and *abis-blajar* precede and contrast with the tense-marked finite form *su-tulis*.

(9) skul   nang abis-pi, mulbar abis-blajar, Farida nyanyi-atu   su-tulis.
    school P   ASP-go   Tamil   ASP-learn   Farida song-INDEF   PAST-write
    'Having gone to school and learned Tamil, Farida wrote a song (in it).'

The phrase structure of the complex tense and aspect-marked finite SLM verb is found in (10).

(10) MATRIX TENSE AND ASPECT-MARKED VERB
     Farida nasi-yang su-makan-abis.   (SLM)
     Farida rice-ACC   PAST-eat-ASP
     'Farida has finished eating the rice.'

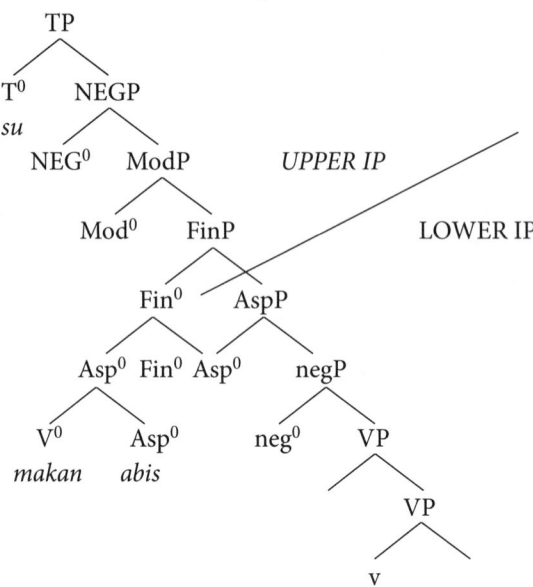

3.1 Deriving negated constructions

The negated counterpart of the sentence in (10) is *Farida nasi-yang tərə-makan-abis* ('Farida has not finished eating the rice') with the finite negation marker *tərə* generated in NEG⁰. The finite SLM verb raises no higher than the bottom of the upper (i.e. finite) region within the inflectional domain. The phrase structure posited is based on more than one type of empirical evidence. The syntactic evidence is the relative position of functional morphemes (aspect morphemes, which are pre-verbal in non-finite contexts, and post-verbal in finite contexts). The morphological motivation for positing different negation positions within the split IP domain is the actual shape of the element and whether or not it can be reduced. FinP is the interface between the two subdomains of IP. There is a separate functional head located in each of these domains, including one for finite negation (NEG^0: *tər, tərə, tra*), which is in the higher inflectional domain, and for nonfinite negation (neg^0: *jang, jeng, jangan*), which is in the lower inflectional domain. This reflects a surface distributional contrast. Finite negation always appears to the left of the verb when aspect appears to the right of the verb. The verb left-adjoins to aspect in finite contexts.[12] A negation element does not attach to the right of the lexical verb as does aspect (*abis*), because the verb only adjoins to (little) neg^0 in finite (i.e. [+tense] contexts, at which point that neg^0 is empty).[13] The two negation morpheme types described here are not allomorphs of each other. Their phonological shapes in fact bear no similarity to each other. The fact that SLM has evolved this contrast is due to the presence of a Functional Stacking Constraint (FSC) (Slomanson 2005, 2006, 2007) in SLM which blocks the co-occurrence of functional morphemes in pre-verbal position. This means that overt independent markers of tense, modality, and aspect cannot co-occur with negation, although portmanteau elements are possible, provided that a checking relationship is possible. For example, modality and negation cannot co-occur if NEG raises to tense before modality does, since the raising of tense would then incur a minimality violation (skipping over the trace left by NEG). Having a lower non-finite negation projection circumvents the problem of raising to tense altogether, since the verb will not raise to tense in tenseless syntactic contexts.

It is significant that the negation system in SLM differs not just from what we find in MT and Sinhala in the Sri Lankan sprachbund, but also from MJ. SLM is the only language in the Sri Lankan sprachbund in which the negation system distinguishes categorically and uniformly between finite and non-finite constituents, with a single morpheme, *jang*, marking *all* non-finite verb types in the language: infinitives, participles, and imperatives. In MT, a verb that is itself tense-marked cannot be negated. Rather, the infinitive itself is negated (11), in what would otherwise be a tense-marked

---

12. The descriptive generalization captured is the fact that aspect is always suffixal in finite contexts. We know these contexts are finite because a tense prefix on the same lexical verb is always grammatical in the same contexts, and because aspect is always marked pre-verbally in SLM participles (where tense morphology is ungrammatical).

13. I have not provided an example of a negated sentence in the adjunction structure in (10), however I have rendered the non-finite negation projection visible in the tree, regardless of the fact that it is technically absent in the sentence exemplified. This is so that the reader can see where non-finite neg^0 is located in IP for constructions in which non-finite negation *is* present, for example, the infinitival construction *jang tidur* meaning 'not to sleep'. In that construction, the verb is non-finite and the phonological shape of the neg^0 element is the only visible reflection of the fact.

matrix verb.[14] Unlike in SLM, no finiteness contrast is marked on the negation morpheme. If this negation morpheme itself were to contain a finiteness feature, we would have to account for the fact that the lexical verb which it negates bears an infinitival affix (-*nna* in (11)). The only way to do this is to treat negation as a verb. This is not possible in describing SLM, since there is no morphological indication of lack of finiteness on the negated SLM main verb, *other than the negation prefix itself*. It might be reasonable to simply treat the tense feature in MT as more closely associated with negation than with the verb itself. Ironically, this works better for SLM than it does for MT though, because the relevant complex is spelled out at the left edge of the verb in SLM, and at the right edge of the verb in MT. On an antisymmetric account of the inflectional domain, it follows that the MT verb is adjoined to this complex, whereas the SLM verb is merely adjacent to it. This disjunction is impossible where there is clear evidence of suffixation to the verb, as there is in MT. This is a part of the analysis of SLM verb morphosyntax schematized by the phrase marker in (10). Whenever that construction is negated (*tərə-makan-abis*), then finite NEG⁰ (left-)adjoins to tense, independent of the lexical verb.

(11) NEGATION OF MATRIX VERB
Farida shattyam pa-nn(a) illə erəcci tim-b-aa ɛndu.   (MT)
Farida promise AUX-INFIN NEG meat eat-FUT-SF COMP
'Farida did not promise to eat meat.'

By contrast, there are different types of non-finite negative suffixes in MT, depending on the verb form (i.e. for an imperative or a conjunctive participial adjunct). The commonality is the constraint blocking tense-negation agglutination in both languages. Standing apart from the facts in MT, closely-related Dravidian languages and SLM, negation in Sinhala always occurs with explicit tense-marking, as in (12).

(12) NEGATION OF MATRIX VERB
Farida porondu unɛ   nææ / mas ka-nnə   (Sinhala)
Farida promise AUX.PAST NEG.MAT meat eat-INFIN
'Farida did not promise to eat meat.'

3.2 A Sinhala near parallel with SLM

Sinhala negates verbs in non-matrix contexts in a manner distinct from the negation of matrix verbs. This is illustrated by comparing the examples in (12) and (13). Both non-finite verbs and participles are treated as a subset of non-matrix verbs, however unlike in SLM, participles are overtly tense-marked (past and non-past), using a combination of apophony and (post-verbal) inflection. Also unlike in SLM, there is a verb

---

14. In some approaches to Tamil morphosyntax, this negation element is analyzed as an auxiliary verb.

movement contrast in the two types of negation, with the negator appearing as a prefix (*no-*) on the verb in non-matrix contexts. The embedded verb can be tense-marked (14). Only in matrix contexts does the verb (left-)adjoin to negation (*-nææ*). SLM verbs do not raise across both aspect and negation, in that order, as they do in Sinhala, but only across aspect. This is consistent with the generalization that SLM, like MJ, does not feature the extent of verb movement associated with both MT and Sinhala. Sinhala, in permitting prefixation of negation in non-matrix contexts, is intermediate between the grammars of SLM and MT in this respect. The string *hondə næ̃æ* ('(is) not good') in (15) shows us that Sinhala adjectives are negated in the way that verbs are. SLM adjectives conversely frequently employ the post-verbal negated auxiliary form *tər-aɖa*, which is frequently reduced to *tra*.

(13) NEGATION OF INFINITIVAL NON-MATRIX VERB
    Farida porondu unaa / mas no-ka-nnə.   (Sinhala)
    Farida promise AUX.PAST meat NEG.NONMAT-eat-INFIN
    'Farida promised not to eat meat.'

(14) NEGATION OF NON-MATRIX TENSED VERB
    oyaa no-ya-nəwa   nam hondə-yi   (Sinhala)
    you NEG.NONMAT-go-PRES if good-PRED
    '(It's) good if you don't go.'

(15) NEGATION OF TENSED PARTICIPLE
    no-gihin   hondə næ̃æ   (Sinhala)
    NEG.NONMAT-go.PASTPART good NEG.MAT
    'Not (having) gone is not good.'

In the following SLM examples ((16) through (18)), we see that the salient contrast in that language's negation morphology is the finiteness of the verb, rather than its matrix vs. non-matrix status as in Sinhala.

(16) NEGATION OF NON-FINITE MATRIX CLAUSE
    Farida daging jang-makang   nang su-tidur.   (SLM)
    Farida meat NEG.NONFIN-eat P PAST-sleep
    'Farida slept without eating meat.'

(17) NEGATION OF NON-FINITE SUBJECT CLAUSE
    daging jang-   makang nang baiə.   (SLM)
    meat NEG.NONFIN eat P good
    'Not eating meat is good.'

(18) NEGATION OF FINITE MATRIX CLAUSE
    Farida daging tərə-makang.   (SLM)
    Farida meat NEG.FIN-eat
    'Farida does not eat meat.'

As stated above, the Sinhala/SLM parallel in the distinct negation of infinitives and participles is only a *weak* parallel, since it is based in Sinhala on non-matrix status, rather than on non-finite status as in SLM. The tense-marking of conjunctive participles in Sinhala adjunct clauses shows us this. In SLM, the analogous participles bear an aspectual prefix in the pre-verbal position, whereas the aspect marker must be suffixed to a [+tense] verb. This is how we know that SLM participles are [+tense] as they are in Sinhala.

Although SLM is clearly a mixed language in global terms, the negation system itself can be characterized as mixed, given the fact that negation morphology is uniformly pre-verbal, rather than uniformly post-verbal, as it is in MT. This reflects verb movement facts from MJ, the source of the SLM lexical inventory, and the language's historical predecessor, likely through the convergence of "genetic" and non-genetic (L2-based) varieties.

4. The SLM perfect construction as biclausal

The SLM perfect construction (19) is modeled on an analogous construction in MT and Sinhala, as in (20) and (21). There is no semantic accretion from MJ to SLM because perfect aspect is frequently marked in MJ, by *su(da)*, which has been reanalyzed as a past tense marker in SLM. The development of the SLM perfect construction does not add a new semantic contrast, only a formal device for encoding the contrast (compensating for the reanalysis of *su* as a past tense prefix). The contrast between simple past tense reference and perfect meaning is quite salient and explicit in the Sri Lankan sprachbund. I will show that facts pertaining to the finiteness contrast in SLM negation support a biclausal analysis of the perfect construction.

(19) *Farida nasi (abis-)makan-aḍa.* PERFECT (SLM)
Farida rice (ASP-)eat-AUX[15]
'Farida has eaten rice.'

(20) *Farida shor tin-d-iikkiy-aa.* PERFECT (MT)
Farida rice eat-PAST-AUX-3SF
'Farida has eaten rice.'

(21) *Farida bat kaala tiyɛnəwa.* PERFECT (Sinhala)
Farida rice eaten AUX
'Farida has eaten rice.'

---

[15]. The auxiliaries in (19) through (21) are all etymologically existential verbs. They are still employed as existential verbs, apart from their function as auxiliaries in the perfect construction.

4.1 Negating different clause types

Negation in SLM appears to the left of a verb in all other contexts, whether or not the verb is finite. Negation markers unambiguously indicate by their phonological shape whether the associated verb is finite. This fact is a useful diagnostic. The examples in (22) through (25) demonstrate non-perfect negation contexts in SLM. The generalization is that all non-finite verb forms are negated by *jang*, and *jang* is the only marker of non-finiteness on negated verbs. This has entered the language through the reanalysis of the homophonous negative imperative marker in MJ.[16]

(22) SIMPLE MATRIX CLAUSE
    Farida nasi tərə-makang.   (SLM)
    Farida rice NEG.FIN-eat
    'Farida didn't eat rice.'

    morphosyntactic analysis of *tərə-makang*:
    upper IP: NEG + T
    lower IP: V + FIN
    V does not adjoin to T

(23) PARTICIPIAL ADJUNCT CLAUSE
    nasi jang-makang, Farida ruma-ka su-duduk.   (SLM)
    rice NEG.NONFIN-eat Farida house-LOC PAST-stay
    'Not having eaten rice, Farida stayed at home.'

    morphosyntactic analysis of *jang-makang*:
    lower IP: NEG V
    V does not adjoin to NEG

(24) NON-FINITE NOMINALIZED CLAUSE
    Tariqa-nang nasi jang-makang (kiyang) Farida su-bilang.   (SLM)
    Tariqa-DAT rice NEG.NONFIN-eat COMP Farida PAST-say
    'Farida told Tariqa not to eat rice.'

(25) IMPERATIVE
    nasi jang makang!   (SLM)
    rice NEG.NONFIN eat
    'Don't eat rice!'

---

16. The homophony with the MJ element is variably lost, due to the new morphosyntactic facts which variably impinge on the phonology of the form. Atonic left-adjacent functional elements in SLM have a tendency to weaken phonologically. This process affects disyllabic morphemes as well as monosyllabic ones. For example the modal prefix *bolɛ-* can be reduced to *bələ-* and *bər-*. The monosyllabic element *jang-* can be realized as *jə-*.

In the completive past construction in (26) and (27), we can see the complex verb, with the verb itself adjoined to aspect. The adjacency of verb and *abis* cannot be interrupted, so aspect is a suffix here. The negation morpheme *tər* that we see in (27) is [+tense], and only appears in finite contexts. It can only appear on the lexical verb, rather than on *abis*, as we can see in (28). *Abis* can also function as a predicate adjective (meaning 'finished' or 'over'), but it cannot function as a verbal auxiliary.

(26) *Farida nasi su-makan-abis.* (SLM)
Farida rice TENSE-eat-ASP
'Farida has finished eating rice.'

(27) *Farida nasi tər-makan-abis.* (SLM)
Farida rice NEG.FIN-eat-ASP
'Farida has not finished eating rice.'

(28) **Farida nasi makan tər-abis.* (SLM)
Farida rice eat NEG.FIN-ASP
'Farida has not finished eating rice.'

(29) **Farida nasi makan jang-abis.* (SLM)
Farida rice eat NEG.NONFIN-ASP
'Farida has not finished eating rice.'

Straightforward participial adjunct clauses assume the form of the leftmost clause in (30) and in (31).

(30) *(Farida) nasi abis-makang, skul nang su-pi.* (SLM)
Farida rice ASP-eat school to PAST-go
'Having eaten/finished eating rice, Farida went to school.'

(31) *(Farida) nasi jang-makang, skul nang su-pi.* (SLM)
Farida rice NEG.NONFIN school to PAST-go
'Not having eaten/finished eating rice, Farida went to school (i.e. anyway).'

In the examples of the perfect construction in (32) and (33), the aspect marker is also at the left edge of the verb, since *nasi abis-makan* here is also an adjoined non-finite participial clause. (Finiteness determines the surface position of the aspect marker *abis*. Finite verbs take post-verbal *abis*, while non-finite verbs take pre-verbal *abis*.)

(32) *Farida nasi abis-makan aḍa.* (SLM)
Farida rice ASP-eat AUX
'Farida has eaten rice (at some time).'

(33) *Farida nasi abis-makan tər-aḍa.* (SLM)
Farida rice ASP-eat NEG.FIN-AUX
'Farida has not eaten rice.'

Certain facts about the perfect construction should lead us to view that construction as having more in common with participial adjunct clauses as in (30) and with its negated counterpart in (31), rather than with the completive past construction in (34) and its negated counterpart in (35). It is an areal feature that periphrastic perfect constructions contain a participial form of the lexical verb (and an auxiliary). The existential auxiliary *ada* can be preceded by a negation element, whereas the same is not true of the aspect marker in the completive past construction in (34) and (35). Due to the finite status of the negation element marking the auxiliary, that verb can be analyzed as the matrix verb in the construction, and the structure containing the lexical verb as a separate clause. The negation element that attaches to *ada* is always *tər*, the finite negation element. We also know that *tər* attaches to *ada* rather than to *makan* because atonic affixes in SLM always attach to the left, and this generalization applies exceptionlessly to *tər*, whose tonic form is *tra*.

(34) *Farida nasi su-makan-abis.* (SLM)
      Farida rice PAST-eat-ASP
      'Farida has finished eating rice.'

(35) *Farida nasi tər-makan-abis.* (SLM)
      Farida rice NEG.FIN-eat-ASP
      'Farida has not finished eating rice.'

4.2 Verb ellipsis as evidence for biclausality

Additional evidence for the constituent status and separability of the structure to the left of the auxiliary and the auxiliary itself is found in the fact that the entire structure containing the lexical verb can be elided in response to a question, as in (36). The negation morpheme remains with the auxiliary.

(36) *Farida nasi abis-makan ada? (tər-)ada.* (SLM)
      Farida rice ASP-eat   AUX (NEG.FIN-)AUX
      'Has Farida eaten rice? (She) has (not).'

4.3 The position of the aspect marker as evidence for biclausality

In addition to the position of negation to the immediate left of *ada*, as well as the finite form of the negation morpheme, the motivation for a biclausal analysis lies in the distribution of the aspect marker *abis*, which obligatorily appears to the right of the verb in finite contexts, through adjunction of the lexical verb. Being able to show that the auxiliary is finite creates a conflict in which we would otherwise expect to see the form in (37).

(37) *Farida nasi makan-abis tər-ada. (SLM)
    Farida rice eat-ASP   NEG.FIN-AUX
    'Farida has not finished eating rice.'

This construction is manifestly ungrammatical, however, which demonstrates that the lexical verb is not finite, and is not the main verb in the construction. Since matrix clauses cannot be infinitival in SLM, this too demonstrates that *ada* is a free-standing auxiliary, rather than an aspectual suffix.

(38) NEGATION OF PERFECT CONSTRUCTION
    Farida nasi abis-makan tr-ada. (SLM)
    Farida rice ASP-eat   NEG.FIN-AUX
    'Farida has not eaten rice (before).'
    (*tər-ada* can be reduced to *tra*)

(39) *Farida nasi tər-makan ada. (SLM)
    Farida rice NEG.FIN-eat AUX
    'Farida has not eaten rice (before).'

(40) *Farida nasi jang-makan   ada.* (SLM)
    Farida rice NEG-NONFIN-eat AUX
    'Farida has not eaten rice (before).'

We can see in (40) that independent (non-finite) negation of the lexical verb is an option, albeit an infrequently realized one. The highest verbal element (i.e. the one on the right) is ultimately tense-bearing, and since the lexical verb in the perfect construction can be negated independent of the presumably tense-bearing auxiliary, this might simply be constituent negation of VP within the matrix clause, rather than negation of an adjoined clause, as in the biclausal analysis proposed. Again we can use the phonological shape of negation in SLM as syntactically diagnostic. All constituent negation in SLM is accomplished with *bukan* (41),[17] however this is completely ungrammatical in the negation of the lexical verb in the perfect construction, as in (42).

---

17. Constituent negation is unusually flexible in SLM. In English and other languages, constituent negation with negative polarity items is ungrammatical (M. den Dikken, p.c.), yet this is not the case in SLM.

Farida su-kasi sapa-nang pun cuma buk-atu   bukan,   tapi
Farida PAST-give who-DAT NPI only book-DET CONSTNEG but
kəmbang-pədə su-kasi. (SLM)
flower-PLUR PAST-give
* 'Farida gave not a book to anyone, but flowers.'

(41) *Farida bukan   makan, bukan   minung su-suka, tapi tidur*
     Farida CONSTNEG eat   CONSTNEG drink   PAST-like but sleep
     arə-suka.
     PRES-like
     'Farida liked not eating, not drinking, but sleeping.'

(42) **Farida nasi bukan-makan   aḍa.*   (SLM)
     Farida rice NEG-NONFIN-eat AUX
     'Farida has not eaten rice (before).'

5. Temporal contrasts in finite negation morphology

The functional contrast between *t*-negation (negation elements beginning with the segment *t*, which are finite) and *j*-negation (negation elements beginning with the segment *j*, which are non-finite) is not sufficient to render tense contrastive in SLM. This is significant because the FSC, which blocks the stacking of SLM functional prefixes based on the MT/Dravidian tense-negation constraint, renders tense contrasts invisible. Other Dravidian languages have circumvented this in various ways.

5.1 Constraint circumvention strategies in Dravidian and SLM

As we have seen, unlike Sinhala, in which negated main verbs are overtly tense-marked by both apophony and affixation (43), the major Dravidian languages, including but not limited to Tamil, have (had) in common that negated verbs cannot be tense-marked (44). The ban on tense morphology in negated verbs led to strategies across Dravidian for morphologically differentiating between tenseless forms of verbs. In Tamil (including MT) for example, the negated form of a main verb commonly bears an infinitival affix and no tense morphology (45), though the use of a participle can indicate non-past reference (46), and there is a habitual/future negative auxiliary (47). While the negated infinitive favors past interpretation in Tamil, it indicates futurity in Malayalam (48). In Kannada, the negated past involves suffixation of the negator to an infinitive (49), while both present and future are expressed with negated participles (50). SLM, as a member of this linguistic area, has instantiated a past/non-past opposition by selecting from the set of two [+finite] portmanteau *t*-negation elements (*tra* versus *tuma*), based on the temporal status of an associated verb. The element *tuma-*, as we will see, can encode habitual meaning, and *tər-* does not refer to unrealized events. This is necessary because in SLM, as in MT, explicit contrastive tense morphemes (i.e. *su-*=past) and negation morphemes cannot co-occur. The FSC in SLM, referred to previously, is related to the Dravidian constraint described. The elements *tra* and *tuma* now encode both negation and temporal feature values. Their contrastive use in place of tense-negation agglutination suggests a strategy for circumventing the FSC.

(43) NEGATION OF MAIN VERB (AUXILIARY)
 Farida porondu <u>unɛ   næœ</u>   mas   ka-nnə   (Sinhala)
 Farida promise <u>AUX.PAST NEG.MAT</u> meat eat-INFIN
 'Farida did not promise to eat meat.'

(44) NEGATION OF MATRIX VERB (AUXILIARY)
 Farida ʃattyam <u>pa-nn(a)   illɛ</u> erəcci tim-baa ɛndu.   (MT)
 Farida promise <u>AUX-INFIN NEG</u> meat eat-FUT QUOT
 'Farida did not promise to eat meat.'

(45) NEGATED INFINITIVE AS PAST MAIN VERB
 Farida kozumbu-kku <u>poo-və-illɛ</u>   (MT)
 Farida Colombo-DAT <u>go-INFIN-NEG</u>
 'Farida did not go to Colombo.'

(46) NEGATED PARTICIPLE AS EXPLICITLY NON-PAST MAIN VERB
 Farida kozumbu-kku <u>poo-v-atu   illɛ</u>.   (MT)
 Farida Colombo-DAT <u>go-0-NOMNLZ NEG</u>
 'Farida doesn't go to Colombo.'

(47) SUPPLETIVE HABITUAL/FUTURE NEGATIVE AUXILIARY
 Farida kozumbu-kku poo-və   <u>maatt-aa</u>.   (MT)
 Farida Colombo-DAT go-INFIN <u>NEG.HAB</u>
 'Farida does/would/will not go to Colombo.'

(48) NEGATED INFINITIVE AS FUTURE MAIN VERB
 Farida avane patippikk-uka-yilla.   (Malayalam)
 Farida him teach-INFIN-NEG
 'Farida will teach him.'

(49) NEGATED GERUND AS PRESENT MAIN VERB
 Farida bar-uvud(u)   illa.   (Kannada)
 Farida come-GERUND NEG
 'Farida does not come.'

(50) NEGATED INFINITIVE AS PAST MAIN VERB
 Farida bar-al(u) illa.   (Kannada)
 Farida come-INF NEG
 'Farida did not come.'

Non-finite SLM negation parallels finite negation by encoding both negation and finiteness features, as [+negative] and [–finite], and by occurring in complementary distribution with temporal (here aspectual) prefixes. The non-finite negation element *jang* is in complementary distribution with the participial/aspectual prefix *abis-*, and with the infinitival marker *mə-*. The fact that SLM requires an independent non-finite negation marker, (*jang-tulis*='not to write'), rather than concatenating the historical Malay negator *tra* and the infinitival marker ((*<u>tra-</u>)<u>mə</u>-tulis*), is a consequence of the historical extension of the FSC to non-finite verbs (and to modal prefixes, which cannot co-occur with negation prefixes), making it stronger than the Dravidian constraint. Negation and reflexes of non-finite status co-occur unproblematically in historic Dravidian languages, including MT. No analog of the FSC is present in Sinhala, in which negated verbs bear tense morphology or morphology indicating non-finite status, and contrastive negation morphology marks matrix versus non-matrix status, rather than finite versus non-finite status, as we see again in (51) through (53).

(51) NEGATED NON-MATRIX (INFINITIVAL) VERB
Farida porondu unɑ: mas no-ka-nnə.   (Sinhala)
Farida promise AUX.PAST meat NEG.NONMAT-eat-INFIN
'Farida promised not to eat meat.'

(52) NEGATED NON-MATRIX (TENSED) VERB
oyaa no-ya-nəwa   nam honda-yi   (Sinhala)
you NEG.NONMAT-go-PRES if good-PRED
'(It's) good if you don't go.'

(53) NEGATED MATRIX VERB
Farida porondu unɛ   nææ   mas ka-nnə   (Sinhala)
Farida promise AUX.PAST NEG.MAT meat eat-INFIN
'Farida did not promise to eat meat.'

5.2 The communicative utility of constraint circumvention

The circumventing of an areal constraint across Dravidian, and more recently in SLM, suggests that certain types of morphosyntactic change are at least partly motivated by universal cross-linguistic tendencies; in this case, by the communicative utility of finding a strategy for morphosyntactically encoding tense and finiteness contrasts in negated verbs, i.e. *across* verb types, particularly in those languages some of whose verb types already have this functional morphology in unnegated contexts, such as the major Dravidian languages and SLM. Constraint-circumventing strategies for the encoding of tense contrasts in negated verbs are very old in historic Dravidian languages. The fact that SLM is *not* an old language (it is at most 350 years old), and the fact that its discrete contrastive finite/non-finite negation affixes developed independently, shows that under the influence of MT, SLM has responded to tendencies that are predictable in the region, only more rapidly. (Contrastive tense and finiteness morphology are available, so strategies for expressing the contrasts in multiple contexts appear over time.)

The negative prefix *tuma-* (*tama-*, *təmau-*) can be analyzed as non-past, since it occurs in future and present tense contexts as well. For Colombo SLM speakers,[18] *tər-* and

---

18. The statement "for Colombo Malay speakers" should be taken to mean "for the subset of Colombo Malay speakers with whom I have worked". There is considerable interfamilial

tuma- may alternate in present tense reference, depending on context. This alternation is governed by the presence or absence of habitual aspectual interpretation. Non-past *tuma* can be described as a fused negative habitual marker, which by definition refers to unrealized events (i.e. I do not, would not, will not). This alternation is paralleled in the *-illɛ/maaṭṭ-* alternation in MT, in which *maaṭṭ-* can be used for the habitual present (as in other colloquial Tamil varieties, see Schiffman 1982; and Asher & Annamalai 2002), and can be regarded as new linguistic evidence for SLM convergence on the grammar of that language. As in MT, the habitual *tuma-* can also be used to express emphatic meaning. Nevertheless, these readings are not available to all speakers of MT. SLM *tuma-* on the other hand is strongly habitual, and many speakers reject the use of *tər-* as a negator of present tense verbs, accepting only *tuma-*.[19, 20] The verbs in (54) and (56) are negative habitual, whereas the verbs in (53) and (55) are negative non-habitual (and non-future). Habitual forms can also be construed as emphatic.

(54) NEGATIVE HABITUAL
 naan tamul paḍi-kka maaṭṭ-en. (MT)
 1s Tamil study-INFIN NEG.ASP-1s
 'I don't (generally, ever) study Tamil.'

(55) NEGATIVE NON-HABITUAL
 naan tamul paḍi-kka-llɛ. (MT)
 1s Tamil study-INFIN-NEG
 'I am not studying Tamil.'

(56) NEGATIVE HABITUAL
 sɛ mulbar tuma-blajar. (SLM)
 1s Tamil NEG.ASP-study
 'I don't (generally, ever) study Tamil.'

(57) NEGATIVE NON-HABITUAL
 se mulbar tərə-blajar. (SLM)
 1s Tamil NEG-study
 'I am not studying Tamil.'

---

variation in Colombo, since regional variants have a tendency to be perpetuated within families there. Relatively isolated Malay communities, such as the SLM-speaking village of Kirinda, display some interfamilial variation, but to a far lesser extent, since there is relatively little in-migration there from other areas.

19. A lexical subclass of adjectives is ordinarily negated with *tər-* by all speakers, however (Slomanson 2006: 141).

20. Verbs marked with *tuma-* are not contrastively tense-marked, and *tuma-* cannot be suffixed to the verb as aspect markers are suffixed to formally finite verbs. This suggests that there is an additional aspectual projection in the upper IP domain, and that the lower aspectual head is associated with completive aspect only. I will treat this contrast in depth in later work.

This parallel between the functional split between on the one hand a general negation marker -(*I*)*llɛ* for non-habitual and non-emphatic main verbs in (Muslim) Tamil and a contrasting auxiliary *maaṭṭ-*, which marks habitual and future forms of verbs, and on the other hand an analogous opposition in SLM, represented by *tər-* and *tuma-*, is another of the striking parallels between MT and SLM (along with the tense/negation constraints themselves), which suggests a primary contact relationship between those two languages in the glottogenesis of SLM. It is important to emphasize that spoken Sinhala does not share the Dravidian constraint, does not morphologically encode future tense, and does not morphologically encode habitual aspect in a manner that parallels the Tamil contrast described.

6. Conclusion

We have seen that the development of the contact language grammar of SLM has yielded a new finiteness contrast, which is encoded in the phonological shape of negation elements across non-finite verb types. All non-finite negation in SLM can be expressed using *jang*, etymologically a negative imperative marker. This categorical contrast between the form of finite negation morphology and the form of non-finite negation is not found in MT or in Sinhala. The morphosyntactically instantiated finiteness contrast is itself an example of complexification in the grammar of SLM and the negation contrast an innovative elaboration of that system. This morphological opposition in the phonological shape of negation elements makes it easier to contrast non-finite and finite verbs, since the morphology of SLM, like the morphology of MT, cannot simultaneously mark negation and tense contrasts, and since negation morphology in SLM marks bare stems only. In that sense, a communicative advantage has accrued under the present system. The presence of [the SLM version of] the Dravidian constraint blocking simultaneous contrastive morphological instantiation of negation and tense is strong grammatical evidence for a primary role for MT in the glottogenesis of SLM. The finiteness opposition in the phonological shape of SLM negation elements also makes it easier for us to see that the SLM perfect construction, also a contact linguistic development, is biclausal. The functional contrast between *tər(ə)-* (past and present non-habitual) and *tuma-* (future and present habitual) suggests the circumvention of a morphosyntactic constraint across major Dravidian and Dravidian-influenced languages. There is no a priori reason to expect inexorable typological drift in which SLM loses all structural vestiges of an earlier Malay grammar. Furthermore, the categorical finiteness contrast in the SLM negation system, an innovation that is nevertheless not typologically discordant with MT grammar, suggests that a future SLM grammar with no remaining retentions from its Austronesian past will not be a relexified variety of another South Asian language. It will remain a mixed Austronesian-Dravidian language with predominantly Malay etyma.

References

Adelaar, Karl Alexander. 1991. Some Notes on the Origin of Sri Lanka Malay. *Papers in Austronesian Linguistics.* A-81.1: 23–37.

Asher, Ron E. & Annamalai, E. 2002. *Colloquial Tamil.* London: Routledge.

Bakker, Peter. 2000. Convergence intertwining: An alternative way towards the genesis of mixed languages. In *Languages in Contact,* Dicky Gilbers, John Nerbonne & Jos Schaeken (eds). Amsterdam: Rodopi.

den Besten, Hans. 1989. From Khoekhoe foreignertalk via Hottentot Dutch to Afrikaans: The creation of a novel grammar. In *Wheels within Wheels,* Martin Putz & Rene Dirven (eds). Frankfurt: Peter Lang.

Gumperz, John & Wilson, Robert. 1971. Convergence and creolization: A case from the Indo-Aryan/Dravidian border. In *Pidginization and Creolization of Languages,* Dell Hymes (ed.), 151–168. Cambridge: CUP.

Hussainmiya, B. A. 1987. *Lost Cousins: The Malays of Sri Lanka.* Bangi: Penerbit Universiti Kebangsaan Malaysia.

Hussainmiya, B. A. 1990. *Orang Rejimen: The Malays of the Ceylon Rifle Regiment.* Bangi: Penerbit Universiti Kebangsaan Malaysia.

Paauw, Scott. 2004. A Historical Analysis of the Lexical Sources of Sri Lanka Malay. MA thesis, York University.

Schiffman, Harold. 1982. Negation and semantic aspects. *South Asian Review* 6(3).

Slomanson, Peter. 2005. The Verbal Morphosyntax of Non-canonical Contact Languages – Malay-derived Constraints and the Inflectional Domain in Afrikaans and Sri Lankan Malay. PhD dissertation, City University of New York.

Slomanson, Peter. 2006. Sri Lankan Malay grammars: Lankan or Malay? In *Structure and Variation in Contact Languages* [Creole Language Library 29], Ana Deumert & Stephanie Durrleman (eds.). Amsterdam: John Benjamins.

Slomanson, Peter. 2007. The perfect construction and complexity drift in Sri Lankan Malay. *Lingua* 118(10).

Contact language formation in evolutionary terms*

Umberto Ansaldo

The aim of this paper is to present a view of contact language formation in which language creation in multilingual ecologies follows the same principles as language maintenance in monolingual ecologies, i.e. selection and replication of features available to speakers in a given environment. In order to do so, I introduce the foundations underlying an evolutionary framework to contact language formation and the views they offer for our understanding of language contact and change. The view of grammar as an evolving system, I believe, can be best appreciated in a functional-typological theory of language. For this reason, I first introduce the basic functionalist, usage-based linguistic theories required for an evolutionary framework. I then synthesize a view on language contact and change in evolutionary terms based on Croft (2000, 2006a) and Mufwene (2001). Finally, I apply the views presented here to a case of contact language formation, namely the evolution of case markers in a variety of Sri Lanka Malay. These are particularly interesting as, from a classic or orthodox view, they might be seen as 'complex', 'marked' or at least 'unexpected' instances of contact-induced change. The evolutionary framework however can explain these as natural acts of linguistic replication in multilingual settings, thus avoiding exceptionalist explanations. Instead, an evolutionary framework offers an integration of socio-historical and functional-typological observation, something that our current approaches to language change still largely lack (Croft 2006b). Among the advantages of the framework applied here, as discussed in the concluding section, is the suggestion that overall structural complexity, however defined, does not change as a result of contact language formation: a new grammar is simply the result of a recombination of grammatical features of the input languages.

---

* I would like to thank Enoch Aboh for his useful comments on this paper.

1. **Introduction**

One of the most fascinating aspects of linguistics is the diversity that is found, albeit decreasingly, in the languages of the world. One question that is still, in my opinion, a fundamental one in linguistics is: How did all these languages come about? Different answers are possible here but it seems clear that any answer will have to be able to account for one thing: the divergence (and convergence) of different languages. In other words, my aim is to contribute to our understanding of language speciation, which is ultimately a window into human history. In doing so, I assume that in the early history of humankind, there have been many episodes of communities being newly created, because of geographical separation, encounters with other populations, etc. Therefore, the study of how new languages emerge offers an important field for understanding how and why language speciation happens.

The area under investigation in this paper is the formation of new grammatical structure salient in – but not exclusive of – contact-induced change as can be observed in the formation of contact languages. Following Thomason (2003), no significant difference is assumed in the processes that lead to the traditional 'types' of contact languages (pidgins, creoles and mixed bilingual languages). In this sense, and following, among others, Mufwene (2001) and Ansaldo and Matthews (2007), such labels, where used, are purely for socio-historical identification. What I argue for in this paper is simple: (a certain version of) an evolutionary framework of language, change and contact offers an illuminating take on what to look for when diagnosing causes and effects of contact language formation (henceforth CLF). It may not force us to abandon other more orthodox approaches, but it adds a new dimension to our current understanding, in particular in offering an integrated approach to both socio-historical and functional-typological analysis. The rationale behind the wish for such a model of CLF rests on three, related ideas:

1. Whichever theory of language and grammar we subscribe to, we view language as a set of cognitive patterns that all humans have in common.
2. Multilingual ecologies have always been and to some extent still are the norm in human societies. The patterns of language use and language change observed in such environments, which include CLF, must be absolutely 'normal' and should not require exceptionalist explanations (Ansaldo and Matthews 2007).
3. It is widely acknowledged that language change and contact-induced change are brought about by speakers; thus, if we want to understand grammatical outcomes of language contact, we must integrate grammatical analysis with sociolinguistic theory.[1]

---

1. Even 'internal' types of change must be ultimately be brought about by speakers, i.e. through idiolectal variation (see Mufwene 2001).

The framework presented here can be seen as a synthesis of already existing proposals.[2] My intention is simply to offer a non-exceptionalist scenario of CLF, i.e. to account for contact-induced change in 'normal' terms (see Section 5; DeGraff 2001, 2003, 2005; Ansaldo and Matthews 2007). Exceptionalism and contact linguistics are closely related as a result of two problematic assumptions common within (historical) linguistic approaches: (i) that the types of change observed in monolingual environments, with normative sociolinguistic tendencies (e.g. standardization) and institutionalized education, are 'normal'; and (ii) that, in reconstructing CLF, whatever cannot be attributed to the lexifier or the substrates must be UG. These, I argue, are questionable assumptions: as stated above and as argued, among others, in Mufwene (2001) and Ansaldo and Matthews (2007), schooling and linguistic homogeneity are recent, modern, ideological reflections of societies from which we should only theorize with extreme care (see also Bakhtin 1981; Kroskrity 2000). In addition, in many cases of CLF, we do not have a full set of documentation available in order to reconstruct the ecology in which a new grammar evolves. What cannot be reconstructed does not necessarily indicate UG, universal cognitive patterns or other abstractions, but may simply indicate a gap in our knowledge (Arends 2001; Ansaldo and Nordhoff this volume). Instead, let us derive generalizations on CLF from well-documented cases where we do have reconstructions of almost complete ecologies. These generalizations can help us establish a not-too-speculative model that will help us reconstruct the process of CLF where ecological information is not fully available.

2. On the history of evolutionary frameworks in linguistics

Evolutionary theory in the history of (historical) linguistics is offered a brief and critical treatment by Janda and Joseph (2003: 7–11). As the current study falls within that apparently problematic tradition, a few words are required to orientate the reader. Perhaps not surprisingly, Janda and Joseph (2003) offer a critical view of organic metaphors of language arising in 19th century Europe (von Schlegel, Bopp, Schleicher, etc.) as basically mistaking language for a natural organism. With respect to these views, they oppose the enlightened view of language as a historical entity expressed, among others, by Bonfante (1946). A little more credit is given to a later attempt found in Lass, most likely the first in modern historical linguistics to present a view of "language as a population of variants moving through time and subject to selection" (Lass 1997: 377). But even Lass attracts their criticism, based on Milroy's (1999) paper which basically identifies the major weakness in Lass's proposal, namely the absence

---

[2]. Moreover, it is a 'lighter' evolutionary scenario than the ones presented so far, as I only pursue the analogies between different types of evolution to the minimally necessary requirements; for example, I do not talk of competition, exaptation, memes, etc. This is a choice derived, in part, from what are a number of negative reactions to evolutionary analogies pushed too far (e.g. Andersen 2006).

of the role of speakers in language change. Janda and Joseph however fail to appreciate what is the fundamental intuition in Lass, which, far from echoing organic metaphors of the past century, tunes in to very contemporary notions of evolutionary theory. Lass (1997) expresses a belief in a theory of a 'historically evolved system', in which both biology and language fall. In Lass's view (1990, 1997), evolutionary theory may help us explain language change, not because languages are seen as biological systems, nor because language is seen as a genetic feature (in the Chomskyan sense). Lass's idea, rather, is that linguistics and biology may be seen as systems that are in some ways similar, most notably in the fact that they evolve over time.[3] The most important question we should worry about, as he aptly puts it, is the non-essentialist one:

> ...which (kind of) facet is the best one to look at given the particular epistemic game one happens to be playing? From this point it doesn't really matter if one is a realist or an instrumentalist, if one wants to grant priority to one particular facet or another. The point always is fruitfulness, not 'truth'. We are Model Builders. We are not (or should not be arrogant enough to think that we are) in the truth Business. (Lass 1997: 384–385)

Lass was partly inspired by Dawkins (1976), who suggested that his work on evolutionary biology could be applied to the evolution of cultural systems. The idea therefore is not that language, change and contact are the same as biological evolution, but rather that they share interesting, common properties worth exploring.

In a critical take on evolution applied to linguistics, Andersen (2006) highlights a number of mismatches between analogies drawn in the fields of evolution of language (change) and biological evolution. This is a common approach that fails however to understand (a) that it is not necessary to attain a total overlap between explanatory models in order for the analogies to be useful (Croft 2000, 2006a, b), and (b) that, at least in the sense of Croft (2000), it is the field of *conceptual evolution* – and not biological evolution – that provides the necessary foundations for a linguistic framework (see Dawkins 1976; Hull 1988). Moreover, Andersen reveals a strong belief in typical products of European historical linguistic scholarship, such as the *Stammbaum* model and the possibility of clearly distinguishing between mechanisms of change, e.g. neologisms, extension, reanalysis and adaptation. It is clear by now that the *Stammbaum* model cannot easily account for the speciation that has occurred in all language families (see e.g. Dixon 1997 for Australian languages), and competing models have existed for a long time (e.g. *Wellentheorie*). Regarding mechanisms of change – which are not discussed in this paper as I believe it is premature to generalize on this aspect of the model – a note is required: typical mechanisms such as the ones listed above, are extremely difficult to keep apart in actual analysis, as can be seen in Andersen's own treatment (2006: 68, 72, 73), which reveals a certain awareness of how blurred

---

3. Note also that Croft (2000) develops a strong usage-based theory of change, recognizing the speaker as the central element, one of Joseph and Janda's (2003) *desiderata*.

these notions can be. Moreover, these mechanisms may serve us to some extent in discussing the histories of languages with relatively uncomplicated, prevalently monolingual ecologies and well-documented histories. This is however clearly not the case in CLF; if we proceed to generalize a set of tools developed to 'fix' 'marked' aspects of speciation (i.e. speciation of written traditions) to fit more 'normal' cases such as CLF, we would be moving in the wrong direction according to point (2) in Section 1 above. From this short historical introduction, we derive three important criteria for a framework of (contact-induced) change:

i. It needs to recognize the historical dimension in language;
ii. It needs to recognize the role of the speaker;
iii. It should be fruitful in offering new insights through novel domains of analysis.

3. Necessary theoretical asides

My framework is inspired by Croft's (2000) Theory of Utterance Selection (see Section 4.2), which builds on Hull's (1988) generalized theory of conceptual evolution. I also re-interpret the notion of Feature Pool in language contact – developed in particular in Mufwene (2001) – in a purely functional-typological perspective. The theoretical foundations are functional-typological (following Bybee 1998, 2006; Croft 2000, 2006a) and usage-based (Tomasello 2003). The latter is a choice that derives from a philosophical orientation and is not a must; in other words, it should be possible to adjust the framework to different theoretical beliefs, as addressed further below.

3.1 Usage-based linguistics

> Language can be viewed as a complex system in which the processes that occur in individual usage events, [...], with high levels of repetition, not only lead to the establishment of a system within the individual, but also lead to the creation of grammar, its change and its maintenance within a speech community.
> (Bybee 2006:730)

Not so long after Chomsky's (1959) review of Skinner, it had already become evident (to some) that the notion of competence was too limited to account for what really constitutes the knowledge a speaker needs in order to be really competent (Gumperz 1964, 1968; Hymes 1971, 1972). In being concerned with what is normally termed 'performance', these and other authors looked at how to seriously integrate variation and diversity in a theory of language. Hymes (1971) for example replaces Chomsky's notion of competence as tacit knowledge of grammatical rules with that of communicative competence, and brings back a behavioral dimension of acquisition of competence. In this tradition, the unit of analysis is the linguistic community or speech community (Gumperz 1968), within which typically a number of varieties are represented; language is therefore regarded as a heterogeneous phenomenon and it is its diversity that becomes a prominent aspect of study (Hymes 1971).

In functionalist and cognitive theories of grammar, linguists do not isolate the structure of language from language use, as grammar is intended as the cognitive organization of a speaker's experience with language (e.g. Givón 1979; Langacker 1987). Grammar in both cognitive and functionalist theories is seen as a set of cognitive representations that rely on general cognitive abilities of categorization, generalization, representation, etc., and are therefore not language-specific. While this view has until recently not been the dominant one in linguistic theory, as opposed to the orthodox, structuralist view of grammar developed in Chomskyan linguistics, in recent years a number of trends have been accumulating substantial evidence in favor of what is clearly a usage-based theory of language, in particular the field of grammaticalization studies, language acquisition and functional-typological linguistics (Bybee 1998). As noted in Bybee (1998), a very important discovery that these approaches share relates to how living languages create new grammar. Research in these areas over the past two decades shows that grammar evolves naturally out of pre-existing lexical material in language use, as is abundantly documented in the literature on grammaticalization (Hopper and Traugott 1993). Grammar is a constantly evolving system in this view and "there is every reason to believe that all existing grammar came about in just the same way we observe in the documented cases at our disposal…" (Bybee 1998:250). Grammar therefore can be seen as an emergent system, complex and dynamic, similar to other complex systems observed in biology (Lindblom, McNeilage and Studdeert-Kennedy 1984; Hopper 1987).

Probably the most systematic and compelling arguments to date in favor of a usage-based view of language can be found in the work of Tomasello (late 1980s onwards) in which sound empirical psycholinguistic evidence and serious theoretical engagement lead to a definition of linguistic competence that recognizes three phases (Tomasello 2003): (i) phylogenetic, as the biological adaptations enabling members of a species to communicate linguistically; (ii) historical, i.e. the process through which a set of conventions emerge in a given speech community; and (iii) ontogenetic, in the sense of the development that leads an individual to acquire full competence during life. Unlike generative grammar, which recognizes a 'periphery', a superficial domain of language that changes over time, and a 'core', the linguistic competence often referred to as UG, Tomasello presents a usage-based approach that recognizes the essence of language in its symbolic dimension, i.e. the ways in which humans use linguistic symbols for interpersonal communication. In accordance with much work in cognitive-functional grammar (e.g. Bybee 1985; Langacker 1987; Givón 1995; Croft 2001), patterns of usage are ritualized (or grammaticalized) into constructions, and new generations inherit such constructions through exposure. The ability of abstracting general grammatical rules, Tomasello shows, is enabled by biological cognitive skills that are not language-specific, but fall under the categories of 'intention-reading' and 'pattern-finding'. Grammar is not a biological adaptation but a historical and ontogenetic process. Crucial to this view is the notion of dual inheritance, which emphasizes that organisms inherit both their genes and their environments (e.g. Durham 1991). This applies to humans as well, but with a twist, as humans are adapted both for pre-existing structures in their environments as well as for acquiring completely new knowledge from the socio-cultural context (Tomasello, Kruger and Ratner 1993). Therefore humans acquire language because they are biologically prepared for it and because they are exposed to their own linguistic culture.

3.2 On usage and the role of frequency

The above-mentioned approaches to language all share the basic assumption that structural aspects of language need to be explained by also making reference to linguistic function, or usage. This is because, as argued above, in usage-based linguistics, grammar is seen as a dynamic system which varies within the life-span of adult speakers; in this view, phenomena of language use influence the representations of grammatical knowledge. In particular, there is wide agreement that frequency plays a dominant role (Langacker 2000; Croft 2000, 2001; Bybee 2001, 1998, 2006). Frequency of usage is responsible for the depth of entrenchment and the degree of abstract generalization of grammatical rules in the evolution of grammar (Bybee 2006; Croft 2006a). As we will see below, frequency is a determining factor in CLF, as it allows us to understand what gets replicated and how the replication happens (see Sections 4.1, 4.2, 5.1, 5.2).

Bybee (2006) offers a review of frequency effects relevant to processing and storage of grammar:

1. High-frequency words and phrases undergo phonetic reduction at a faster rate than low and mid-frequency sequences, e.g. *do not* > *don't*. This can be explained by the fact that articulatory representation depends on neuromotor routines which increase in fluency when repeated. The increase in fluency can lead to a group of words being identified as a single unit (also Anderson 1993).
2. High-frequency strings become more entrenched in their morphosyntactic structure and more resistant to restructuring. Frequency strengthens the memory representation of words, phrases and syntactic structures alike making them easier to access and more conservative (Bybee and Thompson 1997). Bybee (2006: 715) offers the example of high-frequency irregular verbs in English such as *keep, kept* that maintain the irregularity while low-frequency ones such as *reap, reaped* are more prone to regularize.
3. Related to the above, high-frequency strings can lose semantic and syntactic transparency and become autonomous (e.g. words with derivational affixes that increase in frequency lose transparent relations to their base forma, Bybee 1985).

Based on exemplar theory developed in particular for representation of phonetic variation (Pierrehumbert 2001, 2002), Bybee (2006) suggests the following observations about the relation between use and cognitive organization:

i. Organization, or storage in memory is probabilistic, not categorical. While an adult who experiences a new string will be only minimally influenced as s/he already possesses a wealth of older, more entrenched strings, a child, for whom most items are new, will be more influenced in its organization. Repetition or ritualization increases ease of access (Haiman 1994).
ii. Repeated linguistic experiences, just as experiences of other kinds, leads to strong memory of such experiences and loss of non-repeated ones (Goldinger 1996).
iii. Linguistic memories do undergo reorganization.

Frequency effects, as argued here and below, play a significant role in the evolution of grammar, independently of the ecological environment in which such evolution takes place. In particular, we can talk about two broad types of frequency (this is elaborated in Sections 3.3, 3.4 and 4 below, see also Croft 2000):

I. Token-frequency, i.e. the frequency of a linguistic item in discourse, texts etc.
II. Type-frequency, i.e. the frequency of a certain construction in grammar(s).

3.3 Functionalism, variation and language change

From a functionalist perspective, language and grammar are historical entities; it is necessary to embrace this view if we want to seriously embrace the dimensions of variation and diversity that characterize language use, in particular in multilingual, heteroglossic environments typical of contact languages. In Croft (2006a), language change is simply seen as variation at a broader level; his model distinguishes between three different orders of variation. First-order variants are individual variants that occur in all subdomains of grammar (phonological, semantic, syntactic etc.). When first-order variants take on a sociological significance in a community, they become second-order variation. When second-order variation becomes conventionalized in a speech community and leads to divergence, we have third-order variation (i.e. variation across languages). Here, as will be shown below, the study of grammaticalization and typological congruence becomes a central part of the explanation of new grammar creation.

4. A generalized view of change

To understand how we arrive at an evolutionary view of language and language change, we need to first understand the origins of a theory of evolution applied to conceptual systems in general (and not limited to biology). An evolutionary synthesis of complex, evolving systems can be found in Hull (1988); the essence of Hull's position is presented below, followed by an application of his theory to language change as proposed in Croft (2000).

4.1 Selection and replication

Hull (1988) is first and foremost aimed at resolving a number of controversies in evolutionary biology, specifically regarding the objects of selection in the neo-Darwinian debate. At the same time, Hull intends to offer a view of selection that transcends biology and can be applied to conceptual systems at large. For the purpose of this study, and for a general framework of language contact in evolutionary terms, it is not necessary to grasp the actual debate which gives rise to Hull's view, but rather to highlight the product of his work and how it relates to language change and language contact.

i. The nature of change: As an evolutionary model, Hull (1988) is concerned with change by replication; change by replication is one of two (or more) possible types of change, the other being inherent change. While inherent change refers to transformation over time, replication is basically a type of copying. However, copying is not always perfect, as change can enter the replication process in various ways, resulting in *variation* and *differentiation*. In evolutionary biology, copying is an iterative process that is cumulative in nature and that results in a varied set of replicators, due to random mutation.

ii. The trigger for change: The most important aspect of *differential replication* is *selection*. Selection is a consequence of the adaptations that occur through the *interaction of an organism with its environment*. We can therefore generalize with Hull (1988) as follows: iterated copying produces variation; environmental interaction can lead to differential replication.

iii. The locus of change: Hull (1988) assumes a population theory of species. In a population theory, a population is defined as *a set of interbreeding individuals who are reproductively isolated from other populations*; it is within the species that change takes place. This is a departure from an essentialist view of species where a species is identified on the basis of a set of constant structural properties. A population is spatio-temporally bound; there are no inherent properties that define the set but rather relational properties between members of the set.

With these basic notions in mind, let us see how they can be applied to language change, following Croft (2000, 2006a, b).

4.2 Croft's evolutionary model of language and change

Based on Hull's model of change by replication, Croft (2000) proposes the following generalizations (my adaptation). As we can see, points (a) to (e) derive directly from Hull's generalizations presented in the previous sections, as applications of his notions of change, replication and population to language:

a. In language, as in other complex evolving systems, change is caused by replication.
b. In communicating, speakers replicate linguistic features they have been exposed to. This replication can be more or less faithful, resulting in 'normal' or 'altered' replication. Altered replication means change.
c. Change happens at a population level. A population is a set of linguistically interbreeding individuals. The locus of language change is therefore the speech community or the social network.
d. Specifically, a language is interpreted as a population of utterances in a speech community (functional, usage-based theory of language, see Section 2).
e. Grammars are spatio-temporally bound; they are basically idiolects and each speaker's knowledge may include more than one grammar.

Following from the above and from Hull (1988), a population can split into 'varieties' because of geographical isolation; this allows us to conceptualize a phylogenetic classification of languages. We can see that what is appealing in a population view of language is the fact that a close linguistic equivalent of a biological population can be found in the notion of speech community (Croft 2000: 17–20).

In communication, simply put, Croft proposes that speakers engage in the following activities: they select (features of) utterances for replication; they replicate, and in doing so they might replicate identically or innovatively (i.e. 'altered replication', Croft 2000: 38 and Chapter 3.3);[4] finally, they are involved in the propagation of replications within the speech community (2000: 4 and Chapter 7.3). His view of language change is summarized in the *Theory of Utterance Selection* (TUS) (2000: 39):

– TUS does not preclude other selection processes from occurring at other levels of language.
– TUS does not require a specific set of causal mechanisms for the selection of utterances.
– TUS puts linguistic convention at the centre of language change: normal replication means conforming to conventions of the speech community, altered replication means departure from those conventions, i.e. innovation.

From the point of view of TUS, utterances matter, not sentences, meaning that it is the actual occurring linguistic features (texts, dialogues, etc.) that are relevant, not the potential instantiations of grammar. This is obviously a theoretical stance on what constitutes a grammar/ language. In Croft's (2000) view, and in accordance with the theories illustrated in this section, languages are best understood as constantly evolving systems that defy taxonomic categorization. In this sense, language can be seen as a population of linguistic features and grammar as a combination of idiolects (Sec-

---

4. It can be claimed that replication is never exactly 'identical', in the sense that there are not two identical idiolects of a language out there (Mufwene 2001). Therefore 'identical' here needs to be taken in the relative sense of a replication which only minimally modifies the input.

tion 4.3): communication thus entails interbreeding of different idiolects. This means that, when speakers interact, they exchange utterances; in such an exchange, they may replicate the linguistic features of their environment (their community, network, tribe etc.) identically, or they may replicate them with alterations, innovations, etc. An *identical* replication is what we might expect in an environment with a high degree of monolingualism and strong normative tendencies, e.g. a clear notion of standard, compulsory, institutionalized education, etc. Note that language change nonetheless does occur in environments where contact is not present – or salient – which means that altered replication happens in language transmission between speakers in a homogeneous environment. It should follow then that, in a highly multilingual environment with low normative tendencies, an *altered* replication is in fact quite likely (Ansaldo 2008). In other words, in a typical situation of language contact, where speakers afford multilingual competence and where negotiation among different linguistic codes is the norm, altered replication can be expected to occur with rather high frequency. It seems therefore clear that, in order to understand CLF, we need to focus our attention on the dynamics of altered replication.[5]

For a framework based on selection and replication, it is important to clarify the following definitions:

1. The distinction between innovation and propagation is a crucial one that is absent in much literature on language change (but see Lightfoot 1999; Croft 2000; Ansaldo 2008). The general idea is that innovation is something that an individual speaker may do, potentially instantaneously, while propagation is something that happens to innovation at the level of population. The latter is, in accordance with functional-typological theory and grammaticalization studies, gradual.
2. Selection (and propagation) is not functional adaptation. Recall that Hull (1998) is not an evolutionary theory in the strict Darwinian sense; therefore there is no notion of selection and competition as 'survival of the fittest'. In accordance with abundant sociolinguistic literature, selection of variables is socially determined, and may be related to issues of accommodation, imitation, differentiation etc.
3. The mechanisms of innovation are predominantly functional-typological (see Section 3.3).

---

5. I want to stress how this is a theoretical stance that is, as all theoretical stances are, a matter of one's philosophy of language. As Lass reminds us, we are not into the Truth Business; therefore a different take, say, a formal one, may also be possible. As we will see below, Croft (2000) identifies the utterance as the relevant unit that undergoes change in language use. This can be easily replaced by 'sentence' in a different theoretical orientation, and allows for other types of generalization to be invoked.

4.3 CLF as innovative replication

In an evolutionary view of CLF, speakers in a multilingual community have a very heterogeneous set of utterances from which to extract material for replication. This framework assumes that an extremely low level of multilingual competence is sufficient for different linguistic systems to interfere in a speaker's use of language (already in Weinreich 1953), and that new language creation is the natural, creative process that typifies CLF (see Heine and Kuteva 2005).[6]

From what we have seen so far, an evolutionary view of CLF leads us to pay attention to the mechanism of replication and the types of the replication that occur, in particular altered or innovative replication. It also highlights selection and propagation as important areas to look into in order to understand how new variables move within a population. Following Hull (1988) and Croft (2000), and echoing views found, among others, in Thomason and Kaufman (1998) as well as Janda and Joseph (2003), an evolutionary view of contact-induced change acknowledges that it is speakers who change languages, not languages that change themselves. The main area of analysis for a proper understanding of language contact is therefore the socio-historical (and political, economic, cultural dimension). However, as suggested in Croft and as argued below, there is one phase of the process that can be looked at as partially independent from socio-historical dynamics, namely innovation. For the purpose of simplification, let us visualize the main phases of CLF as follows:

I. Selection: Whether speakers select certain features over others is predominantly a matter of social dynamics. There is plenty of literature on this topic, from variational sociolinguistics to the study of ethnolinguistic vitality to show that different forms of prestige play a role in CLF. For example, in the formation of Singapore English, notwithstanding the fact that English is a powerful lexifier with economic capital and institutional support, speakers selected abundant material from Sinitic varieties, due to the fact that these represent a substantial part of the population and do carry both overt and covert prestige (Ansaldo 2004; Lim 2007). Moreover, a few features from Malay were also selected at a point in time where Malay-based contact languages were present in the ecology of Singapore English, and due to founder effects they survive to this day (Mufwene 1996; Ansaldo 2009; also Ansaldo, Lim and Mufwene 2007).

II. Innovation: How variables interact with one another depends, at least in part, on their typological and functional properties (Croft 1995). This phase can thus be – to some extent – investigated on its own terms, though it is never completely independent from socio-historical principles. As I will argue below, frequency

---

6. This is not meant to imply that every multilingual society must lead to CLF. Obviously in societies where standardized varieties are institutionally supported and normative tendencies are enforced, the linguistic ecology may be stable and not particularly prone to high degrees of innovative replication.

needs to be identified as a central factor behind creation of grammar, and related effects such as salience and congruence need to be taken into account. For example, in accounting for the emergence of case in Sri Lanka Malay, we can see how token frequency, i.e. frequency of occurrence, and type frequency, i.e. frequency that emerges out of typological congruence of two adstrates, lead to case features being selected in the replication process (Aboh and Ansaldo 2007; Ansaldo 2009; and Section 5).

III. Propagation: Propagation happens at the broader level of social organization, and requires that we take into account social network dynamics such as density and multiplexity (Milroy and Milroy 1992). The observations here vary, from suggesting that small, tight-knit communities are more conservative to opposing views suggesting that change can spread fast in such communities (cf. Nettle 1997; Trudgill 2002). I suggest that both views are correct, in the sense that *small, tight-knit communities afford a higher control on usage*, and can therefore intervene successfully on maintenance or change, depending on socio-historical situations. More importantly, speed relates to community type, as propagation can be fast in smaller and tighter groups, but is slower in large, diffuse communities. This explains why CLF, most typical of medium to small and often tightly-knit groups, has been often described as 'rapid' in the literature (see also Matras and Bakker 2003; Ansaldo and Nordhoff this volume).

Remember that the three 'processes' listed above are not really separate phases with a hierarchical ordering, as clearly explained for evolving systems in general in Hull (1988). Nor can we treat them as referring to different domains of analysis: just as the interaction between replication and evolution is independent of the levels of organization in evolutionary biology, so can selection, propagation and innovation occur simultaneously and iteratively at any level of organization. In particular, selection and propagation are really concomitant processes, and innovation is abstracted in order to allow functional-typological analysis to take place.[7]

Thus far, we have addressed two important questions. The first question is the *what*-question: what are we looking for when investigating CLF? This has been answered in evolutionary terms, identifying the process of replication as the driving mechanism of change and suggesting that differential replication, i.e. innovation, constitutes one of the salient aspects of CLF. We have also specified *where* such processes can be found, i.e. in the speech community and in language use (this leaves us with

---

7. Note that I do not explicitly bring in the notion of competition in this approach. Obviously a type of competition takes place at least in the social (and political, economic, cultural) domain, which does impact on the selection of certain variables over others. One could also claim that frequency patterns do indeed represent a form of competition, as higher frequency items seem to 'win' over lower frequency ones. However, for the purpose of this paper, the notion of frequency seems sufficient to capture the dynamics of CLF I have in mind. We will surely need more on competition in the future.

a number of possible analytical domains, see the next section). The *how*-question, I have argued, needs to be answered in functional-typological terms: since the relevant domains of enquiry are usage and diachrony, we look at functional-typological properties of language as well as grammaticalization patterns (as a holistic study of emergence of new grammar). There is a fourth question that needs to be answered, for any framework to be worth considering, and this is the *why*-question. This will be addressed in the concluding section.

4.4 The typological matrix and ecology

The notion of the typological matrix (TM) is intended here as the total set of linguistic variables available to a group of people related by shared patterns of communication (a linguistic network / a speech community). The reader may recognize here previous proposals such as Croft's (2000) notion of Lingueme Pool and Mufwene's (2001) Feature Pool. Some minor differences between TM and these alternative notions are the following:

1. Croft's notion of Lingueme Pool is justified by the desire to keep the genetic analogy as tight as possible and implies the notion of 'lingueme' (2000:29) as the linguistic replicator. In genetics, it is recognized that genes come in highly organized structures (e.g. DNA strings) but, as Croft suggests, language change may not show such an organization. This applies even more so to CLF, where attempts to identify (typological) constraints have so far largely failed (Heine and Kuteva 2005; Koptjevskaja-Tamm to appear). Though I am not suggesting that there are no organizational constraints whatsoever in the TM, I want to suggest that there are few and very flexible ones.
2. Mufwene's Feature Pool is a looser concept than Croft's, implying issues of markedness as significant factors in determining the outcome of this process. Moreover, there is also a dimension of discourse salience (e.g. 'perceptual salience' and 'semantic transparency' in Mufwene 1991) that plays a role in the selection process. These are partly useful notions, as I will show below, but in the TM, frequency substitutes for markedness and salience.

The notion of TM simply suggests that, in CLF where typically variables of different typological origins interact, if it is not in the social history of speakers, it is in typological analysis that we find the key to understanding *how* new grammar emerges. This is particularly relevant in the context of this volume as a TM-based approach predicts that the output of a contact ecology is largely dependent on the input (see also Mufwene 2001). In other words, according to the TM, complexity or simplicity however defined do not dramatically increase or decrease in CLF, as the output is a recombination of variables of the input. Moreover, TM provides a convenient way to identify this particular version of evolutionary frameworks of CLF.

The notion of TM offers a convenient abstraction for the purpose of function-form analysis, and allows us to distinguish between socio-historical investigation, which is required to understand selection and propagation, and actual innovation, i.e. different patterns of recombination of variables. Remember however that these phases are not entirely independent from one another and that innovation does depend on selection and successful propagation.

In analyzing TMs, the most salient factor is frequency. As we saw in Section 2, from a functional-typological perspective, frequency is the dominant factor in evolution of grammar, and it comes in two types (Croft 2000, 2006a):

i. Token-frequency: This can be seen as discourse frequency. Linguistic items that are frequent in discourse may be those that are grammatically obligatory, semantically salient or pragmatically more relevant (Aboh and Ansaldo 2007). One such case is Experiencer marking in SLM, as will be shown in Section 5.
ii. Type-frequency: Linguistic items that are type-frequent in CLF are those constructions that are more common ('unmarked') in a specific grammar, for example, because of typological congruence, where the occurrence of the same type in two adstrates reinforces its presence in the TM, as in the case of Dative markers in SLM, as will be seen in Section 5.[8]

Note that frequency patterns, as argued in Haspelmath (2006), can usefully replace the typological notion of markedness in all its linguistically relevant uses, whether in the sense of common, complex, overtly marked or otherwise. It therefore also replaces my earlier use of 'local markedness' as *relative to a single linguistic system*, in CLF (Aboh and Ansaldo 2007).

5. Application

In this section, I look at cases of altered replication involved in the formation of Sri Lanka Malay. By applying the notions of selection, propagation and innovation introduced above, I account for the emergence of what appear as 'complex' constructions as predictable instances of innovation given the ecology of the contact language and its related TM. First the (subset of the) TM of a variety of Sri Lanka Malay, namely Kirinda Java (KJ), is identified based on the principles of selection. Then the relevant domain of the TM is investigated to show its internal dynamics. As we will see, the evolutionary framework is particularly suited to unveil the interaction between the socio-historical principles and the functional-typological dynamics that characterize the three 'phases' introduced above.

---

8. This proposal was still being developed at the time of writing. See Ansaldo (2009) for a fuller account.

5.1 Kirinda Java

Kirinda Java (KJ) is the southernmost variety of Sri Lanka Malay (SLM) (Ansaldo 2005a, 2008). Though the differences between varieties of SLM may not be overwhelming (Nordhoff in preparation), the Kirinda community is a distinctive speech community clearly 'isolated' from other communities (Lim and Ansaldo 2006). As first noted in Hussainmiya (1987), the restructured Malay spoken in Sri Lanka has a fully-developed case system, a marked feature for Malayic languages which typically lack case altogether. Ansaldo (2005a, 2008) describes the Malay of Sri Lanka as a mixed language of trilingual base, in order to capture the fact that this is a heavily 'restructured' variety that evolves in a multilingual situation where Sinhala, Tamil and Malay mix in almost all aspects of grammar. Lexically these varieties show heavy maintenance of Malayic words and a pronominal system of clear pidgin-Malay-derived nature (PMD, see Adelaar and Prentice 1996). These are pronominal forms originally from Hokkien (Sinitic) found in many contact varieties of Malay in the region, a strong evidence of a Founder Principle effect in this case (Mufwene 1996). From the point of view of complexity, as already argued in Aboh and Ansaldo (2007), as well as Ansaldo and Nordhoff (this volume), a case system is clearly a 'complex' type of development in CLF and is typologically marked within Austronesian languages (see also Dahl 2004). This study however is not a full description of the case system of KJ (see Ansaldo 2005a; Aboh and Ansaldo 2007; as well as Smith et. al 2004 for general SLM case features). I focus here only on the core cases in KJ, in order to apply an evolutionary framework to the evolution of case in CLF.

5.2 What goes into the matrix

As argued above, speakers and their socio-history are the salient factors behind change, which occurs through replication. The environment in which KJ evolves is a multilingual speech community without particular segregation between the Malay, Sinhalese and Tamil ethnic groups. The history of the early Malays in Sri Lanka is one of active interethnic exchange and communication (Hussainmiya 1987, 1990); in an evolutionary sense, this means free mixing as elements from the three different languages are and were present in the every day communication between speakers of Malay, Sinhala and Tamil.[9] Therefore, a priori, we must assume that Malay (colloquial Malay), Sinhala and Lankan Tamil features were all available for selection and replication to the (early) Malay immigrants in Sri Lanka.

---

9. Interbreeding is strictly communicative; it does not suggest actual sexual mating between the different groups. Though this is also a possibility, it is, in the case of Sri Lanka Malay, a very unlikely one based on historical documentation (see Ansaldo 2008, cf. other proposals, e.g. Smith et al. 2004).

However these features were not *equally* available for selection. In Sri Lanka, Sinhala was and is the language of the majority, with political and economic prestige. Because of numbers and prestige, we have to assume that Sinhala features had very high frequency in the ecology in which Sri Lanka Malay evolved; frequency was identified in Section 3 as the dominant force behind usage and therefore replication. This means that Sinhala features were more likely to be selected. At the same time, we cannot disregard the potential vitality that the ancestral language, in this case colloquial form(s) of Malay, carries in many contact environments, i.e. the wish to maintain features of one's own ethnic variety. Therefore, so far, we may want to assume good reasons for early Malay speakers to accommodate to Sinhala, considering the basic tendency of speakers to accommodate to the stronger 'norm'; in other words, selection of Sinhala features by Malay speakers should be expected.[10] But we also need to factor in a potential counter-tendency: the wish to maintain one's own language, i.e. selection of Malay features. The third language, Tamil, was, just as it is today, in an inferior position to Sinhala, numerically and economically, as the language of a predominantly lower-class minority, and was therefore undoubtedly less prestigious (Ansaldo 2008). Tamil is thus also present in the ecology and, though less likely to be a candidate for selection, cannot be totally excluded.

Let us now abstract the dimension of functional-typological analysis and reflect on innovation: what can happen in the TM of KJ, where Sinhala, Malay and (to some extent) Tamil features 'interact'? Sinhala has high token-frequency (numerical dominance), which results in salient discourse presence of Sinhala features. Here Tamil starts playing a role, as Sinhala and Tamil have converged typologically over the past thousand years and share many areal features (Masica 1978). From the typological point of view, Tamil reinforces the type-frequency of Sinhala features, where the grammars correspond. For example, Sinhala is SOV, Tamil is SOV, and Malay is SVO. A TM with these word orders would clearly imply the possibility that the output be an SOV language, because one of the SOV orders is numerically dominant in discourse, and the two congruent orders 'gang-up' and are selected (as well as propagated). Indeed the basic word order of KJ (and other varieties of Sri Lanka Malay) is SOV (though variation occurs, of course). Another example is found in morphological processes: the TM has [inflectional (Sinhala) + inflectional (Tamil) + mildly agglutinative (Malay)] morphology; the outcome is an inflecting language, as argued for KJ in Ansaldo (2005a) and other SLM varieties in Ansaldo and Nordhoff (this volume). Where they do not show congruence, this may either undermine the frequency, by offering another alternative for selection, or simply be irrelevant. Moreover, we have to consider functional properties of specific features, i.e. whether they are obligatory in discourse or highly regular, as this increases frequency or 'visibility' in terms of selection (Aboh and Ansaldo 2007 and below).

---

10. I do not mean to suggest that overt prestige is the only form of prestige that matters in CLF. Covert prestige can be just as influential in selection, but it does not seem to apply to this particular scenario (see also Ansaldo 2008).

Table 1. Case alignment in Kirinda Java

Case	Main function	Behavior
Nominative	Agent [+ control]	
Dative	Experiencer/Patient/Goal [control] (Sin. and Tam.)	obligatory
Accusative	+ Animate (Sin.) + Definite (Tam.)	optional

5.3 Selection and innovation

In KJ Nominative case is used primarily for prototypical agents and is zero-marked. Dative is the most frequently expressed and functionally diverse case, marking predominantly Experiencer roles (the 'non-nominative subject' of South Asian languages, see Bhaskararao and Subbarao 2004). Accusative case is highly optional, mostly used for definiteness and/or emphasis (see examples (1)–(3) below). As mentioned above, case is not a feature of Austronesian typology and is absent from Malay varieties. It is clear that case features enter the TM of KJ from Sinhala and Tamil. The functions of core cases in these languages is summarized in Table 1.

As we can see, there is a significant functional overlap between the cases of Sinhala and Tamil and the ones of KJ. Cases are realized as post-nominal suffixes, showing at least partial structural overlap as well, as in examples (1)–(3):

(1) *master=nang pena mau*
 teacher=DAT pen want
 'Teacher wants a/the pen'

(2) *pohong=yang potong*
 Tree=DOM[11]   cut
 '(I) cut the tree'

(3) *go=dang minum mau*
 I=DAT drink want
 'I want/ would like a drink'

We can say that the grammar of case is 'Lankan' (Sinhala/Tamil) but the case suffixes are of Malay origin. *-nang* (in (1)) is a directional preposition in Malay; *-yang* (in (2)) is most likely derived from a Malay colloquial definite marker *-nya* (Uri Tadmor p.c. 2004; for more on this see Ansaldo 2005a; Slomanson 2006); *-dang* (in (3)) is a variant of *-nang* found in the pronominal system (most likely due to Animacy, see below). It is clear that case-marking in KJ evolves as innovative replication in a TM in which case becomes a very frequent option, in the sense that it reflects the linguistic usage of a

---

[11]. Following Ansaldo (2005a, b) what is normally seen as Accusative case is here glossed as 'definite object marker', with possibly emphatic function.

majority of speakers because it is high in both token- and type-frequency. The specific frequency patterns in this TM can be explained as follows:

i. Dative case is assigned identically in Sinhala and Tamil: we have a complete functional overlap as it covers the same semantic roles of Experiencer, Goal and (certain types of) Patient (see Ansaldo and Aboh 2007). This gives it high type-frequency and therefore high visibility. It is obligatory (or regular), which results in extremely high discourse (or token-) frequency and strengthens its dominance. Moreover it is used to encode the Agent-Experiencer opposition, which seems like a rather salient communicative function; this means visibility to the speaker.

ii. Accusative case shows only partial semantic overlap in the adstrates and is highly irregular; therefore, while token-frequency may be high because of a numerical dominance of Sinhala (and to a lesser degree) Tamil utterances in the environment, type-frequency is much lower than Dative. This is related to and enhanced by the fact that the functions it marks are less communicatively crucial. Animacy in Sinhala is usually only marked in high-register variants (Gair and Paolillo 1997) and definiteness is not a constantly salient feature (Accusative marking cross-linguistically is mostly optional, Blake 1994); this also reduces the token-frequency of the Accusative.

The result is that, in the grammar of KJ, Dative case is a regular, frequent and robust feature, while Accusative is a highly irregular, elusive, optional feature, as shown in examples (1) and (3) above. From these observations we derive that a framework such as the one tested here seems to allow us to reflect not only on what is realized through the innovation process but also on how specific features may be realized.

Finally, it is important to note that spatial adpositions are recognized as the most common source of case markers in grammaticalization studies; in this case, as assumed in general in this paper, there is no difference between the processes of change that occur in CLF and elsewhere in historical linguistics (Hopper and Traugott 1993). Moreover, the construction follows predictable typological motivations: the postnominal position of case markers is coherent with the verb-final word-order.

5.4 A note on propagation

Having reflected on selection and innovation, we now briefly consider propagation. As noted above, there is another crucial dimension to propagation, namely network type. Considering the case system as a whole, it may appear remarkable that such a system may evolve in 300 years of history. Indeed, as also discussed in Ansaldo and Nordhoff (this volume), such a complex set of features is not supposed to arise 'quickly' in evolution of grammar (Dahl 2004), and not at all in CLF (McWhorter 2005). But, as argued in Section 3, propagation is a matter of social dynamics, not a structural process with an inherent clock. The Malay communities of Sri Lanka are, to this day, small, tightly-knit but open communities. In such communities, I suggest (and see Matras and Bakker 2003 for similar claims on 'mixed languages') that enforcement of usage is highly effective, whether it is innovative or conservative (cf. Nettle 1997; cf. Trudgill 2001; and see Ansaldo 2009). This suggests that speed is to a large degree relative to type and size of speech community.[12]

5.5 Summary

The evolution of a complex feature of grammar such as case in CLF can be accounted for within an evolutionary framework based on principles of selection, innovation and propagation, with the help of functional-typological analysis of the matrix. In this way, sociohistorical dynamics and functional-typological features are integrated within the same framework. By relying on theories of grammatical evolution and sociolinguistic principles that underlie communication at large, an evolutionary framework suggests that the process of language creation is the same across societies, but that different ecologies lead to diverse outputs. A generalized approach like this is not only desirable; it is necessary if we still subscribe to the view that communication, and therefore language change, including CLF, is a basic human feature that we all share and that functions according to some, perhaps very few, universal principles. The principles invoked to account for case in KJ are in harmony with those presented in Sections 1–3, namely:

1. In CLF, a salient aspect is differential replication, as we are trying to account for the emergence of new structure (and new languages).
2. We look at language as a population of utterances or speech community – in CLF this means a dynamic, heteroglossic population; its functional-typological make-up may, for convenience of analysis, can be abstracted as the Typological Matrix.
3. In CLF, selection, innovation and propagation occur iteratively and feed into one another. The most likely candidates for selection and propagation are determined based primarily on sociohistorical analysis and typological make-up, within which frequency patterns play a dominant role.

The notion of TM suggests that the output in CLF can be fully made sense of by looking at the input languages; I do not necessarily hold that other types of change, such as internal or independent changes, may not occur. For example, I have hypothesized that an earlier stage of the Dative-Accusative case system may have seen a conflated case that then split into the two cases we have today (Ansaldo 2005a, b). The reason for such an hypothesis was the fact that, in the history of languages, we have at least one attested case of such a diachronic pattern, where an adposition grammaticalizes first into a more generic marker and then specializes, namely Persian (Blake 1994).

---

12. It may be the case that relatively unmarked variables might move faster through a community than marked ones, but then again it may be the case that highly infrequent variables do not get selected at all, which makes this difficult to prove.

But it is a rare change and we do not have appropriate historical evidence available to prove it or disprove it, so it is ultimately a little futile to discuss it. However, I believe that 'invisible hand' changes should be treated very carefully, as a last resort in trying to account for CLF, and we should always be aware of the possibility that, more often than not, these hypotheses arise from imperfections in the data and/or in our knowledge and understanding of the TM. A case in point is the pronoun system of KJ that shows Animacy effects, as pronouns are marked by the suffix *-dang* (rather than *-nang*, see Ansaldo 2005a, b, 2008). This we could label an independent innovation of KJ; at the same time, Animacy is a feature present in various domains of Sinhala grammar. In a sense, therefore, Animacy is present with the TM in which KJ evolves; calling it 'independent' may simply be a way to say that, for now, we cannot make sense of why it is selected and then realized as innovation within the pronominal system.

6. Concluding remarks

At this point let us consider the *why*-question: 'do we really need all this in order to talk about CLF?' The answer, I believe, is a clear 'yes'. In contact-linguistics, in particular in the field of language creation, there has been relatively slow progress in crucial areas of investigation. As this volume (and others, e.g. Ansaldo, Matthews and Lim 2007) shows, for example, the field has struggled with notions of complexity, notwithstanding the alarm bells rung as early as Muysken (1988) that a proper discussion on the matter of complexity would have to be based on a clear and shared theory of what is really grammatically complex and what is not. The approach presented above offers a theoretical domain in which complexity can be properly investigated in terms of input-output relations. The views of transmission proposed in the field often assuming some kind of 'failure' on the part of speakers in CLF, or at least some imperfect or abnormal process at play (imperfect acquisition, rapid change etc., see Ansaldo and Matthews 2007), have been criticized for ideological bias as well as theoretical shortcomings (DeGraff 2001, 2003, 2005). The framework presented above offers a neutral approach to CLF in which sociohistorical and functional-typological analysis find integration. Work on alleged universal properties of contact languages such as Creoles have made a number of controversial claims (e.g. McWhorter 2005); such claims, I believe, can be more thoroughly investigated within this framework, and promise less controversial solutions, that can be integrated into general linguistic theories of language rather than requiring exceptional treatment.

References

Aboh, Enoch O. & Ansaldo, Umberto. 2007. The role of typology in language creation: A descriptive take. In *Deconstructing Creole* [Typological Studies in Language 73], Umberto Ansaldo, Stephen Matthews & Lisa Lim (eds), 39–66. Amsterdam: John Benjamins.

Adelaar, Karl Alexander & Prentice, J. D. 1996. Malay: Its history, role and spread. In *Atlas of Languages of Intercultural Communication in the Pacific, Asia and the Americas*, Stephen A. Wurm, Peter Mühlhäusler & Darrell T. Tryon (eds), 673–693. Berlin: Mouton de Gruyter.

Andersen, Henning. 2006. Synchrony, diachrony and evolution. In *Competing Models of Linguistic Change: Evolution and Beyond*, Ole N. Thomsen (ed.), 59–90. Amsterdam: John Benjamins.

Anderson, J. Robert. 1993. *Rules of the Mind*. Hillsdale NJ: Lawrence Erlbaum.

Ansaldo, Umberto. 2004. The evolution of Singapore English: Finding the matrix. In *Singapore English: A Grammatical Description*, Lisa Lim (ed.), 127–149. Amsterdam: John Benjamins.

Ansaldo, Umberto. 2005a. Typological admixture in Sri Lanka Malay. Ms, University of Amsterdam.

Ansaldo, Umberto. 2005b. Contact-induced morphologization. Motivations for the emergence of case in Kirinda Java. Presented at New Reflections on Grammaticalization 3, Santiago de Compostela, Spain, 17–20 July 2005.

Ansaldo, Umberto 2008. Revisiting Sri Lanka Malay: Genesis and classification. In *Lessons from Documented Endangered Languages: A World of Many Voices*, David K. Harrison, David S. Rood & Arienne Dwyer (eds), 13–42. Amsterdam: John Benjamins.

Ansaldo, Umberto. 2009. *Contact Languages. Ecology and Evolution in Asia*. Cambridge: CUP.

Ansaldo, Umberto, Lim, Lisa & Mufwene, Salikoko S. 2007. The sociolinguistic history of the Peranakans: What it tells us about 'creolization'. In *Deconstructing Creole* [Typological Studies in Language 73], Ansaldo, Umberto, Stephen Matthews & Lisa Lim (eds), 203–226. Amsterdam: John Benjamins.

Ansaldo, Umberto & Matthews, Stephen. 2007. Deconstructing creole: The rationale. In In *Deconstructing Creole* [Typological Studies in Language 73], Ansaldo, Umberto, Stephen Matthews & Lisa Lim (eds), 1–18. Amsterdam: John Benjamins.

Ansaldo, Umberto, Matthews, Stephen & Lim, Lisa (eds). 2007. *Deconstructing Creole* [Typological Studies in Language 73]. Amsterdam: John Benjamins.

Ansaldo, Umberto & Nordhoff, Sebastian. 2008. Complexity and the age of language. In Arends, Jacques 2001. Social stratification and network relations in the formation of Sranan. In *Creolization and Contact*, Norval Smith & Tonjes Veenstra (eds), 291–307. Amsterdam: John Benjamins.

Bakhtin, Michael M. 1981. *The Dialogic Imagination*. Translated and edited by C. Emerson and M. Holmquist. Austin TX: University of Texas Press.

Bhaskararao, Peri & Subbarao, Karumuri Venkata (eds). 2004. *Non-nominative Subjects*, 2 Vols. Amsterdam: John Benjamins.

Blake, Barry. 1994. *Case*. Cambridge: CUP.

Bonfante, Giuliano. 1946. 'Indo-Hittite' and areal linguistics. *American Journal of Philology* 67: 289–310.

Bybee, Joan. 1985. *Morphology: A Study of the Relation between Meaning and Form* [Typological Studies in Language 9]. Amsterdam: John Benjamins.

Bybee, Joan. 1998. A functionalist approach to grammar and its evolution. *Evolution of Communication* 2: 249–278.
Bybee, Joan. 2001. *Phonology and Language Use*. Cambridge: CUP.
Bybee, Joan. 2006. From usage to grammar: The mind's response to repetition. *Language* 82(4): 711–733.
Bybee, Joan & Thompson, Sandra A. 1997. Three frequency effects in syntax. *Berkeley Linguistic Society* 23: 378–388.
Chomsky, Noam. 1959. Review of *Verbal Behaviour* by B. F. Skinner. *Language* 35: 26–58.
Croft, William. 1995. Autonomy and functionalist linguistics. *Language* 71: 490–532.
Croft, William. 2000. *Explaining Language Change: An Evolutionary Approach*. London: Longman.
Croft, William. 2001. *Radical Construction Grammar: Syntactic Theory in Typological Perspective*. Oxford: OUP.
Croft, William. 2006a. Evolutionary models and functional-typological theories of language change. In *Handbook of the History of English*, Ans van Kemenade & Bettelou Los (eds), 68–91. Oxford: Blackwell.
Croft, William. 2006b. The relevance of an evolutionary model. In *Competing Models of Linguistic Change: Evolution and Beyond* [Current Issues in Linguistic Theory 279], Ole N. Thomsen (ed.), 91–132. Amsterdam: John Benjamins.
Dahl, Östen. 2004. *The Growth and Maintenance of Linguistic Complexity* [Studies in Language Companion Series 71]. Amsterdam: John Benjamins.
Dawkins, Richard. 1976. *The Selfish Gene*. Oxford: OUP.
DeGraff, Michel. 2001. On the origins of creoles: A Cartesian critique of Neo-Darwinian linguistics. *Linguistic Typology* 5(2–3): 213–230.
DeGraff, Michel. 2003. Against Creole exceptionalism. *Language* 79: 391–410.
DeGraff, Michel. 2005. Linguists' most dangerous myth: The fallacy of creole exceptionalism. *Language in Society* 34: 533–591.
Durham, William. 1991. *Coevolution, Genes, Culture and Human Diversity*. Palo Alto CA: Stanford University Press.
Gair, James & Paolillo, John. 1997. *Sinhala*. Munich: Lincom.
Givón, Talmy. 1979. *On Understanding Grammar*: New York NY: Academic Press.
Givón, Talmy. 1995. *Functionalism and Grammar*. Amsterdam: John Benjamins.
Goldinger, Stephen D. 1996. Words and voices: Episodic traces in spoken word identification and recognition memory. *Journal of Experimental Psychology: Learning, memory and cognition* 22(1): 1166–1183.
Gumperz, John J. 1964. Linguistic and social interaction in two communities. *American Anthropologist* 66(6): 137–153.
Gumperz, John J. 1968. The speech community. In *International Encyclopedia of the Social Sciences*, 381–386. New York NY: Macmillan.
Haspelmath, Martin. 2006. Against markedness (and what to replace it with). *Journal of Linguistics* 42(1): 25–70.
Heine, Bernd & Kuteva, Tania. 2005. *Language Contact and Grammatical Change*. Cambridge: CUP.
Haiman, John. 1994. Ritualization and the development of language. In *Perspectives on Grammaticalization*, William Pagliuca (ed.), 3–28. Amsterdam: John Benjamins.
Hopper, Paul J. 1987. Emergent grammar. *Berkeley Linguistic Society* 13: 139–157.
Hopper, Paul J. & Traugott, Elizabeth C. 1993. *Grammaticalization*. Cambridge: CUP.

Hull, David L. 1988. *Science as a Process: An Evolutionary Account of the Social and Conceptual Development of Science*. Chicago IL: University of Chicago Press.
Hussainmiya, B. A. 1987. *Lost Cousins: The Malays of Sri Lanka*. Kuala Lumpur: Universiti Kebangsan Malaysia.
Hussainmiya, B. A. 1990. *Orang Rejimen: The Malays of the Ceylon Rifle Regiment*. Kuala Lumpur: Universiti Kebangsan Malaysia.
Hymes, Dell. 1971. *Pidginization and Creolization of Languages*. Cambridge: CUP.
Hymes, Dell. 1972. On communicative competence. In *Sociolinguistics*, Janet B. Pride & John Holmes (eds), 269–293. Hardmondsworth: Penguin.
Janda, Richard & Brian, Joseph. On language, change and language change – or of history, linguistics and historical linguistics. In *Handbook of Historical Linguistics*, Joseph, Brian & Richard Janda (eds), 3–180. Oxford: Blackwell.
Koptjevskaja-Tamm, Maria. To appear. Linguistic typology and language contact. In *The Oxford Handbook of Typology*, Jae-Jung Song (ed.). Oxford: OUP.
Kroskrity, Paul V. (ed). 2000. *Regimes of Language*. Santa Fe NM: School of American Research Advanced Seminar Series.
Langacker, Ronald. 1987. *Foundations of Cognitive Grammar*, Vol. 1. Stanford CA: Stanford University Press.
Langacker, Ronald. 2000. A dynamic usage-based model. In *Usage-based Models of Language*, Michael Barlow & Suzanne Kemmer (eds), 1–63. Stanford CA: Center for the Study of Language and Information.
Lass, Roger. 1990. How to do things with junk: Exaptation in language change. *Journal of Linguistics* 26: 79–102.
Lass, Roger. 1997. *Historical Linguistics and Language Change*. Cambridge: CUP.
Lightfoot, David. 1999. *The Development of Language: Acquisition, Change and Evolution*. Oxford: Blackwell.
Lim, Lisa. 2007. Mergers and acquisitions: On the ages and origins of Singapore English particles. *World Englishes* 26(4): 446–473.
Lim, Lisa & Ansaldo, Umberto. 2006. Keeping Kirinda vital: The endangerment-empowerment dilemma in the documentation of Sri Lanka Malay. *Amsterdam Center for Language and Communication Working Papers* 1: 51–66.
Lindblom, Björn, McNeilage, Peter & Studdeert-Kennedy, Michael. 1984. Self-organizing process and the explanation of phonological universals. In *Explanations for Language Universals*, Brian Butterworth, Bernard Comrie & Östen Dahl (eds), 181–203. Berlin: Mouton.
McWhorter, John. 2005. *Defining Creole*. Oxford: OUP.
Masica, Colin. 1976. *Defining a Linguistic Area: South Asia*. Chicago IL: University of Chicago Press.
Matras, Yaron & Bakker, Peter (eds). 2003. *The Mixed Language Debate: Theoretical and Empirical Advances*. Berlin: Mouton de Gruyter.
Milroy, James. 1999. Roger Lass, historical linguistics and language change. *Diachronica* 16(1): 179–191.
Milroy, Leslie & Milroy, James. 1992. Social network and social class: Towards an integrated sociolinguistic model. *Language in Society* 21: 1–26.
Mufwene, Salikoko S. 1991. Pidgins, creoles, typology and markedness. In *Development and Structures of Creole Languages: Essays in Honor of Derek Bickerton* [Creole Language Library 9], Francis Byrne & Thom Huebner (eds), 123–143. Amsterdam: John Benjamins.

Mufwene, Salikoko S. 1996. Creole genesis: A population genetics perspective. In *Caribbean Language Issues Old and New*, Pauline Christie (ed.), 168–209. Kingston: University of the West Indies Press.
Mufwene, Salikoko S. 2001. *The Ecology of Language Evolution*. Cambridge: CUP.
Muysken, Pieter. 1988. Are Creoles a special type of language? In *Linguistics. The Cambridge Survey*. Vol. 2. *Linguistic Theory: Extensions and Implications,* Frederick Newmeyer (ed.), 285–301. Cambridge: CUP.
Nettle, David. 1997. *Linguistic Diversity*. Cambridge: CUP.
Nordhoff, Sebastian. In preparation. A Grammar of Sri Lanka Malay. PhD dissertation, University of Amsterdam.
Pierrehumbert, Janet. 2001. Exemplar dynamics: Word frequency, lenition and contrast. In *Frequency and the Emergence of Linguistic Structure* [Typological Studies in Language 45], Joan Bybee & Paul J. Hopper (eds), 137–158. Amsterdam: John Benjamins.
Pierrehumbert, Janet. 2002. Word-specific phonetics. In *Laboratory Phonology* 7, Carlos van Gussenhoven & Natasha Warner (eds), 101–140. Berlin: Mouton de Gruyter.
Slomanson, Peter. 2006. Sri Lankan Malay morphosyntax: Lankan or Malay? In *Structure and Variation in Language Contact* [Creole Language Library 29], Ana Deumert & Stephanie Durrleman (eds), 135–158. Amsterdam: John Benjamins.
Smith, Ian, Paauw, Scott & Hussainmiya, B. A. 2004. Sri Lanka Malay: The state of the art. In *Yearbook of South Asian Languages 2004,* Rajendra Singh (ed.), 197–215. Berlin: Mouton de Gruyter.
Thomason, Sarah. 2003. Contact as a source of language change. In *Handbook of Historical Linguistics,* Brian Joseph & Richard Janda (eds), 687–712. Oxford: Blackwell.
Thomason, Sarah & Kaufman, Terence. 1988. *Language Contact, Creolization and Genetic Linguistics*. Berkeley CA: University of California Press.
Tomasello, Michael. 2003. *Constructing a Language. A Usage-based Theory of Language Acquisition*. Cambridge MA: Harvard University Press.
Tomasello, Michael, Cale Kruger, Anne & Horn Ratner, Hilary. 1993. Cultural learning. *Behavioral and Brain Sciences* 16: 495–552.
Trudgill, Peter. 2001. Contact and simplification. Historical baggage and directionality in linguistic change. *Linguistic Typology* 5: 372–375.
Trudgill, Peter. 2002. Linguistic and social typology. In *The Handbook of Language Variation and Change,* Jack K. Chambers, Peter Trudgill & Natalie Schilling-Estes (eds), 707–728. Oxford: Blackwell.
Weinreich, Uriel. 1953 [1968]. *Languages in Contact: Findings and Problems*. The Hague: Mouton.

PART V

Evaluating simplification and complexification

Economy, innovation and degrees of complexity in creole formation*

Marlyse Baptista

This paper explores the idea that in contact situations, there exists a process whereby so-called morpho-syntactic simplification is correlated to semantic complexification. In examining this process in the verbal and nominal domains, we show that a given morpheme may actually carry in Cape Verdean Creole (CVC) and Guinea-Bissau Creole (GBC) a cluster of semantic feature values where the European language only has one. In order to measure degrees of simplification versus complexification, this paper uses Kusters' (2003) complexity evaluation metrics involving inflectional morphology specifically. This paper also shows to what extent two sister creoles such as CVC and GBC, assumed to have emerged from the same source languages, display similarities and distinct differences in their morphological properties.

1. Introduction

1.1 Scope of this paper

Given the focus of this volume on *Complex Processes in New Languages*, the main objective of this paper is to highlight how in Cape Verdean Creole (henceforth, CVC) and Guinea-Bissau Creole (henceforth, GBC), apparent morpho-syntactic simplification with respect to the lexifier actually results into semantic innovation and complexification vis-à-vis the European language. By semantic innovation and complexification, I mean that a given morpheme may actually carry a cluster of semantic feature values where the European language only has one. This is illustrated in Section 4.

---

* I am indebted to Enoch Aboh, Sally Thomason and the Contact Group at the University of Michigan for valuable comments and observations that helped clarify many aspects of this paper. I am also grateful to both Enoch Aboh and Norval Smith for the opportunity to contribute to this volume.

In broader terms, this paper wishes to explore to what extent creolization involves processes of simplification or complexification and identify some of the grammatical domains in which such processes occur (see Thomason 2008). I hope to show that in contact situations, there exists a process whereby so-called morpho-syntactic simplification is correlated to semantic complexification. Here, I wish to clarify that it is not my assumption that in the initial stages of their genesis, the lexifiers were actually target languages that the creoles may have tried to model themselves after. I assume, instead, that the two creoles under study have emerged from contact between source languages without the original speakers necessarily aiming at acquiring and mastering the lexifier language. This means that to talk about *simplification* is a misnomer, as this would entail that the creoles are simplified vis-à-vis their lexifiers. This paper tries to demonstrate not only that it is erroneous to view creoles as simpler versions of their lexifiers given that I do not assume that such lexifiers have been a target in the case of these two languages. I also try to provide evidence that in some areas where they appear simpler than the European source language (for those who insist on using such a yard stick), they are actually more complex semantically.

In order to measure degrees of simplification versus complexification, I use Kusters' (2003) complexity evaluation metrics involving inflectional morphology specifically. I introduce these metrics in detail in Section 3. A second and related goal is to show to what extent two sister creoles such as CVC and GBC which are assumed to have emerged from the same source languages display similarities and differences in their morphological properties. Finally, I explore in Section 4 the concept of *bareness* in the nominal domain of creole languages in general. There, I argue that this so-called bareness should not be equated with deficiency or simplicity, as a number of variables must come into action to yield the same range of interpretive options available to languages with overtly full determiner paradigms, McWhorter (2001). The set of semantic operations intervening makes the process of generating the correct interpretation all the more complex. Such questions will be explored within the frameworks of language contact.

This paper is organized as follows: Following the introductory section, I draw in Section 2 a brief socio-historical sketch of the conditions under which these two creoles emerged demonstrating that in spite of common source languages and history, their morpho-syntactic properties are quite distinct from each other. This would suggest that source languages as well as innovation and UG-based tendencies are involved in creole genesis. In Section 3, I introduce Kusters' (2003) evaluation metrics of complexity based on verbal inflectional morphology. In Section 4, I take his complexity evaluation metrics to task, and apply it not only to the verbal domain in those two creoles but also to the nominal domain, and investigate their inflectional morphology in those two areas. In the verbal domain, I focus in particular on verbal inflections such as the anterior marker *ba* and the passive markers *du/da*. I also examine free standing Tense, Mood and Aspect markers and argue that in spite of not being inflectional morphemes, they are symptomatic of a more complex clausal architecture for the two creoles under study. In the nominal domain, I study the only inflection, that of the plural marker *-s* and will show that this particular morpheme carries more feature values than its European counterpart. I base my comparative analyses on the works by Kihm (1994) for Guinea-Bissau Creole and on my own (Baptista 2002, 2007a, 2007c), Lucchesi's (1993), Quint's (2000) and Veiga's (1996, 2000) for Cape Verdean Creole. Once the comparative and descriptive analysis of some of the morphological properties in these creoles is laid out, I reflect on how morpho-syntactic simplification or bareness correlates with semantic complexification and extra-clausal clues.

2. A brief socio-historical sketch[1]

The creole spoken in the Cape Verde islands (referred to as *Kriolu*) is historically and linguistically intimately related to the creole spoken in Guinea-Bissau (locally known as *Kriyol*). For this reason, one must explore the history of Cape Verde and of its language in conjunction with that of the western coast of Africa, particularly that of Guinea.

The coast of Gambia, Casamance, and Guinea-Bissau is believed to have been discovered in 1446. Black slaves were captured and brought back to Portugal in the second half of the 15th century (Teyssier 1959; Carreira 1983).

As for the exact nature of the language spoken by the black slaves in Portugal, two hypotheses have been proposed: according to the first one, slaves spoke a *reconnaissance language* deliberately taught to the Blacks by the Portuguese so that they could communicate with each other. This would have allowed the Portuguese to use the slaves as interpreters during the expeditions on the African continent. Kihm (1994) proposes that travel back and forth between Portugal and West Africa could have given rise to a Portuguese pidgin that served as the foundation for the proto-creole that developed in Senegambia and Cape Verde. Finding out where CVC originated is a controversial issue and three hypotheses have been proposed so far: some scholars believe that CVC emerged in Portugal (Naro 1978), others in Guinea, and a third group in Cape Verde (Kihm 1994; Peck 1988; Lang 1990: 185).

The *lançados* (also called tangomãos), settlers of Portuguese origin, are said to have formed a dynamic trading force (exchanging goods and slaves) between the Portuguese and the local populations. Settling on the African mainland, they married local women and are believed to have actively contributed to the formation of Cape Verdean Creole. Boulègue (1987: 117) reports that indirect reference to them was made in a royal letter dating back to 1500, which leads to the conclusion that *lançados* appeared in the first decades of Portuguese settlement. Cape Verdeans themselves played an active role in the Atlantic economy between the archipelago and the neighboring African coast (Boulègue 1987: 142) and seem to have formed a distinct economic force from the *lançados*. From these facts, one can easily imagine a scenario where the interaction between the Cape-Verdean traders and the *lançados*

---

1. Versions of this section appeared in Baptista (2002) and Baptista (2006).

all contributed to the formation of two distinct but related creoles, one with its roots on the African mainland, and the other on the archipelago.

The languages which have contributed to the genesis and formation of *Kriolu* and *Kriyol* are varied. Besides Portuguese, which contributed to its lexicon, the African element is mostly represented by Niger-Kordofanian languages: West-Atlantic languages (Wolof, Fula, Serer, Balanta, Manjaku, Mankan, Dyola, and Bola to mention a few) and Mande languages (Malinke and Bambara among others) (Brásio 1962). Lang (1990:185) isolates three languages in particular as having played a particularly important role: Wolof, Temne, and Mandinga (including Bambara and Dyola).

In the following sections, I focus on to what extent creolization involves processes of simplification or complexification by laying out Kusters' (2003) tenets of complexity and take it to task when examining in Section 4 inflectional morphology in the two creoles under study.

3. Kusters' (2003) metrics of evaluation of complexity

Kusters (2003) argues that some languages are more complex than others from an outsider's point of view. More precisely, the outsider learning a new language seems to be the best judge of its complexity, and Kusters contends that the best locus for evaluating complexity is inflectional morphology. The following two quotes best illustrate Kusters' stand on the issue of complexity and more precisely on *who* measures it and *how* it is evaluated:

- Kusters (2003:6): "There is no way to define complexity without being specific about to whom a language is or is not complex... Complexity is not a simple predicate attributable to language but a relation between two entities: a language and someone who evaluates the language."
- Kusters (2003:19): "Inflection is found on verbs and nouns... I will restrict this study to the form of inflection that is most wide-spread, namely verbal inflection... generally, more categories are expressed in verbal inflection than in nominal inflection, and therefore, more complex elaboration, fusion, and splitting occur with the verb. Verbal inflection therefore provides a better opportunity for research on complexity."

Kusters' rationale for choosing inflectional morphology as the locus of complexity is that it helps define language typologies in terms of isolating, agglutinative, flexional and incorporating languages. Hence, inflectional morphology alone allows for the classification of languages into distinct types.

Kusters identifies three dimensions of language processing where outsider complexity plays a role. Put simply, these three dimensions are along the lines of ease of learnability for the outsider, ease of perception and ease of production. Kusters argues that:

a. "An outsider is someone who learns the language in question at a later stage, and is not a native speaker. Therefore, phenomena that are relatively difficult for a second language learner in comparison with a first language learner are more complex under my definition. Phenomena that are easy to acquire for a second language learner but difficult for a first language learner are less complex."
b. "An outsider does not have much shared (linguistic and non-linguistic) background knowledge with other members of the speech community in question. She will therefore make progress with a language that is relatively easy to perceive and understand. In contrast, production difficulties of a language are less hindering for an outsider. A language in which perceptual processing is relatively easy in comparison with production is therefore less complex under my definition."
c. "An outsider is primarily interested in clear transmission of information, and less interested in learning a language for all kinds of symbolic meanings, such as expressing personal and group identity and aesthetic feelings. Therefore, phenomena that do not have a mainly functional purpose are considered more complex under my definition."

Crucially, Kusters' definition is not built on any particular theory but is based on the complexities as experienced by an outsider, i.e., an outside language learner.

Whether one judges a language as simpler or poorer on the basis of the lexicon, or on the basis of inflectional morphology, as Kusters does, this particular paper will take a different stand on this issue. Even if a language is judged as simpler on the grounds of inflectional morphology, we will instead proceed in another direction, best expressed by Aitchinson (1991: 214), in assuming that "a language which is simple and regular in one respect is likely to be complex and confusing in others. There seems to be a trading relationship between the different parts of the grammar." This paper will make this assumption more precise by showing that apparent morphosyntactic simplification can actually be correlated with semantic complexification. There may indeed be some areas of the grammar in which one feature value in the European language (i.e., [+PL] on nouns) may correspond to a cluster of feature values in some creoles. In this sense, the information density carried by the plural morpheme in the creoles under study is heavier than in the lexifier. In addition, we will demonstrate that in the passive domain, one inflectional rule in the Portuguese language does not correspond to a set of rules in the creoles but corresponds instead to more complex analytical constructions in CVC and GBC[2] (see Kusters (2003: 17) on this correspondence issue).

In the following section, I take Kusters' metrics to task and compare a set of grammatical morphemes in the verbal and nominal domains of GBC and CVC emphasizing the different and similar morphological behaviors in these two languages. In so

---

2. Although technically *ba* in GBC does not qualify as an inflectional morpheme and therefore should not be considered as a diagnostic for complexity, the semantic and syntactic parallelisms between CVC inflectional *-ba* and GBC free standing *ba* justify its consideration.

doing, I compare them to their lexifier, as creole languages are typically measured against the European source languages when evaluating their degree of complexity or rather comparative simplicity. This will illustrate that this type of comparison is misdirected.

4. Aspects of verbal and nominal morphology in GBC and CVC

In this section, I examine synchronically inflectional and free standing post-verbal morphemes[3] in the verbal domain as well as inflectional post-nominal morphemes in the nominal domain.

4.1 Verbal inflection

4.1.1 *The case of ba/-ba*
In the domain of TMA markers, both GBC and CVC display the same anterior marker *ba* that is distributionally distinct from other aspect and mood markers in that it occurs post-verbally; the other markers precede the verb. Semantically, *ba* in both languages conveys anteriority of the event it modifies. Stative verbs modified with *ba* are interpreted as simple past and active verbs as past-before-past. The parallel between the GBC *ba* and the CVC *-ba* stops, however, there. Indeed, the following subsections will show that while *-ba* in CVC can only modify verbs and always appear as an inflection cliticized to the verb stem, GBC *ba* may modify verbs as well as types of predicates and is free standing.

4.1.1.1 *Ba* in GBC. In Guinea-Bissau, the distribution of *ba* is much less restricted than in CVC. Consider the following examples from Kihm (1994), in which *ba* may appear in a post V + Clitic position as in (1), or following a verb stem (2), a series of verbs in a serial verb construction (3), a noun predicate (4) and (5) and a negated noun (6):

(1) N konta u **ba** kuma nya pirkitu karu de. (Kihm 1994:99)
    I tell you PAST that my parrot expensive DE
    'I had told you though that my parrot is expensive.'

(2) *A! N diskisi **ba**.*
    ah I forget PAST
    'Ah! I had forgotten!'

---

3. This is in contrast to the Barlavento islands where the anteriority marking morpheme *tava* is actually preverbal.

(3) *Mandingas kontinwa nega **ba** rasa.*
    Mandings continue refuse PAST pray
    'The Mandings kept on refusing to pray [in the Muslim way].'

(4) *Pa   ley   i yera   un prosesu...ley i un prosesu **ba**... un tarbaju*
    COMP read it be+PAST a process read it a process PAST a work
    difisil.
    difficult
    'Reading was a process … it was a process … a hard job.'

(5) *Kil omi **ba** i kin.*
    that man PAST it who
    'Who was that man?'

(6) *I ka   el   **ba**.*
    it NEG s/he/it PAST
    'It wasn't her/him/it.'

In every case, *ba* is structurally postverbal which is reminiscent of the Sotavento varieties of CVC where clearly, -*ba* is a verbal inflection,[5] as will be shown in 4.1.1.2. Kihm also notes (1994: 103) that *ba* in GBC is extended to all verb stems irrespective of the original morphological class of the verb. In *Kriyol*, *ba* spreads to all kinds of predicates and non-predicates losing its verbal affix status. According to Kihm, its status as a /CV/ easily segmented syllable contributed to it being reanalyzed as a self-standing element.

In summary, the best way to characterize the distribution of *ba* with regard to the other TMA markers in GBC is found in Kihm (1994: 104):

> The tense marker *ba* differs from the aspectual auxiliaries *na* and *ta* in three ways: (i) it follows rather than precedes the item it modifies, (ii) it does not have to be adjacent to this item, (iii) this item may be a noun predicate, or even an element that is not a predicate.

Kihm (1994: 99) notes a puzzling distribution of *ba* in the presence of two adjacent verbs. As illustrated by examples such as (7), *ba* may appear after the first verb (7b) or after the second verb (7a) without triggering distinct semantic interpretations:

(7) a. *Mandingas kontinwa nega **ba** raza.*
       Mandings kept refuse PAST pray
       'The Mandings kept on refusing to pray.'
    b. *Mandingas kontinwa **ba** nega raza.*
       Mandings kept PAST refuse pray
       'The Mandings kept on refusing to pray.'

Another interesting distributional note: Only monosyllabic complements can intervene between the verb and *ba* although that distribution seems marked for many speakers:

(8) a. *i kunpra pon ba (??).* (Kihm 1994: 104)
he buy bread PAST
'He had bought bread.'
b. *i kunpra ba pon.*
he buy PAST bread
'He had bought bread.'

In the next subsection, we turn to the semantics and distribution of *-ba* in CVC.

4.1.1.2 *-Ba in CVC.* In contrast to its Guinea-Bissau congener, CVC *-ba* is clearly an inflection that only suffixes to verbal stems, and typically yields a past interpretation to a stative verb and a past-before-past interpretation to a non-stative verb. These are its most basic functions,[4] as illustrated by (9) and (10) respectively:

(9) *Joao staba duenti to ki' N odja-l.*
Joao was sick when COMP I see+him
'Joao was sick when I saw him.'

(10) *Kel mininu kumeba tudu kel katxupa to ki' N txiga.*
The child eat+ANT all the katxupa when COMP I arrived
'The child had eaten all the katxupa when I arrived.'

Interestingly in CVC, just as in GBC, in the presence of a serial verb construction, *-ba* may appear suffixed to the first (11a), second (11b) or third (11c) verb without triggering any discernible semantic varying interpretations.

(11) a. *Mandingas kontinuaba nega raza.*
Mandings kept+PAST refuse pray
'The Mandings kept on refusing to pray.'
b. *Mandingas kontinua negaba raza.*
Mandings kept refuse+PAST pray
'The Mandings kept on refusing to pray.'
c. *E ta torna ben tomaba konta.*
he TMA turn come take+PAST charge
'He would have come back to take charge again.'

---

4. This is a very basic portrayal of the function of *-ba* in CVC, as the marker can combine to other TMA markers to convey a complex and exhaustive range of aspectual, modal and temporal interpretations (see Baptista 2002 for a detailed treatment).

Table 1. Anterior marker *ba*

	Free standing	Post verb stem	Post different predicates	Modifies verb 1 or 2
CVC	–	+	–	+
GBC	+	+	+	–

No element, irrespective of syllabic composition, may intervene between the verb and the anterior marker *-ba*, as shown in (11). This is in contrast to the GBC example in (1) above in which the clitic intervened between the verb stem and *ba*.

Just as in GBC, the other aspect and modal markers are preverbal in CVC, as illustrated by sample TMA markers in (12) and (13).

(12) N ka sta ta spera ma N pode.   (MCG-FO)
     I NEG TMA TMA expect that I can
     'I don't expect that I can do it.'

(13) Es ta sta ta briga.
     they TMA TMA TMA fight
     'They are fighting.'

The anterior marker is the only marker that appears in a postverbal position either as a suffix in CVC or free standing in GBC. However, another set of postverbal inflections may be found in the verbal domain with passives. GBC and CVC display the same passive morpheme *-du* with the difference that CVC has two passive markers, one for the present passive *-du* and one for the past passive *-da*, as discussed in the following section.

Table 1 summarizes the common points and differences between CVC and GBC *ba*.

In conclusion to this section, in light of Kusters' complexity evaluation metrics, if one compares the role of *-ba/ba* with respect to its Portuguese counterpart *-va*,[5] the imperfective marker for the first conjugation of Portuguese verbs, one observes that the use of the creole of inflection carries more information weight. It conveys not only information on modality (punctual) and tense (anterior) but also interacts with the stativity status of a given verb to convey a past reading for stative verbs and a pluperfect reading for non-stative verbs. In addition, *ba* is able in GBC to convey a past reading to multiple types of predicates, not just verbal predicates, in contrast to Portuguese.

---

5. A typical use of *-va* in Portuguese is illustrated in the example (i):

(i) Amava os meus pais. (Portuguese)
    loved the my parents
    'I loved my parents.'

4.1.2 The passive

In this subsection, I examine passive morphology in both GBC and CVC and highlight the common points and differences between the two creoles.

On the one hand, both GBC and CVC use the passive inflection *-du*, derived from its Portuguese counterpart *-do* but the parallel stops there. While GBC passives exhibit no copula, CVC passives may or may not under conditions to be outlined below; furthermore CVC displays a present and a past passive.

4.1.2.1 The passive in GBC. Consider the following example from GBC:

(14) E   purpara pa ba vinga   se   kunpanyerus   (Kihm 1994: 243)
     they   prepare for go avenge their comrades
     ku   matadu na Manden.
     who   be-killed in Manding
     'They prepared to go and avenge their comrades who had been killed in the Manding.'

The passive marker *-du* (derived from Portuguese *-do*) modifies all transitive verbs and as Kihm observes, regularization has affected all verb types irrespective of whether or not they are irregular in Portuguese. For instance, irregular Portuguese passive *feito* from *fazer* 'to do' translates into the regular form *fasidu* in *Kriyol*. Kihm does not assume a zero copula in GBC in spite of the obligatory presence of the copula in Portuguese. *Kriyol* passive verbs behave like their active counterparts, being interpreted as perfective when bare, and being modified by the same tense and aspect auxiliaries, as shown in (15):

(15) I   na   bin   dadu   karton di konvidya   (Kihm 1994: 243)
     it ASP and-then be-given   card   of invitation
     a   tudu artistas ku   toma parti.
     to   all   artists   who   take part
     'Invitation cards will be given to all participating artists.'

Kihm views all examples of passives as being agentless passives. The agent is left unexpressed either because it is unknown or because the speaker considers it irrelevant. Passive constructions with a by-phrase demoting the expressed agent to the status of an adjunct belong to Portuguese-influenced registers.

In the case of double object verbs such as 'give' 'lend', Kihm observes that *Kriyol* behaves like English and unlike Portuguese, since both objects may be promoted to subjecthood, with a distinct preference for the indirect object:

(16) a. Dinyeru pistadu el.   (Kihm 1994: 245)
         money   be-lent him
         'Money was lent to him.'

b. *I pistadu dinyeru.*
he be-lent money
'He was lent money.'

Kihm notes that passivization in *Kriyol* is quite different from how it works in Portuguese. For instance, in the following example, only the main verb and not the causative auxiliary is passivized. The passive marker cannot modify both the main verb and the causative auxiliary, as seen by the ungrammaticality of (17b):

(17) a. *Un dia nyu Kornobif   manda comadu.*   (Kihm 1994: 246)
one day Mr. Corned-Beef cause be-called
'One day, they had Mr. Corned-Beef called.'
b. **Un dia nyu Kornobif   mandadu   comadu.*
one day Mr. Corned-Beef be-caused be-called

A possible explanation Kihm provides for such data is that *manda comadu* is analyzed by the creolophone speaker as one predicate head made up of a complex verb.

In summary, Kihm observes that all inner arguments of a transitive or ditransitive verb and adjuncts can become subjects of passive constructions. He proposes that which argument or which adjunct gets selected for subjecthood is subject to the Obliqueness Hierarchy whereby more oblique arguments come first as preferred subjects.

4.1.2.2 *The passive in CVC.* In CVC, passivization is encoded through both impersonal and personal constructions.[6] Typically, the impersonal passive has a null expletive as its subject (18).

(18) a. *Ta   txomadu so   di noti.*   (RS)
TMA called   only of night
'We were only called at night time.'
b. *Ta   fladu si, ta   fladu ku   boka.*   (RS)
TMA said yes TMA said with mouth
'It is said indeed, it is said openly.'

The personal passive takes an overt NP in subject position, as in (19). This type of construction is characterized by the absence of a copula linking the subject to the past participle and the absence of an agentive prepositional phrase.

(19) a. *Bonba ta   dadu dentu di kaza.*   (RS)
spray TMA given inside of house
'The house was sprayed.'

---

6. The data in this section are taken from Baptista (2002).

b. ***Nu podu** tudu na trabadju.* (RS)
   CL put all in work
   'We were all put to work.'

In a number of cases, personal passives may involve subject verb inversion under the condition that the subject be a full NP (20).

(20) a. *Dipos dja ki **pegadu kel rapas**.* (RS)
      after then that caught the young man
      'It is only afterwards that the young man was caught.'

b. *Ka ta **fazedu kaza di padja**.* (RS)
   NEG TMA made house of thatch
   'Thatched houses are not made.'

Such inversion is not allowed with clitic pronominals (21).

(21) a. **Dipos dja ki **pegadu e**.* (RS)
      after then that caught CL

b. *Dipos dja k' e pegadu.* (RS)
   after then that he caught
   'It is only afterwards that he was caught.'

Copulaless passive predicates are perfectly acceptable in CVC although the passive structures in (19) is not found in Portuguese, where the presence of the copula is required, as in (22):

(22) *O Brasil **foi descoberto** em 1500.* (Portuguese)
    the Brazil was discovered in 1500
    'Brazil was discovered in 1500.'

Passivization strategies are varied in CVC dialects. They include structures that are identical to Portuguese, as in (23), as well as structures with no copula and no past-participles of the *-du* type, as illustrated in examples (24) and (25) below.[7]

---

7. Let us note that in examples (23)–(25), the copula *e* cannot appear adjacent to the aspectual marker *ta*, otherwise, the sentences become ungrammatical:

(i) **Es stòria e ta kontòd pa un psóa.*
   this story COP ASP told by one individual

(ii) **Es kantíga e ta kanta oj.*
    this song COP TMA sung today

(iii) **Ali, e ta fala Kriol.*
    here COP TMA spoken Kriol

Barlavento

(23) Es stòria e **kontòd** pa un psóa.   (S. Nicolau)
    this story COP told by an individual
    'This story is told by an individual.'   (Cardoso 1989: 68)

Absence of copula and absence of passive marker:

(24) Es kantíga **ta kanta** oj.   (S. Nicolau)
    this song TMA sung today
    'This song is sung today.'   (Cardoso 1989: 74)

(25) Ali, **ta fala** Kriol.   (S. Nicolau)
    here TMA spoken Kriol
    'Here, Kriol is spoken (or here, one speaks Kriol).'   (Cardoso 1989: 74)

Unlike Portuguese, CVC also has the option of expressing passivization by using a dedicated past tense morpheme -*da* in the Sotavento varieties.

(26) Dja' N **flada** pa-m ka baba.   (Quint 2000: 235)
    TMA I tell+PASTPASSIVE for I NEG go+PAST
    'I was told not to go.'

Quint analyzes -*da* as being the product of a cross between the passive marker -*du* and the past marker -*ba*, a plausible hypothesis. Note, however, that -*du* may be used in past passive sentences, as illustrated by the following example in (27) taken from Veiga (2000: 192):

(27) Katxupa foi **kumedu** pa mi   (Veiga 2000: 192)
    katxupa was eaten by me
    'Katxupa was eaten by me.'[8]

Finally, the CVC counterpart to the GBC example in (17) and involving two adjacent verbs seems to allow (depending on the speaker) the appearance of the passive marker on the right-most verb (28a), the left-most verb (28b), or both (28c).

(28) a. Un dia Nho Kornobif manda **comadu**.   (CVC)
    one day Mr. Corned-Beef cause be-called
    'One day, they had Mr. Corned-Beef called.'
    b. Un dia Nho Kornobif **mandadu** coma.
    one day Mr. Corned-Beef be-caused call
    'One day, they had Mr. Corned-Beef called.'

---

8. This sentence seems more representative of acrolectal varieties in the language.

c. *Un dia Nho Kornobif   mandadu comadu.*
   one day Mr. Corned-Beef be-caused be-called
   'One day, they had Mr. Corned-Beef called.'

In summary, passivization in GBC entails agent or agentless copulaless constructions using the passive marker *-du*. In adjacent or serial type of verb constructions, *-du* appears on the rightmost periphery verb in GBC but seemingly in both rightmost and leftmost places in CVC. In the case of ditransitive verbs, both objects may be promoted to subjecthood, contrary to Portuguese. In contrast to GBC, in CVC, passive constructions accompanied with the passive marker *-du* may appear with or without a copula depending on the variety. The agent may or may not be expressed, also depending on dialectal variation. In some cases, the passive construction appears with no copula and no passive marker (as in (25) above). In addition, CVC has a past passive that does not exist in GBC or Portuguese. In contrast to Portuguese that typically displays one type of passive construction (see Portuguese example (22) above), GBC and CVC display a wide range of structures. They differ from each other in that they may include or exclude the copula, include or exclude the participle marker, and display the passive suffix on V1 or V2. In addition, CVC is endowed with a present and a past participle marker, the latter being inexistent in Portuguese.

It should be pointed out that it is possible that the various passivization strategies portrayed in this section may reflect distinct semantics, stylistic register or pragmatic conditions but teasing them apart is not the purpose of the current paper. The following table summarizes the similarities and differences between CVC and GBC in the area of passive constructions.

Although Kusters considers verbal inflectional morphology exclusively, the next section will consider nominal inflection in the two creoles under study, for the sake of completeness and exhaustivity.

4.2 Nominal inflection

As inflectional morphology is typically taken as the best locus of measurement for language complexity, this section examines inflectional plural marking in GBC and CVC, in other words, inflection in the nominal domain. It aims at showing that plural marking is a highly productive process regulated by principled licensing conditions in these two creoles in spite of the presence of multiple grammars in both languages. The variables that will be shown to play a role in some grammars of GBC and CVC are animacy, definiteness and tense (see Baptista 2003 for a more elaborate study).

Table 2. Passive marker

	Pres. passive	Past passive	*du* on V1 and V2	Copula present	Copula absent
CVC	+	+	+	+	+
GBC	+	–	–	–	+

4.2.1 Plural inflection in GBC[9]

Just like many of its congeners, Guinea-Bissau creole (GBC) may express generic with no marking, as shown in (29):

(29) **Lubu ta branku.**
 hyena TMA white
 'Hyenas are white.' (Kihm 1994: 91)

GBC may also use plural marking economically whereby the presence of a numeral may allow the following noun to appear bare, as shown in (30):

(30) **Kwatru dia**
 four day
 'Four days.' (Kihm 1994: 62)

When it comes to number inflection, plural usage is complex, as GBC seems equipped with two alternate grammars. One is similar to Portuguese and is expressed with the following principle (Kihm 1994: 132):

(31) Plural Marking Principle I: Use plural morphology on a noun whenever more than one token of the entity it denotes is relevantly present in the world shared by the participants.

This is illustrated by (32) where agreement takes place between the plural noun and the modifying adjective. Presumably, this type of agreement occurs in some varieties of the language.

(32) a. **Sapatus altus** ku bonitu sin.
  shoe+PL high+PL that nice so
  'High-heel shoes that are so nice.'
 b. Kil mas **perigozus bandidus** di Italya.
  that more dangerous+PL gangster+PL of Italy
  'Those more dangerous gangsters from Italy.' (Kihm 1994: 132)

---

9. Other versions of this section appeared in Plag (2003) and Baptista (2007). In this subsection, the acronyms in parentheses stand for the name of the informant, kept anonymous, and the informant's island of origin. ST stands for the island of Santiago, and FG for the island of Fogo.

The alternate grammar is more basilectal and seems regulated by the principle in (33) (Kihm 1994: 132):

(33) Plural Marking Principle II: Use plural morphology on a noun whenever more than one token of the entity it denotes is relevantly present in the world shared by the participants, unless the entity is conceived of in non-specific terms and/or its plurality is explicitly indicated by a specialized lexical item.

As the last clause of PMP II states, a noun will not be marked as a rule if it is modified by a numeral or a quantifier already implying plurality. This is illustrated in (34) and (35) respectively.

(34) Dus **galu** ka ta kanta na un kapwera.
 two cock NEG TMA sing in a chicken-yard
 'Two cocks won't crow in one yard.' (Kihm 1994: 133)

(35) a. Kil omi ten manga di **minjer**.
 that man have lot of woman
 'That man has lots of women.' (Kihm 1994: 133)
 b. Es li i ciw ba **minjer**.
 this here he much PAST woman
 'This guy here had a lot of women.' (Kihm 1994: 100)

The second inference from Kihm's principle is that plural marking occurs on definite or specific nouns, relevant to the world of the speaker and hearer. In addition, Kihm notes that whenever specific tokens of a given entity are viewed as an undifferentiated group or mass, plurality is not marked. This option generally affects things or non-individuated animals. As a result, '**only nouns denoting humans or personified animals are regularly marked as plural when PMP II is active (my emphasis)**' (Kihm 1994: 133). Such observation crucially acknowledges animacy as a definite factor in the plural marking of nouns and the absence of individuation becomes a stronger cognitive motive for not marking plurality than mere non-redundancy or simple linguistic economy.

To sum up, the key proposal to be retained of Kihm's characterization of plural marking is that definitess and, crucially, animacy are the essential predictors of plural marking. When viewed as plural entities, [+human / +animate] nouns tend to take a plural suffix. In summary, this section has shown that the two variables that are the strongest predictors of plural marking in GBC are animacy and definiteness. These two variables may combine or exclude each other in the case of animate entities. Inanimate items become potential candidates for plural marking when they are specific. Plural marking strategies in GBC are summarized in Table 3.

Table 3. Pluralization strategies in Guinea-Bissau Creole

Bare noun
Quantifier + noun
Quantifier + noun + -s
Noun + -s

4.2.2 *Plural inflection in CVC*

One of the standard strategies in marking number in CVC is via determiners (36), deictics (37), numerals (38) and floating quantifiers (39) while the nominal stem, as a rule, remains bare, making plural marking generally non-redundant.

(36) a. ***un** rapariga*   (indefinite determiner)
'a young woman'
b. ***uns** rapariga*
'some young women'

(37) a. ***kel** rapariga*   (demonstrative/definite determiner)
'that young woman'
b. ***kes** rapariga*
'those young women'

(38) ***Tres*** *rapariga staba ta spera-l.*   (numeral)
three young women were ASP wait+him/her
'Three young women were waiting for him/her.'

(39) ***Tudu*** *rapariga staba ta txora.*   (quantifier)
all young women were ASP crying
'All the young women were crying.'

CVC is endowed with a wide range of quantifiers conveying plural interpretation to the noun they modify. In addition, as in a number of other creoles, bare nouns in CVC may yield a generic interpretation (40) or be interpreted as plural (41):

Generic reading

(40) ***Omi*** *ten pe di katxor.*   (idiomatic)
men/man have foot of dog
'Men are always out.' **or** 'Man is always out.'

(41) ***Kaza*** *d'es rua ta parse bedju.*
house of this street ASP look old
'The houses in this street look old.'

In addition, nominal stems may carry a plural suffix (as in (42)).

(42) *Raparigas   txiga   sedu.*
young women arrive early
'The young women arrived early.'

Finally, in the case where a noun is preceded by a determiner such as a possessive, the determiner may remain singular and the noun may carry the plural suffix. Furthermore, in some rare instances, both the determiner and the noun may carry the plural marker but only when the referent is [+human]. These two additional strategies are illustrated in (43) and (44) respectively:

(43) a. *nha mininus* (FG)
'my children'
b. *nha kolegas* (FG)
'my colleagues'

(44) *Ah! Kes djentis la* (FG)
'Oh! Those people'

The samples of monolingual speech make the triggers of plural marking quite clear in these particular grammars. In all the examples listed below, plural marking only affects animate nouns (for a variationnist account of plural marking in CVC showing preference for animacy marking, see Ferreira (to appear)).

(45) *Dja   la   nu podu na trabadju,* (S-ST)
COMP there we put   at work
*trabadju duru mi ku   nos **mininus***
work   hard me with our children
'There, we were put to work, me and our children.'

(46) *Bu trabadja ku   nha **povus**.* (S-ST)
you work   with my people
'You worked with my people.'

(47) *Ami nha **mininus**, es   fika tudu la   pa fora.* (S-ST)
me my children they stay all   there for outside
'As for me, my children, they all stayed out there.'

(48) *Sen   nada   i   sen   **pesoas**.* (RSS-ST)
without nothing and without persons
'Without anything or anyone.'

In the realm of animate entities, it is important to emphasize that plural marking is illustrative of a very strong tendency but it is a tendency nevertheless. It is, for instance, possible to find examples where a definite animate plural noun may not be marked with the plural suffix, as in (49):

(49) **Mininu** sta so miodu, mininu inda ka pode trabadja, (WH-ST)
children are only small children still NEG can work
e mi so ki sa trabadja.
COP me only COMP TMA work
'(my) children are all small, my children cannot work yet, I am the only one to be working.'

While number inflection in some speakers' speech exclusively targets animate entities, other monolingual varieties may mark inanimate items under two conditions. These items must either be definite/specific, or be framed in the context of episodic tense, in other words, be relevant to the speaker's past or present experience. Definite inanimate items tend to be found in the realm of time units or monetary currency, as shown in (50) and (51).

(50) *Oras ki da...* (ST)
hours that gave
'Whenever the times were good...'

(51) *Vinti anus* (ST)
twenty years
'Twenty years'

Episodic tense is illustrated in examples (52), (53) and (54):

(52) *Ka tene kondisons* (ST)
NEG have conditions
'There aren't the appropriate conditions...'

(53) *Nu fika t' atxa brokinhus na tera.* (FG)
we stayed ASP find holes in earth
'We kept finding holes in the ground'.

(54) *El ta uza kuzas mariadu.* (FG)
he ASP uses things problematic
'He uses problematic things.'

(55) *Ka ten lugares.* (FG)
NEG have places
'There are no places.'

(56) *Tenba txeu ki tinha maneras.* (FG)
was a lot that had manners
'A lot of them had manners.'

In summary, number inflection on inanimate objects is sensitive to definiteness and Tense (episodic tense versus generic tense). As for animate entities, animacy and definiteness are the two features that target them as prime candidates for plural

Table 4. Plural marking in CVC

uns / kes + bare noun

kes + noun-s (infrequent)
nha + noun-s
noun-s

bare noun (generic or specific reading)

quantifier (of various types) + bare noun

marking. The examination of my corpus shows that plural suffixation is used in monolingual speech and that it is sensitive to variables such as [±animate; ±human] and [±definite].

In a nutshell, the data just considered reveal the presence of multiple grammars among the speakers. Nouns, as a rule, will not carry plural marker if modified by a numeral or a quantifier already implying plurality. This is not, however, always the case. Furthermore, entities that tend to be pluralized are those that carry a [+human] feature. As language is a cognitive faculty, it could be argued that if a given speaker considers things or [−human] entities as an undifferentiated mass for which individuation is irrelevant, then plural marking does not take place. This was clearly the case for some monolinguals in the sample.

We can tentatively propose a hierarchy among the variables affecting NP-marking. Entities are more likely to be marked with the plural suffix if they are [+animate/+human]. They may not require to be definite to be pluralized. Inanimate entities are more often than not unmarked with the plural suffix, but a prerequisite to pluralization is that they be definite, or uttered in the context of episodic tense.

The four-way plural marking strategies in CVC are summarized in Table 4.

For the purpose of this paper, it is worth emphasizing that where the Portuguese plural morpheme conveys only a single [+PL] {more than one} feature, the creole inflection -s conveys four features, which may be summarized by the following bracketed schema:

[+PL, +Human, +Specific, +Episodic Tense]

Another way of looking at this is to argue that the determining factor is that of "uniqueness". Uniqueness may be determined on the basis of the discourse, assuming that D-linking for definiteness and T-binding for episodic tense mainly allow for the indexation or selection of an entity out of a set of other potentially relevant entities. To adopt this formulation makes it possible to have the following contrast between Portuguese and the creoles:

Table 5. Bare nouns interpretive variation

Creole	Specific interpretation		Non-specific interpretation		Plural interpretation	
	SG	PL	SG	PL	overt	non-overt
AAE	yes	no	yes	yes	yes	yes
Berbice Dutch	yes	no	yes	yes	yes	yes
Cape Verdean	yes	yes	yes	yes	yes	yes
Guinea-Bissau	yes	yes	yes	yes	yes	yes
Haitian	no	no	yes	yes	yes	yes
Jamaican	yes	yes	yes	yes	yes	yes
Lesser Antil.	yes	yes	yes	yes	yes	yes
Mauritian	no	no	yes	yes	yes	yes
Mindanao	yes	no	yes	yes	yes	yes
Palenquero	yes	yes	yes	yes	yes	yes
Papiamentu	yes	yes	yes	yes	yes	yes
Réunionnais	yes	yes	yes	yes	NA	yes
Santome	yes	yes	no	yes	NA	yes
Seychellois	yes	yes	yes	yes	yes	yes
Sranan	yes	yes	yes	yes	NA	yes

Portuguese DP is sensitive to ±count
CVC DP is sensitive to [±count; ±specific; ±unique], assuming that uniqueness does not imply specificity.[10]

In this sense, the informational density carried by the morpheme "-s" in the creoles under study is heavier and arguably more complex than in the European language. In the final section, I will further argue that the absence of inflectional morphemes altogether on nouns does not make them semantically any simpler.

4.2.3 *On the implication of morphological bareness for semantic complexification*

This particular subsection offers some reflection on the concept of bare categories in creoles as not necessarily involving simplification. Baptista & Guéron (2007b) offered a cross-linguistic examination of determiner systems in creole languages and highlighted the fact that no two creoles display an identical system because the use of bare nouns conveys a wide range of interpretive options across creoles. Table 5 shows that a bare noun may be interpreted as specific (definite or indefinite) singular or plural, non-specific (definite or indefinite) singular or plural, whether or not the noun bears plural morphology. Their interpretation also relates to the definite or indefinite status

---

10. I am grateful to Enoch Aboh for this highly plausible analysis of the Portuguese/CVC contrast.

of the bare noun. Table 5 presents a cross linguistic examination of creole bare nouns and their interpretations adapted from Baptista & Guéron (2007b).

As a result of the bareness on the nouns displayed above, Baptista and Guéron (2007b) showed that other variables in the sentence or discourse must be taken into account. Such variables involve the consideration of tense (generic versus episodic), distribution of the nominal expression (subject or object), and the animacy and specificity status of the noun. This shows that an interpretation that is not immediately available through an overt morpheme carried directly on the noun or present in its local environment (like a determiner) must be conveyed via other domains. This renders the interaction between various components of the sentence/discourse all the more intricate and multi-levelled, hence more complex.

5. Conclusion

These observations show that in the domain of verbal and nominal morphology, what looks like morphological simplification with regard to the lexifier language, actually results in semantic complexification in the creole language.

In the case of the plural marking, not all head nouns are modified with the plural marker in the two creoles under investigation but instead of conveying the single meaning of [+plural] like Portuguese, plural marking conveys a [+animate] and a [+definite] feature in these two creoles.

In the case of the anterior marker *-ba*, in spite of a lack of inflectional variation in the verbal conjugational paradigm, *-ba* actually refers to a punctual past event for stative verbs and past-before-past events for nonstative verbs. In GBC, the marker has the ability as marking all types of predicates as having occurred in the past, contrary to Portuguese where this is confined to verb stems. CVC on the other hand, has developed two distinct passive markers, one to refer to present passives and another for past passives.

The study of this limited morphemic sample shows that inflectional suffixes adopt innovative semantic and distributional properties, distinct from those of the lexifier, and carry their own set of informational values. More importantly for the purpose of this paper, they may carry heavier informational weight, involving more values per feature. Inflectional morphology may therefore not provide a reliable or a sufficient evaluation metric for measuring language complexity.

References

Abney, Steven. 1987. The English Noun Phrase in its Sentential Aspect. PhD dissertation, MIT.
Aitchinson, Jean. 1991. *Language Change: Progress or Decay*? Cambridge: CUP.

Baptista, Marlyse. 2002. *The Syntax of Cape Verdean Creole: The Sotavento Varieties* [Linguistik Aktuell/Linguistics Today 54]. Amsterdam: John Benjamins.
Baptista, Marlyse. 2003. Inflectional plural marking in creoles and pidgins: A comparative study. In *The Phonology and Morphology of Creole Languages*, Ingo Plag (ed.), 315–332. Tübingen: Niemeyer.
Baptista, Marlyse. 2006. When substrates meet superstrate: The case of Cape Verdean Creole. In *Cabo Verde – Origens da sua Sociedade e do seu Crioulo*, Jürgen Lang, John Holm, Jean-Louis Rougé & Maria João Soares (eds.). Tübingen: Narr.
Baptista, Marlyse. 2007a. On the syntax and semantics of DP in Cape Verdean Creole. In *Noun Phrases in Creole Languages: A Multi-faceted Approach* [Creole Language Library 31], Marlyse Baptista & Jacqueline Guéron (eds), 61–106. Amsterdam: John Benjamins.
Baptista, Marlyse & Jacqueline Guéron. 2007b. *Noun Phrases in Creole Languages: A Multi-faceted Approach* [Creole Language Library 31]. Amsterdam: John Benjamins.
Baptista, Marlyse. 2007c. Feature selection and competition in creole formation: A case study. *Penn Working Papers in Linguistics* 13(2). Paper selected from the conference proceedings of NWAV 35: 38–50.
Boulègue, Jean. 1987. *Le Grand Jolof*. Paris: Karthala.
Brásio, António.1962. Descobrimento, povoamento, evangelização do archipélago de Cabo Verde. *Studia* 10: 49–97.
Cardoso, 1989. *O crioulo da ilha de S. Nicolau de Cabo Verde*. Lisboa: Instituto de Cultura e Língua Portuguesa.
Carreira, Antonio. 1983. *O crioulo de Cabo Verde: Surto e Expansão*. Lisbon: Europam.
Ferreira, Fernanda. To appear. Marcadores de plural no português brasileiro e crioulo caboverdiano. In *Português em Contato*, Ana M. Carvalho (ed). Madrid/Frankfurt: Iberoamericana/Vervuert.
Kihm, Alain. 1994. *Kriyol Syntax: The Portuguese-based Creole Language of Guinea-Bissau* [Creole Language Library 14]. Amsterdam: John Benjamins.
Kusters, Wouter. 2003. *Linguistic Complexity: The Influence of Social Change on Verbal Inflection*. Utrecht: LOT.
Lang, Jürgen. 1990. A categoria número no crioulo caboverdiano. *Papia* 1: 15–25.
Lucchesi, Dante. 1993. The article systems of Cape-Verde and Sao-Tomé Creole Portuguese: General principles and specific factors. *Journal of Pidgin and Creole Languages* 8: 81–108.
McWhorter, John. 2001. The world's simplest grammars are creole grammars. *Linguistic Typology* 5: 125–165.
Naro, Anthony. 1978. A study on the origins of pidginization. *Language* 54: 314–347.
Peck, Stephen. 1988. Tense, Aspect and Mood in Guinea-Casamance Portuguese Creole. PhD dissertation, UCLA.
Plag, Ingo. 2003. *The Phonology and Morphology of Creole Languages*. Tübingen: Niemeyer.
Quint, Nicolas. 2000. *Grammaire de la Langue Cap-verdienne*. Paris: L'Harmattan.
Teyssier, Paul. 1959. *La Langue de Gil Vicente*. Paris: Klincksieck.
Thomason, Sally. 2008. Does language contact simplify grammars? Plenary talk given at the annual meeting of the Deutsche Gesellschaft fur Sprachwissenschaft. Bamberg, February 27.
Veiga, Manuel. 1996. *O Crioulo de Cabo Verde: Introdução a Gramática,* 2nd edn. Praia: Instituto Nacional do Livro e do Disco, Instituto Nacional da Cultura.
Veiga, Manuel. 2000. *Le Créole du Cap-Vert*. Paris: Karthala.

Competition and selection
That's all!

Enoch O. Aboh

This paper demonstrates that the notion of *simplicity* as often used in creole studies is completely irrelevant to the understanding of the structure, as well as the genesis, of creole languages. This is because creole languages are linguistic hybrids in the biological sense. They emerge from the recombination of linguistic features from different languages. Given this perspective, it appears that what could be of some relevance to the study of language change is rather the notion of complexity. Within the framework of Competition and Selection as proposed in Mufwene (2001ff.), and adopted in this paper, creole languages develop opaque syntactic and semantic features. These could not have arisen solely in the context of their source languages. Accordingly, the common claim that creoles are simplified versions of their sources is a fallacy, just as it would be to claim in biology that hybrids are genetically simplified children of their parents.

1. Introduction

Notions such as simplicity and complexity in the domain of morphosyntax have always played a crucial role in the characterization of creole languages. Already in the thirties, creoles had been defined as fully-fledged languages that developed from pidgins, the latter being corrupted, reduced, or simplified linguistic systems without native speakers. Given this view, the supposedly simplified or less complex features of creoles are congenital with regard to their sources: the pidgins.[1]

In terms of Bickerton's (1981, 1988, 2008) approach to creolization, where creoles developed from a 'macaronic' pidgin, this characterization does make sense. As he argued in various work, Bickerton suggests that language change may take two paths: *gradual change* or *catastrophic change*. The first is seen as an everyday phenomenon triggered by progressive divergence from the source or target language due

---

1. I'm very grateful to Umberto Ansaldo, Michel DeGraff, Salikoko Mufwene, and Norval Smith for their very helpful comments and criticisms on previous versions of this paper.

to language contact (e.g., immigrants learning the language of the host country and injecting new features in it). As suggested by the term, the second is a more dramatic (or abnormal) phenomenon. It may be characterized by situations where a group of intruders forces a new language on an already existing multilingual society, or where a new society emerges whose members are of different ethnic origins and have no common language.

Creole plantation societies seem to fit in this last scenario because African slaves of different origins were deported to the New World to serve their European masters. The received wisdom assumes that as the number of slaves grew and outnumbered that of Europeans colonists (sometimes to a ratio of three to one as in Jamaica, see Chaudenson 2001, 2003; Mufwene 2001, 2003a, or even ten to one as in the case of Saint-Domingue/Haiti toward the end of the 18th century, Singler 1996), the newcomers (i.e., the bozals) had less access to the target language and therefore had to learn restructured varieties of the target from each other. The acquisition of restructured varieties led to a *dilution* of the target language characterized by the loss of a great number of lexical and morphosyntactic properties that eventually led to the pidgin: the ground zero of language degeneration (e.g., Bickerton 1988; McWhorter 1998, 2001). While this view appears quite popular within some exceptionalist circles, the analysis of feature recombination proposed in this paper shows that things are not this simple.[2]

Bickerton (1988: 273), assuming the *catastrophic change* scenario, further concluded that "Children with no prior language experience but with their native language capacity to guide them, will take that same input and make good any deficit between it and a natural language." However skilful they are in creating a new language, children faced with such a degenerated input such as a pidgin cannot create a full-fledged language that is comparable to the non-diluted target language in terms of semantic, morpho-syntactic, or lexical complexity.[3] This characterization is compatible with Bickerton's (1988: 274) observation that "creole grammars are in some elusive sense simpler than the grammars of older languages." One can further conclude that, in addition to being young languages and genetically handicapped, creoles have not existed long enough to be able to overcome their handicap and develop the complexities found in older languages.

While this debate opposed Bickerton to various scholars in the eighties (e.g., Muysken 1988), McWhorter's (2001) recent claim that "the world's simplest grammars are creole grammars" and his effort to establish an adequate metric of evalua-

---

2. See also Aboh (2005a, 2009a) for some critiques on this view based on socio-historical considerations.

3. In Bickerton (1999: 52ff.), for instance, one reads that the deported slaves "attempted to learn fragments of [...] those languages that were socially dominant or that had the highest numerical representation. What this gave rise to was a macaronic jargon, a form of communication that employed words from several languages." This macaronic jargon later on served as input to a first generation of children who then created the creoles.

tion of simplicity/complexity has promoted this issue again to the top ten lists of 'hot topics' in creolistics. But what if complexity/simplicity as understood in the analyses mentioned is irrelevant for understanding creole genesis and creole structures?

Though this may look like swimming against the tide of common claims in creolistics, this paper proposes a theory of creole genesis that does without notions such as language dilution, simplification, complexification etc. Adapting Mufwene's (2001, 2003a, b, 2005) biological approach to the evolution of syntactic features/patterns, it is shown that what may be superficially described as simple often hides more complex structures that derive from a recombination of the features of the source languages. The result of this analysis is that creoles appear more 'mixed' than often assumed in the literature (Aboh 2006a, 2007; Aboh and Ansaldo 2007). If creoles, like any contact language, are 'mixed' to the extent that they are not always structurally distinguishable from aspects of their source languages, then we reach a non-trivial conclusion: a research project that starts out to evaluate creoles against their source languages in order to prove their simple grammar and explain their genesis is bound to fail. Section 2 briefly presents aspects of Mufwene (2003b, 2005) that are relevant for the present discussion. Section 3 introduces the reader to the version adopted here with regard to syntactic structures, while Section 4 evaluates the proposed framework on empirical data from the Suriname creoles, Saramaccan and Sranan. Section 5 concludes the discussion.

2. Languages as biological species

A central theme of Mufwene's work on the Ecology of Language Evolution is that "a biological approach to evolution is applicable to languages" that may help understand the hypothetical life cycle of a language as described in (1) (Mufwene 2005: 1).

(1)   Phase 1   Phase 2   Phase 3
      Language creation/birth… Language change… Language death

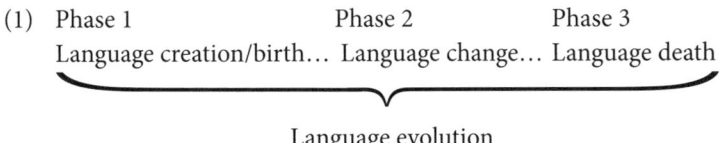

Language evolution

Given the notion of competition and selection as used in biology, these different phases are seen as the results of different ecologies. By analogizing languages to species rather than organisms, Mufwene (2001, 2005) clearly indicates that the question of why certain linguistic "species" disappear to the benefit of others resides in the linguistic ecologies. This view also implies that not every single newly born language will go through the three phases described in (1). It is conceivable that a new language can fade out in a very short period of time because it cannot survive in a particular linguistic ecology. Pidgins, for instance, are often cited as such examples because they tend to disappear along with the function they serve. We can infer from this that the act of language creation itself is contingent on the linguistic ecologies of its creators.

Setting aside social and political matters, we can informally say that such an ecology primarily consists of the interaction of a speaker of a language (Lx) with speakers of other varieties of the same language (i.e., $Lx_1 \ldots Lx_{n+1}$) or speakers of other languages (e.g., Ly, Lz). This interaction feeds a process of competition and selection that opposes the grammars in contact and eventually leads to phases 1, 2, or 3 as described above.

How the competition and selection operates exactly on language structural properties (i.e., in the mind of the speaker) is not clearly established in Mufwene (2001, 2005) who mainly considers these notions at the population level. Yet, the following quotes under (2) and (3) give some indications of his thoughts, and help me fine-tune my own suggestions as to how competition and selection may operate as far as (morpho)syntax is concerned. According to Mufwene (2001:28),

(2) A creole is a restructured variety of its lexifier. The latter was primarily a colonial variety which was spoken by the European colonist and was itself developing from the contact of diverse metropolitan dialects. It has often been identified as a koiné.

Given however that creoles do show uncontroversial traces of substrate influence (e.g., predicate fronting with doubling, topic and focus marking, Aboh 2006a, b, 2007), Mufwene is careful enough to supplement this quote by the following:

(3) It is as necessary to invoke substrate influence from the Celtic languages to account for the speciation of Latin into the Romance languages as it is to invoke African substrate influence to account for the evolution of French and Portuguese into various creoles [....] Both cases are clear instantiations of Pyrrhic victory – where the prevailing language is so clearly affected by the displaced ones. (Mufwene 2005:12)

2.1 Unchaining the competitors

The quotes in (2) and (3) meet two goals in Mufwene's framework. First, creole genesis is regarded as just a(n) (extreme) case of the normal competition and selection process that is typical of language contact situations. Under this view, creoles are only special due to their special ecologies, which in turn derived from the exceptional conditions under which the creole communities were formed (e.g., slavery, plantation society, segregation). Second, that creoles share significant similarities with both their lexifier and substrate languages is accounted for. In a sense, the particular linguistic ecology that led to creole formation also provides us with the *raison d'être* of their particular *phenotype* (i.e., the way they look or sound compared to their source languages).

While I tend to generally agree with this research framework, close scrutiny reveals an imbalance between (2) and (3) that is worth discussing. We may infer from

(2) that the slaves switched to their owner's language and engaged in acquiring the lexifier koiné to some extent (Chaudenson 2001, 2003; Mufwene 2001). This learning process eventually led to the death of the African languages in the colonies, but the battle (or competition) between the displaced African languages and the lexifier koiné was fierce. Accordingly, the prevailing language, that is, the approximation of the lexifier koiné which we now refer to as creole, still shows signs of this period. Such signs are analysed as a consequence of imperfect second language acquisition sometimes allowing L_1 or substrate transfer. Given this description, one has the feeling that right from the beginning the (changing) ecology favored the lexifier. Chaudenson's (2003:199) claims that "*les substrats ne peuvent pas passer en force* [substrate languages cannot forcefully infiltrate the lexifier language]" perfectly illustrates this view, and suggests that the substrate languages can only make their way in the grammar of the lexifier koiné if the former and the latter show converging structures. This, in turn, means that the linguistic ecology in which the creole emerged favoured the lexifier language but constrained the substrate languages. Accordingly, substrate influence appears limited to areas of convergence.[4]

This view may look reasonable if one considers political and sociolinguistic factors (e.g., the oppressing power forcing a linguistic policy on the slaves and prohibiting African languages). Yet, things might not be so obvious. There is indeed abundant evidence that African languages were spoken for some period in the colonial Caribbean (e.g., Long 1774; DeGraff 2002 footnote 45). This would mean that linguistic features from the African languages could be selected by the creole even though they might not converge with the target language. In this regard, note that the process of competition and selection proposed by Mufwene (2001, 2003a, b) assumes that linguistic features of the competing languages form a feature pool on which selection operates. Under this view, it is not clear to me how the ecology of such a language contact situation, in which the lexifier represents the target language, constrains selection inside the feature pool such that non-converging substrate linguistic features are strongly disfavoured (if not excluded). If we adopt a minimalist approach to the study of human knowledge of language, it appears that factors that concern speakers' linguistic ecology or practice are external to the human language capacity. The latter, however, is subject to the competition and selection process, which affects various linguistic modules during the development of the idiolect in the mind of the speaker. Following DeGraff (1999:9) therefore, I assume a distinction between E-creole, that is, an abstraction of the linguistic codes of a creole community, and I-creole, which refers to "the development in individual speakers' minds/brains of a grammar that shows a certain typological distance from the grammars of the languages in contact".

Adopting this distinction, I propose that ecological factors directly operate on E-creole (in a way that still needs to be understood) while competition and selection

---

4. As suggested to me by M. DeGraff, Chaudenson's position can hold only if we have a clear definition of convergence such that we are able to reconstruct the distinctive features that may converge in the competing languages. See Aboh (2009b) for some discussion.

of syntactic features affects I-creole. Given this view, it seems to me that ecological factors, however powerful they may be, cannot impose a ranking of linguistic features on the syntactic module of grammar. This module, I claim is opaque to such external factors. Therefore, competition and selection in core syntax happens freely between features and patterns of the languages in contact. This amounts to saying that even though the speaker's linguistic activities may be (dis)favourable to the competing languages (e.g., workplace language, household language, ritual language vs. poetic/stylistic language) and therefore to certain patterns, the competition and selection that opposes linguistic features and patterns in the mind of the speaker, that is parameter setting in the syntactic sense, is immune to external social factors.[5] I conclude that linguistic features (i.e., syntactic features) are "free" in the mind of the speaker, in this case, the creator of the creole. This axiom, I suggest, can be phrased as in (4).

(4) Competition and selection of linguistic (i.e., syntactic) features is free.

This axiom, which is compatible with Mufwene's general framework, has the advantage that the question of why creoles share certain similarities with their source languages (lexifier or substrate) reduces to the more interesting issue of why certain features are selected over others, or why they are always combined in some particular way. The latter question obviously relates to even more difficult questions such as why the process of competition and selection does not affect all components of a module (e.g., VP, IP, CP, DP in syntax) or all modules of the grammar the same way. A fascinating example discussed in DeGraff (2002, 2005) concerns word order. Most Kwa languages, the major substrate languages for the Suriname creoles and Haitian (Smith 1987; Lefebvre 1998), show VO versus OV alternation in specific aspectual contexts (e.g., progressive, Aboh 2004, 2005b, 2009c). No such aspect dependent word order variation is found in Haitian, Saramaccan, or Sranan. This is surprising since the Kwa speakers being numerically dominant in this context and having this feature in their E-language must have influenced the feature pool with this strong Kwa linguistic feature. Nevertheless, this putatively strong feature of the feature pool did not make it to the emerging creoles (e.g., Sranan, Saramaccan). One could think that the OV order was simply selected against, because the alternative VO order was congruent with that of the lexifier. But it is worth noting that in the case of the Suriname creoles, OV fails to be selected even in contexts where both the superstrate and the substrate converge (e.g., in nominalizations: 'street sweeper', àliò zà-tɔ́ street/sweep/person vs. figi-**strati**-man sweep/street/person, van den Berg 2007: 175). Similarly, DeGraff (2005) indicates that French has alternative OV order with clitics and this was also not selected in Haitian creole. In this language, the object must follow the verb linearly.[6]

---

5. This need not mean that certain external factors (e.g., communication settings) may not favor certain linguistic patterns, which because of their frequency or discourse prominence may in turn favor other linguistic features and their associated parameters.

6. I thank M. DeGraff and S. Mufewene for their suggestions on this issue.

These facts underscore the point made here that the dynamics of the competition and selection must be more complex and to some extent blind to certain external factors that may have to do with say, number of speakers, prestige, etc. Clearly, there must be some independent internal reason to the system such that OV is excluded even when all external factors would seem to favor it.[7]

Similarly Aboh (2006a, b, 2007) has shown that while the Gbe languages have influenced the expression of the Complementizer and Determiner systems in the Suriname creoles to some extent, the same does not hold of other syntactic areas such as the clausal inflectional domain (IP) or even when it comes to modification inside the noun phrase. More study is needed before we understand how linguistic features of competing languages are recombined in the emerging language and I hope to come back to these issues in future work.

In terms of the present discussion, however, the recombination of linguistic features in an I-creole (i.e., idiolect), the replication of such I-creoles, and the emergence of a community of speakers of similar I-creoles leading to the birth of the E-creole (i.e., a new language) is comparable to the evolution of a population in biology. The latter may consist of the mutation of a gene and the selection/reproduction of individuals carrying such gene which eventually leads to a population change. Other striking parallels between biological species and languages (e.g., the analogy between successful communication and biological interbreeding in Mufwene 2005:15) lead me to propose that

(5) Languages are species whose phenotypes – the linguistic features on which typological classifications are based – correspond to genotypes, in this case, syntactic structures.[8]

---

7. DeGraff (2005:353, n. 32) speculates about certain external factors that may have played a role in favoring the rise of VO in Haitian creole in contexts where certain French varieties use VO. As usual, the problem here too is to identify the right varieties and find out whether they are relevant for the genesis of Hatian creole. I leave these issues for future research.

8. This claim appears in contradiction to Mufwene (2005:15, and footnote 13) who argues that "Languages are species whose phenotypes – the linguistic features on which typological classifications are based – correspond to no genotypes […] Clearly languages and idiolects cannot have genotypes, because they are not biological systems."

It is important however that the reader keeps in mind that even within the theory developed here, it cannot be assumed that all phenotypic properties of languages are rooted in the distinctive linguistic features as defined here. What this paper tries to do, instead, is to identify which linguistic features have typical realizations (i.e., phenotypic effects) and how such features recombine with other linguistic features in a situation of language contact.

In terms of (5), syntactic features are expressions of structures (i.e., syntactic projections) that are comparable to genotypes.[9] The next section discusses this issue.

3. Syntactic projections are genotypes

Mufwene's observation that linguistic features correspond to no genotypes is compatible with his other proposal that languages should be compared to a species not to an organism. However, if we take the biological approach to evolution, we have to admit that language evolution results from the recombination or mutation of linguistic features that are part of an idiolect (in this case the I-creole) and the selection of such idiolects. Extended to the domain of syntax this would mean that the recombination *or mutation of syntactic features observed in the phenotype* is a consequence of the recombination or mutation of syntactic structures that is strictly parallel to the recombination/mutation of genotypes.

3.1 The DNA approach to clause structure and syntactic projections

With this in mind, I assume – following Rizzi (1997), Cinque (1999), and much related work in the cartographic approach – a description of clause structure as informally illustrated in (6). The distinct articulations in (6) represent functional projections that have rudimentary semantic content (e.g., focus, interrogative, negation, tense, mood, aspect) and embed specific parameters (some specifications of which are in between parentheses). See Pollock (1989), Haegeman (1995), Aboh (2004), Aboh & Pfau (forthcoming) for discussion.

(6)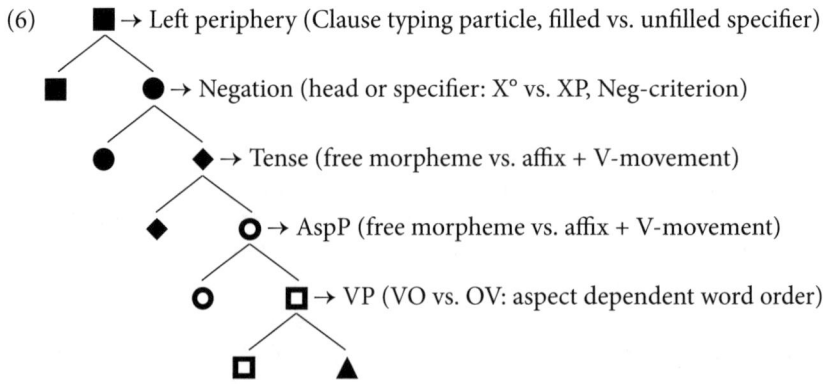

■ → Left periphery (Clause typing particle, filled vs. unfilled specifier)
● → Negation (head or specifier: X° vs. XP, Neg-criterion)
♦ → Tense (free morpheme vs. affix + V-movement)
○ → AspP (free morpheme vs. affix + V-movement)
□ → VP (VO vs. OV: aspect dependent word order)

---

9. The view developed here is different from that proposed by Croft (2000) where the units of selection (or linguemes) represent utterances.

Under this view, while the clause structure is similar to the DNA in containing all the syntactic features as well as their formal licensing properties (i.e., the parameters), the projections are comparable to genes in that they encode specific information about specific syntactic features and parameters only. If we grant this description, then we can further say that manifestations of linguistic features, which Mufwene correctly treats as phenotypes are expressions of a combination of syntactic nodes according to how the associated parameters have been set in the development of the I-language, in this case the I-creole. The conclusion is therefore that linguistic features correspond to genotypes. This point leads us to propose that the only goal of the competition and selection process is to favour or disfavour such syntactic features. Under this view therefore, the overt manifestation of linguistic systems, which we refer to as a language (or a creole) is nothing but the spell-out of specific recombination of linguistic genotypes. The relation between these two entities is represented under (7).[10]

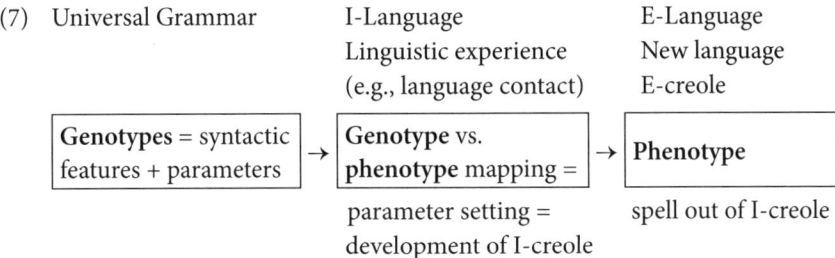

What this description suggests is that the process of competition and selection as well as the recombination of syntactic features happens in the middle box during the mapping of genotype and phenotype. This actually corresponds to parameter setting in generative framework (see Ladiere 2000, 2005 for some discussion). Under this view, the languages in contact provide the speaker with the right triggers for parameter setting. Taking this line of thought seriously, the only difference between contact languages or creoles and other languages is that the input for parameter setting is too diverse and diverging in the case of creoles. As a result, several possible options compete for the fixation of one and the same parameter (e.g., VO vs. OV, affixal TMA morphology vs. free morphemes, specificity vs. definiteness) and the recombined syntactic features that this competition gives rise to in the I-language are also very diverging, when compared to the source languages. This is so because the range of variation

---

10. As Michel DeGraff remarks (p.c), it is clear from this description that a certain amount of "reverse engineering" qua linguistc analysis is necessary to uncover the genotypes that are reflected in the phenotype (i.e., the overt manifestation of linguistic system). This exercise is obviously not a simple one given that not all the properties of the phenotype relate to distinctive linguistic features that are subject to competition and selection. Though further research is needed, questions of this sort show the complexity of the issue at stake, and cast serious doubts on theories of creoles that assume a trivial complex versus simple opposition where the presence versus absence of morpheme types plays an important role (e.g., McWhorter 2001).

set by the typologically diverse competing languages on a plantation exceptionally confronts the speakers with a wide range of combinatories that are not commonly possible in nearly monolingual settings. This conclusion, it seems to me, is compatible with the observation shared by most creolists that creole languages only differ from other languages with regard to the socio-historical contexts in which they came into being. This social context brought together – at a certain point in time and in an isolated geographical location – typologically different languages which otherwise would not have encoutered each other (see also Mufwene 2003a for some discussion).[11]

3.2 Syntactic recombination

The idea that syntactic features are properties of syntactic projections (i.e., genes) that are sensitive to the competition and selection process characterizing the development of the I-language (i.e., I-creole) further suggests that, in a situation of language contact, such linguistic genomes can be combined in various ways across various modules.[12] The following two tables illustrate a recombination of syntactic features that led to the emergence of Saramaccan (see Aboh 2006a, b, 2007; Aboh & Ansaldo 2007 and references cited there).

As discussed in previous work, Table 1 indicates that Saramaccan and Gungbe match in all respects with regard to the morphosyntax of their left periphery to the exclusion of English. I take this to show that the Gbe features of the complementizer layer (or genes to keep the biological approach) have been selected. The phenotype of these features (that is their overt manifestations) makes Gungbe and Saramaccan left periphery similar (even though not isomorphic). For instance, the two languages have markers for question, focus, topic, and mood that realize distinct functional heads within the left periphery. Yet, to the exception of the focus marker wè, which is morphologically, phonologically, and syntactically similar to that of Fongbe and

---

11. On a more general note, the description in (7) assumes that syntactic features have a formal component (i.e., licensing properties) and a semantic component (e.g., discourse function, meaning). Each component can be copied separately or independently during the recombination process that leads to the new language. In terms of this hypothesis, language change boils down to the study of recombination of linguistic features. In addition, if by adopting this view, we are able to isolate syntactic features to the extent that we can distinguish between dominant (i.e., semantically prominent) and weak (i.e, semantically empty) syntactic features, then we may have an answer to why certain features are often found in the recombinations of first generation speakers (e.g., creoles). This predicts that the weak features of such creoles may become dominant under new recombinations. I hope to come back to these issues in future work.

12. This view also implies that the recombination of syntactic genes may lead to changes across syntactic paradigms. For instance, the specification of tense as (free morpheme) may have consequences in the development of mood and aspect markers and the blocking of verb movement. This of course strengthens the comparison between genes and syntactic structures, but I leave the issue for further research.

Table 1. A comparison of the left periphery of Saramaccan, English and the Gbe languages

	Gungbe	Saramaccan	English
Irrealis Mood Comp	✓	✓	*
Deontic Mood Compl	✓	✓	*
Focus particle	✓	✓	*
FocP: XP$_i$-wɛ [$_{IP}$ ...t$_i$...]	✓	✓	*
Verb focus + V-copy V$_i$- wɛ [$_{IP}$ ...V$_i$...]	✓	✓	*
Event relativization V$_i$- Rel [$_{IP}$ ...V$_i$...]	✓	✓	*
Focusing the clause [$_{IP}$ ......]$_i$-wɛ ...t$_i$...	✓	✓	*
Analytic Wh-question words	✓	✓	*
Topic particle	✓	✓	*
Topicalization of the clause V$_i$- wɛ [$_{IP}$ ...V$_i$...]	✓	✓	*
Sentence-final yes-no question particle	✓	✓	*

Gungbe, most Saramaccan markers derive from English (and retain the morphosyntax of English to some extent). Maintaining the analogy between languages and biological organisms, I claim that this is akin to gene recombination where the Gbe linguistic features became dominant (Aboh 2006a, 2007).

Though these languages show strong parallels, when it comes to the complementizer system, other modules of the grammar may be differently affected due to competition and selection.

Table 2 on the syntax of the noun phrase shows this: the determiner in Saramaccan and Gungbe display semantic parallels but differ with regard to syntax (Aboh 2006a, 2007). This table therefore suggests that while we could argue that the selected semantic features are from Gbe, their morphosyntactic realization follows English rules. By analogy again, this would mean that the features (or genes) selected from Gbe became weak under recombination. Alternatively, one could propose that the competition and selection for the feature specific versus non-specific implied two choices: one for the semantics of the feature and one for the syntax of that feature. Accordingly, both competing language types (e.g., Gbe vs. Germanic) won part of the battle here: Gbe-type languages won on the semantic side and English won on the syntax side. This is what Mufwene refers to as "pyrrhic victory" in (3).

Under the competition and selection process as I interpret it here, these facts indicate that creoles or contact languages are not (approximate) replicas of existing linguistic systems. Instead, these *new languages* are syntactically hybrid.[13] As such, their emergence is comparable to speciation (e.g., the emergence of a new species), which arguably derives from cumulative recombinations of different syntactic features in various modules of the grammar during the formation of the I-creole.

---

13. See Whinnom (1971) for another view of creoles and pidgins as hybrid languages.

Table 2. Distributive properties of the noun and its modifiers

	Saramaccan	English	Gungbe
Bare NPs: generic and (in)definite	✓	✓ [indefinites]	✓
Definite vs. indefinite	*	✓	*
D: specific vs. non-specific	✓	*	✓
D precedes N	✓	✓	*
N precedes D	*	*	✓
N precedes that/this; here/there	✓	✓	✓
That/this precedes N	✓	✓	*
Rel. clause precedes D	*	*	✓
D precedes Rel. clause	✓	✓	*
Adjective precedes N	✓	✓	*
N precedes Adjective	*	*	✓

In the following section, I show how the process of competition and selection as conceived of here helps account for semantic and syntactic recombination in the Suriname creoles.

4. Semantic and syntactic recombination

As argued for in previous sections, creole languages emerge from the recombination of various semantic and syntactic features derived from the competing languages (see Smith, this volume for issues of feature recombination from the perspective of phonology). Keeping to this line of thought, the following sections discuss two instances of recombinations. I start with the verb 'eat' which translates in Gungbe and Saramaccan as *ɖù* and *njan* respectively.

4.1 Eating poison

Consider the verb *ɖù* 'eat' in Gungbe, a Kwa language of the Gbe sub-family, which as Smith (1987) and much related work has shown, played a major role in the emergence of the Suriname creoles in the late 17th and early 18th centuries.

In Gungbe, and most languages of the Gbe sub-family, this verb is to some extent comparable to the so-called inherent complement verbs (ICV). These verbs require an object in their citation form (8), see Avolonto (1995), Essegbey (1999) and references cited there for discussion.

(8) a. Kòfí ɖó wèzùn
        Kofi plant race
        'Kofi ran.'

    b. Kòfí ɖó   *gbàdó*
        Kofi plant corn
        'Kofi planted maize.'
    c. *Kòfí ɖó ...
        Kofi   plant
        'Kofi planted maize.'

As the examples under (8c) indicate, an ICV requires a complement to its right. More importantly, the contrast in (8a-b) indicates that ICV's mainly consist of light verbs whose semantics also depends on that of the noun phrase that they select for. Like ICV's the Gungbe equivalent of the verb 'eat' requires a complement to its right as shown in (9a) and (9c).

(9) a. Kòfí ɖù *nú*
        Kofi eat thing
        'Kofi ate.'
    b. Kòfí ɖù *làn*
        Kofi eat thing
        'Kofi ate meat.'
    c. *Kòfí ɖù ...
        Kofi eat

Going back to the contrast in (9a–b), we observe that example (9a) only denotes the semantics of 'to eat' not 'to eat thing' while (9b) can only mean 'to eat meat'. Compared to the examples in (8) where one has the impression that it is the following noun phrase which mainly contributes to the semantics of the ICV, the examples in (9) suggest *ɖù* has the basic meaning of *ingest/consume* somehow subsumed in the English verb 'eat'. Yet, this ICV occurs in various contexts where it is hard to invoke the meaning of ingesting something. Consider the following examples and their various meanings:

(10) a. Tà   ɖù   *mì*
         Head eat 1SG
         'I have a headache.'
     b. Kòfí ɖù *kwέ*   *cè*
         Kofi eat money my
         'Kofi spent my money.'
     c. Kòfí ɖù *àlè*
         Kofi eat benefit
         'Kofi made a benefit.'

Other expressions include:

(10) d. dù àxɔ́
eat debt
'To go bankrupt.'
e. dù gbɛ̀
eat life
'To enjoy.'
f. dù xwè
eat year
'To celebrate.'
g. dù àɖi
eat poison
'To be angry'.
h. dù wìnyán
eat shame
'To be ashamed.'
i. dù nù gò
eat mouth PREP[at]
'To boast.'
j. dù gán
eat chief
'To become chief.'
k. dù yà
eat pain
'To suffer.'

While the examples under (10) might look diverse and unrelated at first sight, the underlying meaning seems to be one whereby the logical subject experiences a state or feeling (e.g., (10b) to (10k)). In addition, it should be noted that these examples are not fixed (or idiomatic) expressions because they are quite productive and allow further combinations. Consider, for instance, (11) with the meaning to enjoy something, where the specifying noun follows *gbè* 'life'. Such constructions are comparable to double object constructions.[14]

(11) a. Mí dù gbɛ̀ Kòfí tɔ̀n
1PL eat life Kofi POSS
'We enjoyed staying with Kofi.'
b. Mí dù gbɛ̀ mótò lɔ́ tɔ̀n
1PL eat life car DET POSS
'We enjoyed the car.'

---

14. One also finds *dù mè jí*: eat someone on => to win over someone, *dù gú*: eat inheritance => to inherit etc.

Finally, the facts in (10) indicate that the verb ɖù in Gungbe poses no particular Agentivity or Animacy restriction on its external argument and the internal argument, which could be both theme and experiencer. These data suggest that the lexical entry corresponding to English 'eat' in the Gbe languages covers a wide range of meanings of which English 'eat' only expresses a tiny part. Similarly, that this verb is an ICV in Gbe indicates that it is strongly transitive, and therefore has a different argument structure than English 'eat' which is either transitive or intransitive depending on the context. The 'genotype' of V-*eat* in the two language types is represented in (12).

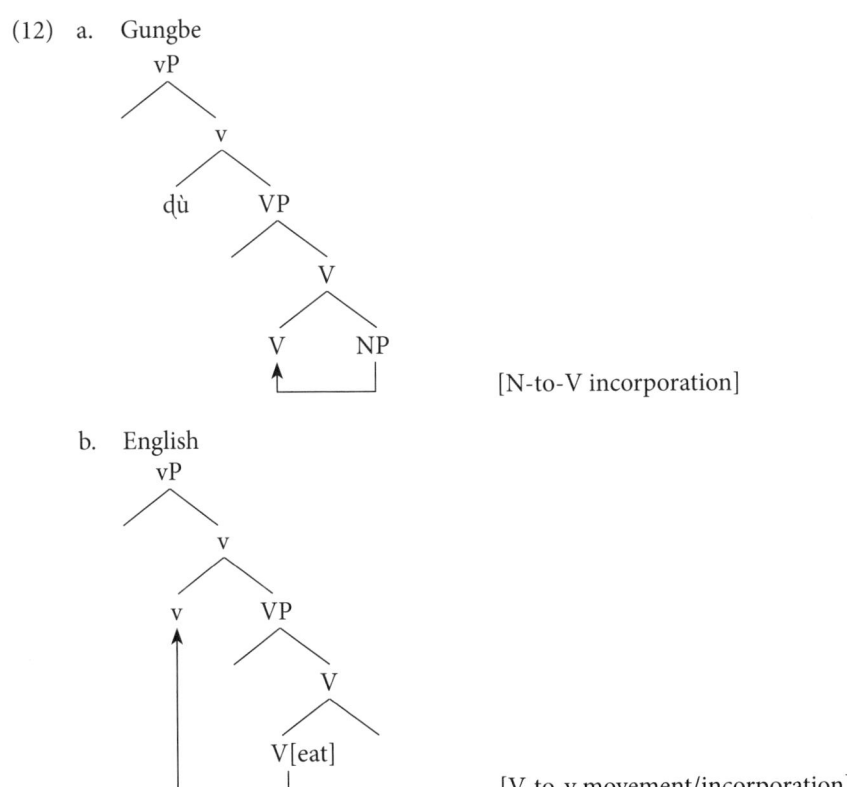

Without entering the intricacies of the formalism, the description in (12a) suggests that ICV's in Gbe are genuine light verbs that merge in little *v* and select for a VP whose head is a transitive empty V. Such empty V's, I claim, select for an NP complement creating as such an incorporation context where the head N is incorporated into V (Baker 1988; Hale and Keyser 1993; Aboh & Dyakonova 2009). We therefore reach a situation where it is the incorporated N that lexicalises V. Given that little *v* is a light verb, the semantics of the ICV derives from the complex *v* + N (that has been incorporated in V). In the case of the examples discussed, I conjecture that *v-ɖù* has the vague meaning of *to get* (either by ingestion of X, association with X or being affected by X).¹⁵ I further conclude that it is the selection of the appropriate complement that further specifies the meaning of the complex *v*+N. In case N is a dummy element as *nú* 'thing' in (9a), the verb gets the generic meaning of ingestion on the basis of the context.

English in (12b), on the other hand, displays a lexical V-*eat* that is specified as either transitive or intransitive and merges under V from where it raises to little *v* under current minimalist approach (e.g., Chomsky 1995). Contrary to the situation in Gungbe, English *eat* seems to have the basic meaning of ingestion for the purpose of feeding oneself or someone else.

With this description in mind, let us consider the corresponding verb *njan* 'eat' in Saramaccan. With regard to syntax, Saramaccan *njan* exhibits the same behaviour as English *eat* in that it can be transitive or intransitive. This is illustrated by the following examples. The sentence under (13) indicates that like English *eat*, this verb may take an internal argument.

(13) Amato njan di bakuba
 Amato eat DET banana
 'Amato ate banana.'

The example in (13) is obviously compatible with the Gungbe example (9b) where the light verb *v-ḍù* selects for a complement. Accordingly, there seems to be no clear difference between Gungbe, English, and Saramaccan in this respect. Yet, when we contrast example (13) to those in (14), taken from Rountree & Glock (1982:43), we realise that Saramaccan *njan* may lack a complement just as English *eat* (14a–b) and unlike Gungbe *ḍù* (9c).

(14) a. I njan kaa no?
  2SG eat already Q
  'Have you already eaten.'
 b. Ai mi njan (kaa)
  yes I eat already
  'Yes I have eaten (already).'
 c. Ai mi njan soni
  yes 1SG eat something
  *'Yes, I ate (something [non-specific]).'
  ✓'Yes, I ate something [specific].'

In addition, the ungrammaticality of Saramaccan (14c) under the relevant reading, as opposed to the Gungbe example (9a) indicates that Saramaccan *njan* cannot select for a dummy noun phrase. This clearly indicates that this Saramaccan example has the same argument structure (and therefore syntax) as English verb *eat*. I therefore

---

15. For instance as in "I got some food"; "I got money"; "I got malaria".

conclude that the syntax of *njan* in Saramaccan maps onto that of English *eat* as represented in (12b).

Yet, Saramaccan *njan* occurs in sequences such as those in (15), many of which (e.g., to spend, to suffer, to boast, to have a headache) are found in Gbe as illustrated in (10).

(15) a. Hédi tá   njan mí
       head PROG eat 1SG
       'I'm having a headache.'   (Rountree & Glock 1982: 39)

   b. Nján búka
      Eat   mouth
      'To boast.'   (Donice & Voorhoeve 1963: 80)

   c. Kofi ta   njan suti buka
      Kofi PROG eat sweet mouth
      'Kofi is boasting.'   (Haboo, p.c.)[16]

   d. Njan moni
      eat money
      'To spend money.'

   e. Njan pena
      eat pain
      'To suffer.'

   f. Njan yai
      eat year
      'To celebrate.'

Assuming that the representation in (12b) holds for the verb *njan* in Saramaccan and *eat* in English, the question arises how Saramacan speakers developed the same usages (or semantics) in (15) as in Gbe. Two options seem possible here. One could propose that such expressions in Saramaccan are calques adopted from Gbe into the creole where they are comparable to fixed idioms such as '*kick the bucket*' in English. But this view is unlikely given that the sequences in (15) are highly productive and the verb can take additional arguments as indicated in (15g).[17]

(15) g. Kofi ta   njan Gaanma   a   baka
       Kofi PROG eat Grandman PREP back
       'Kofi gossips about the chief.'

Another possibility, which I would like to explore here is to suggest that the verb *njan* in Saramaccan combines semantic properties of both Gungbe *dù* and English *eat*.

---

16. I thank Vinje Haboo for providing me with these examples.

17. Interestingly, the usage and meaning in (15g) does not seem to exist in Gbe, but I stand open for correction.

More specifically, I claim that the usages in (15) represent an extension of the semantic specifications of *eat* in English, under the influence of Gbe. A look at the entry *eat* in The New Oxford Dictionary of English (2001) provides us with very interesting examples as in (16), which recall the Gbe usages and could have served as the transmission belt for combining English and Gbe semantics of 'eat'.

(16) a. Eat one's heart out [i.e., suffer from excessive longing, especially for someone or something unattainable].
 b. What is eating you? [i.e., What is worrying or annoying you?]

These examples are clearly similar to the Gbe examples in (10a), (10i) and indicate that both in Gbe and in English the lexical entry for 'eat' may have an experiencer internal argument. Under this description, Saramaccan *njan* maps the semantic properties of English and Gbe 'eat' onto the syntax of English. Accordingly, the linguistic feature of Saramaccan *njan* could be represented as in (17): a new recombination.

(17) *njan* $\begin{cases} \text{Semantic properties (Kwa/English)} \\ \text{Syntactic properties (English)} \end{cases}$

I now turn to another type of recombination involving derivational morphemes.

4.2 *Àzé-tɔ́* versus *aze-man*

Van den Berg & Aboh (2001) show that Gbe languages (e.g., Gungbe) and Suriname creoles (e.g., Sranan, Saramaccan) display nominal sequences that look superficially like simple X-Y adjunctions, where X and Y are heads (e.g., noun). The sequences in (18) provide us with such compounds.[18]

(18) a. Àjàkà dò [Gungbe]
 rat hole
 'Rat hole.'
 b. arátta-oso [Sranan]
 rat-house
 'Rat hole.' (Schumann 1783:6)

These compounds co-exist alongside with sequences involving *-man* in Sranan/Saramaccan or /tɔ́/-nɔ́/ in Gungbe, which one could imagine involve X-Y adjunction structures too.

---

[18]. See van den Berg & Aboh (2001) and references cited there for discussion of other types of compounds.

(19) a. Blέdì nɔ́ [Gungbe]
       bread person
       'Bread seller/baker'
   b. helpi-man [Sranan]
       help person
       'Midwife' (van den Berg 2003: 242)
   c. Àzé tɔ́ [Gungbe]
       witchcraft person
       'Witch'
   d. aséh-man (Schumann 1783: 8)
       witchcraft person
       'Witch'

However, a number of facts about these sequences suggest that -tɔ́/-nɔ́/-man are affixes within a predicate structure. One such fact is that the Sranan/Saramaccan elements -man (derived from English man) and the Gungbe forms -tɔ́/-nɔ́, which literally mean 'father' and 'mother' respectively, appear unspecified for gender in compound head position, unlike when they occur in isolation. Therefore, while the examples in (19) can refer to both male and female persons, those in (20) have gender specification and only refer to either a male or female person.[19]

(20) a. (Ò)tɔ́ cè
       father my
       'My father.'
   b. (Ò)nɔ́ cè
       mother my
       'My mother.'
   c. Man-Ningre / Ningre uman
       man black   black woman
       'Black man/black woman.'

An immediate conclusion here is therefore that the elements -man (Sranan/Saramaccan) and -tɔ́/-nɔ́ (Gungbe) do not function as lexical items when they occur in compound head position. Instead, they are somehow semantically bleached and behave like derivational affixes (or grammaticalized items) that attach to the element on their left. This description finds immediate support in examples such as those under (21), where these morphemes attach to a verb phrase.

---

19. See van den Berg (2003: 244) for similar examples.

4.2.1 VP-tɔ́/nɔ́ versus V-man/VP-man

In Gungbe, the morphemes -tɔ́ and -nɔ́ can attach to nominalised verb phrases only. In such contexts, the object must precede the verb as indicated in (21), (see Aboh 2004, 2005b for discussion).

(21) a. Ùn mɔ̀n [[hún kùn tɔ́] lɔ́]
 1SG see engine drive person DET
 'I saw the engine driver [i.e., the driver].'
 b. Ùn mɔ̀n [[nùkún tɔ́n nɔ́] lɔ́]
 1SG see eye pierce person DET
 'I saw the blind person.'

That the noun can be modified as in (22) suggests that it heads a phrase.

(22) a. Ùn mɔ̀n [[hún **gbó** kùn tɔ́] lɔ́]
 1SG see engine big drive person DET
 'I saw the engine driver [i.e., the driver].'
 b. Ùn mɔ̀n [[nùkún **dòkpó** tɔ́n nɔ́] lɔ́]
 1SG see eye one pierce person DET
 'I saw the blind person.'

It appears that the VP-tɔ́/-nɔ́ sequences in (21) and (22) are complex phrases part of which is a VP. This is indicated by the fact that the whole VP-tɔ́/-nɔ́ sequence can take a determiner and function as argument of a verb. This latter property leads me to conclude that the whole VP-tɔ́/-nɔ́ sequence is a determiner phrase (DP): where D embeds a nominalised verb phrase.

The Gungbe facts are replicated in Sranan/Saramaccan where the morpheme -*man* attaches to a VP as attested both in early and contemporary Sranan (Bruyn 1995a, b).[20]

(23) a. Loecke-man (CR 1745)
 see-man
 'Medicine man'
 b. Hakisi-man (Van Dyk 1765)
 ask-man
 'Inquisitor'
 c. Figi-strati-man
 sweep street man
 'Street orderly'
 d. Sibi-strati-man [Contemporary Sranan]
 sweep street man
 'Street sweeper'

---

20. Smith & Veenstra (1998) observed similar examples in Saramccan.

At this stage, it is worth noting that the word order in Saramaccan and Sranan (i.e., VO) is different from that of Gungbe (i.e., OV). Despite this difference in word order, the situation in Sranan/Saramaccan is very much like that in Gungbe in the sense that -*man* has affixal properties.[21] With regard to morphology, for instance, the elements -*tɔ́/-nɔ́* and -*man* display a reduced form, which underscores the proposed analysis in terms of affix. Empirical data from Gungbe and Sranan/Saramaccan support this point. As discussed in Aboh (2005c) Gungbe noun phrases have an initial vowel (*a-* or *o-*) as indicated in (26).

(26) a. Òhún 'drum'
     b. Àgbán 'plate'

The prefix *o-* can be dropped, while *a-* cannot.

(27) a. Kɔ̀kú xɔ̀ (ò)hún ɖé
        Koku buy drum a
        'Koku bought a drum.'
   b. Kɔ̀kú xɔ̀ *(à)gásá ɖé
        Koku buy crab a
        'Koku bought a crab.'

Both *o-* and *a-* must drop in compound nouns, when the noun they attach to occurs as head. This is illustrated in (28) and (29).

(28) a. (Ò)hún kpòtín
        drum stick
        'Stick to play drum.'
   b. Sìn-(*ò)hún
        water drum
        'Water drum (played at funerals).'

(29) a. Àgásá fɛ̀n
        crab foot
        'Crab foot/pincers'

---

21. This issue merits further attention and I hope to come back to it in future work. As mentioned in Section 2, it is remarkable that while nominalised verb phrases display OV order in both Gbe and English the Saramaccan equivalents maintain VO order. This correlates with the facts discussed in DeGraff (2002), and Aboh (2006a) where it appears that even though most Kwa languages exhibit VO versus OV alternations in the context of aspect, none of their supposedly related creoles has such alternation. These facts cannot be accounted for in terms of universals, since the observed alternations are context-dependent and do not imply a different head parameter (Aboh 2004, 2005b).

    b. Xùmὲ-(*à)gásá
       sea   crab
       'Sea crab'

The same constraints holds true of the source nouns òtɔ́ 'father' and ònɔ́ 'mother' which fail to retain their initial vowel in compound head position (30).

(30) a. *Hún kùn òtɔ́ lɔ́
       car engine person DET
       'Driver'
   b. *Nùkún tɔ́n ònɔ́
       eye pierce person
       'Blind person'

Accordingly, the morphemes -tɔ́ and -nɔ́ 'person' are reduced forms of the nouns òtɔ́ 'father' and ònɔ́ 'mother'.

The facts in Sranan are similar even though less straightforward. Here, one finds the alternation *man* versus *-ma* in certain sources, which suggests that the reduced form *-ma* is an affix, while the full form *man* is a lexical item.

(31) a. *Ase-ma(n)*
       witchcraft-person
       'Witch'
   b. *Joe ben zi hem na da man disi zire boeki.*
       you PAST see him PREP the man REL sell book
       'You have seen him at the man who sells books'.
       [Gy hebt hem by myn Boekverkooper gezien]   (Van Dyk 1765: 31)

Smith and Veenstra (1994, 1998) report a similar alternation in Saramaccan, where the form *-ma* represents an affix, while the free form *mánu* is a noun. Smith (p.c.) notes that the form *-ma* bears no high tone of its own, which further suggests that it belongs to a functional category.[22]

(32) a. *édi-ma*
       head-man
       'Boss/headcase'
   b. *téi-mánu-ma*
       take-man-man
       'Man eater'

---

22. As already reported by Bruyn (1989), Schumann spells the corresponding suffix in 18th century Sranan as *-man* and the free form as *mann*.

Taking these facts seriously, I conclude that -tɔ́/-nɔ̀ and -ma(n) represent affixes that attach to the phrase to their left.

Summarizing, therefore, we have observed that in the Gbe languages and the Suriname creoles, the lexical elements that correspond to 'father/mother' or 'man' can be used derivatively to form new phrases. The next question that I now turn to is what the structure of such phrases is.

4.2.2 X-tɔ́/nɔ̀/man as predicate structure

A fact that one immediately notices about the sequences X-tɔ́/nɔ̀/-man is that they express a relation such that X, a noun phrase, denotes an abstract entity, property or quality that predicates over -tɔ́/nɔ̀/-man. When X represents a verb phrase, however, it expresses an event of which -tɔ́/nɔ̀/-man is an agent. The formed X-tɔ́/nɔ̀/man sequences can be used in equative constructions such as in *John is X-tɔ́/nɔ̀/man* which could mean 'John is wealth-person (i.e., rich)' or 'John is drive-person (i.e., driver)'.

Following Aboh's (2005c) analysis of similar sequences in Gungbe, I propose that the Gungbe sequence *àzé-tɔ́* in (19c) and Sranan *aséh-man* in 18th century Sranan (19d) (see van den Berg 2007) involve a structure of the type in (33) where the item to the left is the subject of the nominal predicate expressed by the head *-tɔ́* or *-man*. The two elements are linked by the inflectional element F° (Kayne 1994; den Dikken 1998).

(33)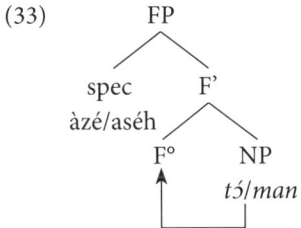

Under this representation, the head N *tɔ́/nɔ̀/man* incorporates into F° where it functions as an affix. Put differently, incorporation of N into F° explains the morphological change of the full form corresponding to the lexical entry *man*, *òtɔ́* 'father', *ònɔ̀* 'mother' into the reduced form -tɔ́/nɔ̀/-ma(n), as discussed previously. Given this view, the sequences involving a (nominalised) verb phrase in (21) for Gungbe and (23) for Sranan can be derived as in (34).

(34)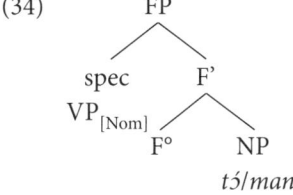

Sranan and Gungbe differ in the sense that the Sranan VP realizes VO order or may contain the verb only. In Gungbe, however, the nominalization of the VP requires OV order. This difference aside, what we see here is that the Sranan forms *aséh-man* or *sibi-strati-man* map on the (Gbe) structures (33) and (34) where *man* has been substituted for *tɔ́/nɔ́*.

The case of *aséh-man* is illuminating in this respect because it raises an interesting issue with regard to language acquisition. Indeed, for the creators of the Suriname creoles to be able to match the English lexemes with the Gbe structures, they have to make the right assumption that *tɔ́/nɔ́* corresponds to *man*, that is [mən], in its compound-head use in English examples such as póst[mən] and políce[mən]. This usage which could be said to involve a clitic compound element (Smith p.c.) reinforces the development of the derivational morpheme *-man*. The end result of this combination is that the Suriname creoles appear structurally mixed both with regard to (morpho)syntax and semantics.

5. Back to complexity and simplicity

The conclusion of this paper is obvious: the notion of *simplicity* is completely irrelevant to the understanding of the structure and the genesis of creole languages, and therefore to the study of language change or language evolution. This is because creole languages are linguistic hybrids. They emerged from the recombination of linguistic features from different languages. While this is the normal situation in every instance of language change and language evolution (see DeGraff 2001; Mufwene 2001, 2008), the case of creoles looks striking at first sight simply because the recombination involves linguistic features from typologically different languages. This means that creoles are noticeable only because of their (contrasting) phenotypes. Nothing in their structures singles them out as a (proto-)type.

As the irony goes, it seems instead that it is the notion of complexity which might be relevant to the description of these languages. Indeed, under the competition and selection approach argued for here, creole languages develop opaque syntactic and semantic features which could not have arisen solely in the context of their source languages. Though interesting, I will not follow this line of argumentation, because I feel it is not more insightful than approaches that argue for simplicity as congenital to creoles.

Coming full circle again, I would like to stress once more that the claim that creoles are *simplified* versions of their sources is a fallacy, just as it would be to claim in biology that hybrids are genetically *simplified children of their parents*. Indeed, the framework argued for here clearly implies that a creole can only derive combinations of a subset of the features competing in the Feature Pool but not all. Why this is so in nature does not seem to me a linguistic question.

References

Aboh, Enoch O. 2004. *The Morphosyntax of Complement-head Sequences: Clause Structure and Word Order Patterns in Kwa.* Oxford: OUP.
Aboh, Enoch O. 2005a. Pattern and feature competition: Toward a syntactic account to contact-induced transfer. Conference on Creole language structure between substrates and superstrates. Leipzig, 3–5 June.
Aboh, Enoch O. 2005b. Object shift, verb movement and verb reduplication. In *The Oxford Handbook of Comparative Syntax.* Guglielmo Cinque & Richard Kayne (eds), 138–177. Oxford: OUP.
Aboh, Enoch O. 2005c. The category P: The Kwa paradox. *Linguistic Analysis* 32: 615–646.
Aboh, Enoch O. 2006a. The role of the syntax-semantics interface in language transfer. In *L2 Acquisition and Creole Genesis: Dialogues* [Language Acquisition & Language Disorders 42], Claire Lefebvre, Lydia White & Christine Jourdan (eds.), 221–252. Amsterdam: John Benjamins.
Aboh, Enoch O. 2006b. Complementation in Saramaccan and Gungbe: The case of c-type modal particles. *Natural Language and Linguistic Theory* 24(1): 1–55.
Aboh, Enoch O. 2007. La genèse de la périphérie gauche du saramaka: Un cas d'influence du substrat? In *Grammaires créoles et grammaire comparative,* Karl Gadelii & Anne Zribi-Hertz (eds.), 73–97. Saint-Denis: Presses Universitaires de Paris.
Aboh, Enoch O. 2009a. Tous coupables…et responsables. Talk presented at the research seminar GRGC, Paris 8, March 2.
Aboh, Enoch O. 2009b. Serial verb constructions: A trans-Atlantic Sprachbund? Ms, University of Amsterdam.
Aboh, Enoch O. 2009c. Clause structure and verb series. *Linguistic Inquiry* 40: 1–33.
Aboh, Enoch O. & Dyakonova, M. In press. Predicate doubling and parallel chains. *Lingua.* 119: 1035–1065.
Aboh Enoch O. & Ansaldo, Umberto. 2007. The role of typology in language creation. In *Deconstructing Creoles* Umberto Ansaldo & Stephen Matthews (eds.), 39–66. Amsterdam: John Benjamins.
Aboh Enoch O. & Pfau, Roland. Forthcoming. What's a wh-word got to do with it? In *Mapping the Left Periphery,* Paola Benincà & Nicola Munaro (eds). Oxford: OUP.
Arends, Jacques & Perl, Mathias. 1995. *Early Suriname Creole texts. A Collection of 18th Century Sranan and Saramaccan Documents.* Frankfurt/Madrid: Vervuert/Iberoamericana.
Avolonto, Aimé. 1995. Pour une approche minimaliste des verbes à objets inhérents en Fongbe. PhD dissertation, University of Quebec at Montreal.
Baker, Mark. 1988. *Incorporation: A Theory of Grammatical Function Changing.* Chicago IL: The University of Chicago Press.
Bickerton, Derek. 1981. *Roots of Language.* Ann Arbor MI: Karoma.
Bickerton, Derek. 1988. Creole languages and the Bioprogram. In *Linguistic Theory: Extensions and Implications, Linguistics: The Cambridge Survey* 2, Frederick Newmeyer (ed.), 268–284. Cambridge: CUP.
Bickerton, Derek. 1999. How to acquire language without positive evidence: What acquisitionists can learn from creoles. In *Language Creation and Language Change*, Michel DeGraff (ed.), 49–74. Cambridge MA: The MIT Press.

Bickerton, Derek. 2008. *Bastard Tongues: A Trail-Blazing Linguist Finds Clues to our Common Humanity in The World's Lowliest Languages.* New York NY: Hill and Wang.

Bruyn, Adrienne. 1989. De nominale constituent in het 18e Sranan. Een Bescrijving van Grammaticale Elementen en Morfosyntactische Processen. MA thesis, University of Amsterdam.

Bruyn, Adrienne. 1995a. Grammaticalizaion in Creoles: The Development of Determiners and Relative Clauses in Sranan. PhD dissertation, University of Amsterdam (Amsterdam: IFOTT, Studies in Language and Language Use 21).

Bruyn, Adrienne. 1995b. Noun phrases In *Pidgins and Creoles. An Introduction* [Creole Language Library 15], Jacques Arends, Pieter Muysken & Norval Smith (eds), 259–269. Amsterdam: John Benjamins.

Chaudenson, Robert. 2001. *Creolization of Language and Culture.* Routledge. London.

Chaudenson, Robert. 2003. *La créolisation: Théorie, applications, implications.* Paris: L'Harmattan.

Chomsky, Noam. 1995. *The Minimalist Program.* Cambridge MA: The MIT Press.

Cinque, Guglielmo. 1999. *Adverbs and Functional Heads, A Cross-linguistic Perspective.* Oxford: OUP.

Croft, William. 2000. Explaining Language Change: An Evolutionary Approach. London: Longman.

DeGraff, Michel. 1999. *Language Creation and Language Change.* Cambridge MA: The MIT Press.

DeGraff, Michel. 2001. On the origin of creoles: A Cartesian critique of neo-Darwinian linguistics. *Linguistic Typology* 5: 213–310.

DeGraff, Michel. 2002. Relexification: A reevaluation. *Anthropological Linguistics*: 44: 321–414.

DeGraff, Michel. 2005. Morphology and word order in "creolization" and beyond. In *The Oxford Handbook of Comparative Syntax*, Guglielmo Cinque & Ricard Kayne (eds), 293–372. Oxford: OUP.

Den Dikken, Marcel. 1998. *Predicate Inversion in DP.* In *Possessors, Predicates and Movement in the Determiner Phrase* [Linguistik Aktuell/Linguistics Today 22], Artemis Alexiadou & Chris Wilder (eds), 177–214. Amsterdam: John Benjamins.

Donicie, Anton C. R. & Voorhoeve, Jan. 1963. *De Saramakaanse Woordenschat..* Amsterdam: Bureau voor Tallonderzoek in Suriname van de Universiteit van Amsterdam.

Essegbey, James. 1999. *Inherent Complement Verbs Revisited: Towards an Understanding of Argument Structure in Ewe.* Wageningen: Ponsen & Looijen.

Haegeman, Liliane. 1995. *The Syntax of Negation.* Cambridge: CUP.

Hale, Ken & Keyser, Samuel J. 1993. On argument structure and the lexical expression of syntactic relations. In *The View from Building 20. Essays in Linguistics in Honor of Sylvain Bromberger* [Current Studies in Linguistics], Kenneth Hale & Samuel J. Keyser (eds.), 53–109. Cambridge MA: The MIT Press.

Kayne, Richard S. 1994. *The Antisymmetry of Syntax.* Cambridge Ma: The MIT Press.

Ladiere, Donna. 2000. Mapping features to forms in second language acquisition. In *Second Language Acquisition and Linguistic Theory*, John Archibald (ed.), 102–129. Malden MA: Blackwell.

Ladiere, Donna. 2005. On morphological competence. Ms, Georgetown University.

Lefebvre, Claire. 1998. *Creole Genesis and the Acquistion of Grammar.* Cambridge: CUP.

Long, Edward. 1774 [2002]. *The History of Jamaica*. Montreal: McGill-Queen's University Press.

McWhorter, John. 1998. Identifying the creole prototype: Vindicating a typological. *Language* 74: 788–818.

McWhorter, John. 2001. The world's simplest grammars are creole grammars. *Linguistic Typology* 5: 125–165.

Mufwene, Salikoko. 2001. *The Ecology of Language Evolution*. Cambridge: CUP.

Mufwene, Salikoko. 2003a. *Créoles, écologie sociale, evolution linguistique*. Paris: L'Harmattan.

Mufwene, Salikoko S. 2003b. Competition and selection in language evolution. *Selection* 3: 45–56.

Mufwene, Salikoko S. 2005. Language evolution: The population genetics way. In *Gene, Sprachen, und ihre Evolution*, Günter Hauska (ed.), 30–52. Regensburg: Universitaetsverlag Regensburg.

Mufwene, Salikoko S. 2008. *Language Evolution. Contact, Competition, and Change*. London: Continuum.

Muysken, Pieter. 1988. Are creoles a special type of language? In *Linguistics: The Cambridge Survey*, Vol. 2: *Linguistic Theory: Extensions and Implications*, Frederick Newmeyer (ed.), 285–301. Cambridge: CUP.

Pollock, Jean-Yves. 1989. Verb movement, Universal Grammar, and the structure of IP. *Linguistic Inquiry* 20: 356–424.

Rizzi, Luigi. 1997. The fine structure of the left periphery. In *Elements of Grammar*, Liliane Haegeman (ed.), 281–337. Dordrecht: Kluwer.

Rountree, S. Catherine & Glock, Noami. 1982. *Saramaccan for Beginners* [Languages of the Guianas 5]. Paramaribo: SIL.

Schuchardt, H. 1914. *Die Sprache der Saramakkaneger in Surinam*. Amsterdam: Johannes Müller.

Schumann, Christian. 1783. *Neger-Englisches Wörterbuch*. [MS published in Kramp, André. 1983. Early Creole Lexicography: A Study of C. L. Schumann's Manuscript Dictionary of Sranan, 44–305. PhD dissertation, University of Leiden.]

Singler, John Victor. 1996. Theories of creole genesis, sociohistorical considerations, and the evaluation of evidence: The case of Haitian Creole and the Relexification Hypothesis. *Journal of Pidgin and Creole Languages* 11: 185–230.

Smith, Norval. 1987. The Genesis of the Creole Languages of Surinam. PhD dissertation, University of Amsterdam.

Smith, Norval & Veenstra, Tonjes. 1994. Affixation in a radical creole. Linguistics Society of America/Society for Pidgin and Creole Linguistics, Boston, January 1994.

Smith, Norval & Veenstra, Tonjes. 1998. Synthetic compounds in a radical creole: abrupt versus gradual change. Creole Conference, Regensburg, 24–27 June.

Van Dyk, Pieter, n.d. c1765. *Nieuwe en Nooit Bevoorens Geziene Onderwijzinge in het Baster Engels, of Neeger Engels* Amsterdam: Wed. Jacobus van Egmont. (Republished in Arends, Jacques & Perl, Mathias. 1995. *Early Suriname Creole Texts*, 93–239. Frankfurt/Madrid: Vervuert/Iboamericana).

Van den Berg, Margot. 2003. Early 18th century Sranan -*man*. In *Phonology and Morphology of Creole Languages*, Ingo Plag (ed.), 231–251. Tübingen: Niemeyer.

Van den Berg, Margot. 2007. A Grammar of Early Sranan. PhD dissertation, University of Amsterdam.

Van den Berg, Margot. & Aboh, Enoch O. 2001. Compounding and derivation in two morphologically 'poor' languages. Morfologiedagen Utrecht, 13–14 December 2001.

Voorhoeve, Johannes. 1980. *Tinadri. Een praktische cursus om Surinaams te leren in 13 lessen*, 2nd edn. Amsterdam: Centrum Anton de Kom.

Whinnom, Keith. 1971. Linguistic hybridization and the "special case" of pidgins and creoles. In *Pidginization and Creolization of Languages*, Dell Hymes (ed.), 91–115. Cambridge: CUP.

Woordenlijst Sranan Nederlands English met een lijst van planten- en dierennamen 1980. No author, Stichting Volkslectuur. Paramaribo: VACO.

Complexity and the age of languages

Umberto Ansaldo and Sebastian Nordhoff

This paper addresses the issue of complexity in language creation and the time it takes for 'complex' structures to emerge in the history of a language. The presence of morphological material is often equated to a certain degree of complexity or is taken to signify a certain time-depth in the history of a language (e.g. Dahl 2004; McWhorter 2005). Though this assumption may be seen as trivial in the absence of a theoretically-based definition of complexity (Muysken 1988), or even misleading (Aboh and Ansaldo 2007; Farquharson 2007), we here put it to a test by looking at morphology in a relatively 'young' language, namely Sri Lanka Malay (SLM). SLM is a mixed language which shows considerably more morphological material and other signs of old age than 'prototypical' creoles. We explain this by arguing (a) that structural output in language genesis is closely motivated by the typology of the input languages and (b) that our understanding of rate of change needs to be revised to take into account ecological matters.

1. Foreword[1]

In this paper, we engage with the alleged relationship between a certain type of structural complexity and the time it takes in the history of a language for such structure to evolve. At least one of the above-mentioned authors has argued against an objective notion of linguistic complexity and so have many others (for a comprehensive discussion see *Linguistic Typology* 2001 vol. 5.2–3); in general, in order to be measurable, complexity needs to be defined on the basis of a specific theoretical module (Muysken 1988). It seems that, for the moment, there is no agreement amongst linguists as to what such a definition should be. For example, it is a clear

---

1. We would like to express our gratitude to the following people/ bodies: the Kandy and Upcountry Malays for their support and collaboration in our fieldwork; the Volkswagen Stiftung's initiative for the Documentation of Endangered Languages (DoBeS) for funding our research on the project 'The documentation of Sri Lanka Malay'; Lisa Lim and Anthony Grant for feedback to the paper.

result of a Eurocentric linguistic theory to view tone languages as phonologically complex; as we will see below, precisely such an assumption is part of one of our current definitions of complexity (e.g. McWhorter 2005).[2] It is legitimate to doubt how phonologically complex tone languages actually are to, say, a Thai child. Conversely, to claim that case morphology is 'complex' may suggest that it is more difficult to acquire a case paradigm than a set of adpositions to indicate grammatical relations. More importantly, it is unclear how complexities within different modules of language interact with one another, i.e. whether we can talk of a morphologically simple but semantically complex language vs. a morphologically complex but semantically simple one and which wins in the overall assessment. Finally, it may be the case that complexity of production leads to simplicity of parsing and vice versa, which makes it difficult to talk about complex and simple languages as a whole.

In what follows, we do not address the issue of how complexity should (or should not) be understood; in Section 2, we assume the validity of, in particular, one view of complexity, namely the one put forward in Dahl (2004), that allows us to at least entertain the possibility that certain types of structural features may require time in order to emerge. In Section 3 we look for signs of age, i.e. 'mature' features in Dahl's sense, in Sri Lanka Malay (SLM), a language that, as we show, is historically relatively 'young'. The concepts of young and old are related to the issue of rate of change in Section 4. In the light of all the observations gathered, Section 5 reviews the notion of complexity that emerges from McWhorter's 'creole prototype' idea, and evaluates its relevance for our understanding of the relationship between age and structural properties in language (McWhorter 2005).

2. On complexity and new language formation

In *Defining Creole*, McWhorter (2005) presents the fundamental argument that links his notion of simplicity to time-depth. For McWhorter, "creoles are indisputably new languages" (2005: 10) *because* they all share the common feature of lacking signs of old age. Typical features of old grammars in McWhorter's view are:

1. Inflectional affixation intended as a morphological, as opposed to an abstract, UG feature, which arises over time if a free morpheme is reanalyzed as grammatical and becomes bound;
2. Tone systems, which emerge through tonogenesis from phonetic erosion, specifically grammatical tone systems involving contrastive monosyllables and grammatical functions;
3. Derivational noncompositionality, arising through semantic drift.

---

[2]. We refer here to McWhorter (2005) as a collated exposition of his previous work on the Creole Prototype.

These features are allegedly by-products of language change but they are not necessary for basic communication as *they are not inherent to UG* (McWhorter 2005). Therefore, they only grow over time and are an indication of emergence of complexity (or overspecification). What makes new languages such as creoles 'simple' (see McWhorter 2001) is the fact they they typically lack all or most of these features. Conversely, presence of these features can be used as a metric of complexity.

In a broader investigation of complexity, Dahl (2004) identifies a series of 'mature' phenomena in languages. Maturity is defined by Dahl (2004: 105) as follows:

> x is a mature phenomenon iff there is some identifiable and non-universal phenomenon or a restricted set of such phenomena y, such that for a language L, if x exists in L there is some ancestor L' of L such that L' has y but not x.

The types of mature phenomena that can be identified according to this definition include (see Dahl 2004: 114–115):

1. Complex word structure (inflectional/ derivational morphology, incorporation)
2. Lexical idiosyncrasy (gender, INFL classes, case)
3. Syntactic phenomena depending on inflectional morphology (agreement, case)
4. Word order rules over and above internal ordering of sister constituents
5. Specific marking of subordinate clauses
6. Morpheme and word level features in phonology

However, Dahl also notes that, while it may be possible to reason about old age, it is quite unlikely that we may ever be able to reason about the youth of a language. In discussing pidgins and creoles, he notes that:

> in order to be defined as a creole, a language must have as its primary historical source a language which has a sufficiently simplified grammatical structure [a pidgin]. No grammatical property of a language can therefore be a counterexample to the thesis that creoles have the world's simplest grammars, because in order to be a creole, the language has to originate from an earlier language state which did not have that property (a pidgin), and if it has it there are only two logical possibilities: either that stage did not exist, in which case it is not a creole, or the property has been acquired later, in which case it is not a counterexample either, since it just means that the language is on its way to losing its creole character.
>
> (2004: 111)[3]

---

3. The fact that McWhorter's assumption equating lack of specific features to youth would be hard to test has been a recurrent criticism of the model (see e.g. Arends 2001a; Ansaldo 2007), and counterexamples of non-young languages showing the same 'simplicity' (e.g. Gil 2001; Grant 2007) as well as creoles with inflectional morphology (DeGraff 1999, 2001; Farquharson 2007) have been put forward.

In what follows, we present an example of a contact language that can be taken as 'young', being at best 350 years old, which would make it comparable to 'prototypical creoles', but which has a substantial amount of signs of old age. This is not intended as a counterexample to McWhorter specifically, for two reasons:

1. As explained by Dahl (see above), and contrary to McWhorter's own claim (e.g. 2005: 140), the Creole Prototype idea is *not* falsifiable.
2. A language which is structurally similar to SLM,[4] namely Sri Lanka Creole Portuguese, is described by McWhorter as having inherited its features of age through intimate contact with the inflected adstrates (Sinhala and Tamil).

Indeed we agree with the characterization provided by McWhorter in (b) above also in relation to SLM. What we aim to show is that this line of reasoning can be extended to all types of contact languages, and that the relation between time and form is not insensitive to, but rather dependent on, the typological ecology of the contact situation.

3. Complexity in Sri Lanka Malay[5]

SLM can be said to show signs of 'age' in at least six different domains:

1. Bound affixes from former free forms: these affixes can be stacked yielding an agglutinative structure;
2. Inflectional/ derivational morphology;
3. Signs of incipient agreement;
4. Arbitrary subcategorization;
5. Complex negation patterns;
6. Difference between main clauses and subordinate clauses.

In what follows we discuss the different manifestations of complexity in turn.

3.1 Agglutinative structure

SLM has substantial bound morphology that is arranged in an agglutinative way. Example (1) shows use of a nominalizing suffix, an infinitive marker, case marking and coordinating association, all expressed by bound morphology:

---

4. But crucially not easily comparable in terms of genesis (Ansaldo 2009).
5. The data in this paper come from the Upcountry variety of SLM.

(1) Rani=pe   thaandak-an=na=le   Farook=pe   nyaani
    Rani=POSS   dance-NMLZR=DAT=ASSOC   Farook=POSS song
    mə-dingar=na=le   suuka⁶
    INF-hear=DAT=ASSOC   like
    'I like Rani's dancing and to hear Farook's singing.'

(2) paasir mə-kumpul-kan=nang=jo   se Dubai=nang em-pi
    sand   INF-much-CAUS=DAT=FOC   1s Dubai=DAT   PAST-go
    'It was to collect sand that I went to Dubai.'

If we accept the view that languages start off as simple and acquire accretion (or 'grammatical junk') over time, the expression of several concepts – up to a total of four (e.g. 2) – in one phonological word is not something that we would locate in the early stages of a language's development.

3.2 Inflectional/derivational morphology

It can be argued that example (1) shows derivational morphology, which according to McWhorter (2005) does not necessarily qualify as a sign of old age. The same holds for clitics, which are less 'morphological' than true affixes. But that still leaves us the infinitive marker *mə-*, which is clearly inflectional. The prefix *mə-* shown in example (1) is of Malay origin (either from transitivizer *meN-*, or from a volitive modal, Slomanson 2006)[7] but has been reanalyzed to serve the infinitive function it has today. While Sinhala and Tamil both make use of infinitive constructions, it should be noted that the SLM infinitive differs in its distribution from both languages. The infinitive is used in Sinhala and Tamil as the complement of all modals, which is not the case in SLM (compare (3) with (3') and (3")).

(3)   Se masthi (*mə-) pi   (SLM)
      1s must   INF   go
      'I must go.'

(3') Mama yanḍa oonä   (Sinhala)
(3") Naan poha veṇum   (Tamil)
      '1s   go.INF must.'

---

6. The SLM examples use a practical orthography, which is based on the orthography of Indonesian, with the following additional conventions: <th> and <dh> mark dental articulation (not aspiration), <ḍ> and <ṭ> mark retroflex articulation, <v> or <w> mark a labiodental approximant. When digraphs are geminated, only the first letter is doubled (<tth>, not <thth>, <nny> not <nyny>).

7. Smith and Paauw (2006: 173) also propose the debitive *mesti* as a possible origin.

Table 1. Some Sri Lankan Malay TMA markers

Past	Conjunctive Participle (CP)	Non-past
ana-, su-	*s-*	*ara-*

As shown in Table 1, other inflectional affixes are also found in SLM, in particular TMA markers.

Example (4) shows the use of the CP[8] and the progressive prefixes. Examples (5) and (6) show the other prefixes.

(4) nyaakith oorang pada s-pi   thaangan ara-cuuci
    sick   man   PL   CP-go   hand   NON.PAST-wash
    'The patients come and wash their hands.'

(5) kitham=pe aanak=pada=le   karang bae=nang   cinggala su-blaajar
    1PL=POSS child=PL=ASSOC now good=DAT Sinhala PAST-learn
    'Now our children learn Sinhala well.'

(6) Se ana-laaher   inni ruuma=ka=jo
    1s PAST-be.born this house=LOC=FOC
    'It was in this house that I was born.'

Considering that no other Malayic language shows TMA prefixes (see Slomanson 2006), these would have evolved in SLM in the last 350 years. We can still find traces of the unbound proto-forms, as we can see in Malay **ada* 'exists' > *ara-* and Malay **habis* (habitual marker) > *s-*. It should be noted that *anna-* is already an archaic form, as younger speakers tend to realize only either the first or the second syllable, the most reduced forms being *e-* and *n-*. These phenomena can be classified under (i) in Dahl's list, namely instances of complex word structure.

3.3 Agreement

An excellent example of grammatical accretion is agreement. There is no semantic need to express a referent twice to communicate propositional content, yet this is precisely what agreement does. In SLM, we can observe incipient agreement. Next to the subject NP, the subject can optionally be expressed by an additional cliticized pronoun (Corbett 2003: 99f.). This clitic can be proclitic (7) or enclitic (8):

(7) Dr Draaman dua thawon blaakang incian=se-nniinggal
    Dr Draaman two year after 3S.POLITE=PAST-die
    'Dr Draaman died two years later.'

---

8. Conjunctive participles are an areal South Asian feature. This form expresses that the action denoted by the verb in the participle clause took place before the action denoted by the verbs of the following clauses. A rough equivalent is English *'having done X…'*.

Table 2. Subcategorization of modals. The first two columns show whether the modal assigns nominative or dative case. The next two columns indicate whether it is used preverbally or postverbally. The last columns show whether the verb appears in the infinitive or the bare form when combining with the modal.

	Assigns		Position		Verb form		
	Nom	Dat	Prevbl.	Postvbl.	Inf.	Bare	Engl.
masthi	+	−	+	−	−	+	must
anthi	+	−	+	−	−	+	IRR
boole	−	+	+	+	(−)	+	can
therboole	−	+	+	+	+	−	cannot
mau	−	+	+	+	+	−	want

(8) spaaman awuliya su-jaadi=spaaman
 3S.POLITE saint PAST-become=3S.POLITE
 'He became a saint.'

This type of agreement is not attested in the other Malayic languages. While agreement is still rare in the SLM of today, and only found in few speakers, it is the beginning of a phenomenon that can be classified under (iii) in Dahl's list, i.e. inflectional morphology for syntactic phenomena.

3.4   Arbitrary subcategorization

Another example of 'maturation' is the arbitrary subcategorization of lexemes. There is no communicative usefulness in, for example, certain German prepositions requiring the dative (*mit* 'with') and others the accusative (*ohne* 'without').[9] The same is true for the SLM modal particles. Modal particles are a class of lexemes that carry modal information; in SLM their distribution is completely arbitrary: for example, *boole* 'can' and *therboole* 'cannot' pattern in a different way, as shown in Table 2.

This behavior can of course be attributed to negation, since asymmetric negation is common in the languages of the world (Miestamo 2005), but this does not explain why *mau* 'want' patterns with the negative form and not with the positive one. Moreover, as shown in Table 2, *masthi* 'must' patterns in a third way, which is different again. In this respect, it behaves exactly like *anthi* 'IRR', but there seems to be no semantic motivation behind this morphological similarity. As Table 2 clearly shows, SLM modals have an idiosyncratic subcategorization pattern, which can be regarded as accretion. Again, it should be noted that the modal subcategorization pattern cannot be attributed solely to Sinhala or Tamil influence, as both these languages have

---

9. The distinction between ACC and DAT is more transparent with local prepositions in German, where DAT denotes Essive and ACC Allative.

conflated the categories of desire and obligation into one morpheme (Sinh: *oonæ*/ Tam: *veṇum*), illustrated below in (8) and (8'):

(8)   *Mama yanḍa oonä*   (Sinhala)
(8') *Naan poha veṇum*   (Tamil)
     1s   go.INF must/want
     'I must go/want to go'[10]

This is not the case in SLM, where obligation is expressed by *masthi* and desire by *mau*.[11] As is clear from Table 2, these two particles show a quasi complementary behavior in their subcategorization patterns. Nearly everywhere where *masthi* has a +, *mau* has a – and vice versa. At least one of these patterns must thus represent a language-internal development. Since we can be sure that the language of the first Malays in Sri Lanka had neither case marking nor infinitive, this subcategorization pattern must have developed within the last 350 years. We can see this as an instantiation of idiosyncratic lexical selection, Dahl's second criterion.

A second instance of lexical idiosyncracy is the subcategorization of highly transitive verbs, of which some select the accusative (9) and some the dative (10):

(9) *Se Farook=yang ara-buunung*
     1s Farook=ACC PROG-kill
     'I kill Farook.'

(10) *Se Farook=nang (*=yang) ara-puukul*
     1s Farook=DAT ACC   PROG-hit
     'I hit Farook.'

3.5 Negation

Yet another example of mature structure can be found in the highly complex system of negation in which the parameters of tense, mood and verbal, nominal or adjectival predication type play a role in the choice of negative morphemes.

Table 3 illustrates some negative morphemes in SLM, while (11)–(15) provide examples from natural discourse:

---

10. Some grammars suggest that the use of a Dative pronoun in Sinhala (*maṭa*) conveys desire while the Nominative conveys obligation, but this has not been confirmed by Sinhala/Tamil informants. Obligation is marked by a focus clitic on the verb instead.

11. It should be noted that some younger speakers permit the use of *masthi* for desire. However, *mau* is never possible for obligation.

Table 3. Negative morphemes

	Verbal	Nominal	ADJ
Past	*thera*-V	N *bukang*	ADJ *thraa*
Perfect	V *thraa*	N *bukang*	ADJ *thraa*
Present	*thama*-V	N *bukang*	ADJ *thraa*/*thera*-ADJ
Future	*thama*-V	N *thama jaadi*	*thama*-ADJ

(11) *Puaasa muusing thəra-duuduk=si*
    Fasting season NEG-stay=INTERR
    'You were not here in the fasting period, were you?'

(12) *Invitations daapath thraa*
    invitation get NEG
    'They had not received the invitations.'

(13) *Mulbar thama-oomong*
    Tamil NEG.NONPAST-speak
    'They do not speak Tamil.'

(14) *Sindbad the Sailor hatthu muslim, mlaayu bukang*
    Sinbad the sailor one Moor Malay NEG.NONV
    'Sindbad the Sailor was a Moor, he was not a Malay.'

(15) *Kluumbu bissar thraa*
    Colombo big NEG
    'Colombo was not big.'

Sinhala and Sri Lankan Tamil have two different negation strategies for verbal and non-verbal predication (Gair and Lust 1998).[12] If we disregard *bukang* and the nominal predication as also found in other Malayic varieties, and therefore not of more recent development, we still have to explain why SLM makes use of three different negative morphemes for verbal predications, where Sinhala uses only one, *nää*, and Tamil two, *ille* and *maṭṭeen*. Additionally, there is the suppletive form *mau/thussa*[13] 'want/don't want' and *jon=*, which marks negation in nonfinite clauses (participle, infinitival and imperative (Slomanson 2006); this adds up to six different negative morphemes. It is clear that this differentiation is a sign of maturation that typically involves a certain amount of redundancy. As for the previous cases of morphological elaboration, these negation patterns would have evolved within the last 350 years.

---

12. The Tamil variety Gair discusses is spoken by Hindus in Sri Lanka. Some pilot research (2007) into Muslim Tamil varieties points to the conflation in Muslim Tamil of the two markers Gair found in the Hindu varieties. Standard Indian Colloquial Tamil shows this conflation as well.

13. Note that *thussa* is also likely of Malay origin [to'sa] = 'don't need/ have to'.

3.6 Subordination markers

A final example of maturity, captured in Dahl's fifth criterion, is specific marking of subordinate clauses. This clearly exists in SLM in the form *katha* given in (16):

(16) *Se=pp   orang thuuwa pada ana-biilang [kitham=pada*
     1S=POSS man   old   PL   PAST-say   1PL=PL
     Malaysia-dring   ana-dhaathang katha]
     Malaysia-ABL   PAST-come   QUOT
     'My elders told me that we had come from Malaysia.'

We can see that the clause final *katha* marks the non-matrix sentence. We now move on to consider what this all means for our understanding of structural complexity in language creation.

4. Discussion

With regard to data such as those presented in Section 3, McWhorter comments that "Creoles with a moderate degree of inflection ... have long existed in intimate contact with inflected superstratal or adstratal languages" (2005: 317). As we mentioned in Section 2, we fully agree on this point. Following up on it, we put forward a related claim as its logical extension:

> Creoles with clearly isolating morphology have long existed in intimate contact with isolating superstratal or adstratal languages.

The implication of our claim is that the 'typical' structural features of a number of creoles are first and foremost a result of the input languages in the contact situaton.[14] This claim is highly plausible in the light of gradualist models of genesis which, at this point in time, appear to be well grounded in historical and typological investigation (Arends 1989, 2001b; Chaudenson 2001; Ansaldo 2008), as opposed to abruptist models which, by now, has been seriously called into question (as shown in Roberts 1999, 2000; Ansaldo 2009).

In what follows, we would like to go beyond Dahl's scepticism regarding whether it is possible to talk about youth of language, and propose that it is questionable whether one can talk about age of language – in relation to structural properties – at all. In order to do so, we need to start with the crucial distinction between change

---

14. As pointed by Anthony Grant (p.c. September 2007), there are still contact phenomena that appear to fall out of this generalization and therefore require alternative explanations. For example, Chinook Jargon owes most of its basic vocabulary to Chinook, which is highly inflected, but none of Chinook's inflections are used productively in Chinook Jargon.

in I-language, i.e mental grammars, and change in E-languages, i.e. socio-historical entities (Lightfoot 1999; DeGraff 2001). Such a distinction is crucial in order to understand rate of change in new language creation.[15]

4.1 Rate of change

Weinreich, Labov and Herzog (1968) already distinguish between the individual and the community as clearly different levels of linguistic analysis. Elaborating on this, in a biological view of language change, one can distinguish between grammar as a generative, 'mental' concept, and language as a population of idiolects and/ or utterances (Paul 1880; Keller 1990/1994; Lass 1997; Lightfoot 1999; Croft 2000). Based on this distinction, one can identify two different levels of analysis: (a) the psychological,[16] and (b) the social. As already pointed out in Lass (1997: 370), in discussing rate of change, it is imperative to clearly identify which domain is being analyzed. Though there may be a relation between what goes on in the minds of speakers and the verbal interaction in which they engage, it is difficult to imagine that the principles that underlie I-language would be identical to those underlying E-languages. The former, however defined, would pertain to the realm of the psychological, or the cognitive (biological grammars in Lightfoot 1999: 101); while the latter would be defined by social and historical contingencies.

Ansaldo (2009), following a suggestion in Lightfoot (1999), argues that change in I-language may be viewed as either abrupt or gradual, depending on the generative framework that is being upheld.[17] When we turn to changes that affect a language as a social construct on the other hand, we are really talking about *propagation* of variables (Croft 2000). Propagation is by definition a gradual phenomenon; whether it occurs more or less rapidly depends simply on (a) the size of a community, (b) the type of social network and (c) the presence or absence of normative constraints on the natural creativity of speakers (such as cultural scripts, educational institutions etc.; see also Milroy and Milroy 1985; Trudgill 2001; Ansaldo 2009). In other words, a given change can register and stabilize in a small group of close-knit individuals who do not share or uphold specific normative contraints within one generation. On the other hand, for a change to spread and be registered in a large, diffuse population, several generations will be necessary.

---

15. Whether E- and I-language can actually be taken as viable conceptual notions or not is not at stake here; the distinction is introduced in order to clarify the potential (if at all) locus of rate of change and its nature.

16. Or cognitive level (we do not commit to a definition of this as we are not aware of any concrete/accepted one).

17. For example, Lightfoot (1999) argues for abrupt change as a matter of parameter-resetting, while Newmeyer (1988) suggests an adaptationist view that implies gradual evolution of grammar.

Rate of change is crucially linked with age of language, as time is regarded as a prerequisite of complexity from an evolutionary point of view (DeGraff 2001). Note that whether it really makes sense to talk of 'a language' in discussing E-languages has been repeatedly questioned (e.g. Lightfoot 1999; DeGraff 2001), and there is good reason for this. What we are really referring to when we talk about the age of, say, English, is extremely arbitrary as it rests on a number of historical and cultural assumptions that are neither objective nor linguistically indisputable.[18] Be that as it may, let us assume that we somehow know when a language is a language, and that we want to determine whether it is young or old. So let us compare a typically 'old' language with the 'young' SLM we have discussed above.

4.2 Old and young

Chinese is considered a very old language, having existed for at least two and a half millennia – what does this mean? It means that we have documents available written in a logographic script that is the precursor of Chinese characters; these texts have been historically ascribed to the beginning of Chinese civilization. Note that there is plenty of structural change between what has been reconstructed as Ancient Chinese and modern varieties. These changes affect phonology, morphology and syntax, to the point that, as is the case for all the languages for which we have good historical documentation, questions of external contact and doubts about genetic classification have been raised (e.g. Sagart 1994; Ansaldo 1999, for Sinitic).[19] The cultural continuity of Chinese is likewise questionable: the earliest texts available, partly attributed to the Daoist school of thought, portray an anarchic social structure with a prominent role of divination and naturalist philosphies, while later, Confucian and Mohist texts, decribe well-organized feudal states, the rule of law and centralized authority. In short, the idea of Chinese being an old language is a historical and cultural construct; we would have the same idea about Mongolian if the Mongol dynasties that ruled China for over a millennium had stayed in power to this date, and if they had displayed a more colonial linguistic policy. The age of Chinese does not exist objectively or in abstraction. What exists is the time span between the present and the earliest records available.

Sri Lanka Malay can be considered young because no SLM diaspora existed until four hundred years ago, when people of Malay/Indonesian origin were brought to Sri

---

18. A typical example of this may be seen in the controversy regarding New English varieties, where some are considered as legitimate modern English varieties, e.g. Australian and New Zealand English, while others are still regarded as 'external' to the family, e.g. Indian English. This is clearly not a matter of linguistic similarities between each new variety and, say, RP, but rather an expression of cultural and racial differences.

19. Similar issues regarding the evolution of English and possible 'creolization' are discussed in Thomason and Kaufman (1988).

Lanka. To be careful, we suggest an age of roughly 300 years for the language. What we claim, based on socio-historical analysis, is that the alleged complexity of SLM would have taken 300 years to evolve. Claiming that it might have taken even less would only strengthen the claim that 'complexity' is not a sign of old age; in the case of SLM, however, we do not see any reasons to invoke rapidity. What does this mean? It means that SLM has been spoken in various forms, probably involving more Malayic elements first, and progressively substituting these with Lankan features, for roughly that period of time. It is the SLM diaspora (also some kind of socio-historical construct) that can be said to be roughly 350 years old. Therefore the variety that emerged as a result of the socio-cultural focussing (Le Page and Tabouret-Keller 1985) that characterizes the SLM diaspora may have roughly the same age. Does this make it a young grammar? If we view grammar as I-language, it doesn't really matter, as each grammar is created anew in the speaker, and we can therefore not compare different mental grammars in terms of age (unless we compare child to adult grammar, see Lightfoot 1999). The very notion of UG denies the possibility that it would take speakers of different languages more or less time to acquire their own variety, especially in the light of present-day relativistic stances regarding the notion of markedness (Rizzi 2001; Haspelmath 2006). If we view grammar as a social and historical construct, SLM may be young, but, as we show, this says nothing about the *grammatical properties* of such language, since similar properties exist in languages that we are perfectly comfortable in calling 'old', e.g. Malay, Dravidian and Indo-Aryan languages.

If we are tempted to still think that it seems like it all happened a bit too fast, we need to remember that propagation of new variants in a relatively small, dense and non-normative ecology does proceed more smoothly than in the written histories of national languages (Nettle 1999; Croft 2000). As noted in Ansaldo (2009), in the study of language histories, abruptness may also be a reflection of the lack of gradual evidence, i.e., as Darwin suggested, a measure of our ignorance. In other words, 'E-change' must always be more or less gradual,[20] as processes of grammaticalization and/or reanalysis proceed in steps, and as each new feature needs to pass from user to user until all or most have accepted it; this will be quick if few and close speakers are involved (say a family), slow if we track the propagation of an innovative feature across generations and countries (say a language family).[21] Age, we suggest, should always be related to the external history of a language, and never attributed to grammatical features of the language, since age of 'grammar' is but an epiphenomenon of the length of documented histories (in the sense of E-language), or identical for all languages (in the sense of I-language).

---

20. The more or less may depend on the relative markedness of a specific variable within the community.

21. See also Arends (2001b).

5. Final remarks

5.1 On type of grammar and typology

Let us recall Dahl's (2004) definition of 'mature' phenomena given in Section 2, which may be loosely interpreted as the accumulation of (redundant?) material (lexical and or morphosyntactic) in a grammar G' that was not present in the grammar of G. This accumulation can – in a way in which age and structure are relatable – be explained in various ways, including the increase of accuracy of a certain utterance, the weight that the utterance may signal to the hearer, etc. (see Dahl 2004: 5–17). It may also be historical accident, e.g. the layering of variables coming from regional varieties, social contingencies that lead to stable ditaxia etc. (Ansaldo 1999). Surely this type of maturation is possible in an environment where grammars of similar typological make-up have been, because of the socio-political histories of their speakers, connected to one another horizontally as well as vertically. This is however not necessarily so: for example, the history of Chinese does not show many of the signs of maturation discussed in Dahl (2004). Why would this be the case? The list of mature features presented above is repeated here for convenience:

1. Complex word structure (inflectional/ derivation morphology, incorporation)
2. Lexical idiosyncrasy (gender, INFL classes, case)
3. Syntactic phenomena depending on inflectional morphology (agreement, case)
4. Word order rules over and above internal ordering of sister constituents
5. Specific marking of subordinate clauses
6. Morpheme and word level features in phonology

As we would expect, features (1)–(3) are largely absent in Chinese, as the language is strictly isolating and, rather than morphology developing over time, there is significant evidence that there is morphological loss in the (pre)history of Sinitic (Sagart 1999). There is however an attested history of development of stricter word-order rules as well as development of word level features in phonology. What this shows is that, though it may be possible that certain features of a grammar are signs of accumulation of historical layers, whatever accumulates depends on the basic typology from which we depart; in other words, the types of features that accumulate are, at least in part, language-type-specific. Let us see what this means for languages with a younger history.

5.2 On age and creoles

We have seen that SLM shows considerable 'complexity', intended as accumulation of mature features according to Dahl (2004), in several domains of its grammar. It seems unwarranted to call SLM a simple language, independent of any definition of simplicity, even allowing for the possibility of such a definition to be valid objectively. While certainly being far from the morphological intricacies of Georgian or Tuscarora, we must not shy away from a comparison with some older languages like other Malayic varieties (or English for that matter) as far as complexity is concerned.

We know that the language the first Malay immigrants to Sri Lanka used for in-group communication did not show the features that are discussed in this paper. Of course, early SLM migrants had command of their own native language, which might have been complex or not, but one of the codes that was available to the early migrants as a means of inter-ethnic communication, and would feed into SLM, was a reduced one, Trade Malay. Trade Malay had the main characteristics of a pidgin, i.e. a reduced function, namely communication for commercial purposes, and morphological and stylistic poverty. In today's SLM, we find lexical traces from a number of places in the Indonesian archipelago (Adelaar 1991; Paauw 2004), but grammatical traces are very rare. There is no classifier system, no reduplication, and a complete absence of diathesis as a grammatical category. If we count from the time when the Dutch conquered Ceylon in 1656, when we know for certain that the SLM ancestors started arriving in Sri Lanka, this gives us the time span of 350 years for today's morphology to emerge.

Let us now investigate the sample[22] used by McWhorter in developing the notion of Creole Prototype (McWhorter 1998); note that, crucially, the sample consists mainly of languages *older* than 300 years (with the exception of Tok Pisin). Out of 8 languages investigated, all have a Indo-European lexifier (4 Germanic, 4 Romance), 7 have a West-African substrate, only Tok Pisin has no West African substrate, and Mauritian has Bantu and Malagasy influence besides West African. The nature of this sample is of course due to the fact that little is known about 'young' languages in other parts of the world, but this justification does not add to the validity of the sample. If we took Chinese, Lao and Thai to show that languages older than 1,000 years do not have inflection, this would obviously be seen as an opportunistic sample. The sample would have been chosen in order to satisfy the hypothesis, and furthermore it would have a strong areal and genetic bias. If a serious claim about the correlation between age and simplicity has to be undertaken, then a sample has to be employed that is genetically and areally more stratified than this one (see Dryer 1989, 2000, 2003).

From a typological perspective, McWhorter's sampling method is clearly biased: West African languages are not known for their rich inflectional morphology, neither are English or Dutch.[23] A language that develops in contact with those languages should not be expected to have rich morphology. The claim that the languages he investigated are simple according to his criteria is likely to be an artefact of the sample to begin with. As we have shown in this paper, and as is predicted in Section 4, had the sample included young languages in a morphologically rich environment, like South

---

22. Ndjuka, Tok Pisin, Saramaccan, Haitian, St. Lucian, Mauritian, Fa D'Ambu and Negerhollands.

23. The Romance languages have somewhat more morphology in their written form, although this is not necessarily so in the varieties spoken by the colonizers (Chaudenson 2001).

Asia, we might have never related 'simplicity' to young languages. And indeed, the one language that developed in an ecology rich in morphology, namely Tok Pisin, shows more morphology at the age of only roughly 100 years than the other languages after 300 years. Ecology has a far greater influence than the time elapsed since the birth of the language (Mufwene 2001) for the structural input-output relation.

What this study has shown is that an objective notion of simplicity has not been put forward so far. Conversely, it is questionable whether we have an appropriate definition of complexity. What we do see is that typology matters; in an evolutionary framework for language change (Croft 2000; Mufwene 2001), the notion of Feature Pool supports the idea that in contact environments speakers derive their new grammars by a process of competition and selection of existing features. Therefore, in a morphologically rich environment, morphology will emerge. In a typologically isolating environment, this would obviously not be the case.[24] Just as simple does not imply 'creolization' (Ansaldo and Matthews 2001; Sampson 2006), 'complex' does not seem to imply old age. We have also supported claims against abrupt language creation, showing how both generative and sociohistorical frameworks of language change converge in disallowing the possibility of essentially differential speed in the development of grammar; speed correlates with size and type of community, but not with abstract structural processes.

References

Aboh, Enoch O. & Ansaldo, Umberto. 2007. The role of typology in language creation: A descriptive take. In *Deconstructing Creole* [Typological Studies in Language 73], Umberto Ansaldo, Stephen Matthews & Lisa Lim (eds), 39–66. Amsterdam: John Benjamins.

Adelaar, Karl Alexander. 1991. Some notes on the origin of Sri Lankan Malay. In *Papers in Austronesian linguistics No. 1* [Pacific Linguistics A-81], Hein Steinhauer (ed.), 23–37. Canberra: The Australian National University.

Ansaldo, Umberto. 1999. Comparative Constructions in Sinitic: Areal Typology and Patterns of Grammaticalization. PhD dissertation, Stockholm University. (Stockholm: Allduplo Tryckeri AB).

Ansaldo, Umberto. 2007. Review of John McWhorter 2005, Defining Creole. *Journal of Pidgin and Creole Languages* 22(1): 170–176.

Ansaldo, Umberto. 2008. Sri Lanka Malay revisited: Genesis and classification. In *Lessons from Documented Endangered Languages: A World of Many Voices* [Typological Studies in Language 78], K. David Harrison, David S. Rood & Adrienne Dwyer (eds), 13–42. Amsterdam: John Benjamins.

---

24. This does not necessarily imply that specific simplification processes do not occur in certain contact situations: Siegel (2000) for example provides a good overview of processes involving also reduction of morphological inflection commonly observed in a number of pidgins. However, even in pidgin formation simplification is locally conditioned, i.e. it is a matter of typological input, as shown in Foley (2006) for the case of New Guinean pidgins.

Ansaldo, Umberto. 2009. *Contact Languages. Ecology and Evolution in Asia.* Cambridge: CUP.
Ansaldo, Umberto & Matthews, Stephen. 2001. Typical creoles and simple languages. The case of Sinitic. *Linguistic Typology* 5(2/3): 311–326.
Ansaldo, Umberto, Matthews, Stephen & Lim, Lisa (eds). 2007. *Deconstructing Creole* [Typological Studies in Language 73]. Amsterdam: John Benjamins.
Arends, Jacques. 1989. Syntactic Developments in Sranan. PhD dissertation, University of Nijmegen.
Arends, Jacques. 2001a. Simple grammars, complex languages. *Linguistic Typology* 5(2/3): 180–181.
Arends, Jacques. 2001b. Social stratification and network relations in the formation of Sranan. In *Creolization and Contact*, Norval Smith & Tonjes Veenstra (eds), 291–308. Amsterdam: John Benjamins.
Chaudenson, Robert. 2001. *Creolization of Language and Culture.* London: Routledge.
Corbett, Greville. 2003. *Agreement.* Cambridge: CUP.
Croft, William. 2000. *Explaining Language Change: An Evolutionary Approach.* London: Longman.
DeGraff, Michel. 1999. *Language Creation and Language Change: Creolization, Diachrony and Development.* Cambridge MA: The MIT Press.
DeGraff, Michel. 2001. On the origin of creoles. *Linguistic Typology* 5(2/3): 213–210.
Dahl, Östen. 2004. *The Growth and Maintenance of Linguistic Complexity.* Amsterdam: John Benjamins.
Dryer, Matthew S. 1989. Large linguistic areas and language sampling. *Studies in Language* 13: 257–292.
Dryer, Matthew S. 2000. Counting genera vs. counting languages: A reply to Maslova. *Linguistic Typology* 4: 334–350.
Dryer, Matthew S. 2003. Significant and non-significant implicational universals. *Linguistic Typology* 7: 108–128.
Farquharson, Joseph. 2007. Creole morphology revisited. In *Deconstructing Creole* [Typological Studies in Language 73], Umberto Ansaldo, Stephen Matthews & Lisa Lim (eds), 21.38. Amsterdam: John Benjamins.
Foley, William. 2006. Universal constraints and local conditions in pidginization. Case studies from New Guinea. *Journal of Pidgin and Creole Languages* 21(1): 1–44.
Gair, James & Lust, Barbara C. (eds). 1998. *Studies in South Asian Linguistics: Sinhala and Other South Asian Languages.* Oxford: OUP.
Gil, David. 2001. Creoles, complexity and Riau Indonesian. *Linguistic Typology* 5(2/3): 325–370.
Grant, Anthony. 2007. Admixture, structural transmission, superficial and substantive creolization. In *Deconstructing Creole* [Typological Studies in Language 73], Umberto Ansaldo, Stephen Matthews & Lisa Lim (eds), 109–139. Amsterdam: John Benjamins.
Haspelmath, Martin. 2006. Against markedness (and what to replace it with). *Journal of Linguistics* 42(1): 25–70.
Keller, Rudi. 1990/1994. *On Language Change: The Invisible Hand in Language.* London: Routledge. (Translation and expansion of *Sprachwandel: Von der unsichtbaren Hand in der Sprache.* Tübingen: Francke).
Lightfoot, David. 1999. *The Development of Language: Acquisition, Change and Evolution.* Oxford: Basil Blackwell.

Le Page, Robert & Tabouret-Keller, Andrée. 1985. *Acts of Identity: Creole-based Approaches to Language and Ethnicity*. Cambridge: CUP.
McWhorter, John. 1998. Identifying the creole prototype: Vindicating a typological class. *Language* 74: 788–818.
McWhorter, John. 2001. The world's simplest grammars are creole grammars. *Linguistic Typology* 5(2/3): 125–166.
McWhorter, John. 2005. *Defining Creole*. Oxford: OUP.
Miestamo, Matti. 2005. *Standard Negation: The Negation of Declarative Verbal Main Clauses in a Typological Perspective*. Berlin: Mouton de Gruyter.
Milroy, James & Milroy, Leslie. 1985. Linguistic change, social network and speaker innovation. *Journal of Linguistics* 21: 339–384.
Mufwene, Salikoko S. 2001. *The Ecology of Language Evolution*. Cambridge: CUP.
Muysken, Pieter. 1988. Are creoles a special type of language? In *Linguistics. The Cambridge Survey*, Vol. 2: *Linguistic Theory: Extensions and Implications*, Frederick Newmeyer(ed.), 285–301. Cambridge: CUP.
Nettle, Daniel. 1999. *Linguistic Diversity*. Oxford: OUP.
Newmeyer, Fredrick. 1988. On the supposed 'counterfactuality' of Universal Grammar. Some evolutionary implications. In *Approaches to the Evolution of Language*, James R. Hurford, Michael Studdert-Kennedy & Chris Knight (eds), 305–319. Cambridge: CUP.
Paauw, Scott 2004. A Historical Analysis of the Lexical Sources of Sri Lanka Malay. MA thesis, York University.
Rizzi, Luigi. 2001. Broadening the empirical basis of universal grammar models: A commentary. In *Language Creation and Language Change: Creolization, Diachrony and Development*, Michel DeGraff (ed.), 453–472. Cambridge MA: The MIT Press.
Roberts, Sarah J. 1999. The TMA system of Hawaiian Creole and diffusion. In *Creole Genesis, Attitudes and Discourse: Studies Celebrating Charlene J. Sato* [Creole Language Library 20], John Rickford & Suzanne Romaine (eds), 45–70. Amsterdam: John Benjamins.
Roberts, Sarah J. 2000. Nativization and genesis of Hawaiian Creole. In *Language Change and Language Contact in Pidgins and Creoles* [Creole Language Libarary 20], John McWhorter (ed.), 257–300. Amsterdam: John Benjamins.
Sagart, Laurant. 1994. Old Chinese and Proto-Austronesian evidence for Sino-Austronesian. *Oceanic Linguistics* 33(2): 271–308.
Sagart, Laurant. 1999. *The Roots of Old Chinese* [Current Issues in Linguistic Theory 184]. Amsterdam: John Benjamins.
Sampson, Geoffrey. 2006. Does simply imply creole? In *A Man of Measure: Festschrift in Honor of Fred Karlsson on his 60th Birthday*, Mickael Suominen (ed.), 362–374. Turku: Linguistic Association of Finland.
Siegel, Jeff. 2000. Introduction: The processes of language contact. In *Processes in Language Contact: Studies from Australia and the South Pacific*, Jeff Siegel (ed.), 1–11. Sant-Laure Quebec: Fides.
Slomanson, Peter. 2006. Sri Lankan Malay morphosyntax: Lankan or Malay? In *Structure and Variation in Language Contact* [Creole Language Library 29], Ana Deumert & Stephanie Durrleman (eds), 135–158. Amsterdam: John Benjamins.
Smith, Ian & Paauw, Scott. 2006. Sri Lanka Malay : Creole or convert? In *Structure and Variation in Language Contact* [Creole Language Library 29], Ana Deumert & Stephanie Durrleman (eds), 159–183. Amsterdam: John Benjamins.

Trudgill, Peter. 2001. Linguistic and social typology. In *Handbook of Linguistic Variation and Change*, Jack Chambers, Peter Trudgill & Natalie Schilling-Estes (eds), 707–728. Oxford: Blackwell.

Thomason, Sarah & Kaufman, Terence. 1988. *Language Contact, Creolization and Genetic Linguistics*. Berkeley CA: University of California Press.

Weinreich, Uriel, Labov, William & Herzog, Marvin. 1968. *Empirical Foundations for a Theory of Language Change. Directions for Historical Linguistics*, Winifred Lehmann Yakov Malkiel, 95–195. Austi, TX: University of Texas Press.

PART VI

Postscript

Restructuring, hybridization, and complexity in language evolution*

Salikoko S. Mufwene

1. Preliminaries

1.1 What this essay covers

My primary aim in this chapter is to be provocative, hoping to arouse further discussion of concepts and positions that deserve more attention than they have received either in the present volume or in much of the literature on the emergence and the general architecture of creoles. Much of this has to do with whether or not creoles have simpler grammatical systems than the languages they have emerged from. This may be termed, for convenience sake, as the "complexity" question, to which we have been redirected forcefully by DeGraff (2001a, 2001b) and Dahl (2004), in response to McWhorter (2001a), and, more recently, by McWhorter (2008), among other references. It is difficult to address the question without also bringing up that of "creole exceptionalism" (DeGraff 2003, 2005; see also Mufwene 2001, 2008). The latter is also connected to another question arising from McWhorter (1998), viz. whether creoles' structural properties (questionably identified by some as "creole features") distinguish them typologically from other languages whose origins are putatively not contact-based.

In order to address these questions, one must first answer the following others: (1) How do features mix during the recombinations that yield new language varieties out of the languages in contact? (2) If naturalistic language "acquisition" is individual-based and every learner aims at communicating (successfully) with the extant speakers of the target language, how do new communal norms emerge? The first may be termed the "hybridization" question (thanks to Aboh 2006, this volume) and the second the "normalization" question, having to do with the emergence of communal

---

* I am very grateful to the editors for inviting me to write this postscript and challenging me to reflect globally on the central themes of this book. I am also deeply indebted to Michel DeGraff and Enoch Aboh for precious feedback on, respectively, the original and last drafts of this essay. I assume alone full responsibility for the remaining shortcomings.

norms (Mufwene 2008).¹ It is in the latter context that one would like to consider the role of the "invisible hand" (Keller 1994; Mufwene 2001, 2008; cf. also Ansaldo, this volume; Kouwenberg, this volume). As presented here, these questions indirectly explain the title of this essay. The first position assigned to *restructuring* in the subtitle indicates what my discussion will start with.

1.2 Conceptual clarifications

This book includes quite legitimately essays on three Asian contact-based varieties, Solomon Islands Pijin (SIP), Sri Lanka Malay (SLM), and Mindanao Chabacano, which I personally would not call "creoles," especially not the former two, because they are not true to the colonial history in which the term *creole* was used in reference to either people or language varieties in layman's language (Mufwene 1997a). I restrict my usage of the term *creole* typically to vernaculars that evolved out of language shift by non-European majority populations enslaved in exogenous European plantation settlement colonies (as defined by Chaudenson 1979ff.) in favor of the relevant colonial European language, albeit an emergent koiné in itself.²

I will reluctantly include in this category a few other varieties that have also been recognized as "creoles" by linguists but whose origins may be considered atypical based on the above stipulation. They are spoken in endogenous settlement colonies such as Macao and Korlai (India), where the Portuguese traders mixed with the local populations, and where the latter not only Christianized but also shifted to the European language as their vernacular and concurrently evolved into a kind of mixed ethnic group both genetically and culturally. Being distinct from the traditional indigenous population, the new groups have been likened to Creole populations of the New World and the Indian Ocean, and their indigenized varieties of the European vernacular (see below) have also been identified as "creoles." This practice by linguists to liberally name all such new nonstandard vernaculars associated with settlement colonization "creoles" muddles the epistemic usefulness of CREOLE as a historic concept (in reference to populations, see also Stewart 2007). At best, the practice highlights the significance of the factor of RACE (socially construed) in the identification of such vernaculars (Mufwene 2001, 2008).

Nonetheless, the inclusion in this volume of chapters on SLM, and SIP, and the like shows how much creoles share with other "contact language varieties" both in the restructuring processes and the ecological factors that determined their emergence. On the other hand, as argued in Mufwene (2001, 2005, 2008), one must wonder

---

1. I owe the term *normalization* itself to Chaudenson (1979ff.). In Mufwene (2005, 2008), I just problematize its significance in the divergence process that has produced creoles.

2. Krio, which some creolists may claim to be an endogenous variety, is certainly a transplanted creole whose origins lie in the New World, especially Jamaica, although it has inevitably evolved into a separate language variety in its new, Sierra Leone ecology.

what modern language does not have its origins in the contact of populations and of languages. The account of the dispersal of Homo Sapiens proposed by, e.g., Cavalli-Sforza (2001) suggests that modern human populations have been colonizing each other at least since the advent of agriculture, and quite likely since before then. Thus, regardless of whether a language is characterized as "creole" or otherwise, what we learn about the contact setting of its emergence should help us develop a better understanding of language evolution, including the process of speciation. Indeed, this book contributes substantially to this subject matter, especially regarding how restructuring works. I return to this below, as promised above.

I use the term *evolution* because, along with DeGraff (2003, 2005), I do not subscribe to the position that creoles have developed in any exceptional way. Indeed, as observed above, I have argued that contact of dialects and/or languages, or of any lects for that matter, has been a catalyst in the evolution of all languages in human history, certainly since the dispersal of Homo Sapiens out of Africa (Mufwene 2008, 2009). Because the present book focuses on language varieties whose origins lie in population contacts associated with European colonization since the 15th century, my comments apply to all of them, naturally subject to peculiarities that are specific to local ecologies of contact and/or language practice.

As explained in Mufwene (2001), the notion of LANGUAGE EVOLUTION applies, among other things, as much to structural changes traditionally dealt with in historical linguistics (viz., Unit/Rule X → Unit/Rule Y in Environment Z) as to the speciation of languages into new dialects or languages, for instance, the diversification of Vulgar Latin into the Romance languages. Accordingly, we need not fuss over the political or social ideological issue of whether the language varieties discussed in this book are separate languages, as usually claimed by creolists, or whether they are new, colonial dialects of the languages they have evolved from, as assumed by some of their speakers, at least in places like coastal South Carolina, Louisiana, and Jamaica. Note that in the latter polity, even the official political ideology is ambivalent (Irvine 2004), promoting Jamaican Patwa alternately as a dialect of English (albeit a nonstandard one) and as a separate language.[3]

---

3. The identification of these varieties as separate languages is much easier in polities such as Surinam, where the acrolect is different from the lexifier, or those such as Sierra Leone, where the creole has been transplanted. In places where the creoles coexist with their lexifiers, creolists should beware of the fact that these vernaculars could have been called nonstandard dialects of their "lexifiers." The occasional identification of creoles by their speakers as separate languages reflects linguists' own "miseducation" of the relevant populations, telling them, contrary to their traditional beliefs, that they speak separate languages (Mühlhäusler 1985; Mufwene 1988). As racist as local European settlers were in disowning these varieties as "bastard" or "adulterated" (witness the continuation of the practice among the Bekés of Martinique and White Creoles of Louisiana), at least they did not deny the genetic connection of the language varieties to their "lexifiers." Not even Adam (1883) and Gonzales (1922), among others, in their racially derisive accounts of the emergence of Creole in Guyana and coastal

Since linguists have to date not come up with any sound structural criteria for distinguishing DIALECT from LANGUAGE, at least not evolutionarily, I will completely ignore claims that deny creoles any genetic connection to their lexifiers. As a matter of fact, along with Posner (1985, 1996) and (Trask 1996), I think they are legitimate offspring of their lexifiers on a par with other new colonial varieties that have evolved from the same European languages (Mufwene 2001, 2005, 2008; DeGraff 2009.) Thus, they should also count as Indo-European language varieties (Mufwene 2007). Although this position may be dismissed now as a confused minority's ideology (influenced particularly by Francophone creolists, according to Bickerton 2004; Siegel 2008), what matters, among other things, is how speciation and the restructuring processes that produced these vernaculars as specific byproducts of European colonial history have proceeded.

In connection to this, it is also useful to remember that Hall's (1962) "life-cycle," which is embraced by those who assume that creoles have pidgin ancestors, predicts that (incipient) pidgins, or "restricted pidgins" according to Siegel (2008), rarely survive. After the contact settings that produced them have changed, they either die or evolve into expanded pidgins, such as Tok Pisin and Cameroon Pidgin English, which some claim to have "creolized" (e.g., Holm 1988), simply because their communicative functions have vernacularized and their structures are as complex as those of creoles. To wit, compare, for instance, Féral's (1989) description of the grammar of Cameroon Pidgin English with Bailey's (1966) description of Jamaican Creole's morphosyntax. They are equally complex, in the sense advocated below.

Treated as evolutionary transitions, true pidgins (different from expanded pidgins) may as well be kept out of the picture in discussions that address the question of whether creoles have simpler structures than the languages they have evolved from. This is precisely what I will do here, although for two different reasons: (1) I maintain, as in Mufwene (2005, 2008), that both creoles and pidgins evolved by basilectalization-cum-divergence from closer approximations of their lexifiers (see, for instance, the evidence provided, perhaps unwittingly, by Christine Jourdan in this volume); and (2) the structural simplicity of true pidgins (each relative to its particular lexifier) is a consequence of the settings of sporadic inter-ethnolinguistic contacts in which they emerged and of the reduced communicative functions they had to serve. They may also reflect the extent of structural differences among the languages in contact, although this takes us to the question of whether the emergent variety should not be considered a koiné in this particular case. (See the relevant discussion in Mufwene 1997a.) Regardless of our respective positions on the role of pidgins in the emergence of creoles, we may as well focus on the end points and address the following question: How do creole and non-creole vernaculars (as varieties used for communication in

---

South Carolina went that far. As argued in Mufwene (2001, 2005, 2008) and DeGraff (2003, 2005, 2009), the emergence of creoles and their genetic kinship to their lexifiers is not affected by how linguists account for the restructuring and speciation processes (viz., by invoking the bioprogram, substrate influence, etc.)

day-to-day interactions with the individuals one lives with) compare with each other regarding structural or systemic complexity, as explained below?

2. Restructuring and hybridization

2.1 What does RESTRUCTURED LANGUAGE (VARIETY) mean?

RESTRUCTURING appears to be a notion that creolistics has appropriated uniquely under the bias of an ideology reluctant to consider an alternative interpretation of the emergence of creoles (in the historic sense discussed above), viz., what we continue to learn about the evolution of creoles under the corresponding contact conditions is prompting us to reopen the books about many things we have taken for granted about the putative uniparental evolution of non-creole languages. The latest example of this reluctance may be seen in, e.g., Siegel (2008), which, although enlightening on the debate about the emergence of creoles, continues to refer to these vernaculars as "restructured" varieties. By this, he appears to mean nothing more than 'having fundamentally changed systems compared to their lexifiers'.

Unfortunately, he ignores the relevant discussion of the process in Mufwene (2001). By the criterion of 'fundamental systemic change' (about which I say more in Part 3), modern Romance languages can also be referred to as "restructured" varieties, in relation to Latin, from which they are now very different. Although one may want to invoke the by now classic argument that it took over 1,000 years for these European languages to become mutually unintelligible with their lexifier, it should be pointed out that the same lack-of-mutual-intelligibility argument could have been applied 200 years or so after the Romans had abandoned their western Empire, even before Old Romance varieties had emerged already as distinct from Vulgar Latin. Polomé (1983) observes that even in the third and fourth centuries (before the collapse of the Empire), there were distinguished members of the elite class in the provinces who did not speak good Latin. According to him, Latin was then spoken almost exclusively in the city, and by the local elite and merchants only. We just do not know whether two centuries or so after they had left their western Empire the Romans did not complain about poor, or lack of, mutual intelligibility with the vernacular Latin varieties spoken in the former provinces. (See also, e.g., Adams 2007 for a lot of invaluable information about regional variation during the early Roman Empire.)

On the other hand, as we should know by now, at least those of us who have paid careful attention to the nonstandard lexifiers of creoles, the mutual intelligibility argument depends on which specific creole and which particular lect one discusses and how the comparison is made. Gullah, whose phonology is closer to North American English varieties than its Caribbean creole counterparts, can be understood to some extent by speakers of nonstandard varieties of American Southern English, insofar as 100%, perfect mutual intelligibility cannot be guaranteed even between two native speakers of the same language variety. As pointed out in Mufwene (2001), one must factor in the hearer's familiarity with the speaker's lect.

Familiarity with a particular variety will permit partial understanding even of a foreign language, whereas lack thereof may impede satisfactory understanding of an alleged dialect of one's own language. Many readers will remember the classic example of Cockney English in London about which even people who have never heard it spoken repeat the myth that it is unintelligible to other English speakers. East End London, with which the variety is associated, is not a politically isolated, self-contained socio-economic community. As stigmatized as it is, Cockney has survived because its speakers can communicate with other people in London. Likewise, many Americans complain they do not understand Amish or Appalachian English. In any event, despite these claims, no linguist to my knowledge has characterized Cockney or either of these varieties as a "creole" or as a separate language. Yet Old Amish and Appalachian Englishes are also outcomes of language shift, therefore language contact, under colonial conditions, just like creoles.[4] We should ask ourselves whether we have fully emancipated ourselves from the 19th-century ideology that treated creoles as aberrations or historic anomalies simply because they are spoken primarily by populations that are not (fully) of European descent. No linguist to my knowledge has ever articulated the threshold past which a "contact-based" vernacular becomes a creole (Mufwene 2003).

Efforts to operationalize the notion of CREOLE by invoking linguistic-structural features have failed to a point where even McWhorter (1998, 2008) had to resort to prototype categorization to disputably support the usefulness of his criteria, viz., lack of "contrastive tones" in the grammar or the lexicon, lack of inflections, and lack of "non-compositional derivational" morphology. Putatively, we could thus speak of languages that are more or less creole, while we cannot speak of languages that are more or less Germanic, more or less left-branching, or more or less serializing.

We should obviously consider the more neutral definition of RESTRUCTURING that literally means 'replacement of one structure or system by another', which makes it a truism to characterize a new language variety as a "restructured" one. As explained in Mufwene (2001, 2008), the restructuring that produced the vernaculars socially disenfranchised as "creoles" is the result of accumulations of ever-divergent feature recombinations during "language acquisition" and of practice by populations segregated socially or geographically from those whose languages were being appropriated. The new speakers wound up developing their own separate norms, thanks to what

---

4. Those who may want to argue that these varieties are not associated with plantations, nor with slave or contract laborers, should remember that there are "creole" varieties, such as Papiamentu and Cape Verdean Creole (Mufwene 2008), that are not associated with plantations. This is likewise the case for Guinea Bissau Creole discussed by Marlyse Baptista in this volume. There is also Hawaiian English Creole, which is not associated with slavery, just as there are the "creoles" of Macao and Korlai (noted in section 1.1.), which are not associated with contract laborers.

Chaudenson (1979ff.) has characterized as "autonomization" and "normalization" of the new language variety. I return to the normalization question below.[5]

2.2 Lectal and language contact breeds hybridity

In this particular context, it is useful to consider the notion of "HYBRIDITY" invoked by Aboh (2006, this volume), which should not too hastily be confused with Whinnom's (1971) invocation of "primary," "secondary," and "tertiary hybridization" to explain the cross-generational stages of mixing, spread, and entrenchment of elements from different languages within a population. Related to Mufwene's (2001ff.) notion of FEATURE RECOMBINATION, Aboh's notion of HYBRIDITY sheds light on how osmosis makes it possible for features originating in the lexifier and the substrate languages to mix into a new system. It is also consistent with Meillet's (1921, 1929/1951) and Hagège's (1993) position that "language acquisition" is a reconstruction process. See also DeGraff (2003ff.).[6]

System-(re)construction is a process that applies as much to L1 as to L2 "acquisition." We are somewhat driven to our wits' end when we address the reconstruction process at the level of communal language varieties, on which diachronic linguistics focuses. This is also where genetic creolistics belongs. All this conjures up what has often been derided as the "Cafeteria Principle." One of its major shortcomings as attributed to substratist explanations is that it does not account in a principled way for how contributions from different languages could be integrated into a new linguistic system. Assuming uniparental language genesis as the normal way languages evolve, universalists such as Bickerton (1981, 1984, 1999) saw no alternative but the bioprogram and the agency of children to account for the emergence of creoles. However, as argued in Mufwene (1996a, 2001, 2005, 2008), in support of Hjelmslev (1938), mixedness is real in the genesis and evolution of all modern languages, and the challenge for believers in the "Cafeteria Principle" like myself is to explain the principles that guide selection from the available menus, that is from within the linguistic feature pool of the contact setting. The competition-and-selection alternative (Mufwene 1996a-ff) was proposed to address this issue.

---

5. As is evident from Baptista's, Hagemeijer's, and Kouwenberg's chapters in particular, a certain amount of reanalysis is involved in the feature recombination process. As I argue below, this does not necessarily entail loss of complexity.

6. Mufwene (2008, Section 7.2) actually also speaks of "Hybridism in the normal and natural development of creoles," arguing that this is to be found in the formation of any idiolect, under the polyploidic influence of the learner's/speaker's community of practice. Charitably, I can now note that Adam (1983) may not have been completely off the mark in submitting his "hybridologie linguistique" to account for the divergence of French creoles from their lexifier; it is rather his particular characterization of the process as a peculiarity of "inferior races" that made his exceptionalist hypothesis infamous.

With the "hybridity" idea (I would prefer "hybridization," focusing on the process itself), Aboh (2006, 2007, this volume) leads us, on the model of Lewontin (1970) in evolutionary biology, to address the question of what the "units of selection" are in the first place. Whereas Mufwene (2001ff.) argues that selection applies to linguistic features (units or combinatorial rules), Aboh (2006, this volume) shows that the units of selection can be smaller details often masked by the partial congruence (see especially Corne 1999; Chaudenson 2001; Mufwene 2001) that obtains between different languages. He is quite clear on this when he shows that while the Saramaccan Determiner exhibits semantic properties more akin to those of Gungbe than those of English, its morphosyntactic properties are those of the latter, the lexifier. There is indeed no particular reason why the significance of the syntactic properties should be subordinated to that of the semantic properties, although the literature has exploited the features that support divergence to promote exceptionality at the expense of continuity in the emergence of creoles (Corcoran & Mufwene 1999). The case for hybridization is made more forcefully with the analysis of the Saramaccan verb *nyan*, whose basic alternation between transitive and intransitive uses makes it more like its counterpart in English than in Gungbe. However, it exhibits influence from Gungbe and genetically and/or typologically related languages in the idiom *nyan* X *a bak* 'gossip about X' (lit. 'eat behind X' or 'bite X's back').

Aboh's approach sheds light on what most of the other chapters contribute to this book. For example, Peter Sloamanson shows that the negative construction in Sri Lanka Malay (SLM) is patterned on Southern Dravidian languages, not on the Java Malay that was brought to this polity. However, although this particular morphosyntactic pattern is areal, the constraints on its application are largely determined by Muslim Tamil. The question we should endeavor to answer is why.

Another interesting example comes from Silvia Kouwenberg's chapter, which shows that fewer of the building blocks for the grammar of Berbice Dutch (BD) originate in Eastern Ijo (EI) than had been assumed in earlier work. This is very informative, especially because BD is one of the rare New World creoles to exhibit incontrovertible contributions from a substrate language comparable to those attested in Melanesian expanded pidgins. What she shows is that where EI elements have been selected into BD's grammar, they do not replicate faithfully the patterns of the donor language, owing largely also to the fact that they must have been reanalyzed by those who were not native speakers of EI.[7] Noteworthy here, among a number of things, is the fact that a

---

7. This actually opens up another interesting fold in the chapter, as it appears that, contrary to Kouwenberg's position and in the absence of archival textual evidence from the early 18th century, BD could have evolved gradually by basilectalization, later rather than earlier in the history of the colony, probably without an antecedent pidgin either, and, admittedly, in a non-uniform way from one part of the Berbice colony to another. According to Kouwenberg herself, the first one hundred years of the Dutch colonization consisted of homesteads (specializing in the cultivation of coffee, cotton, and cacao) rather than the large sugarcane plantations that would become its trademark since the late 18th century. Since a lot of the slaves also originated

certain amount of reanalysis definitely took place as the different materials were being integrated into the emergent grammar, also dividing the labor among them.

This explanation is undoubtedly going beyond my own position that what the new morphemes recruited to play particular grammatical functions can do and how they can do it is determined not only by their current meanings but also by their lexical categories. For example, it is more likely for speakers to exapt a preposition, which can be used predicatively, to function as a modal predicate rather than to do the same with a noun.[8] My showpiece in Mufwene (1989a, 1996b, 2008) was the bifurcated evolution of the preposition *for* as a complementizer (in a way not significantly divergent from the *for-to* complementizer in nonstandard English) but also as an OBLIGATION modal in the resultant creoles, unlike in the lexifier. Coincidentally, Aboh (this volume) uses this same example to explain the subtle ways in which, the internal mechanisms of the emergent grammars of Surinamese creoles could have innovated this particular phenomenon, although the significance of Fon-Gbe influence in favoring this evolution (by partial congruence) cannot be completely ruled out.

As the same bifurcated evolution has also been attested in French creoles, with *pu*'s functions as a preposition, an IRREALIS complementizer, and OBLIGATION modal (Corne 1980, 1999), it is an open question whether or not one may also invoke universals of emergent grammars. One must of course also ask why not all languages have developed it.[9] We must definitely ask ourselves the following question: How do

---

in the Nigerian interior (as Chaudenson 1992ff. generally observes against invocations of the West African coast as the origin of slaves), outside the EI-speaking area, the picture about the agents of restructuring is admittedly more complex than the literature has suggested to date. Kouwenberg is apparently justified in concluding that "EI speakers were not the primary agents in the formation of BD, even though their language was the primary source of functional material." Like elsewhere, every speaker had their role to play and that is where the action of the "invisible hand" has to be explored.

8. To my knowledge, most creoles, and many languages, which allow copula-less predicate phrases not headed by a verb still insert a copula when the semantic head of the predicate phrase is a noun. This makes it difficult to recruit a noun that denotes OBLIGATION or POSSIBILITY to grammaticize into modal marker. As becomes evident in the main text, even Haitian Creole, which is exceptional regarding this typological observation (DeGraff 1997), allows *pu* to function modally but not any noun that could convey the OBLIGATION meaning predicatively. More relevant to the discussion of complexity in Section 3, using a noun predicatively without a copula in Haitian Creole is only an alternative to using it with a copula, but the copula-less option appears to be ruled out when the predicate noun is delimited by an ante-posed or post-posed determiner, as in *Nuriel *(se) yon bèl gason/Nuriel *(se) bèl gason an* 'Nuriel is a handsome boy'. In contrast, there are no constraints on using adjectives predicatively, as predicate adjectives are still used without a copula even when they are modified by an intensifier. The grammar of predication in Haitian Creole is thus more complex than it may appear at first glance.

9. To be sure, one must turn here to typology and see whether languages with isolating morphosyntax have a tendency to grammaticize some prepositions in the same way. Especially

the different units and rules influence each other and define each other's functions in the emergent system, independent of the legacy from the lexifier and influence from the substrate languages? I return to this question tangentially in the discussion of complexity below in relation to the option of conceiving of grammars dynamically as emergent patterns.

2.3   The ecology influences the evolutionary trajectory of a language

With den Besten's chapter, one can also better appreciate the significance of the influence of the external ecology on the restructuring process. It does not seem possible to understand adequately the development of demonstratives in Afrikaans without factoring in the fact that Dutch in South Africa came in contact not only with non-European languages but also with French (brought in by the Huguenots), German, and English.[10] The evolution of a tripartite PROXIMAL/MEDIAL/DISTAL demonstrative system in Afrikaans, from a bipartite PROXIMAL/DISTAL distinction in Dutch, is a curious phenomenon. It is compounded by the fact that demonstratives have become bimorphemic (e.g. *hierdie*) in a way similar to *ce* N *ci/là* in French and *this* N *here* and *that* N *there* in some nonstandard English dialects (as in *this boy here* and *that boy there*). Interestingly, Jamaican Creole has such two-word alternatives to conceivably single-word, equally bimorphemic markers, viz. *disya* N 'this' (< *dis* 'this' + *ya* 'here') and *dade/daya* N 'that' (< *da(t)* 'that' + *de* 'there'/*ya* 'here'), as in *dis-ya/da-de bway* 'this/that boy', although such constructions are marked as "archaic" in Cassidy & Le Page's (1981) *Dictionary of Jamaican English*. In any case, the Afrikaans phenomenon illustrates restructuring in the direction of semantic and morphological complexification, compared to Dutch.

---

noteworthy in the case of English and French creoles is the fact that some nonstandard dialects of their lexifiers have/had time reference expressions such as COPULA + *pour* V$_{INF}$ and COPULA + *after* V-*ing* which differ from the creole constructions essentially in that the lexifiers require a copula before a predicative preposition whereas the creoles do not. Otherwise, the semantics of the AUXILIARY use of the preposition shows various degrees of similarity in all the relevant languages. This is akin to standard English use of COPULA + *going to* V$_{INF}$ for FUTURE where Jamaican Creole and Gullah use *gwain* + V without a copula. Obviously, as pointed out by Chaudenson (1992ff), the legacy of the lexifier is far from being negligible in the evolution of these constructions in creoles.

10. It is unclear to me whether Portuguese must be completely ruled out of the picture. The Cape of Good Hope was originally a Portuguese colony and the Portuguese traded for especially ivory and slaves on the southeastern coast of Africa. Did the Portuguese stop trading in the Cape areas after the Dutch claimed it as their colony? After all, the traditional claim that the English and their slaves all left Surinam after it had become a Dutch colony has proved to be disputable if not false. Political events have not always been coextensive with economic acts in colonial history.

As will become obvious in Section 3, evolution by morphosyntactic complexification is neither unique to Afrikaans nor rare in creoles in general. This is precisely also part of what emerges from Peter Slomanson's chapter, in which the morphosyntax of SLM in the domain of time reference in negative constructions appears to be more complex than in Java Malay, owing to the influence of the Dravidian languages that the latter lexifier came in contact with. Some years ago, Kapanga (1991) argued that Shaba Swahili, the "contact variety," has a richer tense-aspect system than ethnic Swahili, spoken in coastal Tanzania, does. The reason he gives for this is the influence of the central Bantu languages that Swahili came in contact with; they make more morphological distinctions in the domain of TENSE-ASPECT. It is also common knowledge that Melanesian English pidgins (the expanded varieties) have complexified their pronominal systems relative to their lexifier both in morphosyntax and semantics. This provides food for thought regarding the claim that pidgins and creoles evolve uniformly in the direction of simplification, an issue to which I return especially in Section 3.5.

2.4 Hybridization and feature recombination

Overall, hybridization and feature recombination boil down to the same thing. Given the fact that human languages share a lot of features already (which is why we can speak of Language, in the singular, as applicable indiscriminately to mankind), the following questions are relevant: How much of what distinguishes a new language variety from its LEXIFIER (a concept to which I return in a moment) comes from the lexifier itself as it was spoken in the contact setting? How much comes from elsewhere, including the substrate languages and exaptive innovations from the emergent variety itself?

Discussing the regularization of the transitive marker in Solomon Islands Pijin (SIP), Christine Jourdan refers to the latter as "system-internal innovation[s]." Traditionally principles related to markedness, or ranking in Optimality Theory (Fill 2004), have been invoked to account for such developments. Our explanations remain nonetheless incomplete and I hope that research in this direction will make some progress. What seems obvious from the chapters in this book is that simplistic and exclusive accounts assuming only the bioprogram, relexification of some substrate language(s), or universals of second language acquisition will not do. Regardless of whether or not the approach is called the complementary hypothesis (see Mufwene 2001, Section 2.2.1), what the studies in this volume show is the need for more eclectic accounts.

What the studies also show is that it is a mistake to assume that the languages identified for convenience sake as *lexifiers* have bequeathed only their vocabularies to the new vernaculars with their morphosyntactic principles originating elsewhere (Thomason & Kaufman 1988; Thomason 2001). (See especially Chaudenson 2003 for an apt discussion of the topic.) Enoch Aboh in particular shows that even in the case of creoles that would be the prime candidates for relexification or for prevalent substrate influence (viz., Sranan, Saramaccan, and Haitian Creole) grammatical continuities from the lexifier are not only undeniable but very significant.[11] They corroborate DeGraff's (2001a, 2001b, 2009) conclusion that French itself played a central role in determining Haitian Creole's grammar. What we should also remember is an observation made earlier by Whinnom (1971), viz., that no modern language has preserved intact the legacy of its earlier stages and is immune from the effects of contact with other languages.

One can actually develop similar arguments based on Christine Jourdan's and Peter Slomanson's chapters, both of which show that the structural features selected from the substrate languages into the emergent varieties are adapted by regularization to the new systems. Boretzky (1993) had already argued in this direction, remarking that substrate influence in creoles need not be expected to replicate faithfully the patterns of the donor languages.

2.5 Both creoles and pidgins have evolved by gradual basilectalization

It is also informative to note in Christine Jourdan's chapter that earlier SIP appears to have been structurally closer to English than today's SIP is, which suggests that even pidgins have evolved by basilectalization, diverging further and further away from their lexifiers as they were increasingly being learned and practiced as L2 varieties by wider and wider proportions of the indigenous populations speaking them also among themselves (Mufwene 2005, 2008). The systemic "complexification" (see below) that Jourdan discusses need not be associated with nativization; it more generally reflects the vernacularization of SIP, responding to the greater communicative needs of its speakers.

AGE and IDEOLOGY appear to be secondary and incidental factors in the ecology of the evolution of SIP, compared to the factor that appears to be more significant in this case: the deterministic role of the substrate languages which are related typologically and to some extent genetically (Keesing 1988). As noted in Mufwene (2001), little is invented *ex nihilo* in the structural systems of creoles and pidgins. They reflect recycling-cum-exaptation of materials (including structural patterns) from languages previously spoken by some of the speakers, underscoring the significance of Aboh's (2006, this volume) implicit invitation that we endeavor to (better) understand how the selection and recombination of features into an emergent system proceed.

2.6 "Creolization" and "pidginization" as indigenization

Even if we argue that creoles represent extreme cases of restructuring and hybridization, the fact remains that they are new varieties of European languages appropriated

---

11. This should not be surprising. After all, the lexifier was the target language in the contact setting, as heterogeneous as it undoubtedly was, *pace* Baker (1990, 1997).

by non-European populations at times when the European colonists were typically demographic minorities segregated socially from the populations of new speakers. These are the conditions which favored the process that Chaudenson (1979ff.) identifies as "autonomization," i.e., independence and divergence from the metropolitan norm. The literature on the emergence of non-creole English varieties typically spoken in former exploitation colonies has used the term *indigenization* for the same process, a term that incidentally has resonance with one of the ways that Hall (1966) characterizes nativization as a factor that distinguishes creoles from their putative pidgin ancestors. According to Hall, the European vernacular then became indigenous to the contact setting.

In Mufwene (in press), I argue that INDIGENIZATION is the adaptation of a language to the new ecology of its users as it is influenced by the previous communicative habits of some of its speakers and meets new communicative needs of theirs. Every transplanted language appropriated as a vernacular indigenizes in its new ecology. If we assume, for convenience sake, that the lexifiers were the same (viz., Dutch, English, French, Portuguese, Spanish, to restrict ourselves just to colonial languages from Western Europe), then what we must also explain is whether creoles are more divergent from the nonstandard colonial European koinés from which they have evolved than their non-creole counterparts, how, and why. The "why" has to do with peculiarities of social interactions and language "transmission," notwithstanding the specific languages that the lexifiers came in contact with and the demographic strengths of their speakers during the critical stages of their formation. This is in fact what makes the inclusion in this volume of chapters on non-creole languages, at least by my definition, so relevant to addressing this question.

2.7 "Off target?"

Aboh (2007) brings up another important question, whether in the first place the populations that produced creoles really intended to "acquire" the lexifier or just communicate (my emphasis). Baker (1997) had already addressed this question, answering it incorrectly in arguing that the relevant populations created "means of interethnic communication" and did not care to learn the relevant European languages. As pointed out in Mufwene (2000), this is an answer that makes sense only ideologically but is neither consistent with how plantation settlement colonies of the New World and Indian Ocean evolved nor with the pressure felt by the initial slave populations, the first Creole slaves, and, later, the rapidly growing majority Bozal populations of the plantation phase to use the dominant colonial language as a vernacular.[12] Shifting

---

12. As explained in Mufwene (2004, 2005, 2008), for the Bozal slaves of especially the plantation phase in the development of the colonies, the pressure to shift to the European colonial vernacular came not so much from the European populations with which they interacted minimally as from the Creole slaves who spoke it as their mother tongue and served as models in the acculturation process.

to the European language reflects less the oppression under the conditions of slavery than the need to be able to communicate successfully in a new setting and using a language that appeared to be the most practical (see below). As a matter of fact the slaves were not alone in doing this, as some Europeans who had not spoken the dominant European colonial language also shifted to the latter, especially among the indentured servants (Mufwene, in press).

While I agree with Aboh that overall people anywhere are more interested in establishing communication than inventing a new language, I must also underscore the fact that people everywhere also adopt ad hoc solutions when they have no common language. Typically, by the principle of least effort, they identify one that is dominant politically, socio-economically, or demographically, a variety that they recognize as (potentially) useful, and they target it. Indeed, they do not spend time trying to create or invent a new one. No natural language has ever emerged by deliberate invention, and everywhere around the world, the artificial standard varieties fabricated by academies or other institutions have failed to displace the more natural nonstandard ones. The case of Israeli Hebrew remains a notable exception, but even this often cited example of planned language creation appears to have benefited from an important share of natural evolution.

Contrary to Baker, we need not be concerned about whether the divergence of the emergent language variety from the target language is tantamount to failing to "acquire" it. In the first place, not even native speakers replicate the language of their social environment (indeed, their target language) perfectly; this is precisely the condition of language "transmission" that validates the notion of IDIOLECT as an individual speaker's "system" that enables him/her to communicate with other users of the communal language (a variable construct) but is identical with no other idiolectal system. In other words, even *native* speakers' idiolects, which have been claimed to reflect "perfect acquisition," show structural differences among themselves, producing intra-communal variation.

The segregated conditions of language practice of the plantation phase naturally fostered divergence, with the varieties spoken by the slaves reflecting selective deterministic influence of some of their substrate languages. In this respect we must of course face the challenge of the Cafeteria Principle, as we must figure out and articulate the particular deterministic factors that bear on the setting-specific recombinations-cum-hybridizations that produced particular creoles. Recall that they are not only structurally similar to, but also different from, each other in various ways. Interestingly, Mintz (1989) underscores this family-resemblance aspect of Caribbean creole cultures taken together, displaying both similarities and differences among themselves.

2.8 Against the discontinuity hypothesis

Important evidence in support of the hypothesis that the slaves targeted one particular language lies in the overwhelming prevalence of the vocabulary that the lexifiers have generally bequeathed to the new vernaculars. This fact argues strongly against the assumption of break in the transmission of the lexifier. Along with Bolinger (1973), I submit that syntax is a consequence of regularities in the way words are used in sentences. It is with words that we typically start learning a language, especially when we already speak one, and we pay attention to how speakers of the target language use them, although the learners' perceptions and interpretations of the patterns are not always accurate. Where more than one target was available in the population, such as in Surinam, the competition between the targets is also reflected in the mixed core vocabulary of the emergent vernacular, as in the case of Saramaccan, which has not only a substantial proportion of words of Portuguese origin in its vocabulary but also some grammatical markers from the same language, alongside the dominant lexical and grammatical selections from English.[13] The significance of the vocabulary of Eastern Ijo in Berbice Dutch may likewise be associated with the time when the Eastern Ijos appear to have constituted either the demographic majority or a substantial proportion within the slave population. It is in settings where koinés developed that the issue of target language becomes a moot one. What most chapters in this volume contribute in support of my hypothesis is the realization that even the grammars of the new vernaculars maintain a substantial legacy from their lexifiers.

I like directing attention to seemingly simple facts such as some differences between, for instance, English and French creoles regarding the position of the DETERMINER and ADJECTIVE and regarding PIED-PIPING and PREPOSITION STRANDING. They reflect patterns observable in the lexifiers rather than in the dominant substrate languages, even when there are similarities that are attributable (partly) to substrate influence in patterns such as the restructuring of the NP or DP regarding INDIVIDUATION, or PREDICATION WITHOUT A COPULA (see Holm & Patrick 2007). Our assessments have generally been biased by partial analyses that have overlooked many structural features that creoles naturally share with their lexifiers, especially when these are not congruent with those of the relevant substrate languages. Creolists may have exaggerated the significance of the respects in which creoles differ from their lexifiers, compared to those in which they remain similar, bearing in mind that the lexifiers are nonstandard European colonial koinés of the 17th and 18th centuries about which we still need more information. In some cases, the consequence of the practice has been an exaggerated statement of differences between some creoles and their lexifiers, as pointed out by Corcoran & Mufwene (1999). This is precisely why many chapters in this volume are so invaluable.

---

13. As Bunting (in press) also shows, we must equally be prepared to acknowledge the influence of Dutch in the grammar of Sranan.

As is obvious from Christine Jourdan's discussion of prepositional verbs in SIP, for instance, even a variety where substrate influence has been so incontrovertible still leaves room for an important legacy from the lexifier. Note, incidentally, that the order of major constituents in SIP is the same as in the lexifier and different from that of substrate languages (Keesing 1988). Unfortunately space and time limitations prevent me from elaborating on this interesting topic. I will simply conclude this part of my discussion with the wish that Aboh's hybridization hypothesis will receive the positive response it deserves. I also hope more detailed studies will complement some of the chapters in this volume, showing various ways in which elements from both the lexifier and the substrate languages can contribute selectively to the grammar of the emergent language variety even in those cases where the lexifier contributes the lion's share. In connection to this, note Tjerk Hagemeijer's chapter in particular, which shows that competition and selection apply even among the substrate languages (see also Mufwene 2001, 2005, 2008). He demonstrates in this case how both Bantu and Edoid languages have influenced the structures of Gulf of Guinea creoles in different ways.

3. Complexity in creoles' systems

3.1 A striking omission

Glaringly omitted from almost all the chapters in this book are discussions of COMPLEXITY. This is both surprising and disappointing because the title of the book is *Complex processes in new languages*. The authors were invited to contribute variously, certainly in complementary ways, to the subject matter, and it is normal to expect them to have reflected on what complexity means. Although all the contributors are creolists and presumably aware of the special issue of *Linguistic Typology*, vol. 5, # 2&3 (2001) devoted to the topic of whether creoles are the world's simplest languages, there are almost no references to this publication or to Dahl's (2004) book-length and more general discussion of complexity in language. In the former publication, John McWhorter's lead article, which articulated the focus of the double issue, received various responses. The most elaborate and informative of these is a lengthy, 99-page rebuttal by Michel DeGraff in which various interpretations of COMPLEXITY are adduced to bear on his fundamental counter-thesis that Haitian Creole, then considered to be a prototypic one according to McWhorter (1998), has a morphosyntax that is largely selected from that of French, its lexifier.[14] Although Haitian Creole has also

---

14. DeGraff's position is in fact partly corroborated by Tonjes Veenstra's chapter, about Mauritian Creole, which also shows the extent to which other formative pressures have modified some of the features selected from the lexifier, such as the variable position of the negator *pa*, which precedes the verb when time reference is to PAST but follows when it is to HABIT.

been richly innovative, most of its derivational morphemes – including much of their morphosyntax and semantics, not all of which is transparent – have been selected from the lexifier. As noted above, this is contrary to the usual claim that while the vocabulary of creoles is predominantly from their lexifiers, their grammars originate elsewhere. The extensive discussion is also a forceful rebuttal of a stronger claim in McWhorter (2001b) that creoles' grammars had been created *ex nihilo* after the alleged pulverization of their lexifiers' systems. This is a thesis germane to the break-in-transmission hypothesis disputed in Mufwene (2001, 2005, 2008).

One would thus expect creolists invited to contribute thoughts on these issues to clarify, like Siegel (2008), what conceptions of COMPLEXITY they find the most adequate or relevant to their discussions. In this volume, only the editors and Anthony Grant address this question explicitly. I received and read the editors' introductory chapter only at the proofs stage, too late for me to comment on, except to remark that their perspectives overlap with mine below. Grant associates "complexity" with "the addition of features which were not previously present [in the lexifier] and of exceptions with previously exceptionless rules." He also attributes complexity to "the concomitant addition of variation between structures of similar meanings where there was none before." More concretely, Grant argues that Zamboangueño (Zam) owes the "complexification" of its verbal, pronominal, and phonemic system to the Philippine languages that Spanish came in contact with. Unfortunately, he says very little about the grammar of the relevant Spanish that was spoken in the Philippines when the islands were colonized by the Spaniards.[15]

I must also note that we are in an era when a particular emergentist perspective on self-organization is growing, when a discipline of complexity theory is already established and has been embraced in various research areas, including the social sciences, and when quantitative, or variationist, sociolinguistics has shown that grammatical features fluctuate a lot in usage. We may want to ask whether there is any particular reason to expect grammatical systems either at the idiolectal or at the communal level to be static, or whether it is high time we developed a dynamical conception of them and treated them as agent-driven complex adaptive systems (Holland 2005).

3.2 Grammars as emergent systems

If the reader agrees with most of everything discussed in the previous sections, especially with the thesis that creoles' systems emerged gradually and spontaneously, i.e., as unplanned phenomena, while speakers just focused on communicating in the target language, then it is not far-fetched to conceive of grammars as emergent systems

---

15. Grant also provides no clear demonstration of how this evolution took place, although one may surmise that the mechanisms involved cannot be that different from the feature-recombination analysis adopted by Enoch Aboh for Sranan, Saramaccan, and Haitian and by Umberto Ansaldo for SLM.

(à la Hopper 1987). They are therefore collective outcomes of adaptations constantly being made independently by individual speakers as they exapt some extant structures to new communicative needs (just what Holland 2005 advocates). At the communal level, grammars reflect the action of the "invisible hand" (to which I return below).

This position does not of course mean that nothing is continuous and stable in the architecture of a language, nor that everything is chaotic and there are no cross-idiolectal similarities in how the various idiolects are structured, nor even that speakers constantly resort to *ex nihilo* innovations in producing their utterances. It simply means that speakers do not always find ready-made structures or constructions to express their thoughts or feelings; they are creatively exaptive. One can observe the power of analogy in the way they extend some extant structures to convey new meanings, bearing in mind that not all innovations are successful, are repeated, and spread within a population. Rather, consistent with the non-linguistic literature on complexity cited below, it is as if both idiolectal and communal systems were in constant search for new equilibria, as speakers attempt to meet new communicative needs and/or adjust their extant communicative systems to those of their interlocutors in order to communicate more successfully.

However, as explained in Mufwene (2001, 2008), what one speaker gives up may be what another finds useful in another situation. Synchronically, one has no real sense of how this flux of give-and-takes settles at the communal level. This is of course in the domain of the "invisible hand," which produces inter-idiolectal interactive complexity, which in turn influences the choices that speakers make when they communicate, bearing in mind that not all aspects of one's system are concurrently affected. For instance, the basic constituent order in the sentence or within particular phrases may not change but the actual uses of particular constructions can be atypical and innovative. Evidently, this behavior, which has been characterized as "chaotic" (i.e., as in constant search for new equilibria) is not unique to creoles but may be more conspicuous in places where variation has mistakenly been associated with "decreolization" qua debasilectalization.

The idea here is that in reality speakers, who in naturalistic multilingual settings do not wait until they have received classes in a specific language, do not plan to invent a language they will speak thereafter, *pace* Baker (1997). Least of all, slaves in the New World and the Indian Ocean, where our epistemic prototypes of creole vernaculars evolved, did not plan at the outset of their captive conditions in the colonies or at any other time to develop exclusive or secret language vernaculars unintelligible to their masters,[16] although the literature on African American English (see, e.g., Morgan 1993) shows that some counter-languages did indeed evolve later on,

---

16. As a matter of fact, it is thanks to what their "masters" (e.g., Charles Baissac, Lucien Adam, Sam Matthews, and Ambrose Gonzales) wrote, reflecting their typically stereotypical understanding of the emergent vernaculars, that we now can develop a less speculative perspective on how they evolved. The writers are among those who produced the first texts that we can now consider archival, giving us an idea of features of the earlier stages of some creoles, although it

albeit as parasitic systems based on the regular vernaculars that creolistics has traditionally focused on. Rather, like migrant workers in Germany and France in the 20th century, they attempted to communicate in the economically dominant language, just like many European indentured servants also did for that matter, with the difference that the socially mixed living conditions of the slaves did not allow most of them to continue using their African languages as their vernaculars.

Past the normal interlanguage stages, the slaves generally acquired enough command of local European colonial vernaculars to communicate in them, each generation of learners (locally born children and Bozal slaves) having a more divergent target than the earlier one (as argued by Chaudenson 1979ff. in terms of "approximations of approximations"), although it really depended more on whom one was learning the European language from and what were the learners' own individual skills at learning a foreign language if they were African-born. As explained in Mufwene (2005, 2008), the divergence that sets creoles apart as different linguistic systems from their lexifiers did not really proceed differently from those that set, say, the Romance languages apart from Vulgar Latin. It is in this perspective of INDIGENIZATION as explained above that one must also invoke emergentism, dealing with the emergence of new structures in the stead of extant ones (see below).

3.3   Complexity emerging from rule interactions

Thus, along with DeGraff (2001, Section 5.3), I submit that it is more informative to assess complexity more interactively than just from the perspective of whether a paradigm in a particular language includes more units than its counterpart in another (and is therefore "richer" – Dahl 2004), whether a grammatical rule specifies more constraints than another (and is therefore harder to learn), or whether a grammatical system has (many) more rules than another even if they are capable of expressing the same meanings or information contents. We cannot ignore the fact that linguistic systems consist of complementary modules, and this is as true of creoles as it is of other languages. From an interactive perspective, the interface of the modules is what generates complexity, in terms of several processes taking place as one produces or processes an utterance, in any language. Since the loads of work assumed by the different modules are not distributed uniformly from one language to another, it is very difficult to develop a constant cross-linguistic measure of the complexity of various languages.

In addition, the communicative capacity or potential of a particular language must be assessed relative to the communicative needs of the population speaking it rather than relative to the needs of another population. Moreover, how a particular population chooses to package different pieces of information and how it adapts to

---

is debatable whether the materials are faithful representations of how the emergent vernaculars were spoken (Corcoran & Mufwene 1999).

new communicative needs varies from one cognitive domain to another and certainly from one culture to another. As the reader should be reminded of by Bettina Zeisler (this volume), it is too easy to introduce a cultural bias in comparing different languages regarding some abstract measure of complexity. What DeGraff (2001a) exposes in particular is the Schleicherian bias that sought to celebrate the European populations as linguistically the most evolved, for instance, through the stipulation that languages with fusional morphosyntax represent the most advanced level in the evolution of language(s). As a matter of fact, Schleicher's (1863) perspective turned out to be as embarrassing as Darwin's (1871) discussion of human populations; Darwin ranked some as more, or less, evolved than others (hardly explaining how), although he condemned slavery.[17]

3.4 Creoles are not unique structurally

As pointed out by DeGraff (2001a), there are so many "older languages" (McWhorter's terminology) such as Chinese and Vietnamese that have morphosyntactic structures similar to those of creoles. One may also note that while McWhorter (1998, 2008) excludes them from the category of simple languages, because they have developed "contrastive tones" over millennia of evolution, one could also point out the interesting fact that Western European languages are curious in not having evolved "contrastive tones," while a number of them also have morphological structures that are not much more complex than those of Haitian Creole.

The reality is that since the dispersal of Homo Sapiens out of Africa 60,000–50,000 years ago, modern human language has diversified along various evolutionary trajectories, ending in a number of alternative morphosyntactic types today that need not be associated with age. Whether a particular language became tonal or adopted a stress system, or became agglutinating or otherwise, among other typological options, need not be correlated with how old a language is. Note, for example, that Papiamentu, which is not older than other Caribbean creoles, is as tonal as most Niger-Congo languages, whereas Swahili, a Bantu language which, on McWhorter's (1998) terms, is much older, is not tonal. Lingala and Kikongo-Kituba developed probably not before the late 19th century out of the contacts of primarily Bantu, tonal languages, but only Lingala is fully tonal. Kituba is typologically mixed in this respect (Mufwene 1989b, 1997b).

What a number of chapters in this book show is that the extent of morphological complexity (in terms of range of distinctions) retained by a "contact language" largely reflects the morphological structures of the target language and the particular languages that it came in contact with. As pointed out by Chaudenson (2001, 2003), the alleged morphosyntactic poverty of creoles is a reflection of that of their

---

17. See Mufwene (2008, Ch. 6) for an elaborate discussion of this position which is ably denounced by Gould (1993) and Radick (2002), among others.

lexifiers themselves compounded in some cases with the particular isolating morphosyntax of the substrate languages they came in contact with. One may likewise attribute the absence of "contrastive tones" in creoles to the absence of these in their own lexifiers, especially if it is accurate that they have inherited many important structural features from the same languages. These are all evidence that support the position that creoles evolved in settings where the slaves did indeed target particular languages, *pace* Baker (1990, 1997), and they actually learned a great deal under their segregated living conditions in which black Creoles and seasoned slaves were the primary "transmitters" of the colonial language. Evidence in support of this continuity hypothesis may also be found in the conservative nature of their segmental phonetics, as they have maintained various pronunciations that are in fact informative windows into how the European lexifiers were spoken in the colonies, especially in the 17th and 18th centuries, which specify the "unity of time" invoked in Chaudenson's (1992ff.) historical definition of creoles. Patrick (1999), for example, is a good introduction to this subject matter in Jamaican Creole.

Thus, McWhorter's (1998) global typological proposal which singles out creoles by arbitrarily denying them the long genetic history they do indeed share with their lexifiers is question-begging. There is no modern language variety that is not young and there isn't a single evolutionary trajectory that all languages are supposed to have followed. Although the role of probability regarding how different features combine (Gil 2007) cannot be ignored, we must still take very seriously Chaudenson's (2001ff.) position that the kind of morphological reduction exhibited by creoles is largely an extension, by generalization and regularization, of processes that were already taking place in their nonstandard lexifiers. Indeed, Modern English has a less rich inflectional system than Middle English and certainly much less than Old English. The same is true of modern Romance languages in comparison with earlier stages of their evolution. On the other hand, there are nuances that the modern varieties can express with their periphrastic systems that must have been difficult to encode inflectionally, for instance, *The book may (not) have (not) been being considered for publication at that time.* The construction may be difficult to parse with the two negatives used concurrently but is not nonsensical. There must be healthier ways of discussing variation in complexity that can be more informative about how Language as an exclusive property of mankind works and how it varies typologically. It is to this aspect of discussions of complexity that I now turn, taking advantage of current research in other disciplines.

3.5   Against "bit complexity"

A convenient starting point is heeding DeGraff's (2001a) rejection of "bit complexity," which amounts to "richness" of units at any level (Dahl 2004), viz., phonological, morphological, and lexical. A language with a larger phonemic inventory is not necessarily more complex if the sounds do not produce more words than a language with a smaller phonemic inventory. Both may actually exhibit the same extent of complexity, depending on how many different constraints regulate their combinatorics and allophonic variation within their phonemic systems. (For that matter, there are some non-creole languages that have smaller phonemic inventories than creoles but are not considered simple.) How many different words a language can generate depends on other factors, such as word length, syllabic peak dissimilation, and, more fundamentally, how many concepts the speakers find necessary to express (non)compositionally.

Note also that although creoles have typically been claimed to dispense with consonant clusters, this particular evolutionary process has not been universal either system-internally or from one creole to another. Many of the most common clusters have survived in Gullah (which also happens to have a voiced bilabial fricative, a typologically marked consonant), for instance, in *small, try, greed, blood, bottle, bunch, inside, outside, vex* [βɛks ~ vɛks], and *simple*. Word length seems to be subject to the same constraints as in English, where polysyllabic words of more than three syllables as attested in Bantu languages (often thanks to derivational sequencing, compounding, and reduplication) are avoided.

On the other hand, a language with a richer derivational and/or inflectional inventory is not necessarily more complex overall than one that can have the same job done by compounding, and/or by the use of a finite set of free grammatical morphemes to modify various paradigms of lexical morphemes, subject to language-specific constraints. Gullah and Guyanese Creole certainly illustrate this well with their explicit grammatical expression of HABITUAL events with /dəz/ ~ /dɔz/ (as in /haw yu dəz kuk ʌm/ 'How do you [usually] cook it?' – Gullah), including in their time reference system a distinction which many dialects of their English lexifier cannot express unequivocally. Recall that, in English, context (provided by the discourse or the situation in or about which the discourse is taking place) determines whether the verbal inflections for the "present tense," including zero marker, refers strictly to the PRESENT, NEAR FUTURE, or a HABIT. Guyanese Creole goes even further in distinguishing periphrastically between two nuances of PROGRESSIVE/DURATIVE delimitations: *mi de taak* 'I am talking' is different from *mi de a taak* 'I am <u>busy</u> talking'. While the translation with *busy* in English captures the meaning, the expression is not grammaticized in the way the combination of grammatical morphemes *de* and *a* is in Guyanese.[18]

Many similar examples can be adduced to show that loss or reduction of inflections in creoles did not amount to loss or reduction of systemic complexity, which can also be considered dynamically, from the perspective of how different constitu-

---

18. This further illustrates one of the points made by DeGraff (2001a: 257) when he argues that "the *terminus ad quem* will be more complex in certain grammatical domains than the *terminus a quo* in other cases (…)" Although the balance of losses and gains in morphosyntactic distinctions made in individual creoles varies from one vernacular to another, they also remain consistent with DeGraff's (2001a: 263) other observation that "there is no reason to expect complexity qua number of distinctions (…) to increase [or decrease] in lockstep across all levels of grammar."

ents and rules interact with each other. In this volume, informative examples can be cited from, for instance, Marlyse Baptista's discussion of *ba* as an ANTERIOR marker in Guinea Bissau Creole. If its evolution is interpreted as a case of reanalysis, whereby an inflection was reanalyzed as a free morpheme whose position is VP-final, then one can also see that variation in its position and scope is almost a mirror image of that of English in constructions such as *I think he did not come* vs. *I do not think he came*. As Baptista points out, there is also a constituent weight constraint among some speakers, which introduces even more complexity, as it determines what can separate *ba* from the head verb.

Thus, while loss or reduction of inflections compared to the Portuguese lexifier may be interpreted as simplification, there is also syntactic variation that introduces systemic complexity, revealing that there is more to a grammatical system than morphological richness. What goes on here is certainly more than morphological simplicity being matched by complex semantic interpretation rules, although this is certainly the case in the temporal interpretation of predicates, as has been extensively demonstrated in the literature on time reference in creoles.

The same is true of the process of lexical-category shift or zero derivation (traditionally dealt with in creolistics as "multifunctionality") which converts verb particles into autonomous transitive verbs in SIP, as discussed by Christine Jourdan (this volume). Note that in *Mami bae* **insaetim** *kaleto* (Mother FUTURE take-inside laundry) 'Mother will take [the] laundry inside' the prepositional predicate *insaet* 'inside' is regularly transitivized with the suffix *im*, like any regular verbal predicate. The transitivizing suffix licences the presence of the object NP to the right of the predicate.

Multifunctionality, which is a common property of languages with isolating morphosyntax, attested also in what McWhorter (2001a) considers languages with older histories, is itself evidence of interactive and therefore systemic complexity. One must pay attention to the morphosyntactic environment to determine the lexical category of a categorially ambiguous item, where languages relying on particular inflections make the process more transparent and apparently simpler to process context-independently. Thus, out of discourse or other pragmatic context, *I saw her ducks* is not ambiguous, thanks to the PLURAL suffix on *duck*, which shows that it is a noun. Interpreting it as a verb would make the utterance ill-formed. In contrast, *I saw her duck* is ambiguous, as the morphosyntactic environment is not helpful. In this respect, English is no better off than most of the creoles that have evolved from it. Indeed, the creole counterpart of *I saw her ducks* would also include a nominal plural marker, although it is not inflectional. The critical difference is thus typological, not in systemic complexity.

Generally and going beyond the present book, I would be remiss not to underscore DeGraff's (2001a) warranted denunciation of a Eurocentric bias in the way that (lack of) systemic complexity of creoles has been assessed in the literature since the 19th century. There is no sound evidence that justifies equating the restructuring which produced "creoles" – as a sociohistorical rather than a structural category of vernaculars (Mufwene 2000) – with simplification, although there is evidence of morphological reduction in several cases, for instance, the general loss of tense inflections from verbs and nominal number inflections from nouns. However, as noted above, Chaudenson (1992ff.) and Corne (1999) in particular have pointed out, focusing on French creoles, that this process is largely an extension of a morphological regularization process that had been taking place in "les français populaires" (nonstandard French), accelerated by partial congruence with the isolating morphosyntax of some of the substrate languages they came in contact with.

Here, one can observe the power of the "hybridity" account of language "acquisition" that Aboh (2006, this volume) is articulating. In the specific case of these particular examples, it appears to me that the functionality of the lexifier's time reference system could not survive the loss of inflections. The substrate languages' isolating verbal morphosyntax underlain by STATIVE/NONSTATIVE distinction in the articulation of TENSE and ASPECT oppositions would lead to what the literature has typically interpreted as the "creole TMA system." As it turns out, this prerequisite semantic distinction is not at all new to French, for example. It underlies an important difference in the APECTUAL interpretations of, on the one hand, *je travaille au bureau* 'I work at [my] desk/in [my] office', and, on the other, *je pense au problème* 'I am thinking about the problem'. In the former case, a NONSTATIVE verb is interpreted HABITUALLY, whereas in the latter, a STATIVE verb is interpreted as CURRENTLY IN PROCESS. Since loss or reduction of inflections is compensated for by the enhancement of a different factor in the lexifier's system, interpreting the restructuring process unequivocally as simplification begs the question, especially when one factors in distinctions which a creole may have added to the system that are not attested in the lexifier. Recall that I assume that creoles are unbroken, gradual evolutions from their lexifiers, as I know of no evidence that supports the discontinuity hypothesis.

3.6 Hybridity, "featurization," and gradual system emergence

It is difficult to make sense of the "hybridity" account without factoring in what Dahl (2004, Ch. 9) explains with "featurization," which amounts to more and more abstract accounts of language change in which different features are assumed to have evolved separately, although they have influenced each other. It seems to me that a language changes not because its (new) speakers decide to change its structures globally at one time but because at different times different features (at the level now articulated by Aboh) undergo various changes initiated independently by different speakers. As time goes by, some of the changed features spread from the idiolects that initiated them to the communal language and their incremental accumulation produces evolution.

That is, while different components of a language do not evolve concurrently, structural features of the new variety emerge non-linearly out of the particular interactions of the changes. The new grammar emerging out of the communicative activities of speakers influences the ways that features selected from the different languages in contact are integrated, dividing the labor among them. An example of this can be found in Aboh's demonstration of "hybridity" in the way features from the lexifier and from the substrate languages mix to produce new patterns in a creole. As noted above, he shows in his chapter, that the Determiner system and the verb *nyan* in Saramaccan do not faithfully replicate their counterparts in either group of languages. One may say that the evolution of English into Saramaccan is a function of the ecology-specific ways in which its features have changed, sometimes concurrently with those of the substrate languages that influenced the restructuring process. Features from the substrate languages are often as much modified as those inherited from the lexifier, as is also obvious from Sylvia Kouwenberg's chapter in this volume. The recombination of features from the different sources in the same subsystem or even in the same lexical entry is part of the feature change itself, making the feature-change process more complex. In addition, the evolution is also a function of how the different feature-changes interact with each other and converge to produce the emergent language variety.

According to some of the literature on complexity outside linguistics (e.g., Heylighen 1996; Byrne 1997; Mikulecky 2001; Taylor 2003; Casti 2008), this is indeed how system complexity emerges out of the interaction of various components, generating features that can hardly be traced intact to one single source. As they generally put it, "the whole is more than the sum of its parts." To quote Mikulecky (2001: 342), "complex (real) systems cannot be successfully reduced to material parts without loss of some significant attributes in the process." Emergence, a diachronic/evolutionary phenomenon, is an important part of complexity. That is, we must also address the question of how (systemic) complexity as a property of self-organization arises, while the emergent system remains in constant flux, in search of some elusive equilibrium. In the case of language, this is owing especially to inter-idiolectal variation and the consequent adaptations speakers make both to new communicative needs and to each other's characteristics (usually identified as "mutual accommodations").

3.7 A dynamical interpretation of complexity

Most practitioners of complexity theory and emergentism underscore the dynamical aspect of these phenomena, as complexity emerges from the various ways different components, parts, or modules interact with each other. Perhaps these considerations provide an explanation for Umberto Ansaldo's observation that "language and grammar are historical entities," i.e., as currently spoken, they are outcomes of particular evolutionary processes, some of them recent and some older. However, as observed in Mufwene (2001, 2005, 2008), every language is being reshaped as it is spoken, never reaching a particular equilibrium in complexity theory terms. Normalization (Chaudenson 1992ff.) as the emergence of stable communal norms is a convenient fiction; Paul (1880/1891) was not so off the mark when he referred to communal norms as some sort of statistical averages among convergent idiolects.

In this respect, one may point out that creoles are not lacking in complexity compared to other language varieties, although they have evolved more toward isolating morphosyntax. However, structure and function must be approached jointly relative to specific ecologies of their emergence and practice. For instance, serial predicate constructions cannot be seen as less complex than subordination just because the former strategy lacks markers that are associated with the latter. They are alternative ways of forming complex sentences in which several predicate phrases overlap, sharing some of their arguments (Mufwene 1989a). As a matter of fact, serialization relations do not exclusively amount to a coordinate-structure style of sentence expansion; they may involve embedding, such as when one says /ʌ traʸ go/ 'I tried [to] go' as a variant of /ʌ traʸ fə go/ in Gullah (Mufwene 1990). With data from Gbe and Khoisan languages, Aboh (2003, 2009) clearly shows that syntactic relations in serial predicate constructions are much more diverse and complex than they look on the surface. Incidentally, both syntactic strategies involve recursion, an essential factor in the production of structural complexity.

3.8 Creoles as complex adaptive systems

An interesting aspect of creoles as complex adaptive systems, which all human language varieties are for that matter, is that they have not emerged from scratch, *pace* McWhorter's (2001b) claim that they emerged from the pulverization of the target language (and of course the shift from the languages previously spoken by the slaves). As altered as their systems are compared to those of their lexifiers, creoles have also maintained noteworthy fundamental morphosyntactic properties of the nonstandard varieties they have evolved from. Focusing on English creoles alone, note, among many features, the following which make them quite Germanic and in a number of ways unlike the substrate languages often invoked to account for their divergence: the prenominal position of the determiner and adjective in the noun phrase, the basic structure of the relative clause introduced by an invariant complementizer *wɛ*, the stranding of the preposition in questions and relative clauses, the insertion of the verbal object before the particle in constructions such as *pick* NP *up*, the fronting of the question word to the beginning of the sentence, and the use of Clefting for focus constructions (bracketing the focus constituent with the counterpart of *it's ___ that* in English).

To be sure, there are always a couple of substrate languages that happen to display one or two of such features. For instance, according to Aboh (2005), Gbe languages have something very similar to preposition-stranding and they front the question word to the beginning of the sentence. We can conclude that the congruence of these facts (Corne 1999; Chaudenson 2001; Mufwene 2001ff.) must have favored the English construction patterns in creoles such as Sranan and Saramaccan. However, there are also all those other English creoles where the constructions have prevailed without (strong) reinforcing influence from these particular substrate languages, for instance Gullah and perhaps also Jamaican Creole. Moreover, as part of the competition among various possible substrate influences, we cannot ignore the fact that many of the relevant languages simply just do not exhibit these features. We can thus assert quite confidently that the relevant structures could have evolved in different typological directions in English creoles if the lexifier did not have these features at all. To wit, French creoles generally show no evidence of preposition-stranding in questions and in relative clauses, of a pre-nominal determiner, or, as observed by Frajzyngier (1984), of a complementizer that has grammaticized from a main verb SAY. Yet, Fon-Gbe languages are claimed to have influenced, though they did not exclusively determine, the structures of Haitian Creole to some extent, certainly in the ways argued by Aboh (2006).

Many more of the structures of the lexifier have survived, albeit with modification in some cases, even if one overlooks features that the lexifier shared with many of the languages it came in contact with, including the basic major constituent order in a sentence. However extensive, the restructuring that produced various creoles in different contact ecologies illustrates how complex systems actually change, especially when, as is evident from Christine Jourdan's chapter, the divergence process appears to have been gradual. Sometimes the effects of the alterations remain quite local, as in the case of number delimitation within the noun phrase. In some other cases, however, the changes affect more than one subsystem, such as when prepositions can also be used predicatively and therefore can also evolve to function as TENSE-ASPECT or MOOD markers or when the serialization of predicates can lead some verbs to evolve COMPLEMENTIZER functions. This is precisely how I interpret Silvia Kouwenberg's observation that some of the changes in the structure of Berbice Dutch are motivated system-internally. It is a good illustration of how complexity emerges.

In Berbice Dutch, as in other creoles, one can also notice that substrate influence is not evenly distributed in all modules of grammar. Likewise, Aboh (this volume) argues that substrate influence applied non-uniformly in Saramaccan and Sranan too. According to complexity theory, the different components or modules of a system can adapt independently to new conditions and therefore undergo modifications that are not equally extensive. The challenge is of course the variable role of ecological factors in conditioning the changes.

If McWhorter (2001a) is correct, as it indeed seems, that creoles get rid of redundant features that are not so essential for a language to function,[19] and since both the economic histories of the territories where these colonial vernaculars evolved and the archival records suggest that they must have evolved gradually (see in fact Baker 1995), then we must wonder how the restructuring producing the reduction of the redundant features occurred in the first place. In other words, what are the

---

19. This observation is not an endorsement of McWhorter's strong position. As a matter of fact, I have in mind phenomena such as grammatical gender, Noun + Adjective or Subject + Verb agreement, and the copula, which are not discussed in McWhorter (1998). My statement is simply a recognition of the fact that at the morphosyntactic level some markers have been done away with. One must still bear in mind that, as demonstrated by DeGraff (2001a, 2001b) many derivational morphemes have been retained. Also, as argued above, alternative strategies have been adopted in lieu of inflections (to mark especially nominal NUMBER and TENSE-ASPECT), and, in some other cases, even new distinctions have been introduced.

particular cross-subsystemic or intra-systemic interactional pressures that led to the reduction? This seems to me to be a more significant question than the assessment of surface complexity that is not particularly informative about how meaning is expressed in a language. The measure of bit complexity becomes even more elusive as there are non-creole languages which, owing apparently to the role of probability (Gil 2007), have been able to satisfy the communicative needs of their speakers without the putative redundant features.

3.9 The work of the "invisible hand"

I will close this part of the chapter with a short discussion of another aspect of complexity, which may appear to be tangential to the above considerations but is nonetheless relevant to understanding how little we still know about normalization in a population. Like language "acquisition," linguistic performance, which contributes to habit-forming in the emergence of idiolectal characteristics, is individual-based, not community-based. It is also during this practice that individual speakers copy from each other, not necessarily symmetrically, features that they find advantageous for one reason or another. In the process they align themselves with various speakers in ways that eventually produce communal norms, without excluding variation along various social parameters and even some resilient, idiosyncratic inter-idiolectal variation. This is basically where one can also claim that the "invisible hand" (misinvoked in this volume by Umberto Ansaldo and Silvia Kouwenberg) works, as every speaker behaves in ways that serve their individual communicative interests but winds up converging with other community members toward the eventual production of the communal norms (Mufwene 2008; after Smith 1776 and Keller 1994).

Given the ways in which the typically dyadic or triadic patterns of human communication change during our social interactions, it is not clear how the averaging to which Paul (1880/1891) alludes in his characterization of communal norms emerges. This is especially significant because, as pointed out in Mufwene (2008), the literature on naturalistic L2 "acquisition" clearly shows that the learners do not all produce identical sets of deviations. Unfortunately no study of these varieties has pointed to the emergence of some communal norms associated with a migrant workers' community. The reason appears to lie in the fact that typically the migrant workers do not use their interlingual approximations to communicate among themselves, as they live in segregated neighborhoods, where they can remain ethnolinguistically homogeneous and socialize among themselves in their heritage languages.[20] In creolistics, where we

---

20. *Pace* Plag (2008), neither did the slaves on the plantations that produced creoles communicate among themselves using just interlanguages, as if they all had arrived at the same time in a plantation that had been set up overnight, and no children were born in or imported to these colonies. This is one more hypothesis about the emergence of creoles, disconnected from the history of the gradual peopling of the relevant colonies and the gradual development of plantations, that we could have been spared.

have been discussing communal vernaculars that emerged recently rather than individual L2 varieties, I wonder whether we can continue to dodge this emergence question, especially in the usage-based approach adopted by Ansaldo. I have no suggestion to make about how to approach the question at present. However, normalization appears to be the outcome of a very complex process of population-level feature convergence through competition and selection. Some features are (virtually) eliminated from the feature pool while others spread (or "propagate" – Ansaldo, this volume) within the population. Part of what makes the normalization process so mind-boggling is that no speaker communicates with every other speaker in their community, our typically dyadic and triadic patterns of interaction change repeatedly, and the networks in which we operate overlap in ways that typically involve only small subsets of all the relevant speakers. Here too, it appears to me that creoles are evolutionarily not different from other languages. The normalization question boils down to that of how different idiolects trade off features toward convergence without nonetheless losing their individualities. There's so much complexity involved both in the polyploidic influences that shape idiolects and in the competition-and-selection processes that produce communal norms. In this respect, creoles are not different from other languages, either in how they evolved or in how they function synchronically.

4. Conclusions

The evolution of the structures of creoles and other so-called "contact language varieties" is far from reflecting a simple, straightforward, and (uni-)linear trajectory. As new studies such as in this volume contribute more facts about the sociohistorical ecologies of the emergence of some of these vernaculars in the Caribbean, the Indian Ocean, and elsewhere (notably Norval Smith and Silvia Kouwenberg in the present case), the complexity of the evolutionary scenarios increases more obviously, although it remains difficult to interpret unequivocally. There is no single local or regional history for which the informed reader could not think of alternative interpretations of the same facts. This simply means that an honest debate must go on that may shed better light on the significance of various ecological factors. These have to do chiefly with periodized demographics, patterns of population growth, changing population structures, the identities of the languages in contact, the patterns of typological variation among them, who may have been the most critical agents of restructuring, and how the invisible hand works during the gradual normalization of the emergent language varieties.

Likewise, more detailed structural approaches on specific constructions, as illustrated by the majority of the contributions to this volume, will help us understand how new structures arise, where specific aspects of these complex structures originate, and how they have contributed variously to produce the peculiarities associated with creoles and other "contact language varieties" today. This book is a compelling invitation for more fine-grained investigations of the evolution and structures of these vernaculars, on a par with similar studies on other languages. This is central to the contribution that the study of language contact can make to general linguistics and toward the better integration of this research area in linguistics. Such scholarship will help us understand how, now as before, a new form of linguistic diversity is replacing what the expansion of some languages at the expense of others is feared to be reducing, lending new meaning to evolution by emergence. Together the chapters also validate Umberto Ansaldo's statement that languages are historical phenomena, displaying complexity in the very sense that most interest students of complexity theory and emergence.

References

Aboh, Enoch. 2003. Les constructions à objet préposé et les series verbales dans les langues kwa. In *Typologie des langues d'Afrique et universaux de la grammaire*, Vol. 2: *Benue-Kwa, Soninke, Wolof,* Patrick Sauzet & Anne Zribi-Hertz (eds), 15–40. Paris: L'Harmattan.

Aboh, Enoch. 2005. The category P: The Kwa paradox. *Linguistic Analysis* 32: 615–645.

Aboh, Enoch. 2006. The role of the syntax-semantics interface. In *L2 Acquisition and Creole Genesis. Dialogues* [Language Acquisition & Langauge Disorders 42], Claire Lefebvre, Lydia White & Christine Jourdan (eds), 253–275. Amsterdam: John Benjamins.

Aboh, Enoch. 2007. Le genèse de la périphérie gauche du saramaka: Un cas d'influence du substrat? In *Grammaires créoles et grammaire comparative,* Karl Gadelli & Anne Zribi-Hertz (eds), 73–97. Paris: Presses Universitaires de Vincennes.

Aboh, Enoch. 2009. Clause structure and verb series. *Linguistic Inquiry* 40(1).

Adam, Lucien. 1883. *Les idiomes négro-aryens et malayo-aryens: Essai d'hybridologie linguistique*. Paris: Maisonneuve.

Adams, J. N. 2007. *The Regional Diversification of Latin 200 BC – AD 600*. Cambridge: CUP.

Bailey, Beryl Loftman. 1966. *Jamaican Creole Syntax: A Transformational Approach*. Cambridge: CUP.

Baker, Philip. 1990: Off target? Column. *Journal of Pidgin and Creole Languages* 5: 107–119.

Baker, Philip. 1995. Some developmental inferences from the historical studies of pidgins and creoles. In *The Early Stages of Creolization* [Creole Language Libarary 13], Jacques Arends (ed.), 1–24. Amsterdam: John Benjamins.

Baker, Philip. 1997. Directionality in pidginization and creolization. In *The Structure and Status of Pidgins and Creoles* [Creole Language Library 19], Arthur K. Spears & Donald Winford (eds), 91–109. Amsterdam: John Benjamins.

Bickerton, Derek. 1981. *Roots of Language*. Ann Arbor MI: Karoma.

Bickerton, Derek. 1984. The language bioprogram hypothesis. *Behavioral and Brain Sciences* 7: 173–221.

Bickerton, Derek. 1999. How to acquire language without positive evidence: What acquisitionists can learn from creoles. In *Language Creation and Language Change: Creolization, Diachrony, and Development*, Michel DeGraff (ed.), 49–74. Cambridge MA: The MIT Press.

Bickerton, Derek. 2004. Reconsidering creole exceptionalism. *Language* 80: 828–833.

Bolinger, Dwight. 1973. Getting the words in. In *Lexicography in English*, Raven McDavid, Jr. & Audrey Duckert (eds.), 8–13. New York NY: New York Academy of Science.

Boretzky, Norbert. 1993. The concept of rule, rule borrowing, and substrate influence in creole languages. In *Africanisms in Afro-American Language Varieties*, Salikoko S. Mufwene (ed.), 74–92. Athens GA: University of Georgia Press.

Bunting, Jacqueline. In press. Give and take: The role of *gi* in the ebb of one Sranan dative alternation. *Journal of Pidgin and Creole Languages*.

Byrne, David. 1997. Complexity theory and social research. *Social Research Update* 18. <http://sru.soc.surrey.ac.uk/SRU18.html>.

Cassidy, Frederick Gomes & Le Page, R. B. 1981. *Dictionary of Jamaican English*. 2nd edn. Cambridge: CUP.

Casti, John L. 2008. Complexity. *Encyclopedia Britannica Article*. CD.

Cavalli-Sforza, Luigi Luca. 2001. *Genes, Peoples, and Languages*. New York NY: North Point Press.

Chaudenson, Robert. 1979. *Les créoles français*. Paris: Fernand Nathan.

Chaudenson, Robert. 1992. *Des îles, des hommes, des langues: essais sur la créolisation linguistique et culturelle*. Paris: L'Harmattan.

Chaudenson, Robert. 2001. *Creolization of Language and Culture*. London: Routledge.

Chaudenson, Robert. 2003. *La créolisation: théorie, applications, implications*. Paris: L'Harmattan.

Corcoran, Christine & Mufwene, Salikoko S. 1999. Sam Matthews' Kittitian: What is it evidence of? In *St. Kitts and the Atlantic Creoles: The Texts of Samuel Augustus Matthews in Perspective*, Philip Baker & Adrienne Bruyn (eds), 75–102. London: University of Westminster Press.

Corne, Chris. 1980. A re-evaluation of the predicate in Ile-de-France Creole. In *Generative Studies in Creole Languages*, Pieter Muysken (ed.), 103–124. Dordrecht: Foris.

Corne, Chris. 1999. *From French to Creole: The Development of New Vernaculars in the French Colonial World*. London: University of Westminster Press.

Dahl, Östen. 2004. *The Growth and Maintenance of Linguistic Complexity* [Studies in Language Companion Series 71]. Amsterdam: John Benjamins.

Darwin, Charles. 1871. *The Descent of Man*. Amherst MA: Prometheus Books.

Degraff, Michel. 1997. Nominal predication in Haitian and in Irish. In *Proceedings of the 16th West Coast Conference on Formal Linguistics*, Emily Curtis, James Lyle & Gabriel Wenster (eds), 113–128. Stanford CA: CSLI.

DeGraff, Michel. 2001a. On the origin of creoles: A Cartesian critique of neo-Darwinian linguistics. *Linguistic Typology* 5: 213–310.

DeGraff, Michel. 2001b. Morphology in creole genesis: Linguistics and ideology. In *Ken Hale: A Life in Language*, Michael Kenstowicz (ed.), 53–121. Cambridge MA: The MIT Press.

DeGraff, Michel. 2003. Against creole exceptionalism. Discussion note. *Language* 79: 391–410.

DeGraff, Michel. 2005. Linguists' most dangerous myth: The fallacy of creole exceptionalism. *Language in Society* 34: 533–591.

DeGraff, Michel. 2009. Language acquisition in creolization (and language change): Some Cartesian-uniformitarian guidelines. *Language and Linguistics Compass* 3. <http://www3.interscience.wiley.com/journal/122464861/abstract>.

Féral, Carole de. 1989. *Pidgin-English du Cameroun*. Paris: Peters/SELAF.

Fill, Alwin. 2004. Review of Mufwene 2001. *Journal of Pidgin and Creole Languages* 19: 199–203.

Frajzyngier, Zygmunt. 1984. On the origin of *say* and *se* as complementizers in Black English and English-based creoles. *American Speech* 59: 207–210.

Gil, David. 2007. Creoles, complexity and associational semantics. In *Deconstructing Creole* [Typological Studies in Language 73], Umberto Ansaldo, Stephen Matthews & Lisa Lim (eds), 66–108. Amsterdam: John Benjamins.

Gonzales, Ambrose E. 1922. *The Black Border: Gullah Stories of the Carolina Coast (with a glossary)*. Columbia SC: The State Co.

Gould, Stephen Jay. 1993. *Eight Little Piggies: Reflections in Natural History*. New York NY: W.W. Norton & Co.

Hagège, Claude. 1993. *The Language Builder: An Essay on the Human Signature in Linguistic Morphogenesis*. Amsterdam: John Benjamins.

Hall, Robert A., Jr. 1962. The life-cycle of pidgin languages. *Lingua* 11: 151–156.

Hall, Robert A., Jr. 1966. *Pidgin and Creole Languages*. Ithaca NY: Cornell University Press.

Heylighen, Francis. 1996. What is complexity? *Principia Cybernetica Web*, Dec. 9. <http://pespmc1.vub.ac.be/COMPLEXI.html>.

Hjelmslev, Louis. 1938. Etudes sur la notion de parenté linguistique. *Revue des Etudes Indo-Européennes* 1: 271–286.

Holland, John. 2005. Language acquisition as a complex adaptive system. In *Language Acquisition, Change and Emergence: Essays in Evolutionary Linguistics*, James W. Minett & William S.-Y. Wang (eds.), 411–435. Hong Kong: City University of Hong Kong Press.

Holm, John. 1988. *Pidgins and Creoles*, Vol. 1: *Theory and Structure*. Cambridge: CUP.

Holm, John & Patrick, Peter L. 2007. *Comparative Creole Syntax*. London: Battlebrige.

Hopper, Paul J. 1987. Emergent grammar. In *Proceedings of the Berkeley Linguistics Society*, Jon Aske, Natasha Beery, Laura A. Michaelis & Hana Filip (eds.), 139–157. Berkeley CA: Berkeley Linguistics Society.

Irvine, Alison. 2004. A good command of the English language: Phonological variation in the Jamaican acrolect. *Journal of Pidgin and Creole Languages* 19: 41–76.

Kapanga, Mwamba Tshishiku. 1991. Language Variation and Change: A Case Study of Shaba Swahili. PhD dissertation, University of Illinois at Urbana-Champaign.

Keesing, Roger M. 1988. *Melanesian Pidgin and the Oceanic Substrate*. Stanford CA: Stanford University Press.

Keller, Rudi. 1994. *On Language Change: The Invisible Hand in Language*. London: Routledge.

Lewontin, Richard Charles. 1970. The units of selection. *Annual Review of Ecology and Systematics* 1: 1–18.

McWhorter, John H. 1998. Identifying the creole prototype: Vindicating a typological class. *Language* 74: 788–818.

McWhorter, John H. 2001a. The world's simplest grammars are creole grammars. *Linguistic Typology* 5: 125–166.

McWhorter, John H. 2001b. *The Power of Babel: A Natural History of Language*. New York NY: Times Books.

McWhorter, John H. 2008. Deconstructing creole. Review article. *Journal of Pidgin and Creole Languages* 23: 289–306.

Meillet, Antoine. 1921. *Linguistique historique et linguistique générale*, Vol. 1. Paris: Champion.

Meillet, Antoine. 1929. Le développement des langues. In *Continu et discontinu*. Paris: Bloud & Gay. (Reprinted in Meillet 1951: 71–83).

Meillet, Antoine. 1951. *Linguistique historique et linguistique générale*, Vol. 2. Paris: Klincksieck.

Mikulecky, Donald C. 2001. The emergence of complexity: Science coming of age or science growing old? *Computers and Chemistry* 25: 341–348. <www.elsevier.com/locate/compchem>.

Mintz, Sidney W. 1989. *Caribbean Transformations*. New York NY: Columbia University Press.

Morgan, Marcyliena. 1993. The Africanness of counterlanguage among Afro-Americans. In *Africanisms in Afro-American Language Varieties*, Salikoko S. Mufwene (ed.), 423–435. Athens GA: University of Georgia Press.

Mufwene, Salikoko S. 1988. Why study pidgins and creoles? Column. *Journal of Pidgin and Creole Languages* 3: 265–276.

Mufwene, Salikoko S. 1989a. Equivocal structures in some Gullah complex sentences. *American Speech* 64: 304–326.

Mufwene, Salikoko S. 1989b. La créolisation en bantou: Les cas du kituba, du lingala urbain, et du swahili du Shaba. *Etudes Créoles* 12: 74–106.

Mufwene, Salikoko S. 1990. Serialization and subordination in Gullah. In *When Verbs Collide: Papers from the 1990 Ohio State Mini-Conference on Serial Verbs* [Working Papers in Linguistics 39], Brian Joseph & Arnold Zwicky (eds), 91–108.

Mufwene, Salikoko S. 1996a. The Founder Principle in creole genesis. *Diachronica* 13: 83–134.

Mufwene, Salikoko S. 1996b. Creolization and grammaticization: What creolistics could contribute to research on grammaticization. In *Changing Meanings, Changing Functions*, Philip Baker & Anand Syea (eds), 5–28. London: University of Westminster Press.

Mufwene, Salikoko S. 1997a. Jargons, pidgins, creoles, and koinés: What are they? In *The Structure and Status of Pidgins and Creoles* [Creole Language Library 19] Arthur K. Spears & Donald Winford (eds), 35–70. Amsterdam: John Benjamins.

Mufwene, Salikoko S. 1997b. Kituba. In *Contact Languages: A Wider Perspective* [Creole Language Library 17], Sarah G. Thomason (ed.), 173–208. Amsterdam: John Benjamins.

Mufwene, Salikoko S. 2000. Creolization is a social, not a structural, process. In *Degrees of Restructuring in Creole Languages* [Creole Language Library 22], Ingrid Neumann-Holzschuh & Edgar Schneider (eds), 65–84. Amsterdam: John Benjamins.

Mufwene, Salikoko S. 2001. *The Ecology of Language Evolution*. Cambridge: CUP.

Mufwene, Salikoko S. 2003. Genetic linguistics and genetic creolistics. Short note. *Journal of Pidgin and Creole Languages* 18: 273–288.

Mufwene, Salikoko S. 2004. Language birth and death. *Annual Review of Anthropology* 33: 201–222.

Mufwene, Salikoko S. 2005. *Créoles, écologie sociale, évolution linguistique*. Paris: L'Harmattan.

Mufwene, Salikoko S. 2007. Les créoles: De nouvelles variétés indo-européennes désavouées? In *Actes du colloque "Créolisation linguistique et sciences humaines,"* Marie-Paul Ansie (ed.), 59–70. Paris: Presses Universitaires Haïtiano-Antillaises.

Mufwene, Salikoko S. 2008. *Language Evolution: Contact, Competition and Change*. London: Continuum.

Mufwene, Salikoko S. 2009. 'Protolanguage' and the evolution of linguistic diversity. Festschrift for William S.-Y. Wang, 1–33. Hong Kong: City University of Hong Kong Press.

Mufwene, Salikoko S. In press. The indigenization of English in North America. In *World Englishes: Problems, Properties, Prospects. Selected Papers from the 13th IAWE Conference*, Thomas Hoffmann & Lucia Siebers (eds.). Amsterdam: John Benjamins.

Mühlhäusler, Peter. 1985. The number of pidgin Englishes in the Pacific. *Papers in Pidgin and Creole Linguistics* No. 1 *Pacific Linguistics*, A-72.25–51.

Patrick, Peter. 1999. *Urban Jamaican Creole: Variation in the Mesolect* [Varieties of English around the World G17]. Amsterdam: John Benjamins.
Paul, Herman. 1880. *Prinzipien der Sprachgeschichte*. Halle: Niemeyer.
Paul, Hermann. 1891. *Principles of the History of Language*. Translated from the second edition of the original by H. A. Strong. London: Longmans, Green, and Co.
Plag, Ingo. 2008. Creoles as interlanguages. Column. *Journal of Pidgin and Creole Languages* 23: 307–328.
Polomé, Edgar. 1983. The linguistic situation in the western provinces of the Roman Empire. *Principat* 29: 509–553.
Posner, Rebecca. 1985. Creolization as typological change: Some examples from Romance syntax. *Diachronica* 2: 167–188.
Posner, Rebecca. 1996. *The Romance Languages*. Cambridge: CUP.
Radick, G. 2002. Darwin on language and selection. *Selection* 3: 7–16.
Schleicher, August. 1863. *Die darwinische Theorie und die Sprachwissenschaft: Offenes Sendschreiben an Herrn Dr. Ernst Häckel*. Weimar: Böhlau.
Siegel, Jeff. 2008. *The Emergence of Pidgin and Creole Languages*. Oxford: OUP.
Smith, Adam. 1776. *The Wealth of Nations*, Vol. 1. Oxford: Clarendon Press.
Spears, Arthur K. & Donald Winford (eds). 1997. *The Structure and Status of Pidgins and Creoles* [Creole Language Library 19]. Amsterdam: John Benjamins.
Stewart, Charles (ed.). 2007. *Creolization: History, Ethnography, Theory*. Walnut Creek CA: Left Coast Press.
Taylor, Mark C. 2003. *The Moment of Complexity: Emerging Network Culture*. Chicago IL: University of Chicago Press.
Thomason, Sarah G. 2001. *Language Contact: An Introduction*. Washington DC: Georgetown University Press.
Thomason, Sarah G. & Kaufman, Terrence. 1988. *Language Contact, Creolization, and Genetic Linguistics*. Berkeley CA: University of California Press.
Trask, Robert Lawrence. 1996. *Historical Linguistics*. London: Arnold.
Whinnom, Keith. 1971. Linguistic hybridization and the 'special case' of pidgins and creoles. In *Pidginization of Creolization of Languages*, Dell Hymes (ed.), 91–116. Cambridge: CUP.

Language index

A

Afrikaans   201–210, 212–217, 245, 376–377
  Khoekhoe Afrikaans   202, 208–209, 213–215, 217
Akan   54, 58, 152
Aluku   61–62
Ambonese Malay   *see* Malay
Ampuku   58
Ancient Greek   5
Angolar   *see* Ngola
Arawak   115, 120–122, 150–156

B

Bahasa Ternate   224
Balti   *see* Tibetan
Bantu   30, 32–34, 40–41, 43–44, 52, 54, 59, 69, 106–109, 173, 175, 359, 377, 382, 386, 388
Basque   18
Bemba   106, 175
Berbice Dutch (BD)   72, 115–117, 121–132, 134–137, 141–156, 313, 374–375, 381, 393
Bisayan languages   225–227, 230, 237
Burushaski   88, 93

C

Cameroon Pidgin English   370
Cape Dutch   *see* Dutch
Cape Dutch Pidgin   201–202, 210, 214, 216
Cape Verdean Creole   293–295, 297–307, 309–314, 372
Caviteño   224–228, 240
Cebuano   225, 227–228, 236, 241
Central Philippine languages   223, 226, 228–230, 237

Chinese
  Hokkien   225, 230, 241, 280
  Middle Chinese   86
Cotabateño   224–225
Creolese   *see* Guyanese Creole

D

Davaueño   224–225
Dingri   *see* Tibetan
Dju-Tongo   57
Dutch   16–17, 56, 115–116, 121–123, 127–128, 137, 145, 147, 149–154, 156, 201–211, 214–217, 245, 359, 376, 379, 381
  Cape Dutch   207, 216

E

Edo   33, 41, 48, 54
English   5, 7, 10, 12–14, 18, 33, 56–59, 69–70, 164–167, 178–181, 189, 191, 194, 196, 203, 223, 225, 228, 230–231, 233, 236–237, 240–241, 258, 271, 276, 302, 326–329, 331–335, 337, 340, 356, 359, 369, 371–372, 374–376, 378–379, 381, 384, 387–389, 391–392
  Appalachian English   372
  Cockney   372
  Early Modern English   12, 16
  Old Amish English   372
  Old English   13, 387
  Philippine English   225, 241
  Singapore English   276
  Southern English   371
English lexifier creoles   376, 381
Edo   33, 48, 54
Edoid   33, 41–45, 382
Ermiteño   224

F

Fa d'Ambô   30–32, 34–35, 37–40, 43–45, 48, 50
Fongbe   51–55, 57–59, 61, 66–68, 326, 375, 393
French   5–7, 18, 100–103, 124–125, 173–175, 178–185, 188–189, 195–197, 234, 246, 320, 322–323, 373, 375–376, 378–379, 382, 390
French lexifier creoles   20, 29, 34, 99–100, 103, 109, 121, 173, 376, 381, 390, 393

G

Gbe   54–55, 57–58, 153, 173, 175, 323, 326–328, 331, 333–334, 337, 339–340, 392
  Eastern Gbe languages   52, 55
German   18, 109, 210–212, 214–215, 351, 376
  Early Modern German   212
Germanic   3, 6, 11–13, 201–202, 327, 359, 372, 392
  Proto-Germanic   13
Gulf of Guinea creoles (GGC)   19, 29–45, 48–50, 382
  Proto-GGC   30–32, 35–39, 41, 43–45
Gothic   12–13
Guinea Bissau Creole (GBC)   293–304, 306–309, 313–314, 372, 389
Gullah   371, 376, 388, 392
Guyanese Creole (Creolese)   121, 129, 133, 388
Gungbe   6–7, 175, 196, 326–340, 374

402 Language index

H
Haitian Creole 99–100, 104–105, 110, 124, 313, 322–323, 359, 375, 377–378, 382–383, 386, 393
Hiligaynon 226–230, 232–233, 239–241
Hokkien *see* Chinese

I
Ijo
  Central Ijo 148
  Eastern Ijo (EI) 115–116, 120–125, 127–128, 131–132, 145–156, 374–375, 381
  Kalabari (KA) 122–141, 143–151
  Okrika (OK) 115, 132, 147–149
  Proto-Ijo 148
Ijoid 42, 122
Indo-European 11, 13, 237, 359, 370
  Proto-Indo-European 11, 13
Indo-Iranian languages 78, 88–89, 92–93
  Indo-Aryan 89, 94, 246, 357
  Iranian 86
Indo-Portuguese creoles 40

J
Jakarta Malay *see* Malay
Jamaican Creole (Patwa) 7, 121, 153, 313, 369–370, 375–376, 387, 392
Javanese 246

K
Kalabari *see* Eastern Ijo
Kannada 8, 246, 259–260
Kenhat *see* Tibetan
Kham *see* Tibetan
Khapulu *see* Tibetan
Khoisan 392
Kituba (Kikongo-Kituba) 386
KiKoongo (Kikongo) 34, 48, 51–55, 57–70, 153, 192
  KiNtandu 59–65
  Mazinga 60, 64
  Myila 62
  Ndibu 61

Kimbundu 33–34, 40
KiNtandu *see* KiKoongo
Kinyarwanda 106
Kirinda Java *see* Sri Lanka Malay
Kirundi 106
Kriyol *see* Guinea Bissau Creole
Kromanti 58
Kwa 41, 322, 337
Kwinti 60–63

L
Ladakhi *see* Tibetan
Latin 5, 227, 234, 320, 371
  Vulgar Latin 369, 371, 385
Leh *see* Tibetan
Lesser Antillean Creole 103
Lingala 386
Lokono *see* Arawak
Louisiana Creole (LA) 99–100, 103–105, 113
Lung'ie (Principense) 29–35, 37–41, 43–45, 48–50

M
Makhuwa 106–109
Malay
  Ambonese Malay 247–248
  Jakarta Malay 244, 247
  Moluccan Malay 224, 244, 247
  Sri Lanka Malay *see* Sri Lanka Malay
Malayalam 259–260
Manila Bay creole Spanish 224, 226–228, 241
Mauritian Creole (MC) 17–18, 99–100, 104–111, 173–197, 234, 313, 359, 382
Mazinga *see* KiKoongo
Media Lengua 246
Melanesian Pidgin English 374, 377
Middle Chinese *see* Chinese
Mindanao Chabacano 223–224, 226–227, 239–240, 313
Mohawk 17
Moluccan Malay *see* Malay
Mwera 106
Myila *see* KiKoongo

N
Ndibu *see* KiKoongo
Ndyuka 12, 52, 54, 57, 60–61
Ngola (Angolar) 30–34, 37, 40, 43–44, 48, 50
Niger-Congo 122, 386
  West African Niger-Congo 54

O
Okrika *see* Eastern Ijo

P
Papa 58, 62
Papiamentu 227, 235, 313, 372, 386
Philippine Creole Spanish 223–224
Philippine English *see* English
Philippine Spanish *see* Spanish
Portuguese 29–36, 38–40, 42–45, 48, 57, 224, 227–228, 296–297, 301–307, 312–314, 320, 368, 376, 379, 381, 389
  Brazilian Portuguese 39
  Old Portuguese 31
  Tonga Portuguese 33–34
Portuguese-lexifier creole 57, 224, 227, 239–240
  Indo-Portuguese *see* Indo-Portguese creoles
  Malayo-Portuguese *see* Malayo-Portuguese creole
  Portuguese pidgin 295
  Sri Lanka Creole Portuguese *see* Sri Lanka Creole Portuguese
Principense *see* Lung'ie
Proto-Germanic *see* Germanic
Proto-Gulf of Guinea Creole *see* Proto-GGC
Proto-Indo-European (PIE) *see* Indo-European
Proto-Tibetan *see* Tibetan
Purik *see* Tibetan

Q
Quechua 246

Language index

R
Romance languages 6, 179, 320, 359, 369, 371, 385, 387
Russian 6–7

S
Sanskrit 5, 224
Santome (Santomense) 30–34, 36–37, 40, 43–44, 48–50, 313
Saramaccan 9–10, 12, 37, 51–55, 57–70, 155, 227, 319, 322, 326–328, 332–338, 359, 374, 377, 381, 383, 391–393
Setswana 107
Shamskat *see* Tibetan
Shigatse *see* Tibetan
Shina 90, 92
Sinama 225–226
Singapore English *see* English
Sinhala 22, 243–247, 249, 251–254, 259–261, 263, 280–283, 285, 348–350
Skardo *see* Tibetan
Skepi Dutch
Solomon Islands Pijin (SIP) 159–168, 368, 377–378, 382, 389
Spanish 18, 35, 101–102, 117, 223–232, 234–237, 239–240, 246, 379, 383
    Philippine Spanish 226–227, 383
Spiti *see* Tibetan
Sranan 4–5, 12, 52, 54–61, 66–70, 313, 319, 322, 334–340, 377, 381, 383, 392–393
Sri Lanka Malay (SLM) 243–263, 265, 277, 279–281, 286, 288–289, 345–346, 348–354, 356–359, 368, 374, 377, 383
    Kirinda Java (KJ) 279–285

Sri Lanka Creole Portuguese 348
Sri Lankan Sprachbund 244, 249, 251, 254
Sri Lankan Tamil 280, 353
    Hindu Tamil 353
    Muslim Tamil (MT) 243, 245–249, 251–254, 259–263, 353, 374
Swahili 377, 386

T
Tagalog 223–230, 234, 236–237, 239–241
Tamil 22, 246–247, 249–250, 252, 259, 262–263, 280–283, 348–349, 351–353
Ternate *see* Bahasa Ternate
Ternateño 224–225
Themchen *see* Tibetan
Tibetan
    Amdo Tibetan (AT) 77, 80–81, 83, 85, 88, 93
    Archaic Tibetan 78, 87–88, 93
    Balti 77, 81, 90–93
    Dingri 92
    Central Tibetan (CtrT) 75, 75, 78, 80, 83, 89–93
    Classical Tibetan (CT) 79–82, 84, 88–93
    East Tibetan 88
    Kenhat 89–91, 93–94
    Kham 77, 83
    Khapulu 90
    Ladakhi 77, 81, 90, 92, 93
    Leh 91, 93
    Lhasa Tibetan (LT) 77, 80–82, 85–86, 91–93
    Modern Tibetan *see* Lhasa Tibetan
    Old Central Tibetan 93

Old East Tibetan 88, 92–93
Old Lhasa Tibetan 86, 90
Old Northern Trade Tibetan 93
Old Tibetan (OT) 75, 78–85, 87–94
Old West Tibetan 93
Proto-Tibetan 79, 87
Purik 81, 89–92
Shamskat 81, 89–93
Shigatse 92
Skardo 90
Spiti 89, 93
Themchen 82
West Tibetan (WT) 78, 80–81, 83, 85, 88–93
Zanskar 89, 91
Tibeto-Burman 78, 87–88, 94
Tok Pisin 167, 359–360, 370
Tonga Portuguese *see* Portugese

W
West African creoles 77
West Greenlandic 4–5
West Himalayan 88, 92–93

X
Xhosa 17

Y
Yaka 65
Yao 106
Yombe 62–63
Yoruboid 41

Z
Zamboanbgueño (Zam) 224–237, 241, 383
Zanskar *see* Tibetan
Zhangzhung 86, 88
Zulu 107–108
!Xóõ 16

Subject index

A
Abaísa 59
Ablaut 11, 83–84
Accretion 248, 254, 349–351
Adstrate 100, 105, 228, 237, 277, 279, 283, 348
Advanced Tongue Root (ATR) 38, 41, 42
Affixes 257, 261, 271, 335, 338, 348–350
African element 52, 296
Agreement 7–8, 51, 130–131, 179, 307, 347–348, 350–351, 358, 393
Agglutination 19–20, 29–36, 38–39, 41–45, 252, 259
Agglutinative language
  Agglutinative 54, 76, 152, 281, 296, 348
Alternation 10, 12–13, 20, 42, 75, 83–84, 89–92, 99–100, 105–106, 108–111, 229, 262, 322, 337–338, 374, 397
Amerindian slaves 119, 151–152
Argument 6, 8, 21, 100, 104–105, 107, 109–111, 124, 173, 175, 177–179, 190–193, 195–196, 303, 331–334, 336, 392
Argumental 21, 173, 178–179, 191, 196
Article 6, 19, 21, 29, 30, 32, 36, 44–45, 51, 67, 124, 126, 173–175, 177–180, 181, 183, 187–189, 194–197, 212, 215–216, 233

B
BaKoongo 55, 67
Basilectalization 370, 374, 378
Beké 369
Basic lexicon 116, 121, 240
Basic variety 102–103, 109

Biclausality 244, 257
Bight of Biafra 53, 120–121
Borrowings 20, 51, 57, 231

C
Cafeteria Principle 373, 380
Case 6–9, 221, 261, 265, 277, 279–285, 346–349, 351–353, 358
Case morphology 6–7, 346
Change 2, 12, 14, 21–24, 29, 65, 69, 77, 81, 86, 90, 94, 122, 159–162, 165–167, 195–196, 201–202, 207, 209–214, 223, 229–231, 235–237, 244–247, 249, 261, 265–270, 272–278, 280, 283–285, 317–319, 323, 326, 339–340, 345–347, 355–357, 360, 369–371, 384, 390–391, 393–395
Class prefix 34, 54, 64, 66–67
Class prefixes 34, 54, 55, 59, 60–64, 65–67
Clusters 6, 41, 42, 44, 45, 55, 60, 66, 77, 79–82, 84, 86, 88, 90, 91, 123, 126, 230, 388
Competitors 117, 320
Complementizer 9, 126, 176, 213, 323, 326–327, 375, 392–393, 398
Complex adaptive systems 383, 392
Competition and selection 23, 196–197, 317, 319–323, 325–328, 340, 360, 373, 382, 395
Completive past construction 256–257
Complex consonant onset 77
Complex consonant coda
  Coda 77, 79, 81, 209, 231
Complex languages 1, 162

Complex structures 23, 319, 345, 395
Complexification 1, 21–22, 51, 69, 75, 94, 159–162, 165, 223, 226, 229–231, 234, 243–244, 247, 263, 293–297, 313–314, 319, 376–378, 383
  Semantic complexification 22, 293–295, 297, 313–314
Complexity 1, 3–8, 10–12, 14–20, 22–24, 51–52, 70, 75–77, 79–80, 82, 91–93, 161–162, 229, 236, 243–244, 247, 265, 278, 280, 285, 293–294, 296–298, 301, 306, 314–314, 317–319, 325, 340, 345–348, 354, 356–360, 367, 371, 373, 375–376, 382–389, 391–396
  Lexical complexity 11, 76, 318
  Morphological complexity 4, 7, 11, 20, 92–93, 247, 386
  Phonological complexity 11, 16, 80, 82
  Semantic complexity 14
  Structural complexity 11, 22, 76, 265, 345, 354, 392
Compounds 15, 54, 90–91, 155, 334
  Compounding 3, 14–15, 388
Compositional semantics 7
Congo 30, 41, 52–54, 122, 386
Congruence 272, 277, 279, 281, 374–375, 390, 392
Conjunctive participle 254, 350
Contact 2, 19–20, 22–24, 29–31, 44–45, 57, 67, 75, 77–78, 88–89, 92–94, 106, 122, 124, 148–152, 155, 161, 163, 166–167,

197, 223–225, 228–231, 236, 247–248, 263–276, 278–281, 285, 293–294, 318–323, 325–327, 341, 343, 348, 354, 356, 359, 367–373, 376–379, 383, 386–387, 390, 393, 395–396
Contact situation 2, 20, 22, 23, 75, 78, 122, 149–150, 155, 196, 197, 293–294, 320–321, 348, 360
Contact language 22, 24, 106, 228,248, 263, 265–266, 272, 276, 285, 279, 319, 325, 327, 348, 368, 395–396
Contact language formation 22, 265–266
Continuity 356, 374, 387
Constraint circumvention 259, 261
Convergence 176, 223, 243–246, 254, 262, 266, 321, 395
Copula 12, 126, 134, 225, 230, 232–235, 302–307, 375–376, 381, 393
Creole genesis 72, 111–113, 115, 158, 169–170, 197, 289, 294, 319–320, 341–343, 362, 396–397, 399
Creole prototype 346, 348, 359
Creolization 1–3, 11–12, 19–24, 33, 44, 56, 75, 92, 99–100, 103, 105, 161, 165, 173, 231, 294, 296, 317, 356, 360, 378

D

Definite 19–21, 29, 32–35, 44–45, 51, 67, 126, 173–183, 185–186, 188–197, 212, 229, 239, 282–283, 306, 308, 310–314, 325, 328
Definiteness 21, 34, 173, 175, 177–182, 185, 189–190, 194, 196–197, 282–283, 306, 308, 311–312, 325
Definite article 19, 29, 32–35, 44, 51, 67, 126, 173, 178, 180, 183, 196–197, 212, 229
Deixis 89, 179, 182–184, 187, 197
Demonstrative 21–22, 174, 177, 181–185, 187, 189–190, 194–195,

200–204, 206–211, 213–214, 215–217, 239, 376
Derivational morphology 14, 347–349, 372
Determiner 6, 21–22, 34, 70, 126, 173–180, 181–183, 190–193, 195–199, 294, 310, 313, 323, 327, 336, 374–375, 381, 391–393
Developmental path 2
Dialect mixture 51
Discontinuity 20–21, 115, 151, 381, 390
Disjoint/Conjoint 106, 107, 108, 111
Dislocation 10, 142
Diversification 369
DNA 278, 324–325

E

Ecology 267, 276, 278–279, 281, 319–321, 348, 357, 368, 376, 378–379, 391
Economy 293, 295, 308
E-creole 321–323, 325
E-language 322, 355–357
Embedding 132, 143, 161, 249, 392
Emergentism 385, 391
Emergentist 383
Ethnicity 56
Eurocentric bias 389
Evolution 22–24, 71, 76, 198, 265–269, 271–280, 283–284, 319–320, 323–324, 340, 355–356, 360, 367, 369–371, 373–378, 380, 383, 386–391, 395–396
Evolutionary theory 267–268, 275
Exceptionalism 267, 367
External network relations 56

F

Feature 8, 16, 21–24, 29–30, 34, 36, 40–45, 54, 60, 70, 75–77, 81–82, 84, 90, 116, 134, 166–169, 173–174, 176–177, 179, 181–182, 185–187, 189, 192–194, 196, 210, 213–214, 216, 224–231, 233, 236–237,

240, 243, 248, 252–253, 257, 259–260, 265, 269, 274–278, 280–284, 293, 295, 311–312, 314, 317–319, 321–328, 334, 340, 342, 346–350, 354, 357–360, 367, 372–374, 377–378, 381–384, 387, 390–395
Feature Pool 269, 278, 321–322, 340, 360, 373, 395
Feature Propagation Propagation 274–277, 279, 283, 284, 355, 357
Feature recombination 318, 328, 372–373, 377
Featurization 390
Focus 8–10, 107–109, 122, 126, 142, 203, 249, 320, 324, 326–327, 352, 357, 392
Focus construction 8–9, 392
Focus marker 9–10, 122, 126, 326
Fon 25, 46, 51–59, 61, 66–68
Formally parsed 69
Francophone 370
Free standing morpheme 244–249, 258, 294, 297, 298, 301
Free standing 301
Frequency 11–12, 167, 271–272, 275–279, 281, 283–284, 287, 289, 322
Functional-typological theory 265, 275
Functional stacking constraint 251

G

Gender 8, 29, 34–36, 38, 43–45, 51, 55, 59–60, 68–69, 165, 173, 175, 184, 202, 217, 335, 347, 358, 393
Gene recombination 327
Genotype 323–325, 331
Generic 21, 128, 161, 173, 183, 188, 192, 194, 306, 309, 311–313, 328
Gold Coast 53, 58
Grammatical complexity 3
Grammaticalization 131, 165, 168, 175, 187, 190, 195, 270, 272, 275, 278, 283, 357

H

Habitual/future negative auxiliary 259–260
Homo Sapiens 369, 386
Historical demographics 116
Human language faculty 7
Hybrid languages 327
Hybridization 24, 367, 371, 373–374, 377–378, 380, 382
   Hybridity 373–374, 390–391
   Hybridism 373
Hyperpolysynthetic 4–5

I

I-creole 321–327
Ideolect
I-language 325–326, 355, 357
Immediate after verb position 107
Importation of slaves 53, 66
Incorporation 173–174, 183, 195–196, 331, 339, 347, 358
Indian Ocean 24, 368, 379, 384, 395
Indigenization 378–379, 385
Infinitival marker 260
Infinitive 12–14, 22, 89–90, 101, 111, 235, 243, 251, 254, 259–260, 348–349, 351–352
Inflection 3–5, 12, 14, 20, 22–23, 54, 67, 69, 76, 92, 99–100, 103, 128, 131, 135, 175, 179, 243–245, 247, 250–252, 281, 293–294, 296–302, 306–308, 309–312, 314, 323, 339, 346–349, 351, 354, 358–360, 372, 387–390, 393
Inflectional morphology 4–5, 20, 23, 54, 67, 99–100, 103, 111, 175, 240, 247, 293–294, 296–297, 306, 314, 323, 339, 346–349, 351, 354, 358–360
Information structure 8–10, 113
In-group code 56
Inherent complement verb (ICV) 328–331
Innovation 35, 43, 70, 88, 155, 160, 165–168, 227, 244, 263, 274–277, 279, 281–285, 293–294, 377, 384

Interface 1, 3, 5–8, 10, 19–20, 111, 176, 197, 251, 385
Invisible hand 115, 150–151, 285, 368, 375, 384, 394–395
Irregularity 4, 11–12, 14, 69–70, 271
Isolating language 4–5, 12

J

Jang 244, 247, 251, 253, 255–256, 260, 263

K

Kind reading 21, 62, 65, 70, 112, 173, 178, 179, 191–194, 196,
Kirinda Java 279–280, 282
Koiné 320–321, 368, 370, 379, 381
Korlai 368, 372

L

Lángu 58–59
Language acquisition 2, 17, 77, 101, 109, 195–196, 229, 270, 321, 340, 372–373, 377
Language Biogram Hypothesis 17
Language contact 22, 24, 77, 88–89, 93, 158, 166–167, 196, 247, 265–266, 269, 273, 275–276, 294, 318, 320–321, 323, 325–326, 362–363, 372–373, 396
Language genesis 23, 218, 345, 373
Language evolution 24, 71, 200, 289, 319, 324, 340, 343, 362, 367, 369, 399–400
Language shift 86–87, 92, 368, 372
Language type 17, 246, 327, 331
Left periphery 9, 324, 326–327
Lexical Africanisms 121
Lexical complexity 11, 76, 318
Lexicon 2, 4, 15–16, 33–34, 40–41, 46, 51–52, 54, 66, 70, 92, 115–116, 121, 150–152, 156–157, 162, 169, 173, 176, 194, 203, 224, 227, 236–237, 296–297, 372

Lingua franca 20, 75, 78, 87–89, 91–94, 225
Linguistic contact 20, 57, 75, 78, 88, 92, 94
Linguistic feature 23–24, 236, 274–275, 317, 321–327, 334, 340, 373–374
Loango 52–53, 58
"Local" simplifications 68
   Short alternation 100, 106, 109–111
Louisiana 99–100, 103–105, 369

M

Macao 368, 372
Marronnage 57
Martinique 103, 369
Matjáu 59
Mature features 358
Medium of Interethnic Communication 55–56, 70
Metrics of evaluation of complexity 296
Minimal language 2
Monosyllabic 16, 31–32, 45, 54–55, 60–61, 255, 300
Morphological bareness 313
Morphology 3–8, 10, 14, 19–20, 22–23, 54, 59, 67, 69, 75–76, 78, 83, 85, 87–89, 91, 95, 99–101, 103, 175, 191, 196, 236, 243–245, 247–248, 251, 253–254, 259, 261, 263, 281, 293–294, 296–298, 301, 306–307, 313–314, 325, 337, 345–349, 351, 354, 356, 358–360, 372
Morphosyntax 4–5, 16–17, 21–22, 159–160, 162, 165, 166–168, 244, 247, 252, 317–318, 326–327, 370, 375, 377, 382–383, 386–387, 389–390, 392
   Above-word morphosyntax 4–5, 16
   Below-word morphosyntax 4–5, 16
Morphosyntactic complexity 4, 7, 243

N

Nasal cluster 55, 60
Nativization 155, 160, 378–379
Normalization 367–368, 373, 391, 394–395
Negation 17–18, 21–22, 40, 90, 104, 115–116, 122, 126–127, 132–143, 149–151, 243–261, 263–264, 324, 348, 351–353
   j-negation 258–259
   t-negation 259
   Verbal negation
Negative habitual marker 262
Negative polarity items 258
New languages 2–4, 19, 152, 169, 246, 266, 276, 284, 293, 318–319, 323–327, 346–347, 355, 367, 372–373, 377, 380–382
New World 318, 368, 374, 379, 384
Nominal inflection 69, 296, 306
Nominal sequences 334
Nominalization 124, 322, 339
Nouns 6–7, 21, 32–33, 41–44, 51–52, 55, 59–60, 65–68, 89, 92, 121, 123–124, 143, 163, 166–167, 173–180, 182–184, 186–188, 190–192, 194–196, 202, 213–214, 217, 225, 296–297, 308–314, 337–338, 390
   Bare nouns 6, 21, 173–175, 178–180, 182–183, 188, 190–191, 195, 200, 309, 313–314
   Count nouns 21, 173–175, 177–179, 182–184, 188–189, 190–192, 194–196
   Mass nouns 21, 33, 173–174, 178–179, 186–192, 195–196
Noun-class 19–20, 33–34, 51, 54–55, 59, 61, 70
Noun roots 54–55
Normal languages 2
Normative ecology 357
Numeral 43, 176–178, 194, 196, 307–309, 311–312

Number 20–21, 34–36, 51–52, 67–69, 77, 179, 182–187, 189–190, 192–197, 307–311, 392–393

O

Old age 345–349, 357, 360
Older languages 2–4, 8, 17–19, 318, 359, 386
Onset 17, 55, 77, 79, 80, 230
Optimality Theory 11, 377

P

Papadorp 58
Parsability 51
Participial adjunct clauses 249, 256–257
Personal pronoun 201, 205–206, 229
Petrification 59
Phase 99–100, 109–111, 270
Phenotype 19, 320, 323–326, 340
Pidgin 1–3, 21–22, 70, 75–76, 92, 111, 159–162, 167–168, 201–202, 208, 210, 213–217, 235, 238, 245, 264, 266, 280, 295, 317–319, 327, 347, 359–360, 370, 374, 377–379
Pidginization 1, 161, 245, 378
Plural 13, 21, 35, 42, 51, 54–55, 59–69, 101–102, 124, 126, 165, 167, 170, 173–175, 177–179, 183–186, 188–191, 194–196, 201–202, 215, 295, 297, 306–314, 389
Plural prefix 42, 51, 59–65
Polysynthetic language 4–5, 19
Poor morphology 3, 14
Portmanteau elements 251, 259
Predicate 6, 8, 10, 21, 103, 128–130, 133–135, 144–145, 167, 177–179, 181, 188, 191, 193, 196, 236, 248–249, 256, 296, 298–299, 301, 303–304, 314, 320, 335, 339, 375, 389, 392–393
Predicative 173, 175, 177, 179, 188, 196–197, 375, 393
Predicate structure 335, 339

Prefix 20, 33–34, 41–42, 44, 51, 55, 59, 60–70, 83, 85, 88–90, 212–213, 235–236, 248, 251–252, 254–255, 259–261, 337, 349–350
   b-prefix 89–91
Prefixless 61, 63, 64, 90
Primary language 56–57, 160
Prosthesis 30, 33

Q

Quantification 175, 180–183, 187, 194, 196
Quantificational determiner 175, 182–183, 187

R

Rate of change 23, 345–346, 355–356
Reanalysis 19–20, 44, 115–116, 122–123, 125, 131–132, 145–146, 149, 151, 155–156, 164, 194–196, 244, 254–255, 268, 357, 373, 375
Recombination 22–24, 265, 278–279, 317–319, 323–328, 334, 340, 367, 372–373, 377–378, 380, 383, 391
Reduction
   Reduction in morphology 82, 91–92, 165, 271, 387–390, 394
   Reduction in phonological complexity 82, 91–92, 165
   Reduction in morphological complexity 92
Redundancy 70, 196, 308, 353
Reduplicated 54, 79
Restructuring 22, 44–45, 271, 367–372, 374, 376, 378, 381, 389–391, 393–395
Resultative construction 143–144, 146, 150

S

Selection 22, 265–267, 269, 273–284, 312, 317, 319–328, 332, 340, 352, 360, 373–374, 378, 381–382, 395

Semantic transparency 3, 14, 278
Sierra Leone 368–369
Simple languages 1, 162, 346, 386
Simplification 1, 19–21, 23, 51, 69–70, 75–78, 80–82, 86, 88, 92–94, 159–162, 210, 276, 293–297, 313–314, 319, 360, 377, 389–390
Simplicity 1–4, 8, 11–12, 14, 16–17, 23–24, 70, 76–77, 160–161, 278, 294, 298, 317, 319, 340, 346–347, 358–360, 370, 389
Singular 13, 21, 32, 34–35, 42, 44, 51, 54–55, 59–64, 66–69, 79, 101–102, 126, 173–175, 177–179, 183–189, 191–192, 194–197, 202, 205–207, 212, 215, 310, 313, 377
Slave 2, 20, 30, 32, 36, 40–41, 43–44, 52–53, 56–60, 66, 115, 117–121, 151–156, 184, 195, 215, 228, 295, 318, 320–321, 372, 374, 376, 379–381, 384–387, 392, 394
Slave Coast 52–53, 56
Slave trade 43, 52, 120
  Dutch slave trade 52, 120
Social network 274, 277, 355
Speciation 266, 268–269, 320, 327, 369–370
Specificity 21, 173–182, 184–187, 190–196, 307–308, 311–314, 325–328
Spell-Out Domain 99–100, 110–111
Split IP domain 251
Subcategorization 138, 348, 351–352

Subordination 138, 392
Substrate 11, 20–21, 33–34, 40, 45, 52–54, 77, 91, 99–100, 103, 105–107, 109, 115–116, 122–123, 127–128, 131–132, 143, 146, 150–151, 156, 159–161, 166–167, 173, 175, 195–196, 210, 216, 228, 237, 247, 267, 320–322, 359, 369, 373–374, 376–378, 380–382, 387, 390–393
  Substrate transfer 122, 132, 143, 156, 321
Suffixes 40–42, 64, 83, 116, 126–128, 130–131, 252, 282, 300, 314
Superstrate 11, 21, 34, 77, 100, 103, 105, 109, 127–128, 151, 157, 159–161, 196, 228, 237, 314, 322, 341
Suprasegmental features 76, 82
Suriname 12, 23, 51–56, 58–66, 68–70, 115, 120, 122, 153, 319, 322–323, 328, 334, 339–340, 369, 375–376, 381
Syllable structure 16–17, 20, 40, 55, 75, 77, 80, 82, 126, 231
  Syllabic structure 82
  Nucleus 55
  Coda 77, 79, 81, 209, 231
Syncopation 104–105
Syntactic features 40, 319, 322, 324–328
Syntactic projections 324, 326
Synthetic language 4–5

T
Target shift 103, 109
Template 54–55, 236
Tense Mood Aspect 20, 115, 125, 324

TMA 1, 18, 103–104, 127–131, 151, 227, 239–240, 298–301, 303–305, 307–308, 325, 349–350, 390
Tone language 346
Trisyllabicity 65–66
Typological matrix 278, 284

U
Universal grammar (UG) 17–18, 176, 267–270, 294, 325, 346–347, 357, 362
Upper IP domain 262
Usage-based theory 268, 270, 274

V
Verb ellipsis 257
Verb focus 108, 327
Verb morphology 20, 75
Vernacularization 378
Vowel harmony 36, 40, 42
V-to-I movement 104

W
West Africa 52, 54, 56, 77, 173, 227, 295, 359, 374–375
West Central Africa 52
Windward Coast 53
Word class 20, 168
Word shape 54
  Word shapes 54
  Word length 51, 77, 388
Word order 10, 122, 130, 132, 138, 141, 150, 161, 173, 281, 322, 324, 337, 347, 358
Word structure 77, 347, 350, 358
Written language 80, 88

Y
Young language 23, 318, 345–347, 359–360

In the series *Creole Language Library* the following titles have been published thus far or are scheduled for publication:

35   ABOH, Enoch O. and Norval SMITH (eds.): Complex Processes in New Languages. 2009. vii, 409 pp.
34   SELBACH, Rachel, Hugo C. CARDOSO and Margot van den BERG (eds.): Gradual Creolization. Studies celebrating Jacques Arends. 2009. x, 392 pp.
33   MICHAELIS, Susanne (ed.): Roots of Creole Structures. Weighing the contribution of substrates and superstrates. 2008. xvii, 425 pp.
32   HUBER, Magnus and Viveka VELUPILLAI (eds.): Synchronic and Diachronic Perspectives on Contact Languages. 2007. xii, 370 pp.
31   BAPTISTA, Marlyse and Jacqueline GUÉRON (eds.): Noun Phrases in Creole Languages. A multi-faceted approach. 2007. x, 494 pp.
30   SIEGEL, Jeff, John LYNCH and Diana EADES (eds.): Language Description, History and Development. Linguistic indulgence in memory of Terry Crowley. 2007. xv, 514 pp.
29   DEUMERT, Ana and Stephanie DURRLEMAN-TAME (eds.): Structure and Variation in Language Contact. 2006. viii, 376 pp.
28   CLEMENTS, J. Clancy, Thomas A. KLINGLER, Deborah PISTON-HATLEN and Kevin J. ROTTET (eds.): History, Society and Variation. In honor of Albert Valdman. 2006. vi, 304 pp.
27   ESCURE, Geneviève and Armin SCHWEGLER (eds.): Creoles, Contact, and Language Change. Linguistic and social implications. 2004. x, 355 pp.
26   MOUS, Maarten: The Making of a Mixed Language. The case of Ma'a/Mbugu. 2003. xx, 322 pp.
25   MIGGE, Bettina: Creole Formation as Language Contact. The case of the Suriname Creoles. 2003. xii, 151 pp.
24   MÜHLEISEN, Susanne: Creole Discourse. Exploring prestige formation and change across Caribbean English-lexicon Creoles. 2002. xiv, 332 pp.
23   SMITH, Norval and Tonjes VEENSTRA (eds.): Creolization and Contact. 2001. vi, 323 pp.
22   NEUMANN-HOLZSCHUH, Ingrid and Edgar W. SCHNEIDER (eds.): Degrees of Restructuring in Creole Languages. 2001. iv, 492 pp.
21   McWHORTER, John (ed.): Language Change and Language Contact in Pidgins and Creoles. 2000. viii, 503 pp.
20   RICKFORD, John R. and Suzanne ROMAINE (eds.): Creole Genesis, Attitudes and Discourse. Studies celebrating Charlene J. Sato. 1999. viii, 418 pp.
19   SPEARS, Arthur K. and Donald WINFORD (eds.): The Structure and Status of Pidgins and Creoles. Including selected papers from meetings of the Society for Pidgin and Creole linguistics. 1997. viii, 461 pp.
18   ESCURE, Geneviève: Creole and Dialect Continua. Standard acquisition processes in Belize and China (PRC). 1997. x, 307 pp.
17   THOMASON, Sarah G. (ed.): Contact Languages. A wider perspective. 1997. xiii, 506 pp.
16   CLEMENTS, J. Clancy: The Genesis of a Language. The formation and development of Korlai Portuguese. 1996. xviii, 282 pp.
15   ARENDS, Jacques, Pieter MUYSKEN and Norval SMITH (eds.): Pidgins and Creoles. An introduction. 1994. xv, 412 pp.
14   KIHM, Alain: Kriyol Syntax. The Portuguese-based Creole language of Guinea-Bissau. 1994. xii, 310 pp.
13   ARENDS, Jacques (ed.): The Early Stages of Creolization. 1996. xvi, 297 pp.
12   BYRNE, Francis and Donald WINFORD (eds.): Focus and Grammatical Relations in Creole Languages. Papers from the University of Chicago Conference on Focus and Grammatical Relations in Creole Languages. 1993. xvi, 329 pp.
11   BYRNE, Francis and John HOLM (eds.): Atlantic Meets Pacific. A global view of pidginization and creolization. 1992. ix, 465 pp.
10   WINFORD, Donald: Predication in Caribbean English Creoles. 1993. viii, 419 pp.
9   BYRNE, Francis and Thom HUEBNER (eds.): Development and Structures of Creole Languages. Essays in honor of Derek Bickerton. 1991. x, 222 pp.
8   BAILEY, Guy, Natalie MAYNOR and Patricia CUKOR-AVILA (eds.): The Emergence of Black English. Text and commentary. 1991. x, 352 pp.
7   FABIAN, Johannes (ed.): History from Below. The "Vocabulary of Elisabethville" by André Yav: Text, Translations and Interpretive Essay. With the assistance of Kalundi Mango. With linguistic notes by W.

Schicho. 1990. vii, 236 pp.
6   **SINGLER, John Victor (ed.):** Pidgin and Creole Tense/Mood/Aspect Systems. 1990. xvi, 240 pp.
5   **JACKSON, Kenneth David:** Sing Without Shame. Oral traditions in Indo-Portuguese Creole verse. 1990. xxiv, 257 pp.
4   **LIPSKI, John M.:** The Speech of the Negros Congos in Panama. 1989. vii, 159 pp.
3   **BYRNE, Francis:** Grammatical Relations in a Radical Creole. Verb Complementation in Saramaccan. With a foreword by Derek Bickerton. 1987. xiv, 293 pp.
2   **SEBBA, Mark:** The Syntax of Serial Verbs. An investigation into serialisation in Sranan and other languages. 1987. xv, 218 pp.
1   **MUYSKEN, Pieter and Norval SMITH (eds.):** Substrata versus Universals in Creole Genesis. Papers from the Amsterdam Creole Workshop, April 1985. 1986. vii, 311 pp.